CW01021175

THE EXPANSION OF EURO

MANCHESTER
1824
Manchester University Press

MANCHESTER MEDIEVAL STUDIES

SERIES EDITOR Professor S. H. Rigby

The study of medieval Europe is being transformed as old orthodoxies are challenged, new methods embraced and fresh fields of inquiry opened up. The adoption of inter-disciplinary perspectives and the challenge of economic, social and cultural theory are forcing medievalists to ask new questions and to see familiar topics in a fresh light.

The aim of this series is to combine the scholarship traditionally associated with medieval studies with an awareness of more recent issues and approaches in a form accessible to the non-specialist reader.

ALREADY PUBLISHED IN THE SERIES

The commercialisation of English society, 1000–1500
Richard H. Britnell

Reform and the papacy in the eleventh century
Kathleen G. Cushing

Picturing women in late medieval and Renaissance art
Christa Grössinger

The Vikings in England
D. M. Hadley

A sacred city: consecrating churches and reforming society in eleventh-century Italy
Louis I. Hamilton

The politics of carnival
Christopher Humphrey

Holy motherhood
Elizabeth L'Estrange

Music, scholasticism and reform: Salian Germany 1024–1125
T. J. H. McCarthy

Medieval law in context
Anthony Musson

Medieval maidens
Kim M. Phillips

Gentry culture in late medieval England
Raluca Radulescu and Alison Truelove (eds)

Chaucer in context
S. H. Rigby

The life cycle in Western Europe, c.1300–c.1500
Deborah Youngs

MANCHESTER MEDIEVAL STUDIES

THE EXPANSION OF EUROPE, 1250–1500

Michael North

Translated by Pamela Selwyn

Manchester University Press
Manchester and New York
distributed exclusively in the USA by Palgrave

Copyright © Eugen Ulmer KG, 2007

The right of Michael North to be identified as the author of this work has been asserted by him in accordance with the Copyright, Designs and Patents Act 1988.

Published by Manchester University Press
Oxford Road, Manchester M13 9NR, UK
and Room 400, 175 Fifth Avenue, New York, NY 10010, USA
www.manchesteruniversitypress.co.uk

First published in 2007
First English-language edition publication in 2012

Distributed in the United States exclusively by
Palgrave Macmillan, 175 Fifth Avenue, New York,
NY 10010, USA

Distributed in Canada exclusively by
UBC Press, University of British Columbia, 2029 West Mall,
Vancouver, BC, Canada V6T 1Z2

British Library Cataloguing-in-Publication Data
A catalogue record for this book is available from the British Library

Library of Congress Cataloging-in-Publication Data applied for

ISBN 978 0 7190 8020 3 hardback
ISBN 978 0 7190 8021 0 paperback

First published 2012

The publisher has no responsibility for the persistence or accuracy of URLs for any external or third-party internet websites referred to in this book, and does not guarantee that any content on such websites is, or will remain, accurate or appropriate.

Typeset in Monotype Bulmer
by Koinonia, Manchester
Printed in Great Britain
by TJ International Ltd, Padstow

CONTENTS

LIST OF MAPS

LIST OF GRAPHS AND FIGURES

Graphs

Figures

LIST OF TABLES AND GENEALOGICAL TABLES

Tables

Genealogical tables

ACKNOWLEDGEMENTS

In *The Expansion of Europe*, I have chosen an individual approach to European history. The book begins in the thirteenth century, a time when the developments that would come to characterise the early modern period around 1500 were already present. To that extent it was a welcome challenge for me, as a historian normally at home in the early modern period, to search for the roots of modernity in earlier centuries. The fact that the present volume ends in the early sixteenth century owes much to the conceptualisation of the German series in which it originally appeared, which features a separate volume on the period 1500–1648. That being said, every historical work constructs its own history; this one, encompassing the period between the thirteenth and sixteenth centuries, is defined primarily by intense cultural exchange in Europe. Processes of cultural exchange – especially in the fields of art, music and literature – accordingly occupy a relatively prominent place here. In my attempt to present an outline of politics, constitutional issues, economics and society in all European countries as well I soon reached the limits of the possible, since a single historian can scarcely gain, let alone process, an overview of the literature and the most recent scholarship.

If the author learned a good deal in the process, and enjoyed himself as well, I owe much to the continual encouragement of Peter Blickle, on the one hand, and the generous assistance of the members of the University of Greifswald's Research Training Group 'Contact Zone Mare Balticum' and the Comitato Scientifico of the Datini Institute in Prato on the other. Colleagues in Greifswald, throughout Europe and in the USA, read parts of the manuscript, corrected some of my interpretations and kept me informed of the latest scholarship. I am extremely grateful for their help, and would like to thank them individually here: Reinhold C. Mueller (Venice) and Edward English (Santa Barbara) read my chapters on Italy, while Volker Reinhardt (Fribourg) also cast a critical eye on the Italian and Swiss chapters. Pierre Monnet (Paris) commented on France, Markus Cerman (Vienna), Anti Selart (Tartu) and Matthias Niendorf (Greifswald) helped with east-central Europe and Russia, while Claudia Rapp (Los Angeles) updated south-eastern Europe. Jens Olesen and Horst Wernicke (both Greifswald) emended the sections on Scandinavia and the Hanseatic League, while the chapters on western Europe and European economic history benefited from the comments and revisions of Wim Blockmans (Leiden and Wassenaar), Erik Aerts, Herman Van der

Wee (both Louvain) and Bruce Campbell (Belfast). Bartolomé Yun (Seville and Fiesole) brought me up to date on the Spanish scholarship. My discussions about the fifteenth century with Larry Epstein (London) were extremely stimulating. His sudden and untimely death in 2007 meant that he never got to see the finished product.

Finally, Klaus Oschema (Berne and Heidelberg) inspired my research on 'the Europe of the historians', while Karl-Heinz Spieß (Greifswald) provided a wealth of advice on the late Middle Ages in Germany, as well as additional material for the chapter on Society and the review of the literature. Georg Schmidt (Jena) offered suggestions on the Holy Roman Empire and Wolfgang Weber (Augsburg) on Universities and the Character of the Epoch. I also profited from the expertise of Volker Mertens (Berlin) on literature, Walter Werbeck (Greifswald) on music and Matthias Müller (Mainz) on the visual arts.

The book gained much from the critical comments of Peter Blickle, Martin Krieger and Stephen Rigby as well as the translating skills of Pamela Selwyn. The University of Greifswald generously covered the cost of translation. I owe a debt of gratitude to Doreen Wollbrecht and Robert Riemer, who enthusiastically tackled the details of book production for the original German edition. They prepared the manuscript, bibliography and index together with Maik Fiedler, Christian Fricke, Arne Last, Jens Leuteritz, Matthias Müller, Jörn Sander, Lasse Seebeck and Hielke van Nieuwenhuize. The last-mentioned assisted above all with intensive proof reading.

Greifswald, 2010 Michael North

INTRODUCTION: THE EXPANSION OF EUROPE

The Europe of the historians

Each era constructs a history of its own. Since the fall of the Berlin Wall in 1989 and the subsequent expansion of the European Union we have witnessed a huge increase in attention to the history of Europe. In recent years, many historians have written European history as a long process of unification. Frequently, they have appeared unaware of the teleological nature of their enterprise in seeking historical evidence for a preoccupation with Europe.

This approach has its origins in the post-war era, especially in the 1950s, when, in the wake of wartime destruction and a divided Europe, historians in search of an ideal community of nations (the European idea) harked back to a Carolingian Core Europe.[1] While Byzantium and eastern Europe were largely absent from this vision, they returned in the 1990s – parallel to EU eastward enlargement – in the form of south-eastern and east-central Europe, and attracted the interest of historians and the public alike, for example in the 27th Council of Europe Art Exhibition 'Europe's centre around AD 1000'.[2]

In the discussions over Turkey's membership in Europe, and against the background of alleged Islamisation, historians like Jacques Le Goff and Michael Mitterauer have invoked and constructed a Christian Europe in the Middle Ages, or rather a specifically European path of agrarian and family structures.[3]

Meanwhile, according to Eurosceptics like Timothy Reuter or Felipe Fernández-Armesto, medieval Europe existed at most in the minds of historians.[4] They shared this viewpoint with older colleagues for whom medieval Europe represented a purely geographical designation.[5] In recent years, younger colleagues have challenged this interpretation and pointed to processes of identity formation within Europe in the Middle Ages, for instance by analysing the strategies underlying the ways in which the notion of Europe has been used.[6] Against this backdrop, exploring the (self-) image of Europe as it has come down to us, and as it has been constructed by historians, is a worthwhile enterprise.

The idea of Europe

> But now that the city of Constantinople is fallen into the hands of the foe, now that so much Christian blood has been spilt and so many people driven into slavery, the Catholic faith has been deplorably violated ... If truth be told, Christianity has suffered no greater disgrace than this for many centuries. For in bygone days we were defeated only in Asia and Africa, that is in foreign lands, but now we have been brutally struck down in Europe, that is, in our own fatherland, our own house, our own abode.[7]

This oft-cited anti-Turkish oration by the Italian humanist Enea Silvio Piccolomini, the future Pope Pius II, at the imperial assembly of 1454 in Frankfurt is generally regarded as the first articulation of the political notion of Europe. Piccolomini, who also collected descriptions of countries and peoples in his *De Europa* (1458), conceived of Europe as the common religious, cultural and political umbrella covering the peoples and realms of the Occident.[8]

Since the 1430s, the threat to Greek and Latin Christendom from Islam had inspired efforts to unify the Church. In the same context, the term 'Europe' came to be used more frequently in a variety of media. Thus in 1438, Pope Eugene IV charged the German king Albrecht with the task of liberating the territories occupied by the infidels. Not long thereafter, King Władysław III organised the Polish-Hungarian defence against the Turks, which ended in 1444 with the defeat near Varna and the king's death. The humanist and chancellor to King Sigismund, Pier Paolo Vergerio, had already emphasised Hungary as a bulwark against the infidels. The pinnacle of Enea Silvio's stylisation of Europe came in 1453 and 1454; having invoked Europe frequently in earlier letters, his pathos now waned. In his 'European' political writings, he equated Europe with *Christianitas* and clearly distanced it from the pagan Asia of the Turks. He also spoke of *Europaei* for the first time, thus creating a collective term for all of the peoples living in Europe which, however, would only gain wider currency in the sixteenth century.[9]

In the mid-fifteenth century, Europe, which older geographies had treated as an appendage of Asia, became the centre of Catholic Christendom. Once Byzantium, the second eye of Europe (*alterum Europae oculum*), had fallen as a bulwark against the Ottomans, an old problem was solved. The conflict between the Roman and Byzantine empires, between Latin and Greek Christianity, disappeared. While the very title of 'master of Asia and Europe' suggests Mehmed II the Conqueror's efforts at westward expansion, the Holy Roman emperors at first limited their ambitions to Europe, although they found new fields of endeavour in the struggle against Islam both within and beyond the continent.

The notion of Europe had already been deployed to help create identities in the earlier conflicts surrounding the Crusades and the Mongol invasion. Thus in his *Gesta Regum Anglorum*, William of Malmesbury translated Pope Urban II's well-known speech at the Council of Clermont (1095), which launched the first Crusade, for his readers, lamenting the expansion of the infidels and the resulting driving back of Christians to a small, diminished Europe. But even in their retreat area of Europe, the Turks and Saracens (*Turchi et Saraceni*) continued to threaten war on Christendom.[10]

In the mid-thirteenth century, King Bela IV of Hungary, or his chancery, took this idea up again in a letter to Pope Innocent IV complaining that the Mongols had been able to lead their troops into Europe without the European princes coming to the aid of an imperilled Hungary.[11]

Apart from its rise in political and cultural status, in the Middle Ages Europe always played a role in geography and the history of salvation, at least to the extent that people were aware of the categories proposed by Isidore of Seville, 'Divisus est autem orbis trifarie, e quibus una pars Asia, altera Europa, tertia Africa nuncupatur' (The earth is divided into three parts, one being called Asia, one Europe and the third Africa).[12]

Authors such as the Venerable Bede (*c.* 673/674–735), Otto of Freising (*c.* 1112–1158) or Martin of Opara (d. 1278) also opened their chronicles of the world with comments on the division of the earth. The Icelander Snorri Sturluson (*c.* 1178/79–1241), too, began his *Chronicle of the Kings of Norway* (*Norges Konge-Krønike*) with a description of Europe.

Taking up earlier traditions, authors like Gervase of Tilbury (b. *c.* 1152, d. after 1220) linked Europe with the biblical Table of Nations in Genesis 10 and portrayed the continent as a region settled by the sons and descendants of Noah's son Japheth, from which he deduced the immediately Christian character of Europe. By the thirteenth century, however, scholars were also familiar with the ancient Greek myth of the abduction of the princess Europa by Zeus.[13]

This literature hardly conveyed geographical knowledge or economically useful information about Europe, since world chronicles and maps served a different function in the Middle Ages: they were intended to lend visual form to the Christian world order. The centre of the medieval world, as portrayed on the late thirteenth-century Ebstorf map, for example, was Jerusalem, the site of the evidence of the life, death and resurrection of Christ. There was no alternative.

There was thus no need to comprehend Europe geographically, especially because this part of the world was never congruent with a political or ecclesiastical entity. Since the divisions of the empire in late antiquity, a significant portion of the European continent had belonged to the Byzantine Empire, whose capital city was still on 'European' soil. Only the Turkish threat and the fall of Constantinople in 1453 as well as the increasing awareness of Asia set in motion the discourse on Europe sketched above in respect to terminology. In the course of these discussions, clerical humanists and kings also presented plans for Europe, but we should not misunderstand them as forerunners to the present-day European Union, especially since the word 'Europe' rarely appears in this context.

Thus, for instance, authors continued to address the dichotomy between alleged Asian servitude and noble European liberty, which Nicholas Oresmius (*c.* 1320–1382) had already noted in the fourteenth century.[14] Examples from antiquity, such as the struggle of the Athenians against the Persian kings, remained popular.[15] The hope of recovering the Holy Land also motivated calls for European unity such as that made by the French political pamphleteer Pierre Dubois (*c.* 1250/55–1320) in his 1306 *De recuperatione terrae sanctae*.[16] He was inspired by the French interest in a *pax gallicana*, but the rejection of imperial or papal notions of universality like those projected by Dante Alighieri (1265–1321) in *De Monarchia* (1311) also played a role. The European plan developed by the French-born diplomat Antoine Marini on behalf of George of Poděbrady, king of Bohemia (1420–1471), pursued both personal and pan-European interests. The 'heretic king' Poděbrady sought in this way to secure a place among Europe's rulers by suggesting to France, Burgundy and Venice that they form a coalition of European nations to defend Europe against Islam and at the same time circumscribe the universal powers of the pope and the emperor.[17] This topos of a European peace as a precondition for the struggle against Islam reappears periodically into the eighteenth century.

The late fifteenth century then saw the earliest articulation of the political idea of a Europe of states, with which such authors as Philippe de Commynes (1447–1511) identified. By the late fifteenth century, however, regional authors also began to position themselves within Europe. In their 'Descriptions of Switzerland', learned men such as the Zurich municipal physician Conrad Türst or the dean of Einsiedeln Abbey Albrecht von Bonstetten sought to locate the Swiss cantons (*Orte*) within Europe, with Einsiedeln Abbey in one case and Rigi Mountain in the other serving as the centre of Europe. This invention of an autonomous Swiss nation (in distinction to the Holy Roman Empire, to which Switzerland belonged) would become typical of the (expanding) Europe of states.[18]

One proponent of this concept was Niccolò Machiavelli (1469–1527), who went a step further and suggested that a plurality of states was characteristically European. Thus Europe with its republics and kingdoms had produced 'countless excellent men' (*uomini eccelenti sanza numero*), while the number of such exemplary individuals in Asia or Africa was allegedly negligible.[19] While a few great kingdoms dominated Asia and Africa, it was precisely the multiplicity of and competition between states (kingdoms and republics) that would become the signature of an expanding Europe from the fourteenth century. Expansion entailed another aspect as well: increasing – cultural – exchange between states, regions and individuals.

Practical geography: Border-crossings I

Alongside geography that explained the world according to the criteria of a history of salvation, there also existed a practical geography, which was constantly pushing forward the exploration of the temporal world to meet the needs of trade and travel. While the geographical knowledge of the chroniclers stagnated, the horizons of mariners and merchants were expanding apace. Seafarers passed on their knowledge orally at first, but beginning in the late twelfth century it was also written down in the so-called *portolans*. The oldest of these, the *Liber de existencia riveriarum et forma maris nostri Mediterranei*, was compiled in Pisa around 1200 and contained an account of the Mediterranean coasts as well as of the passages of the Black Sea.[20] In the second half of the thirteenth century, a Byzantine sailor wrote a navigation manual, the *Compasso di navigare*, which described routes in the Mediterranean and contained information on distances, course, water depth and characteristics of the coastline.[21] The successors to these manuals, the portolan charts, usually consisted of maps, which became increasingly precise. For the Hanseatic region, a fifteenth-century Low German log book has come down to us, which describes navigation not just in the North and Baltic Sea region, but also the Atlantic route all the way to Cartagena in Castile.

In the Mediterranean region, the siege of Acre (1291) by the Muslim Mamluks and the papal ban on trade with the Saracens encouraged the Genoese (who dominated trade in both the western Mediterranean and the Black Sea) to consider for the first time exploring a sea route around Africa. Although the late thirteenth-century expedition by the Vivaldi brothers probably did not get much farther than North Africa, their undertaking shows the early geographical presence of the continent. It owed much to interest in the legendary Prester John, whom Europeans searched for in Ethiopia.

In the fourteenth century the Genoese, Catalans and Majorcans then pressed forward into the Atlantic, where, probably before 1350, they discovered the Canary Islands, possibly the Madeira group and perhaps even the Azores. To be sure, the mariners' reports were often so sketchy that they could easily be compiled in geographical representations together with ancient topoi (mythical creatures). Certain examples, however, such as the Catalan world atlas of 1375 with a map of the waters of the Black Sea, the Mediterranean and the Atlantic coast already feature precise indications of distances and coastlines, so that one could use this map for orientation when steering a ship.[22]

Travel accounts and perceptions of foreign lands

Such relatively precise maps were probably based on various portolan charts, but oral accounts by missionaries, diplomats and merchants also turned Venice and Genoa, as well as Florence, into centres of geographical knowledge. After all, European expansion did not begin in 1492, but was a long process promoted by traders and travellers, with voyages sometimes leading to discoveries, and discoveries to conquests.[23] While the twelfth and thirteenth centuries witnessed the penetration of the peripheries of Europe and their subjection to the rule of Latin Christendom, the Mongolian expansion – based on the *pax mongolica* (*c.* 1200/50–1350) opened up contacts and commerce with the lands occupied by the Golden Horde, and even with China, for European rulers, travellers and traders. One of the first to travel to Karakorum in Mongolia was the knight Baldwin of Hainaut, who was sent on a diplomatic mission to the Mongols in the years 1243–44 by the Latin Emperor Baldwin II. At nearly the same time, Pope Innocent IV sent the Franciscan Giovanni di Pian di Carpine (*c.* 1182–1252) to the Mongol empire to gain support against Islam.

In 1254, the Flemish Franciscan William of Rubruck (*c.* 1220–1270) was also supposed to seek Mongol aid against the Muslim incursion on behalf of the French king, the pope and the Latin emperor, while at the same time testing the waters for a possible mission to the Mongols. Unlike his predecessors, Rubruck composed a report containing precise descriptions not just of Mongolian customs and manners, but also of the geographical conditions of his journey.[24] His account, written in Latin, reached a far smaller audience than that of Marco Polo (1254–*c.* 1324), however. The travellers of the Polo family were the best known among the many northern Italian merchants who traded in China or Asia. Marco Polo's father Nicolò and his uncle Matteo had already visited China on several mercantile expeditions between 1250 and 1269 before Marco Polo embarked on his own journey in 1271, which would take him through Seljuk Asia Minor, the empire of the Persian Ilkhans, over the Silk Road to the residence of the Kublai Khan in China. While Marco Polo entered the service of the Khan, his kinsmen continued their mercantile activities. They left China in 1292.[25]

Based on the knowledge of Asia available in northern Italy, Francesco Balducci Pegolotti, who earned his spurs as a commercial agent of the Bardi company on Cyprus, was able to provide a detailed account of his journey from the Genoese colony of Tana on the Sea of Azov to Peking in his 1338 *Pratica della Mercatura*. In keeping with the function of a mercantile manual, he devotes the most space to comments on safety during the journey and to exchange rates.[26] A good century after Marco Polo, another Venetian merchant, Niccolò de' Conti (1385–1469), reported mainly on the geographical, religious, social and economic situation in India. In so doing he influenced the cartographic work of the monk Fra Mauro, who in 1459 created the first map of the world reflecting a realistic notion of Africa on a commission from the Portuguese king Alfonso V. Although still produced in the form of a *mappa mundi*, it was already largely based on the practical knowledge of seafarers and merchants. In contrast, the Florentine Paolo dal Pozzo Toscanelli (1397–1482) – like other humanists – based his maps on the study of Ptolemaic spatial abstractions. His incorrect calculation of the dimensions of Asia later caused Columbus, who had been most strongly influenced by the accounts of Marco Polo, to seek the sea route to India by sailing westward.[27]

Nevertheless, it was only a small step from here to the systematic expansion beyond Europe's borders undertaken by the kingdom of Portugal and later also the Catholic kings of Castile and Aragón in the fifteenth century (see the country chapters in Part I). This expansion, which would take explorers into the Old and the New World via the Canary Islands, revolutionised European knowledge. The authority of the authors of classical antiquity and the Middle Ages was undermined when Europeans discovered, first in the Canaries and then in the Caribbean, previously unknown peoples who truly lived in their own, new world. The eyewitness accounts of the explorers brought it home to Europeans that they were living on the edge of a new world inhabited by millions of savage, naked heathens.[28]

Mobility: Border-crossings II

Apart from crossing physical boundaries, which acquainted Europeans with the 'Stone Age societies' of the Canary Islands and later the Caribbean as well as the advanced civilisations of Asia, they also had a multiplicity of internal borders to overcome, all of which reveals the ambiguity of the whole notion of borders.[29] These borders were part of a bundle of perceptions with which neighbouring societies with differing customs, languages or ethnic identities confronted one another. They interacted to the degree that they distanced themselves from each other peacefully or even violently. This type of mental border encompassed above all those religious frontiers and places where Christendom or Latin Christendom found itself under threat. In this respect, the differences and thus the religious delimitations appear rather to have increased in the course of the fourteenth and fifteenth centuries. This does not apply only to conflicts between Orthodox and Latin Christendom in Russia and Poland-Lithuania, respectively. In the Mediterranean region, where religious coexistence among Jews, Christians and Muslims had often been possible during the twelfth and thirteenth centuries, officially fomented segregation intensified, as occurred on the Iberian Peninsula in the course of the fifteenth century. In contrast, the borders between German and Slavic peasants, for instance, who lived within sight of each other in the settlement territories of the east, appear to have levelled out socially. These regions featured extensive wilderness as a sort of 'no-man's-land', leaving enough space for settlement and border-crossing.[30] The migration from areas with relative overpopulation and underemployment to those with a shortage of labour made for trans-regional equilibrium.

We thus should not underestimate population mobility during the Middle Ages. Despite the emergence of royal and noble residences toward the end of the fifteenth century, kings and princes were constantly travelling. The hope of gaining salvation by making long-distance pilgrimages, for example on the Way of St James to Santiago de Compostela, kept nobles and burghers on the move. Even after they had become settled, merchants continued to take training abroad, and they frequently had to visit the great fairs. Journeymen artisans also covered long distances. In this way they were supposed to learn new skills; specialists with particular abilities were deliberately recruited (technology transfer). Even peasants were mobile, for example hauling communion wine or salt over long distances for their landlords as part of their feudal services. Unfortunately, the meagre sources rarely provide much information on these peasant carting services. At any rate, thirteenth- and fourteenth-century invoices show that the Bavarian

Benedictine abbey of Scheyern had dependant peasants transport wine from its South Tyrolean vineyards.[31]

What is more, many people throughout Europe took to the roads in the wake of major enterprises of expansion and settlement such as the Crusades, the German settlement of the east and the Iberian *Reconquista*, but also the Anglo-Norman colonisation of Ireland.[32] To be sure, only a small minority of Europeans settled in the Holy Land or Syria after the First Crusade (1096–1102), but they already included peasants alongside knights, traders and clerics. Just as the cities at home required continual migration from the countryside, the territory of the Crusades depended on continuous migration from Europe. The Fourth Crusade, which the Venetians conducted in 1204 to conquer Constantinople, saw the establishment of several 'Frankish' states on Byzantine soil settled by monastic and chivalric orders. Venice was anxious to secure maritime trade routes, and the acquisition of land and settlement of coastal towns by Venetians served this purpose. The *Reconquista* in Spain also followed the idea of the Crusades. Peasant settlements secured the knights' conquests. The chivalric orders played a leading role in the *Reconquista* and the *Repoblación*. Although increasing numbers of people participated in the inland colonisation of the recaptured territories, and peasant mobility southward led to a labour shortage in northern Spain, the total number of new settlers remained small. Many villages were abandoned, along with irrigation-intensive Muslim agriculture, which was replaced by stock-breeding and olive-growing.

Internal colonisation developed independent of the Crusades and provided a further impetus to mobility in medieval society. Thus the German settlement of the east began with the investiture of Count Adolf of Schauenburg in Holstein (1110), of the Ascanian Albert the Bear in the Northern March (1134) and of Conrad of Wettin as margrave of Meißen and Lusatia (1136), since they invited peasants and burghers from the west to populate their lands. At first, security concerns were paramount, since uprisings by the local Slavic population represented a constant threat, which it was hoped the settlement of German peasants and the foundations of towns under Germanic law would counteract. The prospect of more favourable living conditions (larger farms burdened with less onerous feudal duties, inheritance rights, personal freedom, village self-administration under an *Erbschulze* or village mayor) lured a sufficient number of settlers. Since the settlement of peasants liable to taxes and the founding of tax-paying towns promised higher revenues than the previous payment in kind and services of the Slavic population, the Slavic rulers of Silesia, Pomerania,

Mecklenburg, Bohemia and Moravia as well as the Cistercian order and the Teutonic Knights in Prussia and Livonia also adopted the model of Germanic law settlement. Above all after the devastating Mongol incursions of the early thirteenth century, however, peasants from the old area of settlement were resettled in the recently colonised lands. Nevertheless, we should not overestimate the quantitative importance of eastern settlement. Of the three million increase in population during the high Middle Ages, no more than 200,000 people moved to the east. In comparison, the internal colonisation of the old area of settlement in the west probably involved ten times that number.[33]

Nonetheless, these settlement processes offered the European peripheries, for example Sicily or the southern Baltic region, the possibility of integration through grain production into the emerging European division of labour.

New horizons in the economy

Along with the growth of geographical knowledge about the wider world, the gradual process of internal transformation within Europe also deserves our attention. As early as the thirteenth century, Europe was expanding not just geographically, but also socially, economically and culturally. Thus the actual process of European expansion into the island world of the eastern Mediterranean, the Black Sea and above all the Levant was already under way in the high Middle Ages, when the maritime cities of Genoa and Venice founded colonies there. There were sugar plantations using imported slave labour. Over the centuries, the plantations were then transferred westward from the eastern Mediterranean until finally, in the course of Portuguese expansion, they were introduced to Madeira, the Azores and later the island of São Tomé in the Gulf of Guinea as well as Brazil.

German merchants also broadened the scope of their activities. They formed close relationships with Italy and the western Mediterranean and dominated mining in the Carpathian region. The Hanseatic League expanded their trade area in north-western Europe not just by stabilising the Novgorod–Lübeck–Hamburg–Bruges route in east–west trade, but also extending to the Bay of Biscay and Lwów. The maritime trade would prove especially resistant to crisis. While the continental trade was adversely affected by the wars of the second half of the fourteenth and the fifteenth century, the maritime trade in the North and Baltic Seas flourished.

The precondition for the expansion of trade was the so-called commercial revolution of the twelfth and thirteenth centuries. This term refers to the fundamental changes in business methods and the organisation of trade with which Italian merchants rationalised and improved the efficiency of mercantile enterprises in the thirteenth century. Italians no longer bought Flemish cloth at the fairs in Champagne, but established themselves permanently in the areas of production, especially at Bruges. This process followed the growth of the southern European trade in luxury goods, which rendered a division of labour in trade both necessary and lucrative. Long-distance merchants no longer had to accompany their goods to the fairs by trade caravan or ship, but could direct their business affairs from counting houses in Genoa, Florence or Pisa. Commercial agents who bought and sold on the spot settled in the areas of production and markets of the trading world of the day, while carters or mariners transported the goods – which could now be insured during transport – from the sites of production to the points of sale. A permanent presence in several places at the same time demanded large amounts of capital compared with merchants who travelled from fair to fair, since the geographical and quantitative expansion of trade meant that it now took longer for invested capital to bear interest. New forms of business partnerships, bookkeeping and payment transactions became necessary.

The revolution in trade practices was accompanied by an increase in status for merchants. While the Church Fathers had condemned trade because it arose from greed and forced merchants to lie, cheat and deceive, and because the effects of commerce were socially unjust, from the thirteenth century theologians increasingly found arguments in favour of commercial enterprise. As a rule, they now regarded it as a legitimate occupation associated with hard work and risk, and emphasised the role of trade in supplying people with necessary goods.

Mercantile activity now focused on items of everyday use rather than luxury goods, which also offered opportunities for producers in the north and the east to participate with their commodities such as grain, wood, fish, metals and furs (see 5.12). Mentalities changed as well. Aristocratic entrepreneurs in the Baltic region discovered cereal production as a new source of income, while the English gentry and yeomen farmers actively engaged in sheep farming, enclosing common pastures.[34] By specialising in high-quality products and tapping the resources of their hinterlands, many cities, including smaller ones, also succeeded in participating actively in regional and international trade.

The monetary economy expanded along with trade. The founding of towns in the less urbanised regions such as the Baltic and the emergence of urban landscapes played a role here. The accompanying expansion of peasant production for the market in the west and the east put money in the hands of broader segments of the population, new mints were opened and new coins were minted in silver and, for the first time in 500 years, in gold. Although several of the mints were closed again during the bullion famine of the fourteenth century, the second half of the fifteenth century saw an expansion of gold and silver minting, which was reflected in the opening of numerous new regional mints all over Europe.

Communication

Structures of communication changed markedly as a consequence of the expansion of domestic and foreign trade. Let us recall that in medieval times, communication and the dissemination of news were largely oral. Nevertheless, oral and written communication were closely interrelated. From the twelfth century, waves of textualisation revolutionised the way people communicated with one another, but also the organisation of political authority, the economy and knowledge. Knowledge could now be stored permanently and distributed independent of place.[35] The invention of printing with movable type, put into practice for the first time by Gutenberg in 1455/56, unleashed a further communication revolution. By the end of the fifteenth century, printing shops had sprung up in some 250 towns, offering new opportunities to disseminate and preserve information and exchange ideas in the medium of the book as well as broadsides and pamphlets.[36]

Individual communication also became a good deal faster from the thirteenth century. While kings, princes, bishops and monasteries had always used couriers, it was only in the twelfth and above all the thirteenth century that we find evidence of European cities, merchants and universities using their services. Italian merchants created a network of regular communications spanning the region from the Mediterranean to Bruges and London, with letters leaving daily from Barcelona for Florence, every three days from Bruges for Milan, and about every six days from Venice for Constantinople.

Thus the Datini correspondence from the years 1380 to 1410 shows that western and southern Europe and the Near East were already closely connected by communication networks, with a letter from Venice to Bruges (25 days) or London (33 days) taking not much less time to arrive than one to Rhodes (29), Constantinople (38 days) or Acre (33).[37]

The first evidence of regular princely courier services comes from the rule of the Visconti in Milan. Their successors, the Sforza, set up a regular relay service in the fifteenth century, featuring a network of posts where couriers could change horses. This made it possible to send mail day and night, and significantly accelerated delivery. Other states adopted the Lombard system, and the founding of an imperial post by Maximilian I in 1490, under the entrepreneurial aegis of the house of Taxis, also followed this model. And so, in the first decade of the sixteenth century, a quasi-public institution with regular service and an organised system of tariffs, soon to be known as the 'ordinary post', emerged from dynastic communications. The heart of this early postal system was the continental route Antwerp–Brussels–Augsburg–Innsbruck–Venice–Rome–Naples, which was served once a week by municipal couriers from a number of cities.

Deliberations on how to increase the speed of service arose with the introduction of the post or relay system. They coincided with theoretical discussions about time on the one hand and increasing time management in urban societies and economies on the other. While for the rural population sunrise and sunset as well as the growing seasons defined the seasonal organisation of labour, from the late fourteenth century the urban day was organised by mechanical clocks and divided into hours. The invention of clockwork with a wheel mechanism, which marked twenty-four hours of equal length, played a central role here. We know that there was a clock of this type in the Church of San Gottardo in Milan in 1335, but in the years that followed Padua (1344), Genoa (1353), Florence (1354), Bologna (1356), Ferrara (1362) and Paris (1370) also installed municipal clocks. In north-western Europe, too, as well as in the north German Hanseatic cities, municipal clocks were constructed everywhere in the second half of the fourteenth century, with town governments vying with one another for the most prestigious new devices. Time could now be measured so precisely that traders and merchants could use it for orientation as well as for structuring the working day. With the aid of tables, merchants calculated the time zones or the differences between the various time zones or time systems, which could vary from one town to another. Without this knowledge, they could not, for example, abide by the expiry date of a bill of exchange in international trade. Alongside the official municipal division of time, which emerged largely from the interests of trade, one also finds the beginnings of a theoretical interest in speed, for instance in the work of the above-mentioned Nicholas Oresmius or in Chaucer's (*c.* 1340–1400) observation that 'time is wasting'.[38]

The state expands outward and inward

Alongside the discovery and conquest of new territories outside of Europe, a wide range of expansion processes also occurred within Europe in the fourteenth and fifteenth centuries. In western Europe, they led to the establishment of national kingdoms that ruled over a fixed state territory and began to pursue the expansion of state power within their borders as well. In the east, the decline of Mongol rule left Poland-Lithuania and Russia with extraordinary opportunities to enlarge their territories, of which they also made extensive use, while the intensification of political rule was naturally less marked. Which paths the monarchies chose depended on internal factors such as access to resources and the resistance of rival forces, especially the aristocracy. The great success of this process of expansion and consolidation is evident in the fact that many European countries, such as England, France, Spain, Portugal, the Czech Republic, Hungary or Denmark have virtually the same borders in the twenty-first century as their predecessor states did in the fifteenth century. Characteristic of this process is the fact that England could not establish a permanent presence on the Continent, and that future expansion was orientated toward its immediate neighbours in Ireland and Scotland. The French kingdom, in contrast, expanded by recapturing territories previously occupied by the English. They were joined by newly acquired territories such as Provence or the Dauphiné, whose estates and parliaments promoted the integration of the regions into the kingdom.

Kingdoms could expand both in cooperation with and at the expense of the aristocracy. Thus the Danish monarchy expanded by centralising resources (palaces and offices) in the fourteenth and fifteenth centuries at the expense of previously noble privileges, while eastward expansion in Poland and Lithuania occurred in close collaboration with the noble magnates. The Muscovite state, in contrast, which extended its territory northward and westward by nearly 2.5 million square kilometres between 1460 and 1530, integrated the boyars as a service nobility, while incorporating the republics of Novgorod and Pskov into its realm.

Republics also expanded, however. Thus the Italian city-states of Genoa, Florence and Venice succeeded in subjugating numerous neighbouring city-states and asserting themselves as major powers in conflicts with the similarly expanding princely states of Milan and Naples as well as the Papal State. Other republics, such as the Swiss Confederacy, also enlarged their dominions, just as their individual members, for instance Berne, acquired and ruled over large territories.

In the Holy Roman Empire – to which Switzerland, despite its growing autonomy, still belonged, along with the Netherlands – the expansion of monarchical rule proceeded in the form of institutionalisation. The imperial reform of 1495 created a body, the imperial diet, in which electoral princes, princes and cities, in cooperation with the emperor, assumed responsibility for maintaining the peace in the Empire, defending it against its enemies and supplying the necessary resources to do so. Efforts at integration and institutionalisation within the Holy Roman Empire were sparked by the threat of expansion by the Hungarians under Matthias Corvinus and the Ottomans, but also by Duke Charles the Bold of Burgundy.

While the processes of expansion originated in the individual monarchies and republics, they were interrelated. Overseas expansion was promoted by the rivalry between the Iberian monarchies of Spain and Portugal, just as competition between the maritime republics of Genoa and Venice had shaped the politics of the eastern Mediterranean two centuries earlier. The expansion of Poland-Lithuania occurred in competition with Muscovy at the expense of Mongol rule, with Muscovy cooperating with the Mongols in the struggle against Lithuania and to neutralise its Russian rivals (Tver). The French monarchy could only expand after the English appetite for expansion had been restricted to the British Isles. Finally, in northern Europe, the expansion of the Kalmar Union (the kingdoms of Denmark, Norway and Sweden) collided with the interests of the Hanseatic League. The consolidation of rule in the Holy Roman Empire, too, however, led to the expansion out of the empire of the Swiss Confederacy and later of the Netherlands, since they did not wish to be integrated.

Expansion in the social and cultural fields

Social structures also began to shift. Members of the high nobility (counts and princes) sought to distance themselves from the lower nobility, and a social hierarchy took shape in the towns. Efforts at social closure and exclusivity, which increased in this period, may be interpreted as consequences of society's relative openness to mobility.

Despite a falling population, high consumer demand fostered the trades and manufactures in the towns. Sumptuary regulations like the Scottish Sumptuary Law of 1447 tried in vain to limit clothing expenditures among the lower strata, who were no longer satisfied with plain grey woollens, but now demanded haberdashery goods such as hats, purses, pins and buckles.[39]

Furthermore, social and political revolts served on the one hand to enforce the participation of the self-confident artisan strata in town government, and on the other to defend urban interests successfully against a central authority, as we can observe in the urban landscapes of Italy and the Netherlands, but also in the Swiss Confederacy and the Hanseatic region.

In the Church, new religious orders and reform movements questioned the universality of the pope at least intermittently. Many phenomena, which generally began in Italy in the twelfth and thirteenth centuries and spread over time to the other regions of Europe, show that the Church was in the midst of a long-term process of reform. One could mention the conciliar movement here, which initiated a reform of the Church, 'head and limbs', after the Great Schism. There was also a lay movement from below, which sought to reach the common people through pastoral activities, hymns and popular homilies. These efforts focused on the Christian individual's turning to God and a 'new inwardness', which took up the themes of medieval mysticism. Although this *devotio moderna* did not yet challenge dominant theological doctrine and religious practice, we find many elements here and in the conciliar movement that are generally only associated with the actual early modern period around 1500, although they in fact began long before.[40]

The *devotio moderna*, for example, exerted a lasting influence on the spread of Christian or biblical humanism, which arose as a symbiosis of Italian scientific humanist methods and the Christian spiritual ideals, and demonstrates Europe's great cultural openness in the fourteenth and above all the fifteenth century. Although the Reformation was long considered an era of cultural transfer, one would be hard pressed to find a period before that was as open as the fifteenth century to cultural exchange in the Mediterranean region, but also between southern, western and central Europe. At that time scholars, artists and artisans shared scientific knowledge and cultural goods on a global scale for the first time in personal encounters and commissions but also with the aid of manuscripts and the new printed medium of the book.

Although the Gothic style had already put its characteristic stamp on Europe, it was not until the expansion of Italian architecture and literature during the Renaissance that a European culture arose, which was enriched equally by Netherlandish panel painting and the Franco-Flemish vocal music of the *ars nova*.

The need for 'Europeanisation' through culture was especially great in the expanding states of east-central and eastern Europe, which, like

Hungary, Poland or Russia, recruited Italian architects and sculptors to demonstrate the prestige of their rulers.

This process of social and cultural expansion was surely not a one-way street leading straight to the modern era. The plague or the so-called crisis of the late Middle Ages represented quite significant stumbling blocks along the way. As a consequence, some historians have interpreted the late Middle Ages as a period of depression. In doing so, they overlook the fact that the crisis affected different European countries to varying degrees, just as the innovations of the thirteenth, fourteenth or fifteenth centuries evoked varied responses. I shall treat this diversity of an expanding Europe below in both the country chapters and those devoted to structural issues.

Notes

1 Heimpel, 'Europa und seine mittelalterliche Grundlegung'; Fischer, *Oriens-Occidens-Europa*; Hay, *Europe: The emergence of an idea*; Barraclough, *European unity*.

2 Karageorgos, 'Der Begriff Europa', 141–50, 163–4; Wieczorek and Hinz (eds), *Europe's centre around AD 1000*; Boia, 'Les frontières de l'Europe'.

3 Le Goff, *L'Europe est-nelle née au Moyen Age?*; Mitterauer, *Warum Europa?* Other historians like Walter Laqueur even spread gloom and doom, as in his 2007 *The last days of Europe*.

4 Reuter, 'Medieval ideas of Europe'; Fernández-Armesto, 'A European civilization'. See also Burke, 'Did Europe exist before 1700?', and 'How to write a history of Europe'.

5 Fischer, *Oriens*, 115; Hay, *Europe*, 51–2.

6 Schneidmüller, 'Die mittelalterlichen Konstruktionen Europas'. The expert in this area is doubtless Klaus Oschema, whom I thank for letting me read a number of his as yet unpublished essays. See Oschema, 'Der Europa-Begriff', as well as 'Europa in der mediävistischen Forschung', 'Eine Identität in der Krise', 'Medieval Europe – object and ideology' (forthcoming), and 'L'idée d'Europe et les croisades'.

7 Piccolomini, 'Aufruf zum Kreuzzug', 40–2, 11. For the original Latin, see Piccolomini, *Opera quae extant omnia*, 678–89.

8 On the idea of Europe, see Schmale, *Geschichte Europas*, 17–19, 28–32. On the Middle Ages, see Schneidmüller, 'Die mittelalterlichen Konstruktionen Europas', 5–24; Hiestand, '"Europa" im Mittelalter'; and Karageorgos, 'Der Begriff Europa'.

9 Oschema, 'Der Europa-Begriff', 191–235, here 222–6.

10 William of Malmesbury, *Gesta Regum Anglorum*, Vol. 1, 600. Cf. Oschema, 'Eine Identität in der Krise', 28–30.

11 Oschema, 'L'ideé d'Europe et les croisades', 16.

12 Isidor of Seville, *Etymologiarum sivi originum libri*, IX, 2. The quotations are from Hiestand, '"Europa" im Mittelalter', 33.

13 Oschema, 'Der Europa-Begriff', 200–4.

14 Menut (ed.), *Maistre Nicole Oresme*, 146–50.

15 Fuhrmann, *Europa*, 17–21.
16 Kéry, 'Pierre Dubois'.
17 On the concept of Poděbrady, see Monnet, 'Le projet de federation de Georges de Podiebrad'.
18 Oschema, 'Identität in der Krise', 33–5.
19 Oschema, 'Der Europa-Begriff', 229–30.
20 Gautier Dalche, *Carte marine et portulan au XIIe siècle.*
21 Motzo, *Il compasso da navigare.*
22 Verlinden and Schmitt (eds), *Ursprünge der europäischen Expansion*, 57–8.
23 Reichert, *Erfahrungen der Welt*, 227–8.
24 Verlinden, 'Boudewijn van Hennegouwen', 122–9; Jackson, 'William of Rubruck in the Mongol Empire'.
25 Marco Polo, *The description of the world*; Rachewiltz, 'Marco Polo went to China'; Larner, *Marco Polo and the discovery of the world*; Latham (ed.), *The travels of Marco Polo.*
26 Pegolotti, *La pratica della mercatura.*
27 Cattaneo, 'Fra Mauro', 19–48, and Gentile, 'Umanesimo e cartografia', 3–18, both in Ramada Curto, Cattaneo and Ferrand Almeida (eds), *La cartografia europea.*
28 Abulafia, *The discovery of mankind*, 306–13.
29 Abulafia, 'Introduction: Seven types of ambiguity'.
30 Ibid.
31 Jenks, 'Von den archäischen Grundlagen', 38–9.
32 Erlen, *Europäischer Landesausbau.*
33 Jenks, 'Von den archäischen Grundlagen', 39–40.
34 Dyer, *Making a living in the Middle Ages*, 344–9.
35 Keller, Grubmüller and Staubach (eds), *Pragmatische Schriftlichkeit.*
36 North (ed.), *Kommunikationsrevolutionen*; Eisenstein, *The printing press as an agent of change.*
37 Melis, 'Intensità e regolarità'.
38 Dohrn-van Rossum, *Die Geschichte der Stunde*, 106–63; Dyer, *Making a living*, 318; Behringer, *Im Zeichen des Merkur*, 55.
39 Dyer, *Making a living*, 322–3.
40 Oberman, *The two Reformations*, 17–19, and 'The long fifteenth century', 1–18.

PART I

The history of the European states, 1250–1500: Countries and regions

1

The British Isles and Ireland

1.1 England: The emergence of a national kingdom

In the late Middle Ages, England's territory became increasingly English. The English and French Crowns had been closely connected since 1066, when William of Normandy conquered England, and only in the course of the Hundred Years War would the two kingdoms distance and emancipate themselves from one another. In the thirteenth century, the French kings laid claim to part of England's dominions in northern France (Normandy). The king of England remained in possession of Gascony, however, albeit as a vassal of the French king (1259 treaty of Paris).

The French King Philip IV, known as the Fair, sought to undermine English influence in the south of the country by encouraging English subjects in France to appeal directly to Paris. In this way, Gascony became a continual bone of contention, which led to war between the two countries in 1294. French ambitions toward Flanders, which was closely tied to England through the woollen trade, created another centre of conflict. While England stood by Flanders, the French King supported Scotland against English expansion.[1] These conflicts could only be resolved if both monarchs succeeded in establishing 'national' kingdoms without foreign dependencies. In order for this to happen, however, the dynasty in England had first to become English.

Henry III (1216–72) lived in a wholly French world. His parents were of French origin, he surrounded himself with French advisors at court, married Eleanor of Provence and spoke French. He reigned, however, at a time when Robert Grosseteste and Roger Bacon were advancing English scholarship and tendencies toward cultural isolation from the Continent were increasing in England. Parallel to this growing cultural autonomy, a process of 'parliamentarising' political structures also began. In response to the monarchs' permanent need for money, the English baronage developed representation to limit the king's power. In 1265 a parliament was convened in which for the first time two knights of each shire and two burgesses of each borough attended as representatives. This development stabilised in the fourteenth century. Although Edward III (1327–77) was the first king to speak English well, his grandfather Edward I (1272–1307) had already set the course for future development. Edward I had recognised that a successful kingdom relied on the successful exploitation of economic resources in consensus with Parliament. Edward I, who was permanently at war with Scotland and Wales, needed a steady supply of funds, which he initially received from Italian creditors until Parliament awarded him an export duty of 6 shillings 8 pence for each sack of exported wool in 1275. This raised his yearly revenues by several tens of thousands of pounds. He also regularly requested Parliament's assent to taxation, and Parliament eventually became a permanent institution.[2]

The consensus achieved between Parliament and Crown came with compromises, such as the expulsion of the Jews from England (1290) under pressure from the nobility. With this act, the monarch could portray himself as a Christian ruler over Christian subjects, and he found emulators, for instance in Philip the Fair of France (1306).[3]

Dynastically, the two kingdoms remained closely allied. The peace treaty of 1297 between England and France stipulated that the son of Edward I, the future Edward II (1302–27), should marry Isabella, the daughter of Philip IV. In 1311, the nobility forced a baronial regime on the weak Edward II, which he was able to cast off eleven years later by eliminating his adversaries. He was murdered in 1327 on the initiative of the Queen and her lover Roger Mortimer. The pair acted as regents, since King Edward III (1327–77) was still a minor, but he disposed of them in 1330.[4] Edward III sought to reach a consensus with the high nobility, and tried to integrate them into the kingdom with the aid of tournaments and investitures.

As the grandson of Philip IV, Edward III benefited from the end of the Capetian dynasty in France. In order to prevent him assuming the French Crown, the French devised so-called Salic Law, according to which the throne could only be inherited in the male line. Edward initially recognised the new ruler, a nephew of Philip IV, as King Philip VI (1328–50), but then changed his mind and in 1337 began a war that would ultimately last more than one hundred years.[5] At first, the conflict was centred on Flanders and France's ally Louis II, Count of Nevers. In a strike at French interests, Edward III had banned wool exports in 1336, which did great harm to the Flemish textile trade and sparked a revolt of the Flemish towns under

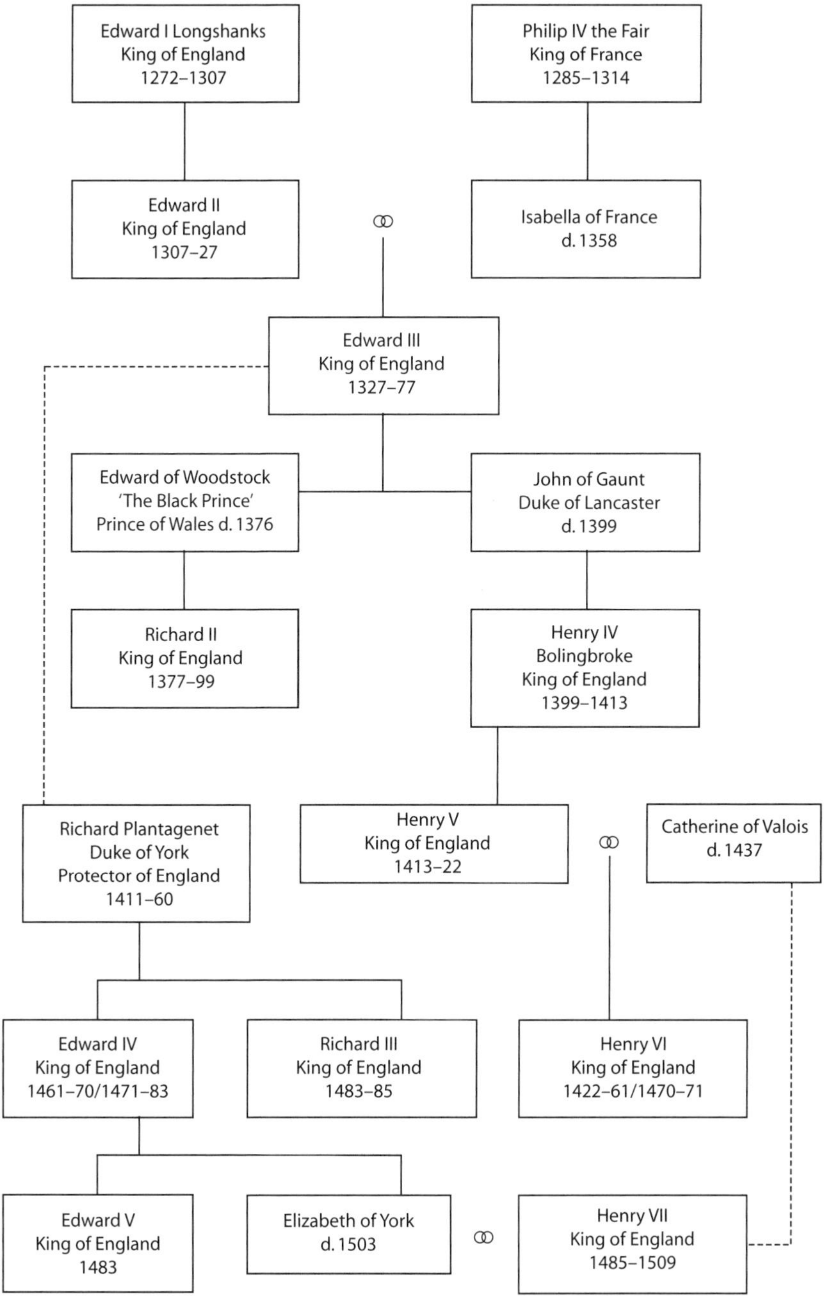

Genealogical table 1 The kings of England 1272–1509

Jacob van Artevelde. After the English fleet vanquished the French navy at Sluys in 1340, Flanders became an English ally and the King lifted the export ban on wool. The English troops proved themselves superior to the French (Crécy 1346), and succeeded in capturing Calais, a bridgehead that England would defend until 1558. In the years that followed, the English armies led by Edward III's son, Edward the Black Prince, would prove so successful on the Continent that they managed to capture even the new French King, John II (1350–64). In 1360 the English gained sovereignty over an expanded Gascony as well as a substantial ransom of 400,000 écus for John II. In exchange, Edward III renounced his claim to the French throne.

England had trouble holding onto these expanded dominions on the Continent, however, in the face of the aggressive policy of conquest pursued by the new King, Charles V. The Black Prince's introduction of a hearth tax met with local resistance in France, which could be broken only with massive force. This came in addition to numerous conflicts in the British Isles. Aside from wars against Scotland and Ireland, the English nobility also had to face Wat Tyler's peasant revolt (see 12.3). The Black Prince's son Richard II (1377–99), still a minor when he ascended the throne, also sought to consolidate the monarchy's position in the 1380s by strengthening his authority over the nobility and developing an efficient administration. He made himself increasingly unpopular as the century neared its end. One of his opponents was Henry Bolingbroke, Earl of Derby (house of Lancaster). When Richard challenged him over the inheritance of the house of Lancaster, Bolingbroke allied with another of the King's critics, the archbishop of Canterbury, and had the King imprisoned in the Tower. Richard was forced to abdicate, and Parliament made Henry Bolingbroke King, as Henry IV (1399–1413).

The new King was legitimised by Parliament and the Church. He won their support by taking decisive action against the followers of John Wycliffe.[6]

In the years that followed, his chief tasks were to unify the country and better coordinate policy in the previously dominant problem areas of war, royal service and finances. Military success stabilised the kingdom politically as well. Thus it was only a matter of time before the war against France flared up again. Henry IV's successor, Henry V (1413–22) saw himself as King of France, which he documented in the splendid victory at the Battle of Agincourt (1415).[7] His alliance with John the Fearless, Duke of Burgundy, who had brought large areas of France, including Paris, under his rule, also played a role. After his successor Philip the Good turned Paris over to the English in 1419, the Burgundians and Henry V agreed in the 1420 treaty of

Troyes that Charles VI would remain King of France, but that the Crown would fall to England after his death. The treaty became moot, however, with the deaths of both Charles VI and Henry V in 1422. Inspired by the Lorraine peasant maid Joan of Arc, the disinherited Dauphin Charles VII had himself crowned at Reims in 1429 and set out to recapture his kingdom. When Burgundy changed sides and became reconciled to Charles VII in 1435, England no longer had any reliable allies on the Continent. Although the English troops put up a vigorous resistance, Normandy fell into French hands in 1449 and the greater part of Gascony in 1451. Of England's continental possessions, only Calais remained. In England, meanwhile, these defeats exacerbated the conflicts at court as well as the baronial rebellion. Deadly rivalries between the houses of Lancaster and York led to the Wars of the Roses and the house of Tudor's rise to a royal dynasty.

The Wars of the Roses – so called after the roses on the badges associated with the two opponents – between the houses of York and Lancaster were an expression of the destabilisation of the kingdom. Since King Henry VI proved incapable of enforcing royal authority at home or abroad, groups of magnates usurped power.[8] The Wars of the Roses were fought by small private armies, which generally did not disrupt economic life in the towns or countryside. The casualties were relatively low, and English society continued much as usual. Because of the incapacity of Henry VI of the house of Lancaster, Edward of York managed to have himself crowned king in 1461. As Edward IV (1461–83) he gradually asserted his prestige with the states on the Continent as well. Instability returned with his unexpected death in 1483, however. His sons were still children, which his brother Richard of Gloucester used as a pretext to have himself crowned Richard III (1483–85). Richard, still a well-known figure today through Shakespeare's play, had his nephews thrown in the Tower, where they met their end. This sparked more struggles among the high nobility, who rallied to the last heir of the house of Lancaster. Henry Tudor, Earl of Richmond, had been taken to safety on the Continent just in time. He vanquished Richard III at the Battle of Bosworth and married Edward IV's daughter Elizabeth, thereby uniting the houses of Lancaster and York. Since he fathered legitimate male heirs (Arthur, b. 1467 and Henry, b. 1491), the new dynasty appeared secure. It had, however, to contend with pretenders to the throne. Lambert Simnel, son of an Oxford carpenter, and Perkin Warbeck, son of a boatman from Tournai, posed as Edward's sons and fought against Henry VII with some French and Scottish support. Thus it is only from the retrospective view of the sixteenth century that Henry's reign appears as a turning point in English history. For contemporaries,

Map 1 England at the time of the Wars of the Roses 1455–85

his blood bonds and thus his claim to the English throne were weaker than those of most other kings.

Nevertheless, Henry VII, like his successors, succeeded in extending the royal monopoly on the use of force and thereby curbing the influence of the magnates. Instead of the high nobility, he relied above all on the royal councillors and members of the royal household, who were dependent on him. He regarded the nobility as his proxies in local affairs. In this way, they could assert themselves as representatives of the country or local society. Further structural foundations of his power were cooperation with Parliament, the economic rise of the metropolis of London and the close ties between the Crown and the Church.[9]

1.2 The rise of parliament

By the end of the thirteenth century England had a far more extensive administration than those of other European monarchies. This process of institutionalisation continued in the years that followed, for instance through the strengthening of Parliament or the development of Common Law. 'Under normal circumstances, the constitution of late-medieval England was perfectly workable.'[10] An incapable and indeed incapacitated king, however, could prove a weakness for the constitution and the country, as had occurred during the Wars of the Roses.

The English monarchy still possessed a sacred character. Thus in the coronation ceremony the king was anointed with holy oil before the bishop handed him the sword. Afterward he was dressed in the *pallium* or cloak, crowned with the crown blessed by the bishop, and given the ring, sceptre and rod. In the view of many contemporaries, these regalia conferred superhuman powers on the consecrated ruler, which allowed him to cure scrofula by the laying-on of hands.

Despite this prominent position, according to the (few) existing political treatises the English kings remained bound by the law. They were also often called upon to listen to the counsel of the people or their representatives. Thus the royal justice John Fortescue distinguishes in his *On the governance of England* between undiminished royal dominion (*dominium regale*) in France and political and royal dominion (*dominium politicum et regale*) in England, where the 'people' were involved in decisions concerning new laws and taxes.[11] The participation of the people was to be guaranteed by the royal council, which by the fourteenth century was already distinct from Parliament, and encompassed the royal officers of state such as the chancellor and the treasurer as well as representatives of the high clergy and nobility. The councillors played an important role when the king was weak or still a minor.

The royal administration increasingly proved to be a stabilising factor. This included the Chancery, which in the late thirteenth century was capable of issuing hundreds of written documents each week and offers an example of the more frequent pragmatic use of the written word in a secular context. The chancellors were generally bishops or archbishops with many years of administrative experience. The keepers of the royal seals also occupied a prominent position. The most important office apart from the Chancery, however, was the treasury, which drew up the budget and controlled the accounts of tax collectors and the expenses of military captains alike.

Alongside this the king's household or Wardrobe developed into a significant instrument of royal rule. Originally the repository for the king's clothes, hence the name, it became the department of finance and accounting for the court, which administered the financial reserves for victualling, clothing and equipping armies. Kings like Edward I or Henry V accordingly used the Wardrobe mainly to fund their wars, and it was only in the late fifteenth century, in the light of the dire financial situation, that it waned in importance. The administration of the country's desolate finances was now left to the treasury, which sought to increase revenues by expanding the royal domains. The king also depended on the cooperation of Parliament to authorise new taxes. Parliament, often after laborious negotiations, consistently agreed to only a portion of the sum demanded. Thus, for example, in 1512 the royal chancellor William Warham asked for £600,000, but received only about £127,000. In addition, taxes amounting to one-fifteenth or one-tenth of movable property were only levied in times of extreme financial need, with current or planned wars against France consistently leading to the approval of disproportionately high taxation (1413/17, 1472/75, 1488/92).[12]

The Crown's financial requirements led to the institutionalisation of Parliament, which in the thirteenth century was still coterminous with the royal council. If the need arose, for example when a trial or decisions about scutage or subsidies were pending, the council was enlarged by a few bishops, archbishops, earls and barons. The term 'parliament' was occasionally used for these assemblies, for example in 1237, when a tax was requested in exchange for confirmation of the Magna Carta.[13]

In 1258 a committee of barons and royal councillors resolved in the so-called Provisions of Oxford that a parliament composed of fifteen royal councillors and twelve representatives of the baronage would henceforth meet three times a year. In the years that followed, these parliaments would become a stage for the King (Henry III) on the one hand and his baronial opponents on the other, who occasionally convened parliaments simultaneously at Windsor and St Albans. During the reign of Edward I, if the King was in the country, parliaments were regularly held twice yearly. They devoted themselves chiefly to responding to large numbers of written petitions. Under his successor Edward II, the participation of selected representatives of the estates in the assemblies now generally referred to as parliaments became increasingly important. As a consequence, the Parliament developed from an enlarged council to a body representing the kingdom that helped to make policy for the country, and after 1325 representatives of the shires or counties and boroughs were summoned to Parliament on a regular basis. They formed the commons, separate from the high nobility and clergy, who were summoned personally. This development was associated with a certain division of labour, with the commons submitting petitions as representatives of the country while the magnates decided upon them. The bills brought forward by the commons formed the basis of royal legislation. Thus, for example, sixteen of the forty-one general bills submitted during the first Parliament under Edward III in 1327 became law as statutes issued in the King's name. While at first the commons' bills were subject to the assent of the king and lords, in the fifteenth century a multi-stage process was instituted in which both the lords and the commons voted. The lords had only developed as an upper house in the course of the fourteenth century, when the lords spiritual and temporal began to deliberate in Parliament. While all members of the higher nobility, the peers, were summoned to Parliament, the number of lords temporal varied because of new creations, extinctions, minorities or service abroad. For that reason, after 1400 the lords spiritual, the archbishops of Canterbury and York, the fifteen English and four Welsh bishops and the twenty-seven abbots and priors normally made up the majority of the upper house.[14]

The sessions of Parliament at Westminster followed a fixed ritual. Parliament opened with a joint session of the lords and commons in the so-called painted chamber. Then the lords withdrew to the adjacent white chamber to deliberate, while the commons gathered in the chapter house or the refectory of Westminster Abbey. In cases where war or rebellion was on the agenda, the kings might find it advisable to convene the lords alone as Great Councils. The legislative function of the lords should not be underestimated. In some parliaments the lords proposed legislation although, according to a judgment of 1489, a bill submitted by the lords could not become law without the assent of the commons. Only the commons, as the representatives of the country, bound the king's subjects to the laws. Thirty-seven shires sent two representatives each, as did the parliamentary boroughs, often royal towns. Only London was accorded four representatives. The focus of parliamentary representation was in the south of the country. For instance, in 1471 only fifty members of the commons came from the north, while the rest of the 245 members of the commons came from the south. Only a few hundred persons in each shire were eligible to vote, of whom a few vied for parliamentary seats, if local magnates did not decide who would represent the shire in the commons. Deputies usually had well-established local networks behind them, and tended to be landowners, often in the king's service. The speakers of the commons also generally came from these circles, since the representatives of the cities and boroughs were usually lower in status than those of the shires. The cities were generally represented by their own burgesses, while for reasons of cost, the boroughs offered the places to patrons, many of them from elsewhere.

Most of the topics of parliamentary debate, such as the problem of taxation, had only tenuous connections to local politics. For that reason, the representatives who owed their election to a particular magnate still had a good deal of scope in their parliamentary activities. Ideally, Parliament was supposed to bring together ruler and ruled. Thus in dynastic matters Parliament frequently affirmed the status quo and followed the politics of the reigning monarch, albeit reluctantly at times, and in this way Parliament affirmed Richard III's usurpation in 1484, whereas the first Parliament of the reign of Henry VII revised the decisions of its predecessor. Apart from current political and dynastic affairs and tax legislation, Parliament also made decisions on the levying of export duties. These included export duties on wool and cloth as well as the tunnage duty on wine imports and the poundage duty on all other imports and exports. While customs duties were permanent, Parliament reserved the right to grant the kings subsidies for certain limited periods only. Richard II had already been granted the wool subsidy for life in 1398, however. In 1465, Edward IV was granted the proceeds of customs duties for life, and in 1484 Parliament made the same pledge to Richard III. Henceforth, kings could expect Parliament's assent to customs duties as a matter of course; Henry VII was granted these revenues in 1485 and Henry VIII in 1510 without further discussion.[15]

The ties between king and country (ruler and ruled) were also created through petitions, which private individuals submitted to Parliament, and which could attain legal status in the form of royal statutes. More important than this statutory law, however, was the 'unwritten' customary and case law known as Common Law.[16] The latter had been transmitted in part in written treatises, but usually orally through a highly developed system of precedent. The decisions of the three royal Common Law courts at Westminster contributed to this system, as did the training of jurists in the Inns of Court in London. Here future lawyers repeated the arguments of older legal cases in dialogue form while gaining insights into the practice of the courts of Westminster by observation. The future lawyers could also read the records of the administration of justice in so-called year books written in antiquated Law French, which had been compiled for study purposes since the reign of Edward I. Judges were not, however, bound by the decisions of their predecessors.[17] Since legal costs were also low, a relatively large proportion of the population made frequent uses of the courts. The jury system meant that the inhabitants of even the most remote boroughs had some knowledge of legal disputes. They were generally settled outside the courts or by the non-appearance of one of the parties. Although Common Law had become more rigid by the end of the fifteenth century, contemporaries lauded it as predating Roman rule and thus superior to all other legal systems, as we can see in John Fortescue's famous didactic treatise *De laudibus legum Angliae* (In praise of English law). In fact, the standardisation of the law began earlier in England than in most of the continental monarchies – not, to be sure, in antiquity, but in the thirteenth century.[18]

1.3 Agriculture and the expansion of trade

Culturally, socially, politically and above all economically, England relied on its own resources and was rooted in its own traditions. In 1086 more than three-quarters of all income derived directly from agriculture, but by 1500 this proportion had fallen to less than 60 per cent. While 90 per cent of the population still lived in the countryside in 1086, the figure in 1500 was still around 80 per cent.[19]

Land was more than merely a productive factor, though. It conferred status, power and wealth, but also brought with it a number of responsibilities. Agriculture was in every respect the very foundation of the economy, feeding the population in town and country. It produced and maintained the animals (horses, oxen) who provided power for the entire economy and supplied the manufacturing sector with organic raw materials such as wood, wood products, textile fibres, dye plants, wool, furs, skins, fat, tallow, wax, grain (among other things for the brewer's trade) and straw.

A portion of these raw materials, such as wool, skins, grain, wood and the metals tin and lead were exported or traded for other commodities such as wine and luxury goods. Up to the fourteenth century, England was still on the margins of a Mediterranean-dominated European economy. Only in the late Middle Ages, when the English began to process wool into woollen cloth and the Atlantic presented itself as an alternative trade region, was England increasingly integrated into the European economy.[20] This was not a linear process, however.

Because of its agrarian foundations, England, like all other countries in Europe, was subject to the old European cycle of a disproportionate development of population and arable land. Around 1300, with 4.5 to 5 million inhabitants, England reached its highest population up to that point. It had tripled since the era of the Domesday Book (1086). The markets supplying the population had also increased greatly. At the same time, the trades and manufactures, particularly the production of woollens and the trade in wool, had strongly expanded, and ports on the east coast such as King's Lynn and Boston had grown through shipping and the woollen trade into large cities. This economic upswing was brought to a halt by harvest failure, war, heavy taxation, and scarce money and credit in the 1290s. In 1315–17 serious harvest failure was greatly aggravated by Scottish raids deep into northern England and the English Lordship of Ireland. The European cattle panzootic of 1315–25 (which struck England in 1319–20) destroyed an estimated 60 per cent or more of the national cattle herd, including around half of all draught animals. The scarcity of working animals greatly deepened and prolonged the agrarian crisis. Grain prices rose and small tenant farmers in particular suffered in the famine, while the wealthiest demesne producers, such as the bishop of Winchester, were enriched by the sky-high grain prices of the famine years.

In November 1348 the plague broke out, first in London and in the spring of 1349 in rural England. In some regions the population fell by 50 per cent and more, but not all segments of society were equally affected. The plague gradually changed the structure of labour on the great estates, in particular. By the last quarter of the fourteenth century the high prices for agricultural produce and low wages that had made it possible to run estates profitably had become a thing of the past. The great landowners were compelled to switch from direct management of their demesnes to a leasehold system because the remaining peasants were generally unwilling to take over the land under the old conditions. The Peasants Revolt of 1381 also deterred landlords from re-imposing labour services and emboldened tenants to refuse to perform them. Since there was more land than there were peasants to work it, the size of peasant holdings grew and new forms of tenure (tenure at will or copyhold) replaced old forms of personal dependence.[21]

The focus of agriculture shifted from arable land to pasture. The rise of sheep farming in some regions, e.g. the chalk downlands of southern England, was accompanied by its decline elsewhere, e.g. much of the north of England, where it was cattle that gained most from the relative expansion of pasture farming. Also, increased sheep numbers on demesnes often came at the expense of reduced numbers on tenant holdings and vice versa.[22] As a result, England gradually became an exporter of wool and woollens. After the collapse of the domestic market more than 40,000 cloths were exported annually by the late fourteenth century. The demand for English cloth initially had a positive effect on urban textile production, but later promoted the emergence of rural manufactures. Domestic consumer demand rose again around 1450,[23] while the real upswing in wool and above all cloth exports only came in the 1460s. Wool exports via the staple of Calais increased only slowly, but exports of finished cloth rose by leaps and bounds. The devaluation of currency by Edward IV in 1464/65, in particular, lowered the price of English cloth on the Continent to the detriment of the competition in Brabant. Around 1500, exports had already surpassed the 80,000 unit mark (see Graphs 1 and 2).

English cloth was sold as far away as Spain and Portugal, and certainly in France. The most important purchasers were probably south German merchants who brought their metals to the fairs of Antwerp and Bergen op Zoom and sold English cloth in Germany and east-central Europe. Antwerp thus became the entrepôt for English, south German and later also Portuguese merchants. While cloth exports represented the greatest asset of England's foreign trade balance – wool exports declined again after 1500 – exports of lead and tin to the Continent also continued to rise. Many English ports participated in the growing export trade, but London profited most from the export boom. Thus a good 50 per cent of English cloth exports were shipped from the Thames in 1465–69 and nearly 80 per cent in 1524–28, much to the benefit of the privileged Company of Merchant Adventurers. To be sure, the Merchant Adventurers traded as individuals, but the Company chartered ships, organised loading and negotiated cargo prices and port fees in London.[24]

London's population recovered during this period, but it would be some time before it reached the figure of 80,000 from the period around 1300. Around 1400 the population of London had probably fallen to approximately 40,000, and only at the end of the century did the number

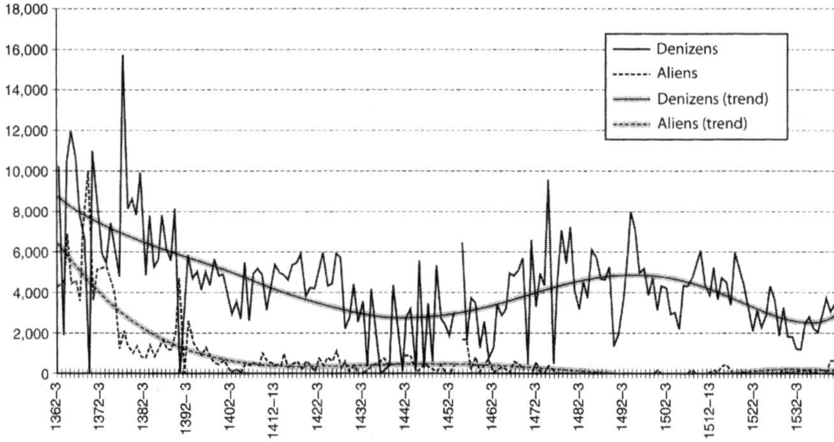

Graph 1 London wool exports in sacks 1362–1543

rise from 50,000 to approximately 63,000 (1535). In 1550 London probably again had a population of 80,000.[25] The disproportionate expansion of London's population was stimulated not just by the booming export trade; growth in domestic trade as well as London's role as a government centre attracted people to the city. London's demographic and economic growth was thus not representative of the kingdom as a whole. Southampton's cloth exports, for example, grew only as long as Londoners traded from there. Exeter, in contrast, profited from the revival of trade with Spain, Gascony and northern France. Other ports on the east coast lost out in competition with Hanseatic merchants and above all with Londoners.

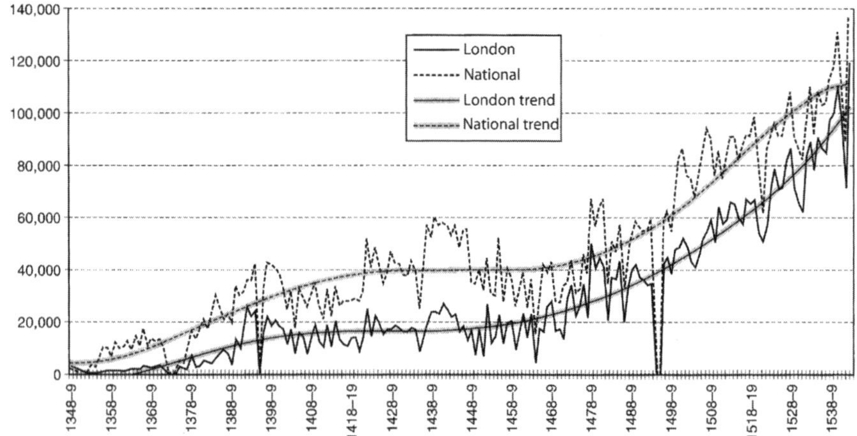

Graph 2 English cloth exports by piece 1348–1589

England's trade and shipping did not target the Continent alone. They also took advantage of the new opportunities offered by the Atlantic trade. In 1497, for example, the Venetian citizen John Cabot (Giovanni Caboto, *c.* 1450–98), having been snubbed in Spain and Portugal, set off from Bristol to find a sea route to the legendary Cathay. He probably reached the coast of Newfoundland, but died during his second expedition in 1498. Henry VII showed great interest in these early voyages and gave Bristol merchants, the so-called Society of Merchant Venturers, support for an expedition to Newfoundland. Initially, however, only fishermen benefited from the fishing grounds there. John's son Sebastian (1472–1557) tried to sail to Asia along the same route (1508–9). Increasingly, however, it was now intellectuals rather than merchants who expressed an interest in the New World.[26]

1.4 Society

The Norman Conquest long influenced English society, at least at the top. Even one and a half centuries after the invasion, the nobility were therefore more Anglo-Norman than English. According to the Domesday Book, twenty years after the Conquest, some 170 great barons closely allied with the king controlled 50 per cent of the land in England, while William the Conqueror reserved 17 per cent of the land as his own domain. The Church received one-quarter, and minor royal officials and landowners shared the remaining 8 per cent.

The barons differed according to their wealth and the size of their landed holdings. Unlike the dukes or margraves of the Holy Roman Empire, the Anglo-Norman aristocracy could not maintain their leading position in the long run. One contributing factor was the fact that the lands of these families were scattered geographically across a number of counties, if not across the whole country, which made it more difficult to consolidate their territorial power base. In addition, a large portion of the Anglo-Norman families died out in the centuries that followed. They were replaced by a new high nobility, created in some cases by the king, which arose alongside a gradually diversifying stratum of knights made up of 4–5,000 individuals. At the top of this relatively compact new political elite were the peers, including barons and eventually viscounts, as well as dukes, marquises and earls, some 70 families in all. What set them apart from the rest of the landed nobility was that their members were personally summoned to Parliament. Under them were the gentry, ranging from wealthy knights and squires at the top to gentlemen at the bottom of the scale, where this landed aristocracy mixed with farmers. The members they elected represented the shire in Parliament. The gentry have been estimated at 2,500 politically significant families, with about 50–60 families per county.[27]

The high clergy – the archbishops, bishops, abbots and priors of the great monasteries – existed alongside the high and lower nobility. The lords spiritual not only wielded substantial power within the Church, but also sat in Parliament, served in the royal administration and were wealthy landowners. To that extent their interests were identical to those of the lords temporal.

The power of this small group of nobles, the lords spiritual and temporal, was based on wealth, privilege and the exercise of authority. All lords had some manner of retinue, whether servants and villeins or, in the case of the great earls and dukes, hundreds of servants, officials, knights and squires. The ties between lords and their dependents were created in a multiplicity of ways – oaths of loyalty and fealty, contracts of tenancy and fealty or particular service contracts. Some historians have used the term 'bastard feudalism' to refer to these specific characteristics of English society and politics.[28] Despite the power these nobles wielded they depended on the Crown to secure their titles and inheritance. The economic basis was landed property, whose extent varied widely and changed over time. According to a tax assessment of 1436, some 230 large landowners controlled around 20 per cent of arable land, while some 7,000 middling landowners used 25 per cent, the Church 30 per cent and the Crown 5 per cent. Smaller non-noble landowners with one or two estates worked the remaining 20 per cent of the land. The exclusive use by the high nobility reflected in the Domesday Book had thus clearly diminished in the intervening centuries in favour of broader strata of society.[29]

The peasantry had also changed markedly over the centuries.[30] While the majority of the peasant population, the so-called *villani*, *cottarii* or *bordarii*, were originally only partially free – they coexisted with a smaller group of bonded peasants or serfs (*servi*) – from the mid-fourteenth century, in the wake of the plague, the differences between free and dependent peasants waned in significance. Lords were now compelled to lease their land to serfs and villeins, which led to a social and economic levelling process within the peasantry. Many manors, however, saw an increasing polarisation of land ownership and wealth within peasant society, as some peasant families accumulated land and others opted for wage labour and industrial employment.[31] Such tenants were always well integrated into the village community, their status within which they could also improve by marriage. It was therefore mainly increased fiscal pressure that pushed peasants to rebel in 1381 (see 12.3). The revolt further promoted peasant mobility, and many peasants left their home villages in search of higher wages or better conditions of land use.[32]

For town dwellers, the plague opened up the possibility of rising into the lower nobility by purchasing land. The Church offered a very specific route to mobility, as the Black Death left many ecclesiastical livings vacant. In 1500, there were some 38,000 priests and members of monastic orders alongside 500 members of the high clergy. In 1300, the former figure had been 50,000. Education, in particular, could ease a clerical career. The weaver's son Thomas Beckington (*c.* 1390–1465), for example, became bishop of Bath and Wells. Even the sons of the serfs and tenants of ecclesiastical manors had opportunities to go to school and better their social position. Among the boys at Winchester College, for instance, were sons of peasant farmers, who went on to study at Oxford and thus had good chances of a career, even if only patronage led to benefices and higher positions.

Apart from the Church, the merchant profession also offered numerous routes to social mobility, which could take the ambitious well beyond the towns of their birth. Thus Michael de la Pole from the Hull merchant family of the same name became royal chancellor in 1383 and just two years later was created Earl of Suffolk. The average London merchant or draper from a middle-sized town was probably wealthier than many members of the gentry. In the fifteenth century, the export trade in particular promised substantial profits. Many merchants were involved in manufacturing as well. The social and productive structures correspondingly differed from town to town. While in Colchester, for instance, the textile trade was still dominated in the late fourteenth century by many small artisans, in the fifteenth century a process of concentration occurred. Weavers, carders and dyers became dependent wage labourers who produced on the putting-out system for merchants or other middlemen, the drapers. This development occurred within, outside and alongside guild structures.

Since the guild system emerged relatively late in England, smaller towns in particular did not have enough masters to establish a guild administration.[33] In London, in contrast, many tradesmen did not need a guild structure because the market there offered other opportunities. Where guilds were strong, they helped to balance the interests of apprentices, journeymen and masters or to resolve conflicts among producers, consumers and the municipal authorities. Besides guilds and fraternities, along with charitable giving, parish assistance, almshouses and the like performed an important welfare function in an era lacking in any systematic national system of poor relief. Furthermore, especially when they also served as religious fraternities, guilds played a central role in the cultural life of the towns. This included not just participation in processions, but also theatrical performances and other festivities.

Not all conflicts could be resolved in this manner, however. As elsewhere in Europe, tensions arose between the elite strata, the guilds and naturally also the urban poor, for example during the Peasants' Revolt of 1381 or Jack Cade's Rebellion in 1450. Disputes also exploded during mayoral elections when the candidates were tradesmen.

1.5 The emergence of an English cultural sphere

England's various cultural traditions repeatedly entered into a symbiosis with foreign influences. What, then, was specifically English about English culture, and did English identity grow in the course of the late Middle Ages? For centuries, English kings had ruled a unified realm whose institutions ensured loyalty to the Crown. Parliament and the Common Law, in particular, were recognised as the guarantors of a specifically English liberty. Despite this emerging English identity and a certain antipathy to continental monarchies, antagonisms existed, for example between north and south. The differences between English dialects were substantial, but by the fifteenth century a standard written language based on English as it was spoken in and around London had spread throughout the country. The advent of the printing press accelerated this process from about 1470. The tendency toward linguistic standardisation continued across the Scottish border as well. In Wales, the royal administration and marriages between the English and Welsh also changed the use of the Welsh language. Despite the widespread use of a standard English for royal documents, Latin remained dominant in diplomacy, the Church and jurisprudence. The use of Law French also persisted in the last, but knowledge of French was otherwise relatively limited in Britain by 1500. A strong process of Anglicisation had been under way since the time of Edward I.

The Anglicisation process is evident in literature as well, which in the twelfth and thirteenth centuries was more shaped by French influences than any other area. To be sure, in those days the English court was a literary centre, but this literature was written in French or Latin, not English. Only in the fourteenth century, with Geoffrey Chaucer (*c.* 1343–1400), did an English courtly literature emerge, but it continued to absorb continental influences. Thus the first larger work by the diplomat and royal official Chaucer, *The book of the duchess*, was still based on French models, while his later works such as *The parliament of fowls* and finally the unfinished

Canterbury tales reveal the influence of Dante and above all of Boccaccio. With his friend John Gower (*c.* 1330–1408), who wrote in Latin, French and English, Chaucer also became the protagonist of so-called Ricardian poetry, an efflorescence of English lyric poetry during the reign of Richard II. Chaucer's poems in particular influenced the English courtly poets of the fifteenth century, who continued to publish their works under Chaucer's name.[34] In Scotland, Chaucer retained his influence into the sixteenth century through the work of William Dunbar and Gavin Douglas. In the late fifteenth century, however, printed English literature increasingly had to compete with translations of foreign authors or adaptations of classical texts.

This development is clearly associated with the spread of humanism in England. Although the Duke of Gloucester's collection of ancient manuscripts and its donation to Oxford University in 1444 at first had little influence on university teaching, humanist training also developed in England from the 1470s. William Grocyn (*c.* 1446–1519), Thomas Linacre (1460–1524) and John Colet (1466–1519), in particular, all of whom had studied Latin and Greek as well as medicine and law in Italy, taught in Oxford after their return to England. In 1496, Colet introduced textual criticism using the example of the New Testament. This was very much in keeping with the ideas of Erasmus, who arrived in England for the first time in 1499, stayed again in 1505, and on several occasions between 1509 and 1519, teaching in Cambridge between 1511 and 1514. In 1517, the bishop of Winchester, Richard Fox, founded the humanist-orientated Corpus Christi College at Oxford, and one year thereafter Richard Croke, who had studied in Paris, Louvain and Cologne, began his lectures on the Greek language at Cambridge. From there the teaching of Latin and Greek spread to the grammar schools. This led to changes in spoken Latin, in which the Italian manner now became very evident.[35]

English authors composed their literary prose in Latin, as Thomas More (1478–1535) did his *Utopia*, and even the most important poet of the era, John Skelton (1460–1529), wrote in both English and Latin as poet laureate and later as *orator regius*. He also translated from the Latin. In the fifteenth and early sixteenth centuries, men of learning and politicians like Thomas Wolsey or the kings who transmitted an English identity to their subjects at home scrupulously cultivated their international status and eagerly adopted southern and western European culture. Thus those concerned for their reputation sat for one of the fashionable Flemish painters in Bruges. In the 1430s, Cardinal Henry Beaufort had his portrait painted by Jan van Eyck, while in 1446 the Suffolk nobleman and diplomat Edward Grimson was painted in the Burgundian style by Petrus Christus.

Altars were also commissioned from Hugo van der Goes, Hans Memling and other artists from the Continent.[36]

In comparison to English literature, English medieval architecture long appears to have been rather insular. It too, however, absorbed a variety of influences and recast them in a typically English manner. The most intense influences came from the French Gothic but, as numerous journeys to Rome or the Burgundian motherhouses of the Cistercians document, clerics from the Low Countries or the Rhineland also brought new inspiration to the country. The so-called decorated style, which influenced less the architecture than the ornamentation of fourteenth-century English churches, developed out of the reception of these models. An example is Ely Cathedral, which represents the kingdom of heaven in ornamental form with a wealth of decorative elements carved in stone. From the decorated style, which took up French ideas and reworked them into a specifically English style, the perpendicular style emerged in the final phase of English medieval architecture. The penchant for covering every surface with decorative elements was already widespread in the fourteenth century, but in the perpendicular style ornament became the absolute focus. This style continued to develop into the sixteenth century in both secular and ecclesiastical contexts, without any admixture of Renaissance elements. Examples are the chapel of Henry VII in Westminster Abbey and Eltham Palace in Kent or Oxburgh Hall in Norfolk. This artistic development is still visible today in the chapel of King's College, Cambridge.

Despite its strong indigenous traditions, England did not permanently resist Renaissance influences. The first objects to arrive were portable items such as Italian manuscripts, printed books and other *objets d'art*, and eventually patrons became interested in seeing these stylistic elements translated into sculpture and ornamentation. The Florentine sculptor Pietro Torrigiano was commissioned to design the tombs first of Henry VII's mother Margaret Beaufort (1511), and then of Henry VII himself and Elizabeth of York (1512). That is why we find an Italianate tomb in the wholly un-Italian setting of the Perpendicular chapel in Westminster Abbey. Cardinal Wolsey, too, planned Italian tombs for himself and Henry VIII, but they were never completed. Wolsey did, however, commission Giovanni da Maiano to create a series of Roman terracotta busts to adorn Hampton Court Palace. Apart from these signs of enthusiasm for the Italian Renaissance, which were stimulated by such mercantile companies as the Bardi and the Cavalcanti, French and Burgundian models also played a role in art and design. Paintings were not the only works of art imported from Flanders, but also tapestries from Bruges, Tournai or Brussels.[37]

In music, influences ran in the opposite direction, since composers like Lionel Power (1380–1445) and John Dunstable (1390–1453) were very popular on the Continent, and may have inspired Guillaume Dufay (1400–74) and Gilles Binchois (1400–60) to change their styles of composition. The careers of Power and Dunstable show some similarities, but their music differed markedly. Both spent most of their musical careers in royal service. Nearly all of their known compositions are settings of Latin liturgical texts, with a focus on the cyclical composition of the order of the Mass (*Kyrie*, *Gloria*, *Credo*, *Sanctus*, *Agnus*), as for example in Dunstable's mass *De gaudiorum premia* or in *Rex saecolorum*. This cyclical mass, which Power and Dunstable apparently cultivated intensively for the first time, set the standard for liturgical composition among their successors Walter Frye (1420–75), John Plummer (1410–84) and Robert Fayrfax (1464–1521). The creations of a number of lesser-known English composers reflect the whole range of musical offerings. The richness of English music can both be admired in the choirbooks of the colleges (Eton Choirbook of 1490–1502, Lambeth Choirbook of 1510 and Caius College Choirbook of 1520) and enjoyed in the bravura performances of the great chapel choirs.[38]

1.6 Ireland

After an Anglo-Norman invasion from South Wales into Ireland in 1169, the 1175 Treaty of Windsor divided Ireland between Henry II and Rory O'Connor, high king of Ireland. Thus was established the English Lordship of Ireland, England's first and oldest colony. Henry granted Ireland to his youngest son, John. When John became king in 1199 the Irish Lordship therefore became part of the English realm. It was John who built Dublin castle, established an English-style administration, introduced English law and minted the first Irish coinage. Large numbers of English settlers were also lured to Ireland by the prospects of cheap land and improved social status. For its first 100 years, the Lordship of Ireland was a runaway success story. It was accompanied by far-reaching ecclesiastical reforms within the conquered and occupied territories. Thus was initiated England's long and tortured involvement with Ireland and the internal divisions and dichotomies within Irish society that have persisted to this day. It was Edward I who neglected, exploited, and disastrously weakened the Lordship of Ireland in his quest to create a single Empire of Britain via the conquest of first Wales and then Scotland.[39] He drew upon Irish money, men and provisions to advance his territorial and political ambitions first

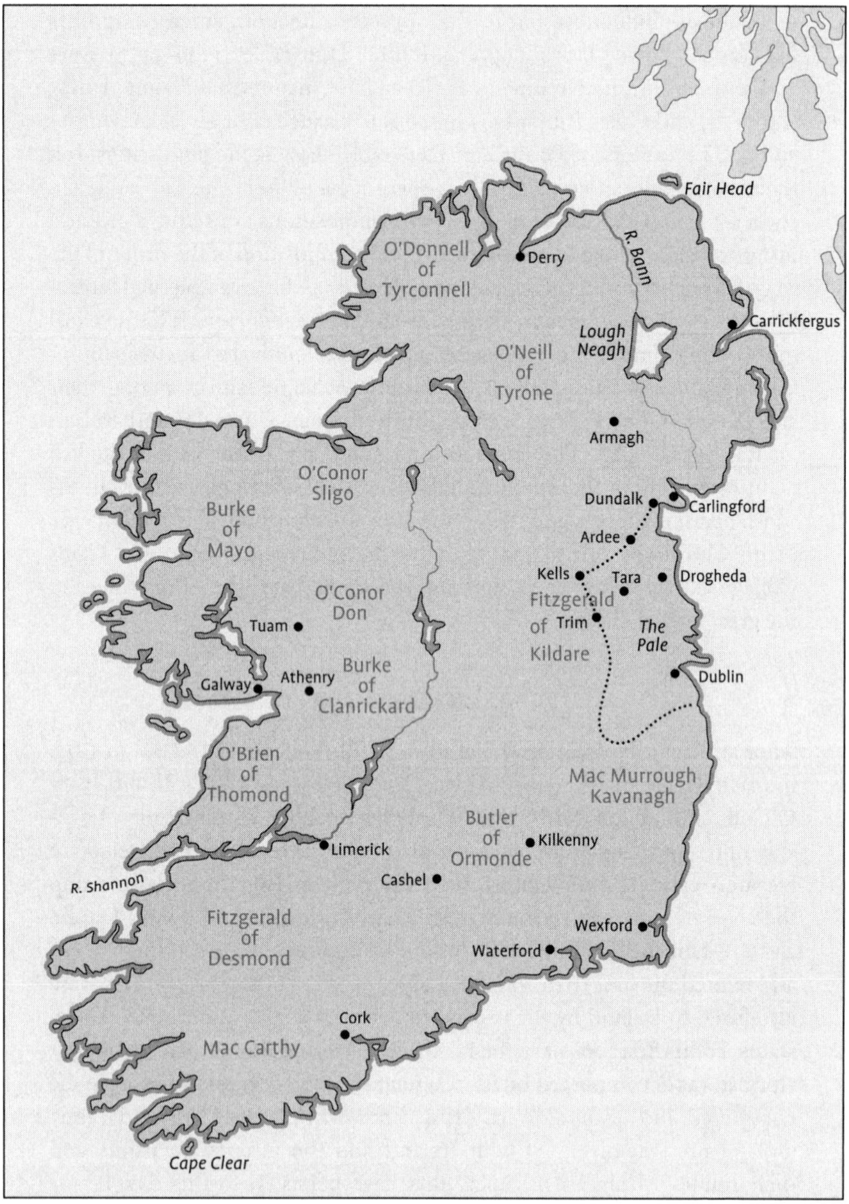

Map 2 Ireland in the fifteenth century

in Wales and then in Scotland. Despite the English incursion into lowland Scotland, the Scots preserved their independence.

By the late thirteenth century, the Anglo-Norman settlement of Ireland was in decline since the population was insufficient to expand settlements and the English Crown was not in a position to support the conquest militarily because of commitments in Scotland and France. The Gaelic Irish, or rather their leaders, used this situation to recapture territories occupied by the Anglo-Normans. The relative strength of the Gaelic Irish on the one hand and the several-generation-long presence of the Anglo-Normans on the other rendered a political, social or ethnic integration impossible.

A Dublin-based parliament of the English Lordship of Ireland established legal apartheid, making only the Irish of Anglo-Norman origin subject to Common Law. This population group was then advised to distinguish themselves in appearance from the Gaelic Irish, who were excluded from the use of Common Law. Fears of assimilation were substantial. The first half of the fourteenth century was marked by the Scottish invasion of 1315–18 that devastated the Lordship of Ireland and compounded the social and demographic effects of bad weather and crop failures. Ireland's cattle-based economy was also seriously affected by the cattle panzootic of 1321–25.

Although the Scottish enterprise ended in 1318, Anglo-Irish rule profited little from this withdrawal in the fourteenth century. The drastic fall in population – from 1.4–2 million around 1300 to 700,000–1 million around 1400 – changed Ireland socially, economically and also politically. Central political, administrative and legal control could not be maintained because of under-population. The fragmentation of the country continued apace, as is evident in the growth of Gaelic influence in the fourteenth and fifteenth centuries. This rise in Gaelic Irish power and culture derived from the unbroken tradition of clan and family rule and was fostered by the dependence of Anglo-Irish domination on cooperation with the Gaelic Irish lords. Contrary to the hopes of the English Crown, the Anglo-Norman elites even succumbed to Gaelicisation, as expressed in a preference for bards and Gaelic musicians and even for the Gaelic language and dress. To be sure, the Anglo-Irish parliament sought to counter this trend with the 1366 Statute of Kilkenny, which forbade marriage, concubinage and fosterage between the Anglo-Irish and Gaelic Irish. This prohibition, however, like stipulations concerning the use of the Irish language and customs, only serves to show how far the assimilation process had already gone. The Irish Church played a particular role here. While in the English

Lordship ecclesiastical reforms such as the establishment of parishes, clerical celibacy and the advent of continental religious orders had made significant progress, in the north and west, where older religious traditions persisted with a continuity of ancient sites, rituals und superstitions, little changed. In the fourteenth and fifteenth centuries it was still common here for priests to marry and to pass their parishes on to their sons. People also married outside the Church and divorce was apparently not uncommon, even spreading to all parts of Ireland. So the dichotomy within the Irish Church mirrored the dichotomy within Irish society.[40]

Economically, the decrease in population made itself felt in lower agricultural production and the expansion of pastoralism as well as the decline in trade and the urban economy. On the one hand, the towns were disproportionately affected by the plague, while on the other Ireland's declining population had less need of urban services. As a consequence, many smaller towns disappeared in the fourteenth and fifteenth centuries, and the remaining ones shrank in size. Ireland's share of international trade also fell. Flanders no longer had any demand for rough Irish wool, which now had to compete on the European market with high-quality English and Scottish wool. The other products of the pastoral economy, such as skins and pelts, also offered no advantage. Only fish exports (herring and salmon) proved to be a growth sector, although herring was caught by foreign fishermen and brought to shore on the west coast of Ireland.

Political structures were only weakly developed. The will and ability of regional clan leaders to enforce their power claims militarily determined the political balance of power. The Anglo-Irish territorial lords could only assert their status by paying protection money to the Gaelic provincial rulers. Despite several attempts to reassert English domination in periods of armistice on the Continent, by the mid-fifteenth century the territory under Anglo-Irish rule had shrunk to a small area in the east around Dublin, the so-called Pale.

In the second half of the fifteenth century, the Wars of the Roses over the English throne overshadowed conditions in Ireland. The 5th Earl of Ormond supported the house of Lancaster, while the house of York enjoyed the backing of the 7th Earl of Kildare. These conflicts fostered the self-confidence of the Anglo-Irish lords, who were loath to involve themselves unconditionally in English power struggles. Thus in 1460, the Anglo-Irish parliament at Drogheda declared its independence from the English Parliament. Though subject to the English Crown, they were only bound by the regulations and laws of the realm to the extent that the Irish parliament also assented to them. After the victory of the house of York, the 7th Earl of Kildare, Thomas Fitzgerald, became governor of Ireland in 1462, expanding his power by building clientele relationships with both Gaelic and Anglo-Irish lords. Thus after the victory of the Lancastrians in 1485, the Kildares could continue to maintain their position. To be sure, Henry VII tried to cement English rule in Ireland through his envoy Edward Poynings, but he, too, found himself compelled to accept the existing power structure and reaffirm the position of the Earls of Kildare in 1496. They would hold onto this position largely undisturbed until being toppled in 1534.[41]

1.7 Scotland

Unlike the political structure of Ireland, that of Scotland in the thirteenth century appears comparable to that of England. The country was a unified hereditary monarchy whose aristocracy had Anglo-French leanings. The kings sought connections in and also married into society south of the border. Nevertheless, they could not prevent the English monarchs from meddling in disputes over the succession. Scottish magnates also formed alliances with the English king to press their interests. Thus for example they offered the Scottish Princess Margaret in marriage to the future Edward II, heir to the English throne, but the plan was thwarted by her early death in 1290. Edward I consequently claimed feudal suzerainty and the right to decide on potential successors to the throne. Since Edward's candidate John Balliol did not function as the King expected and entered into an alliance with France, Edward I and later his son tried to assert English interests several times by invading Scotland. The new King, Robert Bruce, however, achieved Scottish independence in 1314 through victory at the Battle of Bannockburn. It was recognised in 1324 by the Pope and in 1328 in the Treaty of Edinburgh.[42] This re-established the Scottish monarchy, which after the extinction of the new royal line in 1371 fell to the hereditary stewards. This dynasty, the Stuarts, would endure until 1702 and rule both Scotland and later England.

This was not the end of conflicts with England, however. As France's allies in the Hundred Years War, Scottish troops fought frequently on the Continent. In the fifteenth century the events of the war shifted largely to the French mainland, while relative calm reigned in Britain, which helped to stabilise the Scottish kingdom under James III and James IV. In 1468/69 Scotland acquired the Orkney Islands as part of the dowry of Margaret of Denmark. The marriage between James IV and Margaret Tudor, daughter of Henry VII, temporarily improved the relationship between England

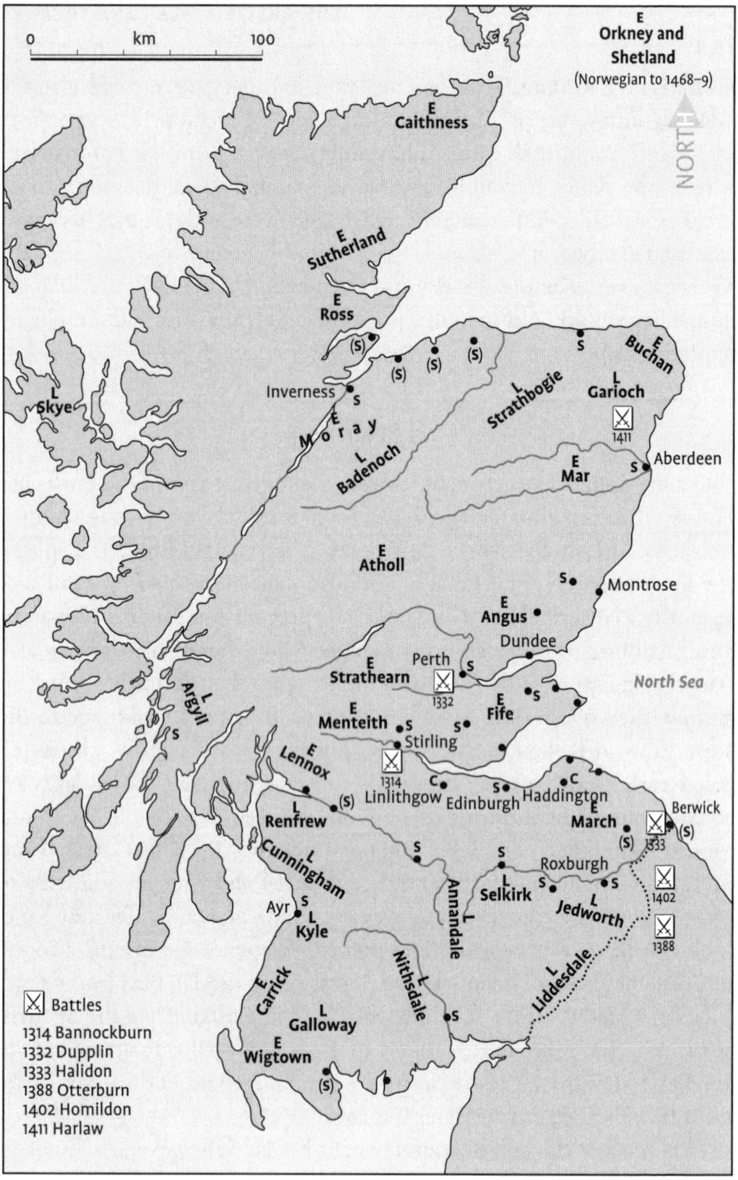

.... Inter-regional boundary (to 1468 excluding Berwick)

E Earldom

L Lordship

• Important burgh, either administratively or commercially

S Seat of a sheriff (except in sheriffdom of Argyll)

(S) Seat of a sheriff for part of the period, or of a sheriffdom incorporated into an earldom or lordship

C Constabulary within sheriffdom of Edinburgh

Map 3 Fourteenth-century Scotland

and Scotland, which the confessional conflicts of the second half of the sixteenth century would disrupt again.

Despite such strong monarchical personalities as James III or James IV, political rule in Scotland remained largely decentralised.[43] The noble families were accorded substantial influence on both the regional and local level, as this was the only way of keeping their constant feuds under control. For the magnates, this freedom meant that it was unnecessary, as in English 'bastard feudalism', continually to seek new lords, especially since they owed their positions of power mainly to their provincial standing rather than to royal mandate.[44]

Scottish economic life was shaped above all by pastoralism. From the thirteenth century arable farming, textile manufactures, salt harvesting on the coast and coal mining also played a role. Accordingly, wool, cloth, hides, salt and coal were the most important export products. The overlap with the range of English exports is striking, although Scottish trade differed structurally from its English counterpart. While English merchants sold wool, cloth, salt and hides wholesale in the port cities of the Continent, the Scots distributed their products, for example their lower-quality woollen cloth, to individual retail customers. Thus in the hinterlands of the North and Baltic Sea ports a Scottish trading system developed in which pedlars supplied the rural population with all manner of everyday goods. Some of these Scottish traders would eventually settle in Poland or the duchy of Prussia in the sixteenth century.[45]

Notes

1 Keen, *England in the later Middle Ages*, 27–57; Prestwich, *War, politics and finance*.
2 Ormrod, 'State building and state finance'.
3 Stacey, 'Parliamentary negotiation'.
4 Keen, *England in the later Middle Ages*, 58–81.
5 Vale, *The Angevin legacy*; Rogers (ed.), *The wars of Edward III*; Contamine, Giry-Deloisin and Keen (eds), *Guerre et société*.
6 Taylor and Childs (eds), *Politics and crisis*.
7 Allmand, *Henry V*.
8 Griffiths, *The reign of King Henry VI*; Carpenter, *The Wars of the Roses*.
9 Chrimes, *Henry VII*.
10 Carpenter, *The Wars of the Roses*, 252.
11 Burns, 'Fortescue and the political theory of "dominium"'; Gross, 'Unending conflict: The political career of Sir John Fortescue'.
12 Britnell, *The closing of the Middle Ages*, 112–13.
13 Fundamental works on parliament include Harriss, *King, parliament and public finance*; Sayles, *The king's parliament*; Spufford, *Origins of the English Parliament*; Davies and Denton (eds), *The English Parliament*.

14 Brown, 'Parliament, *c.* 1377–1422', 116.
15 Britnell, *The closing of the Middle Ages*, 115.
16 Caenegem, *The birth of the English common law.*
17 Baker, *The legal profession.*
18 Baker, *The legal profession*; Fortescue, *De laudibus legum Angliae*, 38–40; Britnell, *The closing of the Middle Ages*, 167–70.
19 Fundamental here are Hallam, *The agrarian history of England and Wales II*; Miller (ed.), *The agrarian history of England and Wales III.*
20 Campbell, 'England, Scotland and the Hundred Years War'.
21 Bailey, 'Demographic decline'; Hatcher, *Plague, population and the English economy*, and 'Mortality in the fifteenth century'.
22 Campbell and Overton, 'A new perspective', 76–80.
23 Dyer, *Making a living*, 322–3.
24 Carus-Wilson and Coleman, *England's export trade*; Carus-Wilson, *Medieval merchant venturers.*
25 Keene, 'London from the post-Roman period', 194–5; Barron, 'London 1300–1540', 396–7.
26 Sharp, *Discovery in the North Atlantic*, 39–56; Macpherson, 'Pre-Columbian discoveries and exploration', 66–9.
27 Given-Wilson, *The English nobility in the late Middle Ages,* 14. See also Coss, 'An age of deference', 31–73.
28 The term was first used by Plummer in his introduction to J. Fortescue, *Governance of England*, 15–29, here 15–16. McFarlane takes it up again in *The nobility of later medieval England.* For an overview of the scholarly debate, see Hicks, *Bastard feudalism.*
29 For an overview, see Rigby, *English society in the later Middle Ages*, 17–144.
30 Campbell, 'The land'; Raftis, *Peasant economic development*, 65–78.
31 Whittle, *The development of agrarian capitalism,* 167–224.
32 Fryde and Fryde, 'Peasant rebellion', 768–97.
33 Kermode, 'The greater towns', 450–1.
34 Rigby, *Chaucer in context.*
35 Schoeck, 'Humanism in England'.
36 Richmond, 'The visual culture of fifteenth-century England', 188–9.
37 Coldstream, 'Architecture'; Sicca, 'Consumption and trade'.
38 Sandon and Page, 'Music'.
39 Davies, *The first English Empire.*
40 Simms, 'Bards and barons'; Nicholls, *Gaelic and Gaelicised Ireland*; Duffy, Edwards and Fitzpatrick (eds), *Gaelic Ireland.*
41 Ellis, *Tudor Ireland*, 85–108.
42 Duncan, 'The war of the Scots'.
43 MacDougall, *James III*, and *James IV.*
44 Wormald, 'Scotland 1406–1513', 527–8.
45 Rorke, 'English and Scottish overseas trade'; North, 'The role of Scottish immigrants'.

2

France

2.1 A European power in the making

The rise of the French kingdom to a national monarchy began under Philip II Augustus (1180–1223) and was brought to a preliminary conclusion by his grandson Louis IX (1226–70). Commonly known as Saint Louis, he strengthened centralised royal power by expanding the *parlement* of Paris as a royal law court and thus an instrument for the juridification of his own rule. Louis also succeeded in establishing French feudal suzerainty over the English possessions in Gascony. The great prestige he enjoyed in Europe also transferred to France, which for a time was even accepted as an arbitrator in dynastic disputes. His personal piety and close ties to the papacy were evident in his participation in the Sixth Crusade, during which he fell captive to the Arabs. Freed upon payment of a ransom, he took part in the Seventh Crusade and died at Tunis in 1270. This circumstance contributed to his posthumous reputation, as did the internal peace and economic prosperity that made Louis' reign appear as a golden age, particularly when viewed from the war- and crisis-ridden fourteenth century.[1]

His successors Philip III and Philip IV the Fair (1285–1314) were keen to preserve Louis' achievements, but above all to ensure France's rise as a European power. The country soon ran up against its own limitations, however. Philip III succeeded at first in securing the counties of Poitou and Toulouse for the French Crown through marriage. The interests of France and Aragón collided in the Mediterranean region, however, and Philip could not prevent Aragón from taking Sicily in 1282. French hopes of territorial expansion in the Mediterranean and on the English Channel proved illusory. Philip's son and successor Philip the Fair accordingly turned his attention to Flanders and English-dominated Gascony. As

Duke of Aquitaine, the English king was no more accepting of French suzerainty than was the count of Flanders. Both regarded themselves as de facto on a par with the French king and rejected the interventions of French royal officials in Flanders and Aquitaine alike. In this situation, Philip the Fair, having reached an agreement with Aragón, provoked war against England from 1294–97, and against Flanders between 1302 and 1304. While he was willing to reach a settlement with England despite military successes, he remained merciless toward Flanders. In 1302, the infantry of the Flemish towns dealt a stunning defeat to the army of French knights at Courtrai. Only after a subsequent French victory (1304) was a peace treaty signed in 1305 at Athis-sur-Orge, although tensions persisted between France and Flanders.[2] They were overlaid at times by conflicts between France and the papacy, however.

The conflicts with the Pope flared up in 1296 when Philip the Fair attempted to impose a tithe on the clergy. Boniface VIII responded with the bull 'Clericis laicos' of 24 February 1296, in which he affirmed the need for papal consent to taxation and threatened those clerics who paid nevertheless with severe ecclesiastical penalties. The King in turn prohibited the export of gold and silver coins in order to cut Rome off from the French clergy's monies. After an agreement was reached the following year, the dispute was reignited, this time by the excesses of the Inquisition in Languedoc, which made the King fear for his authority in southern France. The Pope then withdrew from all previous agreements and in the bull 'Ausculta fili' proclaimed the supremacy of the Holy See over temporal kingdoms. On 18 November 1302, he took matters a step further in the bull 'Unam sanctam', in which he postulated not just the primacy of the Church over secular princes, but also the power of the Pope over the Church and the world. It was only a matter of time before Boniface VIII excommunicated the French King.[3] The King pre-empted this act, however, by declaring himself the defender of the Church against a pope unworthy of the office and by summoning the latter to a council by force of arms. Boniface VIII did not survive long after this humiliation, and when his successor Benedict XI also died after only one year in office, the cardinals elected the archbishop of Bordeaux, Bertrand de Got, to be the new Pope, Clement V. Failing to assert his authority in Rome, he established himself at Avignon in 1309.[4]

Avignon, originally a stopgap measure, soon became a permanent institution.[5] The papacy fell under French influence, and the Holy See became quasi-French. After initial hesitation, Clement V supported Philip the Fair in his conflicts with the Knights Templar. The Order was accused of heresy,

North Sea
NORTH
England
London
Calais
Flanders
Agincourt (1415)
Crécy (1346)
Picardy
Harfleur
Reims
Caen
Rouen
Formigny
(1450)
Paris
Normandy
Brittany
Maine
Orléans
Anjou
Dijon
Touraine
Poitiers
(1356)
Poitou
Poitiers
Limousin
Bay of Biscay
Saintonge
Périgord
Bordeaux
Castillon
(1453)
Rouergue
Auvergne
Dauphiné
Gascony
Agenais
Quercy
County of
Toulouse
Bayonne
Armagnac
Bearn
Bigorre
0
km
200
Mediterranean
Territory under the rule of the house of Anjou in the late twelfth century
English territory after the Peace of Bretigny, 1360
Territory controlled by England, 1327
Territory under English control in the 1420s
Border with the Holy Roman Empire

Map 4 France in the Hundred Years War

idolatry and sodomy, and under systematic torture some knights confessed to these offences. Many members of the Order were burnt at the stake. When Clement V abolished the Order in 1312 there were no protests. The greater part of the Order's property and lands fell into the king's hands, but the Knights of Saint John and the Spanish orders also profited.[6]

Despite an initially favourable starting position, a succession crisis broke out soon after the death of Philip the Fair. Of his three sons, none survived him long – Louis X reigned until 1316, Philip V until 1322 and Charles IV until 1328 – and none had a male heir. An intensive search for uncles or nephews began. One possible candidate was Philip the Fair's grandson, the son of his daughter Isabella (sister to Louis, Philip and Charles), who in the meantime had ascended the English throne as Edward III. Philip the Fair's nephew Philip of Valois, the son of his brother Charles, however, seemed a more suitable alternative. He was the oldest male member of the dynasty and a French baron, who enjoyed the support of his peers and was recognised as King Philip VI (1328–50). Edward III did not yet harbour ambitions toward the French throne at this time, especially since he had yet to secure his rule in England and Aquitaine.

It was not until 1337 that the domestic political situation had stabilised and foreign relations changed to such an extent that Edward III dared to challenge the position of 'Philip of Valois, who calls himself king of France'.[7] The first theatre of war was Flanders, which was already weakened economically by the embargo on wool exports. In the wake of the rebellion by the artisans of Ghent, who elected the patrician and merchant Jacob van Artevelde captain general of the city, the Count of Flanders called on his French feudal lord for help. The French King thereupon decided to launch a naval assault, but the French fleet suffered a crippling defeat at the Battle of Sluys (1340). Edward III now ruled the seas and had gold coins known as ship nobles issued to mark this naval victory. After Van Artevelde was murdered that same year by the very people who had made him their leader, Flanders was lost as a possible ally. During its next venture in the mid-1340s, England concentrated on the French theatre of war and won a victory at Crécy in 1346. After the death of Philip VI in 1350 his son John II inherited the Crown. He owed his byname 'the Good' to his attentiveness to his clientele rather than any generosity toward the French people, let alone any outstanding qualities as monarch. Suspicious by nature, he frequently ordered the killing of nobles and proved unable to raise the funds necessary for successful military ventures. Militarily, everything that could go wrong for France did. The King could not prevent the successes of the Black Prince and his bowmen.

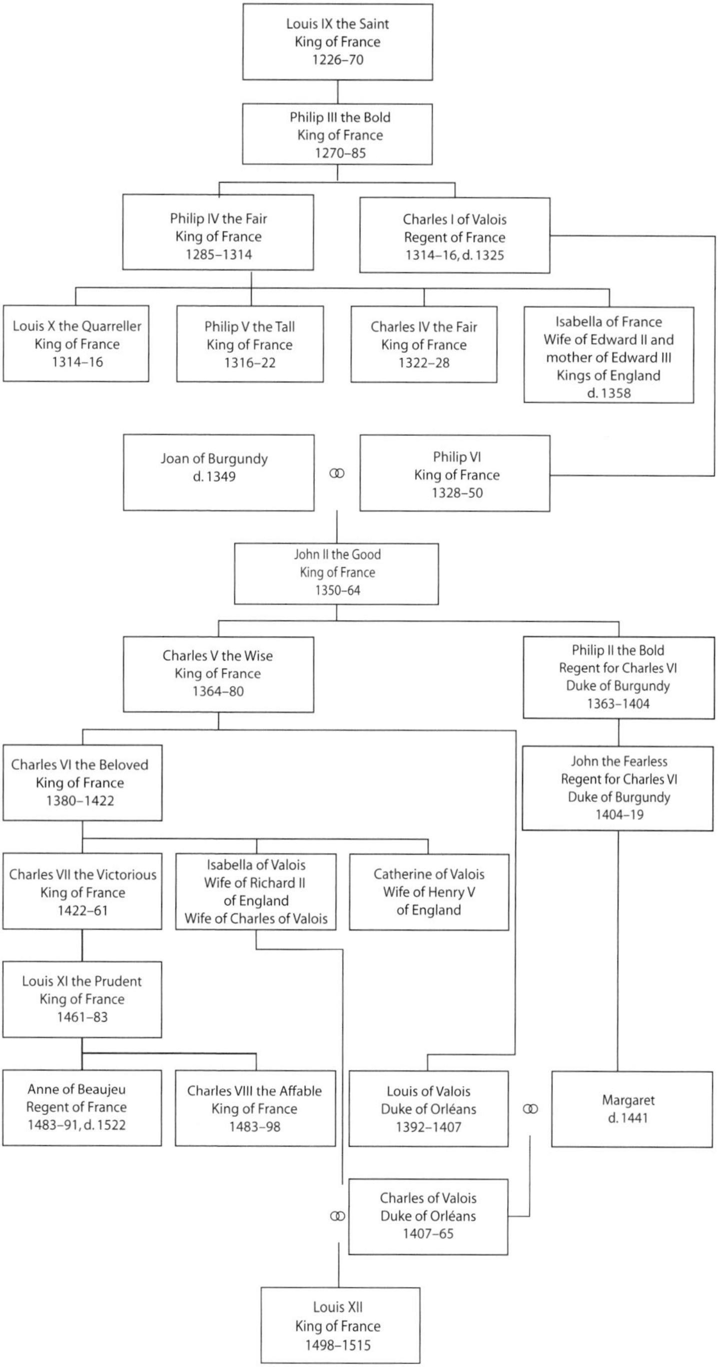

Genealogical table 2 The kings of France 1226–1515

Things went from bad to worse at the Battle of Poitiers near Maupertuis in 1356. John II of France was forced to capitulate and hoped to be ransomed. While he spent the years that followed in Bordeaux and London as a royal prisoner with special privileges, the Dauphin tried to assert himself against the opposition of numerous barons and to wrest agreements to new taxation from the estates general (*états généraux*) in order to finance the war. Reaching a settlement with England, including on the ransom for John's release, remained the foremost priority, however.

This situation of political crisis was accompanied by another area of conflict, the Jacquerie revolt. The movement, which began in 1358 as an uprising of rather well-to-do peasants in Saint-Leu-d'Esserent near Chantilly, spread within only a few days to the Paris Basin, Valois and Brie, and from there to Normandy, Burgundy, Lorraine and the Beauce. The peasants murdered nobles and other landlords, and found a leader in Étienne Marcel, a commoner critical of the King. He used the fervour of the so-called Jacques to plunder the country houses of Paris notables and nobles, for instance. Only after Étienne Marcel was stabbed to death by his enemies on 31 July 1358 was the way open for the Dauphin, the future Charles V, to enter Paris.

At the same time, there was at last movement in the peace negotiations. In London, John the Good accepted England's calls to surrender large sections of France, including Normandy and suzerainty over Brittany, which would have put France's key ports in English hands. The Dauphin, however, refused Edward III's request. An army sent to the Continent to enforce the English demands failed, however, to compel him to accept the imposed settlement. The 1360 Peace of Brétigny was a compromise, in which Edward relinquished his claims to the French throne and in return received an enlarged Aquitaine and Calais in the north. The ransom for John the Good was set at three million *écus*, for the payment of which high-ranking French hostages in London had to stand surety. John was released in October 1360 after a one-time payment of four million *écus*.

On his return, John the Good again began to dominate French politics. He succeeded in gaining approval for a hearth tax of three francs per household, the *fouage*, in order to put the kingdom on a firmer financial footing. In January 1364 he again travelled to London to stand in personally for his second son, who was still a hostage but had escaped. John died there in April of that year. After his death, further consolidating the French monarchy became a central priority. In addition, Charles V (1364–80) repeatedly sought to recapture parts of English Aquitaine. Despite a French naval victory under Genoese command near La Rochelle, the conquest of Aquitaine stagnated, since English cavalries were repeatedly sent to the Continent.

When Charles V died in 1380, his successor Charles VI was still a minor, so that his uncles, including Philip of Burgundy, enjoyed considerable power as the young king's guardians. Philip the Bold, who pursued his own interests in Flanders and Burgundy, continued his autonomous policies even after his nephew reached his majority. Thus he succeeded in arranging a matrimonial connection with the Wittelsbachs and thereby with the counties of Holland and Hainaut. In 1388/89 Charles VI began to rule in his own right, after dismissing his uncle. This ended the phase in which Burgundian and French interests coincided. Four years later, the monarch's increasing signs of madness imperilled French policy, which was in a process of consolidation. The conflict erupting between France's princes (Orléans versus Burgundy) made a unified front against England impossible. When Philip the Bold died in 1404, his son, John the Fearless, assumed regency for the mentally ill French king and entered Paris in 1405.[8]

France now had two rival governments, that of the King's brother Louis of Orléans and that of John the Fearless in Paris. The Paris *parlement* and the scholars of the University of Paris, in particular, supported Burgundy, because they expected reforms in the kingdom. This support dwindled with time, however, and John the Fearless could hold onto power only by murdering Louis of Orléans.[9] In these uncertain times, the English army appeared on the Continent in 1415 and vanquished the French troops at Agincourt. Now John the Fearless, whose men had not been involved in the fight against England, was the only one who had not been discredited. The King sank deeper and deeper into madness and the Dauphin Charles had become the puppet of another baron, Bernard d'Armagnac. Henry V of England continued to pile triumph on triumph. After partisans of Armagnac stabbed John the Fearless to death (1419), his son Philip (the Good) signed the treaty of Troyes with England in 1420. This alliance was directed against the Armagnacs and Dauphin Charles. The marriage stipulated in the treaty between Henry V and the mad king's daughter Catherine of France made Henry V at once the king's son-in-law and the heir to the French Crown. This treaty was to have no future, however, since both Henry V and Charles VI died in 1422, on 31 August and 21 October, respectively. The minor successor to the English King, Henry VI, claimed a large part of northern France through his uncle, the Duke of Bedford. The Dauphin ruled western, central and southern France. Philip the Good of Burgundy, who wisely enlarged his possessions, enjoyed a comparatively stable position.

In this situation, Joan of Arc, the Maid of Orléans, gave new impetus to the process of French unification.[10] At home in Lorraine a vision had told her to travel to 'France', expel the English and crown the Dauphin king at Reims. In March 1429 the Dauphin received her at Chinon, where she renewed his hopes of a strengthened French kingdom. Equipped with weapons, she made her way with a group of soldiers to Orléans, then under English siege. So successful was she in boosting the morale and fighting spirit of the besieged population that the English – hard-pressed by the French relief army – ended the siege in May. The Dauphin, given free passage by the Burgundians, could now set off for Reims, where he was crowned King Charles VII (1422–61) in July. Afterward he began negotiating an armistice with Philip the Good. Joan advanced on Paris at the head of an army but ran up against determined resistance from the English, the Burgundians and the Parisian populace. While the royal army successfully advanced into Normandy, Joan was occupied with smaller operations for the capture of fortified or the relief of besieged towns. She was taken prisoner in May 1430 and sold for 10,000 *livres tournois* to the English, who turned her over to the Inquisition. Charged with heresy in 1431 in Rouen, she only abjured her mission when threatened with death at the stake. As a repentant sinner she was accordingly sentenced to imprisonment in a dungeon instead. After recanting her abjuration only a few days later, she was burnt at the stake as a relapsed heretic and her ashes strewn in the Seine.

This opened the way for an agreement between France and Burgundy, which was reached in the 1435 Peace of Arras.[11] Philip the Good was able to adjust the boundaries of his possessions around Auxerre, Mâcon and Bar-sur-Seine and was freed for his lifetime from fealty to the French king. Now that Burgundy was neutral, Charles VII could set out to recapture the territories occupied by the English. In 1436 Paris opened its gates to the royal army, and in 1444 a five-year armistice was signed at Tours. Hostilities resumed in 1449. One by one, England's Atlantic possessions fell: Rouen, Caen, Cherbourg, Bordeaux and Bayonne. Calais remained as England's last foothold on the Continent. Now nothing stood in the way of the consolidation of the French kingdom, although it still had to contend with aloofness or resistance in the local duchies and counties (Brittany, Foix, Albret).

Charles VII's son and successor Louis XI, in particular, faced constant princely rebellions after his coronation in 1461. The princes rejected his 'reform programme', which aimed to centralise the (financial) administration and strengthen the urban economy and did not stop at meddling with noble privileges (taxation of noble property). In 1465 his opponents joined forces in a *Ligue du bien public* (League of the Public Weal). Aside from political demands such as the convocation of the estates general and the abolition of the *aides* (extraordinary taxes), the League's objective was to depose the King and install his brother Charles of France in his stead. The war unleashed by the League proved indecisive, especially since Paris supported the King for economic reasons.[12] Louis XI made concessions nonetheless, granting Normandy to his brother and parts of Picardy to Charles the Bold, Duke of Burgundy. In the years that followed Charles the Bold managed to consolidate his position, but despite a number of small but costly conflicts between Burgundy and France, resounding success eluded the future Duke of Burgundy. After his death in 1477 at the battle of Nancy and the early demise of his daughter Mary in 1482, the duchy of Burgundy as well as his possessions in Picardy, the Artois and the Franche-Comté fell to France, while Archduke Maximilian of Austria incorporated the Burgundian inheritance of the Netherlandish provinces (for example Flanders, Brabant, Hainaut and Namur) into the Habsburg empire.

Louis XI died in 1483 and his daughter Anne and her husband Pierre de Beaujeu assumed guardianship of the minor Charles VIII (1483–98). The estates general met at Tours in 1484. Among the reforms proposed there were ones benefiting the nobility, the Church and the common people. At the same time, the merchants and traders achieved the lifting of protectionist measures instituted under Louis XI. The central demand for a regular convocation of the estates as a representative body in the kingdom remained unsuccessful. The attempt by some princes to lend a reformist complexion to the new war provoked in 1485 (the *Guerre folle* or Mad War) also failed. The royal side took this opportunity to bring heretofore independent Brittany under their influence. Charles VIII then incorporated Brittany into the kingdom in 1491 by marrying the Breton heiress, Duchess Anne. Having assumed the regency in 1492, Charles VIII was eager for foreign policy successes. He began by concluding a lasting peace with England (Étaples, 1492), then restored Roussillon to the Catholic monarchs of Spain without recompense in the treaty of Barcelona. Finally, in the treaty of Senlis, he ceded the Franche-Comté and the Artois, which had been intended as a dowry in case of his marriage to Margaret, daughter of Maximilian of Habsburg. In return, Maximilian relinquished his claims to Burgundy. Having thus pacified his potential enemies, the Italian adventure could begin.[13]

The Italian campaign was about more than merely reviving old claims to Naples. Bolstered by the fantasies of his advisors, the King even dreamt of conquering Constantinople. What is more, in nearly every territory of northern Italy rivals of the local reigning dynasties hoped for French assistance in promoting their own political interests. The capture of Naples in 1495 went smoothly, but after the King returned to France the French army was annihilated by Aragonese troops. Naples was lost, but it was the beginning of a long-term French engagement in Italy. Louis XII (1498–1515), who succeeded Charles VIII, soon resumed his cousin's Italian policy. Initially and in the years that followed the focus was on Milan, where the old claims of the Visconti (Louis was a grandson of Valentina Visconti) were revived. For a time, the interests of Louis and Emperor Maximilian intersected in northern Italy in the face of the Holy League initiated by Pope Julius II in 1511, whose members Venice, Aragón and England joined forces under the leadership of the Holy See. This alliance, however, proved as short-lived as the French coalition with the Emperor. The new Pope, Leo X, sought reconciliation with France, and in 1514 Henry VIII of England gave the hand of his sister Mary in marriage to the widowed king. Louis XII died three months later, on 15 January 1515. He was succeeded by his cousin and son-in-law, also a grandson of the Visconti, who became Francis I. His renewed claims to Milan were rejected by Emperor Maximilian, Ferdinand of Aragón and the Pope. In 1515, however, France vanquished the opposing army at Marignano, which was made up largely of Swiss mercenaries. Milan was French once again, thus becoming a permanent bone of contention between the Habsburgs and France. In the 1516 Concordat of Bologna, however, France gained official sanction for its ecclesiastical semi-independence from Rome. Meanwhile, the perpetual peace with the Swiss cantons (or *Orte* as they were called at the time) made them long-term allies and a reservoir of soldiers for early modern France (see 4.1, 5.9).

2.2 Taxation and representative bodies

In the thirteenth century, kings, princes and the nobility began to expand their possessions and to consolidate their domains. By the early fourteenth century, the king possessed hundreds of provinces, and the princes and nobility sought to emulate him. The provinces were organised in administrative districts known as *prévôtés* (prevostships) or *bailliages* (bailiwicks) and administered by officials called *baillis* or *sénéchaux*.[14]

In the early fourteenth century, by contrast, the kings at first took only hesitant steps to extend their sovereignty beyond the royal domain. They limited the political and military independence of the smaller lords, whom they taxed heavily. Thus upon the death of a vassal the heirs had to pay a duty known as a mortuary in order to prevent the fief from reverting to the lord. The king also asked his vassals for financial assistance in addition to or instead of military service.

As war became a permanent state of affairs, warfare changed in the fourteenth and fifteenth centuries, and the importance of fortified castles and chivalric military service declined, the duchies and principalities had to establish new financial structures to maintain their mercenary armies, often trading fiefs for administrative and other support. Financiers (merchants) who reformed the territories' financial administrations were also rewarded with significant fiefs. Particularly in the field of taxation, the king and princes tried new tactics. While Philip IV relied on extraordinary *tailles* or *aides* in the royal domains, the princes also sought to secure their finances by levying the *tailles* in towns and villages. In Languedoc, Poitou and the Auvergne, for example, Alphonse de Poitiers levied a variety of extraordinary taxes such as *aides*, *subsides* or *fouages*, collecting large sums above all in the cities; Toulouse and La Rochelle, for instance, yielded 6,000 livres each. In the second half of the thirteenth century Alphonse's brother, Charles of Anjou, Duke of Provence, levied extraordinary taxes in nearly every town and *seigneurie* of his lands, which caused financial difficulties for some villages and cities. In addition, institutions such as the fairs in Champagne also earned a substantial income for their territorial lords, the counts of Champagne. This amounted to 60,000 livres a year in the 1280s, for example.[15]

In the fourteenth century, particularly the latter half, the balance of power shifted toward the kings. Thus the great lords were held directly and indirectly responsible for France's shameful showing at the beginning of the Hundred Years War. Instead of relying on the protection of the territorial lords, the towns organised and armed themselves, levying taxes to this end. In 1358 the Dauphin exploited the situation and placed all fortified cities under royal authority and jurisdiction. New taxes were introduced in 1355 and 1370; alongside the *aides*, the *gabelle* was imposed on salt and the *traites* on imports and exports. In addition, the royal *taille* was levied as a hearth tax. The new system of taxation gave rise to a direct relationship between the king and his subjects. The royal taxes were not levied everywhere, however. Thus the princes of the appanages (Provence, Bourbonnais, Bourgogne, Orléans and Brittany) occasionally refused the collection of royal taxes. Thus it was not until the end of the reign of Louis XI (1461–83) that most of the principalities were fiscally incorporated. The revenues from the royal domain grew parallel to this development, as became evident above all in the process of economic recovery in the second half of the fifteenth century. In this way, Louis XI was able to increase the proceeds of the *taille* from 1.2 million livres in 1462 to 4.6 million in 1481. The amount fell somewhat thereafter and stabilised for the next twenty-five years at an average of between 3.2 and 3.3 million livres, albeit with significant fluctuations from one year to the next.[16]

Unlike in England, the tax levy did not lead to a system of regular estate representation. To be sure, public debates repeatedly addressed the convocation of the estates general on questions of taxation, and the estate assemblies convened under Charles VII between 1421 and 1439 served the purposes of financing his war against England. The estates, however, did not exploit the king's predicament in order to establish themselves as an institution independent of the royal will. In the early fourteenth century Philip the Fair had convoked estate assemblies during his conflicts with the Pope and the Knights Templar, and in the years 1355, 1358 or 1413 the estates general sought to realise their reform ideas vis-à-vis the monarchy. Nevertheless, the assemblies of representatives of the entire country as well as regional assemblies remained extremely heterogeneous throughout the period.

The intervals at which the estates were convoked also grew longer in the course of the fifteenth century. Following the last assembly of the estates general convoked by Charles VII (1439), Louis XI convoked the first and last of his reign in 1468; after that, the representatives of the estates did not come together again until 1484. Since the resolutions of the estates general in 1439 had given Charles VII carte blanche for future tax levies, in tax matters he only convoked the provincial estates or the assemblies of notables – representatives personally invited by the king. This was also the preferred procedure of Louis XI, who met with the estates of the various provinces (1463–64). Accordingly, the convocation of the estates general (1468) can only be explained by the desperate political situation in which the King found himself (see 2.1 above). To be sure, in 1484, too, the public had demanded the convocation of the estates general, but the new King's guardians managed to suggest a modality for sending delegates to the estates general that did not weaken the position of the monarchy. On the one hand, the estates general consisted of elected representatives for the first time, and in some regions even the peasantry had participated in the election. On the other, royal officials whose loyalty ultimately strengthened the monarchy also played a significant role.[17]

Far more important as guardians of the constitution than the estates general were the *parlements*, especially the *parlement* of Paris. Saint Louis had also reserved for himself, as chief justice, the final word in judicial conflicts, and in the early fourteenth century the King claimed sovereignty and the administration of justice for the entire country. The royal council *(conseil du roi)* and the *parlement* were separated from the *curia regis* (royal government), and the *parlement* established as the highest royal court of justice. The *ordonnance* of 1345 divided the *parlement* into three chambers, the *grande chambre* (chamber of appeals), the *chambre des enquêtes* (chamber of inquiry) and the *chambre des requêtes* (chamber of petitions), which were staffed by professional councillors and met in certain rooms in the Parisian *Palais de la Cité*. Widespread acceptance of the court led to a flood of lawsuits in the early fifteenth century, which dried up after supporters of the Dauphin established a second *parlement* at Poitiers in 1418, at a time when Paris was in the hands of the English and the Burgundians. It was, accordingly, only through the reforms of 1454 that the Paris *parlement* was able to work again. At the same time, the founding of provincial *parlements* at Toulouse (1443), Grenoble (1456), Bordeaux (1462), Dijon (1477), Rouen (1499), Aix (1501) and Rennes (1554) took some of the burden off Paris. In a similar manner, provincial *chambres des comptes* (revenue boards) were also established to relieve the central Parisian *chambres de comptes*.[18]

2.3 Economic dynamism in the late Middle Ages

France was part of the secular cycle of European population development. While this goes without saying, the extent of actual demographic changes is open to speculation. A hearth count of 1328 for the French crown domains (without the appanages) has survived, according to which – based on a household size of 4.5 to five persons – the country had an estimated nineteen to twenty-two million inhabitants.[19] This would make France the most populous country in Europe at the time. It is impossible to know with any precision how many people died as a result of the Black Death of the mid-fourteenth century, the plague epidemics that followed or the consequences of the Hundred Years War. In some regions, like Normandy, the figure may have been more than 50 per cent. In the first half of the fifteenth century, too, war and famine claimed further victims in western and central France, so that the population of France around 1450 was probably no more than ten million. The result was a substantial drop in the acreage under cultivation, with cereal-producing regions less affected than the vineyards and orchards of the South. Thus in Languedoc, for example, viniculture on marginal soils was reduced most because it was less profitable. Most of the vineyards there were permanently lost to winegrowing, and at best were planted again during the demographic growth of the sixteenth and seventeenth century, this time with cereal crops. In the villages, landownership began to be concentrated in the hands of only a few families: 'The victims' goods had been joined to those of the survivors'.[20]

At the same time, the depopulation of entire regions set off large waves of migration. The destinations were not just the large urban centres or regions such as the Paris basin, but also the deserted winegrowing region on the Garonne around Bordeaux, which was settled in the second half of the fifteenth century above all by migrants from the Limousin and the Auvergne as well as Poitou, Anjou or the Vendée. Thus speakers of the *langue d'oïl* entered the realm of the *langue d'oc.* It was only around 1470 that population numbers actually began to stabilise, though, peaking in the mid-sixteenth century.

In this period people began to cultivate the deserted land again, and demand for agricultural products corresponded approximately to supply. In the sixteenth century population growth already outstripped agricultural resources, so that everywhere marginal soils had to be planted again, this time with cereals. This reduced the cultivation of specialty crops (common madder, dyer's weed, hemp, hops), which had partially compensated for the falling demand for grain in the fifteenth century. Of similar overall economic importance as cereal cultivation was viniculture, which had already represented an important export branch in the thirteenth and early fourteenth centuries. The main growing region was Gascony, which in its heyday exported up to 100,000 tuns of wine annually, mainly to England. Despite English privileges, wine growing and wine exports from the region did not escape the effects of the Hundred Years War. Thus the Bordeaux wine trade did not recover until the final quarter of the fifteenth century. At the same time, wine growing on the lower Loire was on the rise. Wine from there was exported to England and the Low Countries, mainly via Nantes. Wine consumption in France's large urban centres naturally also played a major role alongside the export trade.

While wine remained the most important French export throughout the Middle Ages, an export-oriented French textile industry developed only in the second half of the fifteenth century. In this period, silk weaving was established at Lyons (1466) and Tours (1470) on the initiative of Louis XI, in addition to a cloth industry aimed at the domestic market. With the help of Italian experts recruited expressly for this purpose, Louis sought to stem the outflow of money to Italy for silk fabric. On this basis, a silk industry organised on the putting-out system developed, which employed some 5,000 persons in Lyons in the mid-sixteenth century. With time,

Nîmes, Montpellier, Toulouse and Paris also built up their own textile trades, with Parisian artisans specialising in silk ribbons and hats. In the same period the production of art and luxury goods also emerged, influenced by the building projects of the Renaissance kings. At Fontainebleau a tapestry manufacture was founded with specialists from Flanders and Italy, but painters, sculptors, clockmakers and goldsmiths also worked for the king, the nobility and the urban bourgeoisie.

During the reign of Louis XI, Lyons was strongly privileged as a centre of fairs and commerce. The city continued a tradition of fairs that had made France a leading entrepôt of international trade in the twelfth and thirteenth centuries with the fairs of Champagne.[21] Thus in the twelfth century, the fairs of Champagne, held on six fixed dates in the towns of Lagny, Bar-sur-Aube, Provins and Troyes, had become a crossroads of trade between southern, western and eastern Europe. Here people traded cloth from Flanders and Brabant, leather, especially kidskin from southern Europe, furs from the east as well as spices (saffron, nutmeg, pepper, ginger, cinnamon, anise) and sugar from the Mediterranean and Asia offered by Italian merchants. It was also here that the rudiments of a cashless payment system developed that would advance trade throughout the Middle Ages.

The fairs of Champagne nevertheless declined over the course of the thirteenth century. The chief contributing factors were the intensification of the sea trade between the Mediterranean and the North Sea – that is, of direct trade between Italy, Flanders and England – the expansion of German–Italian trade along the Alpine route and the development of Italian cloth production, but also the annexation of Champagne by the French Crown and the exploitation of the fairs for fiscal purposes. Moreover, economic progress had also rendered the fairs of Champagne obsolete. The settled merchant banker had replaced the merchant who travelled to the fairs because the former had access to novel business techniques such as bills of exchange, bookkeeping, maritime insurance and new forms of business partnership (see II.3). To be sure, these techniques and thus trade more generally were dominated by Italian merchants, but in the late Middle Ages France also produced a merchant and banker of note in the form of Jacques Coeur (*c.* 1395–1456), a shopkeeper's son from Bourges.

The source of Coeur's rise was the office of *argentier*, the treasurer and purveyor to the royal court, which he attained in 1438. The duty of the *argentier* was to supply the royal family with clothing, jewellery, furniture, horses and weapons. In order to do so, he had to gather the necessary goods in the various trading centres of France and the Mediterranean region. This gave him the opportunity to engage in international trade both on the king's behalf and on his own account. As a source of funds he used the share of tax revenues allotted for the maintenance of the *argenterie*, mingling his own finances with the king's. Later, after he had lost all his offices as the result of an intrigue, he would face legal charges because of this. His banking activities arose from his trading enterprise: Jacques Coeur offered credit to customers and suppliers, made transfers of money from the French bishoprics to Rome and financed the French recapture of Normandy in the final phase of the Hundred Years War. During the fifteenth-century secular shortage of bullion Coeur battled continually with the problem of acquiring money. Thus he attempted to acquire silver for the mints and his Mediterranean trade by mining silver-bearing lead in the region of Lyons. He also had silver coins, jewellery and tableware collected and melted down into bars, since every galley that sailed to Rhodes or Egypt in his name had 3,000–4,000 marks in silver on board to pay for purchases. Coeur was certainly not the only French merchant involved in this trade, but he was probably the most important one.[22]

After the Hundred Years War the French monarchy tried to revive trade in the country, promoting the trade fair city of Lyons with extensive privileges. The primary aim, however, was to stop the outflow of bullion from France to the Geneva fairs. These attempts at first proved unsuccessful, but in October 1462 a royal decree created a new situation: the French were prohibited from attending the Geneva fairs and foreigners travelling to Geneva through French territory were threatened with the confiscation of their goods. The Count of Savoy did not react, since he was involved in a conflict with Geneva at that time. In March of the next year (1463) the King of France founded the four Lyons fairs, which were to take place simultaneously with those in Geneva. The merchants who travelled to the fairs – except the English, 'our old enemies' – were exempted from all taxes and duties, while the Crown dispensed with its right to confiscate the property of merchants who died. The stipulations concerning monetary transactions and payments were more liberal still, which was no small privilege in a time of scarce precious metals and omnipresent restrictions.

No limitations whatsoever were placed on money exchanges or bill transactions; anybody could transfer money abroad or lend money from one fair to the next with the aid of the so-called *deposito*, which the Church still prohibited at that time. All coins including French ones could circulate at the market rate, and bullion could be imported and exported. The official mint regulations were suspended de facto for the period of the fairs, and merchants set their own rates as they saw fit.

The Italian merchants and bankers could not resist such an offer. In

1465 they abandoned Geneva and contributed to Lyons' rise as the leading European fair of exchange. Thanks to the economic potential of southern Germany, Geneva continued as a trade fair city, but would not regain its importance as a centre of international finance until the private banks of the eighteenth century. The symbiosis between French and Italian interests was key to Lyons' success. The Italians regarded the Lyons fairs as a favourable location for reviving their transcontinental trade in luxury textiles and spices. It was not so much the fifteen-day trade fairs, however, that established the international reputation of Lyons. Rather, it was the one-week fairs of exchange that gave Lyons European significance as a 'hinge' in payment transactions between southern and north-western Europe. Since the *foires de change* did not always immediately follow the trade fairs, they gradually developed into an independent institution with their own rituals. Debtors or creditors settled their accounts either directly or through intermediaries who paid the creditors. If their reciprocal claims did not balance out, money had to change hands, or the transaction was put off until the next fair, creating a new obligation that would fall due there. The significance of the Lyons fairs of exchange rested on both the large number of bills of exchange discounted there and the European scope of this clearinghouse, to which the fairs of Brabant and Castile as well as the Italian sites of exchange were subordinated.[23]

The success of Lyons was imperilled by the mid-sixteenth century, however, when the French kings increasingly exploited the fairs to finance the State. This occurred both directly and indirectly. On the one hand, the State raised the duties and taxes levied at the fairs, which rendered them less attractive for merchants; on the other, the Crown used the fairs as a capital market to raise the enormous sums devoured by military adventures.

2.4 A regionalised society

The society of late medieval France was highly regionalised and differentiated, which makes it rather difficult for present-day historians to determine how far we can generalise from the insights offered by regional studies. These regional differences were bridged by ideology, for instance when Philippe de Poitiers drew a rather romanticised picture of the country, citing the old topos of the functional division of society into three orders, when he spoke to the estates general in 1484: the Church should pray, counsel and admonish, the nobility should protect, and the people should support the aforementioned by paying taxes and tilling the soil. His was

Table 1 Ennoblements in France 1317–1498

Ruler	*Period*	*Number of patents of nobility*
Charles IV	1322–1328	31
Charles V	1364–1380	323
Charles VI	1380–1418	527
Charles VII	1436–1461	215
Charles VIII	1483–1498	100
Divided kingdom	1418–1435	76
John the Good	1350–1364	183
Louis X	1314–1316	6
Louis XI	1461–1483	227
Philip the Fair	1307–1314	7
Philip V	1316–1322	45
Philip VI	1328–1350	233

Source: Contamine, *La noblesse*, 67-8. Since from the period when France was divided the documentation on ennoblements by Charles VII remains fragmentary, the number was probably higher.

not an isolated voice, and the constant repetition of this postulate would seem to indicate how distant it was from reality.

As elsewhere in Europe, the nobility had also come under pressure in fourteenth-century France. Alongside pan-European transformations such as the decline of the feudal system or the income losses of landlords, France underwent specific changes that were typical of the country or were felt particularly keenly there. In fourteenth-century France, the nobility made up about 1.8 per cent of the population, some 50,000–60,000 families or 250,000 to 350,000 individuals.[24] The proportion of the nobility differed from region to region. While in the Bordelais 'noble hearths' made up 1 per cent of the households counted, in the Basse-Auvergne the figure was 3 per cent and in the Périgord 2.2 per cent. In the fifteenth century the number of nobles had fallen slightly to 1.5 per cent of the population, i.e. 200,000 persons or 40,000 families, and in the sixteenth century – in the age of the wars of religion– their numbers decreased still further.

The nobility was organised in a strict internal hierarchy. At the top were the high nobility (*barons*) with the princes of the blood, dukes, counts, viscounts and the rest, who were referred to as *sires*. Beneath the high nobility were the mass of knights (*chevaliers*) and squires (*écuyers*), who filled the ranks of Church and State office. Overall, however, the nobility was not as closed as is often claimed. Those who could not afford to live in a manner befitting their rank left the group, while others found opportunities to rise into the nobility. Despite a degree of openness, the hierarchy within the nobility was repeatedly reinforced over the centuries, with the help of dress regulations and sumptuary laws that allowed the various groups of nobles a certain extravagance, which they then demonstrated outwardly. For example, when the king displayed his jewels in the fifteenth century, he did so in a case containing seven *niveaux* (compartments). A duke, in contrast, had only five at his disposal and a count only three.

Despite this pronounced conservatism, changes did occur in the nobility of the fourteenth and fifteenth centuries. While there were between 5,000 and 10,000 *chevaliers* in 1300, their number declined to approximately 1,000 in 1500. As their numbers dwindled their prestige increased, so that in the sixteenth century the *chevaliers* belonged to the middle (and no longer the lesser) nobility. In 1469, Louis XI created the Order of St Michel on the model of the Burgundian Order of the Golden Fleece in recognition of the rising prestige of the *chevalerie*. The size of the high nobility, which in the fourteenth century had consisted of 400 to 800 families, also increased in the late Middle Ages.

In the fifteenth century the nobility regained and outwardly displayed their prestige, which had reached a nadir in the mid-fourteenth century in the wake of military defeat by the English in the Hundred Years War. In those days, anti-noble sentiment was widespread in all strata of society. Resistance came from a group of noblemen under the leadership of the archbishop of Sens, Guillaume de Melun (1345–76), the Richelieu of the fourteenth century, who sought to restore the aristocracy's leading political role. They stabilised the money supply and with it noble incomes after John II's return from English captivity. The introduction of direct taxation – from which the nobility remained exempt – likewise favoured this stratum.

The kings also had to resolve the problem of the extinction of noble families in many territories, and with them the source of royal officials. One example is the Forez, of whose original 215 noble families 66 were already extinct in the male line before 1300; 149 remained, of which 80 had died out by 1400. Of the remaining 69, 38 died out in the fifteenth century, so that by 1500 only 31 of 215 families survived.[25] In 1789 only five families could trace their lineage back to the thirteenth century. It was impossible to compensate for such losses without new ennoblements. The French kings consequently saw themselves compelled to elevate more of their subjects into the nobility.

The French kings issued some 2,000 patents of nobility during these two centuries, with the weaker kings particularly prominent among them. These ennoblements did not suffice, however, to return the nobility to thirteenth-century levels (see Table 1).

A further means of expanding the noble estate was to recognise the bastard children of aristocrats. Thus in the fifteenth century the illegitimate offspring of the high nobility, in particular, were no longer stigmatised. Illegitimate children still could not inherit the appanages or family estates, but they increasingly attained high Church and secular (royal) office. Noble families certainly used bastards to assert or acquire influence through matrimonial alliances or the occupation of administrative functions. The sale of office, however, which was becoming increasingly widespread in the late fifteenth century, did not yet play an important role in ascent into the nobility. To be sure, offices in the financial administration were already being sold in the late fifteenth century, but offices in the judiciary were officially exempt from sale. It was only under Louis XII and Francis I that the sale of office was recognised as a regular source of royal income or revenue. In the course of the sixteenth century the Crown sold numerous patents of nobility for fiscal purposes. The nobility paid correspondingly close attention to who belonged to the *nobles de race* for whom seats in the estate assemblies were reserved by birth, and who belonged to the *anoblis* or *noblesse de dignité*, who continued to form part of the third estate.

Clientele relationships were essential for connections to the Crown and to other nobles. French historians have sought to view this as characteristic of the transition from feudal society to the modern French state. Jean-Philippe Genet, for instance, has applied the English model of bastard feudalism to France, using it to describe the French aristocracy's relationship to the Crown.[26] Although the similarities with fifteenth-century English bastard feudalism appear fascinating for the sixteenth century, especially the era of the wars of religion, it is worth noting that the high nobility, in particular, was far more tightly bound to the monarchy in the sixteenth century than had been the case in the fifteenth century.

The situation of the French clergy was strongly influenced by relations with the papacy. When the Pope moved to Avignon (1309), the curia became largely French, or southern French, and was forced to help finance the Hundred Years War. In the age of ecclesiastical reform and councils in the fifteenth century, France (Synod of 1407) clung to the French monarchy's independence from the Pope and thus to independence from papal provisions and tallage. The University of Paris developed into a centre of the conciliar idea. As a fortunate side effect, graduates of the university were given preference when Church offices were filled (up to 80 per cent of the available positions). The cathedral chapters lost their right to elect the bishop, since the electors were bound by royal recommendation. If several people were competing for candidacy or election at the same time, the stronger man often won. While the popes retained their right to appoint bishops and abbots, they were compelled to accept the king's candidates. At the same time, most bishops came from the high nobility, and – with the acceptance of bastards and the accumulation of offices – veritable dynasties emerged. Thus in 1477 Philip of Luxembourg took over the archdiocese of Le Mans from his father, to which he added the bishopric of Thérouanne in 1496. In 1507 he relinquished Le Mans in favour of his nephew, who was already bishop of Saint-Pons. When the latter died in 1509, he in turn inherited Le Mans and Saint-Pons from him; in 1516 he exchanged bishoprics with his uncle, François de Melun, who gave him Arras in return. In the meantime he had even risen to the rank of cardinal.[27] Similar accumulations are evident among the abbots of monastic orders.

Despite the significant social differences within the lower clergy, they enjoyed notable wealth overall. Thus, for example, the fifty priests in the *doyenné* of Lille had average annual earnings of sixty-eight livres (120 livres in the city), which was more than a master craftsman could earn. Five of these priests were *magistri artis*, and three were still university students. Seventeen of the fifty clerics had dispensations freeing them from residence in their parishes, meaning that they had to pay a proxy to fulfil their duties. Since in other parishes, too, 40 to 50 per cent of priests were absentees, their work was actually done by vicars and chaplains, the so-called poor priests, who had to get along on twenty livres a year and occasional fees for the performance of their duties. As the example of Lille shows, the lower clergy were present in the city in the form of the priests themselves or their proxies, and thus constituted part of urban society. In the course of the fifteenth century the cathedral chapters were also more frequently occupied by the sons of wealthy merchants, some of whom had studied at university and in this way acquired opportunities for a career in the clergy and royal service. Economic thinking gained greater influence above all during the reign of Louis XII, long considered the merchants' King – an exaggeration as we now know. The towns were dominated by merchants and officials equally, whereby the city's character – as the seat of a *parlement*, a trading centre or a university town – influenced the importance of the various strata. In the seats of *parlements*, the members of the high courts and revenue boards as well as the officials of the provincial and municipal administrations were already well represented, but their numbers would rise significantly in the sixteenth century.

As a group, the merchants were influenced by the great long-distance traders or merchant-bankers, joined in Paris, Lyons, Bordeaux or Nantes by numerous Italian, Spanish, Portuguese, Flemish, Dutch and German merchants. Particularly in the sixteenth century, this social mobility often culminated in the transition from the merchant to the office-holding class. Below this elite was the large and internally diverse stratum of artisans. Particularly in the commercial and manufacturing towns, the merchant-entrepreneurs dominated the artisans. Beneath them were dependent employees and day labourers, who would develop into a social problem above all in the sixteenth century. They were always the first to suffer from famines and often died of starvation. We should also not forget the marginalised groups who were excluded from municipal society, but could still be found among various social strata. In 1300 this category included for example some 100,000 Jews, whom Philip IV, however, expelled from France in 1306. Although they received temporary permission to return in the years that followed, they remained the target of repeated persecution. For many years the county of Provence remained untouched, and its cities saw an efflorescence of Jewish life. After the French Crown acquired the region in 1483, the legal situation of the Jews initially remained unchanged. Ultimately, though, anti-Jewish riots in 1498 led to the expulsion of the Jewish population here, too. Italians resident in France were not persecuted, although they provided similar services to the Jews. The 'Gypsies' – often referred to as Egyptians – appeared in the early fifteenth century and initially met with sympathy, since people took them for Christians persecuted by the Turks.

The situation in the countryside was strongly influenced by demographic developments and the effects of war. Most authors have concentrated here on the consequences for the nobility. Thus in his work on the Bordelais, Boutruche stresses the miserable state of the rural aristocracy around 1450. From this impoverishment of the nobility Guy Bois concludes that there was a crisis of the feudal system, which affected first the peasant population and then the entire society (see Chapter 14).[28]

On the whole, the decline in population nevertheless strengthened a comfortable, middle peasantry. In the fifteenth century, their situation depended above all on how quickly the manorial lords returned to the old status quo. To the extent that the population increased and settlement became denser, the holdings of those peasants supplied with land by the manorial lords decreased. The population in the south of the country appears to have recovered more quickly than in the north. When traditional agrarian relations were re-established, this does not mean that the manorial lords directly farmed their own land again. They let their lands in exchange for money rents or medium-term contractual tenancies, although in the sixteenth century short- and medium-term contracts increasingly replaced long-term rents. In this regard, for many the good years ended around 1530. Unlike England, however, France did not yet have any cash-rich tenant farmers around 1500, so that in comparison to its English counterpart, French agriculture retained its feudal structures. Thus a well-to-do middle peasant generally had 5 to 10 hectares of his own land, while the majority worked less than 2.5 hectares of land. There were also a growing number of rural day labourers, who cultivated a small patch of land and profited from their work on other farms. When they were paid in cash they suffered from the loss of purchasing power, but they did relatively well when they were paid in kind. Since agriculture underwent a relatively positive economic development into the sixteenth century, the country was spared such peasant uprisings as the *Jacquerie* from the crisis period of the fourteenth century. Only the burdens of taxation might have provoked a peasant revolt. Although Sir John Fortescue noted during his 1463 sojourn in France that the unfortunate French peasants were hard pressed by taxes, the first tax rebellions in France were only recorded in 1542 as reactions to the extension of the *gabelle* in the western regions of the country.[29]

2.5 Languages and cultural production

Can we speak of a French identity around 1500? To be sure, certain cultural elements were present that can readily be associated with France: the triumphal march of Gothic architecture, the Occitan literature of the troubadours or a refinement of courtly culture such as Johan Huizinga describes in his *Autumn of the Middle Ages*. Joan of Arc's struggle against the English Crown was also long interpreted as an expression of 'Frenchness'. In this view, the Hundred Years War awakened French national sentiment. Bernard Guenée has accordingly claimed that by 1500, despite linguistic differences and varying regional developments, people were convinced that they belonged to a French nation. Even Bishop Bernard de Rosier of Languedoc wrote in his 1450 *Miranda de laudibus Franciae* that France, while consisting of two countries (*pays*) and two languages (Gallican and Occitan), was held together by the Church and the government of the most Christian king.[30]

It was only in the sixteenth century, though, that maps presented a visual image of the French kingdom, which was disseminated with the aid of the printing press. Linguistically, France was still quite heterogeneous. Apart from the main linguistic groups of the *langue d'oc* and the *langue d'oïl*, the inhabitants of France spoke Basque, Breton and Flemish. The *langue d'oc* and Occitan were made up of numerous dialects (Provençal, Auvergnat, Gascon, etc.). For that reason, many parts of the country were unable to understand regulations issued by the central administration in the northern French tongue (*langue d'oïl*), and they had to be translated. The language question was only officially settled in an ordinance of 1539 (Villers-Colterêts), which stipulated that henceforth, all legal matters would be treated and decided 'en langage maternel françois et non autrement' (in the French mother tongue only).[31] With this decision, the southern elites were gradually and generally integrated into the French legal and administrative language and thus into the French language more generally.

Proficiency in northern French became a prerequisite for social mobility. The breakthrough of this language occurred in several stages. In 1488, the consuls of Limoges introduced French as the language of official records. The notaries followed suit in 1518 and the cathedral canons in 1542. The judges at the Toulouse poetry competition chose an Occitan poem for the last time in 1513, after which all prizes went to works composed in French. The jurists of the royal chancery and the *parlements*, in contrast, began using French in the fourteenth century, which paved the way for its entry into literature. In this period, Paris evolved into the centre of intellectual and literary production. University scholars regarded themselves as the heirs of Athens and Rome, and translated classical and medieval Latin texts into French on a grand scale. Thus Nicholas Oresmius (*Nicolas Oresme*), for example, earned a reputation as a translator of Aristotle.[32]

At the same time, courtly poetry became more literary and lyrical. New forms such as the *chant royal*, the *ballade* and the *rondeau* spread as sociable poetry, with Guillaume de Machaut, Jean Froissart and Othon de Grandson emerging as central figures. Literary life flourished in Paris particularly in the peacetime years around 1400, and integrated the high nobility, intellectuals and 'amateurs' alike. Chivalric romances played a role in the theatre, along with historical spectacles and comedies of manners. It is telling that Boccaccio's *Griseldis* was likewise translated and dramatised. Christine de Pizan, a young mother and widow, daughter of the personal physician of Charles V, also became a professional writer.[33] Alongside apologetic texts such as the *Livre des faits et bonnes mœurs du sage roi Charles V* (Book of the deeds and good manners of the wise King Charles V), her works included love ballads but also the *Épître au dieu d'amour*, which unleashed a literary dispute on the misogyny of the popular *Roman de la rose*.[34]

The continuation of the Hundred Years War and the division of the country for some years interrupted literary life, which did not experience a renewed flowering until the second half of the fifteenth century at the courts of Blois, Anjou-Provence and Burgundy. This efflorescence was rather backward-looking, however, and followed traditional models. The reception of humanism was accordingly slow. It took the innovation of the printing press to inject new energy into literary life. Now, both the classical authors – frequently in improved French translations – and the Latin authors of the early Renaissance as well as contemporary fifteenth-century French works were published. Publishers' and printers' catalogues such as that of Antoine Vérard clearly illustrate the scope of these literary offerings. The first fifty titles published by Antoine Vérard between 1485 and 1497 included Boccaccio's works (among them the *Decameron*), collections of novellas (*Les Cent novelles nouvelles*), chivalric romances (Olivier de la Marche's *Le Chevalier déliberé*) and works by Christine de Pizan (*Le Tresor de la cité des dames*) as well as the works of Aristotle in the translation by Nicholas Oresmius, editions of Lucian, Suetonius, Sallust and Flavius Josephus as well as Leonardo Bruni (*Traité des deux amans*) in French.[35] Historical works such as the history of the Franks by the Flemish author Robert Gaguin, a diplomat in French royal service who later held a chair in Latin literature in Paris, were also published. Although Gaguin still wrote in medieval Latin, he attracted the attention of Desiderius Erasmus. More significant figures for the formation and institutionalisation of French humanism were Jacques d'Étaples (*c.* 1460–1536), who became known, among other things, for his commentaries on Paul (1512) and French edition of the New Testament (1523), and above all the jurist and philologist Guillaume Budé (1468–1540). After sojourns in Italy, the latter introduced Greek and Latin textual criticism in Paris. His main interest was in Roman law. He sought to continue the work of the Italian scholars Lorenzo Valla and Angelo Poliziano and reconstruct an 'original text' with the 'original meanings' of Roman law. To this end he studied Roman history and institutions (*De asse*), focusing on Greek and Roman coins as well as weights and measures. From coinage he worked his way to the economy of the Roman Empire, which he compared to contemporary society, and in this way moved from the topic of usury to the incomes of the various professions and arrived at abuses within the Church. He defended the French Crown's Italian policy and justified its claims to Naples and Milan. Despite these national motivations, the scholarship of *De asse* gained him a high reputation in Europe. Apart from his historical endeavours, Budé worked tirelessly to spread knowledge of Greek, Latin and Hebrew in the country. Thus his 1529 commentaries on the Greek language remained a cornerstone of Greek lexicography into the twentieth century. In 1530 he persuaded Francis I to establish royal professorships in Greek, Hebrew, Latin and Mathematics, which would form the heart of the future Collège de France. In the sixteenth century, the *Studia humanitatis* introduced by Budé acquired a strong following among royal officials and members of the *parlements*, the so-called *noblesse de dignité*.[36]

In architecture, Renaissance influences asserted themselves quite late despite the Italian campaigns of Charles VIII and Louis XII. French architecture was dominated by the Gothic style invented here, which, while it underwent changes, probably represented France's most significant cultural export. The early Gothic style had already emerged in the royal domain in the twelfth century as a new type of construction, one that verticalised buildings by using the pointed arch as a structural principle. Like the term Renaissance, Gothic was introduced at a later date to characterise a specific stylistic development. The new cathedrals and abbey churches were built above all in the cities, which still bear their specific stamp today. After beginnings in the crown lands (Morienval 1122, Saint-Denis 1137, Sens 1140), construction commenced on the cathedrals of Laon (1155), Paris (Notre Dame, 1163) and Soissons (1180) in the second half of the twelfth century. In the thirteenth century the Gothic style spread to all regions of France through communication among masters of the medieval building lodges. Innovations introduced in this period include high window openings and thus large surfaces for stained glass. Chartres (begun in 1194), Reims (1211) and Amiens (1220) are the classic examples of the high Gothic style that emerged during the reign of Saint Louis. In the fourteenth century more refined styles developed, which as the *rayonnant* and *flamboyant* styles influenced the French late Gothic.[37] A wider variety of forms and types arose, and tracery as well as more sculptured ornamentation broke up the at times ossified architectural structures. Pillars and arcades also became increasingly important as decorative elements in secular buildings such as the elaborate townhouse of Jacques Coeur in Bourges (1443) or the *parlement* in Rouen (1499–1509). Italian elements, in contrast, first appeared in royal palace architecture as well as remodelled noble residences. Thus from 1495 Domenico Bernabei, known as Domenico da Cortona or Boccadoro, worked at the palace of Amboise, which acquired an important decorative element in the form of an Italian loggia. It was not until 1515, however, that a wing influenced by Italian Renaissance architecture was added to the palace of Blois. Numerous châteaux on the Loire such as Chenonceau, Villandry, Chambord and Blois

Figure 1 Château of Blois: Wing from the reign of Louis XII.

display a specific mix (*style composite*) of Gothic structures and Renaissance decorative elements. This may be interpreted as an autonomous adaptation of contemporary Italian palace architecture while preserving traditional French characteristics.[38]

Italian stylistic elements were also disseminated in the form of monuments, for example in the tomb of Charles VIII, which Louis XII commissioned from Guido Mazzoni. Although Mazzoni, like the Giusti brothers, was not among Italy's most illustrious artists, these craftsmen influenced French sculptors such as Michel Colombe.

Cultural transfer in the field of music, in contrast, ran from France to Italy, and exchange with Italy was also underway in painting. In French music a sophisticated style with a melodic descant developed in the motet genre around 1300. The main protagonists such as Vitry and Guillaume de Machaut wrote the texts to their own music and developed new genres alongside the motet. Guillaume de Machaut (*c.* 1300–77), who had travelled throughout Europe as secretary to King John of Luxembourg, was also the most important poet and composer of his day. His oeuvre consists of hundreds of ballads, *rondeaux*, *virelais* (*chansons balladées*), motets and a complete mass. He had a lasting influence on both poets like Chaucer and Froissart and other composers. In the fifteenth century, a distinct style known as Franco-Flemish, which also integrated Italian elements, emerged especially in the cathedral schools, notably at Cambrai. Nicolas Grenon and above all the Hainaut native Guillaume Dufay, who had spent time in the papal service in Rome, Florence and Bologna, were active there. Dufay was succeeded by numerous singers in the princely and papal chapels, where, like Josquin Desprez (*c.* 1450–1521), they developed into the leading composers of the turn of the century. Although Josquin spent the final two decades of his life as provost of Nôtre Dame in Condé-sur-l'Escaut, his compositions and his fame spread outward above all from Italy until France, the Low Countries and Germany, too, participated in this transfer process.[39]

In French painting it was the manuscript illuminators in particular who grappled with Italian stylistic developments. Thus in the early fourteenth century Jean Pucelle acquainted his courtly audience with the Italian art of the *trecento*, for example in his book of hours for Jeanne d'Évreux, consort of Charles IV. A specifically French version of the genre arose in the late fourteenth- and early fifteenth-century books of hours, although they melded Flemish and Italian elements from artists working in France. The works of the Limbourg brothers for the Duc de Berry, of the Master of the Duke of Bedford and the Boucicaut Master feature not just the first landscapes created north of the Alps, a new dramatic verve among the figures, and the first interiors in central perspective, but also an altered composition of miniatures. During the crisis of the French monarchy in the 1430s, however, this development was interrupted, and it was left to Jean Fouquet (*c.* 1420–*c.* 1480), court painter to Charles VII and Louis XI, to revive manuscript illumination in the second half of the century. At the same time, Fouquet, inspired by a sojourn in Italy, introduced into France a mode of panel painting orientated toward the Florentine early Renaissance and inspired by Flemish models.[40] This development had no sequel in the sixteenth century, since the father and son Jean and François Clouet, though successful as court painters to Francis I, fell short of contemporary Italian, Netherlandish or German painters.

Notes

1 Le Goff, *Saint Louis.*
2 Favier, *Philippe le Bel*, 206–49, and *La France féodale*, 238–44.
3 Chenu, 'Dogme et théologie dans la bulle "unam sanctam"'; Coste, 'Les deux missions de Guillaume de Nogaret en 1303'; Gauvard, *La France au Moyen Age*, 302–4.
4 Favier, *Philippe le Bel*, 250–88.
5 G. Mollat, *The popes at Avignon.*
6 Barber, *The trial of the Templars*; Demurger, *Vie et mort de l'ordre du Temple.*
7 The most important French works on the Hundred Years War are Perroy, *La guerre de cent ans*; Favier, *La guerre de cent ans*; Contamine, *La guerre de cent ans*; and Bove, *Le temps de la guerre de cent ans*. See also Vale, *The origins of the Hundred Years War.*
8 Vaughan, *Philip the Bold.*
9 Guenée, *Un meurtre, une société*; Schnerb, *Les Armagnacs*; Vaughan, *John the Fearless*, 29–48.
10 Pernoud and Clin, *Joan of Arc*; Krumeich, *Jeanne d'Arc in der Geschichte*; and Beaune, *Jeanne d'Arc: vérités et légendes*; Fraioli, 'The literary image of Joan of Arc'; Contamine, *De Jeanne d'Arc aux guerres d'Italie*; Duby, *Histoire de France.*
11 Vaughan, *Philip the Good*, 55–126.
12 Leguai, 'Les états princiers' and 'Emeutes et troubles'; Gaussin, *Louis XI.*
13 Denis, *Charles VIII et les Italiens.*
14 Kerhervé, *Histoire de la France*, 18–23.
15 Goldsmith, *Lordship in France.*
16 Neveu, Jacquart and Le Roy Ladurie, *Histoire de la France rurale,* II: 94–5.
17 Bulst, *Die französischen Generalstände*, and 'Die französischen General- und Provinzialstände'; Guillot, Rigaudière and Sassier, *Pouvoirs et institutions.*
18 Genet, 'France, Angleterre, Pays Bas', 135–54, here 142.
19 Carpentier and Le Mené, *La France du XIe au XVe siècle*, 314–5.
20 Le Roy Ladurie, *Peasants of Languedoc*, 15–29, quotation p. 20.
21 Bautier, 'Les foires de Champagne'; Thomas, 'Beiträge zur Geschichte der Champagne-Messen', and 'Die Champagnemessen'; Epstein, 'Regional fairs, institutional innovation'.
22 Mollat, *Jacques Coeur*; Reyerson, *Jacques Coeur.*
23 Boyer-Xambieu, Deleplace and Gillard, *Monnaie privée*, 147–50, 374–87, 405–10; Bergier, *Les foires de Genève*, 224–33; Gascon, *Grand commerce*, 243–8; North, 'Von den Warenmessen'.
24 Contamine, *La noblesse au royaume de France*, 48–56.
25 Perroy, 'Social mobility among the French noblesse', 27.
26 Genet, *La genèse de l'état moderne*, 268.
27 Derville, *La société française*, 234–5.
28 Boutruche, *La crise d'une société*; Bois, *Crise du féodalisme.*
29 Derville, *La société française*, 251.
30 Guenée, 'Etat et nation en France'; Arabeyre, 'La France et son gouvernement', 255–7; See also Beaune, *Naissance de la nation France*, 393–416.

31 Knecht, *The rise and fall of Renaissance France*, 1–2.
32 Sharp, *Discovery in the North Atlantic*, 39–56; Macpherson, 'Pre-Columbian discoveries and exploration', 66–9; Seymour, *The transformation of the North Atlantic world*, 25–9.
33 Willard, *Christine de Pizan*.
34 Rioux and Sirinelli (eds), *Histoire culturelle de la France*, 251–65.
35 MacFarlane, *Antoine Vérard*, 1–25.
36 Rice, 'Humanism in France'; Grafton, *Commerce with the classics*, 135–83.
37 Aubert, *Cathédrales et trésors gothiques de France*.
38 Müller, 'Die Tradition als subversive Kraft'.
39 Roset, *Josquin des Prez*.
40 Avril (ed.), *Jean Fouquet. Peintre et enlumineur*.

3

The Iberian Peninsula

3.1 The *Reconquista* and the consolidation of monarchical rule

The history of the Iberian Peninsula from the twelfth to the fifteenth century is marked by both the rivalry among the five kingdoms of Castile, León, Navarre, Portugal and Aragón and the *Reconquista*, the recapture of the territories occupied by Muslims. Thus after unifying the kingdoms of Castile and León (Saint) Ferdinand III proceeded with the reconquest of the south: following the capture of Córdoba (1236) and of the Guadalquivir valley (Úbeda, Jaén), Seville fell in 1248 after a long siege. Other cities of Baja Andalucía, such as Jerez, Medina-Sidonia, Cádiz and Arcos de la Frontera were subsequently subject to the Castilian Crown. Only Niebla under Ibn Mahfuz and Granada under Sultan Muhammad I retained their autonomy, but became vassals of Castile. The *Reconquista* was followed by the *Repoblación*. Under royal supervision, the captured lands were distributed among the king's vassals as well as new settlers. The remaining Moors and their property were placed under the Crown. The chivalric orders of Calatrava, Alcántara and Santiago, which had played a central role in the *Reconquista*, also received extensive landholdings, which would become an important source of revenue for the king a few centuries later. The Guadalquivir region, from which most of the Muslim population emigrated, was rapidly resettled in this manner. Overall, Castile-León increased its territory by about one-third.[1]

The much smaller kingdom of Aragón, which was only about one-third the size of Castile-León and had emerged in 1137 out of the union with Catalonia, also pursued territorial expansion. Following the economic interests of the Catalan towns (including Barcelona), under James I (1213–76), the kingdom first set its sights on the islands of Majorca (1229) and Ibiza (1235), the most important centres of shipping and trade with North

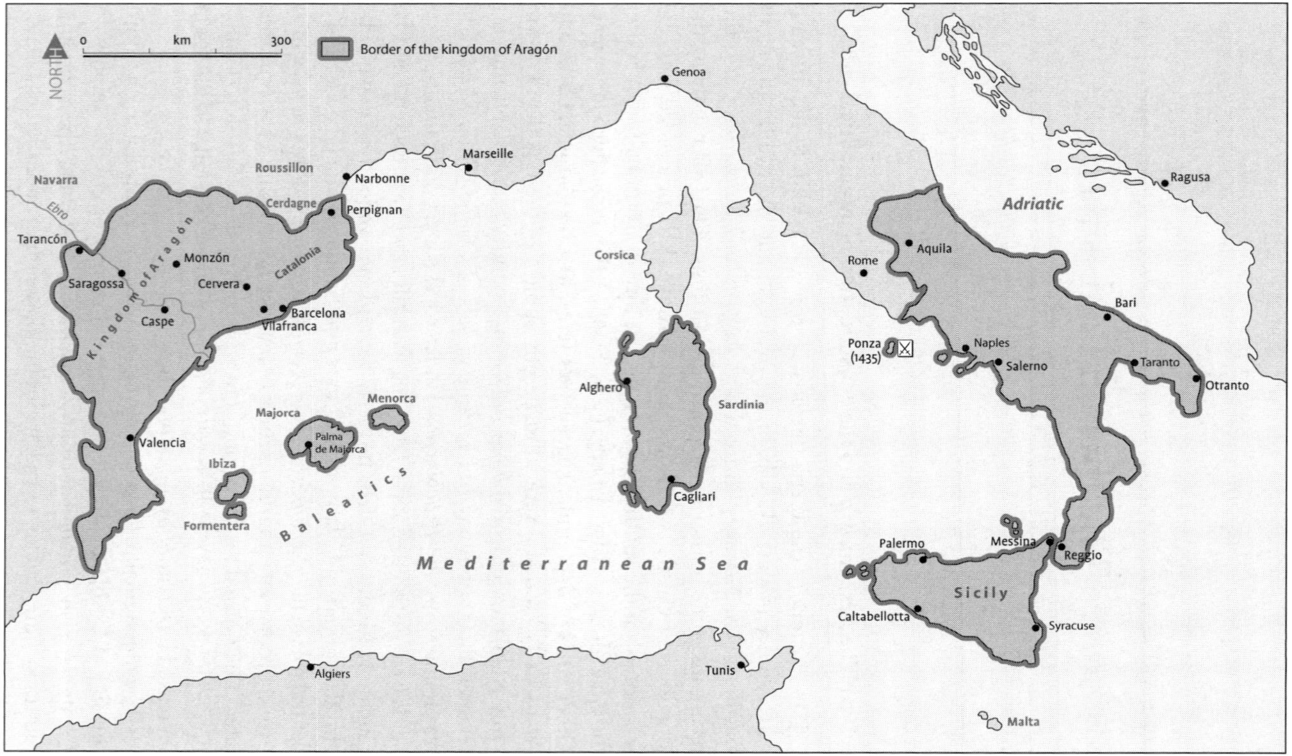

Map 5 The kingdom of Aragón in the fifteenth century

Africa.[2] At the same time, Aragón captured the territory of Valencia. The rural areas were given to the Aragonese nobility for settlement, while – as on the Balearic Islands – the King settled Catalans in the towns alongside the remaining Mudéjar population. This also occurred in Murcia, where Aragón crushed a Mudéjar revolt against Alfonso X of Castile in 1266 and then ceded the town to Castile. During this period Alfonso X (1252–84), known as the Wise because of his diverse intellectual interests and the works written at his court,[3] had to contend with setbacks on many fronts. Apart from the rebellion in Murcia and the war against the Nasrids of Granada, he also had to ward off numerous revolts by the Castilian nobility. Alfonso X's aspirations to the imperial title, which he pursued between 1257 and 1273, proved fruitless. The successor to James I in Aragón, Peter III the Great (1276–85), in contrast, used the Sicilian uprising against the house of Anjou, the so-called Sicilian Vespers of 1282, to win Sicily for Aragón. Further conquests in the Mediterranean followed with Malta, Gozzo, Ischia and Djerba. At home, the King had to fend off a French invasion in the guise of a Crusade. He succeeded, among other things by reaching an agreement with the nobles, who participated in governance in the form of the legislative bodies, the *cortes*. Although James II (1291–1327) relinquished Sicily in the treaty of Agnani (1295) and left it at the Pope's disposal, the dynasty retained Sicily, and Aragón was also compensated with Sardinia and Corsica.

Expansion continued in the fourteenth century, above all in the eastern Mediterranean. Catalan mercenaries entrenched themselves in Greece and placed their territorial conquests at the disposal of the Aragonese Crown which, however, could only hold them until 1379. Cooperation and confrontation characterised contacts with the Muslim world. Thus James II sounded out a possible alliance with the Mongol Ilkhans of Persia against the Mamluks. For a time Aragón joined forces with Granada against Castile, and before the campaign against Granada in 1309 Aragón also formed an alliance with Morocco. Relations with Muslim rulers did not differ significantly from those with Christian neighbours. When the possibility of Crusades was mentioned, it was mainly to acquire papal approval for an expansionist politics in the Mediterranean region. More important still was the financial support of the *cortes* of Aragón, Catalonia and Valencia. This dependence forced Peter IV (1336–87) to focus on the Iberian Peninsula and on conflicts with Castile.[4]

The history of Castile in the fourteenth and fifteenth centuries was marked by numerous power struggles. Although Alfonso XI succeeded after reaching his majority in putting down most of the aristocratic rebellions and in stabilising his power in alliance with the lower nobility, the *caballeros* and *hidalgos* of the towns, these internal struggles reignited under his son Peter I (1350–69), known as Peter the Cruel. Alfonso XI himself had undermined the position of his legitimate successor by bestowing substantial wealth on his seven illegitimate sons by his long-time concubine Leonor de Guzmán. The eldest, Henry of Trastámara, as prince of Asturias, became the adversary of Peter I. In the so-called War of the Two Peters (*Guerra de los dos Pedros*) between Castile and Aragón (1355–66) Peter IV supported the rival of Peter I, who would ultimately vanquish him. Because of his cruelty, Peter forfeited the backing of the old Castilian nobility, the *nobleza vieja*, and English support also proved short-lived. The takeover of power by Henry II (1369–79) led to a lasting alliance between France and Castile, and the old nobility was supplanted by a *nobleza nueva* composed of partisans of the new Trastámara dynasty.[5]

Henry II reached an accommodation with his Iberian neighbours through matrimonial politics. While his successor John I was married off to Eleonore of Aragón, he proposed that his illegitimate son Fadrique Enríquez marry Beatrice of Portugal and offered the hand of his daughter Leonore to Charles III of Navarre.[6] John I's plans to acquire the Portuguese Crown proved unsuccessful. In the wake of these failures the power of the estates increased, particularly in the 1380s. Henry III succeeded – among other things through acts of grace – in eluding any permanent influence by the estates, but this relative stability was threatened by his early death, at which time his heir John II (1406–54) was only one year old. While the regent Ferdinand managed to assert his might through successes in the war against Granada, in the years that followed he had to contend with numerous noble parties of varying composition and aspirations. When John II came to the throne in 1419 the situation resembled the one seventy years before when Peter I assumed power. To be sure, his marriage to Blanche of Navarre improved his position, but it took the single-minded politics of his favourite, Alvaro de Luna, to preserve the King's power. New noble families rose in the wake of numerous government crises and displaced the old high nobility, which had also once been a *nobleza nueva*.

Luna's era came to an end in 1453, when he was arrested on the King's orders following accusations by the Infante Henry, the future Henry IV (1454–74), and executed without trial. This did not pacify Castile, however. On the contrary, in the 1460s the nobility's inability to compromise culminated in a 'civil war' over the royal succession, which even the coronation of Isabella I (1474–1504) did not bring to an end. Aragón was not much more stable. Although the kingdom of Aragón permanently

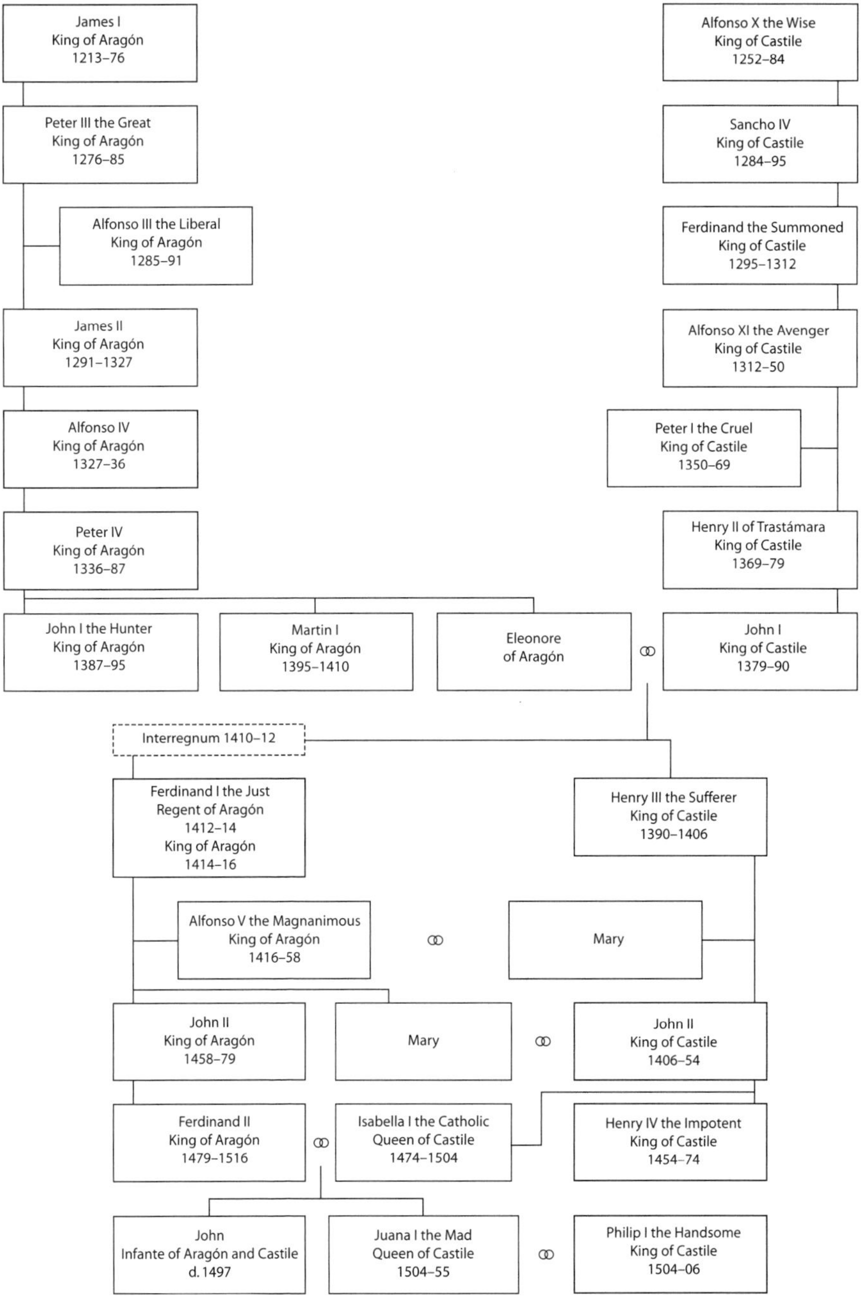

Genealogical table 3 The kings of Castile and Aragón 1213–1516

incorporated Sicily in the early fifteenth century, the simultaneous deaths of King Martin I (1396–1410) and his heir Martin the Younger (d. 1410) threw the royal house into a dynastic crisis. The *cortes* of Aragón chose the Castilian candidate Ferdinand I (1412–16) from the Trastámara to be king. His son Alfonso V the Magnanimous (1416–58) intervened in Castile by supporting the Aragonese anti-Luna faction. Above all, however, he returned to an expansionist foreign policy in the Mediterranean region. He not only invaded Corsica and destroyed the port of Marseilles but also successfully fought for the annexation of Naples (1442) to the Crown of Aragón. While his illegitimate son Ferrante inherited Naples, his successor as King of Aragón was John II (1458–79), who had to fend off an uprising in Catalonia. The economic decline of Catalonia, which had been looming since the late fourteenth century, proceeded apace and caused the focus of economic activities to shift from Barcelona to Valencia. John II found a way out of the crisis, however, by marrying Ferdinand of Aragón to Isabella of Castile (1469).

Developments only took a visibly positive turn in the 1480s, though. Up to that point, conditions in Castile and Aragón remained civil war-like, for in addition to Ferdinand of Aragón, Alfonso V of Portugal and Charles of Valois, Duc de Berry, a brother of Louis XI of France, had also sought the hand of Isabella, sister of Henry IV of Castile. Isabella chose Ferdinand on the advice of the archbishop of Toledo, contrary to her brother's intentions.[7] Thus after Henry's unexpected death, the recognition of Isabella as Queen of Castile became a problem. The question of whether Ferdinand of Aragón would be accepted as King of Castile created a further difficulty. While a segment of the cities and the high nobility pledged their loyalty to the new Queen, the role of Ferdinand, who entered Segovia in 1475, was initially unclear. As the late king's closest male relative, Ferdinand himself could certainly make a claim to the throne. He accordingly sought the regency, and was prepared to exclude Isabella from government if need be. Isabella, however, suggested that the matter of the governance of Castile be put to a commission, composed, not surprisingly, of her supporters. In the so-called Concordat of Segovia the commission stipulated that all documents containing the royal signature were to be issued in the name of both monarchs, with Ferdinand's coming first, but Castile featuring at the head of the titles and coats of arms. Homage was due to Isabella as Queen, who was to appoint all of the officials of Castile, just as she would present candidates for episcopal sees and the position of grand master of the chivalric orders to the Pope. Justice was to be administered in the name of both monarchs, but could also be exercised separately. Although Ferdi-

Map 6
The Iberian Peninsula
in the fifteenth century

nand's power was restricted – he became co-regent of the Queen of Castile – he agreed to the compromise and in the years that followed the so-called Catholic monarchs pursued a politics of mutual agreement.

Castile and Aragón did not fall to the new royal couple without a fight, however, especially since in the western regions partisans of Princess Juana, daughter of Henry IV, carried a good deal of military weight and also enjoyed Portuguese support. The foreign policy constellation – Castile had long been allied with France, Aragón's adversary – did not initially favour Isabella and Ferdinand's rule. On the contrary, France grasped the opportunity to invade Roussillon, and Afonso V of Portugal marched into Castile. The new royal couple suddenly found themselves on the defensive. They played for time, and at the Battle of Toro on 1 March 1476 succeeded in forcing Portugal and Juana's partisans to beat a retreat. Support for Juana crumbled, and her partisans sought a rapprochement with the Catholic monarchs. This settled the domestic situation for the time being, although France continued to fight a war against Castile and Aragón. Portuguese troops still occupied a few fortresses along the border, although the war was largely fought at sea. In 1479 Castile and Portugal finally made peace. Juana entered a convent in Portugal while the Catholic monarchs' eldest daughter Isabella was to be married to the grandson of the Portuguese king.[8]

At least as important as these dynastic agreements was the reconciliation of the interests of the expanding maritime powers in the Atlantic. Castile retained possession of the Canary Islands, while Portugal claimed the right to conquer North Africa and insisted on a monopoly on shipping south of Cape Bojador. Since Ferdinand succeeded his late father John II in Aragón that same year, the old enemies Castile and Aragón were united in a single kingdom for the first time in 1479. Although it seems that the Catholic monarchs, like their Habsburg successors, set their sights on creating a unified state, this was by no means the case initially. Yet even contemporaries had high expectations of the new monarchy. The Franciscan Íñigo de Mendoza, for example, compared Isabella to the Virgin Mary and accorded her the role of saviour of her kingdom's people. Diego de Valera, an author and soldier, in contrast, placed his hopes in the iron hand of Ferdinand of Aragón. The latter, however, had to prove himself not just against Portugal, but later in the revolts of the Catalan cities in Aragón as well.

The introduction of the Inquisition was a step toward internal consolidation. When Ferdinand and Isabella visited Andalucía in 1477–78 to restore control over the large towns, they encountered both nobles and town councillors with certain aspirations toward autonomy, as well as veritable gangs, which it took quite some time to suppress. At the same time, they also confronted a problem they interpreted as a religious one. The prior of the Dominican monastery of San Pablo, Brother Alonso de Hojeda, informed them that the undermining of royal authority in Seville and other parts of Andalucía was caused not just by rebellious magnates and municipal officials bent on asserting their civic freedoms, but also by religious dissent. He particularly drew their attention to the role of converted Jews who had returned to the Jewish faith, painting them as a danger to the rule of Isabella and Ferdinand. This provided the impetus for the reintroduction of the Inquisition in Spain. Unlike the papal Inquisition of the Middle Ages, the Spanish Inquisition was a state institution legitimised by the Pope whose officials were royal appointees. The Inquisition Council, known as the *Suprema*, differed from other institutions in that it united the two kingdoms and rapidly spread throughout Spain as a national, hierarchically structured agency. In 1478 Pope Sixtus IV recommended the appointment of two to three inquisitors in Seville, and in 1480 two Dominicans were appointed as inquisitors in Medina del Campo. The first six heretics were burnt at the stake in February 1481, and additional Inquisition tribunals were established in the 1480s, above all in Andalucía. Once appointed Inquisitor General, Tomás de Torquemada soon established the abovementioned *Consejo de la Suprema y General Inquisición*.

The Inquisition acquired additional mandates as part of foreign policy, especially during the battle against Moorish Granada. In Aragón, however, it met with fierce resistance in many places. After the settlement with Portugal, the foreign policy of the Catholic monarchs focused not just on the south of the country, but also on large stretches of the Mediterranean. Aragón finally acquired the kingdom of Naples in 1504, and on the northern coast of Africa – in competition with Portugal – captured Melilla in 1497, Mazalquivir in 1505, Oran in 1509 and Bugia and Tripoli in 1510. This was the direct consequence of the war against Granada, which had begun with small skirmishes in 1481. That year Abu'l-Hassan, the emir of Granada, occupied the Castilian town of Zahara, while a short time later the Marqués of Cádiz captured the heavily fortified Alhama. The next year Abu'l-Hasan's son Boabdil, who had toppled his father and driven him from Granada, was taken prisoner by the Spanish and, as a vassal of Ferdinand and Isabella, obliged to continue the fight against his father and his uncle, Muhammad al-Zagal. In the period that followed, Boabdil, who seized Granada again, pursued a seesaw policy between Spain and his Nasrid kinsmen. In 1487 the Nasrid kingdom was divided when Málaga was captured after a protracted siege. Small conflicts brought further acquisitions of land, and Boabdil could assert his power only in Granada. It was merely a matter of time before he had to relinquish the city, which had been under siege since 1491. That time came in January 1492, when Granada was surrendered in exchange for a promise of freedom of religious practice. Boabdil went into exile in Fez, where he died in the 1530s. For the Catholic monarchs, the fall of Granada was the most prestigious event of their reign, which they marked with the minting of a commemorative coin, the *Excelente de la Granada*.[9]

The conflict with France in Italy was also significant for the Catholic monarchs. The initial bone of contention was the Neapolitan inheritance, which Charles VIII of France captured in 1495 (see 2.1) but could not hold onto in the long run. An anti-French alliance that the Catholic monarchs sought to create through matrimonial connections played a role here. Their eldest daughter Isabella was married to King Manuel of Portugal in 1496, their second daughter Juana to Philip the Handsome, Duke of Burgundy, and in 1497 the heir to the throne, John, married Margaret of Austria. Unexpectedly early deaths – John died in 1497, Isabella shortly thereafter and her son Miguel in 1500 – left Juana as the sole living heir to the throne. Since she was already showing signs of insanity by 1502 and her husband Philip the Handsome, who had been treated as a possible successor to the Catholic monarchs, was under the political influence of France, foreign policy achievements up to that point appeared seriously imperilled. When Isabella died in 1504 and Philip, whom the nobility had chosen as regent to the incapacitated Queen, followed her in 1506, the Castilian nobility had no choice but to hand the reins of power over to Ferdinand in 1507. In 1510 hostilities erupted again with France, which intervened in northern Italy. Since the King of Navarre, Jean d'Albret, joined forces with France in this situation, Ferdinand took the opportunity to occupy southern Navarre and unite it with the Crown of Castile. This final success of Ferdinand's gave Spain its modern form. His grandson Charles was able to take over an undivided country in 1516 (King Ferdinand having died in 1515). He travelled to Spain in the late summer of 1517 and received his mother Juana's permission to have himself proclaimed co-regent. The Castilian *cortes* refused to recognise him in 1518 and demanded, among other things, that in future Castilian offices not be given to foreigners (Flemings), but only to native sons. Once he had accepted the petition of the estates, the *cortes* paid him homage as co-regent. The Aragonese estates followed suit after protracted negotiations. His position was only truly consolidated after the crushing of the so-called *comuneros* revolt of the Castilian towns in 1521 and the announcement of a general amnesty in 1522.

3.2 The participation of the estates and resistance to royal authority

The parliamentary institutions of Castile and Aragón had a long tradition. The *cortes* of Aragón went back to the thirteenth century, and retained considerable power into the seventeenth century. The Aragonese nobility's rebellion against Peter III in the 1280s had provided the impetus to convoke regular estate assembles in Aragón, which were followed by the *cortes* of Catalonia and Valencia. Despite these later thirteenth-century concessions, the Aragonese *cortes* were only convoked nine times during the reign of James II, while the Catalans convened somewhat more frequently. A certain institutionalisation did take place in this period, and the representation of the estates or *brazos* was determined. The estate assemblies of each province were subdivided into *brazos* or arms. There were four in Aragón and three each in Catalonia and Valencia. Bishops and members of the chivalric orders were represented in the clerical *brazo*, and the *ricos hombres* and *infanzones* or *hidalgos* in the noble or knightly *brazo*. Finally, the fourth *brazo*, the so-called *brazo real*, represented the cities, villages and market towns. In the mid-fourteenth century the financial needs of Peter IV led to frequent estate assemblies, which met for long periods. The *cortes* succeeded above all in establishing control over taxation by means of a permanent *diputació* (1359) set up for that express purpose. These were the beginnings of a contractual regulation of parliamentary participation in all important affairs, which later came to be known as *pactismo* or *pactisme*. It would take effect particularly during the crisis that followed the death of Martin I and during Alfonso V's long absence in the new capital of Naples, and would also become a topic of debates on political theory. At the same time, the nobility used the *cortes* as a forum to expand the rights of lords over peasants, for example sanctioning the *ius maletractandi* (right of mistreatment). Apart from authorising taxes, the estates of Aragón also exercised a right of petition into the sixteenth century.[10]

While the Catholic monarchs were consolidating their power administratively in Castile, Ferdinand still faced substantial resistance in Aragón. Like his father, he had to contend with the problem of the royal domains being occupied and 'alienated' by the cities and nobles in times of weak monarchical rule. In 1480/81 he achieved the first successes in the return of the royal domains, but at the same time he had to restore relations between the ruling elites of Barcelona and the Crown. Ferdinand's attempts to mediate between lords and peasants in particular met with suspicion in the towns. In 1486 Ferdinand decided that the feudal services and dues that were such a bone of contention between peasants and lords could be removed by a onetime payment to the lord, freeing the peasants from their obligations. The situation in the towns could only be pacified – after the failure of previous attempts at settlement – by the introduction of a new constitution in 1493 in Barcelona.

In Castile and León, where the position of the monarchy was generally stronger than in Aragón, the position of the *cortes* appears to have been correspondingly weaker. *Cortes* were already held here in the twelfth century, when representatives of the clergy, nobility and the cities met under royal protection. The estates were not convoked at fixed intervals, although assemblies were apparently held more frequently in certain (crisis) periods such as after 1385 or in the early sixteenth century. The composition and tasks of the estates naturally changed over the fourteenth and fifteenth centuries. Apart from their advisory role in the succession, regency and legislation, their main task was to approve extraordinary taxation. In return, the king had to hear and decide upon petitions presented by the representatives of the estates (*procuratores*). In the fourteenth century, however, the Castilian kings began to circumvent the *cortes* by introducing new duties that were outside the jurisdiction of the estates. Alfonso XI – like Edward III of England – levied a duty on woollen exports and increased the sales tax, the so-called *alcabala*. As a result, the clergy and nobility lost interest in participating in the assemblies and sought other means of asserting their interests. The number of represented towns, which in the fourteenth century had sent up to 100 *procuratores* to the *cortes*, also fell sharply. By the fifteenth century, only seventeen towns were represented, and after the capture of Granada eighteen, including the most important such as Burgos, León, Toledo, Murcia, Seville, Salamanca or Valladolid.

The Castilian estates were nevertheless integrated into the Catholic monarchs' system of rule at the estate assembly of Madrigal (1476). This occurred through the establishment of the *santa hermandad* (holy brotherhood), a peacekeeping organisation. *Hermandades* had already existed in earlier centuries as town coalitions, such as the 1315 *hermandad* of Burgos. What was new about the *santa hermandad* was that it was intended not just to preserve peace and safeguard trade routes, but also to unite all of the towns and villages of Castile in a peacekeeping alliance and at the same time accord them representation. The Crown sent loyal bishops to head the *hermandad*, who were to guide it in the royal interest and also move the towns to participate in financing wars. By the time the towns noticed that integration into the *hermandad* meant relinquishing some of their rights, it was already too late. It was not until 1498 that the monarchs permitted the disbanding of the organisation, which the towns had assailed particularly in the 1480s.[11] Further administrative changes were initiated at the 1480 assembly of the *cortes* in Toledo, and the *consejo real* (later also referred to as the *consejo de Castilla*) was restructured. Originally, the royal council, which had both administrative and judicial powers, was composed of several bishops, noblemen and a small group of educated men of either the lower nobility or non-noble origin, known as *letrados*. These officials could be found on various councils that oversaw the Inquisition, the *hermandad*, the chivalric orders of Santiago, Calatrava and Alcántara and later the Council of the Indies as well. The new royal council was now headed by a bishop and consisted of eight or nine *letrados* in addition to three members of the high nobility.

The power of a further category of royal counsellors was based on political experience and personal influence over the monarch. The reform of 1480 limited the importance of these counsellors, who now were only permitted to participate in the royal council as non-voting observers. The result was the closure as well as the professionalisation of the council, which was now headed by an appointed leading Church dignitary such as Diego Hurtado de Mendoza, archbishop of Seville.

The *cortes* met repeatedly on the invitation of the monarchs, but evolved into an advisory body and one for the acclamation of royal laws. Although the *cortes* were convoked regularly during the turbulent first decade of the sixteenth century, they would never again occupy the position they had held during the reign of John II, for instance.[12]

The revolt of the *comuneros*, which erupted in Toledo in 1520 and was directed against the taxation policies of the new King Charles, represented a final attempt to revive the *cortes*' old rights to a voice in affairs of state. After it was put down, the estates lost their position of power. From now on, Spain's resources could be placed unchallenged in the service of the monarch's universal politics.

3.3 The economy between stagnation and recovery

The economic structures of the Iberian Peninsula were as heterogeneous as its political structures. The individual kingdoms thus felt the effects of the crisis to different degrees. The population density of Spain is more difficult to estimate than that of other countries. The only figures we have came from a survey by the Catholic monarchs of how many Castilians were available to fight the war against Granada. According to this count, there were about 1.5 million hearths or households in the kingdom of Castile. If we estimate 4.5 or 5 persons per household, the population would have been 6 to 7 million. A more precise calculation from the years 1528–36, which also includes the former Nasrid kingdom but not the some 180,000 Basques, estimated no more than 4.5 million inhabitants, however. Thus the figure mentioned above seems too high. Realistically, we can speak of a population of approximately 4 million for Castile in 1500 and something over 1 million for Aragón and Navarre. Portugal probably had about 1 million inhabitants at this period. Naturally this was relatively few, compared to the millions of inhabitants of France. Although many Spaniards lived in towns, only Seville, Barcelona and Valencia belonged to the group of larger European cities with populations numbering in the several tens of thousands.

Spain was sparsely populated in comparison to many other European states. The territory of Castile had constantly expanded as a result of the *Reconquista*, providing ever more land for a population diminished by the plague. Accordingly, a manorial economy developed in which peasants worked the lands of their lords, and the large estates could devote themselves solely to extensive grazing. In Castile and Aragón the main crops were cereals, wine and olives (for oil), with fruit, vegetables and rice being cultivated on a small scale. Grain was the main foodstuff for the Christian population. Christians did not yet cook with olives, or rather olive oil, at this time, since its use aroused the suspicions of the Inquisition as it was considered typical of Muslim and Jewish households. Especially in Andalucía, olive oil was used instead to manufacture soap, which was exported to Flanders and England for the textile trade. Wine was produced for both domestic consumption and export, with specialised wine-growing regions emerging in the area around Seville, including Jerez de la Frontera, and in central Spain on the Duero River and in Rioja.

Typical of Spain and already legendary is the system of transhumance (*mesta*). The term *mesta* originally referred to universally accessible grazing land, but beginning in the thirteenth century it came to refer to an association of sheep breeders and shepherds. They met three or four times a year to organise the migration to the summer and winter pastures. At first these were regional councils, from which the *Honrado Concejo de la Mesta de los Pastores de Castilla* would develop as a nationwide institution. Alfonso X legitimised it in 1273 to serve a number of ends. On the one hand, the King (himself a landowner and sheep holder) wished to promote animal husbandry and wool production, especially from the new merino sheep; on the other, he sought to increase royal revenues through dues and fines. Environmental protection was an additional concern, since the huge sheep drive from the summer pastures in the north to the winter pastures in the south of Castile had to be organised. In 1347 – not surprisingly within the context of the plague – Alfonso XI placed the *concejo's* livestock under his protection, creating a royal association (*cabaña real*), which received privileges for the sheep drive and land use. These principles were reaffirmed by the Catholic monarchs in 1492, and in 1500 the *concejo*, whose membership now numbered some 3,000 sheep farmers, was given a presidency. The compilation of laws in 1492 was intended to avoid competition over pastures among the sheep farmers. Earlier historians such as Julius Klein thus interpreted the *mesta* as a democratic institution.[13] We should nonetheless keep in mind that sheep farming and the wool trade were as a rule dominated by herds of 30,000 and more sheep belonging to nobles, and thus by their owners. The overall population of sheep grew from some 2.7 million in 1477 to nearly 3.2 million in 1519. The conflicts between sheep farmers and peasants, which had always existed, increased accordingly in the late fifteenth century. This can be observed above all in Andalucía, where the population and their need for grazing land for cows and oxen were growing.

The wool from the *mesta* sheep was processed partly in Castile, but mostly exported to western Europe. Unlike England or Flanders, Castile and Aragón did not succeed in establishing an export-oriented trade in textiles or other goods. This focus on wool production and trade also made itself felt in the economic crisis and subsequent recovery on the Iberian Peninsula. All regions were affected by the agrarian crisis of the later Middle Ages, but at different times and to varying degrees. While in Castile the first symptoms of the crisis were already evident in the late thirteenth century and intensified after 1360, the Catalonian economy reached a high point between the late thirteenth and the mid-fourteenth century, only to succumb to a protracted crisis thereafter.[14] While Castile's economy began to recover in the 1420s, Catalonia, Aragón, Navarre and Granada saw a further decline in the fifteenth century, when both Portugal and Aragonese Valencia were growing. Particularly surprising here is the economic recovery of Castile, which profited above all from growth in Andalucía as well as the boom in merino wool exports to Flanders, France, England and Italy. 'Consulates' in Burgos and Bilbao supported this wool export and improved the position of Spanish merchants in the aforementioned countries.

The growth of agrarian production in Andalucía is documented particularly impressively in the figures of the ecclesiastical tithes. According to these records, cereal production in Andalucía rose continually between the 1430s and 1480, only to grow further in the 1490s after a temporary reversal.[15] Seville became a centre of economic growth: the population increased from 15,000 in 1385 to 40,000 in 1490. An important contributing factor was doubtless the presence of Italian merchants eager to participate in the growing involvement of the Guadalquivir region in Atlantic expansion. Catalonia, in contrast, remained mired in crisis. Several problems contributed to this situation. One outward sign was the continual fall in the number of Catalan and foreign ships in the port of Barcelona. The population shrank from some 50,000 in 1340 to 28,500 in 1497. The economic decline of Catalonia benefited Valencia, whose population grew from 26,000 in 1361 and 36,000 in 1418 to 70,000 in 1489, making it by far the largest city in the Catholic monarchs' realm.[16]

The causes of the decline particularly in Catalonia were many. In the fourteenth century, as a centre of manufacturing and commerce, Catalonia had engaged in intensive trade with the Mediterranean region and North Africa, extending as far as Damascus. With the decline in population in the wake of the Black Death, however, the manufacturing base was also reduced. Protectionist measures adopted by the Barcelona town council and the founding of a public bank (*taula de canvi*) could not compensate for numerous monetary crises and company collapses (1381–83 and in the early fifteenth century). Unfortunate royal policies also played a role. Alfonso V's military campaigns deprived the Catalans of their markets in the Mediterranean, which were taken over by the Venetians, Florentines and Genoese. Domestic political conflicts among the so-called *bandos*, i.e., the different factions in the town council, exacerbated the situation. The Biga, the faction of the commercial patriciate, and the Busca, the faction of artisans and exporters, supported different programmes. The former stood for stable money and secure annuity income, the latter for money devaluation and tariff protection. Since the king supported the latter party, commercial activities declined, only to come to a virtual standstill during the subsequent civil war.

3.4 Maritime expansion

The Canary Islands were the first destination of the expansion into the Old and New World that set forth from western Andalucía. Already known in classical antiquity, they had to be rediscovered in the Middle Ages by several expeditions. The first documented voyage was led by Lanzarotto Malocello, a Genoese in Portuguese service. In 1341, another Genoese, Nicoloso da Recco, travelled to the Canaries, and the islands appear repeatedly on maps beginning in this period. Portugal initially laid claim to the Canaries, but in 1477 the Spanish conquest of the islands began with a bill of sale between the Catholic monarchs and the rulers of the Canaries. Gran Canaria was captured in a joint action by the bishop of Lanzarote and the commander of the Spanish forces, Juan Rejón. One year later, Rejón founded Real de la Palma, the first Spanish town on the island of La Palma. Although a Spanish governor was placed over him, Rejón continued to plan further enterprises. Only some years later, in 1492, were the native population, the Guanches, vanquished on the islands of La Palma and Tenerife. The Spanish military campaign was financed by a syndicate of Genoese merchants. It was not until 1496 that the last leaders of the Guanches surrendered to the Spanish, and the Canary Islands were integrated into the kingdom of Castile. The Canary Islands may thus be viewed as a sort of dry run for the later Spanish expansion into the New World. Since the natives could not be regarded as either Moors or Black Africans, a debate arose over the origins of the Canarian population, although the process of assimilation between the Canarians and the Spanish proceeded rather rapidly. The fact that the Canaries were only one week's distance by sea from southern Spain, as well as the marked decline in the native population as a result of the introduction of European diseases, accelerated this development.[17]

As elsewhere in the New World, the motivations of the conquerors were at once economic, political and religious. Thus the efforts of Christian missionaries in the fourteenth century were resumed and ecclesiastical institutions established. Settlers received large estates and small landholdings, where they cultivated cereals and above all sugar. Genoese and Dutch merchants played an important role in the port towns, for it was their capital that built the sugar industry. The islands' population rose again in the wake of these economic activities, and by 1516 some 25,000 people were living on the Canaries. The aboriginal population made up one quarter of the total. Besides Spanish and Portuguese settlers, the rest of the population consisted of African and Moorish slaves brought to the Canaries to work on the sugar plantations.

The Canary Islands represented an important way station for later expansion into the New World, including the first voyage of the Genoese Christopher Columbus. After his plan to find a sea route to India by sailing west met with no success in Portugal, he received support for a time from Andalusian magnates. In the autumn of 1491 Columbus attracted the interest of the Catholic monarchs, which resulted in a written agreement after the surrender of Granada (1492). The Crown was to cover about three-quarters of the expedition costs, or two million *maravedís*, and supply two caravels (the Pinta and the Niña), while Columbus outfitted the Santa Maria. This agreement, which was favourable to Columbus, doubtless came about because neither he nor the Crown knew exactly what he might discover or that Portugal had already made great progress on finding a sea route to India. Columbus was even accorded the title *Almirante del mar Océano*, which corresponded to the hereditary title of an admiral of Castile. His collection of titles became more complete still when he acquired those of Aragonese viceroy (*virrey*) and Spanish governor (*gobernador*) of all the lands to be discovered.

On 3 August 1492 Columbus set sail from Palos for the Canary Islands, which he left on 6 September in a westward direction. On 12 October he landed on the Caribbean island of Guanahani, which he called San Salvador (the present-day Watling Island in the Bahamas). He passed other islands with his ships, sailed along the coast of Cuba and on 6 December landed on an island he dubbed La Española (Hispaniola), the present-day Santo Domingo. On 16 January 1493 he began his return journey, which he was forced to interrupt on both the Azores and in Lisbon because of storms. After being received by the Portuguese King, who laid claim to the newly discovered islands, he reached Spain on 15 March 1493. Here Columbus was received at court in Barcelona, together with the Indians he brought back from the journey. A few months later, on 25 September 1493, he was able to embark on a second voyage with a larger fleet. This voyage lasted until 1496 and took him once again to the Antilles. The expedition discovered Puerto Rico as well as the southern coasts of what would become Cuba, Haiti and Jamaica. Santo Domingo was founded as a Spanish settlement in 1496, presumably on the model of the Portuguese system of military and commercial outposts. The proceeds from the voyage were disappointing, however, although Columbus had Indians sold as slaves at the market in Seville. The meagre profits and the diminishing support of the Spanish court forced Columbus to take a break from his enterprises. Only in 1498–1500 could he make a third voyage, on which he discovered Trinidad and the South American mainland near the mouth of the Orinoco River. Columbus took his fourth and final journey from 1502 to 1504, during which he sought a passage between Cuba and South America which had been discovered in 1498. He sailed along the Central American coast from Honduras to Panama, but had to turn back because of accidents, hunger, disease and mutinies. He died a disappointed man in Valladolid in 1506.[18]

The exploration of the New World continued even without Columbus, however. Amerigo Vespucci explored the coasts of northern South America, which was named after him, and Giovanni Caboto (John Cabot), an Italian in English service, landed in North America in 1497. Cabral discovered Brazil and in 1513 Vasco Núñez de Balboa saw the Pacific Ocean for the first time, which he called the Mar del Sur, while that same year Coelho traversed the Isthmus of Panama. Juan Ponce de León began exploring the coast of present-day Florida, while Juan Díaz de Solís reached the Rio de la Plata in 1516. The demarcation between the Portuguese and Spanish spheres of interest was central to the further course of European expansion. To this end, Isabella of Castile and Ferdinand of Aragón applied to Alexander VI for papal bulls assuring them a monopoly, including the missionary mandate, on territories already discovered as well as future discoveries. John II of Portugal, in contrast, entered direct negotiations with Spain. In the Treaty of Tordesillas signed on 7 June 1494 the two powers agreed to a line of demarcation at 46° West. The line thus ran some 1,200 nautical miles west of the Cape Verde Islands, which meant that Brazil remained Portuguese. Overall the Spaniards and the Portuguese divided up the world in such a way that the New World, with the exception of Brazil, fell to Spain and the Old World to Portugal. Only the circumnavigation of the globe by Ferdinand Magellan (1515–22), a Portuguese explorer in Spanish service, led to a clash of interests between the Spanish and Portuguese in Southeast Asia. In 1527 Spanish ships appeared in the Philippines, which had remained within the Portuguese sphere of influence following a compromise by Emperor Charles V. The Spanish nevertheless entrenched themselves in the Philippines (where they remained until 1898); in the later sixteenth and seventeenth centuries the so-called Manila galleons regularly set sail from Acapulco.

In the Caribbean, the hunger for gold kept alive the Spanish idea of expansion. The riches the explorers found, however, rarely lived up to their expectations. Panning for gold soon exhausted the deposits, and the Aztec and Inca treasures stolen on the American mainland could not provide a permanent economic basis. It was thus only with the discovery of significant silver deposits in Upper Peru and Mexico around 1550 that Spanish America acquired a greater economic weight.[19]

3.5 The society of estates and multi-ethnicity

On the Iberian Peninsula, as elsewhere in Europe, the top of the social pyramid was occupied by the nobility, who in Castile invoked their descent from the aristocracy of the Visigothic kingdom and claimed 'blue blood' as a noble characteristic. In Diego de Valera's 'Mirror of true nobility' (*Espejo de la verdadera nobleza*), for instance, the heraldic colour blue is associated with the sky, divinity, loyalty and justice. Despite this apparently old tradition, changes had occurred over time, beginning with nomenclature. The high nobles referred to since the mid-twelfth century as *ricos hombres* had become the grandees, who as the most powerful social group were close to the king and claimed the highest offices at court for themselves. The knights or lower nobility, the *infanzones*, had become the *hidalgos* who, however, continued to fight on horseback. Both categories of the nobility were originally defined as hereditary, but in the late Middle Ages a distinction was increasingly made between an *hidalguía de sangre* (nobility of descent) and an *hidalguía de privilegio* (nobility of privilege). The latter was bestowed by royal patent and could be attained by *conversos* (converts from Islam or Judaism) as well as artisans, as long as *limpieza de sangre* (purity of blood) was not yet deemed a criterion of exclusion. The status element (noble quality) of the *hidalguía* was exemption from direct taxation by the Crown. Further categories of the lower nobility were the so-called *caballeros burguesos*, who lived in the towns founded during the *Reconquista*, and the *caballeros vilanos* who settled in villages and were obliged to perform military service with their own horses.

The lines between this lower nobility and the *hidalguía* were fluid. The high nobility, too, underwent changes, however, for example during the rise of the new dynasty of Trastámara (1369–79), when the extinct families of the *nobleza vieja* were replaced by others of the so-called *nobleza nueva*. This new nobility stabilised its landholdings with the help of the instrument of *mayorazgo* or primogeniture. It stipulated that the owner of a noble estate, as sole heir, must not divide the inheritance and only pass it on intact.[20] At the same time, the new nobility sought to demonstrate their position through outward representation, for instance by furnishing and decorating their residences, commissioning works of art, endowing foundations and travelling to other European countries.[21] The stratification of the nobility meant that their numerical representation in the population varied. While the high nobility was concentrated in the south and the proportion of aristocrats in the overall population was relatively low (2.5 per cent), in some northern areas, such as Asturias or the Trasmiera region near Burgos, up to three-quarters of the inhabitants were *hidalgos*, many of whom engaged in non-noble occupations.[22] Thus some noblemen, particularly those not in a position to maintain horses and weapons, could lose their status and tax exemption. In all, some 10 per cent of the population in Castile regarded themselves as noble. They were supplied with posts in the royal administration while at the same time taking over certain municipal offices. This was a function of the specific urbanisation of Aragón and Castile, since, with the exception of large cities such as Seville and Valencia, villages and small towns dominated the landscape, and they were ruled by a military aristocracy. The bestowal of offices such as that of *alcaldes mayores* or *alguaciles mayores* also included the right to intervene in and dominate municipal affairs. Alongside their manor houses in the country they also maintained town palaces. At times the influence of these noblemen and their clients in the town councils was so closely intertwined that– as occurred in Seville and Cordoba in the 1470s – the Crown saw itself compelled to remove them from office. A portion of municipal offices (*regidores*) were occupied by the lower nobility anyway, who were the clients of the high nobility and bolstered their power and patronage networks. Those who also had judicial authority possessed further sources of income and power with which royal officials, the *corregidores*, often could not compete. In Aragón, too, the local aristocracy exerted influence over some cities, such as Teruel, Calatayud and Saragossa.

Unlike Castile, Aragón had a strong tradition of municipal autonomy. As in some northern Italian towns, the nobility here did not have the rights of citizens, even if they lived in the city. Accordingly, mercantile and manufacturing interests dominated municipal government, which was intended to impede the king from intervening in town affairs. Where the king was successful, it was only because merchants, notaries, bankers and other townspeople had gradually adopted the values of their noble neighbours.

Ecclesiastical structures in Castile and Aragón were long determined by developments in the high nobility, although the clergy became professionalised in the fifteenth century. Since in the fourteenth and fifteenth centuries bishops largely came from families of the high nobility, they favoured the nobility and often joined noble rebellions against the king, regents or potential successors to the throne. Rulers sought to undermine such political struggles by appointing loyal representatives of the lower nobility or commoners from the towns to vacant Church offices. The precondition was that the king was able to assert himself against the cathedral chapters and above all against the Pope when it came to appointing bishops. The Catholic monarchs, who had still encountered opposition among a segment of the Castilian episcopate before they took power, had increasing success in pressing their interests. In the course of the fifteenth century, a university education in theology also became more and more important for aspirants to episcopal sees. Thus a candidate for a bishopric needed to have studied at the University of Salamanca or later Alcalá or Lleida (Aragón), and perhaps also Paris or Bologna. Moreover, future bishops were expected not just to attend to the pastoral and administrative needs of the diocese, but also to show an interest in classical and liturgical texts as well as patronage in the fields of architecture and art. Not all of the bishops invested during the reign of the Catholic monarchs were university-educated *letrados*, however. To be sure, rulers were generally able to get their way in negotiations with the Pope, but in return they had to swallow a number of papal candidates, and naturally also to observe the interests of the Pope's clientele when filling posts. Thus as Pope Alexander VI, the Valencian Rodrigo de Borja (Borgia) was able to push through his own son Cesare as archbishop of Valencia in 1492 together with two other candidates, and appointed him cardinal one year later. In 1496 he repaid the royal couple by bestowing on them the title of *Reyes Católicos* or Catholic monarchs. Two decades previously, in contrast, Ferdinand of Aragón had encountered great difficulties in installing his illegitimate nine-year-old son Alfonso as archbishop of Saragossa. While this rid the candidate of the stigma of illegitimate birth, he had to wait until his twenty-fifth birthday to gain access to the *temporalia* and *spiritualia* that went with his archdiocese. Such cases were exceptions, however. Of the 132 investitures of bishops by the Catholic monarchs (1474–1516) in Castile and Aragón, 32 were members of the high nobility and 74 of the lower nobility and the stratum of professional jurists, while only 8 bishops came from the lower classes.[23] Twenty had already occupied episcopal sees in Italy and worked in the Roman curia. With the exception of a few noblemen, as a rule all of the appointed bishops had studied both canon and Roman law, and the great majority had served at the royal court. Men who had studied theology were still the exception. Although the episcopal candidates included a few members of orders who had worked in noble households or as royal confessors, most lacked any pastoral experience. Nevertheless, the Catholic monarchs clung to their programme of reform and sought to extend the new standards to the members of the cathedral chapters as well as the canons of the collegiate churches. They were concerned above all to prevent papal influence over the distribution of such benefices and thus their bestowal on non-Spaniards. At the same time, criticism focused on the moral conduct of priests – the *plebanos* (in the towns) and the *abades* (in the country) – as well as monks. This resulted in the *cortes* of Toledo passing a catalogue of penalties for cohabitation with concubines. Meanwhile, the monarchs supported those monastic orders that as *observantes* or *reformados* aimed to preserve or return to the Benedictine, Franciscan, Dominican or Cistercian Rule. A key figure in these reforms, at first in the Franciscan order, then in the regular clergy and later among the secular clergy as well was Francisco Jiménez Cisneros, who as father confessor to Isabella and archbishop of Toledo deeply influenced religious life in Castile and Aragón as well as in conquered Granada.

Relations between lords and peasants in Aragón differed from those in Castile in that the peasant population in the former was highly dependent on the nobility. Unsettled agrarian relations influenced social conditions throughout the kingdom. A major bone of contention was the so-called *remença*, the amount that a peasant owed his lord for redemption from feudal services or for leaving his land. In Catalonia, unlike in Castile and many other regions in Europe, the plague and population decline had not strengthened the bargaining position of subject peasants. Lords continued to demand large sums of money for redemption, and the Crown left the lords' *ius maletractandi* (right of mistreatment) intact. In the fifteenth century, the Catalan peasants often formed illegal alliances, on the one hand to collect money for *remença* payments and on the other to exert pressure on their lords. By the mid-fifteenth century, well-organised groups known as *remenses* had emerged, which hoped to secure royal assistance in asserting their interests. The *remenses* had a socially quite diverse composition, extending from poor peasants in the Pyrenees to the wealthy peasants of the plains. While Alfonso V initially sympathised with the *remenses* and decreed the abolition of seigniorial abuses (*malos usos*), they were reintroduced in 1456. The peasants' chances of combating feudal excesses improved temporarily during the civil war (1462–72), but John II, anxious to reach an agreement with the nobility, abandoned them. His son Ferdinand inherited the problem and tried to solve it once and for all in 1486 by abolishing servitude, while stipulating the payment of high redemption sums to lords. Only rich peasants profited from this policy.

Apart from the aforementioned social distinctions, ethnic and cultural differences were also characteristic of the Iberian Peninsula. No other region in Europe was influenced by so many ethnic groups and religions. In addition to Basques, Galicians, Castilians, Catalans and Portuguese, who despite their linguistic differences all professed the Christian faith, there was also a large Muslim and a smaller Jewish population. This coexistence yielded fruitful cultural exchange, on the one hand, and a great potential for conflict on the other. In the course of the *Reconquista*, the proportion of Muslims and Jews in Christian areas grew, for the conquered Muslim population (for example in Cordoba or Seville) had not been assimilated. In Valencia, for instance, the majority of the population was still Muslim in the fourteenth century, and overall about one-third of the Aragonese population probably adhered to the Muslim faith. Jews made up about 5 per cent of the population in Aragón, but their financial resources meant that they played a role in economic life disproportionate to their numbers. The Muslim population also included numerous slaves, some of them from North Africa, but others from the Balkans or the eastern Mediterranean (Greeks, Tatars). The Balearic Islands in particular had such a large slave population that it was sometimes viewed as a threat. In the fourteenth century Christian rulers sought to limit the growth of the Jewish and Muslim communities. In Valencia, for example, the privileges accorded to Muslims on the occasion of their capitulation in the thirteenth century were respected ever less in the fourteenth century. Although Jews and Muslims generally lived in their own distinct quarters in the large cities of Castile and Aragón, a number of laws, for example concerning clothing and hairstyles, were enacted to separate these population groups. These regulations, such as the introduction of the *garceta* as a specific haircut for Muslim men, proved as unenforceable in the fourteenth century as the strict separation of population groups, however. Christian and Muslim men frequented the same taverns and the same Christian prostitutes. Christians, especially the kings, also availed themselves of the services of Jewish and Muslim physicians. At court Jewish scholars were also highly prized as astronomers, astrologists, cartographers or translators, whether at the 'Toledo School' or in the Aragón of Peter IV.

Public religious expression, in contrast, particularly the muezzin's call to prayer, was restricted in the fourteenth century, and pilgrimages to Mecca were forbidden. Soon, prohibitions that affected Muslim public life were extended to the Jewish population as well. Since the Crown regarded Jews and Muslims as a 'treasure', it enacted corresponding measures solely under pressure from the Church and the nobility and usually only with great reluctance. As everywhere in Europe, the Black Death bred numerous pogroms against the Jews, which often spread from Castile to Valencia, Catalonia and Majorca. Moreover, the Muslim community of Valencia came under suspicion of being a 'fifth column' of the Nasrids in Granada, leading to repeated attacks on this population group.

After the coronation of the Catholic monarchs and their visit to Andalucía, the policy toward Jews and Muslims assumed a new quality. Old ideas of segregation between the Jewish and Muslim population, known as *apartamiento*, were affirmed by the *cortes* of Toledo in 1480, and enforcement entrusted to the royal *corregidores* in the cities. A process of ghettoising (before the advent of the actual ghetto in Venice) the Jewish and Muslim population into *juderías* and *morerías* followed. The result in many cases was a brutal fracturing of urban life and infrastructure. The anti-Muslim mood intensified increasingly during the ten-year campaign against Granada.

At the same time, the scrutiny of the lives of *conversos* by the Inquisition also took on ever more extreme forms. Converts had already been the targets of anti-Jewish politics since the mid-fifteenth century. The success of those *conversos* who had gained power and influence through public office particularly irked their opponents. For this reason, the first statutes on purity of blood (*limpieza de sangre*) were enacted in 1449 and 1467 for potential public (municipal) officeholders and dignitaries. These statutes, however, like accusations of crypto-Judaism, proved unsuccessful in removing *conversos* from office or convincing them to become pious Christians. On the contrary, *conversos* and Christians continued to marry one another in the fifteenth century, for instance in Toledo, and as royal officials, rich *conversos* even married into the Castilian nobility. The offspring of these marriages became merchants and tax farmers, who then invested a portion of their fortunes in the purchase of public offices. *Conversos* were even represented in local ecclesiastical institutions as priests, chaplains and cathedral canons. According to the penances imposed by the Inquisition, some parishes were characterised by a large proportion of or special preference for *converso* families. Certain convents also attracted the particular attention of wealthy *converso* donors, if they did not found new convents altogether.[24] This religious life was brutally interrupted by the Inquisition in the years that followed. A heresy trial in Avila in 1491 accused *conversos* and Jews of ritual murder and desecrating the host, and after the alleged delinquents were burnt at the stake, provided the occasion for the large-scale expulsion of Jews and *conversos* from Spain. On 1 March 1492 the Catholic monarchs published two parallel edicts for Castile and Aragón. All Jews who had not been baptised by 31 July were forced to leave the country. They were not permitted to take goods, horses, mules, precious metals or coins with them. This destroyed the largest Jewish community in Europe, and an estimated 50–70,000 Jews left.[25] They took refuge in the neighbouring kingdoms of Portugal and Navarre as well as in Italy and North Africa. The various edicts employed different arguments. While the Aragonese version repeated traditional Christian enmity toward the Jews, the Castilian edict pointed to the dangers of contacts with the Jewish population for the spiritual and social conduct of *conversos*. In the years that followed, Inquisitorial measures focused on the remaining *conversos*. Nevertheless, the majority of formerly Jewish new Christians probably remained unmolested, for according to estimates only one-tenth of all *conversos* fell victim to the Inquisition, and the most frequent penances imposed by the Inquisition tribunal were warnings and monetary fines. For the Muslim population, nothing changed immediately in 1492, since despite the surrender of Granada they retained the right to practice their religion. A 1499 rebellion by the Muslims of the Alpujarra mountains (Sierra Nevada) gave the archbishop of Toledo and grand inquisitor Francisco Jiménez de Cisneros occasion to cancel the privileges that had been accorded to the Muslims of Granada upon their surrender. A policy of compulsory baptism began, and continued until the *Moriscos* were expelled to North Africa in the early seventeenth century.

3.6 Regional and national culture

The multiethnic population of the Iberian Peninsula made the coexistence and cooperation of diverse cultures typical of this region. At the end of the Middle Ages, a national Spanish culture – parallel to a national Portuguese culture – began to develop with the triumph of Castilian. The rise of the Castilian dialect had begun far earlier, with the court chancery playing an important role in the evolution of a Castilian administrative language, which was used alongside Latin. At the court of Alfonso X at Toledo Jewish, Christian and Muslim scholars translated works of philosophy, mathematics and astronomy from Arabic into Latin, but at the same time a specialised Castilian vocabulary also emerged for the various branches of learning. The King himself wrote poetry in Galician, which in the fifteenth century also gave way to Castilian as a literary language. It was above all the reception of the works of classical antiquity that effected a refinement of Castilian in fifteenth-century literature and science. Juan de Mena (1411–56), the one-time secretary of King John II's Latin chancery, translated Homer's *Iliad*, among other works, and created a new Castilian literary language above all with his poetry. At the end of the century another Andalusian, Elio Antonio de Nebrija, who like Mena had studied in Italy, composed, in addition to his editions of classical and Christian authors and his *Introductiones latinae* (1481), the first Castilian grammar (*Arte della lengua castellana*, 1492), in which he understood language very much as an instrument of political power. This would be put into practice during the expansion of Castile and Aragón into the New World, when Castilian became a global language. But even in the border regions such as the Basque country or French-influenced Navarre, which fell to Castile in 1512, Castilian, which was on its way to becoming Spanish, was gaining ground. In the late sixteenth and early seventeenth centuries prose novels and plays (Cervantes, Calderón, Lope de Vega) would also be written in the language previously known mainly for the lyric poetry of authors such as Jorge Manrique or Juan del Encina.[26]

This would likely have been impossible without the influence of translations from the Latin on the development of a Spanish literary language. After all, unlike in other European countries, the initial focus of Spanish humanists was not on improving knowledge of Latin and Greek, but rather on harnessing and later popularising the legacy of classical antiquity. Some scholars, such as the founder of Spanish humanism and bishop of Burgos Alonso de Cartagena (1384–1456), came from *converso* families. He was well versed in Jewish scholarship, had studied Cicero during a sojourn in Italy in the 1420s, and sought to make his philosophy available at court. Thus he translated Cicero's *De officiis* and *De senectute* for the royal secretary Juan Alfonso de Zamora and later the chief works of Seneca for John II of Castile. He also offered young aspiring scholars the opportunity to pursue their learned interests in his service. One of his disciples was Alfonso de Palencia (1424–92), who went to Seville in 1453 after a longer sojourn in Italy, and arrived at the court of Archbishop Alfonso de Fonseca in 1456. At almost the same time he was appointed to succeed Juan de Mena as Henry IV's Latin secretary. In addition to lexicographical works such as a Latin-Castilian dictionary he wrote mainly historical texts such as the *Gesta hispaniensia*, thereby establishing himself as the historian of his time. His philological successor was the abovementioned Antonio de Nebrija, who found in Cardinal Cisneros a collaborator in establishing the classical languages in Spain.[27]

Cisneros had intended theology to become the main subject of study at the newly opened University of Alcalá, which was founded in 1509, following the model of the University of Paris. In Salamanca, in contrast, the focus was on jurisprudence, on the model of Bologna. In keeping with his humanist views, Cisneros believed that the academic training of the clergy demanded chairs of classical languages and the various schools of theology (Thomist, Scotist and Nominalist); even professorships of Arabic and Chaldæan were planned. The central task was a critical edition of the Bible in the received languages, the so-called Complutensian Polyglot Bible. The first four volumes contained the Old Testament in Hebrew, Greek and Latin as well as the Pentateuch in Chaldæan, and the fifth the New Testament in Greek and Latin. Hebrew and Chaldæan dictionaries and a Hebrew grammar rounded out the enterprise, which was ready for the press in 1517 but appeared only in 1520 with papal permission.

Alongside these humanist critical endeavours, the late scholastic tradition continued to play an important role in Castile, where Francisco de

Vitoria (1483–1546) revived Thomist scholarship. It would reach a final high point in the second half of the sixteenth century with the Salamanca School's studies of social ethics and natural law. Humanist influence appears to have been less intense in Aragón. Although linguistic and artistic exchange flourished at the court of Alfonso V in Naples, and what was probably the most significant literature in Catalan was produced there by Ausias March (1397–1458), this literary tradition had little influence in the mother country.

The kingdom of Aragón cultivated a lively exchange with the Low Countries in the field of sculpture and painting, however. As early as 1431, Alfonso of Aragón sent his court painter Lluís Dalmau from Valencia to Flanders. By 1436 he was again active in the kingdom. In 1439 the Bruges master Luís Alimbrot (Allyncbrood) moved his workshop to Valencia, where he painted a triptych of the Passion influenced by Jan van Eyck. Jan van Eyck himself probably travelled to Valencia with a Burgundian delegation in 1427, and to Portugal one year later. Alfonso V received an important work by van Eyck, the Lomellini triptych, as a gift in 1444. Another painter who worked on commission from Alfonso V was Jaume Baço, called Jacomart, who was active in Valencia and later in Naples.

Valencia was a centre of economic and cultural exchange in the fifteenth century, and Netherlandish painting as well as the arrival of Italian artists such as Paolo da San Leocadio played an important role. Flemish paintings were imported in large numbers, but little concrete documentation of them survives. We do have evidence that the jurors of Valencia purchased Vrancke van der Stockt's *Last Judgment* in 1494, a work that eventually adorned the chapel of the town hall. The Netherlandish style did not penetrate much farther into the kingdom of Aragón than Valencia; Aragonese art and architecture remained dominated by the late Gothic style.

The basis for the reception of Flemish painting seems to have been somewhat broader in Castile.[28] Here, pilgrims en route to Santiago de Compostela and dynastic contacts particularly to the Burgundian Netherlands in the fifteenth century appear to have played a role in promoting Flemish art. Some impulses came via France, Germany and, as in the case of Jorge Inglés, even England. Thus the altarpiece that Inglés created in 1455 on commission from the Marquis of Santillana for the hospital in Buitrago (Guadalajara) belongs to the earliest examples of the reception of Flemish art in Castile, and depicts the donor and his wife in the Burgundian style. Although the themes and techniques of Flemish painting were familiar here,[29] the works were executed on pine rather than oak and in tempera instead of oils. The resulting technical deficiencies were compensated for

Figure 2 Fernando Gallego, *Adoration of the Magi* (on wood, 131×100 cm).

by the rich use of gold and – compared to the Netherlands – the much larger dimensions of the altarpieces in Spanish churches.

While in Aragón urban corporations and religious orders purchased Flemish art as well, in Castile patronage was limited to the royal dynasty and the high nobility. Merchants also had the opportunity to commission paintings or to purchase works ready-made at the fairs. Thus Spanish merchants were prominent among the clients of Hans Memling in Bruges. Paintings by Jan van Eyck, who also visited the Castilian court during his journey to Portugal, had reached Castile even before the works of Memling. In 1459 Henry IV donated the *Fountain of life*, from the workshop of van Eyck, to the monastery of Santa Maria del Parral in Segovia, and a copy of the same work was made around 1500 in Spain. Probably more important than van Eyck were the paintings of Rogier van der Weyden and Robert Campin, which exist in Castile not just as originals but also as Castilian adaptations. John II had already donated a triptych of the Virgin by Rogier van der Weyden in 1445 to the Carthusian monastery of Miraflores, which he had chosen as his final resting place.

Centres of painting orientated toward Netherlandish models were Burgos, where Diego de la Cruz was active, Toledo and above all Salamanca. In the last-mentioned city, Fernando Gallego left behind an extensive opus in the Flemish style. His work is characterised by the realism of his figures and above all the unusual brilliance of his palette. From the 1480s, Pedro Berruguete brought Netherlandish as well as Italian Renaissance influences to Toledo. Berruguete had spent a good deal of time at the court of Federico da Montefeltre at Urbino, and sought to satisfy the wishes of his patrons with his stylistic symbiosis. In numerous works commissioned by Isabella of Castile for the Carthusians of Miraflores, he took up Netherlandish traditions while also adopting decorative elements from the Italian Renaissance as well as Islamic architecture in Mudéjar style, which he used in the backgrounds of his paintings. Apart from her role in commissioning new works Isabella also collected paintings and tapestries and engaged foreign artists as court painters. The first of these was probably Michel Sittow, a native of Reval (present-day Tallinn) who had trained in Bruges and was already active at the court of Castile in 1492.[30]

Sittow's successor was Juan de Flandes, who also painted pictures for the Carthusians of Miraflores. The King was reticent in his reception of Italian elements, and it was not until the sixteenth century, during the reign of Charles V, that Venetian influences gained ground in the Spanish global empire.[31]

Reception of the Renaissance played only a minor role in architecture. New buildings followed the style of the late Gothic. This applied both to Juan de Colonia's design for the cathedral of Burgos and the above-mentioned charterhouse of Miraflores. In other towns of Old Castile many churches, such as San Pablo and San Gregorio in Valladolid, were given Hispano-Gothic façades. In New Castile, Flemish Gothic entered a symbiosis with the Mudéjar style in the hospitals designed by Jan Waas. Waas (known in Spain as Juan Guas) built a new palace in Guadalajara as well as the chapel in San Gregorio in Valladolid. The buildings of Toledo then influenced other structures such as the Dominican monasteries in Avila, Segovia and Madrid. The great architectural event in Andalucía was the construction of the cathedral in Seville, which began in 1402 and was completed in 1506. Numerous craftsmen and artists worked on the cathedral, including the Breton Lorenzo Mercadante and the Frenchman Michel Perrin on the exterior sculptures. The cathedral of Granada also occupied an important place in the architectural programme of the Catholic monarchs. Here, as in the construction of other churches and monastic buildings, the creation of Catholic identity was paramount. At the same time, the palace of the Nasrids, the Alhambra, was also restored. It was only the Catholic monarchs' grandson Charles V who ruthlessly inserted his Italian Renaissance palace into this ensemble. The other great architectural monument of Moorish Spain, the Mezquita of Córdoba, was given its first Hispano-Gothic chapels at this period. Here, too, it was Charles V who undertook major reconstruction.

Spanish medieval music was characterised by the spread of polyphony in the monasteries beginning in the twelfth century and the cultivation of sacred music at the various courts. Courtly secular monody flourished alongside it into the thirteenth century. Sacred and secular court music ensembles established themselves with greater intensity from the fifteenth century. By the time of Peter III and John I of Aragón, musicians were being recruited from the papal residence at Avignon. Above all in the era of Alfonso V close relations existed with the Burgundian court as well as the papal chapel in Rome. In Naples, for instance, Juan Cornago and Pietro Oriola were active alongside the Fleming Ycaert. The music of the Low Countries, for example that of Guillaume Dufay, was well known both here and in Castile. In the late fifteenth century Spanish compositions, as well as instruments, were exchanged with other courts. The Catholic monarchs in particular each had his or her own music ensemble, which in Isabella's case consisted of some twenty singers, twenty-five choirboys and numerous instrumentalists. Ferdinand's ensemble, which was fused with the Castilian ensemble after Isabella's death, was headed by the Bruges-born Juan Urrede (Johannes de Wreede, 1451–82). Other well-known members were Juan Cornago (fl. *c.* 1455–85), Pedro de Escobar (*c.* 1465–*c.* 1535), Alfonso Pérez de Alba (? – after 1519) and Fernando de Tordesillas. Charles V took over the royal musicians when he inherited the Spanish Crown in 1516. As the 'Capilla flamenca', the ensemble recruited mainly Flemish musicians. In 1526, after Charles married Isabella of Portugal, the Queen added her own music ensemble, the 'Capilla española', which was composed of Spanish musicians.

3.7 Portugal

Portugal is one of the few European countries whose shape has scarcely changed since the thirteenth century. In the twelfth century, however, it was a smaller power than Castile-León or Aragón-Catalonia, and had first to consolidate its independence and the legitimacy of its monarchy. In this period Portugal did succeed in substantially expanding its territory in the south through the *Reconquista*, but this led to repeated clashes with Castile. Portuguese rule was already moving gradually southward in the twelfth century, capturing Santarém and Lisbon in 1147 with the aid of a Crusader army. In 1160, the Knights Templar and in 1166 members of the Castilian chivalric order of Calatrava settled in Tomar. They would later establish themselves in Avis, and exert influence on the Portuguese monarchy from there. In 1249 the Portuguese conquered the territory of the Algarve, thereby expanding the foundations of Afonso III's kingship (1248–79). Afonso sought to bolster his power base internally in a process of bureacratisation and centralisation. He could rely on the *cortes* of Leiria, the first Portuguese representative assembly, and not just on the nobility but above all on the urban middle class, which at this time was already engaged in trade with Bruges and England. Since the aristocracy and clergy found access to landed property in the north restricted by the dominance of the royal domain they diverted their interests to the south, where political authority was still open.

Afonso's successor Dinis I (1279–1325) peacefully secured the borderlands with Castile in the 1297 treaty of Alcanices, thus furthering the consolidation of his territory – Castile had already recognised the Algarve as a Portuguese possession in 1267. Dinis, who was chiefly interested in promoting trade, manufacturing and agricultural reorganisation was, however, compelled to resist a number of aristocratic revolts. He succeeded in part by integrating the nobility into royal administrative enterprises. By founding the *Studium Generale* in Lisbon, which would later become the University of Coimbra, he laid the foundations for the training of an administrative elite. The establishment in 1318 of the so-called Order of Christ, which received the property of the suppressed Knights Templar and would soon become a pillar of the monarchy, proved significant for the future.[32]

Like Castile, however, Portugal suffered setbacks. Conflicts repeatedly erupted with Castile, and Portugal was drawn into the Hundred Years War as an ally of Edward III. When the dynasty expired and the nobility and towns joined forces to rebel against Castilian rule – the Queen of Castile,

Beatriz, was King Ferdinand's sole legitimate heir – the late King's half-brother John seized power in 1383. In 1385 the *cortes* in Coimbra declared him John I of Portugal. At the battle of Aljubarrota (1385) John of Avis (so called because of his position as grand master of the Order of Avis) was able to fend off the invasion of Castile. An alliance with England and marriage to the granddaughter of Edward III, Philippa (daughter of the Duke of Lancaster), fortified the position of the monarchy and thus the new dynasty of the house of Avis.[33] John's relatively long reign of fifty years (1383–1433) brought the country lasting peace, further cemented by a treaty in 1411 and a final alliance with Castile. John's sons from his marriage to Philippa, Edward (Duarte), Peter (Pedro) and Henry (Henrique) contributed significantly to expanding Portugal's role in Europe, especially in the Mediterranean and the Atlantic. Edward became King and gained the support of the Portuguese nobility. Peter promoted Lisbon's trade, and Henry, known as the Navigator, was responsible as governor of the Order of Christ for combating the 'infidels'. He used this as an opportunity to promote Portugal's overseas expansion – an expansion that would largely determine Portuguese history in the fifteenth century.

After the premature death of Edward, the monarchy was weakened by a regency government until Afonso V (1446–81) managed to suppress the influence of the high nobility and strengthen the kingdom both internally and externally. This included not just a lasting engagement in North Africa, but also an extensive system of alliances. In concert with Aragón, Burgundy and England, Afonso sought to contain Castile and France and prevent Isabella of Castile from succeeding to the throne. With the defeat at Toro in 1476, however, he suffered a severe loss of prestige among his partisans in the Castilian aristocracy. In the long term, his influence was stronger on domestic than on foreign policy. The *Ordenações Afonsinas* that arose during his reign placed Portugal's legislation on a uniform basis of Roman law at an earlier date than most other European countries. Once printed in the 1521 *Ordenações Manuelinas*, the body of law would gain wide currency, especially in Portugal's overseas territories.

Afonso's son and successor John II (1481–95) could build on his father's domestic policy and end the conflict with the high nobility to his own advantage. He did not shy away from drastic measures, either. Thus in 1481 he gained the approval of the *cortes* to intervene in the privileges of the high nobility (jurisdiction). The rebellion that then broke out under the leadership of the house of Bragança was quelled by executing the Duke. A segment of the high nobility went into exile and their confiscated estates increased the royal domain. When the Duke of Viseu, a brother-in-law and cousin of the king, planned a further plot John stabbed him to death personally, and his alleged co-conspirator, the bishop of Evora, was poisoned in prison. This brutal approach actually gained sympathy for the King among the lower nobility. The 1492 expulsion of the Jewish population from the kingdom of the Catholic monarchs presented Portugal with a serious problem. The Portuguese monarch offered Jews fleeing Spain temporary exile in Portugal for a per capita entry fee of eight *cruzados*, and some 50,000 persons accepted the offer. Only approximately 600 wealthy Jewish families were allowed to settle in the country permanently, while the rest were soon forced to leave or to convert to Christianity. John's brother-in-law and successor – the legitimate heir, his son, had died young in a riding accident – Manuel I (1495–1521) sought a compromise with the banished families of the high nobility, whom he allowed to return, and also decided to expel the Jewish population once and for all. Since he had married the Catholic monarchs' daughter Isabel, it appeared only logical for him to adopt their Jewish policy as well. Thus the Jewish population was faced with the alternative of emigration or conversion, while all Jewish children under the age of fourteen years were to be forcibly adopted by Portuguese Catholic families. This brought with it another wave of conversion, since in the decades that followed the new Christians were not officially persecuted. Pogroms against the Jewish population continued, however, for example in 1506 in Lisbon (see 3.10).

Manuel's foreign policy hopes proved in vain, however, since the Castilian legacy moved beyond his reach with the death of his wife Isabel (1498) and their son Miguel (1500). In fact, after the death of his son John III (1557) and his grandson (1578), the great-grandson of the Castilian kings, Philip II of Spain, became King of Portugal as well in 1580. It was not until the second half of the seventeenth century that the Duke of Bragança, now John IV, would lead Portugal out of the 'Spanish embrace' into independence.[34]

3.8 The power of the estates and centralisation in Portugal

In Portugal, too, representative assemblies emancipated themselves from the royal council *(concelho)* in the thirteenth century. The assembly of Leiria (1254) convoked by Afonso III, to which representatives of the towns were invited for the first time, may be considered the first Portuguese *cortes*. Documenting the growing economic and political position of the mercantile community, the representation of the towns, in particular, was to become characteristic of the development of the Portuguese estates.

It played an important role especially in matters of taxation and the coinage prerogative, as well as in bolstering the towns' position vis-à-vis the clergy and the nobility. The significance of this institution grew particularly after the *cortes* of Coimbra elected John I of Avis King in 1385. Although the new King at first had to make concessions to his noble and clerical supporters, he soon returned to his alliance with the towns. The twenty *cortes* held between 1385 and 1430 frequently treated urban concerns such as price regulation, securing the labour force, town administration, the influence of royal officials in the towns, the privileges of the nobility and clerical jurisdiction. Agreements were reached with the clergy to curtail their privileges and with the nobility regarding the hereditary use of royal land grants *(lei mental)*. The strengthening of royal power in this period is evident from the fact that extraordinary taxes (*pedidos*) could be levied almost constantly without convoking the *cortes*, and that the Crown laid claim to municipal excise taxes (*sisas*). In the years that followed, the kings frequently adopted the general petitions (*capitulos gerais*) of the *cortes*, albeit after a certain delay. Thus the 1439 demand for legal codification by the Lisbon *cortes* was met in the *Ordenações Afonsinas* of 1446. As part of his anti-aristocratic policy, John II also took up old municipal recommendations to expand royal jurisdiction in previously privileged legal spaces and decreed the omnipresence of royal justices, just as he made the confirmation of noble privileges dependent on the provision of documentary proof. These were the beginnings of a progressive centralisation, which ultimately led to the ever less frequent convocation of the *cortes* in the sixteenth century. In its stead, the responsibilities of the 27-member council of state, which advised the king, were expanded, while a cabinet of 6 ministers or secretaries pursued the actual business of governing.[35]

3.9 Long-distance trade and the beginnings of colonial expansion

Portugal's economy was highly dependent on geography and climate. Apart from a northern Atlantic zone with substantial rainfall, the country extended over a southern Mediterranean zone with corresponding agricultural production. Cereals and olives were grown across the country, while the south concentrated on the production and export of figs and almonds as well. In the north and centre, in contrast, viniculture and animal husbandry played an important role. The sea also provided a rich source of fish and salt. Portugal's location promoted shipping and trade between the north and south of the country, but also with the Islamic world of the Mediterranean region. In exchange for textiles, above all from England and

Flanders, Portugal exported fruit, salt, wine and olive oil as well as wax, cork, carmine and leather to western Europe. Exports to the Mediterranean region included dried fish as well. From its Mediterranean trading partners Portugal also purchased spices, sugar, silk, weapons and grain. In addition, Portugal served as an intermediary between western Europe and the Mediterranean region (southern Europe and northern Africa).

Plague and population decline in the fourteenth century also affected Portugal. Despite laws tying peasants and agricultural labourers to the land, many previously cultivated areas of the already sparsely populated country returned to extensive pasturage and hunting. In the towns poverty grew, and the populace found outlets for their dissatisfaction in the unrest of 1371, the rebellion of 1383–85 and further uprisings between 1438–41 and 1449 in Lisbon. A growth in wine and oil production may have compensated somewhat for the decline in agrarian output (cereals). While grain was increasingly imported above all in the fifteenth century, wine exports especially to England developed into an important branch of trade.

Portuguese expansion into northern Africa and the South Atlantic, which assumed ever greater proportions in the course of the fifteenth century, also acted as a social safety valve. The first destination was Ceuta, an important trading centre on the northern African coast, which was connected by caravan routes with the regions south of the Sahara, where it distributed products from the Mediterranean world. The Europeans obtained ivory and above all gold for coins from Ceuta, so that the town appeared as a lucrative prize. After its capture in 1415 the Muslims shifted their trade routes, making it difficult and costly for the Portuguese to provision the city. As governor of the Algarve, Prince Henry, known as the Navigator despite his – with the exception of the passage to Ceuta – scant practical experience at sea, held onto Ceuta while at the same time promoting maritime exploration along the western African coast in order to free Portugal from the monopoly of the caravans.[36] During these voyages first the island of Porto Santo and then neighbouring Madeira were officially rediscovered around 1420. The knowledge of these islands during classical antiquity had been lost, and voyages of discovery in the Atlantic by the Majorcans had also left no traces here. Henry tackled the colonisation of the islands and appointed the Italian-born Bartolomeu Perestrelo, the future father-in-law of Christopher Columbus, as governor. Sugar cane and grape vines were planted on the islands and the settlement of colonists began. In 1427 the Portuguese discovered the first of the Azores, and Henry colonised some of them beginning in 1439. The islands would attain great significance for later voyages to the South Atlantic.[37] In 1433 Gil Eanes took a further step in this direction and sailed around Cape Bojador. Mariners' fears of running up against the Antipodes and monsters near the Equator or of finding the heat there unbearable proved groundless.

By 1448, more than fifty ships must have sailed beyond Cape Bojador; they returned with black slaves and gold from Africa. A trading empire stretching from the African coast near the Cape Verde islands, the Azores and Madeira all the way to the Algarve began to take shape. A trading post was established on the island of Arguin, off the coast of present-day Mauritania.

In the period that followed the forays along the African coast continued. After the death of Henry the Navigator in 1460, the task of discovering new regions was handed over to Fernão Gomes in 1468. He agreed to explore one hundred miles of coast per year in exchange for a trade monopoly. The expeditions of João de Santarém and Pero Escolar accordingly reached present-day Ghana and, not long thereafter, Fernão do Póo arrived at what is now Nigeria and Cameroon. The islands in the Gulf of Guinea – São Tomé, Príncipe and Ano Bom – were discovered around the same time. The mariners named the new coastal areas after the main goods traded there: Costa da Malagueta or do Grão (Pepper or Corn Coast, present-day Liberia), Costa da Marfim (Ivory Coast), Costa do Ouro (Gold Coast, present-day Ghana), Costa dos Escravos (Slave Coast, now Togo and Benin).[38]

A third stage under the command of Diogo Cão led to the discovery of the Congo Delta in 1482 and, on a second voyage (1485–86), to the discovery of what is now Namibia. From there it was not far to the Cape of Good Hope, which Bartolomeu Dias circumnavigated in 1488. He realised that he had reached the southern tip of Africa, thereby finding an open sea route to India. Aside from these discoveries, which culminated in Vasco da Gama's success ten years later, exploration also continued inside Africa. Here the Portuguese searched for gold, spices and Christians, especially the legendary King Prester John.

In the 1480s the Portuguese reached Timbuktu and Mali and in this way gained knowledge of the gold caravan routes. In 1486 the King entrusted João Afonso de Aveiro with investigating the so-called slave rivers in the coastal hinterland, and he received a warm reception from the *oba* (king) in Benin. The contact between the *oba* and the Portuguese royal house remained intact, and the first son of an *oba* was baptised by Portuguese missionaries in 1515. The first missionaries also arrived in the kingdom of Congo in 1490, and in the early sixteenth century the now baptised Prince, Dom Afonso (formerly Nzinga Mbemba) sent his own son Dom Henrique to Portugal to study. Particularly in the Congo region, however, missionary interests vied with those of the slave trade.

The Covilhã-Paiva mission, deputed by John II in 1487 to search for Prester John, was particularly important. One year previously the Portuguese had sent two priests who managed to reach Jerusalem, but their deficient linguistic abilities soon forced them to return home. Pero de Covilhã, in contrast, spoke Arabic after several sojourns as an envoy in northern Africa, and was well qualified for the enterprise. He and Afonso de Paiva disguised themselves as Moorish merchants and travelled via Alexandria and Cairo to Aden, which they reached in 1488. Paiva set off for Ethiopia, where he died, however. Covilhã first boarded a boat to Cannanore and then visited Calicut and Goa. He returned to Cairo via Hormuz and Aden. There he met two Jewish envoys, whom the King had sent to search for him and Paiva. Covilhã submitted his report on the details of the spice trade and on the sea route from Guinea to Madagascar. It is not certain whether John II ever received Covilhã's report, but around the same time, in 1488, an Ethiopian priest travelled via Rome to Portugal, where he was received at court. After the meeting in Cairo, Covilhã continued his journey via Jeddah, Mecca and Medina to Ethiopia, where he reached the supposed court of Prester John. He died there in 1526.[39] On other occasions in the early sixteenth century Portuguese delegations were sent to Ethiopia, but also despatched from there in the opposite direction.

Unlike Christopher Columbus, Vasco da Gama, after departing from Belem on 8 July 1497, was able to travel much of the way to India along known routes. He spent Christmas in a bay beyond the Cape of Good Hope, which he therefore called 'Natal', and with the help of an Arab pilot reached Calicut on the Malabar Coast in May 1498, after crossing the Arabian Sea. The hostility of the Arab traders who dominated the spice trade, and who scented new competition, forced him to divert his journey to the north, to Goa, where he was able to assemble a cargo of spices only with difficulty. Western European products met with no interest there, and in future it would take bullion to buy spices. Nevertheless, even the small amounts of pepper da Gama brought back to Lisbon caused the European pepper market to collapse. A second journey in 1502 was largely dedicated to establishing trading posts and outposts in Asia and to pushing back the Arab competition. The Portuguese succeeded here with military superiority and calculated terror against Arab merchants and pilgrims to Mecca. The yield of pepper was now so large that it unleashed a run on Portugal by southern German and western European merchants and at the same time convinced the King to establish a permanent Portuguese presence in India.

The *Estado da Índia* was founded in 1505 to administer the Indian trade and placed under the authority of Francisco de Almeida. He was given the title of viceroy and the task of building and fortifying outposts on the east coast of Africa and in Goa. He was also expected to set up a blockade of the Red Sea and thus of the traditional pepper route. Although he did not succeed in the latter, at his death – he was killed by Khoikhoi near the Cape of Good Hope in 1510 in the wake of a cattle raid by his crew – Almeida and his successor, Afonso de Albuquerque, had expanded Portugal's position in India, and the latter even captured Malacca, the entrepôt of the spice trade, in 1511. The Portuguese reached Timor in 1515 and a year later Canton, but it was not until 1554 that they established a permanent outpost in China on the island of Macao. With the founding of a Portuguese trading post on the cinnamon island of Ceylon, a network of fortified outposts and unfortified trading posts was largely in place. Portugal also acquired a small amount of territory, which supplied the Portuguese colonial system with consumer goods and people. Albuquerque had already realised that Portugal's own population would not suffice to send new men out to Asia every year, men who remained without legitimate offspring because Portuguese women rarely ventured into these regions. The promotion of marriages between Portuguese men and baptised women of the local upper class proved more effective than sending orphan girls from home. Nevertheless, there were probably never more than 12,000–14,000 men of Portuguese origin in Portuguese India.[40]

The settlement of Brazil, which Pedro Álvares Cabral had discovered and taken possession of in 1500 during his voyage to India, proved more successful. By abandoning among the natives there a sailor who had actually been sentenced to death, he unintentionally laid the groundwork for further colonisation. It was above all the interest of other powers (e.g., France) in expeditions to Brazil and a war of piracy between the two powers that convinced Portugal to begin settling Brazil in the 1530s. Although granting hereditary fiefs with the obligation to recruit settlers proved unsuccessful, the settlement of Brazil did make progress in some regions where the Portuguese lived among the indigenous inhabitants. In those places where economic motivations led to the introduction of sugar cane plantations worked by African slaves, there was also incentive for Portuguese colonisation. A further impetus came in 1559 with the appointment of a governor-general and with it the establishment of a central financial, judicial and military administration as well as the creation of Church structures and the activities of Jesuit missionaries.

3.10 A multi-ethnic society

Like Castilian and Aragonese society, Portuguese society was influenced at once by the western European feudal system, the specific form of the *Reconquista*, and Mozarabic traditions. Accordingly, the feudal system only developed fully in the north of the country; nevertheless, the kings claimed the rights of high jurisdiction for themselves. Moreover, there was a wide range of property rights and thus highly diverse variants of vassality and dependency on the monarch among the nobility. While some families of the high nobility, the so-called *ricos homens*, possessed their land without restrictions, including jurisdiction and the right of inheritance, a second group needed to have their ownership confirmed from generation to generation and by every new king. Although the Crown generally acceded to this request, it held a bargaining chip that it could deploy in the fifteenth century to strengthen the royal domain. The *lei mental* (Mental Law) of 1434, for instance, stipulated that royal land grants could only be passed down within the legitimate line, and otherwise reverted to the king. Since the law could also be applied retroactively and the reversion of landed property was executed in many cases, the royal domain grew in size. John II went a step further, subjecting all nobles, regardless of their tenures, to his sovereignty as vassals. His successors reversed these tendencies, bestowing new titles (such as duke, marquis, viscount and baron) on segments of the high nobility, but at the same time integrating them more tightly into service at court. It was from this group of nobles that the holders of high (administrative) office in the country, and soon the colonies as well, were recruited. Beneath this group was an upper-middle nobility, whose members received a fixed income (*quantia*, *contia*) as vassals of the king, and below them a lower nobility obliged to provide military services, the so-called *fidalgos*, *cavaleiros* or *escudeiros*, who were often indistinguishable from wealthy peasants, but exerted influence on the local level.[41]

The greatest concentration of landed property, however, was in Church hands. Bishops, monasteries and the chivalric orders had large holdings both in the countryside and in the towns. The clergy frequently deployed excommunication to discipline their subjects or assert their interests against royal or municipal officeholders. By the late fourteenth century, however, this instrument had become dulled by overuse. Thus, for example, in 1402 John I won the cities of Porto and Braga, which had previously been dominated by the clergy, for the Crown. In 1472, however, Braga returned to the control of the archbishop of Portugal, whose see it was. Ecclesiastical land ownership was unevenly distributed geographically. While the greater part of the large monasteries were located north of the Tejo, the chivalric orders controlled some 40 per cent of the land between the Tejo and the Guadiana in the southern half of the country as well as 20 per cent in the Estremadura. Although abbots and the grand masters of the chivalric orders belonged to the high nobility, in the fifteenth century kings often succeeded in filling these posts with their confidants and building up a royal clientele. The same was true of bishops. Since up to the late fifteenth century Portugal did not experience the accumulation of benefices typical elsewhere in Europe, bishops required royal favour in order to rise in the episcopal hierarchy. Thus bishops from the lower nobility and the urban middle classes were not uncommon in the less important dioceses. It was not until the sixteenth century that bishoprics were distributed on a larger scale in the royal family as appanages.

The group of commoners was composed of university-trained lawyers, burghers (*boni homines*), artisans and the remainder of the population. In the fifteenth century, the boundaries between the individual strata and between commoners and the nobility became more permeable. Lawyers, in particular, who made up the apparatus of municipal and royal officials, often rose into the nobility. Among the burghers, merchants generally dominated the town councils and also represented the cities in the *cortes*, in which the towns appeared as a unified group and, despite certain criticisms, constituted the king's most reliable supporters. The artisans, in contrast, who were not organised in guilds until the late fifteenth century, and then only under royal pressure, lost their representation in the town councils in most places. They enjoyed social prestige, however, and developed a strong sense of solidarity in the religious confraternities, which distinguished them from the mass of day labourers. Muslims, Jews and slaves existed alongside them as marginal social groups typical of the Iberian Peninsula.

After the conquest of the towns, the Muslim population generally had to retreat to the suburbs, while in the countryside they continued to be tolerated in the villages. Since Muslims, as peasants or small artisans, belonged to the lower classes, there was substantial pressure on them to assimilate. Nonetheless, several thousand Muslims were still living in Portugal in 1497, when they were ordered to leave the country. Most of them emigrated to northern Africa. The Jewish community of some 30,000 persons (3 per cent of the population) was a good deal more visible in the fifteenth century. In the larger towns such as Lisbon or Porto they made up nearly one-tenth of the population. The kings of the Avis dynasty deliberately pursued a different policy toward the Jewish population than their Castilian neighbours. Thus in 1391, perhaps in response to the anti-Jewish riots of 1384 in Lisbon, they expressly affirmed the guarantee of religious freedom and property ownership for Jews. This policy attracted Jewish emigrants from Spain, and the Jewish population grew. In the 1480s, when the Inquisition began its activities in Castile, it was mainly *conversos* who crossed the border to Portugal. Here, however, they encountered resentment from the local population toward 'Spaniards' and also faced the Inquisition tribunal newly instituted by John II. The anti-Jewish mood intensified and the Christian majority's calls for the baptism of Jews became louder. In this situation, the conversion edicts of the Catholic monarchs issued on 31 March 1492 unleashed a new stream of emigration. Although the 600 wealthiest families obtained royal residence permits for the sum of 6,000 *cruzados*, the great majority of the some 30,000 Jews who had emigrated quickly came under pressure to convert. Since some Jews had their children under the age of fourteen forcibly taken away from them and sent to São Tomé for Christian instruction and subsequent work on the sugar plantations, many accepted baptism for themselves and their older children in exchange for the right to remain in Portugal. Although the situation at first seemed to ease under John II's successor, Manuel, he adopted severe measures after marrying into the Spanish royal family in 1497. Once again, Portuguese Jewish children were taken away from their parents. In addition, those Jews lured to Lisbon with the promise of emigration were forcibly baptised. Compulsory conversion mainly affected the Spanish Jews who had only recently chosen emigration over baptism. Since it was no longer possible to emigrate, in the decades that followed Portugal had to live with a strong crypto-judaising population of new Christians.[42]

The black population remained tiny in comparison. Since the first discoveries of the mid-fifteenth century, increasing numbers of African slaves had been sold on the Portuguese slave market, where they replaced earlier Muslim slaves. More than 1,000 slaves were brought to Lisbon from western Africa between 1441 and 1448, and in the years that followed approximately 800 slaves were sold every year in Portugal and either sent to Castile or employed in local households or agriculture. A large proportion of them went to the sugar plantations of Madeira, either directly or via Lisbon.

3.11 Introducing a new world

By the thirteenth century, standard Portuguese had already evolved into a national language used in the composition of numerous texts. Around 1300 it replaced Latin as the official language, and also supplanted it in written

Church communications. Apart from troubadour poetry, which was fading in the fourteenth century, the other literary genres developed only slowly. Translations from the French dominated, and the most significant literary work of the era was perhaps an early Portuguese version of the Spanish chivalric romance *Amadís de Gaula*. Devotional literature was also translated from the Castilian, French or Latin. Other works were compiled around the court of John I, for example a book on hunting (*Livro da montaria*). His sons Edward and Peter produced philosophical treatises and translations of Cicero (*De officiis*), respectively. The focus of prose lay in the field of historiography, in which the royal secretary and librarian Fernao Lopes (1380/90–1460/70) set new standards with his royal chronicles, particularly the unfinished chronicle of John I. More important literary impulses came above all from the court of Manuel I, where Gil Vicente (*c.* 1465–1536) established Portuguese drama under the influence of the Castilian playwright Juán del Encina. Italian-influenced authors such as Henrique Caiado (1470–1509) or Bernardim Ribeiro (1482–1552) acquainted the Portuguese with new poetic forms and themes, but the reception of their work only began in earnest in the second half of the sixteenth century. The same may be said for the spread of humanism, an area in which the philologist and poet André de Resende (1500–73) and the grammarian Aires Barbosa (*c.* 1470–1540) initially remained lone figures.[43] It was not until the 'Lusiads' (*Os Lusíadas*) of Luís de Camões, which presented the Portuguese explorations and conquests in Asia in verse form, that the Portuguese Renaissance had its national epic.

The 'Lusiads' thus exemplify the role that Portugal played in conveying a new view of the world. Initially, this included generating new astronomical and geographical knowledge and disseminating it in Europe. It was no accident that Martin Behaim (1459–1507) had his famous globe fashioned in his home city of Nuremberg in the years 1490–93 after a longer sojourn in Portugal, during which he also sailed down the African coast. Although in so doing he documented the spherical shape of the earth, he still adopted the old legends of the all-consuming heat south of the Equator.

Portugal also spread knowledge of the Old and New World in the form of exotic beasts. One example is the famous rhinoceros that arrived in Lisbon in 1515 aboard the ship *Nostra Señora de Ajuda*. It was the first living example to reach Europe since antiquity and a gift to the Portuguese governor Afonso d'Albuquerque from the sultan of Gujarat. Albuquerque presented the animal to King Manuel I, who sent it that same year as a diplomatic gift to the Medici Pope Leo X (1513–21). This rhinoceros was made famous in Europe by the woodcut of Albrecht Dürer, who never actually saw the creature but received a precise description (possibly with a drawing) from Nuremberg merchants in Portugal. Portugal thus represented an important point of departure for news from the New World and Asia as well as its commercial exploitation.[44]

Elements of Indian and Arabic art also found their way into architecture, for example in the so-called Manueline style. It was developed by the builders of the late Gothic cathedral of Batalha and refined in numerous sacred buildings, such as the monastery of the Hieronymites in Belém or later in the famous tower at the entrance to the city's port, with borrowings from the Italian Renaissance. It was not until the late sixteenth century that Italian architects such as Filippo Terzi left tangible traces in Portugal. In painting, the court painter Nuno Gonçalves appeared suddenly and without any known role models in the second half of the fifteenth century. His famous Saint Vincent Panels in Lisbon Cathedral amount to a group portrait of the Portuguese society of his day. Although his surviving oeuvre is small, the influence of Netherlandish as well as Spanish art is obvious. Despite Jan van Eyck's sojourn at the court of John I, we cannot reconstruct any direct relationship to Portuguese painting. Only toward the end of the fifteenth century is there evidence of the presence in Portugal of Flemish painters such as Francisco Henriques or Frei Carlos, who were orientated toward the figures and spatial conceptions of Old Netherlandish painting. They may have had a joint workshop, perhaps together with Jorge Alfonso, who would profoundly influence the subsequent development of Portuguese painting.[45]

Notes

1 Lomax, *The reconquest of Spain*; Moxó, *Repoblación y sociedad.*
2 Abulafia, *A Mediterranean emporium.*
3 González Jiménez, *Alfonso X el Sabio 1252–1284*; O'Callaghan, *The learned king.*
4 Reilly, *The medieval Spains*, 161–85.
5 Valdeón Baruque, *Pedro I, el Cruel, y Enrique de Trastámara*; Ruiz, *Spain's centuries of crisis*, 72–85.
6 Valdeón Baruque, *Enrique II de Castilla.*
7 On what follows, see Ladero Quesada, *La España de los reyos católicos.*
8 Edwards, *The Spain of the Catholic monarchs*, 243–4.
9 Ladero Quesada, *Castilla y la conquista.*
10 Lalinde Abadía, 'El pactismo'.
11 Lunenfeld, *The Council of the hermandad.*
12 Edwards, *The Spain of the Catholic monarchs*, 39–67.
13 Klein, *The Mesta.*
14 Cabrillana, 'La crisis del siglo XIV'; Vilar, 'Le Déclin catalan'.

15 Ladero Quesada and González Jiménez, *Diezmo eclesiástico*; Comin, Hernández and Llopis (eds), *Historia económica de España*, 39; Yun Casalilla, *Marte contra Minerva*, 20–52.
16 Treppo, *I mercanti cataloni*; Carrère, *Barcelone.*
17 Fernández-Armesto, *Before Columbus*; Abulafia, 'Neolithic meets medieval'.
18 Macpherson, 'Pre-Columbian discoveries', 66–9; Fuson, 'The Columbian voyages'; Weddle, 'Early Spanish exploration'.
19 Reinhartz and Jones, '"Hacia el norte!" The Spanish Entrada into North America'; Fisher, *The economic aspects of Spanish imperialism*; Seymour, *The transformation of the North Atlantic world*, 25–9, 46–8; Sharp, *Discovery in the North Atlantic*, 39–56.
20 Moxó, 'De la nobleza vieja'.
21 Yarza Luaces, *La nobleza ante el rey*, 309–21.
22 Gerbet, *Les noblesses espagnoles*, 218–36.
23 Edwards, *The Spain of the Catholic monarchs*, 194–208.
24 Martz, 'Relations between conversos and old Christians'.
25 Suárez Fernández, *Judíos españoles en la edad media.*
26 Deyermond, *Edad media.*
27 Camillo, 'Humanism in Spain'.
28 Yarza Luaces, 'Flanders and the kingdom of Aragón'.
29 Yarza Luaces, *La nobleza ante el rey*, 224–5.
30 Navascués Palacio (ed.), *Isabel la Católica*, with essays on painting, sculpture and architecture.
31 Maroto, 'Flanders and the kingdom of Castile'.
32 Ackerlin, *King Dinis of Portugal.*
33 Disney, *A history of Portugal and the Portuguese Empire,* I, 122–42; Coelho, *A revolução de 1383*; Caetano, *A crise nacional de 1383–1385.*
34 Disney, *A history of Portugal and the Portuguese Empire*, I, 143–97; Anderson, *The history of Portugal*, 79–98.
35 Disney, *A history of Portugal and the Portuguese Empire*, I, 137–42.
36 Diffie and Winius, *Europe and the world of expansion*, I, 44–56.
37 Disney, *A history of Portugal and the Portuguese Empire*, II, 1–33; Russell, 'Prince Henry the navigator', xi, 3–30.
38 Diffie and Winius, *Europe and the world of expansion*, 57–106.
39 Boxer, *The Portuguese seaborne empire*, 15–38; Diffie and Winius, *Europe and the world of expansion*, 144–65.
40 Disney, *A history of Portugal and the Portuguese Empire*, II, 172–203; Boxer, *The Portuguese seaborne empire*, 39–64.
41 Costa Gomes, *The making of a court society*, 231–52.
42 Edwards, 'Expulsion or indoctrination?'.
43 Saraiva and Lopes, *Historia da literatura portuguesa*, 189–297.
44 Smith and Findlen, 'Commerce and the representation of nature'.
45 Porfirio, 'Portugal and the north'.

4

Italy

4.1 From urban network to equilibrium of states

Because the Italian state has existed only since 1861 (and with the Veneto only since 1866), when applying this term to earlier centuries we must always keep in mind that what is now Italy was once home to a variety of states that underwent different political, economic, social and linguistic developments. When we nevertheless speak of Italy – as the fifteenth-century humanists did – it is in an attempt at a comparative perspective. After all, despite diverse structures, this geographical space was marked in the thirteenth century by the global conflicts between the Hohenstaufen emperors and the papacy, to which the territories responded in quite different ways. By the late twelfth century the northern Italian towns of imperial Italy had joined forces in the so-called Lombard League and offered themselves as negotiating partners to Emperor Frederick I. After the defeat of the imperial forces at Legnano in 1176, Frederick was accordingly compelled to make peace with the cities at Constance in 1183. In return, the cities recognised the Emperor's sovereignty. His grandson Frederick II nonetheless attempted to subjugate the cities to the empire, leading to the formation of a second Lombard League in 1226. The Emperor won out in 1237, and used his victory to exact punishment, particularly through interventions in the autonomy of the cities. In so doing he drove the communes into the arms of the Pope (first Gregory IX, then Innocent IV), so that the cities were gradually lost to the empire. Nevertheless, there continued to be parties of Hohenstaufen supporters within the cities, known as Ghibellines (*ghibellini*) or of their opponents, the partisans of the Pope or of the Guelf dynasty, known as *guelfi*.[1]

The Emperor was not the only danger to the cities' independence, however. Hostility among neighbouring cities also interfered with growing prosperity. For this reason the communes, which profited from the growth of the urban population, sought to increase their territory and fortify the growing urban space with new rings of city walls. The towns also fought over ports and access to the sea. Apart from the coast, Pisa and Genoa vied with one another for Corsica and Sardinia, which repeatedly unleashed fierce wars. In 1284 Pisa bowed out as a maritime power after being defeated at sea by Genoa.[2] Other city-states such as Bologna and Modena, Pavia and Piacenza, or Milan and Cremona were in a permanent state of war. The conflicts between Florence and Siena were especially bloody. In 1260, with support from the Hohenstaufen and the exiled Florentine Hohenstaufen faction (the *ghibellini*), Siena asserted itself militarily against Guelf Florence, and only the intercession of the Florentine exiles, who sought to assume power in Florence, saved the city on the Arno from complete destruction. After the defeat of the Hohenstaufen King Manfred at Benevent in 1266, circumstances were reversed, and the supporters of the Pope (the *guelfi*) gained the upper hand in Florence. A few years later Siena was also vanquished once and for all and disappeared as a political rival. This rivalry did not merely produce military conflicts, however, but was also reflected in artistic achievements. Thus with their construction of a new cathedral beginning in 1296, the Florentines sought to outdo the cathedrals of their competitors Siena and Pisa, to which Siena responded with rebuilding projects of its own.[3]

Rivalries and deadly enmity existed not just between the cities, though, but also within urban societies. The labels Ghibelline and Guelf lost some of their meaning because the cities generally supported the curia, that is, were Guelfic, and, apart from the urban nobility, the Emperor relied mainly on the families of the rural aristocracy, for example in the Po valley. Within the cities the Guelfs often succeeded in asserting themselves over the Ghibelline urban nobility with calls for communal liberty. Here too, however, the labels often became blurred. Thus in Milan the della Torre family belonged to the Guelf faction and as a result their rivals, the Visconti, were Ghibellines. Nevertheless, both factions sought to bolster their position with the Emperor's help. With time Ghibelline and Guelf degenerated into catchphrases of inner-urban partisan conflict, which began to paralyse conditions in the cities. The cities only began to emerge from this stalemate by asking a lord from outside, known as the *podestà* (from the Latin *potestas*, or power), to assume authority and suppress the partisan conflicts. The *podestà* came from another commune and held office temporarily. In 1151 in Bologna and in the years that followed in most other cities, noblemen from elsewhere were appointed to serve as *podestà*, which developed into an attractive profession. Success in one city could lead to appointments as *podestà* in others. In order to be able to remove the *podestà* again, the cities limited his powers and carefully delineated his responsibilities and qualifications. He had to be married already, in order to prevent him from marrying into a local family, and was not permitted to acquire land in the city he administered. At the end of his term, which lasted a year or six months, he had to submit a report.[4]

Despite some successes, the appointment of a *podestà* did not prove to be a permanent solution, since the leading families, or the parties who gained the upper hand in civic conflicts, began to fill the post with their own preferred candidates. This anticipated the development of the *signoria*, a form of urban rule in which the governing lord came from one of the respected leading families. Along the way, however, the *popolo* or people sought to exert their influence, for as the economically active element in society they suffered most from the partisan conflicts. The *popolo* also included the wealthy merchants, bankers and landowners, who – although richer than the urban oligarchy – were denied access to municipal office. Their aim was to curtail the rule of the urban nobility, or to participate in municipal government, by organising themselves in their quarters, neighbourhoods and guilds. In this situation the *popolo* (often also called *pedites*) joined forces by taking an oath as a sworn community (*coniuratio*) of non-nobles in order to assert their demands on the nobility (the *milites*). Such a coalition existed in nearly every city of northern and central Italy in 1250.[5]

The leading representatives of the *popolo* fought for access to lucrative offices as well as to the local cathedral chapters, which monopolised political authority in the cities. Well-to-do artisans and traders represented a second group in the *popolo*. Their demands focused less on access to office than on fair taxation, a proper administration of municipal finances and an impartial justice system that guaranteed personal liberty and the protection of property. They were also interested in the restoration of public order to contain bloody feuds and partisan conflicts among the noble families. In the mid-thirteenth century, the *popolo* began to aspire to political power in a few places. In some cases, noble feuds could only be suppressed with the help of force. One such instance occurred in 1257 in Genoa, when the *popolo* entered an alliance with a leading family and appointed Guglielmo Boccanegra 'captain' of the *popolo* and ruler of the city for a period of ten years.

The *popolo* appears to have pursued a particularly successful politics in Florence, where from the mid-thirteenth century they were represented by an elite of the guilds. Not all guilds were equal, however. Power lay with the seven major guilds, the *Arti Maggiori*, which included the lawyers, judges and notaries (*Arte dei Giudici e dei Notai*) as well as the international cloth merchants and bankers (*Arte di Calimala*), the moneychangers (*Arte del Cambio*) and the cotton and silk merchants (*Arte di Por Santa Maria*). Behind them came the medical doctors and apothecaries (*Arte dei Medici e Speziali*), the woollen merchants (*Arte della Lana*) and the furriers (*Arte dei Vaiai e Pellicciai*). Even in these important guilds, however, only a few masters held positions of power, since the guilds consisted not just of the abovementioned great merchants, but also of saddlers, painters, small traders and the like, as in the *Arte dei Medici e Speziali*. It is thus not surprising that merchant bankers of the *Arte di Calimala*, such as the Mozzo, Spini, Frescobaldi, Bardi, Cerchi, Acciaiuoli and Falconieri also belonged to the Florentine *popolo*. These so-called *popolani grassi* occasionally took up the demands of simple guild members, but their chief objective was to strengthen their own position vis-à-vis the urban oligarchy. The latter was split between the party of the Church (*parte guelfa*) and the party of the Hohenstaufen (*parte ghibellina*), which offered the *popolo* some access to power. Thus in the conflicts of the 1280s, the Guelfs could rely on the *Arti Maggiori*, and the Ghibellines on the minor guilds. In this way the *popolo* acquired the role of arbitrator in 1282. Every two months, six representatives of the seven major and five middle guilds, the *Arti Medie* (butchers, cobblers, smiths, masons and traders), were elected members of the *signoria*, the council that ruled the city. This constitutional reform did little to change the conflicts within the nobility, since noblemen joined the guilds, which meant that the city's de facto rulers were an oligarchy of Guelfs and members of the *Calimala*. In this situation, in 1292, Giano della Bella, a nobleman from an old *Calimala* family, mobilised the *popolo* against the abovementioned urban oligarchy, allying himself with members of both the middle and minor guilds, the *Arti Minori* (bakers, dyers, innkeepers, etc.), and removing the elites from power. His success was short-lived, however, for the leading families struck back in March 1295.[6]

While not typical, Florence was also not an isolated case. Only in a few cities such as Padua, Cremona, Brescia, Genoa, Parma, Bologna or Perugia did the *popolo* achieve effective control over the government for a certain period. In Tuscany – in Prato, Pistoia, Lucca and Siena, in addition to Florence – the movement of the *popolo* was effective, but not lasting.

Internal peace was the rule neither in the thirteenth nor in the early fourteenth century, which made it logical to seek out a strong man or family whose rule could end the city's internal unrest. It is thus not surprising that around 1380 most of the cities mentioned were either ruled by a *signore*

(Padua, Cremona, Brescia or Parma), threatened by a *signoria* (Bologna and Genoa) or had been swallowed up by Florence (Prato and Pistoia). The power of the *signori* lay in their ability to assert themselves within their own faction, but also in their talent for fighting violence in the city with counter-violence, or for bringing about a rapprochement within the elites. Toward the end of the fourteenth century the *signori* then had their position of power affirmed by the Pope or the Emperor (appointment as imperial vicar). The *signoria* differed from one region to the next. A *signore* could rule over both a single city and an entire urban network. Thus from 1300 the Visconti, having wrested control from the della Torre family in Milan, extended their rule to numerous cities in Lombardy (Cremona, Piacenza, Pavia, Lodi, Bergamo and Parma). The Milan family extended their power furthest under Gian Galeazzo Visconti (1378–1402), who as Duke of Milan purchased entry into the estate of princes of the empire and married his daughters to European monarchs. Other *signori* such as the della Scala family in Verona and the da Carrara family in Padua also had to bend to the expansion of his rule.[7] The conflicts between Genoa and Venice gave the Visconti what amounted to free reign on the 'mainland', and only Florence, whose humanists defended republican liberties with their pens, resisted the Milanese embrace.[8]

In the south, the Este set up a *signoria* over Ferrara, Modena and Reggio (Emilia) and temporarily took power in Verona and Mantua. When Azzo VIII died without issue in 1306, the *signoria* collapsed in all of these cities and Ferrara became the scene of a struggle between the Holy See and Venice, both of which sought to seize power. During these conflicts, a branch line of the Este family tried to recapture the *signoria* of Ferrara in 1327, of Modena in 1336 and of Reggio in 1409. Since Venice continued to be a threat, they fortified Ferrara, which under the rule of the Este would develop into one of the culturally richest courts of the Italian peninsula in the fifteenth century.[9]

The Bonacolsi ruled Mantua until Luigi da Gonzaga took over the *signoria* in 1328.[10] Shortly thereafter Luigi was appointed an imperial vicar, and a century later, during his Roman campaign, Emperor Sigismund raised the Gonzaga family into the estate of imperial princes as margraves. This finally legitimised the rule of the Gonzaga, and henceforth they would further increase their prestige through art patronage and international marriages. At the same time, in the Marches, the Montefeltro family succeeded in gaining power over Urbino, Cagli and Gubbio in Umbria, although the Papal State opposed these usurpations.[11] To be sure, the landowning aristocracy dominated most cities in the Papal State, but here the representatives of the Pope's secular power were an important element. Nevertheless, over time some leaders of the urban parties passed their authority on to their sons and in certain cases were appointed papal vicars as well. This was also how the Montefeltro family came to power in Urbino, for example.

With the weakening of the Papal State and the Great Schism, the vicariates, which were initially granted for ten years, became more or less hereditary. Only in large cities such as Rome or Bologna did the Pope succeed in averting such a development and with it the erosion of his power. Not everywhere in northern and central Italy did all paths lead to the *signoria*, let alone to the formation of dynasties such as occurred in Ferrara, Milan, Mantua or Urbino, however.

In Pisa, for instance, outsiders and local families alternated as lords of the city. In Florence, even the short-term *signoria* of Robert of Anjou (1313–21) and Charles of Calabria (1325–28) failed to break the power of the oligarchy. Prato, Pistoia, Volterra and San Gimignano were incorporated into Florentine territory before a *signoria* had a chance to form.

Siena and Venice proved resistant to the model of the *signoria*. Venice would successfully defend its republican constitution until the occupation by Napoleon in 1797. The commune integrated its elected ruler, the Doge, by establishing fixed rules and rituals for the exercise of his authority. Newcomers and social climbers found a place in the commune, just as the territories or possessions in the eastern Mediterranean region offered them opportunities for economic and political activities. As a result, the struggles between *popolo* and oligarchy familiar from other cities were absent in Venice. This comparatively peaceful development was fostered by the circumstance that offices were only bestowed for short periods and could be attained by election. Throughout the thirteenth century, entry into the political ruling class (including the office of Doge) was open above all to rich and powerful non-nobles. For this reason, the Great Council was expanded in 1297 to more than 1,000 members, who elected all holders of public office. Although a small circle of old families, who before 1297 had reserved the majority of offices for their members, continued to enjoy the greatest prestige in the Venetian Republic, networks and clientele relationships that extended beyond these families now gained importance in filling offices. Even the Doge, whose freedom of action the Republic further restricted in the course of the fifteenth century, could shape policy in the Republic only with the cooperation of his peers.[12]

Despite episodes of signorial rule, republican structures also persisted in Florence, with certain families exercising authority either directly or indirectly. At times, the ruling oligarchy conducted their internal disputes by instrumentalising the pressure of the streets for their own purposes. The revolt of the *ciompi* in 1378 is an example. For decades, the *ciompi*, unguilded wool-workers, had been trying to form their own guild, and Salvestro de' Medici, for instance, supported these efforts in order to strengthen his position in the city government. Rumours, discussions and numerous meetings at which other artisans and small shopkeepers joined forces with the *ciompi* awakened hopes of change. These conflicts grew increasingly radical during July 1378, leading to the pillaging of the houses of supposed opponents. The *ciompi* pushed through reforms of the guild statutes and placed one of their own, Michele di Lando, at the head of the city government. Apart from adequate guild representation they called for the abolition of municipal forced loans – but not, interestingly enough, of direct taxes – in favour of a tax on property. Interest payments from the city's publicly funded debt, the *monte*, from which the rich profited, were ended, and the municipal debt was to be amortised over a period of twelve years. At the same time, the *ciompi* tried to introduce a two-year moratorium on private debts as well as better working conditions and wages. They attained some of their demands in the weeks that followed, created three new guilds (dyers, shirt makers and *ciompi*, or wool carders) and agreed on a new system of taxation based on estimated wealth. This lost the *ciompi* some of their supporters among the middle class, who on the one hand held shares in the municipal debt and on the other, as shopkeepers, were often the creditors of the lower classes – a moratorium on debts would have ruined them financially. Their employers, the drapers, reduced their orders, which meant even fewer work opportunities for the *ciompi*. Because of this radicalisation the previously leading guilds were able to win Michele di Lando over to their side. A large sum of money, which later allowed him to set up in business as a woollen cloth merchant in Modena, also helped sway him. With the aid of the guild militias, Michele di Lando put down the protests of the *ciompi*, whose guild was disbanded. The two other new guilds remained. A state of uncertainty persisted for about four years, in which the lower class, the middle class and the oligarchy vied for power. In 1382 the old elites finally regained their influence and adopted harsh measures against anyone they associated with the insurrection. Both Michele di Lando and Salvestro de' Medici were sent into exile.[13]

The commune was now ruled by a network centred around the Albizzi family. It would not be long before the Medici, who portrayed themselves as friends of the 'people', regained power. After the unsuccessful war against Milan, Cosimo de' Medici openly criticised the politics of the

Albizzi, which led to his exile in Padua and Venice. In 1434 the Albizzi were toppled and the Medici called back to Florence. Unlike the Albizzi, Cosimo only indirectly influenced the politics of the Republic of Florence, which attached great importance to its liberal traditions. His means were patronage and clientele relationships within and outside the city, but above all prestigious investments in public buildings as well as support for the arts and charitable foundations. That is how he gained the title of a *pater patriae*, which the city bestowed on him posthumously in 1464. Cosimo's peace policy benefited from the external framing conditions provided by the Peace of Lodi (1454), which allowed Italy to develop for nearly fifty years undisturbed by war.[14]

The prerequisite for the Lodi peace system was a consolidation of the most important Italian states. With the formation of larger territorial states grew the recognition that changes to the status quo were neither opportune nor enforceable by military means. Stabilisation began in the south, where in 1442 Alfonso of Aragón made Naples the centre of his realm, which in addition to the Iberian possessions, with the Balearic Islands and the Kingdom of Naples, also encompassed Sicily and Sardinia.[15] The Papal State likewise had a long process of consolidation behind it. The territorial possessions of the Papal State had eroded during the 'Babylonian Captivity' of the Pope in Avignon. In this power vacuum, a revolt took place in the mid-fourteenth century under the leadership of Cola di Rienzo, which brought the *popolo* to power in Rome in place of the previously ruling noble families. Rienzo's aim was to establish a confederation of Italian states with the Republic of Rome at its centre, but he could not assert himself for long against the nobility. Since he needed funds to finance the war and levied extraordinary taxes to this end, he soon lost support. After his death, the cardinal legate Egidio Albornoz took it upon himself to restore dominance in the Papal State. He largely succeeded in Umbria and Sabina, where the papal position was consolidated externally, for instance through fortresses in Assisi, Spoleto or Orvieto. Bologna was wrested away from the Visconti and integrated into the Papal State. The Pope returned to Rome in 1367. The anti-French movements dashed hopes of a permanent establishment in Rome, however, so that after three years the Pope was compelled to return to Avignon. The stability achieved was short-lived, and the Great Schism ensured that circumstances would not change until the Council of Constance. Thus the new Pope, Martin V, of the Roman Colonna family, had to reside several years in Santa Maria Novella in Florence before making his entry into Rome in 1420.[16] With the help of his family, which assumed important functions in the Campagna, he could assert himself at least in central Italy and Rome. His successor, the Venetian Eugene IV, tried to deprive the Colonna family of part of their recently acquired territories. The strong resistance of the Roman commune forced him to spend the next nine years in Tuscan exile. Only after his cardinal legate Giovanni Vitelleschi had established a 'graveyard peace' in Rome and environs could Eugene return in 1443.

In Milan, after the extinction of the Visconti family in 1447 and the brief intermezzo of the Ambrosian Republic, the Sforza assumed power, which rested on a consensus between the leading strata and the rulers.[17] Both Francesco Sforza and his father Muzzio had earned a good deal of money leading armies of mercenaries (*condottieri*), which at least made them independent of the Milan elites. Francesco Sforza was not quite so independent of Cosimo de' Medici, who had helped make him what he was, and now possessed in him a long-term ally above all against an expanding Venice. After several years of war between Milan and Venice, and serious damage to Venice's interests as a result of the fall of Constantinople and the Turkish invasion in the Mediterranean, lasting peace was established at Lodi in 1454. Piacenza and Parma remained part of the duchy of Milan, while Venice incorporated Brescia, Bergamo and Lodi. With the aim of preserving peace on the Italian peninsula, Milan, Venice and Florence formed a 'holy league', which Aragón and the Pope also joined. This *pax italiae* was, however, already challenged in 1478 by the nepotistic wars of Pope Sixtus IV. In the years that followed, papal attempts to gain a territorial power base for themselves and their families would become the source of new territorial conflicts, which France sought to exploit by intervening in 1494 (see 2.1).

Charles VIII of France's Italian adventure, which aimed to capture the Neapolitan throne after the death of King Ferrante, proved more arduous than expected. After the French arrived in Naples, Pope Alexander VI (Borgia), Emperor Maximilian, Ferdinand of Aragón, Milan and Venice formed an alliance that forced the French king to beat a hasty retreat to northern Italy. After the alliance was crushed in 1495 the Pope, who elevated his son Cesare to Duc de Valentinois, changed sides.

Florence's pro-French policy embroiled the city in protracted internal conflicts. Piero de' Medici was forced to flee the city because of his indulgence toward Charles VIII, and for a time the Dominican friar Savonarola controlled the fate of Florence. Savonarola was burnt at the stake in 1498 after excommunication and a papal interdict, and the Medici could only return to Florence in 1512. A second French invasion in 1501 under Louis XII had only initial success in the kingdom of Naples. The death of Alexander Borgia (1503) led to the collapse of his family's power in northern Italy.[18] In 1504 Aragón conquered Sicily and Naples, in each of which a viceroy represented the king. In the north, Milan became the centre of the conflicts of interest, a state of affairs that persisted until the Peace of Cateau-Cambresis (1559). The Papal State remained directly involved in the conflicts even under Julius II (1503–13), Leo X (1513–21) and Clement VII (1523–34), because of its shifts of alliances between France and the Holy Roman Emperor or Spain.

4.2 Republics and princely states

In his *Civilisation of the Renaissance in Italy*, Jacob Burckhardt coined the term 'Renaissance state', which later historians and political theorists regarded as an immediate antecedent to the modern state. Liberal historians sketched the model of the 'good republic' in contrast to that of the despotic princely state. In the light of more recent scholarship, however, neither the princely state appears to have been as despotic and efficient, nor the republic as democratic, as writers from the fourteenth century on claimed, and as historians later assumed (see 13.1). Thus in the conflicts between Milan and the republics of Florence and Venice, many authors came in on the side of the latter two, and argued on their behalf. Less voluble were the supporters of despotism, whose arguments were not encapsulated until the works of Machiavelli and Guicciardini. While republicans lauded 'liberty' as an ideal, monarchists propagated 'order', 'peace' or 'concord'.[19]

Even a critic of the Florentine Republic like Guicciardini, however, could approve of a moderately oligarchic state such as Venice. The lasting stability of the Venetian constitution, in particular, surprised not just contemporaries but also subsequent generations. Venice was ruled by the Doge, who was elected for life and governed the city together with the privy council or *consiglieri*. The senate, composed of 120 elected members, was responsible for legislation and foreign policy, while the Council of Ten (*dieci*) functioned as a judicial authority. The task of the Great Council (about 2,000 members in the late fifteenth century) was to fill the numerous offices of senators, ambassadors, judges and the like, most of whom served terms of only six months. Life membership in the Great Council and a professional bureaucracy in the chanceries guaranteed continuity.[20] In the Republic of Genoa, which historians generally consider to have been politically weak in the fifteenth century, the government of the Doge and the Council of Elders (*anziani*) was based on consensus. Under the *anziani* the nobility and the *popolo* accordingly had equal representation, and the

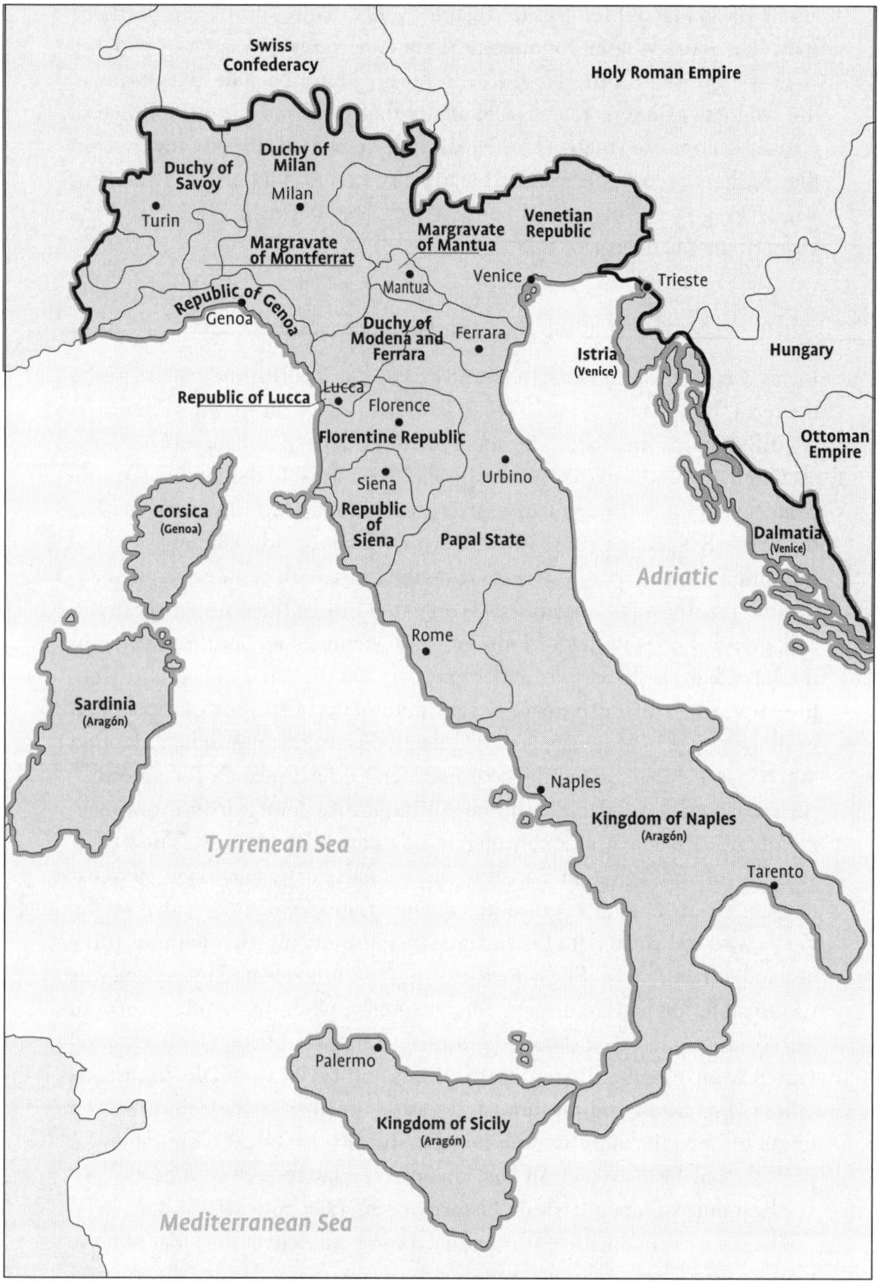

Map 7 Italy in the fifteenth century

popolani were evenly divided between merchants and artisans. When very important decisions had to be taken, ad hoc committees were also formed and citizens' assemblies convoked. The constant search for compromise and frequent changes in the office of Doge made foreign lords such as the Visconti, the Sforza or France appear as alternatives. After numerous changes of ruler, in 1527/28, under Spanish influence (*pax hispanica*), the formally independent Republic of Genoa was restored and the balance of power in domestic policy redistributed among twenty-eight noble clans (*alberghi*).[21]

In Florence, a two-month rotation of the highest government body, the *signoria*, led to a fluctuation of officeholders. Apart from the head magistrate, the *gonfaloniere della giustizia*, the members of the *signoria* included eight priors originally elected by the guilds. Under this body were several councils, the *gonfalonieri*, the *buonomini* and those representing the city's neighbourhoods and administrative divisions with legislative functions. Special committees also existed to deal with law, commerce, war and peace. As in Venice, the chancery with its permanent staff of civil servants lent the administration a certain stability. They were joined by numerous subaltern officers, the *familia* of the *signoria*. They included not just the municipal guard, doorkeepers and messengers but also countless servants, musicians, artisans and a cook. The rotation of office was accomplished not by election, but by drawing lots from a leather pouch. The number of potential officeholders, however, fell in the course of the fourteenth century from about 3,000 originally to 750. And this number, too, was further reduced by a preference for the higher-ranking members of the guilds. By the time of Cosimo de' Medici, only 'the most reliable of their followers were deemed "pouch-worthy"'.[22] Moreover, in the second half of the fifteenth century several new bodies were created, which were supposed to convey a sense of representation to the Florentines. Among them were a Council of the Two Hundred (1458) and a Council of the Seventy (1480), which replaced the former. After the expulsion of the Medici Florence created a Great Council like that in Venice, which was replaced after their return by the Council of the Seventy. After their renewed expulsion in 1527 and return in 1530, the Venetian model was adopted again in 1532. When Cosimo de' Medici took power (from 1537 as Duke Cosimo I, from 1569 as Grand Duke), the republican constitution became obsolete.

Henceforth, Florence thus followed the example of the monarchical or princely states of Milan, Rome and Naples with no apparent distress to the elites. Although in a monarchy the prince alone issued the laws, this did not mean that he dispensed with the counsel and participation of others. Milan, where the Sforza continued to rely on the consent of the old elites, had a privy council and an organization of public administration and justice largely independent of the prince, including courts for the western and eastern provinces and several appellate courts. This increased the demand for qualified jurists in the council of state and the courts. In Naples, too, Alfonso of Aragón established an appellate court and hired six lawyers to work as salaried judges. The King also heeded the recommendations of his counsellors – even if the Great Council had more ceremonial significance – and created a new financial administration. In Rome the College of Cardinals provided advisors to the Pope. As it grew in size, the popes increasingly relied on an inner circle of cardinals and secretaries and entrusted numerous administrative offices in the Papal State to their family members. In addition, the popes also had to find a *modus vivendi* with the powerful Roman families such as the Orsini and the Colonna.

The centre of the monarchies was the court, so that many elements of patriarchal rule persisted alongside a bureaucracy independent of the rulers.[23] There, personal ties to the ruler were often more important than qualifications. With the monarch's consent, positions of trust could very well be passed down from father to son or from uncle to nephew. The inflation of the courts in the late fifteenth and early sixteenth century is especially striking. The Este in Ferrara are a good example. Not only did Duke Ercole I and Duchess Eleonora of Aragón each have his and her own court with staffs of 550 and 110, respectively, but Ercole's brothers and sons also maintained their own residences, each with a small retinue of his own. After the Duke's death in 1505, his successor Alfonso I greatly increased the number of court offices (from 65 to *c.* 300). What is more, his brothers expanded their own staffs from a total of 60 to nearly 200. The personnel of the Este residences continued to expand until the mid-sixteenth century, so that 1,730 servants were on the payroll in the 1550s, one-third more than in 1500. Musicians, singers, painters and other fine craftsmen represented a significant portion, which underlines the creative potential of such a court. This is also reflected in levels of payment. Thus the famous composer Josquin Desprez headed the list of salaries at 632 lire, and many instrumentalists earned more than some ministers. The Flemish tapestry weavers also earned higher salaries than some courtiers, and the secretaries and notaries were outstripped by a harness-maker. Only artists lent a court glory and radiance, while courtiers could be easily replaced.[24]

4.3 Economic ascendancy

Like most European countries, the Italian territories experienced an economic upswing at this time, but it was far more intense than in the rest of western Europe.[25] A great migration to the cities began virtually simultaneously with the expansion of developed land and a sharp increase in population. The consequent urbanisation also set Italy apart from the rest of Europe. Around 1300 Milan, Venice, Genoa and Florence probably had more than 100,000 inhabitants each, and a number of other cities, including Pisa, Siena, Lucca, Bologna, Perugia, Padua, Pavia, Verona, Brescia, and Mantua as well as Palermo, Naples and Messina in the south had populations of between 20,000 and 50,000. The urbanisation process, which was also reflected in countless small cities with 5,000 to 20,000 inhabitants, intensified the division of labour between town and countryside. This development had come to an end by 1340, however, with the famines (1339–40, 1346–47, 1352–53, 1374–75) that were accompanied by numerous wars. The situation was exacerbated by the plague, which came from the eastern Mediterranean via Messina and quickly spread northward over the course of 1348.

Additional, smaller waves of plague further decimated the population in 1363, 1373 and 1382, if not to the same degree as in 1348. In the absence of precise population statistics, we can only estimate from the few figures we do have for individual cities or regions. In San Gimignano (town and surrounding countryside) 2,539 hearths were counted in 1332, which dropped in the years that followed to 1,163 (1350) and then 564 (1428). It has been estimated that the Florentine population fell from 90,000 in 1348 (according to Villani's chronicle) to 30,000 at the end of the fourteenth century, with a rise to 38,000 by 1427. A decline of nearly two-thirds thus appears realistic. In the fifteenth century, however, the population gradually recovered. Thus in the second half of the fifteenth century the number of inhabitants in Florence probably increased from 40,000 to 70,000, but it was not until the eighteenth century that the city's population returned to pre-plague levels. Venice and Naples, in contrast, probably already passed the 100,000 mark in the fifteenth century. The source of this population growth was a steady stream of migrants. In the case of Venice, they included merchants and artisan-entrepreneurs from other northern Italian cities who became citizens, but also a large number of labour migrants from the eastern shore of the Adriatic.[26] Rome, too, owed its increase in population from 20,000 to more than 50,000 over the course of the fifteenth century to migrants from Genoa, Tuscany,

Lombardy and Naples, who were magically attracted to the resurrected heart of Christendom.

Given the relatively large size of Italian cities and the dominance of merchants and artisans, the latter occupied a far more significant position in Italian society than elsewhere in Europe. The concentration of manufacturing and mercantile elements in the cities created a constant demand for grain and thus a strong market orientation in agriculture. The commercialisation of peasant production had accordingly proceeded apace since the twelfth century. Feudal dues, which in mid-thirteenth-century Tuscany consisted of cereals, money and pepper, point to the close market connections of peasant farmers, who after all had to purchase the pepper. Moreover, systems of fixed-term leases had become widespread by the twelfth century, gradually replacing long-term leases for a fixed rent. Landlords favoured the long-standing *mezzadria* or sharecropping system, in which tenants and landlords each received half of the agricultural produce, whether cereals, olives or livestock. One could regard this as a return to the barter economy, but it was more a successful attempt by landowners to participate directly in rising prices for agricultural products at a time of increasing currency devaluation.[27]

Italian agriculture was based on the typical Mediterranean crops of cereals, olives and wine grapes, with the addition in some regions of rice and fruit. In the north, the land under cultivation increased until around 1300 and again in the fifteenth century, when in Lombardy, for example, wasteland was increasingly opened to cultivation and marshes drained. In the fifteenth century Venetians, too, increasingly acquired land in the so-called *Terraferma*, which they cultivated or made arable. In Tuscany the amount of cultivated land shrank between 1300 and 1500 and the number of villages declined. Agricultural recovery here was slow because the remaining peasants suffered under the pressures of Florentine taxation.[28] The south, including Sicily, which had been the breadbasket of Italy before 1300, also experienced a lasting decline in agricultural production. In the mid-fifteenth century the available land there was increasingly used for grazing rather than cultivation, a practice emulated by some noble landowners in the Roman Campagna. Here, too, some villages disappeared, but this did not fundamentally threaten the supply of cereals to Rome. In the sixteenth century Rome would even develop a sophisticated system for supplying the city with grain.[29]

By the eleventh century, the trade in foodstuffs had led to an intensive exchange of goods by ship and overland on the Appenine peninsula. Apart from Emilia, cereals were produced above all in Apulia and

Sicily and transported from southern Italy to the north with the help of Genoese, Pisan and Venetian ships. Livestock from the Po Valley was also an important commodity. This trade was vital particularly for a city such as Florence, which in the early fourteenth century could feed its population from its surrounding countryside for five months a year at best. A trade in finished goods and bullion as well as luxury goods from all over Europe soon arose in exchange for foodstuffs and the raw materials for textiles. Northern Italian merchants quickly opened bases and branches in the south, which they later extended to the other side of the Adriatic and the eastern and western Mediterranean and even the Atlantic and the North Sea, with Genoa and Venice vying for the territories of the eastern Mediterranean and the Black Sea. It was only with the conquest of Constantinople during the Fourth Crusade (1204) and the trade settlements on the Balkan Peninsula and the Peloponnese that Venice gained ascendancy in this region. Genoa continued to assert itself in the Black Sea and the Crimea, but in the second half of the thirteenth century orientated itself westward past Gibraltar toward the Atlantic and the Bay of Biscay.

The incredible growth in trade brought changes now known as the Commercial Revolution (see 11.3). Where the volume of trade on one or several routes had grown continuously, a division of labour began. Merchants no longer had to accompany their wares to market personally by ship or caravan, or to make purchases themselves. Instead, they managed their firms' commercial transactions from their counting houses in northern Italy. Carters or ship owners specialising in transport saw to it that goods found their way from their places of production to the markets. In the foreign branch offices, factors organised the sale of goods or the purchase of raw materials from overseas or north of the Alps on instructions from the central office.

A portion of profits was invested in industrial development, for the Tuscan merchant-bankers were also active as entrepreneurs in the cloth and woollen trade. Thus the new societies established in the fourteenth century, such as the Datini or Medici companies, also distributed their investments equally between woollen cloth and silk production and the long-distance trade, and they founded local banks, which in the case of the Medici would later develop into international banking services and become the most important branch of their business.[30] In a manufacturing city such as Florence, but elsewhere as well, however, commerce and industry were closely intertwined. Particularly the process of manufacturing woollen cloth, with its elaborate division of labour, brought together entrepreneurs (equity owners), overseers, factors, spinners, weavers, dyers or fullers as well as wool cleaners, wool washers, wool combers, cloth shearers and finishers. Spinning the yarn was a task generally delegated to women in the countryside, and the final production of woven and fulled cloth was performed by small dyers' or shearers' workshops, which in turn hired labourers and apprentices. The same was true of silk production. Thus in Florence, up to one-third of the population lived from the textile trades. The city's woodworkers (carving and cabinetmaking), goldsmiths and stonemasons also enjoyed an international reputation.

Lombardy, in contrast, specialised in the production of weaponry. With the transition in military technology in the late fifteenth century, however, the market for swords and armour collapsed, where it had not been taken over by the Nuremberg arms industry (see 10.3). The dukes then promoted the silk industry instead. Alongside the manufacture of fustian in Cremona, Milan or Como, it would become a Milanese specialty. The Lombard stonemasons who contributed to numerous building projects in northern Italy in the fifteenth and sixteenth centuries were another regional trademark.[31]

Genoa distinguished itself as both a seaport and a silk-manufacturing city. Many silk fabrics were produced here, including brocade, damask, velvet, taffeta or so-called black silk for widows and clerics. Paper production and shipbuilding also played an important role in the economy.

As a commercial centre, Genoa profited from the upswing in the thirteenth century, while in the fourteenth century the city suffered from the military conflicts in the western Mediterranean. In the fifteenth century, Turkish expansion robbed Genoa of its trade with the Orient. It was able to expand its position as the most important shipping site in the western Mediterranean and dominated ship traffic with the Iberian Peninsula and France. In the sixteenth century Genoa became the most important hub for Ibero-American silver and a banking centre for the Spanish Crown.[32]

Venice, which focused on trade with the Orient, had gained international renown with its glass industry. On the island of Murano, where the Venetian glass foundries moved in the thirteenth century because of fears of fire in the city, glassmakers manufactured enamels for mosaics, ampullae and also container glass, which found markets both in the Near East and north of the Alps. Shipbuilding and, in the late fifteenth century, the printing press also played an important role. Venice at this time was the most important European book city, with more than 150 printing shops. Trade with the Orient overshadowed all of these manufacturing activities, however. Every summer and autumn numerous galleys left Venice en route to Beirut and Alexandria, from whence they brought back spices, mainly pepper, but also cotton and silk. Venetians paid 300,000 ducats yearly for these commodities in addition to exports of local goods (cloth and glass, among other things). Although the Turkish incursion into the eastern Mediterranean impeded the Venetian Levantine trade, and Portuguese expansion into Asia was also viewed as a threat, Venice retained its important role in the Mediterranean region in the sixteenth century, as evidenced by the continuing presence of German merchants in the *Fondaco dei Tedeschi*.[33]

What of the crises and cycles of the Italian economy? We need to distinguish here between local crises triggered by wars or unexpected monetary, credit or production bottlenecks and major watershed events such as the plague. Although the fragmentary evidence often makes this impossible, it is clear, at any rate, that the late fourteenth century and the first half of the fifteenth century witnessed crisis upon crisis. In Venice, for example, the plague of 1348 (which carried off about one-third of Venetians) left most banks surprisingly robust, while the 1370s, 1420s and the years after the conquest of Constantinople proved fatal to many of them. In most cases, however, the founding of new banks, or the re-founding of old ones by the original proprietor families soon compensated for bank collapses. In Florence, the war against Milan and the return of the plague around 1400 brought the economy to a standstill, causing Francesco Datini to comment in January 1402 that business there was utterly dead.[34]

The annual production of woollen cloth, with 80,000 pieces documented for the year 1338 in Florence, dropped to 30,000 pieces in 1373 and remained below 20,000 pieces in the century that followed. The decline in cloth production, which faced increased competition on the European markets, however, was largely compensated for by the upswing in the silk industry and the growing demand for brocade and silk stuffs at the European courts.[35] There was a palpable labour shortage both in the Florentine countryside, the *contado*, and in the city. The commune tried for that reason to stimulate settlement and immigration by offering tax privileges. Merchants from other cities, such as the Panciatichi from Pistoia or the Borromei from Pisa, enjoyed excellent opportunities for advancement which they used to acquire wealth, according to the *catasto* records of 1427. The Medici, too, succeeded in this period in accumulating a fortune that would allow them to become the city's secret rulers in the decades that followed.[36]

4.4 Clerics and the urban middle classes

In Italy, too, society was organised into estates: the clergy, nobility, townspeople and peasantry. Because of the high degree of urbanisation, however, the occupational classes of the free professions, artisans and shopkeepers played a far larger role within the urban middle classes than elsewhere in Europe. When it came to the traditional clerical estate, Italy appears to have surpassed the rest of Europe both as regards the status and the concentration of clerics. Here, the Pope and numerous cardinals ruled over the archbishops, bishops, abbots and parish priests.

The number of clerics was also relatively high. In Bologna, for example, they made up 5 per cent of the population in the sixteenth century. In Venice in this period monks and nuns alone represented 2 per cent of all inhabitants. The social origins of the episcopate, however, present a picture familiar to us from other parts of Europe. Around two-thirds of bishops were noblemen, some of whom were already made bishops as children to secure the episcopal see for their families. Similarly, Pius II, Calixtus III and Sixtus IV appointed their nephews cardinals, and these men were then elected Pope as Pius III, Alexander VI and Julius II.

Serving as a secretary in the household of a prominent cardinal after studying jurisprudence offered another route to ecclesiastical office. Family and clientele relationships also played an important role in the appointment of parish priests (benefices). The members of religious orders who fulfilled a variety of functions in the cities were especially numerous. Women's orders in particular served as a social reservoir, since putting daughters in a convent was cheaper than providing a dowry when they married. The male members of orders also promoted religious life by preaching publicly, and some of them, like Fra Filippo Lippi and Fra Angelico, participated in the artistic production of the Renaissance.

Nobles were such by virtue of birth or patent of nobility. Venice, for example, registered its aristocratic families in 1297 and thus closed off the noble estate. Between 1293 and 1379 the city had 244 noble families, a number of which died out, however. For that reason, after the 1381 peace of Turin, which ended the war against Genoa, thirty families of the *popolo* were taken into the nobility. Adopting an aristocratic way of life could also ennoble, however. A segment of the nobility still supported themselves by military service. This could lead from service in the Genoese or Venetian navy to a lucrative position as a *condottiere* in the mercenary armies. Another attractive office was that of castellan in the duchy of Milan. In the Papal State and the south, feudal services also played a more important role.

In the republics, in contrast, noblemen had access to numerous unpaid offices, including those of doge in Venice or *gonfaloniere* in Florence. In the princely states noblemen served as officials in the territorial administration. At the same time, the position of courtier became increasingly appealing. Aristocrats also had access to bishoprics and cathedral chapters, especially since the latter were generally monopolised by the city's noble families. The Venetians provided four popes in the fifteenth century, with Angelo Correr (Gregory XII), Gabriele Condulmer (Eugene IV), Pietro Barbo (Paul II) and the Cretan-born Alexander V. Candidates were also needed for five archbishoprics, thirty-eight bishoprics and countless abbeys on Venetian territory alone.

New fields of endeavour for the Italian nobility opened up in the flourishing area of diplomacy as well as the law, which apparently was easily reconciled with the idea of a noble way of life. In Florence, high finance and commerce were also open to the nobility, and the rise of the old aristocratic Pazzi family, who became the most important bankers alongside the Medici in the fifteenth century, provides an eloquent example of this.

Much the same applied to Venice, where the majority of nobles engaged in commerce. Here it was also quite common for patricians to cultivate their own estates in the *Terraferma*, while Florentine aristocrats preferred rural leisure pursuits at their country manors. All nobles shared a code that bound them to *onore* – i.e., to an honourable and reputable way of life. This included courage, loyalty and generosity as well as offices and titles, which contributed to a family's reputation through hospitality and art patronage and thus represented an important inspiration for the artistic achievements of the Renaissance.[37]

In the latter area there were intersections with non-noble townspeople, particularly the merchants and members of the free professions including lawyers, judges, notaries, medical doctors and apothecaries, as well as with government officials. As members of the seven major guilds, they represented what was known in popular parlance as the *populo grasso*, literally the fat people, since leading merchant families like the Medici and a large portion of Florentine wealth were concentrated there. Like the merchants and other professions, the guilds also differed according to their prestige. Thus the legal profession ranked above the mercantile class. Merchants accordingly had their sons trained as lawyers and married their daughters to jurists. The profession of lawyer also appeared attractive to the younger sons of the nobility and the urban elites. For migrants from the countryside, becoming a notary was often a first step up the social ladder. This hierarchy also assumed visual form in the processions, which in Florence were led by the nobles, with the lawyers, merchants and notaries behind them. The trades, represented by artisans and shopkeepers, who in Florence were combined into the *arti minori*, ranked below the liberal professions. Many artisans worked as small-scale entrepreneurs who hired subcontractors or rented workshops or tools to other craftsmen. According to the records of the *catasto*, they often also owned a piece of land. The shopkeepers, for example drapers and grocers, were often wealthier than the average members of the crafts, at the lower end of which were wage labourers like the wool washers. Beneath them were the numerous day labourers who worked in commerce and shipping as well as the many domestic servants and above all representatives of the dishonourable trades and other marginal groups.

Venice, but also Vicenza, offers variations on this picture, which often generalizes from the Florentine perspective.[38] In Venice, the group under the nobility were the *cittadini*, families who had failed to rise into the nobility before its closure. They nevertheless enjoyed many privileges, such as access to the office of High Chancellor or various notary positions. Closely allied with the patriciate in their political activities, their way of life resembled that of the nobility. As a result of the integration of this group of commoners, Venice was spared the kind of conflicts between patriciate and *popolo* that flared up in the Tuscan cities. As *cittadini* with the privilege of being treated as such *de intus et extra*, that is, both inside and outside the city, foreign merchants also had the opportunity to do business and trade like Venetians. Artisans also profited from Venice as a commercial centre, which offered a living to various export-oriented trades. The port and local industry continually attracted foreigners as traders and labour migrants. Not only were German merchants based in the *Fondaco dei Tedeschi*; German bakers, cobblers, textile workers and medical doctors also plied their trades in Venice. Dalmatians, Croats and Albanians worked in shipping and the port, but also as thieves. A large Greek and a smaller Armenian community also existed. Venetian traders brought slaves to the Italian slave markets from the Balkans and in the fifteenth century increasingly from Africa. Slaves worked as domestic servants in all Italian cities and even formed part of dowries. In Venice and its possessions, they were also used to row gondolas and work on the plantations of Crete and Cyprus. The Jewish population was not permitted to live in Venice proper, but was expressly invited to settle in Mestre and the other cities of the Veneto (Treviso, Padua, Vicenza and Verona) in order to replace the consumer credits of Christian usurers at more favourable conditions (see 12.4).

In the years 1382 to 1397 alone, after the end of the war against Genoa, the need for credit in Venice was so great that a Jewish community was able to negotiate a right of settlement at fixed conditions (pawn lending at an interest rate between 8 and 10 per cent). Once the credit situation had relaxed, in 1394, the Venice Senate ordered the Jews to leave the city, effective in 1397. This anti-Jewish policy did not, however, prevent the Senate from inviting Jewish merchants who imported raw silk, and thus served Venice's competitors, to return to Venice in 1408.[39]

The largest social group in Italy, as elsewhere, was the peasantry, which was also highly differentiated both internally and from region to region. Thus in the fifteenth century remnants of serfdom persisted in Friuli and Liguria, and even the free *mezzadri* of Tuscany eked out a bare subsistence from the land. Their tiny market share meant that they did not profit from the late fifteenth-century revival of demand for cereals and rising grain prices. The only beneficiaries were the manorial lords and the large farmers, the so-called *contadini grassi*, who both leased and leased out land. Moreover, peasant incomes largely depended on which part of the feudal rent Florentine landlords claimed as dues, and the Republic of Florence took in taxes.

Thus the Florentine *catasto* records of 1427 show a great concentration of wealth in Florence and a relative impoverishment of the surrounding countryside. Three thousand Florentine families (5 per cent of the population) held more than half of the wealth of the Florentine Republic, while the remaining 57,000 Tuscan households paid taxes on the rest. In Florence, 1 per cent of the population (100 families) held one-quarter of the wealth (one-sixth that of the entire republic). The Strozzi (fifty-three families, 2.6 per cent of municipal wealth) were at the top of the pyramid, ahead of the Bardi (sixty families, 2.1 per cent), the Medici (thirty-one families, 1.9 per cent), the Alberti (eighteen families, 1 per cent), the Albizzi (twenty-four families, 1 per cent) and the Peruzzi (twenty-eight families, 1.1 per cent). Only 14 per cent of households had no taxable income, so that despite a certain concentration of wealth at the top, assets were present well into the lower ranks of society, and artisans and shopkeepers were also potential consumers of luxury goods.[40]

4.5 Renaissance art

From the fourteenth to the sixteenth century, the process of renewal that in the nineteenth century came to be known as the Renaissance shaped the culture of the Italian states (see 13.2). Although it might seem as if the

Renaissance was invented in fifteenth-century Florence, it was influenced by processes of exchange in the Mediterranean region that had begun long before and would continue into the sixteenth century. In the thirteenth century, most Tuscan painters worked in the Byzantine style, and only Cimabue's *Madonna* for the high altar of Santa Trinità (1260/1280) created a spatial illusion. The Sienese painter Duccio went a step further in his *Rucellai Madonna* by giving the figures a human (aristocratic) visage, inspired by French illuminated manuscripts. Finally, in the fourteenth century, Giotto replaced Greek spiritualisation or dematerialisation with diverse embodiments of the human form. In his frescoes in Assisi, Padua and Florence, he found new ways of expressing space and the human body.[41]

Duccio and the fourteenth-century Sienese School he inspired were similarly innovative. Simone Martini, who was much praised by Petrarch, did not merely adapt the influences of French Gothic art, but from the 1330s also contributed to the spread of the Gothic style in Avignon. Sienese painting reached a high point with the Lorenzetti brothers. While Pietro's paintings strike us with their dramatic action and expressive figures, Ambrogio Lorenzetti's frescoes, such as the allegories of *Good and Bad Government* in the Palazzo Pubblico of Siena, are characterised by a perspectival construction of space and, for the first time, a topographical – but still allegorical – representation of landscape and cityscape.[42]

The next developments, however, occurred in Florence. There, in collaboration with Masolino and to distinguish himself from the other artist and his delicate Gothic style, Masaccio ushered in the so-called early Renaissance with the frescoes for the Brancacci Chapel, which are striking for the plasticity of the figures and use of light. In his *Trinity* in Santa Maria Novella, he created the first painted space using scientific central perspective, translating Brunelleschi's language of architectural forms into a painterly idiom. The *Opera Duomo* provided essential inspiration. These workshops produced sculptors and architects such as Nanni di Banco, Brunelleschi, Ghiberti and Donatello, who assumed new tasks in town planning and the fine arts. At the centre were two competitions, to complete the dome of the cathedral and for the second door of the baptistery. Francesco Brunelleschi won the competition for the dome in 1418, and his epochal construction was completed in 1436. The commission for the second (north) door of the baptistery – Andrea Pisano created the first (south door) in 1330–36 – had already gone in 1402 to Lorenzo Ghiberti, who took until 1424 to complete it, however. The goldsmith Ghiberti may well have been the most versatile artist of the Florentine early Renaissance.

As a craftsman well acquainted with the Florentine painters of the *Trecento*, he supplied cartoons for paintings and stained-glass windows. Painters of the younger generation such as Masolino, Uccello and Benotto Gozzoli trained in his workshop. Together with Donatello and other artists he was also commissioned by the guilds to create three monumental figures to adorn the outside of Orsanmichele. In old age, Ghiberti penned theoretical texts as well, reflecting on the art of antiquity in his *Commentarii* and at the same time compiling the first lexicon of artists, before Vasari.

A number of styles coexisted in painting. While Fra Angelico, Benotto Gozzoli and Fra Filippo Lippi remained true to the International Gothic style, Paolo Uccello took perspective to almost grotesque lengths, and Andrea del Castagno painted his series of illustrious men and women in a sculptural style. In the frescoes of the chapels he painted, Ghirlandaio combined religious themes with his Florentine patrons' desire to express their social standing. The Florentine painter most prized by Lorenzo de' Medici (known as the Magnificent), however, was Antonio Pollaiuolo, who painted not just heroes of antiquity for the Medici palace, but also the altar-piece for the funerary chapel of Cardinal James of Portugal in San Miniato del Monte or a portrait of the Duke of Milan. The young Sandro Botticelli, whose mythological early works, with their profane, antique themes – influenced by Flemish tapestries – are still the focus of interest, studied Pollaiuolo's linear style. Above all in the 1480s, Botticelli created important altarpieces, and changed his style in the *Annunciation*, the *Pietà* or the *Nativity*, possibly under the influence of Savonarola's preaching.[43]

Beyond Florence, Piero della Francesca, who was associated with the court of Urbino, gained particular prominence. His interest in matters of perspective, proportion and catoptrics was more than merely theoretical. His portraits of the Duke and Duchess as well as his *Madonna di Senigallia* show the influence of Netherlandish panel painting in their landscape backgrounds and the direction of the light. Andrea Mantegna, in contrast, who spent the last forty-six years of his life as a painter at the Gonzaga court in Mantua, where he decorated the palace – most importantly with the group portraits in the *Camera degli Sposi* – influenced the northern artists Dürer and Paumgartner with his paintings, which were also widely disseminated as prints.

The court of Alfonso of Aragón at Naples is often overlooked as an intermediary between Netherlandish and Mediterranean influences. Alfonso gathered humanists at his court, hiring Pisanello, among other artists, as a medallist, and commissioned a still extant triumphal arch on the antique model from Iberian and Italian masters. He also acquired Flemish tapes-

Figure 3 Triumphal arch of Alfonso V on the Castel Nuovo in Naples.

tries and art, for example Jan van Eyck's *Lommelini Altarpiece*, named after the Genoese client who commissioned it. The mention of the four painters Gentile da Fabriano, Pisanello, van Eyck and Rogier van der Weyden and the three sculptors Lorenzo and Vittorio Ghiberti and Donatello in *De viris illustribus* by the Naples court humanist Bartolomeo Fazio is evidence of this creative atmosphere. Although the passion for collecting waned after the King's death, Antonello de Messina, who had been schooled in Flemish painting in Naples, introduced the Netherlandish technique of panel painting into Venice in the 1470s, and the achievements of Naples artists also stimulated painting in Valencia (see 3.6).[44]

Netherlandish paintings were present at this period in the commercial centres of Genoa, Venice and Florence, where trade contacts provided access to the visual culture of Flanders. Italian merchants served as intermediaries: the Luccan Paolo Poggio supplied the court of Ferrara with these paintings, and himself owned a *pietà* by van Eyck. Another Luccan, Giovanni Arnolfini, commissioned the famous double portrait, and the Genoese Battista Lomellini commissioned a triptych that would later gain renown in the possession of Alfonso of Aragón. The Piemontese de Villa family ordered works from Rogier van der Weyden, just as the Loiani family of Bologna commissioned paintings by Memling and other Bruges masters. Patrons from the circle of the Florentine Portinari family would prove particularly important for artists from Bruges.

In comparison to their counterparts in Genoa and Lucca, Florentine collectors were slow to develop an interest in Flemish painting. The Prato native and papal legate Francesco Coppini, bishop of Terni, made a start during a sojourn in the Low Countries, where he commissioned an altarpiece (*The Resurrection of Lazarus*) from Nicolas Froment, a Provençal painter active there. The next commission would be Memling's *Last Judgment* for Angelo Tani's new chapel in Badia Fiesolana, although the painting ended up in Danzig (Gdańsk) instead in 1473. Ten years later, the Van der Goes triptych ordered by Tommaso Portinari arrived in Florence. Portinari commissioned two further works from Memling, a Passion and a portable triptych (Virgin and Child), of which only the donor portraits survive. In addition, Memling and other artists painted numerous other friends and members of the Portinari family.

Alongside commissions, the purchase of Netherlandish paintings and tapestries on the free market in Antwerp or Florence represents another variant of cultural transfer. Thus in the 1460s, agents of the Medici bought *pannetti dipinti* at the Antwerp fairs. They also ordered tapestries, or purchased cartoons after which they could be woven directly in Florence.

It was also possible, however, to buy tapestries as well as painted *panni* in Florence.[45]

In Venice, Giovanni Bellini ushered in the period of the high Renaissance, which would be influenced by Lotto, Titian, Palma Vecchio and Veronese and began in 1496/97 in Milan with Leonardo's *Last Supper* in Santa Maria delle Grazie. The centre of artistic activities shifted to Rome, however, where the popes set out to lend the city new splendour, for which project they engaged Bramante, Michelangelo and Raphael. In 1480/81 Pope Sixtus IV hired the best artists of his day, including Ghirlandaio, Botticelli, Perugino and Signorelli, to paint frescoes on the walls of the private papal chapel that now bears his name.

Michelangelo and his assistants painted the ceiling in 1508/12 and completed the decoration in 1534 with the fresco of the Last Judgment. Building St Peter's after plans by Bramante, in contrast, would be a matter of centuries. After the death of the architects Bramante (1514), Raphael (1520) and Sangallo (1546), Michelangelo assumed responsibility until 1564 for the architecture of the project, which would only be completed in the second half of the seventeenth century under Bernini with the design of St Peter's Square.[46]

Architecture tackled a wide variety of themes and tasks. Apart from the reception of classical antiquity in the column orders, tectonics and decorative forms, these included the revival of the domed central-plan building, the invention of the imposing city palace and the country villa, and the creation of programmatic public buildings. The first structure in the new style was the Florentine foundling hospital designed by Brunelleschi, who then offered fresh inspiration for the central-plan building with the Pazzi Chapel and for the nave of Santo Spirito. Leon Battista Alberti combined the study of classical authors and their theoretical reflections with architectural practice. He thus introduced the pediments of Roman temples to the façade design for Santa Maria Novella and optically linked the high nave with the lower side aisles using volutes, a stylistic device that his successors would take up repeatedly into the baroque period. A new type of building was the town palace, which fulfilled both prestige and defensive functions and allowed for a new cultivation of interior decoration.

The leading Florentine families commissioned palaces by Michelozzo (as did the Medici and the Pazzi) or Alberti (as did the Rucellai). In Rome, numerous cardinals reinforced their claims to the papal tiara by building palaces, which in case of success entailed substantial extensions to the papal residence.[47] The new palaces confronted their owners and consequently the artists they engaged with new tasks of interior decoration and furnishing. These included not just murals and wainscoting for the walls, but also furnishing the building with chairs, beds, cabinets and chests, which in turn reflected a new richness of form. Framed pictures, mirrors, statues, glass and majolica adorned the rooms and stimulated artistic and artisanal production.

The construction of country villas or noble residences outside the city as well as propagandistic mausoleums and other funerary monuments represented additional attractive architectural projects. The latter frequently constituted a symbiosis of architecture and sculpture. One example is the tomb of Pope John XIII (d. 1419) by Michelozzo and Donatello in the baptistery of Florence. While Pollaiuolo's tomb of Sixtus IV (d. 1484) in Rome, adorned with depictions of the Virtues, was still very much in the tradition of medieval gravestones, the architecture and sculpture of Michelangelo's Medici tombs in the sacristy of San Lorenzo in Florence (1520–34) already exhale the very spirit of the new era.

4.6 The model of Italian literature

With the development of various poetic forms such as the sonnet, the tercet, the ballade, the canzone and the stanza, the Italian literature of the fourteenth to sixteenth centuries became a model for other emerging national literatures. The striving for refined forms of literary expression was still in the forefront, but increasingly took on a life of its own in the sixteenth century. The emergence of a literature in the Italian territories was nevertheless a process of several centuries. The earliest surviving signs of literary activity in the Italian language date from the period around 1230. While Venetian and Lombard authors (Gerardo Patecchio, Bonvesin da la Riva, Giacomino da Verona) wrote didactic and gnomic poetry in a northern Italian vernacular, jurists at the Hohenstaufen court chancery of Frederick II translated the themes of Provençal poetry into a Sicilian-southern Italian dialect, thereby creating a new literary language. Meanwhile, in the second half of the thirteenth century, some 3,000 so-called *laudi* were written in Umbria and Tuscany following Francis of Assisi and his psalm in praise of creation ('Cantico di frate sole'), with the Franciscan Jacopone da Todi gaining renown as an author in the *laudi* genre.

The late thirteenth century is characterised by the emergence of the *dolce stil nuovo* (sweet new style) in Bologna and later in Florence. The borrowings from Sicilian lyric poetry– during his long captivity in Bologna, Frederick II's illegitimate son King Enzo disseminated Sicilian culture in university circles – are unmistakable. Authors such as Guittone d'Arezzo and Chiaro Davanzati not only offered variations on the inexhaustible theme of unrequited love, but also positioned themselves in the contemporary conflicts between the Guelf and Ghibelline factions. Guido Cavalcanti (*c.* 1260–1300) and above all Dante Alighieri (1265–1321) would become the most important protagonists of this new lyric poetry, which was no longer an art reserved for the nobility.

Dante was also drawn into the conflicts between the city-states when, after joining the guild of the apothecaries and medical doctors, he soon garnered the post of prior in Florence. As an opponent of Pope Boniface VIII's claims to power, he was forced into permanent exile when the Pope's partisans came to power in Florence, and he had to seek asylum at various Italian courts, initially in Verona and later in Ravenna. While still in Florence he wrote *La vita nuova* (1293/94), which tells of the poet's love for Beatrice and calls for a renewal in manners and morals. After the never completed 'Banquet' (*Il Convivio*), Dante wrote a Latin work directed at scholars in which he argued for the vernacular (*De vulgari eloquentia*), calling for a unified language that would overcome the multiplicity of dialects and be useful for all purposes and classes of society. Of all the available dialects, only Florentine Tuscan fulfilled the criteria, and Dante's magnum opus, the *Divina Commedia*, as it came to be known, ultimately made it the dominant literary language. This didactic work of world poetry, written around 1320, does not simply provide the first-person narrator with constant opportunities for self-reflection. With its large cast of characters from antiquity as well as contemporary Florence, it also unfolds a broad panorama in which to address the Fall, purification and triumph of Man, who, in the person of Dante, traverses Hell, Purgatory and Paradise, experiencing vice, suffering and triumph.[48]

After Dante died, the number of his followers grew exponentially. His death was already the occasion for countless elegiac sonnets and *canzoni*. Giovanni Villani, for example, added a life of Dante to his Florentine chronicle under the year 1321. Unlike his predecessor Dino Compagni (*c.* 1255–1324), who like Dante was a victim of the political conflicts of his day and compiled his chronicle from his personal point of view, the much-travelled merchant Villani endeavoured to give a sober account of events in Florence and neighbouring regions. After he succumbed to the plague in 1348, his brother Matteo (after 1280–1363) and later his son Filippo (1325–1404) continued the chronicle.

Boccaccio (1313–75), too, made a name for himself as a biographer of Dante. He was the first to draw attention to the *Divina Commedia* (it was he who added the word 'divine' to the title), and he told of a competition over an epitaph for Dante. Unlike his humanist friends such as Petrarch (see 13.1), who placed greater stock in their Latin compositions than in the works they wrote in their mother tongue, Boccaccio fostered the Italian literary language in prose and poetry. After serving at the courts of Ravenna and Forlì in the 1340s, he was caught unawares by the plague in Florence in 1348/49, which inspired him to write the famous *Decameron*. Under the new term 'novella', Boccaccio brought together a variety of short narrative forms, mixing aesthetic, satirical, farcical and edifying elements. Successors such as Sercambi, Giovanni di Firenze or Sacchetti would emulate and diversify this medium.

Although Latin humanism shaped the learned landscape first in Italy and later throughout western Europe, by the mid-fifteenth century so-called vulgar humanism (from *volgare*, the language of the people) had emerged as a movement for the national vernacular. Thus in his 1436 *Vita di Dante*, Leonardo Bruni defended Italian by arguing that as a literary language, it came very close to Latin. Matteo Palmieri (*Della vita civile*, 1432/36) and Leon Battista Alberti (*Della famiglia*, 1434/41) then expressly promoted Italian. It was also in this context that the first printed Italian grammar appeared, the *Regole della lingua florentina*. One of the new literati was Luigi Pulci, who created a novel type of comic chivalric romance in *Il Morgante* and who would inspire many authors of the sixteenth century. Pulci was a client of the Medici family, who, in the form of Lorenzo (*Il Magnifico*, 1449–92), expressly supported literature in Italian alongside the cultivation of the classical heritage.[49] Lorenzo not only wrote poetry, but also commissioned Angelo Poliziano to compile an anthology of Tuscan authors, known as the *Raccolta Aragonese*, for the Aragonese court. Poets around the courts and princely residences also accepted commissions for panegyrics. Francesco Filelfo (1398–1481) penned a *Sforziad* glorifying the Sforza family of Milan. Naldo Naldi (1436–*c.* 1513) wrote an epic poem on the sacking of Volterra for Lorenzo de' Medici, and other authors also used this theme to further their careers.

The Este court in Ferrara also commissioned works of this nature. Tito Vespasiano Strozzi wrote the *Borsias* for Borso d'Este, establishing a series of epics for the family, for the Este revived interest in chivalric epics and started a collection of relevant manuscripts. This was the context in which Matteo Boiardo (1441–94) wrote his epic poem *L'Orlando innamorato* (Orlando in love). In addition, Boiardo produced a three-volume vernacular *canzoniere* containing 150 sonnets and 30 other poems. His *Orlando innamorato* doubtless influenced the *Orlando furioso* of Ludovico Ariosto (1474–1533), who wrote epics in the service of the Este in Ferrara as well.

Between 1517 and 1525 Ariosto also penned seven satires that dealt quite ironically with court life, although they were only published after his death. He may also be regarded as the originator of the Italian Renaissance comedy. Borrowing motifs from Roman comedy, he wrote numerous plays, which he produced in Ferrara with a small ensemble. These comedies, which were addressed above all to the court ladies of Ferrara, distinguished Ariosto fundamentally from another contemporary writer of comedies, Niccolo Machiavelli. Machiavelli, made famous by his call for a modern state under the leadership of an energetic prince in *Il Principe* (The Prince, 1513), addressed the origins of the strife among the Italian states in his dark comedy *La Mandragola* (The Mandrake).

The reception of Machiavelli's *Il Principe* was overshadowed by that of Baldassare Castiglione's (1478–1529) *Libro del cortegiano* (Book of the courtier, 1528). While many critics over the centuries rejected Machiavelli's grim defence of *raison d'état*, the *cortegiano* went on to epitomise the aristocratic courtier and diplomat, and the court of Duke Guidobaldo de Montefeltro at Urbino became the very symbol of Renaissance courtly culture. Quite a different figure was the playwright and polemicist Pietro Aretino (1492–1556) in Rome, whose first comedy *La cortigiana* (The courtesan, 1525/34) is a scathing satire of life in the Papal State as embodied by the career-mad Messer Maco of Siena, who dreams of becoming a cardinal. It was not for nothing that Pope Paul IV, a year after the playwright's death, placed Aretino's works on the index of banned books.[50]

4.7 Secular polyphony and the reception of the *ars nova*

As in all western European countries, monophonic singing was the most widespread form of musical expression in fourteenth- and fifteenth-century Italy. As a rule, melodies were passed down orally, and only a few collections of *laudi* included musical notation with the texts. At the same time, an extraordinarily rich autonomous form of secular polyphony developed in northern Italy, which was closely associated with the emergence of an Italian literary language. Preferred genres such as the *ballata*, the madrigal and the *caccia* were usually composed for two or three voices, tightly adapted to the textual models and set down in their own notation. The primary centres of this music of the Trecento, which Boccaccio writes about in the *Decameron*, were the courts of Milan, Verona and above all Florence.[51] We have virtually no information, in contrast, about the practice of secular polyphony in central Italy. The return of the papal court to Rome from Avignon (1377), though, meant the entry of French elements into the Pope's private chapel. The influence of French music increased toward the end of the century throughout Italy, including the north.

The inspiration came from musicians in the service of Church dignitaries, who came to Rome from western Europe with their employers. In this way the French *ars nova*, with its polyphonic masses and motets, spread in Italy from the early fifteenth century. Motets were composed and performed above all in honour of bishops, doges and other local rulers. In the second half of the fifteenth century it was above all Franco-Flemish musicians and composers, such as Guillaume Dufay and later Josquin Desprez (*c.* 1440–1521), who spent longer periods working in Italy and influenced musical styles there.[52]

Thus a large proportion of Franco-Flemish music was composed and performed in Italy, and survives in the Italian sources. Italian composers, in contrast, are scarcely to be found among the creators of this music before the early sixteenth century. Italian cathedrals lacked the choir schools of their north-western European counterparts, and in the churches, too, polyphonic music was performed mainly by court musicians. Even St Peter's in Rome, where Sixtus IV had intended to establish a choir for polyphonic music, had to wait until the time of Julius II for its realisation. His successor Leo X, himself a musician and composer, had already expressed his musical interests before his election, so that many members of the Mantua choir entered his service. Given the relative scarcity of good musicians in Italy, well-known musicians could command high salaries not just at court, but also in the cities. Thus for example Venice created the office of *maestro di cappella* for the Doge's chapel in San Marco, and filled it in 1491 with the Frenchman Pierre de Fossis, who was followed in 1527 by Adrian Willaert, despite local lobbying on behalf of the assistant Lupato. Music acquired a new impetus in the context of court plays and masques, which were promoted by, among others, the duchesses of Ferrara and Mantua.

At the same time, the madrigal (not to be confused with the Trecento genre of the same name) emerged in the sixteenth century as a symbiosis of polyphonic music by foreign composers and the native literary tradition, a new art form that would become the dominant genre in secular ensemble music as the century wore on.

Notes

1 Toubert and Paravicini Bagliani (eds), *Federico II.*
2 Benvenuti, *Le repubbliche marinare.*
3 Raveggi, Tarassi, Medici and Parenti (eds), *Ghibellini, guelfi e popolo grasso.*
4 Jones, *The Italian city-state*, 408–19.
5 Ibid., 333–583.
6 Raveggi et al.(eds), *Ghibellini, guelfi e popolo grasso*, 245–58, 282–98, 307–9.
7 Varanini (ed.), *Gli Scaligieri*; Hyde, *Padua in the age of Dante*; Kohl, *Padua under the Carrara.*
8 Chiappa Mauri (ed.), *L'età dei Visconti.*
9 Dean, *Land and power.*
10 Vaini, *Ricerche gonzaghesche.*
11 Maire Vigueur, *Comuni e signorie in Umbria.*
12 Cracco and Ortali (eds), *Storia di Venezia.*
13 Brucker, 'The ciompi revolution'; *Il tumulto dei ciompi.*
14 Reinhardt, *Die Medici*; Rubinstein, *The government of Florence.*
15 Ryder, *Alfonso the Magnanimous.*
16 Partner, *The Papal State.*
17 Giusti, *Visconti e Sforza.*
18 Reinhardt, *Der unheimliche Papst.*
19 Jones, 'Communes and despots'.
20 Rösch, *Venedig*, 117–26.
21 Lopez, 'Quattrocento genovese'; Forcheri, 'Dalle regulae'; Shaw, 'Principles and practice'.
22 Reinhardt, *Geschichte Italiens*, 93.
23 Chittolini, Molho and Schiera (eds), *Origini dello stato*, 425–89.
24 Guerzoni, 'The Italian Renaissance court's demand for the arts', 55–70.
25 For an updated overview, see Franceschi, Goldthwaite and Müller, *Commercio e cultura mercantile.*
26 Mueller, '"Veneti facti privilegio"'.
27 Pinto, *La Toscana*, 225–46.
28 Epstein, 'Cities, regions and the late medieval crisis'.
29 Reinhardt, *Überleben in der frühneuzeitlichen Stadt.*
30 De Roover, *The rise and decline of the Medici bank*; Goldthwaite, 'Banking and finance'. On Datini, see Origo, *The merchant of Prato*; Nigro (ed.), *Francesco di Marco Datini.*
31 Leydi, 'Le armi' .
32 Massa Piergiovanni, *Lineamenti di organizzazione*; Jacoby, 'Genoa, silk trade and silk manufacture'.
33 Lane, *Venice, a maritime republic*, and *Venetian ships and shipbuilders.*
34 Mueller, *The Venetian money market*, 121–219.
35 Goldthwaite, *The economy of Renaissance Florence*, 265–95.
36 Brucker, *Renaissance Florence*, 133–67.
37 Burke, *The Italian Renaissance*, 209–17, 241.

38 For a critique of the Florence-centric view of history, see Grubb, *Firstborn of Venice.*

39 Rösch, *Venedig*, 134–9; Mueller, 'The Jewish moneylenders'.

40 Herlihy and Klapisch-Zuber, *Tuscans and their families*, 93–109; Goldthwaite, *Wealth and the demand for art in Italy*, 45–52.

41 Maginnis, *Painting in the age of Giotto*; Bagnoli (ed.), *Duccio*; Bellosi, *Cimabue.*

42 Oertel, *Early Italian painting.*

43 'La pittura in Italia'; Hale, *Italian Renaissance painting* (on what follows as well).

44 Castelfranchi Vegas, 'Der künstlerische Austausch'.

45 Nuttall, *From Flanders to Florence.*

46 Bredekamp, *Bau und Abbau*, and *La fabbrica di San Pietro.*

47 Reinhardt, *Rom: Kunst und Geschichte*, 139–43.

48 Hausmann, 'Anfänge und Duecento'; Hardt, *Geschichte der italienischen Literatur*, 78–130; Bellomo, 'Dante e l'Europa'.

49 Hausmann, 'Quattrocento', 100–3; Branca, 'Boccaccio e l'Europa'.

50 Hardt, *Geschichte der italienischen Literatur*, 273–320; Hösle, *Kleine Geschichte der italienischen Literatur*, 79–82.

51 Huck, *Musik des frühen Trecento.*

52 Lütteken, *Guillaume Dufay und die isorhythmische Motette.*

5

The Holy Roman Empire

The question of what constituted 'Germany' in the Middle Ages and into the early modern era was controversial even at the time. The *Regnum Teutonicum* – German kingdom – and the Holy Roman Empire were inseparably intertwined, as is evident in the designation 'Holy Roman Empire of the German Nation', a term used for the first time in 1474. Several years later, in 1512, Johannes Cochlaeus offered a fairly precise geographical description of Germany, 'Forsooth, I do believe that no realm in Europe has a greater extent than Germany, although Spain may boast of six or seven kingdoms. In the south, it is bounded by Italy and Dalmatia, in the east by Hungary and Poland, in the north by the Baltic Sea and the Great Ocean, but in the west by France and the British Ocean'.[1] He thus described the empire's area in its restricted sense, that part generally north of the Alps known as Germany, or the *Regnum Teutonicum*.

Tied to the German kingdom by personal union were the kingdoms of Burgundy and Italy, so that the empire in fact extended to the south and the west. However, its boundaries overlapped with those of other realms. In the north, Holstein belonged to the empire, while Schleswig, though tied to it by a personal union, belonged to Denmark, and the Danish king also held lands in Holstein. In the west, Frisia, the bishopric of Utrecht, the duchy of Guelders, the counties of Holland and Zealand, the duchies of Brabant and Hainaut, the bishoprics of Cambrai and Liège and a small part of Flanders – the greater part was under French suzerainty – were part of the empire. In the southwest, the Duchy of Luxembourg, the bishoprics of Liège and Toul and the duchies of Bar and Lorraine were the empire's borderlands. The free county of Burgundy and also Savoy, a duchy since 1416, were long able to maintain their independence, although the influence of the French Crown was growing continually there. Only the duchy of Burgundy was able toward the end of the fourteenth century to free itself both from the empire and from France, and to incorporate much of the western part of the empire – the Low Countries.

The Swiss Confederacy too was slowly loosening its ties to the empire, but remained part of it through the end of the Middle Ages. There were also close ties between the German kingdom and northern Italy, the central area of its Italian kingdom. These were of an economic and cultural nature, and did not necessarily reflect the strength or weakness of the German kingdom. The south-eastern boundary, where the duchy of Carniola extended to the Adriatic Sea, was primarily formed by Bohemia and Moravia until 1355, when Bohemia annexed Silesia, thus pushing the border eastward. But here, imperial policy, which was largely driven by dynastic interests, especially in the kingdoms of Bohemia and Hungary, focused to a large extent on regions outside the imperial boundaries. Bohemia, in particular, which belonged to the empire, and Hungary, which did not, but was periodically also tied to it through Habsburg dynastic bonds, were structurally connected to east-central European history. The same is true of the north-east, which was remote from the kingship, and where Pomerania, the bishopric of Kammin and the Neumark (Nowe Miasto Lubawskie) formed the eastern boundary. Here, the activities not of the imperial authority, but of the free and imperial cities, extended far beyond the frontiers of the empire, through their membership in the Hanseatic League.

That institution was only noted by a few contemporary writers, and discussed by fewer still. At the same time, the area of the empire north of the Alps gained new significance with the political paradigm shift between the high and the late Middle Ages. After the failure of the idea of a universal empire, for which Frederick II and his successors in the Hohenstaufen dynasty had struggled, only a concentration on the *Regnum Teutonicum* appeared promising. Future candidacies for becoming German king depended on the electoral princes who chose the King, and on the approval of the Pope.

5.1 Kings and dynasties

In 1273, Count Rudolf of Habsburg was elected German king, since both the electors and Pope Gregory X (1271–76) preferred him to the powerful Bohemian King Ottokar II of the Přemysl dynasty. Although Rudolf remained loyal to those who had elected him as well as to the papacy, he attempted to stabilise his position by regaining the imperial lands frittered away by his predecessors. While that succeeded in Franconia, Swabia and

Map 8 The Holy Roman Empire in the fifteenth century

the territories along the upper and middle Rhine, this 'policy of revindication' provided the opportunity to challenge and defeat Ottokar of Bohemia on the battlefield. Nonetheless, Rudolf did not succeed in gaining the imperial crown, and the establishment of a dynasty became a distant dream.

Count Rudolf was followed by such further 'petty kings'[2] as Adolf of Nassau (1232–98) and Albert I (1298–1308); most of the petty kings were murdered. Only the last of them, Henry VII, made a somewhat greater mark. He had been elected at the behest of his brother Baldwin of Luxembourg, archbishop of Trier, and established a new dynasty by securing for his son John the inheritance of the Premyslids in Bohemia, which he had obtained through his wife Elizabeth. Henry added considerably to the prestige of the Luxembourg dynasty when he was crowned Emperor at Rome in 1312, in spite of an unsuccessful campaign in Italy and his own early death in 1313.

His successor, Louis the Bavarian (1314–47), attempted to renew the imperial policy of the Hohenstaufen dynasty with regard to Italy. At the same time, Louis was the first to pursue dynastic politics on a grand scale, although he later lost out to Charles IV of the house of Luxembourg. The reason was his conflict with the Pope, who by now resided at Avignon, and was unwilling to countenance Louis' Italian ambitions. In 1324, Louis and his supporters were excommunicated, and the interdict pronounced upon their places of sojourn.

Although the German royal electors at the electoral college of Rhense defended themselves in 1338 against clerical attempts to interfere with their electoral prerogatives, no agreement could be reached between the electors and the King. A new alliance between the houses of Habsburg and Luxembourg put Louis the Bavarian on the defensive and in 1346 the electors chose Charles of Luxembourg as counter-king.[3] But Charles IV, too, who was initially considered a 'priests' king' and a product of the clergy, had to defend himself during his early years against a number of counter-kings such as Günther of Schwarzburg, or the 'false Woldemar', with the force of both arms and money. Since Charles IV succeeded during his first Italian campaign in 1355 in being crowned King of Italy and then Emperor in Rome, he could quickly reinforce his position. In addition, he satisfied his princely supporters with the Golden Bull of 1356, which guaranteed them a monopoly on the privilege of electing the king, and stipulated the indivisibility of their electoral realms. The electors were additionally privileged with regard to the other princes, and at the same time Frankfurt was designated as the permanent venue of election, Aachen as the place of coronation, and Nuremberg as the site of the first *Hoftag*, the assembly of the vassals or magnates of the empire.[4]

Despite the constitutional nature of this document, we should not underestimate the contemporary circumstances at the time of its promulgation. The Wittelsbachs were excluded, as were the Habsburgs, who did obtain, by forging the so-called *privilegium maius* in 1358/59, their own promotion to the rank of archduke. Accordingly, the attempt to establish a 'hegemonic kingship'[5] was closely tied to the person of Charles IV. This exceptional position was already beginning to decay under his successor Wenceslas, who was elected in 1376. For one thing, the Great Schism, which might only have been overcome with a major political effort, took place in the very year of Charles's death. In addition, disputes within the empire grew apace, in spite of the perpetual public peace (*allgemeiner Landfriede*) proclaimed in 1389 between the cities, princes and petty rulers. These struggles included the defeat of the Swabian League of Cities at the hands of Eberhard of Württemberg in 1388. Wenceslas also did not succeed in expanding his dynastic power; even in Bohemia, the upper nobility put him on the defensive. Tied up in Bohemia, he was barely capable of action within the empire, and was deposed in 1400 by the Rhenish electors and replaced by Rupert of the Palatinate, who died in 1410.

The Rhenish opposition thus gave preference to another 'petty king', while Wenceslas continued to reside in Bohemia. King Rupert squandered his political capital by a march to Rome in 1401–02, in which he only got as far as Brescia. Moreover, his unilateral attachment to the Pope in Rome prevented Rupert from participating in the efforts to overcome the Schism at the Council of Pisa.[6] After his early death in 1410, both Sigismund of Luxembourg and the leader of the Bohemian nobility opposed to Wenceslas, Jodok of Moravia, were elected king. Jodok's early death cleared the way for Sigismund's unanimous election in 1411. Sigismund (1411–37) initially had no powerful dynastic base, and little time for the empire. What is more, he was forced to strengthen his position in Hungary, which was being threatened by the Turks, and, after Wenceslas' death in 1419, he sought to take over Bohemia. That was initially prevented by the Hussite movement (see 6.1 and 13.4). Sigismund's support in the empire came largely from the imperial cities. The imperial treasurer Konrad of Weinsberg, a financial genius who granted credits to the King by mortgaging future city taxes, played a key role here. He was responsible for expanding the activities of the royal mint, and for taxing the Jewish population.[7]

Sigismund benefited from the support of families close to the king such as that of Count Frederick VI of Nuremberg, of the house of Hohenzollern, who was ultimately rewarded with the margravate of Brandenburg. The transfer of the electorate of Saxony from the extinct Ascanian dynasty to the house of Wettin in 1423 removed the dependence on the Rhenish electors while at the same time unintentionally strengthening the electoral college.[8] Sigismund gained prestige as the initiator and patron of the Council of Constance, which overcame the Schism. The Council of Basle, opened in 1431, was likewise a success for him, since the Acts of Compact achieved a compromise with the Hussites, and opened the way for Sigismund's recognition as King of Bohemia. Under pressure from the Council, Pope Eugene IV had also crowned Sigismund Emperor in 1433.

After Sigismund's death, his Habsburg son-in-law, Duke Albert of Lower and Upper Austria, was elected German king, thus opening an era of dynastic continuity that would last for centuries. However, owing to divisions of inheritance, the Habsburg possessions were distributed among numerous lines. Albert II (1438–39) made defending the Austrian lands against the Turkish peril the priority of his reign.[9] After his early death, he was followed in 1440 by another Habsburg, Duke Frederick III of Styria, Carinthia and Carniola, who reigned for fifty-three years (1440–93), longer than any other German ruler. Apart from his coronation in 1442 and a few conflicts in 1444, Frederick III spent his reign in Wiener Neustadt in the south-eastern corner of the empire, in whose central territory he did not so much as set foot between 1444 and 1471. Nonetheless, the King attempted to activate new sources of income in the inland areas of the empire by issuing privileges, revindications and fiefs.[10] This resulted both in the fiscalisation of the empire and the spread of the king's judicial authority.

Frederick was crowned Emperor in 1452, and in 1463, after the death of his brother and rival Albert, he was able to take over the other Habsburg possessions, with the exception of the Tyrol and Anterior Austria (a number of territories on the upper Rhine), while Hungary and Bohemia became independent. During the 1480s, Frederick was forced to ward off attacks from the Hungarian King Matthias Corvinus, who in 1485 even occupied Vienna. Only after Corvinus's death in 1490 was Frederick able, with the aid of his son Maximilian, to regain possession of Vienna, and also to take over the Tyrol from the near-bankrupt Archduke Sigismund (the Rich). Frederick III was successful in his cooperation with the papacy. From a position of strength, he was not merely able to rapidly seize the imperial crown, but by 1445/46 he had also negotiated control of the investiture of bishops in his dynastic lands, which was confirmed by the Concordat of Vienna in 1448. In 1478, he also secured the privilege of appointing the seventeen bishops of the empire without consultation with the Pope. That put an end to papal interference and political power struggles within the empire. Even earlier, the Emperor had succeeded in arranging for the election of his former chancery secretary, Enea Silvio Piccolomini, as Pope Pius II.

In foreign policy, the marital connections of his heir Maximilian were of great importance. In 1473, Charles the Bold of Burgundy and the Emperor met at Trier to negotiate marriages between the houses of Burgundy and Habsburg, which, in spite of the Burgundian expansions into the western part of the empire, such as the futile siege of Neuß in 1474/75, were successfully concluded in 1477, when Maximilian married Mary of Burgundy in Ghent. The incorporation of the Burgundian heritage (see 5.13), in particular, changed the situation in the western part of the empire. Maximilian's second marriage in 1494 to Bianca Maria Sforza caused the Habsburgs to place a higher priority on the Burgundian Netherlands and northern Italy. Maximilian I (1493–1519), who had already been elected king in 1486, succeeded his father on the throne in 1493. Under him, the Europeanisation of Habsburg dynastic policy continued.[11] The 1496 marriage of Philip the Handsome, Maximilian's son and heir in Burgundy, to Juana of Castile, daughter of the Catholic monarchs Ferdinand and Isabella, laid the foundations for the Habsburg world empire, which could, however, be realised only thanks to the occurrence of several dynastic coincidences on the Iberian peninsula. No less successful were the marriages arranged with an eye to Hungary and Poland. Louis and Anne, the children of Vladislav of Bohemia and Hungary, married Maximilian's grandchildren Mary and Ferdinand in 1521 and 1522, respectively.

Maximilian's domestic policy focused on the imperial reform project. This involved balancing the powers of the Emperor and the estates with the aim of creating a permanent economic base for the empire. In this way, the imperial institutions developed into a second power centre alongside the imperial court, based on cooperation between the holders of power and the enhanced importance of the imperial diet (*Reichstag*).[12]

5.2 The empire and the estates

The empire differed in a number of ways from the western European monarchies, both constitutionally and administratively. Peter Moraw has described these differences as problems of continuity and coherence. Unlike England or France, the electorally constituted empire lacked any dynastic continuity, core land or residential capital. Every switch between the potential royal dynasties – Habsburg, Luxembourg and Wittelsbach – meant a change in the centre of gravity of rule. Accordingly, the coherence of royal action – its ability to implement policy – differed from one region to the next. Hence the king's chances of success were greater in his dynastic lands as well as in the three regions 'near to the king' – Franconia, the middle and lower Rhineland and Swabia – than in the regions 'open to the king', such as the upper Rhine area or the territories of the electors and of the rival dynasties. And in the areas 'remote from the king', such as the northern part of the empire, he had virtually no influence. The king's position in these territories could simply depend on the politics of the day, such as the attitude of individual electors, or the person of the king himself. In addition, the electors and princes built up their own administrations in their territories alongside the king's own administration, which had originally been the only one, so that a dual constitution of the emperor and the imperial estates developed over the course of the fifteenth century. Unlike in France or England, the emperor did not create a unitary state, even if the struggles with the Hussites, the Turks, Hungary and Burgundy contributed toward constitutional and administrative consolidation. This process was preceded by an era of an open constitution characterised by an extremely low degree of institutionalisation of the empire, and a low level of participation of other holders of power. However, the empire could only withstand pressure from the outside if not just the kingship but also other imperial institutions participated in its maintenance. This included a fundamental transformation of the dual administration of the royal authority on the one hand and the territories on the other.[13]

The task of the administration was necessarily to improve and expand the material base of royal rule. While in England, for example, the Tudor monarchs were able to regain the crown lands in the late fifteenth century and use them as their main source of revenue, in the empire the royal court long financed itself through its own dynastic domain. The imperial domain (*Reichskammergut*), which in the early days of the Hohenstaufen dynasty had provided a financial basis for rule, had gradually been alienated during the thirteenth century in the form of gifts from potential candidates for the throne to their constituents. Although the revindications carried out by Rudolf of Habsburg were to some extent successful, his successors began once again to generously distribute the parts of the imperial domain among their followers.

Since by the fifteenth century there was ever less land to dispose of, the rulers turned to temporarily mortgaging parts of the royal domain, although this further restricted their financial leeway. They also devised new means of generating income. Since King Sigismund had already mortgaged the taxes to be paid annually by the imperial cities years in advance, the emperors were forced to impose general imperial taxes – such as the Hussite tax of 1427 and the Turk tax of 1471/74 – which were not always easy to collect. The 'Jewish taxes' that the Jewish population, as vassals of the royal treasury (*Kammerknechte*), had to pay beginning in 1342 therefore proved a secure source of income. This head tax, the so-called *goldener opferpfennig* of one florin, was levied upon all Jews above the age of twelve. The King obtained additional income from coronation fees, extraordinary wealth taxes, special letters of protection for Jews and fines. In addition to these taxes, the remaining royal privileges that had not been transferred to territorial rulers were expanded. These included customs duties and the fiscalisation of the imperial judicial authority. In this way, Frederick III regularly generated new income, imposing new custom duties and granting new market rights, while reserving for himself a share of the revenues.

Royal suzerainty was also used for fiscal purposes. When a fief became vacant and was granted to another person, considerable sums were paid for preparing and issuing the documents. The confirmation of privileges was also costly, and was the business of the royal chancery. Finally, the king used his judicial authority financially by imposing not only court costs, but also fines and penalties for misdemeanours and for the cancellation of imperial bans.[14]

The centre of royal rule was the court, which was a kind of symbiosis of itinerant and residential rule. In addition to his activities in his domains, his dynastic territories, the king had to be at least temporarily present in remote regions as well, and also had to maintain his personal ties in the areas 'near to the king'. The court itself consisted of bodies which were originally loosely constituted, but which were institutionalised over the course of time. In addition to the king's privy council (*Hofrat*), the 'daily council' consisting of the master of the household, the treasurer of the household, the marshal of the court and the chancellor of the court, it included the intricately organised institution of the court chancery (*Hofkanzlei*) and the aulic court (*Hofgericht*). The privy council or royal council, which included the above officials as well as additional councillors appointed by the king, met regularly and also assumed tasks of government. The moves toward bureaucratic professionalisation can best be seen in the case of the court chancery. Thus, the chancery of King Rupert of the Palatinate was already very well organised, with great value placed on the careful formulation, copying and safekeeping of royal documents. During the fifteenth century, a second chancery was created when Frederick III established a distinction between the imperial court chancery and the Austrian court chancery. However, this did not create any clear division of responsibilities, let alone a hierarchy, for competing cliques formed within each of the chanceries and engaged in a struggle for power and influence. The King encouraged these rivalries, since they facilitated his control over his own court.[15]

The chancery officials accompanied the king on his travels until the time of Maximilian I, when the Austrian chancery found a permanent location at Innsbruck. This can certainly be interpreted as a reaction to the centralisation of the imperial chancery in Mainz undertaken by Berthold of Henneberg, archbishop of Mainz and imperial chancellor. The chancellors were experts in the art of administration, and were guarantors of continuity in the electoral empire. The number of documents prepared rose from approximately 10,000 under Charles IV to over 100,000 under Maximilian I.[16] Unlike the court chancery, the degree of institutionalisation of the court treasury, the royal fiscal authority, was low. Its efficacy was largely dependent upon the treasurer, who, like Konrad of Weinsberg, was continually obliged to devise new sources of income.

The aulic court, which accompanied the king on his travels, was also of great significance. A new institution created during the fifteenth century alongside the aulic court was the royal chamber court, a body of royal counsellors and experts which adjudicated under the presidency of the king. Among the experts it called upon, the university-trained lawyers increasingly gained in importance under Frederick III. This constituted the basis for the establishment of the imperial chamber court (*Reichskammergericht*) in 1495. Just as the aulic court was gradually eclipsed by the chamber court, so too did the *Hoftag* gradually yield to a representative assembly, the imperial diet. This development was based on a number of elements. Around the middle of the fourteenth century, the electors alone held a constitutional function, the election of the king, which they used to seize power for the first time in 1394, while King Wenceslas was imprisoned. They gathered at a 'kingless assembly', which was to be followed by other such assemblies called by the electors during the Hussite wars in 1422 and the Council of Basle in 1438. Another precursor to the imperial diet was the royal *Hoftag*, which the King convoked on certain occasions.[17]

Through a process of common law, the symbiosis of these two elements developed into the imperial diet, which met under that name for the first time in 1495. This institution included not just the electors and the other princes and imperial cities, but also the less powerful counts, knights and prelates, who were thus tied into the process of securing peace within the empire. The imperial diet is closely associated with the so-called imperial reform. This concept may sound overly auspicious in the light of today's reform debate, since the imperial reform undertook no fundamental reorganisation of the empire. Rather, the term *reformatio* was borrowed from clerical language and closely associated with the demands of the conciliar movement.

King Sigismund was not alone in wishing to 'bring the affairs of the holy Church and of the Holy Roman Empire into good and fair order';[18] the theologians Job Vener and Nicholas of Cusa also made numerous suggestions for reform. Thus, Job Vener, who had served as a proto-notary and counsellor to King Rupert, believed that the imperial estates should elect an imperial council. Nicholas of Cusa went a step further, and sought to limit the power of the princes and institute an independent judiciary to this end, which would be occupied by the clergy, nobles and commoners. A standing army was to uphold the perpetual public peace and strengthen the royal authority. The anonymous author of the *Reformatio Sigismundi* sought, in the context of ecclesiastical reform, to abolish the feudal rule of Church dignitaries. Early initiatives for royal reform are also documented for the 1430s. At the *Hoftage* held at Frankfurt in 1434 and Eger in 1437, Sigismund was presented with reform demands primarily concerned with abolishing feuds and improving the judiciary. However, it was not until the 1495 imperial diet of Worms that a permanent compromise could be reached with the princely opposition led by Berthold of Henneberg. Heinz Angermeier sees this reform step as merely a compromise in the political power struggle between the Emperor and the imperial estates; however, a certain climate of reform seems to have made this compromise possible. The King did not only encounter opposition in implementing these reforms; he also had partners, such as the imperial cities.[19] Accordingly, Berthold of Henneberg met with most success in reforming the judiciary. The royal chamber court was reorganised, received a permanent venue and was separated from the king's entourage. While the king still appointed the president of the imperial chamber court, he and the imperial estates jointly determined the composition of the body, which consisted of sixteen assessors, half of whom were of noble and half of common origin.[20]

An additional demand was to secure domestic peace. This was proclaimed by the King in 1495 as the perpetual public peace, which made feuds punishable. Its implementation required a monopoly on the use of force, which only the princely states could provide, however. Without the approval of the imperial diet, or of the so-called imperial estates from 1500, the king could neither declare war nor conclude alliances that might burden the empire. Moreover, the financial foundations of the empire were to be improved by means of a tax, a head tax or wealth tax known as the common penny, the success of which was to be guaranteed by the electors, the princes and the cities. Nonetheless, the income from this direct imperial tax proved considerably less than expected, for the electors and princes collected it only reluctantly, fearing that it would make them financially subordinate to the King.

As a result, the dualism between king and princes remained. The further-reaching demands of the estates, such as the establishment of an imperial regime (*Reichsregiment*), to which Maximilian had to accede in 1500 in exchange for imperial support from the estates, were not permanently successful, for an estate-based government was only briefly institutionalised, and thus helped to affirm the concentration of imperial policy, which did not necessarily conform to the interests of the powerful imperial estates.[21] The six imperial circles, which subdivided the empire north of the Alps, with the exception of Switzerland and Bohemia, were originally conceived as electoral districts for the counsellors of the imperial regime. Increased to ten in 1512, they would later develop into bodies above the estates, which secured the peace and subsequently became organs of public policy, with responsibility for such matters as coinage. The right of estates to participate in the imperial diet had a similar effect in the ensuing period, since Maximilian and his successors certainly called on the support of the cities and the lower estates.[22] However, attendance at the imperial diet was one thing, participation in formulating policy quite another. Only the electors and the princes were in a position to do that, inasmuch as they continued to reinforce the structure of their territories as little kingdoms.

The formation of territorial rule was a long-term process that proceeded parallel to royal power, sometimes competing with it for sovereign rights and acquiring or usurping them. Much like the process of 'fashioned concentration' toward which the empire developed during the fifteenth century, the various regional domains also grew more concentrated. Significant elements associated with this include such personal components as manorial lordship and judicial authority on the one hand, and the so-called regalia, such as the rights over coinage, mining and customs duties on the other. The development of territorial lordship required not just territorial acquisition – i.e., the incorporation of castles, towns, villages and court districts into one's own areas of rule. Equally vital was the expansion of influence beyond one's own territory, since relationships within the empire and the holding of imperial office, or the rights of patronage over towns, villages and monasteries and the establishment of extensive vassalage ties could be beneficial to one's domain. Within the territory, rule was stabilised by vassalage relationships, whereby the counsel and aid provided by vassals and the princes' desire to collect general territorial taxes reciprocally shaped the relationship between prince and territorial estates. This relationship was strengthened by the construction of territorial judicial authority, which gradually infringed upon the judicial rights of the towns and village communities. This was accompanied by territorial legislation, in which, for example, local rights were redefined. In addition, the district structure on the one hand and the construction of centralised territorial authorities on the other contributed to the establishment of territorial states.[23]

Around 1300, so-called *Ämter* (districts; singular *Amt*) were established in most German territories. These small districts, often consisting of only three or four parishes, constituted the lowest level of territorial rule. The tasks of the *Ämter* included collecting territorial taxes and duties, judicial authority and police powers, and in some cases recruiting peasant soldiers. In this respect, the *Ämter* may be regarded as the successors to the castles of the high Middle Ages; in fact, they were often direct continuations of the castle districts, and the descendants of the castellans headed the *Ämter*. The immediate superior to the governor of an *Amt* was generally the prince himself, or his counsellors. We have evidence of counsellors as early as the late thirteenth century in various territories including Bavaria, the Habsburg lands, Brandenburg and Württemberg, and during the ensuing period, increasing numbers of princely documents contain the clause '*mit rade unser rete*' – with the counsel of our councillors. During the fifteenth century, the princely council seems to have been institutionalised and to have been permanently in session. The council members included not only close noble trustees of the prince; non-noble scholars too were taken into these bodies as experts. Such important jurists as Gregor Heimburg entered the service of several princes and cities during their careers, since the rulers were eager to boast of a respected scholar.

Alongside the council, the personnel of which changed frequently, it was the chancery that ensured continuity, since it alone represented the memory of the territory. As early as 1300, the archbishops of Cologne established so-called cartularies of the most important documents, so as to secure their rights. During the first half of the fourteenth century, Baldwin of Trier compiled all of the legal titles of his archdiocese and had them copied in triplicate – one each for the archive, the cathedral chapter and his personal use. During the second half of the fourteenth century, registers of incoming and outgoing documents were established in an attempt to cope with the growing flood of such papers. The chanceries now became places of regular work and, in the fifteenth century, additional files were made using the new cheaper material, paper. With the growth in written documents, the German language became increasingly important as an official or chancery language. The old *protonotarius*, the head scribe of a chancery, now became a *chancellor*, which title is attested in many territories beginning in the mid-fifteenth century.

While the *protonotarius* and the early chancellors were generally clerics, by the fifteenth century, lawyers schooled in Roman law were preferred for appointment to the office of chancellor. Backed by the power of the knowledge stored in their chanceries, they often succeeded in crowding the princely counsellors out of the prince's entourage, thus becoming his closest associates.

In addition to the council and the chancery, the princely treasury was the most important authority in the territory. Nonetheless, until well into the fifteenth century, most German territories still disposed of no central exchequer, so that much improvisation was still necessary in this area. As a result, there were repeated financial shortages, some of them seasonal. Many princes who lacked profitable regalia found it difficult to acquire the funds to pay for a lifestyle befitting their rank. Small wonder, then, that such poorer princes as Duke Otto Cocles of Brunswick-Göttingen had his territorial estates guarantee him in 1453 the support of his court, consisting of three chamberlains, two *valets de chambre*, a tailor, a gardener, a cook, a chaplain, three pipers and their knave, two grooms, one stable-boy, one gamekeeper and one forester.[24]

However, the term *Landstände*, territorial estates, is not documented prior to the sixteenth century, and even the term *Stände* (estates; singular *Stand*), established itself in the German language only around 1500; other terms such as *Mannschaft* for the knighthood, and *Landschaft* are more common. The latter term could, as in the Tyrol in 1363, refer to both noble and peasant representatives of a certain valley or court district, while in Württemberg in 1457, only the representatives of cities and *Ämter* were considered to constitute the *Landschaft*. That meant that the composition of territorial estates varied from territory to territory. Unlike the nobility, who were always represented, the cities participated in estate decisions, particularly regarding the granting of taxes, to varying degrees. Sometimes, they might have an interest in having their say; in others, in refusing to do so. Thus, the episcopal cities and free cities were no more interested in being tied into a territorial council of cities than were Brunswick or Lüneburg. The cathedral chapters in the clerical estates were generally also unwilling to be incorporated into the territorial constitution, since they saw themselves as autonomous bodies checking the power of the prince bishops. However, even the acceptance of a territorial constitution remained anachronistic well into the sixteenth century, since regular assemblies of the estates were not yet common. In this context, the approval of imperial taxes by the territories certainly had a constitutional effect.

In the territories, the road from the land tax (*Bede*) of the late thirteenth century to the introduction of the territorial tax during the fifteenth century was a long one. While the land tax had begun as a voluntary tax, and had often been collected together with taxes owed to the lord of the manor by cattle owners, the new taxes were either levied on property, or demanded as consumer taxes on beer or wine. Unlike the land tax, which had become permanent, the new territorial taxes could only be imposed for limited periods after consultation with the estates. Associated with this was the demand for control by the estates over the revenues from taxes. Since the estates generally collected the taxes on behalf of the prince, they soon also demanded a say in how the money was spent, which in the sixteenth century developed into a tax administration by the estates.[25]

5.3 Economic advances

As in most European countries, the population of the *Regnum Teutonicum* had been increasing since the turn of the millennium, with a continual annual growth rate of 0.3 to 0.5 per cent. Around 1300, the limits of population growth had been reached, and the population stagnated at a level of 13 to 15 million. Agricultural production could barely feed the population, so that famines and poor harvests, such as that of 1315–16, decimated the population. In 1348–49, the Black Death broke out in overpopulated Germany, affecting different regions to varying degrees. While port cities like Hamburg were particularly severely affected, Franconia and Bohemia were largely spared (see Chapter 11). The abandonment of villages allows us to estimate demographic decline at between one-fifth and one-third, so that the population was reduced to approximately eight million. Since it did not recover until the fourteenth or fifteenth centuries, the population had risen to only around 9 million by 1500, apart from the densely settled areas of Flanders and Brabant. These losses notwithstanding, several cities grew considerably during the fifteenth century. In the fourteenth century, only Cologne and Prague, with fewer than 40,000 inhabitants each, were comparable with a smaller capital such as London, but not with Paris or the big Italian or Flemish cities, and Milan or Venice had twice as many people, and even Florence, Bruges and Ghent had population levels unattained in the heart of Germany. Such cities as Lübeck, Danzig, Strasbourg, Nuremberg and Vienna had smaller populations; behind them came Hamburg, Frankfurt, Brunswick, Augsburg, Erfurt and Magdeburg. Although Nuremberg, Augsburg and Vienna experienced population increases into the sixteenth century, none of them reached the 50,000 mark. The Hanseatic cities of Lübeck and Hamburg also both grew between 1400 and 1500; Hamburg was in fact to double its population between 1375 and 1450.[26]

In the countryside, demographic recovery took longer, although we need to distinguish here between the abandonment of villages, hides and village fields. Generally, marginal lands were abandoned, while the better lands and the fields nearer to the towns continued to be farmed. The ratio of pasture to farmland also increased. Animal husbandry expanded, leading to a rise in meat production. Meat consumption increased, as did the meat-processing trades in the towns. In addition, more land was planted in such dye crops as madder in the area of Speyer and Worms and along the lower Rhine, and woad in the villages around Erfurt. The increased production of beer also required more hops-growing. In northern Germany, beer brewed from hops replaced wine as the drink of the masses, so that wine production remained concentrated along the middle Rhine and its tributaries, the Moselle, the Nahe and the Main, in the Bergstraße area north of Heidelberg, and in Alsace. 'Rhine wine' and 'Alsatian wine' were the primary export products,[27] and their quality was improved by the introduction of Riesling on the Rhine and Moselle. In addition, fruit and vegetable farming developed on the outskirts of the cities, with the produce transported into town for sale. The main industrial crop was the ubiquitous flax – which, however, generated an important linen industry only in the area around Lake Constance and in Westphalia.

The dominant commercial activity in Germany was the textile trade, which was primarily dedicated to woollens, and secondarily to the production of new types of cloth, such as fustian. Every town had cloth-makers who supplied local customers with simple textiles. In addition, a textile export industry developed, which concentrated on the production of quality woollen cloth. Around the middle of the fourteenth century, Cologne cloth-makers were producing 15,000 to 20,000 woollen cloths per year, along with 8,000 tirtey cloths, a mixture of wool and linen, made possible by a well organised division of labour involving spinners, wool cleaners, weavers, fullers, cutters and dyers. Often, the first stages of the process, such as spinning and even weaving, were farmed out to the areas surrounding the cities, while in some textile towns, nearly one-third of the population worked in cloth production. In addition to the production of woollen cloth, linen weaving – that is, the production of coarse linen cloth – was initially a widespread trade.

From the thirteenth century, special linen regions emerged, most prominently around Lake Constance, including Constance, St Gallen, Ravensburg and Kempten, and during the fifteenth century in Westphalia, including Münster, Osnabrück, Herford and Bielefeld. Later, the Vogtland, Lusatia and parts of Lower Saxony joined them. Even during the thirteenth century, merchants from Constance, Lindau, Ravensburg and St Gallen were exporting Lake Constance linen to the south, and their wares were also traded at fairs in the Champagne region and Frankfurt. Municipal quality control ensured high standards, which opened up the market. During the second half of the fourteenth century, part of the Lake Constance region switched from linen to fustian production. The raw material, cotton, was obtained from Venice via South German merchants. Other cities, such as Regensburg, Augsburg, Biberach, Nördlingen, Ulm and Memmingen, supplied the international market. But the main effect of fustian was to allow South German merchants to gain a foothold with a new product at the fairs of Frankfurt and Brabant. In view of the shift to fustian production – by 1500 it was being produced in more than sixty cities – only St Gallen and Zurich among the old linen-producing towns were able to survive by specialising in high-quality linen cloth. The concentration in certain branches of the textile industry caused the emergence of specialised trade regions, in which town and countryside cooperated in a division of labour.[28]

The same was true of metalworking, where, from the end of the fourteenth century, Nuremberg, together with the Upper Palatinate and the Fichtel mountains, produced the largest range of products, from brass to weapons. But Cologne too invested in the iron and steel trades in the nearby regions of the Eiffel, the Bergische Land, the Sauerland and the Siegerland, where steel, wire, blades, knives, scissors, nails and boxes were produced. Non-ferrous metals were also processed in Liège and Aachen. The usual urban trades that provided food and clothing (tanners, furriers and tailors) were also of considerable significance. Some, such as the breweries in Hamburg, Bremen, Stralsund or Lübeck developed into important export trades.

Accordingly, the cities also dominated commerce, and the export trades and long-distance commerce were closely connected. There were four distinct commercial areas of both domestic and foreign commercial significance:

- The northern German Hanseatic area, which stretched from the Netherlands to Livonia, and southward to Brunswick and Magdeburg
- The Rhineland, which had the advantage of the main trade route, the Rhine, and its position close to the Netherlands, and was dominated by the export trading city of Cologne and the trade-fair city of Frankfurt
- The southern German area, dominated by Nuremberg and Augsburg
- The central German area, which became increasingly important from the fifteenth century because of the Leipzig trade fairs

Owing to their orientation toward the North Sea and Baltic region, and toward Scandinavia, the Hanseatic cities were only loosely connected to the empire, and may be considered a separate political territory (see 5.12). Together with the northern and eastern German Hanseatic cities, Cologne and Nuremberg emerged as the most important export trade and commercial cities. But the Cologne export trade, whose most important product was wine, was orientated toward the Champagne fairs at a very early date – the twelfth and thirteenth centuries, when Cologne merchants first appeared there. In addition, they travelled to the Flemish fairs and to London. The markets along the Danube, too, and the new cities in the Baltic region, Riga and Reval (Tallinn), were supplied with Cologne cloth via the transit stations of Lübeck and Gotland. After the decline of the Champagne fairs, in the fourteenth and early fifteenth centuries Cologne merchants concentrated on the new sales centre of Bruges. In addition, the Cologne merchants visited Antwerp and other textile cities in Brabant. During the second half of the fourteenth century, they established direct trade links between London and the Frankfurt trade fair, which at the time was Cologne's most important trading point in southern Germany. Initial contacts were also made with Venice and later Milan and Lucca.[29]

Relations with Frankfurt were intensified during the fifteenth century, and the city became the entrepôt for the Cologne and Nuremberg trade region. At the Frankfurt fair, Nuremberg merchants purchased the goods they sold in the east: cloth from the Middle Rhine and Hesse, Flanders and England, or linen and fustian from southern Germany. In return, they sold precious and non-ferrous metals from the Carpathians and the Upper Palatinate in Frankfurt, as well as Oriental products imported through Venice; Cologne merchants bought them for sale in the west – the Brabant fairs, Antwerp and Bergen op Zoom. It was not long before the Nuremberg merchants visited these markets directly. Their rise to world market status was aided by the metals and fustian of the south German merchants as much as by English cloth and Portuguese spices. Here, Cologne, Nuremberg and Brabant merchants profited from the resurgence of continental land traffic (see 5.15).

How closely commercial innovations relied on the political backing of the emperor and princes is evident from the example of Nuremberg. There, as in the Hanseatic League, the long-distance trading families sought exemption from custom duties in a large number of cities. Families like the Pfinzings, the Mendels, the Stromers, the Kreßes, the Rummels, the Pirckheimers, the Kolers, the Granatels and the Imhofs assiduously built up trade relations with Italy, Flanders, England and Spain, and especially with east-central Europe. The Nuremberg merchants attained exemption from customs duty even from their competitors in Cologne in 1340 and Lübeck in 1373, and by breaking the Hanseatic embargo of Flanders in 1362, they acquired trading privileges there. Nuremberg also managed to persuade Venice to dispense with trade north of the Alps.

So-called Upper German high finance was especially successful in Hungary, crowding out the competing Italians with the support of King Sigismund during the early fifteenth century, and thus gaining access to the Hungarian gold mines. As administrator-entrepreneurs known as chamber counts (*Kammergrafen*), Nuremberg experts occupied key positions in the Hungarian mines, thereby securing their capital investments.[30] The Nurembergers were innovative in a wide range of areas. In addition to the first paper mill built by Ulman Stromer in 1390, these included developing a new wire-making process, and the so-called *Saiger* smelting process. While the wire-making processes considerably expanded the range of metal products that could be made using iron from the Upper Palatinate, the new smelting process allowed for the separation of silver and copper. That permitted the production of both silver and copper from the silver-bearing copper loads at Neusohl (Banská Bystrica) in upper Hungary (Slovakia) and in the county of Mansfeld in central Germany. This gave Nuremberg companies an incentive to invest in the smelting mills of Eisleben and Hettstedt, while their Augsburg competitors concentrated on Neusohl and set up a consortium with the Thurzo family. By that time, the production of fustian, trade with Italy and financial transactions had laid the foundations for the rise of Augsburg, in which many companies participated. The combination of banking and financial transactions, trade and investment in mining and metallurgy, as demonstrated by the Fugger family, would prove particularly successful. To this end, the Fuggers not only took over a mortgage of the Schwaz silver mines, but also made the money-changing and credit business one of their most important operations. Loans to the Habsburgs were regularly secured by mortgages and privileges. This, however, resulted in a long-term attachment to the house of Habsburg.[31]

5.4 Society

In the empire too, the nobility represented the ruling political and social stratum. Unlike in other parts of Europe, the German nobility was characterised by the existence of the imperial princes and particularly the clerical princes, and by an imperial Church dominated by the aristocracy. Although it constituted only between 1 and 1.5 per cent of the population, the nobility in Germany was not a cohesive social stratum, but was riven by a number of fault-lines. While the 'old' or true nobility was freeborn, and traced its lineage back to the Carolingian nobility, the lower nobility was composed of the non-freeborn ministerials and those who had obtained knightly status since the twelfth century. During the late-medieval process of social closure, 'knight' became the term designating the lower nobility, while the higher nobility no longer emphasised knighthood but rather their freeborn status with such titular terms as 'high-born' or 'well-born'. Proximity to the king also constituted a dividing line. While the king gave fiefs to those nobles who were immediate to the empire, the non-immediate nobility had other princes as their immediate lords.[32]

In the hierarchy of the nobility and the *Heerschildordnung* (literally, the army shield ranking), the electoral princes, with their privilege of electing the king, held the top position. Behind them were the peers as territorial princes, who were considered members of the empire. Their number was increased by the elevation of the counties of Berg, Holstein, Cleves, Savoy and Württemberg. Ahead of them were the clerical princes of the empire, both bishops and archbishops; here, too, there was a hierarchy – at the top was the archbishop of Mainz – but not all bishops in the empire were also prince bishops. Also members of the upper nobility were the counts and barons, who constituted a reliably loyal power base, especially in the territories 'near to the king'. Some of them, like Rudolf of Habsburg, Adolf of Nassau or Henry of Luxembourg, even attained the kingship themselves. During the fifteenth century, these groups, together with the knights, sometimes tried to protect their interests by forming leagues against the power of the great princes. The lower nobility, more numerous than the higher nobility, organised themselves in confederacies, the so-called noble societies. These not only served the purposes of regulating conflicts among their members, but also provided mutual aid in conflicts with cities and subject peasants. In addition, they helped to create a sense of identity among the nobility through festivals and tournaments.[33]

The noble societies had interregional significance. Examples are the Society of St George's Shield of the south-western German nobility and the Swabian League, which emerged from it in 1488 and also incorporated members of the upper nobility.[34] The noble societies also included low-ranking nobles immediate to the empire, who would later be referred to as imperial knights (*Reichsritterschaft*). Although the imperial knights would constitute themselves as a group organised in cantons only in the sixteenth century, the king had a knightly clientele within the Empire as early as the fifteenth century, which provided the armed contingents for the imperial castles. Thus, the imperial castle of Friedberg remained immediate to the empire until its demise at the beginning of the nineteenth century. The greater part of the lower nobility, however, were unable to resist integration into the growing territorial entities. As the princes fortified their position as territorial rulers, a non-immediate nobility emerged, constituted on the basis of feudal ties to their territorial princes. In this way, a large part of even the upper nobility in Bohemia and the Habsburg lands became non-immediate. However, those were exceptions, especially since as a rule the prelates, knights and cities assembled as estates to represent the country vis-à-vis the prince. At the same time, the princes tried to bind local nobles to the court or integrate them. Thus, the Electors Palatine established the Order of the Pelican modelled on the Burgundian Order of the Golden Fleece, and Elector Frederick II of Brandenburg established the Order of the Swan – or, to give it its original name, the Society of Our Lady of the Swan.

The episcopal sees, too, were firmly in noble hands. Since the German kings had only limited authority over the investiture of bishops during the period between the Concordat of Worms and the Concordat of Vienna, the power of the cathedral chapters, which possessed elective rights, grew considerably. This body, composed of members of the regional nobility, ensured that bishops from comital families, and often of lower noble origin, were elected.[35] Only the bishoprics of Cologne and Strasbourg were reserved exclusively for members of the higher nobility. In addition, the territorial princes naturally also influenced the appointment of bishops, when they formed so-called secondogenitures.

While the lower nobility did close itself off from burghers and peasants, just as the higher nobility tried to distinguish itself from the lower nobility, upward social mobility into and within the aristocracy remained possible. A patent of nobility was issued by imperial charter, but could also be undertaken by an imperial official, the *Hofpfalzgraf*, in the emperor's stead. In addition, in 1453 Emperor Frederick III granted the reigning Habsburg archdukes the right of ennoblement. After entry into the nobility, formal elevation to the rank of an imperial prince was the next great leap in status. So strong was the push of the nobles in this direction that by the sixteenth century, virtually all had obtained the title of count, so that the title of baron (*Freiherr*) degenerated to a rank of the lower nobility. At the same time, the status quo was solidified, as higher nobles were entered into registers, land tables, etc., in order to provide information concerning who was eligible to attend estate assemblies, liable for taxes or obliged to provide soldiers in case of war. The territorial estates were fixed in accordance with the property listed in the registers, to which certain sovereign rights were attached.

In addition to the formal act of ennoblement, the new nobles also had to gain acceptance from their peers, which generally took several generations. The criteria demanded ranged from knighthood and participation in tournaments to possession of sovereign rights and marriage ties with noble families.[36] The non-immediate nobility could protect themselves against this intrusion from below only with the aid of greater proximity to the court and active membership in the noble societies. An additional challenge came from attacks in the fourteenth and fifteenth centuries on the economic basis of the nobility, which was much weakened by the so-called agrarian crisis – the drop in agricultural prices, the fragmentation of manors and other factors. It was, however, certainly possible to develop successful counter-strategies, such as expanding domestic production or increasing feudal rents (see 12.3). There were also new opportunities for mercenary service and entrepreneurship, and even robber-baron activities brought short-term financial relief. The highest yields came from service to the princely court. Its officials received a share of the income, and the possibility to advance their careers. The urban middle class was also no competition for the nobility. There is evidence of nobles marrying into the cities as well as becoming citizens. The nobility likewise demonstrated their presence in town palaces and tournaments held in the city. Often, a societal symbiosis emerged between the urban patriciate and the aristocracy of the surrounding countryside.

5.5 Urban society

Urban society was at once more open than rural society and characterised by greater social differentiation. The urban citizenry was composed of men, women and children, each group having its own distinct status.

Only the male head of the household had full citizenship rights; his son could acquire them only by taking the oath of citizenship. A widow, while she might continue her husband's business, could never acquire the same opportunities for political participation. The tenure of citizenship rights was important for the identity of townspeople, to which other constituent elements, such as membership in the parish, guild or confraternity could contribute. A considerable part of the urban population did not possess citizenship rights. Some members of these groups lived legally in the city as *Beisassen*, citizens without full civil rights, or in its environs as so-called *Pfahlbürger*, since they generally lacked the income required for citizenship or the training for guild membership. From the twelfth or thirteenth century, a social hierarchy emerged in which so-called *meliores* or *boni homines*, or 'houses' (*Geschlechter*) appeared. These elite strata originated either in the ministerial class, or consisted of long-distance merchant families who had taken control of the town councils.[37]

Like the *Erbmänner* (honourable men) or patriciate of Münster, the 'houses' claimed a higher, quasi-noble status.[38] In Nuremberg and Cologne, the elite strata already called themselves *nobiles*; there, as in Trier, Metz, Regensburg or Zurich, patrician families built and lived in fortified towers. They set themselves apart from the merchant stratum in order to be able to marry other *nobiles*, or into the landed aristocracy. These urban elites also copied the example of the aristocracy by participating in tournaments and wars, and by acquiring landed property in rural areas and establishing their own clienteles. These families, such as the Weises and the Overstolzes in Cologne, used these clientele revenues for power struggles within the cities, similar to those being carried out in northern Italy. In the urbanisation process, which had been going on since the fourteenth century, both the urban proportion of the total population and social differentiation grew apace.[39]

The development of urban networks and the rise of commerce and manufacturing facilitated social mobility. As a result, the guilds and the rich merchants began to challenge the authority of the ruling elites. The elite strata were also reinforced by the in-migration of members of the lower nobility from the surrounding areas, such as the Paumgartner family in Nuremberg. What is more, the houses – only known as patricians after 1500 – sought to acquire land. Lübeck and Stralsund dynasties with hereditary rights on the councils owned rural villages, which they had in some cases acquired as fiefs from their territorial rulers. The Pirckheimer family in Nuremberg, too, combined merchant activity with aristocratic land tenure and political activities, such as the office of mayor. In addition, by the fifteenth century they were sending their sons to study in Italy, an early example of the reception of humanism in Nuremberg. In the city – unlike the countryside – fortunes permitted continual upward social mobility. A good example was the Fugger family, whose progenitor Hans Fugger settled in Augsburg as a weaver in 1367. It was nearly a century later that Jacob the Elder established the Fugger trading company, which his sons then expanded into a worldwide operation. In 1526 and 1530, the Emperor raised the Fuggers to the ranks of counts of the empire; by contrast, they did not become members of the Augsburg patriciate until the so-called increase of houses (*Geschlechtervermehrung*) in 1538, which expanded the city's shrinking elite to ensure enough members to fill government offices. But the Fuggers' economic activities were far from over at that time.[40]

Contemporary estimates of assets based on tax registers confirm a concentration of wealth in the upper strata. In 1396, for example, 1,202 citizens of Schwäbisch Hall were registered with a total fortune of 262,000 florins. These were headed by twenty-one citizens (2 per cent) who owned 39 per cent of the wealth. In Augsburg, which registered 3,617 taxpayers that same year, half the residents were counted as 'have-nots', while 74 taxpayers (2 per cent) had taxable fortunes of 1,200 florins.[41] However, money was not the sole means of entry into the upper classes; education counted as well. This only became common over the course of the sixteenth century, however, as lawyers, university professors and medical doctors gradually rose in social status. While for guild artisans the guild and possibly the religious confraternity were the centres of social life, the upper strata formed special associations, such as the Compass Society in Lübeck, which distinguished them among urban society. One expression of such exclusivity was the 'Nuremberg dance statute' of 1521, which specified which families were admitted to balls at the town hall, and hence eligible in future for seats on the town council.

Below them were the well-to-do merchants who were barred from political participation, and beneath them the master craftsmen of the guilds. Most cities distinguished between the guilds in terms of reputation, and there were certainly differences of wealth and status within the guilds. Most estimates are that artisan assets declined during the course of the fifteenth century, by contrast with the concentration of large fortunes. At the same time, the craft guilds showed tendencies toward closure. While the son of an artisan could inherit his father's workshop, the problem of upward mobility shifted to journeymen. This led to the organisation of journeyman associations, and to unrest familiar to us from the upper Rhine area and from Hamburg during the fifteenth century.[42] By contrast, the great mass of day labourers were not organised. This group, which is difficult to locate in the sources, constituted the labour force reserve of the cities, and was largely recruited from the surrounding areas. However, day labourers ranked above the economically necessary but dishonourable trades (see Chapter 12).[43]

The Jewish population was under imperial protection, in return for the payment of a large sum of money, but was not integrated into urban society. The situation of the Jews differed from city to city. By the beginning of the fourteenth century, Jewish populations existed in the middle Rhenish regions, in Frankfurt, Würzburg, Nuremberg and in Swabia – Augsburg, Heilbronn and Ulm – as well as Munich, Passau, Vienna and Wiener Neustadt, while very few Jews are documented in the Hanseatic cities. Lübeck expressly forbade the settlement of Jews. The pogroms of the fourteenth century led a considerable proportion of the Jewish population to flee to Poland and Lithuania to escape persecution. During the ensuing period, virtually all imperial cities expelled the Jewish population from within their walls, and only in Frankfurt and Worms – as well as in Prague – did Jewish communities continue to exist. The Jewish settlements now shifted to rural areas, and the Jews sought the protection of the territorial lords.[44]

5.6 Rural society

Rural society was strongly marked by the dissolution of the villication system. With the break-up of the manors, peasants received greater independence, and also more economic autonomy, due to the replacement of corvée labour by payment in money or kind. The manor no longer determined peasant life; the village did. In this process of village formation, there emerged so-called clustered villages (*Haufendörfer*) which farmed their fields according to a mandatory system as part of the spreading open-field farming structure.[45] The peasant house, with husband and wife forming a marital and working partnership, constituted the core of village organisation.[46] Considerable social differences existed within the peasantry, which were primarily reflected in farm size. In addition to the farms of the princes and the nobility, there were the medium-sized holdings of the peasant farmers, and below them the cottars, labourers and gardeners. Within Germany, these small peasant holdings existed in such areas as the upper Rhineland, the middle Rhineland or Franconia, where partible inheritance was the norm. Medium-sized and large farms, on the other hand, existed in areas where primogeniture prevailed, such as Westphalia and Lower Saxony. In the course of the East Elbian colonisation, the new settlers also received larger holdings. The wealthy farmers usually functioned as officials or lay judges. They were also deployed as bailiffs or tax collectors.

The majority of the peasantry lived in feudal dependence; however, there were also a number of groups of free peasants. These included those in the coastal regions of the North Sea, and in the outlying areas, but also those in the regions of eastern settlement, where peasants received personal freedom for clearing land, as well as a hereditary usufruct. The plague and the abandonment of land changed the social situation of the peasantry considerably. While the population was reduced by one-third, farmed land was reduced by only one-fifth. The abandonment of villages, like the reaction of the landlords to it, differed from one region to another. In addition to conversion to animal husbandry and direct exploitation of the demesne, many landlords in the south attempted to compensate for the reduction in their income from rents by increasing dues and services. Those unable to do so were forced to grant reductions in dues in order to retain their peasants, or to resettle their lands. At the same time, many manorial lords in south-western Germany tried to intensify their authority. This included extending the personal dependency (*Leibherrschaft*) of peasants to limit their mobility, which at the same time opened up new revenues for what were often ecclesiastical landlords. For example, the Benedictine monastery of St Blaise in the Black Forest turned what had previously been loosely described dependency into serfdom. Their new sovereign right specified the materialisation of the death dues of serfs as well as the right to inheritance by the monastery in the case of those who died unmarried or childless, which extended to the children of the peasants.[47] In the fragmented territorial structure of south-western Germany, the peasants of a single village could easily have different lords, so that one might be a serf and another not.

In north and east Elbia, the nobility expanded its ownership of abandoned land and took to direct exploitation of the demesne. By the end of the fifteenth century, there were attempts to limit peasant mobility. However, the legal tying of the peasants to the land was only successfully imposed in the course of the sixteenth century, by which time there were enough peasants available again to work the noble estates.[48]

All in all, however, the rural social structure did not change fundamentally between the fourteenth and sixteenth century. Nonetheless, the peasants participated to varying degrees in the rise in agricultural production, as shown by the example of Holstein peasants who specialised in animal husbandry, or the peasants in the areas surrounding the densely settled urban regions of western and southern Germany, who concentrated on supplying urban markets. Market proximity could also affect community structures that were characterised by a long-term transition from 'ruling with the peasants' to 'ruling over the peasants'.[49] Around 1300, the villages were peasant communes that attempted to regulate conflicts between villages over boundary and usufruct rights peacefully. By the fifteenth century, however, the territorial state gradually began to intensify control over rural communities using taxation and judicial authority as the instruments. The manorial lords were transformed into representatives of the territorial ruler, which is also reflected in their integration into the system of territorial administration. The communes, for their part, increasingly lost their autonomy. Moreover, the advance of Roman law reduced opportunities to participate in the judicial process. The communes only attained the right to attend estate assemblies in a few regions, such as the Tyrol and some smaller clerical domains, in which, since there was no nobility, the peasant communes and towns were the only existing estates. The village aristocracy often remained untouched by these developments, and attempted to consolidate their position by cooperating with the new rulers, unless they attempted to resist the intensification of rule by force. Thus peasant revolts were on the increase from the end of the fourteenth century through the beginning of the sixteenth century, reaching a new level of intensity at the turn of the fifteenth to the sixteenth century as a result of the interregional communications of the *Bundschuh* movement along the upper Rhine, the 'Poor Conrad' movement, and the Peasants' War of 1525. Unrest was strikingly concentrated in southern Germany, except for Bavaria, while it was largely absent in northern Germany (see 12.3).

5.7 Culture and humanism north of the Alps

Literature in the German language area was multilingual. Medieval Latin and, since the second half of the fifteenth century, humanistic new Latin, dominated in clerical and scholarly circles; around 1500, fourteen out of every fifteen printed books were in Latin. Even popular materials such as the *Legenda aurea*, written by the archbishop of Genoa Jacob de Voragine (1228/29–98) in Genoese Italian, were initially published in Latin, before numerous German translations appeared from the mid-fourteenth century. In all, the work was published in 150 to 200 editions.[50] The only other book other than the Bible to experience such widespread publication was the *Imitatio Christi* by Thomas à Kempis, and the writings of the Church fathers St Augustine and St Jerome. Other than such 'bestsellers', literary production remained confined to certain court and urban circles. Courtly poetry initially involved retelling tales drawn from French literature, such as the story of the Knights of the Round Table – Parsifal, Lancelot and others – and distributing them in numerous manuscript copies. Rudolf of Ems (1220–54) and Conrad of Würzburg (1220/30–87) authored many courtly novellas, legends and tales for their patrons, such as the story of Troy based on Latin sources. Such popular works as 'Stricker' or 'Helmbrecht' gained their first readers and listeners with novella-like, didactic but also crudely farcical literature. In its final stages, the troubadour song was transformed into poetry to be read. The Zurich citizen Johannes Hadlaub, for instance, not only composed his own songs but also was involved in the compilation of a collection of songs, the most comprehensive book of German poetry, the *Manesse Codex*, named after the Manesse family of Zurich. Oswald of Wolkenstein (*c.* 1376–1445) marked the end of this era. He combined courtly poems with his own experiences and set them to familiar tunes or to his own compositions. The *Meistersinger* poetry of the south German towns in the fifteenth century was institutionalised artisan poetry.[51] Religious literature was dominated primarily by mysticism in a wide variety of genres such as sermons, epistles and devotional books. Master Eckhart (1260–1327/28), Johannes Tauler (1300–61) and Heinrich Seuse are the most important representatives of German-language mystical theology. In addition, there was a wide range of literature intended for the religious education of the laity.

For courtly literature, the princely residences of the large dynasties gained increasing importance from the fifteenth century. They collected courtly epics and orientated themselves in part toward the elevated discourse of humanism. Early prototypes such as the *Ploughman of Bohemia* by Johannes of Tepl (1350–1414) only found emulators in the fifteenth century, when Nicolas of Wyle (*c.* 1410–78) Heinrich Steinhöwel (1412–82) and Albrecht of Eyb (1420–75) began translating Italian literature on a large scale. Eyb's book on marriage, *Whether a man should take a lawful wife or not* closely follows similar Italian genres.[52]

In addition to these translations, German prose romances also reworked medieval themes. Princesses such as Elizabeth of Nassau-Saarbrücken (1390–1456) or Eleanor of Austria (1433–80) penned their own novels based on French and other prototypes. Prose versions of medieval romances appeared, as well as new creations such as the novel *Fortunatus* (published in Augsburg in 1509), which emerged from the urban milieu of southern Germany.

The historiography of the thirteenth through fifteenth centuries is marked on the one hand by the chronicle of the world in the style of Martin of Opava, and on the other by the blossoming of regional chronicles. At the behest of Pope Clement IV, the Dominican monk Martin of Opava compiled a chronicle of popes and emperors, which was translated into German, French and Italian during the fourteenth century and later into Persian and Armenian. Additional universal chronicles were written by Matthias of Neuenburg and Heinrich of Diessenhofen based on older chronicles. Often, as in the case of Martin of Opava, the chronicle of Vincent of Beauvais served as the basis. One of the most interesting compilations, the rhymed world chronicle of one Heinrich of Munich, combined biblical tales with legends and epic literature in the fourteenth century. By contrast, the other world chronicles of the fifteenth century, such as Ulm town physician Heinrich Steinhöwel's *German chronicle from the beginning of the world up to Emperor Frederick*, or the German chronicles of the Nuremberg town clerks Johannes Plattenberger and Theoderich Truchsess, already exude the spirit of humanism. Along with these world chronicles, the numerous regional chronicles also attempted to connect local histories with world history. Thus, some regional chronicles are simultaneously world chronicles, such as that of the Strasbourger Jacob Twinger of Königshofen and the *Thuringian chronicle* of Johannes Rothe. The Bavarian regional chronicle of the fifteenth century also places the history of that country and its dynasty, the Wittelsbachs, in a long-term historical context.[53] The chronicles of the Swiss Confederacy constitute a special kind of regional chronicle, which historically justify the emancipation of the Confederacy from the empire, thus creating a separate identity. For example, the *Berne chronicle* of Conrad Justinger places the history of the city in the context of world history. Published in 1420, it is continued in the illustrated chronicle of Diebold Schilling, which takes it up to the end of the Burgundian wars. The first overall Swiss chronicle was the *Chronicon helveticum* of Aegidius Tschudi (1505–72), who understood it on the one hand as a legitimation of Swiss freedom, and on the other as an example of perfect humanistic literary language.[54]

The reception of humanism in the empire proceeded along several paths. In addition to monasteries and abbots with an interest in humanism, such as Abbot Johannes Trithemius of Sponheim, the courts and the southern German cities played an important mediating role. For instance, Petrarch's communication with Emperor Charles IV and his chancellor Johann of Neumarkt opened the way for a brief episode of humanist influence in Bohemia.

A more permanent effect was achieved approximately 100 years later by Enia Sylvio Piccolomini, the future pope Pius II, whose first position as secretary to Cardinal Capranica took him across the Alps to the Council of Basle. Here, he worked his way up until he was posted to the court of Emperor Frederick III in 1442. From there, the humanist who was named poet laureate in 1442 continued to climb the career ladder in the chancery until being appointed royal counsellor in 1450. At the same time he accumulated bishoprics – Trieste and Siena – and represented the Emperor at several imperial assemblies. In these various functions he contributed to a wide range of cultural transfers. A considerable portion of international royal correspondence was the work of his classically trained hand. Moreover, he maintained an extensive correspondence, of which some 670 letters with 192 correspondents have survived. Most of his correspondents were Italians, including the humanistically orientated Pope Nicholas V. Other recipients of his letters at the curia included the Spaniard Juan Carvajal and the German Nicholas of Cusa.

Relations with the Prague court, with Chancellor Prokop of Rabstein, and the Hungarian court, with the humanist Bishop John Vitez, were intensive. The correspondence with the royal chancellor of Poland Zbigniew Oleśnicki was similarly intensive, as it was with Casper Schlick, chancellor of Frederick III. Some of the letters were collected and compiled *in corpora*, which means that they were also accessible to the public. Copies of this corpus were sent abroad, for example in 1453 to Oleśnicki. Piccolomini also spoke publicly, as he did at the imperial assembly after the fall of Constantinople, where he delivered his Turkish speeches and propagated his idea of a Christian Europe. He also tried his hand as an educator of princes, and wrote treatises for the future Archduke Sigismund of Tyrol and for the Bohemian King Ladislas Posthumus. He earned a reputation as a historian as well, composing the *Historia austrialis* and the *Historia bohemica*, and entered virgin territory with his *Cosmographica*, and its sections on Europe and Asia.[55]

Maximilian I of Habsburg earned a reputation as a promoter of humanist scholarship and literary production by commissioning the epic poems *Theuerdank* and *Weißkunig*, and supporting Konrad Celtis. Other imperial princes such as Joachim of Brandenburg, Philip of the Palatinate and Eberhard of Württemberg followed in his footsteps. The last-mentioned visited Lorenzo de' Medici in Florence in 1482 and thus became acquainted with the Florentine Platonic Academy. Johannes Reuchlin was a member of his entourage. He visited Florence a second time in 1490, and met the leading protagonists Marsilio Ficino and Giovanni Pico della

Mirandola. Another meeting point was Bologna, where for example Duke Bogislav of Pomerania met the jurist Peter of Ravenna and invited him to visit Germany and to teach Roman and canon law at the recently established University of Greifswald. Humanists studying in Italy also brought ideas and contacts to their students. Chief among them was the Dutchman Rudolf Agricola (*c.* 1443/44–85) who, after a long sojourn in Italy, served at the court of Philip of the Palatinate in Heidelberg – at the initiative of Chancellor Johann of Dalberg – and can be regarded as the teacher of Jacob Wimpheling (1415–1528) and Johannes Reuchlin (1455–1522). He also discovered Konrad Celtis (1459–1508), and encouraged him to make a journey to Italy (1486). After his return in 1487, Celtis was crowned poet laureate at Nuremberg Castle by Emperor Frederick III, and Maximilian I repeated the honour a second time after Celtis took up his professorship in rhetoric and poetry at the University of Vienna in 1497.

Beyond the courtly context, certain cities also became centres of humanism. In the second half of the fifteenth century, Schlettstadt and Strasbourg reorganized their schools on the basis of the *studia humanitatis*. Jacob Wimpheling, educated in Schlettstadt and Heidelberg, introduced humanist pedagogy to Strasbourg, which corresponded to the classical interests of the patrician Peter Schott. This fertile climate attracted the preacher Geiler of Kaisersberg and the author Sebastian Brant to Strasbourg. In Augsburg, the first humanists gathered around the patrician Sigismund Gossembrot, who also inspired Konrad Peutinger at the beginning of the sixteenth century. In addition to studies in Italy, the trade contacts of the Augsburg companies such as the Fuggers promoted the dissemination of humanist culture. The actual centre, however, the German Venice, was Nuremberg, where, even before the time of Italian-educated Willibald Pirckheimer, a number of other disseminators of Italian culture, such as Gregor Heimburg, Albrecht of Eyb, and Nicolas of Wyle, were active. The last of these was a translator of numerous Italian works. In addition, a humanist circle formed around the physician Hartmann Schedel, author of the *Nuremberg chronicle*, one of the most important book projects of the late fifteenth century.[56]

There was also a great interest in Nuremberg in the neo-Platonic philosophy of the Medici academy in Florence, and the libraries of Hieronymus Münzer and the Pirckheimer family contained manuscripts and early editions of the works of Ficino. Hartmann Schedel, too, had ordered such works from Italy in 1496. The Nuremberg printer and publisher Anton Koberger, whose first incunabula included the second-century AD *Handbook of platonism* in Latin, which was thought at the time to be the work of Albinus (it has since been attributed to Alcinous), contributed to the growing interest in neo-Platonic literature. He later published Ficino's letters as well. Beyond that, Koberger concentrated on theological works, although he did publish an edition of Virgil in 1491, and the *Satires* of Juvenal six years later. Interesting in this context is Hartmann Schedel's surviving library catalogue of 1498, which, in addition to the traditional disciplines, such as the liberal arts, medicine, jurisprudence and theology, also includes the new category of *arte humanitatis libri*, which in turn contains the following subdivisions:

Opera Tullii
Poete et oratores
Historici Greci
Latini veteres
Moderniores historici
Cosmographi et geographi.

Of interest here is the division of historians into Greeks, Romans and modern historians; the final rubric primarily includes manuscripts and books by Italian humanists.[57]

The universities displayed varying degrees of openness toward the new *studia humanitatis*. The University of Vienna had already established a reputation for itself through such scholars as Georg of Peuerbach, Regiomontanus and Peter Luder, even before the appointment of Konrad Celtis (1459–1508) to a professorship. Thereafter, Heidelberg, Erfurt, Leipzig and Wittenberg rapidly adopted the new curriculum, while Cologne and Ingolstadt remained reticent. The reactions of the German humanists toward Italy were ambivalent, however. While regarding themselves as part of a cosmopolitan movement, most strongly represented in the early sixteenth century by Desiderius Erasmus, many German humanists had an inferiority complex, which they tried to compensate for by re-evaluating the German past. The rediscovery of Tacitus' *Germania* in the Hersfeld monastery in 1445 proved a godsend in that respect, and even Piccolomini used it as a basis for his book of the same title. Celtis' project of *Germania illustrata*, also based on this ancient text, was particularly ambitious. This work was to portray the history of the German nation from its barbaric prehistory up to the humanist culture of his own day in order to pay tribute to what had already been achieved – in line with an Italian example, the 1474 *Italia* illustrated by Flavio Biondo – as well as to inspire further cultural endeavours.[58] But only a prototype of the overall project, the *Norinberga*, would appear in 1495.

At almost the same time, Celtis and others promoted a national panegyric of monarchs. After the Freiburg jurist Ulrich Zasius argued that Emperor Maximilian was a direct descendant of Hercules, and Celtis described him as a second Hercules, Johannes Trithemius (1462–1516) was assigned to demonstrate this relationship, for which purpose it was necessary to invent all the sources. Maximilian himself was intensely preoccupied with the ancient Roman and medieval German past and encouraged the search for material relics.[59] The Alsatian humanists Jacob Wimpheling and Beatus Rhenanus (1485–1547) proved themselves particularly patriotic by constructing a prehistoric Germany that predated Italian classical antiquity, thus separating it from France and Italy. But a humanist such as Konrad Peutinger (1465–1547) in Augsburg, while fascinated by Italy and the study of Pomponio Leto, also tried to connect the Roman remains he found in Augsburg and displayed in his house with the Germanic north. He not only published inscriptions and an edition of Jordanes' *History of the Goths* and Paulus Diaconus' *History of the Lombards*, but also collected German historical sources and engaged in historiography. In addition, Peutinger set up an Italian style *studiolo*, which he decorated with statuettes and small bronze artefacts, as well as contemporary paintings. Like the merchants active in trade with Italy, he thus contributed considerably to the reception of classical antiquity in southern Germany.[60]

The effects of humanist historiography were felt even in regions untouched by the heritage of antiquity, however. One outstanding example was Albert Krantz of Hamburg (1448–1517), who, after serving as professor at the University of Rostock and legal counsellor to the city of Lübeck, earned a doctorate of theology at the University of Perugia. After his return to Hamburg in 1493, he wrote a massive history of northern Europe. Three books were dedicated to the Scandinavian kingdoms, *Chronica regnorum aquilonarium daniae, suetiae et norvagiae*, and three more, *Saxonia*, *Wandalia* and *Ecclesiastica historia sive metropolis*, to the history and the ecclesiastical history of northern Germany. His aim was to present the former greatness of the Hanseatic north German area to the leadership of the Hanseatic League.[61]

5.8 Art

Fine arts in the empire were long dominated by the late Gothic style, especially by its specific expression, the so-called *Sondergotik* (special Gothic) style. In the thirteenth century, the Cathedral of Reims had been reflected in the Church of Our Lady in Trier and St Elizabeth's Church in Marburg;

now, in the ensuing period, simpler forms predominated, with the basilica being replaced by the hall church. The late Gothic hall churches hark back to older styles, such as the Westphalian hall churches, as in Paderborn, Minden and Münster, and presented them in new forms. The new special style was designed by the Parler family in Prague, from where it spread to Nuremberg – the churches of St Sebaldus and St Lawrence – and to Nördlingen, Soest, Munich and finally Annaberg. The Wawel Cathedral in Cracow and the cathedrals in the Polish cities of Gnesen (Gniezno) and Posen (Poznan) were also built or rebuilt as hall churches. One characteristic feature was the double tower façade in Cologne, Strasbourg, Lübeck, Soest and Munich. The façade designs vary from the light, delicate tracery of the stone pyramid in southern Germany to the brick façades on the Baltic coast. Renaissance and Italianate elements are usually present in the decoration of the late Gothic churches. Members of the Vischer school in Nuremberg, or Adolf and Hans Daucher in Augsburg, were already using classical forms. Both the portal of the old vestry of St Anne's in Annaberg and St Anne's in Augsburg were orientated toward Italian models. The Fugger chapel in particular shows an adaptation of Italian stylistic elements mixed with Swabian traditions. Sculpture also borrowed from Italy, for example when sculptors adorned the tombs of scholars. Following the tomb of Kallimachus in Cracow designed by Veit Stoß, which became the prototype for humanist tombs north of the Alps, the Augsburger Hans Burgkmair made a woodcut death portrait of Konrad Celtis based on Roman gravestones. Elements borrowed from antiquity were also used for the epitaphs of Johannes Cuspinian of Vienna and Johannes Aventinus of Regensburg. Tillman Riemenschneider also selected new forms for the Würzburg epitaph of Johannes Trithemius.[62]

Not surprisingly, Nuremberg humanist circles were in the forefront of the reception of Italian art. The humanists active here were in close contact with the native artisans from whom they commissioned illustrations based on ancient or Italian models. For instance, the library of the humanist Sebald Schreier may have been decorated with classical images by workers of the Wohlgemut workshop. Albrecht Dürer was also in close contact with this circle. Not only was he friends with Schedel, Celtis, Schreier and particularly Willibald Pirckheimer, he also illustrated the works of Celtis, published portraits of Pirckheimer and Erasmus, and, together with the humanist Johannes Stabius (*c.* 1460–1522), designed the so-called Triumphal Arch of Maximilian I.[63] On journeys to the Netherlands and Italy, for instance to Venice, he became acquainted with fellow painters, and studied questions of proportion and Italian aesthetic theory. His 'four books on human proportion' cannot be explained without Italian influence, for the question of proportion was closely connected to that of perspective. From his Nuremberg workshop and the painters and engravers associated with it such as Hans Schäuffellein, Hans of Kulmbach, Hans Baldung Grien, Georg Pencz and the brothers Barthel and Hans Seebald Beham, as well as his immense volume of graphic production, Dürer's style spread beyond the Nuremberg area, both to the east and to the west, and with such works as the *Feast of the rose garlands* Dürer was present even in Venice. Here, in the *Fondaco dei Tedeschi*, adorned with paintings by Venetian artists, the south German merchants spared no expense to create an imposing impression. But not all southern German painters followed Italian models. Early Netherlandish painting particularly influenced the schools of the painters Lucas Moser and Conrad Witz in Swabia and the upper Rhenish regions. Rogier van der Weyden proved most influential on their style, as can be seen in the work of Martin Schongauer. Albrecht Altdorfer (1480–1538) could be considered a 'symbiosis'; while he adopted Italian elements, his own landscape style became his trademark.

Musically, Germany was a developing country, which only took up such western European achievements as polyphony at a very late date. In the Church, traditional monophonic Gregorian chant was now joined by newly composed sacred songs with Latin texts, which were used in processions and at mass; in time they would also be translated into German. During the fifteenth century, polyphony developed only slowly. Oswald of Wolkenstein (*c.* 1377–1445) stands out as a lone figure for his original combination of monophonic songs and polyphonic elements adopted from France and Italy. The achievements of Flemish composers such as Guillaume Dufay and others penetrated eastward only in the latter half of the fifteenth century by way of convivial music-making, and their compositions became known in large numbers in the repertoires of princely choirs and in organ tablatures. For the first time, German composers appear: masters such as Heinrich Finck (1445–1527) and Thomas Stoltzer (*c.* 1475–1526), followed by Ludwig Senfl (*c.* 1486–1542 or 1543), who, following the Netherlandish model, especially that of Heinrich Isaacs (*c.* 1450–1517), incorporated new stylistic elements into his own creations. In addition to the Munich court, where Senfl worked, the courts and residences in Vienna, with Arnold of Bruck (*c.* 1500–54), Constance with Sixt Dietrich (1492–1548), Stuttgart with Ulrich Brätel (*c.* 1490–1544/45), Heidelberg with Lorenz Lemlin (*c.* 1485–1540) and the imperial city of Nuremberg with Wilhelm Breitengraser (1495–1542) also deserve mention.

5.9 The Swiss Confederacy

The growing importance of St Gotthard as a pass across the Alps in the thirteenth century meant that both the Hohenstaufen emperors and the Habsburg counts began to develop an interest in the region that would become known in the late eighteenth century as the Swiss Confederacy (*Schweizerische Eidgenossenschaft*). In 1291, the valley communities of the so-called three forest cantons (although the term 'canton' to designate these territories was a later development, and they were referred to as *Orte*) Uri, Schwyz and Unterwalden joined forces to form an alliance for peace, the purpose of which was primarily to put an end to feuds in the valleys. When Duke Leopold I of Austria, who regarded himself as the overlord of the territory, undertook an expedition to punish the confederates for their attacks on the Einsiedeln monastery, he suffered a humiliating defeat at the hands of the Swiss peasants. The three valley communities, which were directly subordinate to the emperor, renewed their alliance against Habsburg attempts to subordinate them. In 1332, the city of Lucerne, which was embroiled in a struggle against its Habsburg overlord, also joined the alliance. An additional alliance was created around Lake Constance, where Zurich was joined by St Gallen, Constance, Schaffhausen, Lindau, Überlingen and Ravensburg, for here, too, the cities were forced to defend themselves against the power of the Habsburgs and other noble families. A third alliance was organised in the Burgundian area by the imperial city of Berne, to which Payerne, Avenches, Murten, Neuchâtel, Biel, Fribourg, the imperial city of Solothurn, and a number of nobles from Valais acceded. During the fourteenth century, these alliance systems cooperated with one another. The cities used the military prowess of the 'herder warriors' of the forest cantons in their battles with neighbouring nobles, resulting in such victories as that at Laupen in 1339.

In 1351, Zurich formed an alliance with the forest cantons, and in the ensuing period, Zug, located between Zurich and Schwyz, and the neighbouring valley community of Glarus, were incorporated into the alliance. In 1353, Berne too formed an internal alliance with the forest cantons. War with Austria broke out again and ended in Swiss victories at the Sempach in 1386 and Näfels in 1388. In 1392, the communities committed themselves to a military pact to protect 'our Confederacy', and in the fifteenth century expanded southward to incorporate and jointly administer the upper valleys of Ticino as far as Bellinzona. Aargau was conquered in 1415, and became a condominium of the eight communities. At the same time, the communities, which were all still directly subordinate to the emperor,

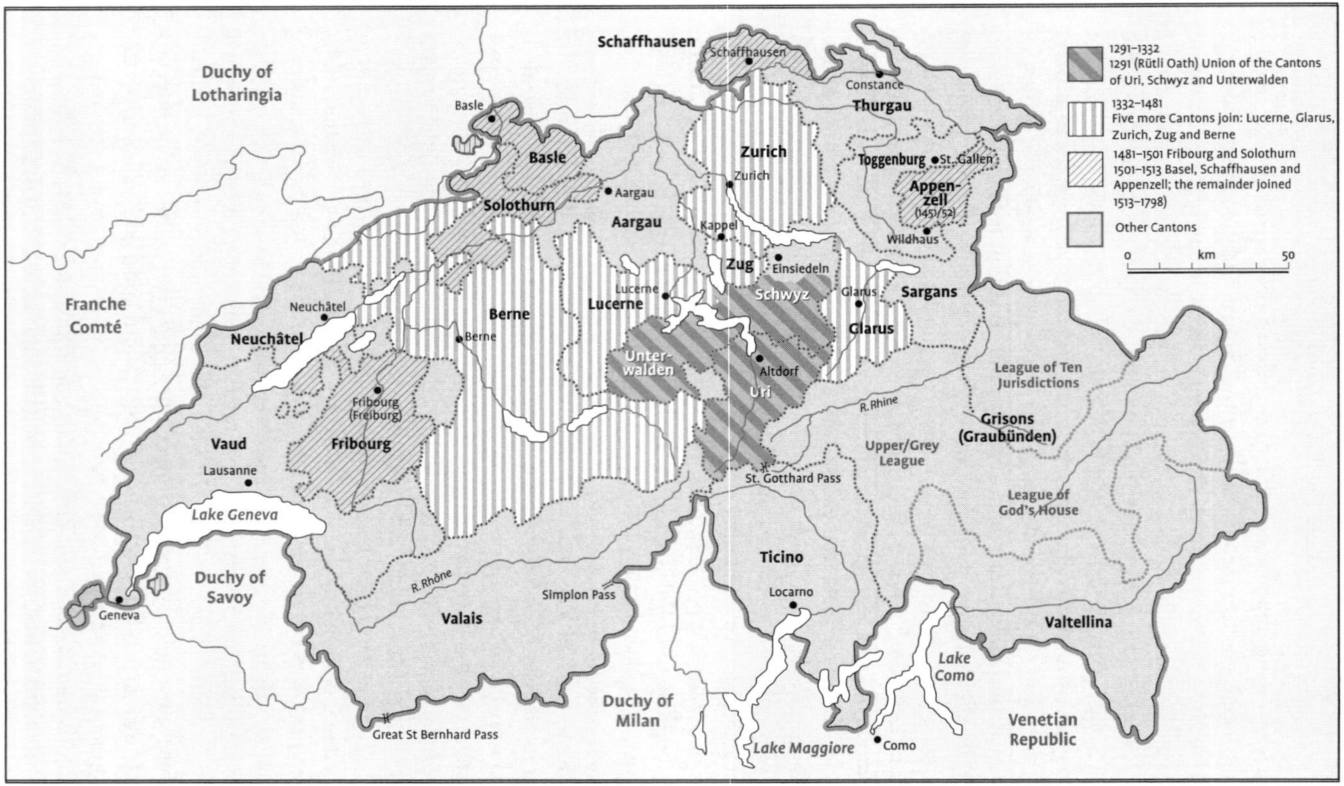
1291–1332
1291 (Rütli Oath) Union of the Cantons of Uri, Schwyz and Unterwalden
1332–1481
Five more Cantons join: Lucerne, Glarus, Zurich, Zug and Berne
1481–1501 Fribourg and Solothurn
1501–1513 Basel, Schaffhausen and Appenzell; the remainder joined 1513–1798)
Other Cantons
0
km
50
Duchy of Lotharingia
Franche Comté
Duchy of Savoy
Duchy of Milan
Venetian Republic
Schaffhausen
Schaffhausen
Constance
Thurgau
Basle
Basle
Zurich
Zurich
Toggenburg
St. Gallen
Appen-zell
(1451/52)
Wildhaus
Solothurn
Aargau
Aargau
Kappel
Zug
Einsiedeln
Lucerne
Lucerne
Schwyz
Glarus
Glarus
Sargans
Neuchâtel
Neuchâtel
Berne
Berne
Unter-walden
Altdorf
Uri
Fribourg
(Freiburg)
Fribourg
Vaud
Lausanne
Lake Geneva
Geneva
R. Rhône
Simplon Pass
Valais
Great St Bernhard Pass
St. Gotthard Pass
R. Rhine
League of Ten Jurisdictions
Grisons
(Graubünden)
Upper/Grey League
League of God's House
Ticino
Locarno
Lake Maggiore
Como
Lake Como
Valtellina

Map 9 The beginnings of the Swiss Confederacy

expanded their territory at the expense of the neighbouring petty nobility. This territorial expansion led to conflicts of interest between competing Swiss communities. From 1418 to 1424, for example, the forest cantons and Berne waged war for control over Valais, while Zurich fought with Schwyz and Glarus over Toggenburg. In this conflict, the old Zurich War (1436–51), one faction in the Zurich government even aligned itself with Austria so that at Birs in 1444, the Swiss barely won a victory over the Armagnacs and the Austrians. Zurich was later reintegrated into the Confederacy, and the alliance was expanded to include such cities as St Gallen, Schaffhausen, Rottweil (now in Württemberg) and Mulhouse (in Alsace). The internal and external expansion continued. Appenzell joined the Confederacy after freeing itself from the abbey of St Gallen; the latter itself joined the Swiss Confederacy in 1451/52. The areas along Lake Constance and the Rhine became border areas.

In European power politics, the Swiss had a persistent opponent in Charles the Bold of Burgundy (1433–77), whom they were able to defeat at the battles of Grandson and Murten in 1467 and at Nancy in 1477. The Burgundian spoils were shared out among the victors, with the Burgundian tapestries making a considerable contribution to cultural transfer.[64] During the following decades, Swiss mercenaries fought in most military engagements, especially in Italy, first for the French, and after 1510 at the head of the so-called Holy League against France. There, they were briefly able to take control of Milan, but a defeat at French hands at Marignano in 1515, and another, in alliance with France, by the troops of Charles V in 1525, forced the Swiss Confederacy out of the contest of the great powers. In 1495, the Swiss had triumphed over Charles's grandfather Maximilian in what was known as the Swiss or Swabian War, successfully resisting integration into his new imperial structure. Since the imperial military campaigns against Switzerland regularly bogged down in the border area, Maximilian was forced to confirm the privileges of the Swiss communities in the Peace of Basle. They remained part of the empire, although no seats were provided for them in the imperial diet. In 1501, the imperial cities of Basle and Schaffhausen, which had remained neutral during the Swabian War, joined the Confederacy. The Appenzellers, who had excelled during the Swabian War, achieved membership in the Confederacy in 1513, which had now grown from ten to thirteen member communities. It was from this time on that the confederates began to see themselves as 'Swiss', a term that had hitherto been a derogatory foreign designation for them, derived from the name of the valley community of Schwyz.[65]

5.10 The communal principle and federal structures

The Confederacy was a system of individual republics united in a federation.[66] They had been forming since the thirteenth century in a process of communalisation based on the purchase of freedom from dependence on nobles and monasteries. Thus the free peasants in Uri or Schwyz became legally and also politically capable of action. In most cases, the families that had originally determined the fate of the communities did not survive the fourteenth century politically. By acquiring land and administering it communally, the valley communities developed popular assemblies of all rural people who organised the shared use of the land. Thus did the *Landsgemeinde*, or cantonal assembly, arise, which elected the leading officers of the community such as the bailiff (*Landammann*). During the fifteenth century, Valais also organised itself communally, with the former episcopal administrative districts, the so-called tenths (*Zenden*), becoming communities with tenth-assemblies, tenth-councils, tenth-bailiffs and tenth-bannerets, where peasants, cities and nobles shared responsibility. The bishop of Sion and the cathedral chapter functioned as the territorial rulers, and were accompanied by a council representing the tenths; only in 1630 did the bishopric become a republic. In Grisons (Graubünden),[67] political representation was based on three leagues, the Upper or Grey League, the League of the House of God and the League of the Ten Jurisdictions, which jointly administered a subject area including Chiavenna, Valtelina and Bormio. Political leadership was in the hands of a federal diet consisting of one or two delegates from each jurisdiction, presided over by the heads of the three leagues. In the cities, the communal movement arose from a rebellion by the artisans, as in the case of Zurich in 1336, where the patrician council was replaced by a guild constitution as the supreme authority. This remained in effect until 1798. In many cities, so-called great and small councils assumed communal responsibility for governing, although this structure did not prevent the emergence of oligarchic ruling classes.[68]

The various members of the Confederacy were bound together by a number of different relationships, which they managed by means of so-called federal letters of the communities (*Zugewandte Orte*) as well as concordats such as the agreement of Stans. During the initial period, the delegates of the participating communities ran federal business as the situation demanded. In the fifteenth century this evolved into a structured system of government. Henceforth, the delegates of the communities met at least once a year for the so-called *Tagsatzung*, or federal diet, the resolutions of which obtained the force of law by ratification in each community.

Eventually, the *Tagsatzung* became a kind of court of arbitration, and, like certain communities, concluded treaties with foreign countries. In addition to the eight old communities, Zurich, Berne, Lucerne, Uri, Schwyz, Unterwalden, Zug and Glarus, which had the greatest prestige, five new communities, Basle, Fribourg, Solothurn, Schaffhausen and Appenzell, became equal members and so constituted the thirteen communities that formed the Swiss Confederacy. In addition, there were so-called associated communities that had formed alliances with the Swiss communities, including St Gallen, Mulhouse, Rottweil, Biel and Geneva, the city and principality of Neuchâtel, the abbey of St Gallen and the county of Gruyère. Also allied to the Confederacy were the abovementioned independent leagues of Valais and Grisons. This alliance did not prevent conflicts of interest between cities and communities, or in foreign policy toward France. One example of this was the *Saubannerzug* (boar banner campaign), carried out by dissatisfied soldiers from the rural communities of central Switzerland who demanded a revision of the distribution of spoils within the communities. To protect themselves against such devastations from the rural communities, the cities of the Confederacy and associated cities allied themselves in civic associations known as *Burgrechte*. Since the rural communities saw such alliances, as well as the attempt to admit the cities of Fribourg and Solothurn to the Confederacy, as attempts to change the balance of power, an open conflict developed. This was settled by a compromise obtained through the negotiation of the hermit Nicolaus of Flüe, in the abovementioned agreement of Stans.[69] Fribourg and Solothurn were admitted, but the civic associations were abolished. Agreement was reached on mutual support and on banning violent attacks upon other members of the Confederacy or their allies. The spoils of war were to be divided fairly in future, and the alliance was to be renewed every five years. In this way, the balance of power was restored at least enough for the cities and rural communities to continue to cooperate with one another in future, although the Reformation soon revived the old conflicts.

5.11 The Alpine economy

Economically, Switzerland differs from many other countries of Europe because of the great importance of animal husbandry, which became the principal economic sector toward the end of the Middle Ages. While farmers in the Swiss plateau had always primarily cultivated grain, and only maintained those animals necessary for agricultural work, the mountain areas had also initially been orientated toward cereal production. Only in the twelfth and especially in the thirteenth century did the communities of central Switzerland and the Bernese Highlands move toward animal husbandry. This development was initially promoted by the monasteries, which introduced cattle rearing in their mountain holdings. Thereafter, the higher mountain areas in particular were used for grazing, and from the thirteenth century, such use is recorded in the form of conflicts between neighbouring valley communities over boundaries and pasturing rights. Cattle, meat, butter and cheese were sold to Italy and also to the north and the west, which explains the interest in developing the Gotthard route. An additional push for the rise of animal husbandry occurred during the economic depression of the fourteenth century, when the last marginal fields still dedicated to crops yielded to pasturage. No longer did grain from the mountains appear on the urban market; meanwhile, butter and cheese from Schwyz were sold to Milan as well as Como, Calmar, Zurich and Constance. The profits obtained from animal husbandry in the sixteenth century motivated urban dwellers to purchase alpine pastures.[70] Since cattle rearing created few jobs, mercenary service became the only important outlet for a growing population, and the most significant economic factor apart from animal husbandry.

Switzerland was linked commercially with the European trade fair and finance system through Geneva and its fairs. Because of the privileges of the merchants of various northern Italian cities in the fifteenth century, the fairs which took place four times a year increasingly specialised in the trade in luxury goods such as silk, pepper, sugar, saffron, furs and weapons. Spurred by the trade in luxury goods in Geneva, the first international fairs of exchange were held there, immediately following upon the trade fairs. Geneva thus became the crossroads of a European system of cashless payment, which was primarily in the hands of Italian bankers such as the Medici. The temporary predominance of Geneva as the centre of exchange is documented by the list of transactions of the Medici branch in the city during the years 1441–45, when the branch was the most profitable in the entire Medici bank; after that, it still took second place after the main office in Florence. However, the profits in Geneva did not prevent the Italians – especially the Medici – from following the clarion call of the French king when he offered generous privileges for the trade fairs at Lyons. In 1465, they left Geneva and aided in Lyons' rise to the leading position among European fairs of exchange. While Geneva continued to exist as a trade fair centre thanks to the economic potential of southern Germany, its significance as an international financial centre was not restored until the founding of private banks in the eighteenth century.[71]

5.12 The German Hansa

Beginning in the thirteenth century, the Hanseatic League, originally an association of travelling merchants, developed into a powerful league of cities which dominated trade, shipping and politics in the North Sea and Baltic Sea regions for three centuries. In Old High German, the term *Hanse* means band or community, and in the twelfth century it referred to long-distance merchants joined in an association who generally came from the same town. There were thus many Hansas before the German Hansa first entered the political stage in the thirteenth century. Initially, the Cologne merchants trading in London formed a company, which in 1175 received the special protection of the king for their trading post (*kontor*), the London Guildhall, and obtained the privilege of free trade throughout the kingdom.[72] More important for the history of the Hansa, however, were developments in the Baltic region during the twelfth and thirteenth centuries: the founding of Lübeck, the founding of cities in the context of the German colonisation of the east, and the emergence of the German 'company of travellers to Gotland'.

The founding of Lübeck between 1143 and 1159 was the first permanent establishment of German long-distance merchants on the Baltic coast, and permitted travelling merchants from Lower Saxony and Westphalia to reach markets in the Baltic region and Russia without recourse to Scandinavian or Slavic middlemen. For example, the peasant-merchants of the island of Gotland had long dominated trade with Russia. For them, the German merchants constituted major competition after the founding of Lübeck. They had greater capital backing, better training and commercial techniques and organisation, and, with the cog, a ship with greater carrying capacity than those of the Gotlanders. As early as 1161, a large group of western German and Lübeck merchants appear to have engaged in trade in Gotland, for Duke Henry the Lion in that year granted permission for trade by Gotlanders in his realm, under the condition that German merchants be granted the same rights in Gotland in return. The first document to mention a German company of merchants who travelled to Gotland (*universi mercatores romani imperii gotlandiam frequentantes*) is a privilege issued by Countess Margaret of Flanders in 1252. Thereafter, there was an association of German Gotland merchants who traded both toward the west and the east, and who increasingly used their trading posts in Visby to gain a foothold in the Novgorod market. Like the Gotlanders, the German merchants also opened a trading post in Novgorod, known as St Peter's Yard, first mentioned in 1191, which served as headquarters for the Hanseatic trade in Russia until it was closed down by Ivan III in 1494. Thanks to its extensive hinterland, which extended to the White Sea, Novgorod was a centre of the fur trade. The trade in Novgorod was supervised from Visby in Gotland; it was here that the remaining money was brought after the conclusion of the trading season. Visby was also the site of the court of arbitration for conflicts in the Novgorod trade. Nonetheless, from the thirteenth century Lübeck increasingly attempted to gain control of the Russian trade, and, with the support of other cities, instituted a rule whereby the money from Novgorod would alternately be sent to Visby and to Lübeck. This was a matter of prestige; it was also stipulated that legal disputes from Novgorod could be heard either in Lübeck or Visby. This development prefigured Lübeck's role as 'patron' of the Russian trade and 'head of the Hansa'.[73]

The foundation of cities inspired by Lübeck and its town charter contributed to this status. Riga, founded in 1201 at the mouth of the Daugava, and a long-distance trading port, was systematically supported by Lübeck. During the thirteenth century, a string of trading cities emerged along the southern shore of the Baltic Sea: Wismar, Rostock, Stralsund, Greifswald, Elbing, Königsberg and Reval (Tallinn). German merchants were even more strongly present in the Scandinavian kingdoms. In Denmark, they were attracted by the yearly swarms of herring off the coast of Scania. Southern Sweden, too, experienced the immigration of German merchants and artisans to its cities, particularly Lödöse, Kalmar and Stockholm, and of German miners to the iron and copper mining areas. Norway was also an important trading partner, as it depended on imports of cereals for its food supply. This was provided by the Lübeck merchants, who came particularly for the stockfish (dried cod), caught in Norwegian waters and dried on sticks on the coast. The most important trading centre was Bergen, where a Hanseatic trading post was established at the so-called German Bridge. It was under the control of Lübeck, which dominated trade with the Scandinavian kingdoms.

However, the German merchants did not trade only with Russia, Scandinavia and the southern shore of the Baltic, but, initially under the leadership of Cologne, with England and Flanders as well. After the privilege bestowed upon the Cologne Hansa in England in 1175, at the beginning of the fourteenth century the *Carta Mercatoria* of Edward I granted foreign merchants freedom from all dues, freedom of residence, and legal protection against harassment by royal officials, and even a promise that there would be no future dues levied against foreigners – all in return for a rise in tariffs. This last provision would prove to be the core of the privilege, for as Edward III proposed an increase in the export duty on textiles in order to finance the Hundred Years War, the Hanseatic League was able, by invoking the *Carta Mercatoria*, to free itself from this duty, which English and other foreign merchants had to pay. Thus the *Carta Mercatoria*, which had originally been granted as a privilege to all foreigners, became a privilege for the Hanseatic League in England. They used the Guildhall as a trading post, and in the ensuing period expanded into the neighbouring Steelyard.[74]

The last and also the most important trading region for German merchants was Flanders, where large quantities of high-quality textiles were produced. The merchants first purchased the Flemish textiles at the markets in Champagne, and later in Bruges, which, thanks to its favourable geographical location, developed into the most important commodities market in western Europe. In 1252, Countess Margaret privileged the German merchants by granting them customs relief. One year later, they were exempted from trial by combat, liability for the debts and misdemeanours of others, and from wrecking (that is, the forfeiture of their goods in case of shipwreck) and other duties, which provided their trading activities with a high degree of legal security. Nonetheless there were repeated conflicts between the city of Bruges and the German merchants, usually involving restrictions on trade. The merchants reacted in 1280/82 by moving to neighbouring Aardenburg, thereby achieving the confirmation of their privileges. In 1347, the German merchants adopted a trading post statute, giving themselves an effective representation of their interests in relations with the city of Bruges and the county of Flanders. The Flemish trade was vital for the merchants, for it was here that they obtained the textiles they sold in Germany, in the Baltic area and on the Russian market. It is for this reason that the structural changes that affected Hanseatic commerce during the late Middle Ages appeared first in the Flemish trade.

In order to be able to counteract violations of their privileges in Flanders, in 1356 the hitherto autonomous Bruges trading post was subordinated to the Hanseatic diet, an organ of the entire Hanseatic League. In this way, the 'cities of the Hansa', which were represented in the diet and first mentioned as such in 1358, could take control of trade policy, which had previously been the purview of Hanseatic merchants locally. The successful trade embargo designed to restore their privileges in Flanders had effectively demonstrated that the Hanseatic League acting in concert was more effective than groups of merchants in foreign trading posts guided by their local special interests.[75] The creation of a general Hanseatic diet as the unified organ of the Hanseatic cities brought to a conclusion a process initiated in the thirteenth century, in which the cities gained ever greater control over the associations of their merchants abroad. The cities supported them in acquiring privileges, created the legal framework necessary for their trade and provided them with legal protection. Henceforth, the cities of the North Sea and Baltic regions represented in the Hanseatic League were to dominate trade and trade policy in this region. To this end, their representatives met regularly at the Hanseatic diet, which made all major decisions. Lübeck, as the head of the Hansa, functioned as their external representative.[76]

During the second half of the fourteenth century, new challenges emerged in the Baltic area, which permitted the league of cities to demonstrate their newly gained capacity for action. In 1360, King Valdemar IV attempted to impose Danish hegemony in the Baltic, and conquered not only Scania, which had temporarily been lost to Sweden, but also Gotland. He raised the tariffs and dues for the Hanseatic merchants, thus burdening the Scanian trade – a cause for war for Lübeck and the eastern Hanseatic cities. The struggle ended with the defeat of the Hanseatic League at sea, and the beheading of Lübeck mayor Johann Wittenborg, who had commanded the fleet. Encouraged by the victory, Denmark ultimately made the passage through the Öre Sound more difficult for the Hanseatic cities of the Zuiderzee as well as the cities of Holland, which were only loosely connected with the Hanseatic League. Thereupon, in 1367, all the Hanseatic cities from the lower Rhine to Reval joined forces with the cities of the Zuiderzee and Holland in the Cologne Confederation for a common attack against Denmark. With this military pressure, the Hanseatic League achieved the Peace of Stralsund in 1370, in which its privileges were restored, especially the right of unhampered passage through Denmark, by both land and sea, as well as payment of damages for the consequences of the war, secured by mortgages on the castles of Helsingborg, Scanör, Falsterbo and Malmö. With the peace of Stralsund, the Hanseatic League was at the pinnacle of its power: the predominance of the Hanseatic cities in the Baltic trade was confirmed.[77] How long it would be able to maintain its privileged position depended on both its control of resources and its skilful use of commercial techniques. For the Hanseatic League was a mercantile community of interest that used political and military means only for the purposes of securing trading privileges.

Trade proceeded from east to west along the main line from Novgorod to Reval, Riga, Visby, Danzig, Stralsund, Lübeck, Hamburg and Bruges to London, and was based on the exchange of foodstuffs and raw materials from northern and eastern Europe for the manufactured products of north-western Europe. However, the merchants went beyond that function of mediating between east and west, on the one hand trading in products manufactured by the Hanseatic cities themselves, and on the other advancing into the hinterlands of the coastal areas. Thus they not only opened up trade relationships with Bohemia and Silesia by way of the Elbe and Oder Rivers, but also moved up the Vistula through Cracow to the copper mining areas of upper Hungary (present-day Slovakia), and connected with the Black Sea trade by way of Lwów.[78]

Demand and production determined the specific regions to which merchants travelled. The range of commodities they traded was broad, and included both items of daily use by the masses of consumers and artisans and luxury goods for a small but wealthy stratum of customers. The most important goods in the Hanseatic trade were wool, woollen and linen textiles, furs and hides, herring and stockfish, salt, wax, cereals, flax and hemp, wood and forest products (ash, pitch, tar), beer and wine. Of these products, furs, wax, cereals, flax, wood and beer went westward, while primarily textiles, salt and wine, as well as metal goods, spices and other luxury products from the Orient were shipped eastward. Fish was sold throughout the Hanseatic area.

In the eastern region, we can define two interconnected economic areas: the Russian trading region around the fur centre of Novgorod, and the region of the Livonian cities, including Reval (Tallinn), Dorpat (Tartu), Riga and the hinterland of the Daugava, which mainly provided flax and hemp. The demand for furs, from the costly mink to cheap squirrel, and for candle wax existed throughout Europe. Likewise, hemp for ropes and flax for canvas were needed in all ports of the Hanseatic region. The east primarily imported Flemish cloth and Atlantic sea salt. An additional trading region existed to the south of Livonia, and was dominated by the state of the Teutonic Knights and the Hanseatic cities of Danzig (Gdańsk), Elbing (Elbląg) and Thorn (Toruń). By way of the Vistula and the Neman, they made the products of the Polish and Lithuanian hinterland available to the Hanseatic trade. From the Lithuanian area came wax, furs, wood and flax; from Poland, chiefly cereals, timber and other forest products. The latter were needed by the shipbuilding trade for masts and planks, by the herring fisheries, and by the brewing and salt refining industries for barrels, while many trades required such products as pitch, tar and ash. The main export product of the Prussian Hanseatic cities however, was grain, which fed a considerable part of the population in the highly urbanised areas of western Europe. Not to be forgotten is the luxury product amber, gathered on the Baltic coast of the Sambia peninsula. The Teutonic Knights had a monopoly on the trade in amber, which they exported to Lübeck and Bruges, where it was used, for example, to fashion high-quality paternosters. Salt, herring and textiles were the most important Prussian import goods.

In the western Baltic Sea area, Sweden provided iron, copper, butter, cattle and hides for the Hanseatic trade, but with the exception of the metals, was overshadowed by Denmark. For Denmark had attained an important position since the fifteenth century as an exporter of horses, oxen and butter. Up to this time, the Hanseatic trade with Denmark had been concentrated primarily on Scanian herring, the swarms of which were said to have been so great in the fourteenth century that one could catch the fish by hand. In the late fifteenth and sixteenth centuries, Baltic herring was increasingly crowded out by fish from the North Sea, so that the Dutch herring fisheries replaced those in Scania. The second provider of fish to the Hanseatic cities was Norway, which also belonged to Denmark, and which was completely dependent on Hanseatic imports. Hanseatic merchants delivered cereals, flour, beer, malt, hops, salt and linen, and mainly exported stockfish and small quantities of fish oil, walrus tusks, hides and other goods. At the end of the fifteenth and in the sixteenth century, consumers began to prefer Icelandic salted and dried fish, so that the Hanseatic trade with Norway waned in importance.

Trade with England was of major long-term importance. Originally, it had been the domain of Hanseatic merchants from the Rhineland and Westphalia, who brought Rhine wine, metals and the dye plants madder and woad to England, and returned with tin and English wool for the Flemish and Brabant textile industries; later, they also exported English cloth. In return, the Hanseatic cities of the Baltic coast provided such typical eastern goods as furs, wax, cereals and timber, as well as fish and metals from Scandinavia. But the Low Countries represented the most important market in western Europe. Flanders and later Brabant were not only the most important textile producers, but they also provided a connection to the Mediterranean trading area. The Hanseatic merchants primarily purchased high- and medium-quality woollen cloth in the cities of Flanders and Brabant, as well as hosiery from Bruges. In addition, they purchased spices, figs and raisins from southern Europe. From France came oil and wine, and also the so-called bay salt, or sea salt, from the Atlantic coastal towns of Bourgneuf and Brouage. Since it was cheaper, it gradually replaced Lüneburg salt to preserve herring. Henceforth, Prussian and especially Dutch ships regularly made voyages into the Baltic area carrying bay salt as ballast, and returned westward loaded with cereals and timber. This undermined the Lübeck monopoly in the trade in Lüneburg salt. In southern Europe, the Hanseatic presence remained sporadic, except for a position in the wine trade of Bordeaux, and also an attempt by the Veckinchusen family to establish a market for furs in Venice.

In addition to these goods traded internationally, manufactured products were of great importance, in both domestic and foreign trade. These included, from west to east, the non-ferrous metal products of Aachen, Rhine wines, tools from the Rhenish regions of Mark, Berg, and Sauerland, ceramics from the Rhineland, cloth and linen from Westphalia, brassware from Brunswick, salt from Lüneburg and beer from Hamburg.

The Hanseatic trade was organised by merchant trading companies. The predominant type was the free company, in which two or more partners invested capital and shared profits and losses in proportion to their capital stock; such companies were generally maintained for one or two years. The great international merchants were generally involved in several such companies, as it allowed them to reduce the risks of trading and maritime travel and increase their product range. The partners in a company were often related, thus providing the foundation of trust that was indispensable for trade on the Hanseatic east-west route. Unlike Italy or southern Germany, the Hanseatic area did not have large, centrally managed trading companies with a substantial number of stockholders that continued for several generations. For this reason, the Hanseatic companies saw no need for double-entry bookkeeping on the Italian model.

The four trading posts in Novgorod, Bergen, London and Bruges represented a higher level of organisation for the Hanseatic trade. Here, the German merchants lived in clearly delimited enclaves such as St Peter's Yard, the German Bridge and the walled Steelyard. Only in Bruges did the Hanseatic merchants live with local hosts. Each trading post had a tight structure, with aldermen elected annually, fixed statutes, its own judiciary, and a treasury and seal. The trading posts were important for the acquisition and retention of trading privileges, for, with the backing of the Hanseatic cities, they represented the interests of the merchants against the princes and cities of the host countries. But they also considerably eased everyday business. They established a regular system of information and couriers linking merchants to their home cities, provided assistance with correspondence, notarisation and accounting, and facilitated loans. The primary purpose, however, was, by means of the compulsory registration of all merchants active in a given area, to achieve a certain level of uniformity among Hanseatic merchants in the purchase and sale of goods, and thus to limit competition within the Hanseatic League.

At the end of the fifteenth century, Hanseatic trade suffered setbacks in all areas. The old trading system based on privileges was no longer viable in a time of growing competition and the consolidation of the great European powers. The Scandinavian kings made great efforts to restrict Hanseatic trade for the benefit of their own merchants. They also played the Hanseatic merchants and their Dutch competitors off against one another. The Hanseatic cities intervened in the power struggles in Scandinavia with naval campaigns and attacks of piracy, in the hope of maintaining their privileges. This was ultimately successful with regard to Christian II of Denmark (1513–23). The closure of the Novgorod trading post by Ivan III in 1494 was also a blow to the Hanseatic League, although the trade could now be relocated to the Livonian port cities of Riga and Reval, which thus experienced a major upswing.

In England, the overall situation also changed, with the import and export of cloth being the central issue, as English cloth merchants were demanding the same rights in the Baltic that the Hansa enjoyed in England. There were certainly internal Hanseatic conflicts, since in the dispute with England Lübeck stubbornly insisted upon its old privileges, while Cologne and the Prussian trading cities were willing to reach a compromise. The result was that after a lengthy period of disputes and the reestablishment of Hanseatic privileges, trade with England entered into a final period of prosperity, which lasted until the mid-sixteenth century.[79]

There was also competition between the Dutch merchants in Holland and Zeeland on the one hand and the Wendish Hanseatic cities such as Lübeck, Wismar, Rostock, Stralsund and Greifswald on the other, since the latter saw their position as middlemen in the transport of commodities along the east-west route threatened. Nonetheless, Lübeck was unable to limit Dutch access to the Baltic Sea, either by peaceful or by military means. On the contrary, the Prussian Hanseatic cities of Danzig, Elbing, Thorn and Königsberg were largely dependent upon Dutch carrying capacity. As early as 1475/76, one quarter of Danzig's seaborne trade was being transported by Dutch ships. While Hanseatic vessels continued to handle the bulk of east-west commerce, the Dutch share increased continually.[80]

The Bruges trading post had de facto been located in Antwerp since 1460, because the merchants were attracted to the Brabant trade fairs there and in Bergen op Zoom. By 1563, when the Hanseatic merchants finally built their kontor in Antwerp, the city's trade had already passed its peak. The decline of the Lübeck-dominated trading post at the German Bridge in Bergen, Norway was ushered in by other Hanseatic cities such

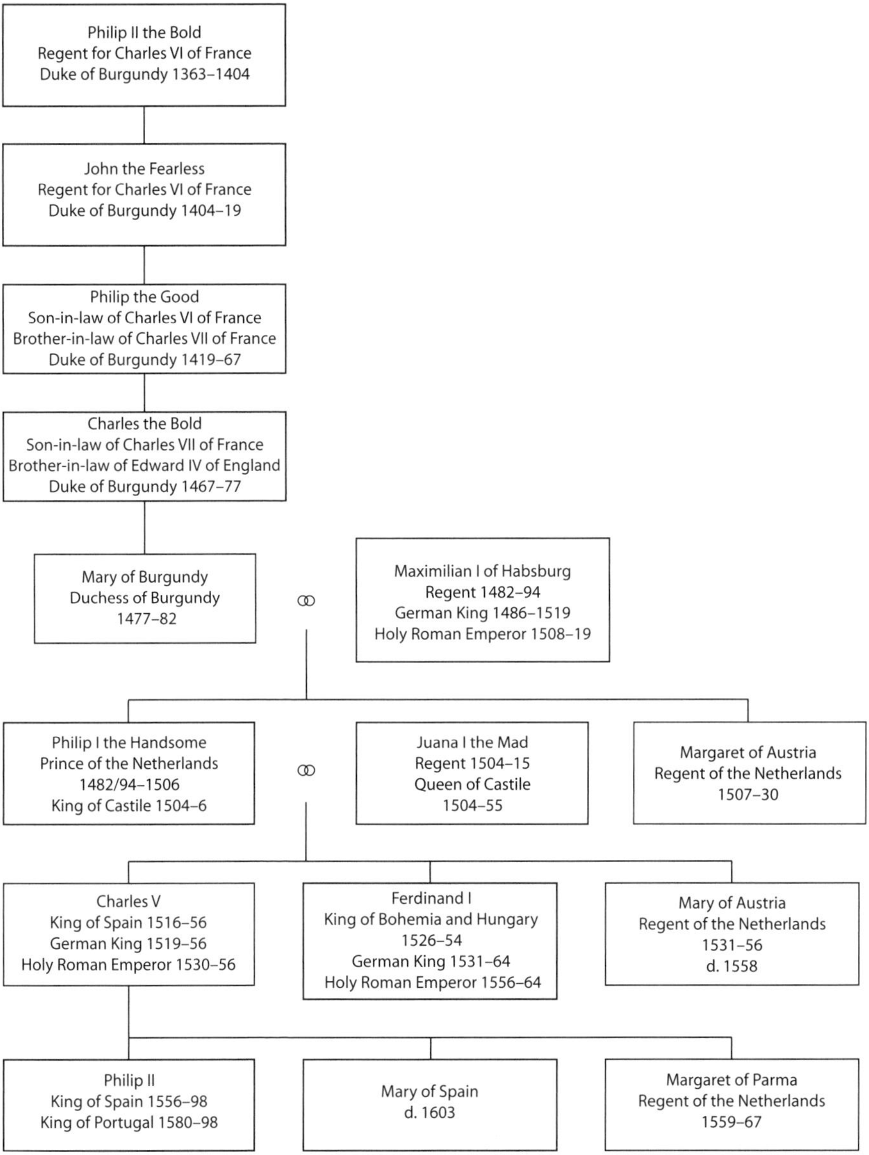

Genealogical table 4 The dukes of Burgundy and the governors of the Burgundian Netherlands 1363–1567

as Hamburg and Bremen, which began to run voyages to Iceland and the Shetland Islands in the fifteenth century.

Signs of the decline of the Hanseatic League were ubiquitous in the sixteenth century. Historians have offered various explanations, such as the rise of the German territorial states and of the Nordic kingdoms, or the superior competition of southern German trading companies and of the Netherlands as a trading nation.[81] However, this picture of decline contrasts starkly with the general rise in European trade during the sixteenth century. While this growth benefited the Hanseatic cities, it also outgrew the rigid framework of the traditional privilege-based Hanseatic trading system which, since the fifteenth century, had been increasingly undermined by the competing interests of the Hanseatic cities as well as by foreign competitors. It was no longer Bruges, Bergen, Lübeck or Novgorod that profited from the expansion of European trade. The future belonged to Amsterdam, Hamburg and Danzig. Just as innovations in shipbuilding and trade had once provided the Hanseatic League with an advantage over the peasant merchants of Gotland, new types of ships and the expansion of commission trading and non-cash payment were now decisive in promoting the rise of the Netherlands as a commercial power.

5.13 The rise of the Burgundian Netherlands

In the Middle Ages, the term Netherlands, or Low Countries, simply referred to the lowlands around the mouths of the great rivers Rhine, Meuse and Scheldt. In this area dominated by marshes and sandy moorlands, independent territories arose early, including Flanders, Brabant, Artois, Hainaut, Namur, Limburg, Holland, Zealand, Guelders and the bishoprics of Liège and Utrecht. An essential element in the history of these territories was political unification by the dukes of Burgundy at the end of the fourteenth and throughout the fifteenth century. From this period, European chanceries began to refer to the Burgundian lands as *pais d'embas* in French, or *Nyderlande* in German – the Low Countries. Not all of the territories belonged to the Holy Roman Empire: Brabant, Liège, Holland, Zeeland and Guelders were part of the empire, while Flanders, except for the Aalst region, was a fief of the French crown. What is more, in the fourteenth century, certain territories such as Flanders and Namur, or Holland, Zeeland and Hainaut, were ruled by the same dynasty.

From the late thirteenth and early fourteenth century, the county of Flanders regularly had to defend itself against attacks from its French liege lord. At the same time, the Counts Guy de Dampierre (1278–1305) and

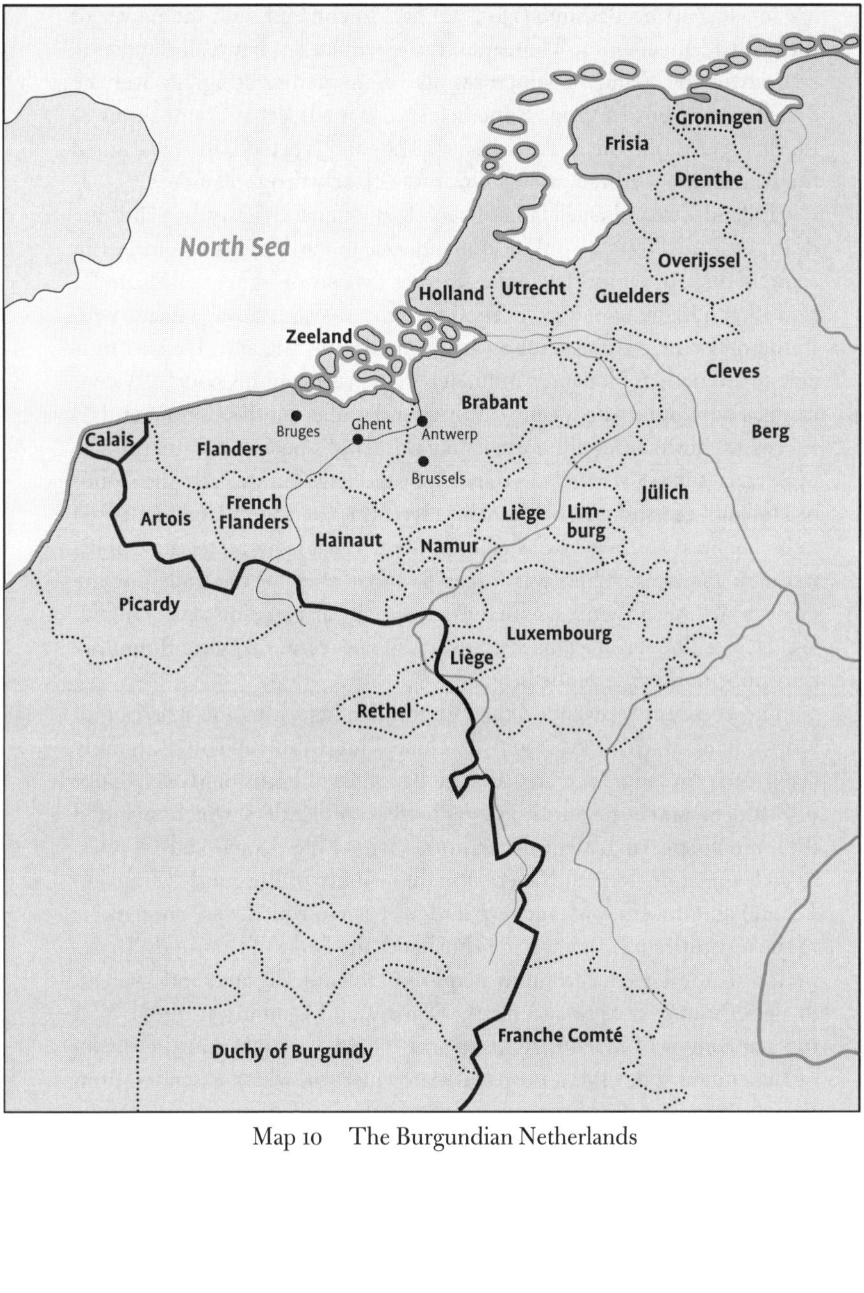

Map 10 The Burgundian Netherlands

his son Robert de Bethune (1305–22) had to contend with the power of the great Flemish cities. Thereafter, rivalry broke out between the duchy of Brabant and Flanders, which resulted in numerous struggles over the Scheldt, their border river. Nonetheless, the marriage of Count Louis of Maele (1332–84) to the Brabant heiress Margaret (1323–80) in 1347 calmed the situation, since Brabant was now more closely tied to Flanders.

Holland-Zealand and Hainaut each had its own dynasty, but after the death of Floris V (1256–96) of Holland-Zealand and of his son John I in 1299, all three provinces fell to the Avesnes dynasty of Hainaut. William III (1305–37) initially hoped for French support, but later allied himself with Emperor Louis the Bavarian and Edward III of England. He was thus able to strengthen Holland's influence in the east, and his court at Valenciennes developed into a centre of England's allies on the Continent. His successes, however, could not maintain Holland's position, so that Albert of Bavaria (1358–89) ruled not only his own duchy, but was also the Count of Holland-Zealand and of Hainaut. Here, the Count of Flanders proved to be his most stubborn external opponent. What is more, because of his frequent absences, Albert was forced to suffer a regime controlled by the cities in all three provinces, with the occasional participation of the nobility and clergy. The death of his successor William VI in 1417 gave Burgundy the opportunity to seize the provinces.[82]

The constitutive event of the Burgundian state was the marriage of Margaret of Maele (1384–1405) to Duke Philip the Bold of Burgundy (1363–1404) in 1369. Margaret was the daughter of Louis of Maele, Count of Flanders, and at his death in 1384 heiress to Flanders, which included the French-speaking Flemish territories with Lille, Douai and Orchies, as well as Artois, Rethel, Nevers, the free county of Burgundy (Franche-Comté) and the cities of Antwerp and Mechelen, which were contiguous to the territories belonging to her husband, the Duke of Burgundy. In the period that followed, Burgundy acquired Holland, Zeeland and Hainaut in 1428, Namur in 1429 and finally Brabant and Limburg in 1430. With the acquisition of Macon, Auxerre and Picardy in 1435, and the duchy of Luxembourg in 1451, a powerful state emerged, which extended from French Burgundy in the south to the Netherlands in the north. Duke Philip the Good furthered the unification of the state structure by means of centralisation.[83] His son and successor, Charles the Bold (1467–77), attempted to realise his father's dream of an independent kingdom of Burgundy between France and the Holy Roman Empire. His personal motivation was the ideal of chivalry, to emulate classical antiquity with great and glorious deeds. He had listened to tales of the heroic deeds of Sir

Lancelot from earliest childhood, and was later fascinated by figures from antiquity, especially the conquerors Alexander the Great, Hannibal and Julius Caesar. Many of his contemporaries saw the conscious imitation of these ancient heroes as the driving force behind his activities, especially his numerous wars. Charles pursued an anti-French policy, as demonstrated by his marriage to Margaret of York, the sister of the English King, in 1468. The conquest of Lorraine, an imperial territory, provided the connection between Charles's lands in Burgundy and in the Netherlands. Nonetheless, Charles's foreign policy was a complete failure. After the failed siege of Neuss in the Rhineland in 1474/75, and the serious defeats at the hands of the Swiss Confederacy at Grandson and Murten in 1476, he was killed in 1477 while trying to recapture Nancy, the capital of Lorraine.[84] With the loss of Lorraine and the French seizure of the core duchy of Burgundy, the centre of gravity of the Burgundian realm shifted to the Netherlands. The beneficiaries of Charles the Bold's debacle were France as well as Charles's son-in-law Maximilian of Habsburg, who succeeded in taking over the Burgundian inheritance against French opposition.[85]

As a result of the 1477 marriage of Archduke and later Emperor Maximilian (1508–19) to Charles's daughter Mary of Burgundy (1457–82), and Mary's early death in a hunting accident, the Netherlands fell to the Habsburgs; in the southern Netherlands, their rule would last until 1795. This and other dynastic coincidences allowed the Burgundian-Habsburg alliance to evolve into the Habsburg world empire.

The basis for this was the marriage, arranged by Maximilian in 1495, of his children Philip the Handsome and Margaret to the children of the Catholic monarchs of Spain, Isabella of Castile (1474–1504) and Ferdinand of Aragón (1479–1516). Philip married their daughter Juana, known as the Mad (1504–16) while Margaret married the *Infante* John. Since John died five months after his marriage, and his sister Isabel, who had married a Portuguese prince, died the following year, Juana inherited the Spanish empire including its overseas territories. After her husband Philip the Handsome died in 1506, their son Charles acceded to the inheritance in the Netherlands in 1515, and a year later, thanks to his mother's incapacity, to the kingship of Spain. In 1519 he was elected German King as the successor to his grandfather Maximilian, and crowned Emperor in 1530. For the Netherlands, being anchored in the emerging Habsburg universal empire, upon which the sun never set, was initially of small significance.

At the death of Charles the Bold, the integration into the Habsburg empire was not yet preordained. After Charles's death, both Mary and Maximilian had to establish their rule in the face of particularist forces in the provinces. Mary was able to mollify the opposition of the cities of Bruges, Ghent, Ypres, Brussels, Antwerp, Maastricht, Valenciennes and others only by means of the Great Privilege of 1477, which gave the estates of the provinces the right to assemble in what were known henceforth as the Estates General at any time, without the invitation of the ruler. Moreover, from now on no wars could be fought and no taxes levied without the approval of the estates.

After the death of his wife, Maximilian even faced the challenge of a political revolution of oppositional Flemish and Brabant cities, which took issue with both his anti-French foreign policy and his domestic policies. After he had been held captive for a time by the Flemish cities in Bruges, Maximilian gradually began to gain the upper hand militarily, with the support of German and Swiss mercenaries. Ghent's capitulation in 1492 put an end to the rebellion, and opened up possibilities for Maximilian to intervene in the politics of the cities, including the establishment of municipal government authorities and the election of the guild masters. In those Dutch provinces, such as Frisia and Guelders, which were not yet under Habsburg rule, opposition continued to mount. Philip the Handsome was also unable to suppress it after Maximilian succeeded his father Frederick III as Emperor in 1493.

Only his grandson Charles, born in Ghent and raised in the Netherlands, would eventually acquire Tournai in 1521, Frisia in 1524, Overijssel and Utrecht in 1528, Drenthe, Groningen and the surrounding lands in 1536, and Guelders and Zutphen in 1543, and incorporate them into the Netherlands, so that the seventeen provinces were now for the first time, albeit briefly, united in a single state.[86]

5.14 Counts and cities

During the fourteenth century, Flanders was at the centre of numerous conflicts involving its bonds of vassalage to France on the one hand, and its important role in international trade on the other. It was also the scene of conflicts between its cities. In 1297, the textile artisans and merchants had gained access to municipal government in a struggle against the old patrician class, which they replaced, leading during the ensuing period to new struggles over the distribution of power between weavers, fullers and merchants. In 1336, as a result of the English embargo on wool exports, the weavers under the leadership of Jacob van Artevelde regained control and switched to a pro-English policy, thus challenging both the Count of Flanders and the King of France. The rule of the weavers, their suppression of a wage rebellion by the fullers and the murder of Artevelde led to their expulsion from the city government, so that only a political compromise between the merchants and the weavers' guild, which distributed the city offices among the participating groups – with the exception of the fullers – produced long-term stability, which then spread to the rest of the country. Under Artevelde the major cities of Ghent, Bruges and Ypres had in fact already ruled Flanders, and it was ultimately left to the new Count Louis of Maele (1346–84) to restore princely authority, although he had to accept the political participation of the cities.[87]

Only Duke Philip the Good (1419–67) succeeded in advancing the internal unification of the various territories into a single state structure. One of his key achievements was the centralisation of the financial and judicial systems. In order to improve the collection of ducal revenues, he expanded the chambers of accounts and restructured their responsibilities.[88] At the same time, the ducal privy council, under the name grand council, became the supreme court of appeal. The Duke countered the

Table 2 Population of the Low Countries *c.* 1470

Region	*Urban population (%)*	*Rural population (%)*	*Total inhabitants*	*Proportion of total population (%)*
Artois	20	80	176,000	7.1
Boulonnais	12	88	31,000	1.2
Brabant	29	71	399,000	16.1
Flanders	33	67	705,000	28.6
Guelders	41	59	133,000	5.4
Hainaut	28	72	202,000	8.2
Holland	44	56	254,000	10.3
Limburg	6	94	16,500	0.6
Liège	26	74	135,500	5.4
Luxembourg	12	88	138,000	5.6
Namur	26	74	17,500	0.7
Picardy	19	81	184,000	7.4
Zeeland	?	?	85,000	3.4
Overall	**32**	**68**	**2,476,500**	**100**

Source: W. P. Blockmans and W. Prevenier, *The promised lands*, p. 152.

resistance of the estates against this policy of centralisation, which took the form of a tax boycott, by regularly convening a representative assembly of his Dutch territories, which was known after 1478 as the Estates General. Although such moves accelerated institutional integration, the political and economic centre of gravity of the Burgundian Netherlands was still in the south of the country, in Flanders and Brabant. The language of the court and administration was French, and the order of the Golden Fleece established by Philip the Good in 1430 included almost exclusively *nobiles* from the southern provinces.

The unique concentration of cities in Flanders and Brabant was decisive for the political and economic significance of the southern Netherlands. Even in the fourteenth century, the major Flemish cities of Ghent and Bruges, with 64,000 and 46,000 inhabitants respectively, were larger than any other western European city aside from Paris. Although these populations declined during the fifteenth century, Flanders and Brabant still boasted the largest cities and the most inhabitants of all the provinces at this time. Around 1500, Ghent and Antwerp had more than 40,000 inhabitants each, and Bruges and Brussels more than 30,000 each, while none of the four leading cities of Holland – Leiden, Amsterdam, Haarlem and Delft – exceeded 15,000 inhabitants, making them smaller than the Brabant towns of Louvain or Den Bosch.

Holland began to close the gap in the fifteenth century, however. The total population of the Low Countries was 2.56 million, with Holland in third place behind Flanders and Brabant. In terms of population density, its sixty-six inhabitants per square kilometre were not far behind the Flemish figure of seventy-eight, and when it came to the urban share of the population, Holland was even ahead of Flanders, an indication of the growing importance of the province's numerous small cities. Nonetheless, international trade, manufacturing, financial resources and political influence remained concentrated in the south, and particularly in the relatively large centres of Ghent, Bruges, Antwerp and Brussels. Accordingly, the major Flemish cities put up the strongest resistance to integration into the Burgundian state. Like the cities of Brabant, they could look back on a 'grand tradition of rebellion' (Blockmans), which had begun in the fourteenth century and reached a provisional highpoint in the Dutch War of Independence in the second half of the sixteenth century. The opposition of the urban elites grew in proportion to the Burgundian state's assumption of the judicial and fiscal responsibilities that had previously been the purview of the cities. Thus interventions in the city's law courts by ducal bailiffs led to the Bruges rebellion of 1436–38, which ended with the penalisation of Bruges. The city not only lost control over its port of Sluys, but also had to pay a fine of 480,000 pounds.

In 1447, Philip the Good attempted to impose a tax on salt consumption, but ran up against the resistance of Ghent and other Flemish cities. The stage was set for conflict once again, which the Duke deliberately permitted to escalate. Interference in the city's autonomy, for instance in the election of aldermen, provoked a strike by craftsmen. After several attempts at negotiation failed because of the Duke's obstinacy, he blockaded the city and defeated the soldiery of Ghent at Gavere in 1453. The penalty imposed followed the precedent of Bruges: a fine of 480,000 pounds. The Duke had made an example of the largest cities, however, without permanently breaking their power.[89]

5.15 A trade hub

The most important trading centres in the Low Countries were Bruges and Antwerp.[90] Even in the fourteenth century, Bruges had become a notable point of trade between southern and western and eastern Europe. Here, cloth from Flanders and Brabant, leather from southern Europe, furs and wax from the east, and spices such as saffron, nutmeg, pepper, ginger, cinnamon and anise as well as sugar from the Mediterranean and Asia were traded. Privileged merchants from Genoa, Florence, Venice, Lucca, Catalonia, Castile and Portugal, as well as English and Hanseatic merchants, settled in Bruges and made the city the most important trading centre of north-western Europe during the late Middle Ages.[91]

In the second half of the fifteenth century, the Brabant trade-fair city of Antwerp finally rose to the status of a European commercial centre. Even at the beginning of that century, the twice-yearly Brabant fairs of Antwerp and Bergen op Zoom became major emporiums for English cloth. The English merchant adventurers often imported it as a semi-finished product to Brabant, where the cloth was dyed and glazed and sold as a finished product to both Hanseatic and the south German merchants. The demand for cloth in southern Germany, like the demand for silver in the Netherlands, attracted Nuremberg and Augsburg merchants and their expanding trade in silver, copper and fustian to the banks of the Scheldt. Here, they encountered not only English, but also Portuguese merchants, with their Asian products and their gold and ivory from Africa. The Portuguese in turn were dependent on southern German metal goods as well as copper and silver for their trade in Africa and India. Thus did English cloth, southern German metals and Portuguese spices constitute the basis for Antwerp's rise as the centre of a European world market during the sixteenth century.[92]

Imports of cheap English woollen cloth damaged the Flemish textile industry, which specialised in high-quality products. The Flemings responded with import bans and the diversification of production. The cloth producers of Mechelen and the cities of Holland, for their part, successfully re-orientated their production toward lighter woollen cloth, the so-called new draperies, which they sold internationally at the fairs. However, not just cloth production, but also beer brewing and above all fishing and shipping, were responsible for the economic rise of Holland during the fifteenth century.[93]

The province's natural conditions were an important prerequisite for that expansion. Since mediocre soils and the high costs of drainage made the cultivation of cereals unprofitable, agriculture in Holland focused on alternatives such as commercial crops and horticulture, and later dairy products. In addition, traditional subsidiary activities such as fishing and shipping were expanded. Since the permanent import of grain had to be paid for by a supply of goods for export, Holland gradually developed the production of beer, cloth and North Sea herring, for which it captured market shares and with which it paid for the imported grain. Often, these products were cheap copies or variations of renowned Flemish and Hanseatic products.[94]

Beyond that, shipping and freight transport provided Holland and Zealand with access to the Baltic area, where shipping capacity was limited. The demand for the shipping capacity of Holland and Zealand rose in step with that for cereal exports in the west. Thus shippers increased their share of the ship traffic in Danzig from one-quarter in 1475/76 to approximately 50 per cent in 1583 (see 5.12).[95]

5.16 Burgundian culture

The culture of the Burgundian Netherlands was a unique symbiosis of courtly and urban elements, in which the aristocratic culture of France and the burgher culture of the Netherlands came together and inspired each other.[96] An independent culture emerged that would dominate north-western Europe from the fifteenth to the seventeenth century.[97]

The character of this culture is nowhere better preserved than in Flemish painting. Centres of artistic production included, most prominently, Tournai, Bruges, Louvain and Antwerp. Tournai dominated during the first half of the fifteenth century. Rogier van der Weyden (*c.* 1399–1464) studied here before attaining success in Brussels together with Robert Campin (*c.* 1378–1444). Bruges excelled with the brothers Hubert (*c.* 1370–1426) and Jan van Eyck (*c.* 1390–1441). Petrus Christus (*c.* 1410/20–*c.* 1473) continued the latter's work as a portraitist. During the second half of the fifteenth and the early sixteenth century, Bruges painting blossomed with Hans Memling (1430–94) and Gerard David (*c.* 1460–1523). In Brabant, the Louvain workshop of Dirk Bouts (*c.* 1420–75) and his sons, and the Antwerp painters Quentin Metsys (1465–1530) and Joachim Patinir (*c.* 1480–1524) deserve mention.

A closer look at Bruges, the most important centre for the visual arts north of the Alps, demonstrates the extraordinary conditions of artistic activity in Flanders, which was based on a constantly increasing demand for works of art. Buyers and patrons included the Burgundian court, the local merchant elite, the colonies of foreign merchants and an extraordinarily broad and prosperous middle class. We should not overestimate the role of the court; the dukes rarely came to Bruges, and most orders came from the local elites and the religious confraternities, in which various social groups came together. Foreign merchants, especially Italians, feature most prominently among the recorded patrons of Hans Memling, before Bruges citizens and confraternities.

Art was at once an export article and promoted the social prestige of the native and foreign merchants settled in Bruges, but also of the local artisan elite, which was organised in confraternities. These customers preferred new forms of self-presentation such as the merchant portrait, which replaced the older tradition of religious themes, or combined portraiture with religious motifs. The city's spatial and social confinement stimulated the rapid dissemination of new ideas, and with them competition in the area of artistic production and social representation. The existing artistic creativity in turn drew talents from the surrounding region, and the various artistic centres vied with one another to attract them.[98]

Similar conditions as those for painting applied to other areas of Flemish art. Manuscripts, sculpture, woodcarving and tapestry as well as instrumental and vocal music were greatly in demand both in the Burgundian Netherlands and abroad. Two of these genres are still directly associated with Burgundian court culture even today: illuminated manuscripts and tapestries. Here, princely patronage stimulated the painting of miniatures to the high degree of artistic refinement visible in the book of hours of the Duke of Berry, the *Très riches heures* by the Limbourg brothers. They initially worked in France, for only Duke Philip the Good fostered the development of a specifically Flemish school of book illumination.

Tapestry weaving flourished in Brussels, Tournai and Arras. Works were commissioned by the court, which for example publicly proclaimed the foundation of the Order of the Golden Fleece with a series of tapestries depicting the legend of the Argonauts. The cities also had tapestries produced for the dukes, with Bruges artists creating the magnificent series of twelve tapestries depicting the Trojan War between 1472 and 1476, the price of which represented the annual wages of 120 skilled labourers. Sculpture and woodcarving were closely tied to princely representation. During the lifetime of Philip the Bold, the Flemish artists Jacob de Baerze and Klaas Sluter (*c.* 1340/50–1405/06) were already commissioned to decorate the mausoleum of the Duke and his wife Margaret of Maele in the Carthusian monastery of Champmol near Dijon; it would later be completed by Klaas van der Werve (*c.* 1380–1439). The Duke and Duchess are everywhere memorialised, both lying on their sarcophagi and kneeling before the Virgin Mary and Christ Child at the church portal. Charles the Bold created a similar link between religion and the Burgundian dynasty by donating a reliquary to St Lambert's cathedral in Liège, which shows him kneeling before St George holding the shrine in his hand.

Alongside the visual arts, a specifically 'Franco-Flemish' style developed in music, which is associated with Guillaume Dufay of Hainaut (*c.* 1400–74), who, after sojourns in Rome, Geneva and Paris, worked in Cambrai, a centre of sacred music. Dufay combined Italian and French elements to create his own style of composition. His notable achievements include four-part harmony, the expansion of the cyclic mass, and the connection of the separate parts of the mass through the use of sacred and secular *cantus firmi* and the rise of the motet, which was now mainly spiritual in content and characterised by a close coordination between word and tone. During the second half of the century, the Fleming Johannes Ockeghem (*c.* 1410/1425–95), who had worked for many years at the Paris court, created a number of mass compositions, some of them using intellectually highly ambitious notation, while the motets receded into the background. All in all, it is certainly true that beginning in the second half of the fifteenth century, the southern Netherlands both created new forms of music and provided the most accomplished performers of this music, so that they largely set the standard for such performance. Countless accounts of choirmasters who travelled to the Low Countries for their patrons, especially from Italy, in order to recruit singers, give evidence of musicians' exchanges in Bruges and Antwerp, where one could hire basses, tenors, altos and boy singers, 'for good singers could best be got in the Low Countries.' At the same time, foreign musicians entered the service of the Burgundian court chapel.[99]

The great demand in Europe for musicians from the Flemish and Walloon Netherlands can be explained by the high quality of their professional training. The choirmasters and singing masters of the great schools at Cambrai and Antwerp must have been extraordinary teachers. The training included not just singing in discant and composition, but also secular music. Thus when Emperor Maximilian I established the Vienna court chapel in 1498, he could demand that his singers be well versed in 'Brabant discant.'

Notes

1 Münch, *Lebensformen*, 27.
2 Moraw, *Von offener Verfassung*, 211–28.
3 Thomas, *Ludwig der Bayer*, 368–70.
4 DuBoulay, *Germany in the later Middle Ages*, 37–43; Hergemöller, *Fürsten, Herren und Städte*; Wolf, 'Das "Kaiserliche Rechtbuch"', 1–32.
5 Moraw, *Von offener Verfassung*, 240–59.
6 Thomas, *Deutsche Geschichte*, 341–76.
7 Fuhrmann, *Konrad von Weinsberg*.
8 Wefers, *Das politische System*.
9 Hödl, *Albrecht II*.
10 Heinig (ed.), *Kaiser Friedrich III.*; Rill, *Friedrich III*.
11 Wiesflecker, *Kaiser Maximilian I.*, I; Meuthen, *Das 15. Jahrhundert*, 48–50.
12 Wiesflecker, *Kaiser Maximilian I.*, II: 201–301.
13 Moraw, 'Verwaltung des Königtums', 23–6, and 'Königliche Herrschaft'.
14 Isenmann, 'The Holy Roman Empire in the Middle Ages', 243–80.
15 Reinle, *Ulrich Riederer*, 463–73.
16 Moraw, 'Verwaltung des Königtums', 41.
17 Ibid., 54–7. See also the more recent fundamental work, Annas, *Hoftag*.
18 Kerler (ed.), *Deutsche Reichstagsakten*, no. 38 (1411), 56.
19 Angermeier, *Die Reichsreform*; for a critique, see Moraw, 'Fürstentum'. For an overview of the literature, see Krieger, *König, Reich and Reichsreform*, 114–18.
20 See Diestelkamp, *Das Reichskammergericht*.
21 Schmidt, *Geschichte des Alten Reiches*, 39.
22 Schmidt, *Der Städtetag*.
23 Willoweit, 'Entwicklung und Verwaltung'.
24 Schubert, *Fürstliche Herrschaft*, 14–19, 27–38.
25 Ibid., 41–9.
26 Reincke, 'Hamburgs Bevölkerung', 170; Reisner, *Die Einwohnerzahl*, 99; Scheftel, *Gänge*, 11.
27 Sprandel, *Von Malvasia bis Kötzschenbroda*, 30–2.
28 Jenks, 'Von den archaischen Grundlagen', 54–9; Stromer, *Die Gründung der Baumwollindustrie*.
29 Hirschfelder, *Kölner Handelsbeziehungen*, 537–48.

30 Stromer, *Oberdeutsche Hochfinanz*, and 'Die ausländischen Kammergrafen'.
31 Pölnitz, *Die Fugger*.
32 Spieß, 'Ständische Abgrenzung'; Hechberger, *Adel*, 38–55.
33 Moraw, *Von offener Verfassung*, 68–78.
34 Obenaus, *Recht und Verfassung*; Carl, *Der Schwäbische Bund*.
35 Holbach, *Stiftsgeistlichkeit*; Fouquet, *Das Speyerer Domkapitel*.
36 Spieß, 'Aufstieg in den Adel'.
37 Isenmann, *Die deutsche Stadt*, 249, 258–9.
38 Lahrkamp, 'Das Patriziat'.
39 Groten, *Köln*; Herborn, *Die politische Führungsschicht*.
40 Pölnitz, *Die Fugger*; Blendinger, 'Versuch', 50, 71
41 G. Wunder, *Die Bürger von Hall*, 269.
42 Schulz, *Handwerksgesellen und Lohnarbeiter*; Göttmann, *Handwerk und Bündnispolitik*.
43 Graus, 'Randgruppen'; Hergemöller (ed.), *Randgruppen*.
44 Toch, *Peasants and Jews in medieval Germany*, and *Die Juden*, 45–68.
45 Rösener, *Bauern im Mittelalter*, 37–8, 54–61, 65–6.
46 H. Wunder, '"Jede Arbeit ist ihres Lohnes wert"', and *Die bäuerliche Gemeinde*.
47 Ulbrich, *Leibherrschaft*, 59–80, 109–13.
48 North, 'Entstehung der Gutswirtschaft'.
49 H. Wunder, *Die bäuerliche Gemeinde*.
50 Cramer, *Geschichte der deutschen Literatur*.
51 Rupprich, *Die deutsche Literatur*, I, 227–35.
52 Ibid., 568–78.
53 Von der Brincken, 'Martin von Troppau'; Johanek, 'Weltchronik'.
54 Bodmer, *Chroniken und Chronisten*.
55 Helmrath, 'Vestigia Aeneae imitari'.
56 Stauber, 'Hartmann Schedel'.
57 Stauber, 'Nürnberg und Italien', 138–9; Worstbrock, 'Hartmann Schedels "Index Librorum"'.
58 Muhlack, 'Das Projekt der Germania illustrata'.
59 Wood, 'Maximilian I as archeologist', 1128–74.
60 Busch, 'Studien zu deutschen Antikensammlungen', 1–16.
61 Stoob, 'Albert Krantz'.
62 Kaufmann, *Court, cloister and city*, 97–115.
63 Schauerte, *Die Ehrenpforte für Kaiser Maximilian I.*; on Cranach's humanist contacts, see Bierende, *Lucas Cranach d. Ä.*
64 *Die Burgunderbeute und Werke burgundischer Hofkunst*.
65 Stettler, *Die Eidgenossenschaft*, 335–50, 386–92.
66 Würgler, 'The league of the discordant members', 29–50.
67 Head, *Early modern democracy in the Grisons*.
68 Blickle, *Kommunalismus*, 32–44.
69 Walder, *Das Stanser Verkommnis*.
70 Bergier, *Wirtschaftsgeschichte der Schweiz*, 87–96.
71 North, 'Von den Warenmessen zu den Wechselmessen', 223–38.
72 Dollinger, *The German Hansa*; North, 'The German Hanse', 57–68.

73 Hoffmann, 'Lübeck'.
74 Lloyd, *England and the German Hanse*, 13–46; Jenks, 'Die "Carta mercatoria"'.
75 Murray, *Bruges, cradle of capitalism*, 219–21.
76 Wernicke, *Die Städtehanse: 1280–1418*.
77 Jörn, Werlich and Wernicke (eds), *Der Stralsunder Frieden*; Fritze, *Am Wendepunkt der Hanse*.
78 Bracker, Henn and Postel (eds), *Die Hanse*, 700–57.
79 Jenks, *England, die Hanse und Preußen*; Fudge, *Cargoes, embargoes and emissaries*.
80 Seifert, *Kompagnons und Konkurrenten*; Schildhauer, 'Zur Verlagerung des See- und Handelsverkehrs'.
81 Bracker, Henn and Postel (eds), *Die Hanse*, 110–95.
82 Blockmans, 'De vorming van een politieke unie', 65–102.
83 Vaughan, *Philip the Good*, and *Valois Burgundy*. More recently, see Brown, *The Valois dukes of Burgundy*; and Cauchies, *Philippe le Beau*.
84 Vaughan, *Charles the Bold*.
85 Blockmans, 'De vorming van een politieke unie', 102–15.
86 Blockmans, *Emperor Charles V*; Blockmans and Mout, *The World of Emperor Charles V*. See also Soly and Blockmans (eds), *Charles V and his time*.
87 Nicholas, 'Economic reorientation and social change', and *Medieval Flanders*; Carson, *James van Artevelde*.
88 Stein (ed.), *Powerbrokers in the late Middle Ages*; Aerts, Rion and Vandenbulcke, *La Cour des comptes entre tradition et innovations*.
89 Blockmans, 'Alternatives to monarchical centralisation'; Dumolyn and Haemers, 'Patterns of urban rebellion'; Boone and Prak, 'Rulers, patricians and burghers'; Boone, 'The Dutch revolt and the medieval tradition of urban dissent'.
90 Stabel, Blondé and Greve (eds), *International trade in the Low Countries*.
91 For Bruges, see Murray, *Bruges, cradle of capitalism*; Van Uytven, 'Stages of economic decline'. The most recent literature on Bruges and Antwerp is summarised in Aerts, 'The stock exchange in medieval and early modern Europe'.
92 Van der Wee, *The growth of the Antwerp market*, 'The Low Countries in transition' and 'Trade in the southern Netherlands'.
93 Munro, 'Medieval woollens: textiles, textile technology and industrial organisation', and 'Medieval woollens: The western European woollen industries and their struggles for international markets'; Van der Wee, 'Structural changes and specialization in the industry of the southern Netherlands'.
94 Blockmans, 'Der holländische Durchbruch', and 'The economic expansion of Holland and Zeeland; Hoppenbrouwers and van Zanden (eds), *Peasants into farmers?;* Van Bavel and van Zanden, 'The jump-start of the Holland economy'.
95 Schildhauer, 'Zur Verlagerung des See- und Handelsverkehrs'.
96 Huizinga, *The autumn of the Middle Ages*; Blockmans and Prevenier, *The Burgundian Netherlands*. See also their *The promised lands*.
97 Arnade, *Realms of ritual*.
98 Blockmans, 'The Burgundian court'; Martens, 'Artistic patronage'; Borchert (ed.), *The age of van Eyck*; Martens (ed.), *Bruges et la Renaissance*.
99 Fiala, 'Les musiciens étrangers'.

6

East-central Europe

The east-central European kingdoms of Bohemia, Poland and Hungary were so closely linked politically, economically and socially that it appears useful to treat them together. Shared structural characteristics included the process of the so-called eastern settlement, based on colonisation by the Cistercians, peasant settlement, and the increased founding of cities based on German law, as well as the emergence of dynasties that established kingdoms: the Přemyslids, who ruled Bohemia until 1306, the Piasts, who reigned in Poland until 1370, and the Hungarian Árpád dynasty, whose rule ended in 1301. Dynastic interrelationships meant that these dynasties and their successors sometimes ruled several east-central European countries simultaneously. Thus, eastern and central Europe were united for the first time in 1305, when Hungary briefly fell under the rule of Wenceslas II, King of both Bohemia and Poland.

When the Přemyslid dynasty was extinguished in 1306 by the murder of Wenceslas III, a new king was selected from the house of Luxembourg. Between 1419 and 1444, this dynasty united the crowns of Hungary and Bohemia under Sigismund of Luxembourg, and later under his Habsburg successors. Previously, the Hungarian magnates had elected a king from the house of Anjou, which led, after the extinction of the Piasts in Poland in 1370, to a Hungarian-Polish union under Louis of Hungary from 1442 to 1444, and again from 1490 to 1526, during which time the Polish kings were simultaneously kings of Hungary. Moreover, the Polish-Lithuanian personal union that lasted from 1385 until 1569 was to become the dominant power in east-central Europe during the transition from the medieval to the early modern period. During this time, the Jagiełłonian dynasty occupied the throne of Poland under Casimir IV (1447–92), and that of Bohemia (1471–1516) and Hungary (1490–1516) under his son Vladislav II.

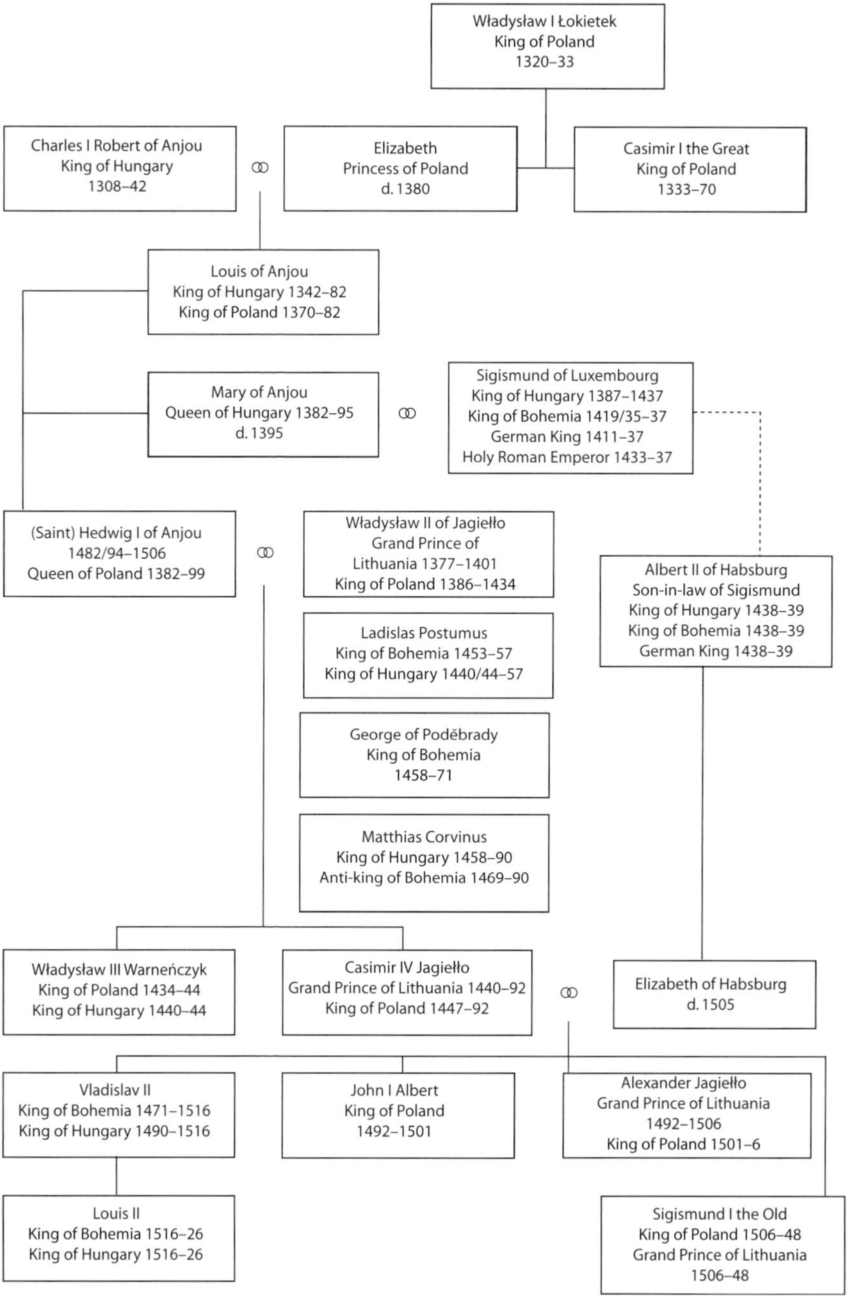

Genealogical table 5 The kings of Bohemia, Poland and Hungary 1308–1548

He was succeeded in Poland-Lithuania by Kings Albert (1492–1501) and Alexander (1501–05).

Also characteristic of the region was the strong position of the nobility. This meant that the estates had an important say in the election of the king and in political decision-making processes.

Another power with a different structure arose alongside these kingdoms during the thirteenth century: the monastic state of the Teutonic Knights. This military-religious order had been founded in Palestine, and was called into the land east of the Vistula to combat and Christianise the heathen Prussians – the so-called mission of the sword that built castles, peasant settlements and new cities into a realm independent of both the emperor and the Pope. In 1236, the Teutonic Order incorporated the Order of the Brethren of the Sword in Livonia, which had hitherto subjugated and missionised the Livonians, Latgalians and Estonians. Since Lithuania resisted these missionary attempts, it became a constant field of conflict for the Order.[1]

6.1 Territorial reorganisation

In all three kingdoms, the thirteenth century was marked by both the terror of the Mongol invasion and the resulting devastation and the disintegration of the kingdoms into petty principalities. Thereafter, at the turn of the thirteenth to the fourteenth century, attempts were made to re-establish the former unity of the kingdoms. For instance, Przemysł II, who was crowned King of Poland in 1295 by Archbishop Jakob Świnka of Gniezno, attempted to forge a larger territorial complex from his power base in Greater (i.e., west-central) Poland. His murder in the following year opened the way for the kings of Bohemia to expand their territory eastward. Wenceslas II was crowned King in 1300 with the support of the nobility and the largely German urban middle classes, who hoped for favourable conditions for their trading activities. However, this Bohemian interlude proved brief, since his successor Wenceslas III, who was also King of Hungary for a short time, was murdered in 1306. A new attempt to unite the kingdom was now initiated in Cracow. Here, Ladislas the Short (Władysław Łokietek) of Łęczyca, Kuyavia and Sieradz had attempted to contest the Bohemians' claim to the Polish inheritance at the end of the thirteenth century. After the death of the Bohemian King, he saw the possibility of uniting the Piast principalities. To this end, he called upon the aid of foreign powers, including the Teutonic Knights, who in 1308 drove the Brandenburgers out of Danzig, but then, to Ladislas' despair, took over the city themselves.

Ladislas had a serious new opponent in the new Bohemian King John of Luxembourg, who, as the heir to the Přemyslids, continued to lay claim to the Polish Crown. A compromise solution could only be achieved by ceding most of Silesia, so that by 1327/29, virtually all Silesian princes were vassals of the Bohemian Crown. Nonetheless, Ladislas succeeded in passing on a partially consolidated kingdom to his son and successor, Casimir the Great (1333–70). Casimir was able to reach a permanent agreement with Bohemia, under which Poland bought back the Bohemian claim to the Polish Crown and also Bohemia's recognition that it held Silesia as a Polish fiefdom. In addition, Casimir acquired Masovia and Kuyavia as his personal domains in 1351. Casimir was particularly successful in the south-east, in so-called Red Russia, where he had claims to the territory of Halich and Vladimir – later to be known as the kingdom of Galicia and Lodomeria. Beginning in 1340, he took advantage of the power vacuum in the region to conquer Ruthenia, the territory of Przemyśl and, permanently, Halyč (Halich) and Vladimir. This required an agreement in the north with Lithuania, which had taken over Volhynia, and in the south with Hungary. Only with the Teutonic Knights did relations remain difficult, so that in the 1343 Treaty of Kalisz Casimir recognised the Knights' claims to Pomerelia, Danzig, Culm and Lubava.[2]

Thus resurgent Poland developed into a Catholic bulwark against both orthodox Christianity to the south-east and against Lithuanian paganism – although Casimir was married to a Lithuanian princess. Casimir's prestige grew when he arbitrated the 1364 Peace of Brno between Louis of Hungary, Rudolf IV of Austria and Charles IV of Bohemia. Casimir secured his position by means of a wide-ranging marital policy: his granddaughter married the King of Bohemia and later Emperor Charles IV;[3] his nephew Louis of Hungary of the house of Anjou succeeded him in Poland.

This dynasty had already succeeded the Hungarian Árpáds seventy years before the extinction of the Piasts in Poland. The last Árpád king, Andrew III, was no longer capable of stabilising his disintegrating kingdom in the face of rival magnate parties. After his death, they supported various pretenders, most of them grandsons of Bela IV. Although one of these, Wenceslas III, did succeed in obtaining the crown of St Stephen, Charles Robert of Anjou, the great-grandson of King Stephen V, was ultimately successful with the support of the Pope, the Hungarian clergy and the middling nobility. Crowned in 1310 at Székesfehérvár, it took him another ten years to finally suppress the rival noble factions in Hungary and Transylvania, but every victory meant another castle in the possession of the Crown, which could now be occupied by a loyal castellan. Since he

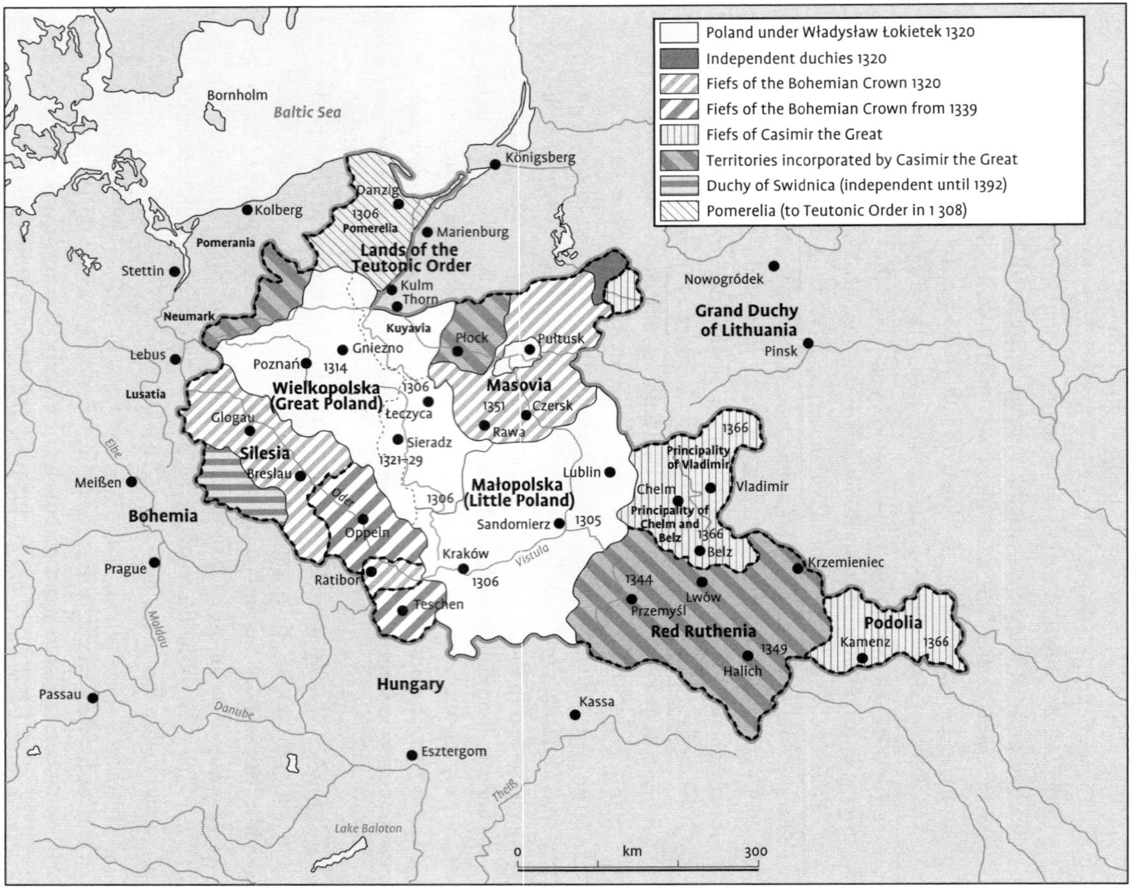

Map 11
The development of Poland in the fourteenth century

also expanded the crown domains, he reinforced his power base, which provided his son Louis with the basis for an expansive foreign policy.[4]

Through his connections with Croatia, his interests were oriented toward the west and south, and rivalry with Venice seemed about to emerge with regard to the Dalmatian coast; this was forestalled, however, by an armistice in 1346. This allowed the King, in alliance with Emperor Louis the Bavarian, to intervene in the Italian peninsula, specifically in the affairs of the kingdom of Naples. In spite of military successes, Louis was forced to recognise that combining these two thrones into a great Adriatic empire was beyond his reach. Instead, he involved himself in Bosnia and Dalmatia, the northern part of which was recognised as a Hungarian possession. In the Balkans, he attempted to limit Ottoman expansion, albeit without any great success.

Louis' priorities changed with his accession to the Polish throne. The king made his mother his regent in Poland, but he certainly had his own goals. These included the incorporation of Ruthenia into the lands of the Hungarian Crown, to which end he appointed the Silesian Duke Vladislav of Opole as regent of the territories of Lwów and Przemyśl. He regarded the crown of Poland primarily as a dowry for his daughters Mary and Hedwig. In 1372 he married Mary to Sigismund, the son of Charles IV, for whom the acquisition of Poland represented the fulfilment of all the territorial desires of the Luxembourg dynasty. Hedwig, or Jadwiga, as she was known in Poland, was provided with Hungary as her dowry, and was to be married to William of Habsburg. These plans sparked considerable resistance among the Polish magnates, whom Louis could only persuade to recognise the inheritance rights of his daughters by granting special privileges. In the so-called Privilege of Koszyce of 1374, he laid the groundwork for the constitutionally powerful position of the Polish nobility, who, like their Hungarian peers, received considerable say in all policy areas, as well as virtually complete freedom from taxation.[5]

Nonetheless, disputes over King Louis's policy continued until his death in 1382, particularly because he was rarely present in the country. As a result, the inheritance remained in dispute until his ten-year-old daughter Hedwig was crowned Queen in Cracow in 1384. Since the dead king could no longer offer the hand of his daughter to her promising Habsburg suitor, the nobility of Lesser Poland offered their queen to Jagiełło, the Grand Prince of Lithuania, their neighbour to the east, with the promise of unification with that huge territory. The Christianisation of Lithuania was an achievement of the Polish Crown, which thus brought Europe's last 'heathens' under the purview of Rome. For the Lithuanians, the Polish marriage was also a promising option, since they hoped it would put an end to the constant vexations and incursions – the so-called 'Lithuanian journeys' – of the Teutonic Knights. Accordingly, in an agreement reached at Krewo Castle in 1385, the Grand Prince promised to accept baptism with his entourage and the entire Lithuanian people, and also to reconquer lost Polish territories. Moreover, the Grand Principality of Lithuania was to be 'associated' with the Polish Crown. Months later, in 1386, Jagiełło was ceremoniously baptised at Cracow, married to the Queen and crowned King. The marriage resulted in territorial gains, the first being that temporarily Hungarian Red Russia was reunited with the Polish Crown, and Lithuania dropped its claims to that territory.

The extinction of the Přemyslids threw Bohemia and Moravia into a dynastic crisis. After the murder of Wenceslas III, the Habsburg Rudolf III, son of King Albert, and Albert's brother-in-law, Henry of Carinthia contested the inheritance. Although Rudolf was killed in the struggle, the Carinthian Duke was unable to achieve any permanent benefit from the situation. Prominent clerics, including abbots of the great Cistercian monasteries and diplomats of Wenceslas II promoted John of Luxembourg, the son of Emperor Henry VII, who was then married to Wenceslas' daughter Elizabeth. Constitutionally, Bohemia was now a vacant fiefdom of the empire, which the Emperor might award as he pleased, regardless of the rights of election claimed and already exercised by the Bohemian nobility. In 1310, John was crowned at Prague, and recognised as King by the nobility the following year in return for a promise of *indygenat*, that is, of privileged access to office for native over foreign nobles. Nonetheless, this alliance did not last long. While the Church – the Cistercian monasteries – the lower nobility and the German patricians of the cities supported John, the upper nobility revolted against him. Not until 1318 was he able to return to Prague with the support of Emperor Louis the Bavarian, and he succeeded in maintaining his position by allowing his adversaries from the high nobility to participate in power as governors. John of Luxembourg nonetheless spent most of his reign outside of Bohemia. He was orientated toward France and Italy, and tried to play a role in imperial and European politics.

John had some foreign-policy successes, gaining the Silesian principalities for the Bohemian Crown, and in the Empire he participated in the victory of Louis the Bavarian over the Habsburg forces at Mühldorf, by which he gained the Egerland (Cheb). He supported the Emperor's policy with regard to the inheritance of the margravate of Brandenburg, as a result of which he regained Upper Lusatia. While Louis the Bavarian withdrew for a time from his alliance with the Bohemian King, those ties were revived in 1330 in an alliance against the Pope. The reason for this was John's support for his uncle Baldwin of Trier, who aspired to the electorate of Mainz and thus the office of arch-chancellor of the empire, which Pope John XXII tried to block. The result was an invasion of Italy and the usual disillusionment. Thus from 1335 John made every effort to win the imperial Crown for himself or his son, while at the same time strengthening his ties to France. The French Crown Prince John (II) married the daughter of the Bohemian King, while the latter, after the death of his wife Elizabeth, married Beatrice of Bourbon, granddaughter of Louis IX (St Louis). The same consideration moved King John to fight on the French side at the battle of Crécy in 1346, although he was already blind by that time. He died in the battle.[6]

John's son Charles, who had succeeded him as regent on the Bohemian throne in 1340, reaped the fruits of his father's foreign policy when, in 1346, he was elected German King against the reigning Emperor Louis the Bavarian with the votes of the three spiritual electors, as well as those of Saxony and Bohemia, and with the support of Pope Clement VI. After Louis the Bavarian died in 1347, Charles IV ruled the empire from Bohemia for three decades. Although he had been raised in France, and was also King of Italy and Burgundy, the land of his birth was Bohemia, and it remained the centre of his life, which had a considerable effect on Bohemian culture and society. He founded Prague's New Town and its university, and engaged in a massive building programme to turn it into a royal capital.[7]

At the administrative level, a distinction should be made between the reinforcement of the imperial central authority on the one hand and the failure to reinforce royal rule in Bohemia on the other. In 1355, Charles failed to pass a law, the *Majestas Carolina*, in the face of opposition from the nobility, and to expand the royal domain. He did, however, succeed in having the lands of the Bohemian Crown, including the associated lands, united into a single territory (*Corona regni*). Charles's dynastic policies must be distinguished from his foreign policies. He acquired Lower Lusatia and Brandenburg as well as the principality of Schweidnitz-Jauer in Silesia. In Italy, where he was crowned in 1355, he was present without overly committing himself.[8] From Bohemia, his goal was to take over Poland, which appeared realistic in view of the marriage of his son Sigismund to Mary (see above); however, such a goal was realised only in Hungary.

His eldest son Wenceslas became King of Bohemia in 1363 and German King in 1376. However, he was unable to combine these two duties in the way that his father had. Economic and social conditions had deteriorated. The noble opposition had gained in strength, and was cooperating with Wenceslas' brother, Sigismund of Hungary, as well as with Margrave Jodok of Moravia.[9] Although the opposition was twice successful in capturing the King – in 1394 and in 1402 – and although Wenceslas' reputation had suffered gravely, for instance as a result of his murder of the archepiscopal vicar John of Pomuk, his removal from the imperial throne had no repercussions in Bohemia. Social and religious tensions would soon erupt, however, in the form of conflicts with the Hussite movement.

All of the countries of east-central Europe were obliged to fight on several fronts during the fifteenth century. While Bohemia, the richest and the most highly developed among them, was bogged down in the Hussite wars, the Hungarian kingdom had to fight the expansion of the Ottoman Empire. But in 1400, Poland-Lithuania, which during the fifteenth century would rise to become the leading east-central European power, still had to face the challenge of both the Golden Horde and the Teutonic Knights. And in all of these conflicts, Emperor Sigismund, as King of Bohemia and Hungary and also Margrave of Brandenburg, played various roles ranging from an alliance with the Teutonic Knights to mediation between them and Poland.

According to the 1385 Union of Krewo, Lithuania was to be permanently tied to the Polish Crown: this, however, proved unrealistic. Lithuania had conquered a number of west Russian principalities, and was thus six times the size of Poland, and distinct from it in language as well as religion and culture. Moreover, Lithuania's interests in the east and south-east determined its relationship with Poland, but also the Teutonic Knights. In 1362, the Lithuanian Prince Algirdas had defeated the Golden Horde, occupied Kiev and conquered the Ukraine as far as the Black Sea. When in 1380 Grand Prince Dmitry Donskoy of Muscovy also defeated the Tartars, Lithuania faced a rival that, through religious and linguistic commonalities, had an easier time 'collecting' Russian lands than did the Lithuanians. Grand Prince Vytautas (Witold), a cousin and energetic competitor of Jagiełło, sought to seize pieces of the defunct empire of the Golden Horde with the support of the Teutonic Knights, but suffered a surprising defeat at the hands of the Tartars in the Battle of the Vorskla River, leading to a partial reorientation of Lithuanian policy.

The Polish-Lithuanian Union was revived in the Unions of Wilna and Radom, which recognised Lithuanian autonomy. At the same time, conflicts broke out again with the Teutonic Knights, with whom an agreement over Samogitia, the borderland between Poland and Livonia, had been reached. The Knights could not hold the borderland against the Samogitian warriors, and launched a propaganda campaign against Poland-Lithuania, whose ruler they attacked as a heathen prince. Poland reacted by accusing the Order of trying to conquer territory under the pretext of Christianisation. Ultimately, military might decided the issue, and the Polish-Lithuanian forces dealt the Order a crushing defeat at the Battle of Tannenberg (Grunwald) in 1410. Although the territorial losses of the Knights under the 1411 Treaty of Thorn were modest, the propagandistic struggle resurfaced at the Council of Constance.[10]

While the ties between Poland and Lithuania were reinforced, the rule of the Teutonic Knights was gradually eroded. The conflict continued at a very low level, and spread to the lands of the Order. Opposition grew among the nobility and in the Prussian Hanseatic cities, leading in 1440 to the formation of the so-called Prussian League, which renounced its allegiance to the Teutonic Order in 1454 and offered the Polish King Casimir IV suzerainty over their lands. After a long war financed primarily by the Prussian cities of Danzig, Elbing and Thorn, the western parts of the Order's lands were subordinated to the Polish Crown as 'Royal Prussia'. The residual state of the Teutonic Order continued to exist until 1525, when in the process of the Reformation it was transformed into a secular duchy under Polish suzerainty, the Duchy of Prussia. In Livonia, the local branch of the Teutonic Order maintained its reign till the 1560s, when Livonia was divided up among Russia, Poland, Sweden and Denmark.[11]

In the east, Poland-Lithuania had to limit itself to defending its own territory in the face of Muscovite expansion. After the death of Vytautas, first his cousin and then his brother succeeded him as grand prince until the election of Jagiełło's younger son Casimir in 1440. Casimir's older brother Władysław III (known in Bohemia as Vladislav and in Hungary as Wladislas), still a child, had succeeded Jagiełło in Poland in 1434, with Bishop Zbigniew Oleśnicki of Cracow acting as regent. After the death of Emperor Sigismund, the pro-Hussite oligarchy of Lesser Poland advanced Władysław III as a candidate for the kingships of Bohemia and Hungary against a Habsburg candidate. In 1438, the moderate faction of the Hussites, the Utraquists, offered him the Bohemian crown, and in 1440 Vladislav (Wladislas) was elected King of Hungary. He led a Hungarian army against the Ottomans, and after initial successes was killed in the Battle of Varna. In Poland, he was succeeded by his brother, the Grand Prince of Lithuania, as Casimir IV. He ruled both kingdoms in a personal union until his death in 1492, and privileged the Polish and Lithuanian aristocracies equally. That had the effect of largely establishing the union of Poland and Lithuania. While the two realms did go their separate ways briefly under his sons, Alexander in Lithuania and John Albert in Poland, unity was re-established in 1501 with the accession of Alexander to the Polish Crown as well.[12] From then on, both realms elected their ruler in common, beginning in 1506, after Alexander's death, when his youngest brother Sigismund (1506–48) succeeded him. In 1569, under the pressure of the constant military threat to Lithuania from Russia, the personal union was made a permanent union by the Treaty of Lublin. From this position of strength, Poland involved itself in the conflicts in eastern and central Europe, albeit often unwillingly. Moreover, certain parties supported the Jagiełłonians as candidates for the throne as an alternative to the Luxembourgs and Habsburgs.

During the first half of the fifteenth century, Bohemia was the most prominent field of conflict in central Europe. Here, the religious, social and national elements that emerged with the Hussite movement, and which fundamentally changed the kingdom, augmented the struggles between the high nobility and King Wenceslas. Jan Hus disseminated Wycliffian ideas and juxtaposed the ideal of a poor Church of the people in the tradition of Jesus Christ to the ruling official Church. His sermons and his efforts to produce a New Testament in Czech challenged both Church officials and the professors of Prague University. Anti-German resentment was combined with religious ideas, and exploited by King Wenceslas for his own purposes.[13]

Hoping to win restoration as German King, Wenceslas sought to overcome the schism with a Bohemian delegation to the Council of Pisa in 1409. Since the archbishop of Prague prevented this, he managed to gain the obedience of Prague University by skilfully exploiting the disputes over Wycliffe's teachings between the Czech magisters and other members of the university. In the decree of Kuttenberg (Kutná Hora), he changed the voting rights of the various national blocks at the university, giving the Bohemian (i.e., Czech) nation three votes, while the other three blocks, the Bavarian, Saxon and Polish nations, were combined into a single 'German' nation with only one vote. In response, the German teachers and students, with the exception of the law faculty, withdrew from Prague, so that the university developed into a regional institution (see 13.3).[14]

John Hus was made rector of the university, which sent a delegation to Pisa. As the conflict in Prague escalated, Hus withdrew to southern Bohemia, and in 1414, with a letter of free passage from King Sigismund, followed a summons to appear before the Council of Constance. Hus was

Map 12 Hungary in the fourteenth century

then burnt at the stake as a heretic in Constance, which evoked a great wave of solidarity. The Bohemian nobles placed Church reform on their agenda, while radical Hussites, including preachers, artisans and petty nobles, revolted openly. Sigismund's attempt to use a crusade to gain the Bohemian crown left by his late brother Wenceslas led to the unification of the various Hussite groupings. In the so-called Four Articles of 1421, they united on a minimum programme that unconditionally demanded the Eucharist in both kinds, the free preaching of the word of God, the renunciation by the Church of all power and property and the punishment of the clergy in case of misdemeanour. Nonetheless, considerable parts of the country, as well as the associated lands such as Moravia and Silesia, remained Catholic. While the Four Articles had been formulated by the moderates, in the course of successful military operations power shifted to the armies of the radical Taborites.[15]

Hussite armies also invaded Bavaria and Franconia, while the Hussite propagandists sent the Four Articles to the European universities in order to gain the attention of the conciliar movement. In 1431, the Council of Basle and the Emperor called for the initiation of negotiations with the Hussites. After the victory of a coalition of nobles and cities over the uncompromising Taborite faction at the Battle of Lipany in 1434, and the acceptance of a moderate version of the Four Articles, the so-called Compacts of Basle, by the Emperor, the way was open for him to obtain the crown of Bohemia. He only held it for one year, since he died in 1437. Although the country was divided between the supporters of the new doctrine, known as Utraquists or Calyxtines, and the Catholics, the position of the nobility was greatly strengthened, while the cities and the lower nobility also retained their representation in the estates. The loser was the Church, which forfeited a considerable portion of its lands. This benefited the nobility, and enabled the rise of new families.

After Sigismund's death, the problems of succession broke out immediately. His son-in-law, the Habsburg heir Albert II, who would die in 1439, was opposed by Jagiełłonian candidates, one of whom proved successful in Hungary. In Bohemia, Albert's son Ladislas Posthumus (1453–57), known as such because he was born after his father's death, was only able to take over during the 1450s with the support of the Utraquist magnate George of Poděbrady; after Ladislas' death, George was elected king by the Bohemian diet in 1458. Although branded a heretic king by the Pope, he maintained himself successfully against Catholic rivals in Bohemia and against Matthias Corvinus of Hungary, and fortified the central authority. Nevertheless – perhaps by design, in order to gain recognition – he attempted to reinforce European cooperation against the Ottomans. His alliance with Casimir IV of Poland-Lithuania was particularly effective. Since founding a dynasty of his own was beyond his power, he offered Casimir's son Vladislav the Bohemian crown.[16] The fifteen-year-old Vladislav II gave generous recognition to the liberties of Bohemia in 1471, including the Compacts. In 1477, Emperor Frederick III affirmed his position. Nevertheless, Matthias Corvinus continued to control Moravia, Silesia and Lusatia. After Matthias's death in 1490, the subsidiary lands were also reunited with the crown of Bohemia, while Vladislav acceded to the crown of Hungary. The privileged position of the nobility was expanded further, and underpinned in the Vladislavian Constitution. In the inheritance compacts of Vienna, Wladislas II (Vladislav) then set the stage for Habsburg accession in Bohemia and Hungary.

In the fifteenth century, Hungary was torn between the Scylla of the Turkish danger and the Charybdis of an increasingly mighty nobility. With the defeat of Serbia at the Battle of Kosovo in 1389 and the failure of the crusade under the leadership of King Sigismund at Nicopolis in 1396, the buffer zone between the Ottoman Empire and Hungary became increasingly narrow, so that the Hungarian border was immediately threatened. Within Hungary, numerous aristocratic rebellions undermined royal power. Sigismund of Luxembourg had to fight for over a decade, first for his marriage to Mary and then for the Hungarian throne. The Hungarian magnates henceforth claimed the right of election, as a potential candidate could only be elected king in return for very considerable promises. Only the founding of the so-called Order of the Dragon and the admittance to this order of Hungarian nobles, who could then administer some of the royal castles, strengthened his regime. This was all the more important as the king spent much time outside of Hungary, especially after his election as German King in 1411. That also pulled Hungary, by way of its ruler, into the problems of the empire, and especially of Bohemia, which resulted in a Hussite invasion of Upper Hungary.

Sigismund attempted to shore up the royal authority by choosing not only great nobles and prelates, but also members of the lower nobility and the urban patriciate as his personal advisers. The unresolved financial situation drove the King to desperate measures. He mortgaged the sixteen richest cities of the Zips region to Poland, which retained control of them until the partition of Poland in 1772. Moreover, Sigismund resorted to the practice of debasing coinage, a ruse also used in other countries. In Transylvania, where feudal rents continued to be demanded in good money, this sparked peasant uprisings. His regulation of the succession met with no better success. While his chosen successor, his son-in-law Albert of Austria (1437–39) like Emperor Sigismund before him, had to sign an electoral capitulation – a promise of *indygenat* for the native nobility – Albert II's early death rendered it ineffective. Now, struggles over the succession broke out in earnest. Albert's widow Elizabeth attempted to save the throne for his son Ladislas Posthumus, and rapidly had him crowned with the crown of St Stephen. However, the Hungarian estates elected Wladislas (Władysław III), the son of Jagiełło of Poland, who called for war against Turkey. Wladislas's brief reign was hence entirely dominated by the resumption of war against the Turks, and the rise of the Hungarian commander in that war, John Hunyadi. Under his leadership, the Hungarians would suffer a devastating defeat at Varna in 1444, where King Wladislas was killed, and again in 1448 at Kosovo, but with a victory in Belgrade in 1456 over Mehmed II, the conqueror of Constantinople, Hunyadi secured a period of relief for the country on the southern front. Moreover, he succeeded in stabilising the country during his regency from 1446 to 1453. Thereafter, Ladislas, released by Emperor Frederick III, took over the Hungarian throne.[17]

After the deaths of John Hunyadi in 1456 and Ladislas Posthumus in 1458, Hunyadi's son Matthias was elected King. Like George of Poděbrady in Bohemia, he was the first great noble to attain the kingship with no blood relationship to any previous dynasty. His reign from 1458 to 1490 is viewed as the last Hungarian golden age. By reforming the system of taxation and of sovereign privilege, Matthias acquired the means to build a mercenary army – which, however, he had to keep constantly occupied. Rather than sending it south to fight the Ottomans or to recapture Dalmatia, which had been lost to Venice, he deployed it to fight against George of Poděbrady in Bohemia and Frederick III in Austria.

Thus, Moravia and Silesia came under Hungarian rule for ten years, as did parts of Lower Austria, including Vienna. This reversal of the military agenda, and the removal of all aristocratic counsellors in favour of new men in his entourage, strengthened the internal Hungarian resistance against the ruler. Meanwhile, an ambitious foreign policy, together with the sponsorship of the arts and sciences, brought Matthias considerable prestige, which he sought to use to secure his succession. He failed to establish a dynasty, however.[18] When Matthias suddenly died in Vienna at age fifty, his son John was only one of the candidates for the succession, and the estates elected the Jagiełłonian Vladislav II of Bohemia (Wladislas II) in his stead. The system of government and defence became weakened, since the upper nobility had no interest in financing it.

At the same time, a treaty of inheritance was concluded between Wladislas and another of his rivals, Maximilian of Habsburg, by which they agreed to ties of marriage between their successors. In 1505, the Hungarian estates thereupon determined that, were the monarch to die without issue, no foreigner could be elected king. That resolution became moot with the birth of Prince Louis, who succeeded his father in 1516. While Hungary was preoccupied with its own affairs, the Ottoman Empire had resumed its expansive course. The hopelessly inferior Hungarian army met the Ottoman forces at Mohács in 1526; the greater part, including Hungary's clerical and secular leadership, died in the battle. The King drowned while fleeing the battlefield, so that everything pointed to a Habsburg succession. First, however, the popular magnate and general John Zapolya was elected King, while Ferdinand of Habsburg pressed his claim as well, on the strength of the treaty of inheritance. Neither succeeded, however, in restoring Hungary, or rather Hungarian unity. After Buda fell to the Turks in 1541, Hungary was permanently divided into three parts. The smaller part in the west and north remained under Habsburg rule, while the Ottoman Empire occupied the central areas. Transylvania, under a successor of Zapolya, was reduced to a vassal state of the Ottoman Empire.

6.2 The path to the aristocratic republic

Like the rulers of most European countries, the kings of east-central Europe did not rule from a fixed residence until the mid-fourteenth century, and surrounded themselves with an initially fluctuating group of advisers. The first Polish royal residences were in Greater Poland, first in Poznań and later in Gniezno, which also became the seat of the Polish archbishop, while Cracow became the capital in the twelfth century. In Hungary, the court and the archbishop initially resided at Esztergom, while the king was crowned at Székesféhervár. The Angevin kings moved their capital to Visegrád; Buda did not become the capital until the fifteenth century under Sigismund. Only Bohemia never had any capital but Prague, although Charles IV resided some distance away on the so-called Karlstein. But even once the capitals began to emerge, the king's travels, accompanied by the court, were not over. Yet the most important officials, such as the palatine or voyevod, the chancellor and the treasurer did not always take part in these journeys. These officials, who formed the royal council together with the bishops and the powerful magnates, were normally present in the country, and only assembled when the king summoned them.

The key element of rule was the royal chancery, whose officials often accompanied the ruler on his journeys in order to be able to issue documents. In Bohemia, the royal chancery, staffed by high Church officials, had existed since the first half of the twelfth century, while in Hungary it was only in 1181 that King Bela III established such an institution, on the Byzantine model. But during this period, the production of documents in Hungary was still relatively low. Only in the thirteenth century did the situation change under the chancellorship of the archbishop of Esztergom and the privileging of new settlers and settlements. The Polish chancery, which went back to the twelfth century, was also assigned extensive new tasks during the course of the eastern settlement, owing to the foundation of new cities and the granting of immunity to nobles after the thirteenth and especially after the fourteenth century; the number of chancery officials also increased considerably. In the process, this office developed from a court office to an organ representing the king in his lands. In Poland, for example, each constituent principality had its own voyevod.[19]

The office of castellan also emerged; at the Cracow court, it would develop into the most important office in the government hierarchy. This position was also instituted in the provinces, and monopolised by the local nobility. In Hungary, the magnates occupied the royal castles, and often incorporated the associated lands into their usufruct areas. During the reigns of the last Árpád kings toward the end of the thirteenth century Hungary thus also disintegrated into autonomous provinces, and only the new King Charles Robert was able to restore royal authority after a long struggle, and in return for 'compensations' for the high nobility in the countryside.[20] After his successful struggle for the Hungarian throne Sigismund, too, had to pay for his absence from the country in Bohemia and other parts of the empire by making concessions and land grants to the Hungarian nobles. As a result, aristocratic associations had considerable influence in the country, to which end they no longer even needed any representation on the royal council. In Poland and Bohemia, the royal council was still an important forum for the magnates. In Bohemia, they fought against King Wenceslas to secure representation in this body. Especially during the period of the interregnum, the royal council played an important role; it also introduced newcomers to the throne, such as Jagiełło of Lithuania, to the country. During the fifteenth century, this institution was transformed into the upper chamber, the senate, of the Polish diet (*Sejm*).[21]

However, the royal council was not the sole source of the development of estates in east-central Europe. In all countries, assemblies of the high nobility and the prelates had existed since the twelfth century; in some cases, the lower nobility and the cities were also included. Usually, the monarch would convene them in matters of peace or war, and sometimes the nobility would only assemble on the battlefield itself, in order to discuss court matters with the king prior to a military campaign. In Bohemia and Moravia, assemblies of the nobles and the higher clergy are attested even in the eleventh and twelfth centuries, and in the thirteenth century (1281), the Bohemian estates were included in an assembly for the first time; of course, they occupied a more important economic position than in other areas of eastern and central Europe. Only in Moravia were the cities not represented in the diet until 1440. During the first half of the fourteenth century, the Bohemian estates assembled frequently but irregularly, in order to address the succession of the Přemyslids (see above). Thus was the nobility able to extract from John of Luxembourg the promise of the *indygenat*. His son and successor, Charles IV, attempted to advance centralisation with the aid of the estates, but he did not succeed in getting his reform code, the *Majestas Carolina*, passed by the diet in 1355. As a result, the estates were only summoned once to adopt the general peace of 1356, and thereafter not until 1419, when they were needed once again to cope with a crisis. The following decades, too, were a time of feverish activity among the estates, during which time the diet, under the leadership of the city of Prague, in fact ruled Bohemia. Sigismund, Albert, Ladislas Posthumus, George of Poděbrady and Vladislav II were all elected to the kingship by the estates, which claimed the right to elect the king and hence regarded themselves as the source of legitimacy.[22]

The Hungarian estates proceeded similarly in 1458, when they elected Matthias Hunyadi king. In Hungary, the estates referred back to the Golden Bull of 1222, in which King Andrew II had promised a general assembly for all nobles. However, at future estate assemblies, he repeatedly had to be reminded of his promise, and in 1351, the estates attained confirmation of the Golden Bull, which every future Hungarian king had to reconfirm prior to ascending the throne. Previously, the estates had already elected Andrew III (1290–1301), who had promised regularly to summon the Hungarian diet and an assembly of the estates of Transylvania. Here, the lower nobility were also represented, so that the diet was able to present its decisions and proposals for legislation to the king and the barons. Charles Robert of Anjou broke with that tradition after his election as king by claiming his right of dynastic inheritance. He relied on the counsel of the high nobility and the prelates, without listening to the diet. After 1323, he never convened the diet again. Only his son Louis was forced to summon the diet once again after the failure of his 1351 Italian campaign. There, by confirming the Golden Bull, he placed the lower nobility on an equal footing with the magnates and freed them from all direct taxation not passed by the diet. Only during the reign of Sigismund, who was frequently absent, would the diet regain its position as an important organ of government. This allowed those nobles who belonged to the clientele of certain magnates, but who occupied important mid-level positions as their seneschals, army commanders or provincial governors, to rise to prominence. During his brief reign, Sigismund's successor Albert II was forced in 1439 to promise expressly not to grant land or offices to foreigners, nor to change the coinage or the country's laws without consulting the Hungarian estates.[23]

In matters affecting their interests, the cities were represented in the diet. Although authorised to do so in 1435, they failed to exercise their rights regularly, as they feared being called upon to pay higher taxes. Moreover, their representatives were often Germans who could not follow the debates in Hungarian. After 1445, the diet assembled annually, since the Ottoman threat required continual military expenditures, and the king now issued edicts only with the approval of the estates. In spite of this strong estate tradition, Matthias Corvinus was able to play the estates against one another in order to reform the tax system, and to use the funds to create a standing mercenary army. As a result, the diet was only rarely summoned; nonetheless, the succession was determined by election.[24] The Hungarian estates elected his successor, Vladislav II of Bohemia, who was not ill disposed to their desires, and his proclivity for saying 'yes' to everything won him the nickname of King Bene.

In Poland, the magnates and prelates had already been meeting sporadically during the period of disunity in the twelfth and thirteenth centuries. Under the last of the Piasts, Władysław Łokietek and Casimir the Great, however, the estates were rarely summoned, since the kings preferred to rule alone. Casimir only sought confirmation from the estates to ratify the Peace of Kallisz with the Teutonic Knights in 1343. As in Hungary, the situation changed fundamentally under the new King, Louis, who was forced to make considerable concessions to the Polish nobility in order to secure his daughters' right of inheritance. In the famous Privilege of Koszyce, he granted them far-reaching freedom from taxation – with the exception of the plough tax – as well as the right of consultation in all important matters of state and the right of *indygenat*. In the ensuing years, questions of succession and military conflicts with the Teutonic Knights provided the estates with frequent opportunities to prove themselves the unofficial government of the kingdom. The diet elected Jagiełło of Lithuania in 1386 and, after negotiations for the recognition of the succession, his sons Vladislav and Casimir in 1434 and 1447, respectively. In exchange, the nobility received the privileges of Warta in 1423, Jedlno in 1430 and Cracow in 1433. Among other things, these privileges secured the inviolability of the person of a nobleman – immunity from arrest without a court sentence – and the nobles' claim to the benefices of the cathedral chapters. They also obtained the right to buy out village mayors. This permitted the nobles to acquire the often considerable landed property accumulated by village mayors since the time of the colonisation, to round out their own estates or establish demesne farms.

The negotiations on the eve of the war against the Teutonic Knights in 1454 went one step further. In order to obtain support for the war, the King promised in future not to wage any war without the agreement of the diet. After Poland's first defeat at the Battle of Chojnice (Konitz), he had to make further concessions. After negotiations with the army contingents of the nobility from the various regions of the country, the Statutes of Nieszawa (*statuty nieszawskie*) determined that the general levy of troops could only be carried out with the approval of the regional diets (*sejmiki*). That strengthened these bodies, which were controlled by the lower nobility, and led to the formation of the parliamentary system based on regional and national diets.[25] At the end of the fifteenth century, the king's proposals were considered first by the regional diets and then by the two national diets – one for Greater Poland and Kuyavia and one for Lesser Poland. Finally, the first combined national diet met in Piotrków on the border of Greater and Lesser Poland. It consisted of delegates from the two national diets and the senate, the former royal council. In 1494, this body adopted such far-reaching resolutions as one tying peasants to the soil. In 1504/05, because of the resistance of the lower nobility against the magnates, the regional diets adopted the *nihil novi* constitution, according to which no new laws could be passed without the approval of the senate and the representatives of the regional diets. This paved the way for the aristocratic republic, for in Hungary (1505) and in Bohemia (1500), too, the constitutions now stipulated the pre-eminence of the estates in legislation.[26]

The monastic state of the Teutonic Knights in Prussia trod a different but structurally similar path. Here, assemblies of the high masters with representatives of the cities or the vassals had been meeting since the thirteenth century. In the 1330s, assemblies of the cities were held at which agreements were taken on common weights and measures. Only from the end of the fourteenth century, as conflicts between the Order, as the sovereign, and the cities and the large landowners increased, do we find more frequent evidence of estate assemblies. Conflicts arose between the cities and the Order over the trading activities of the latter, particularly the monopoly on the trade in cereals, which it would claim at times. Since the Order suppressed all competition in the cereals trade at the same time, the owners of the manors also saw their market for grain endangered. Moreover, the Order periodically confiscated the land of the nobility in order to re-grant it or to turn it into peasant land. This was a threat to the rural land-owning class, which increasingly regarded itself as part of the nobility. Moreover, hunting and fishing rights, which the Order denied the landowners and retained for itself, contradicted their sense of propriety. In this situation, the nobles of the Kulm (Chełmno) countryside formed a society, the so-called Lizards' League, designed to protect them from the Order and its vassals. This league was comparable to the confederations of Polish nobles that formed in 1352 to oppose the confiscation of noble property by royal officials, or in 1406/07 against the tithe demands of the Church in Piotrków. After the suppression of the Lizards' League at the beginning of the fifteenth century, the estates were unable to articulate their interests until 1440, when the cities and nobles founded the Prussian League. Their principal demand was a law court to be staffed in common by the Order and the estates, which would settle disputes over privileges and other conflicts. The Order, as a clerical organisation subject to canon law, could not and would not accede to that, and sued before an arbitration court chaired by the Emperor to achieve the dissolution of the League. When the Emperor ordered that dissolution in 1453, the Prussian estates renounced the suzerainty of the Order, and placed themselves under the protection of the Polish King.[27] This decision could no longer be reversed even by force of arms; on the contrary, in the sixteenth century, the Duchy of Prussia, which succeeded the state of the Teutonic Knights and was under Polish suzerainty, was on its way to becoming an aristocratic republic.[28]

6.3 Population, settlement and integration into the European division of labour

The demographic development of east-central Europe differed markedly from that of western Europe. Because of its low population density, in the course of eastward settlement it profited from population growth in the west. At the same time, east-central Europe was less strongly affected by the Black Death than southern and western Europe, so that demographic changes were less drastic here. Some regions even experienced population growth, while the population in western Europe declined or stagnated. In this way, differences in development between western and east-central Europe were temporarily levelled or even overcome. However, a search for information on population development, to the extent that it exists at all, remains speculative, as it does for other countries. Thanks to the extant Peter's pence registers, the most reliable data exists for Poland, where the population in the mid-fourteenth century has been estimated at between 1.3 and 1.8 million inhabitants. Poland's population density of six or seven persons per square kilometre was thus considerably lower than that of France, with thirty per square kilometre, but still higher than the four per square kilometre in Lithuania. At the end of the fourteenth century, some 2 million people may have lived in Poland, with an additional 400,000 Lithuanians and 1.5 million Ruthenians in the former Red Russia. In the course of the fifteenth century, the population continued to increase, so that Poland and Lithuania had a combined population of 7.5 million.[29]

For Bohemia, for which very little quantifiable material is available, the effects of the plague have been studied. During the first wave of the plague around 1350, owing to its isolated location the population of the country was affected only slightly. In 1380, however, a second wave hit, with a mortality rate of 0.5 per cent during this time, and a greater effect thereafter; even so, the reduction of the population was considerably less than in most other regions of Europe affected by the Black Death. As a result, estimates are that Bohemia (without Moravia) experienced a long-term population rise from 835,000 inhabitants around 1300 to between 2 and 2.3 million around 1400.[30] Over the course of the fifteenth century, the population probably increased again. Only Silesia suffered a serious drop in population during the fifteenth century as a result of the Hussite incursions.[31]

In Hungary, the Mongol invasion of 1241 constituted the greatest demographic break. Even moderate estimates assume a population loss of between 15 and 20 per cent. Accordingly, the Mongol invasion in Hungary seems to have had effects similar to those of the plague in many other areas a century later. Part of this loss could be compensated for even during that century by resettlement, as regional investigations have shown a strong increase in the number of villages around 1320 and again approximately one hundred years later. The population density at the beginning of the fourteenth century is estimated at five to seven inhabitants per square kilometre. The sources testify to some 400,000 taxpaying peasant farms in Hungary around 1430, which would indicate a population of between 3 and 3.5 million, and a population density of ten to twelve per square kilometre. By 1500, Hungary's population had probably risen to at least 7.5 million inhabitants, and 14 to 14.5 persons per square kilometre.[32] In general, the degree of urbanisation was negligible. Bohemia had a denser network of cities than either Hungary or Poland-Lithuania, but the urban share of the population was low overall, for example only about 10 per cent of the population or less in Poland-Lithuania. Around 1500, only Danzig with 35,000 inhabitants, and Prague with 30,000 inhabitants – in the latter, the population had dropped by 10,000 during the fifteenth century – could be considered larger cities. The only other major settlements in the region were Cracow, Lwów, Poznań, Elbing, Thorn and Riga in Livonia, with approximately 10,000 inhabitants each.

The economy and society of east-central Europe were influenced to a large extent by the phenomenon of German eastward settlement. This process has often been interpreted as a process of acculturation and thus of the Europeanisation of eastern Europe. Recently, however, it has tended to be seen more as part of the great wave of medieval inland colonisation, which also included the settlement of the marshlands along the North Sea and the resettlement of the Iberian Peninsula after the *Reconquista*. What distinguishes east-central Europe from these undertakings was perhaps the scope and the sheer amount of land affected, which began in the territories of the Slavic princes within the Holy Roman Empire and extended far beyond its borders.[33] Only in the state of the Teutonic Knights did settlement also involve Christianisation. The other areas had for the most part already become Christian 200 years prior to the beginning of eastward settlement. The motivation for eastward settlement was the desire of princes and other rulers to attract settlers to farm their lands, which generally had a positive effect on peasant freedoms. Since virtually all regions of east-central Europe were under-populated, lords found themselves in stiff competition for the services of peasants. Kings, bishops and nobles in Poland, Bohemia and Hungary therefore supported the settlement of peasants in order to increase their revenues. To this end, they offered privileges to these 'guests' (*hospites*) from the west. These included freedom from rent for a certain number of years, guaranteed inheritance of usufruct rights, personal freedom, and payments in cash or kind instead of labour duties. The self-administration of the peasant communities was also strengthened. These rights, which were collectively known in the thirteenth century as 'German law', were so attractive that even existing settlements, for instance those based on Polish law, were transferred to German law.

The earliest waves of settlement reached those regions, like Silesia or Bohemia, that were relatively close to previously settled lands. There, the

Cistercian and Premonstratensian monastic orders in particular pushed the settlements into hitherto uncultivated marginal forests, since the princes had charged them with clearance missions to benefit the entire country. Often, the monasteries received large contiguous forest areas in addition to their old properties, with the assignment to clear them. Deploying monasteries and religious orders was only a first step, however, and further ones followed in the princely domains. To this end, settlement entrepreneurs, so-called locators, recruited peasant settlers on a large scale. After the original settlement in Silesia, German settlement and German law penetrated many parts of Poland, Bohemia and Hungary. While in Silesia, approximately one-third of the villages were privileged with German law, this was the case for only one-quarter of the villages in Greater and Lesser Poland, while in other areas such as Masovia, old common law continued to prevail. In Bohemia and Hungary, German law exerted a positive influence on land titles, so that by the end of the fourteenth century Bohemia boasted the largest number of peasants who held their land by hereditary right. In Hungary, where large complexes of German settlement appeared in the Zips region of Upper Hungary and Transylvania during the thirteenth century, the law concerning these *hospites* or 'guests' promoted the development of a relatively independent peasant class.

In the state of the Teutonic Knights in Prussia, the new settlers appeared as peasants in village associations, as owners of single farms and, as in other regions, as citizens of the towns. The peasants received farms two hides (*Hufen*) in size, approximately thirty-three hectares, under hereditary quitrent, payable to the landlord – usually the Order. This new Kulm (Chełmno) legal system differed considerably from the legal system under which Prussian peasants used their land. Their holdings were measured not in hides, but in 'hooks' (*Haken*), in other words by the amount of labour power rather than the area, i.e., the land that could be farmed with such an implement. With time, the Prussians, too, were granted measured holdings (two or three hooks of ten hectares each). Moreover, economic pressure to adapt led to the incorporation of Prussian landholdings into the hide system. In addition to the peasants in village societies, so-called greater and lesser freemen, who had to provide mounted military service with heavy or light weapons, respectively, for the army of the Teutonic Order, settled on their own farms. The greater freemen then constituted the noble class, joined in the course of time by other nobles who had been provided land in the service of the Order. These nobles did not initially exploit their holdings directly, but rather settled peasants upon them, while Livonia attracted no German rural settlers.

Urban settlement, with the foundation of cities, mainly under the Magdeburg Law, was a further aspect of eastern settlement. The territorial rulers imported cities under German law on a large scale, which resulted in the disappearance of most of the indigenous towns of the Slavic states.[34] The foundation of new towns by locators contracted by the city fathers of existing cities strengthened the ties between them and to the territory, so that only the larger Hanseatic cities founded under Lübeck Law were able to free themselves from such ties. Meanwhile, attempts were made to block the demands for autonomy of such cities as Cracow, Sandomierz and Poznań. Such cities as Prague during the Hussite period or the Prussian cities during the fifteenth century, in contrast, were able to conduct policy independent of the sovereign.

Urban settlement under German law began in Mecklenburg, Pomerania and Silesia. In Mecklenburg, a total of twenty-six cities were founded between 1218 and 1276. In western Pomerania, twenty-seven ducal, twelve ecclesiastical and five noble cities had been founded by the time Duke Barnim I died in 1278. In the duchy of Breslau, too, the founding of eighty-eight new cities by the duke, the Church and the nobility in the thirteenth century is attested. In Poland, Bohemia and Moravia, in contrast, the city-founding process continued into the fifteenth century, with foundations by the nobility accounting for a larger share. The resettlement of the cities, especially after the Mongol invasion of 1241, played an important role in Hungary. Bela IV issued more, and more extensive, city privileges than his predecessors. In addition to urban autonomy and judicial independence, he especially promoted the migration of artisans from Germany and Italy. Here, many *hospites* communities were transformed into legally recognised cities. This policy, which continued into the fourteenth century, attracted many new settlers. During their conquest of the country, the Teutonic Knights had founded the first two cities, Thorn and Kulm (Chełmno), whose charter, the so-called *Kulmer Handfeste*, served as a model for other Prussian urban charters, and even for Prussian settlement law in general. With this document, the Order granted the town-dwellers the right to elect their judges and thus fostered the emergence of urban constitutional organs: the council, the college of aldermen and the mayor. The Order was present as ruler through its patronage of the city's ecclesiastical livings. However, not every commander (*Komtur*) of the Order observed the autonomy of the city located in his commandery (*Komturei*), and particularly in the fifteenth century conflicts frequently erupted between the city administrations and members of the Teutonic Order.

Some of the cities were founded on hitherto unsettled land and built according to a plan. Some of them – though not in the land of the Teutonic Knights – were based on old Slavic settlements, but even then, the territorial lord might relocate a city, or move it to a neighbouring, more favourable site. This was the case especially if existing settlements bordered on the jurisdictions of the Church or a noble, and the new city founder had to find an unoccupied spot. The territorial lords were particularly interested in founding mining towns, since the revenues they provided from precious metals, copper, lead and salt were indispensable for the treasury. Thus, mining cities were founded during the initial period of urban settlement, for example Freiberg in Saxony in 1168 (silver), Goldberg in 1211 and Löwenberg in Silesia in 1217 (gold), Bochnia or Salzberg in Lesser Poland in 1253 (salt), Schmölnitz *c.* 1338 and Kremnitz in 1328 (gold; both in Upper Hungary), Kuttenberg (Kutná Hora) in the thirteenth century and Iglau (Jihlava) in 1245 (silver; Bohemia) and Schemnitz (Banská Štiavnica), Upper Hungary, *c.* 1240 (silver). Equally important were the mercantile towns, which were founded in addition to existing trading posts, for instance along the Baltic coast, but also on the routes of continental trade with the east.

Economically, east-central Europe was divided into three major production regions. The hinterlands of the Baltic Sea concentrated on the production of cereals, and thanks to its river and maritime routes offered favourable conditions for exporting grain, wool, wood and forest products such as charcoal, ash, pitch, tar, honey and wax. The Carpathian and Sudeten regions, with their silver, copper, lead and salt mines, attracted western European investment. The third region extended from the Black Sea to Hungary, and thanks to its steppe landscape was eminently suited to stockbreeding and exports.[35] These regions provided raw materials for the Italian, Flemish and German cities, into whose productive circuits they were integrated. Such cities as Breslau, Prague, Nuremberg, Danzig and Lvov as well as other Hanseatic cities and also Leipzig and Augsburg played the role of middlemen in the late Middle Ages. The first region, specialised in cereals production, profited greatly from the eastward settlement and the reforms it engendered. These included the three-field system, which spread throughout the central regions of Poland, Prussia and central Bohemia as far as Livonia. Livestock was reared only for local breeding needs. Since the vast majority of peasants during this period paid rent and duties to their landlords, direct exploitation of the land by the nobility was not a major factor beyond production for their own use. Peasant production was at least partially orientated toward an urban market, and a regional and international cereal trade based on the cities developed. Only in the fifteenth century did landlords turn to the direct exploitation of their holdings, with commercial production – beer brewing – emerging as an adjunct to cereals farming. For that reason, peasant labour services were increased, out of which the manorial system would develop in east-central Europe during the sixteenth century. One of the largest cereal exporters during the fourteenth and fifteenth centuries was the state of the Teutonic Order in Prussia which, however, largely exported the excess production of the peasantry, and only secondarily the products of the Order's own demesnes. Intensive forms of agriculture such as orchards and horticulture were generally of only local importance. Hops and dye plants were also cultivated. In Hungary, the intensive cultures primarily consisted of vineyards in the hills around Pressburg (Bratislava) and Sopron, but also north of Lake Balaton and in the so-called Tokaj region. This wine was in demand locally and regionally, and was increasingly exported as well. Only in Hungary did stock-rearing, which had spread in the Hungarian plain thanks to the integration of the nomadic Kumans, achieve an importance that extended beyond the needs of the home region. By careful breeding, the bodyweight of the originally grey Kuman cattle increased to 350 kg by the sixteenth century, and hence met the demand for meat in the west and the south. By the middle of the fourteenth century, Hungarian oxen were being exported to the southern German and northern Italian markets, reaching a peak of 50,000 head annually by the mid-sixteenth century.[36]

In most east-central European towns, commercial production only met local and regional demand. Most trades were present, but specialisation was certainly at a lower level than in the western European commercial centres. While in the beginning of the fifteenth century, a world-class city such as Paris could boast more than 150 different trades, the number of specialised trades even in the larger cities of east-central Europe was generally less than fifty. Cloth, largely Polish cloth, was the only product traded internationally, as evidenced by the numerous complaints of Prussian wool weavers against Polish cloth imports. The state of the Teutonic Order itself exported so-called Marienburg linen to Sweden and England. In Danzig, on the other hand, the reorientation of the cloth trade began only in the sixteenth century with the immigration of Dutch weavers, who revolutionised cloth manufacturing in many towns of the Baltic region.

Economically, east-central European trade was largely local and regional. Its international dimension primarily involved transit trade. Two central trade routes passed through the area, the first from Nuremberg through Breslau or Prague to Cracow, Lwów and the Black Sea, and the second from the Black Sea through Lwów, Sandomierz, Łęczyca and Thorn to Danzig. The staple rights claimed by these cities forced the merchants to visit them and offer their goods for sale at the markets there. These two main routes also included diversions and variations, which were used when necessary. Moreover, such cities as Thorn, Łęczyca, Sandomierz or Lwów constituted intersections at which trade routes from Flanders, Lusatia, Lesser Poland, Bohemia and Hungary crossed the Polish north-south axis or the Black Sea-Baltic axis. The north-south route was used primarily to transport metals north from Upper Hungary, and especially to make the agricultural and silvicultural products of the hinterland available to western Europe by way of Danzig. Even in the fifteenth century, Danzig was the most important trading centre in the Baltic area after Lübeck, and trade with western Europe was its foundation. Until the 1470s, the Dutch share of ships docking in Danzig had never exceeded 10 per cent, but in the last two decades of the fifteenth century, it rose to 30 per cent, and by the second half of the sixteenth century, Dutch ships constituted half of all vessels entering the port of Danzig. Since western European demand exceeded the supply which Royal Prussia could provide, the Danzig merchants moved ever more frequently into the lands of the Polish Crown, particularly Masovia and Kuyavia, to purchase forest products and cereals. At the same time, noble manors and Church domains in the areas along the Vistula began selling wood and cereals to Danzig independently. By 1492, Danzig grain exports amounted to 10,000 lasts (600,000 bushels), although wood exports predominated during this period. The commodities imported to Danzig and then distributed southward on the Vistula or by land included English and Flemish cloth, salt from the Bay of Biscay and Portugal, herring from Holland, wine from France and Spain, and iron from Sweden.[37]

In the Carpathian region, mining was the principal activity. The primary products were salt from Bochnia and Wieliczka for regional use, and precious and non-ferrous metals, which for a time made east-central Europe of key importance to the European economy.[38] Of major importance were the Iglau (Jihlava) silver deposits, newly discovered in the thirteenth century on the border between Bohemia and Moravia; their annual production is estimated at over four tonnes. They were, however, exceeded in the fourteenth century by the silver deposits of Kuttenberg (Kutná Hora) in Bohemia, which provided more than twenty tonnes a year during the first half of the century. Bohemia's wealth of silver made it possible for King Wenceslas II to place his coinage on a new foundation. All mints operating in the country were moved to Kuttenberg, where seventeen workshops processed between 6.5 and 6.8 tonnes of silver a year into coins. Since it would have made no sense, given these quantities, to mint *deniers*, as had previously been the practice, a new larger coin on the southern or western European model was struck, known as the Prague *groschen*, which took its name from the legend on the coin rather than the site of the mint, which was Kuttenberg. However, the silver used for coin at the Kuttenberg mint represented only the king's share of the total annual silver yield from the local mines.[39] The larger portion of the bullion mined there went to the miners themselves, or to the foreign owners of shares in the mines. They marketed their silver directly, often in standardised bars. During the fifteenth century, Kuttenberg silver mining collapsed entirely, and only in the sixteenth century would silver mining be revived at Joachimstal, in the Bohemian part of the Ore Mountains. Gold mining began in the thirteenth century in Bohemia, Silesia and the northern Carpathians, but only in Hungary, and especially in Kremnitz, was production still considerable by the end of the fifteenth century, when 3,000 kg could be mined annually. By this time, however, Hungarian production had already passed its peak. Hungarian gold flowed first of all to northern Italy by way of commercial exchange, and only after 1325 were florins (*gulden*) coined north of the Alps on the Florentine model. Although the image of St Ladislas replaced that of the Florentine patron saint John the Baptist on the coin, the weight and alloy of the Hungarian *forint* emulated the *fiorino*, and would continue to do so until the mid-sixteenth century.

The importance of Upper Hungary as a producer of copper increased during the late fifteenth century. The deposits at Neusohl (Banská Bystrica) had been important even in the fourteenth and fifteenth centuries, but lack of capital and technical problems kept the level of production low. By the end of the fifteenth century, the Fuggers took over the Neusohl copper mines, greatly increased their yield, and brought Hungarian copper to the international market in Antwerp.[40]

6.4 Aristocratic society in east-central Europe

More than any other part of Europe, society in east-central Europe was dominated both quantitatively and qualitatively by the nobility. The share of the nobility in the population amounted to as much as 5 per cent in Hungary, and 10 per cent in Poland. During the thirteenth to the fifteenth century, these countries experienced processes of both fusion and fission within the nobility. In Poland, we can distinguish between two groups.

An older aristocracy stretching back to the origins of the Polish state is referred to in the sources as *nobiles*, *comites* or *principes terre*, or by the corresponding Slavic terms *żupan, pan* or *ksiądź*. The other group were the knights (*milites* or *włodycy*), who acted as a service nobility. From the thirteenth century, these two strata merged into a single estate called the *szlachta*, derived from the German word *Geschlecht*, meaning family or dynasty. The basis for this was the so-called law of knighthood (*ius militare*), which guaranteed the heritability and free disposal of usufruct land. Outside of Silesia, vassalage was not widespread in Poland; only Casimir the Great attempted during the second half of the fourteenth century to use it as an instrument to provide privileges for new strata, such as village mayors, against the counterweight of the existing *szlachta*.[41]

In Hungary, a distinction was initially made between the *nobiles* and the *servientes regis* (the knights), as in the 1222 Golden Bull of Andrew II, but by the end of the thirteenth century the latter group had obtained the same privileges as the magnates. By 1351, when King Louis reconfirmed the Golden Bull, the landlords of Hungary, Transylvania, Croatia, Slavonia and Dalmatia were all considered *nobiles*. Thus the Walachian (Romanian) *knezi*, the Saxon *Graeven* (village headmen) and some of the Szekler guardians of the border rose into the Hungarian nobility. After the Mongol invasion, Bela IV elevated entire communities of free peasants into the nobility as a reward for their wartime deeds.[42] Moreover, throughout east-central Europe, other persons were able to enter the nobility either through adoption or ennoblement by the king. As a result, at the end of the fourteenth century the old Bohemian nobility saw itself threatened by the new nobility from the prosperous towns. The noble class banded together against these social climbers and demanded that royal service no longer constitute the criterion for determining nobility, but rather noble birth and at least two generations of noble ancestry. Accordingly, attempts were made to document aristocratic birth by use of the term *urozený pan* (high-born lord). Not until the fifteenth century did a uniform term for the noble elite, *šlechta*, become common in Bohemia. Prior to that time, distinctions had been made between lords (*pány)*, knights (*rytíře*), squires (*zemany*), *vladyky* (the old Slavic knighthood) and noble vassals (*panoše*).[43]

The situation became complicated when two realms united, as was the case in the Polish-Lithuanian Union. Thus, the 1413 Treaty of Union of Horodło recommended to Polish nobles that they enable their Lithuanian peers to partake of their privileges by way of adoption. Initially this only applied to Catholic Lithuanians, but in 1434, the Catholic and Orthodox aristocracies of Lithuania were placed on an equal footing.

In spite of its closure toward other classes, the nobility was anything but homogeneous, since the magnates, often called *barones*, were clearly distinguished from the mass of the nobility. Thus at the beginning of the fifteenth century the Polish lower nobility ranged from Jan Głowacz Oleśnicki, the grand marshal of the Crown and voyevod of Sandomierz – he was the brother of Zbigniew Oleśnicki – who owned several cities and fifty-nine villages, to the forty-seven *nobiles* who shared ownership of the village of Krzyszkowice in the Ziemia Proszowska area.[44] During the fourteenth and fifteenth centuries, royal service in particular opened the way for enormous upward mobility for the lower nobility. One example is provided by the members of the Kurozwęcki family, who, over the course of two generations under Casimir the Great, rose from bannermen (*podchorąży*) in Sandomierz to voyevods and castellans of Cracow. During the next generation, the family expanded to Greater Poland, benefited from the royal domain and Church incomes, and acquired vast latifundia. They invested the resulting profits in loans to the king and in long-distance trade. Marriage ties to other magnate families such as the Lanckorońskis increased their status. Other leading families such as the Czarnkowskis, the Kmitas, the Melsztyńskis, the Tarnowskis and the Łęnczyńskis also heightened their prestige by international marriages.[45]

The result was a split within the nobility, which opened the door to client relationships. In Hungary, this had already been formalised in the fourteenth century by the institution of the *familiaritas*, under which a petty nobleman would join a baron's clientele as a *familiaris*. In Bohemia, the lower nobility, the squires (*zemane*) and the *vladykove*, who lived on average from the rents of three to five peasant families, also often joined the service of the high nobility in search of additional sources of income, although robber-baron activity was another possibility. In any case, the military conflicts of the Hussite era opened up a new area of activity, for which the leader of the Taborites, Jan Žižka, provides a prime example. Even if the scales did tip back toward the higher nobility over the course of the fifteenth century, at least part of the lower nobility profited from the secularisation of Church domains. One example of this was Nicolas Třcka of Lípa who, despite his origins in an insignificant petty noble family, had by 1450 amassed an estate that included nine castles and manors, fourteen towns and more than 320 villages, thus surpassing many older families.[46]

The nobility was set off from the rest of society by the common and exclusive enjoyment of privileges. Nearly everywhere, nobles enjoyed freedom from the alienation of their property as well as judicial immunity. Only in Hungary could royal officials execute the law on land owned by *nobiles*. Another important privilege was very extensive freedom from taxation. In 1374, Louis of Hungary and Poland limited the tax duty of the Polish nobility to two *groschen* per *łan* (15 ha), a tax that was in any case passed on to the peasants. In Lithuania, an edict of 1434 freed the *nobiles* from paying taxes to the Grand Prince. These guarantees, however, made the king increasingly dependent on further extraordinary tax authorisations by the nobility and strengthened the political position of the latter. In Hungary, the nobility was also exempt from taxation, although here, King Louis imposed new tax demands.

Almost equally important was the privilege of *indygenat*, which the nobility of Poland-Lithuania, Bohemia and Hungary had largely achieved. They also attained other social and economic privileges such as the heritability of landed property in the female line, or the right to buy out the hereditary village mayor and institute direct noble exploitation of the land.

In addition, nobles enjoyed a virtual monopoly on high clerical positions, which laid the foundation for the close relationship between the aristocracy and the clergy. While at the beginning of the thirteenth century it was possible even for those of modest origins to rise to the rank of bishop, such careers became ever rarer during the fourteenth century. By the fifteenth century, the Polish and Bohemian nobles occupied all high clerical positions. Archbishop Mikołaj Trąba, for example, who came from a family of village mayors, was forced to have himself adopted by a noble family. In order to keep cathedral chapter positions open for university graduates, in the fifteenth century certain privileges were reserved for the inhabitants of specific regions (*ziemia*, *terrigenae*). The *nobiles*, however, often interpreted such measures as guarantees of a monopoly. While the members of the religious orders were largely of urban origin, the leadership position of abbot was reserved for noblemen. This situation was legally sanctioned in Poland in 1505, when noble birth was made a requirement for all high official positions, with a few exceptions for university graduates. Beyond that, the close connection of the high clergy to the king and the State must be considered. Thus, such personalities as the cardinal and bishop of Cracow Zbigniew Oleśnicki, as royal chancellor, accumulated not only great wealth, but also extensive personal networks, from which Church officials could be recruited.

In Hungary, membership in such a network, along with a position at the royal court, especially the royal chancery, was a precondition for episcopal office. But even after their investiture, bishops remained politicians, and even commanded the military units raised from their bishoprics. Twelve archbishops and five bishops died at the battle of Mohács in

1526, sword in hand. Nonetheless, the aristocratisation of the bishoprics was less pronounced than in other countries of east-central Europe. Since the younger sons of the Hungarian nobility were not destined for Church office to the same degree, university study was an important prerequisite for recruitment. Half of the bishops and 40 per cent of canons had studied at various universities, particularly Cracow, Vienna and the Italian institutions. The last group, after they returned to the four Hungarian cathedral chapters, passed on the Renaissance culture they had imbibed. Of their 526 members between 1458 and 1526, 138 were *nobiles*, the rest were of burgher or peasant extraction. Accordingly, of the fifty-three bishops invested during this period, fourteen were of non-noble origin.[47] The state of the Teutonic Knights was a special case in this respect, since during the fifteenth century it increasingly became an institution providing sinecures for the impoverished nobility of the Holy Roman Empire.

In the cities of Poland, Bohemia and Hungary, long-distance traders made up the most prestigious upper stratum, which in many cases constituted a closed patriciate. They monopolised municipal government, and primarily passed the burden of taxation on to the lower strata. Normally, they did not mix with the artisan class, or with the lesser merchants, but replenished their ranks through in-migration from western Europe, especially the empire. In many cases, however, the patriciate was forced by violent internecine conflicts to allow representatives of the artisans and lower merchant class to participate in running the city. In 1368, Casimir the Great stipulated that the Cracow town council be composed of equal numbers of merchants and artisans. But only in 1418, when Jagiełło appointed members of this group to a sixteen-member commission to monitor the city's finances, did Casimir's decree become a reality.

In the fifteenth century, economic and social conflicts periodically intertwined with ethnic and religious tensions over city administration, since the patriciate of many towns in eastern Europe was still dominated by Germans. During the Hussite era, Czech artisans and merchants took control of town councils in Bohemia, including Prague, while German inhabitants left the cities. Buda experienced numerous rebellions in the early fifteenth century. In 1402, the old town council was driven out at the initiative of prosperous citizens, and replaced by a new 36-member council, in which the lower strata were also represented. While the uprising was socially motivated, it was manipulated by Italian merchants in a dispute with their German competitors, and was also connected with aristocratic resistance to King Sigismund of Luxembourg. In the ensuing years, the King reinstituted the regime of the council and confiscated the property of the Italian merchants. A second revolt broke out in 1439 in the wake of rivalries between German and Hungarian groups, and was concluded with an agreement providing for future parity between the two parties on the town council.[48] In a further wave of unrest during the 1520s, the so-called 'third orders', the representatives of artisans and smaller merchants, were recognised in Cracow, Warsaw, Lublin and Danzig.

Often, as in the case of Cracow, the patriciate welcomed well-to-do new arrivals. Johann Boner of Nuremberg, for instance, was granted citizenship in 1483, married into the Morsztyn family and was elected to the town council for the first time in 1498. After initial success in the textile trade, he rose to the position of financier of the Crown. Also connected with southern Germany and active in the metal trade were Casper Ber and Leonard Fogelweder. The most significant figure, however, seems to have been the Hungarian Johann Thurzo who, after acquiring citizenship in 1464, turned Cracow into the centre of his trade in Hungarian copper, and, as the patron of Veit Stoß, made a historic contribution to the city's cultural life. In addition to the Germans, the cities of east-central Europe were also home to Italians, Frenchmen and -women, Armenians, Jews and, in the Prussian cities, people of Dutch, Scots and English origin.

Jews had been working successfully in the royal financial administration of Poland, Bohemia and Hungary since the twelfth century. During the thirteenth century, the princes increasingly supported the settlement of Jews as an infrastructural measure to promote trade and credit. In 1264, Bolesław of Greater Poland issued the privilege of Kalisz, in which he proclaimed the Jews chamber vassals of the prince, as the Duke of Austria and Styria and the King of Hungary had done before him; they thus obtained the protection of the prince, in return for a payment. In 1334, Casimir confirmed the privilege of Kalisz. When numerous Jews left the empire during the wave of persecution that followed the plague of 1349, Casimir expressly offered the Jews protection. In 1364 and 1367, additional privileges were granted, which exempted the Jews from the stipulations of German law and placed them directly under the royal voyevods; moreover, they were granted the right to acquire houses and land. As a result, the almost exclusively urban Jewish communities grew rapidly in this period, particularly in Poland, especially since the Jews were temporarily expelled from Hungary under Louis of Anjou. In most cities, 'Jewish streets' appeared, followed by Jewish quarters, which offered a certain measure of protection against attacks by Christians. Since Jews were barred from citizenship, and hence from participation in the administration of the cities, organs of self-administration emerged, such as the *kahal*, a council of elders which regulated the affairs of the community both internally and in regard to the Christian environment. This situation was not, however, as peaceful as it might appear, in spite of the existing privileges. The fifteenth century witnessed regular attacks on the Jews of Cracow, which led in 1494 to their expulsion to the suburbs of Kasimierz.

In this period, no Jewish communities had yet settled in the countryside, where free peasants and their families constituted 85 per cent of the population. Nonetheless, rural society was hierarchical. Beneath the peasantry were the land poor and landless villagers. At the top were the village mayors and well-to-do tradesmen, such as millers and innkeepers. During the colonisation period, the princes or, in the case of Prussia, the Teutonic Order, had given the locators and later the village mayors land usually amounting to between one-tenth and one-sixth of the hides in the village, as free hides, which were heritable property. Accordingly, the village mayors generally farmed their lands with the aid of the so-called 'gardeners'. The most important task of the village mayors, aside from acting as the local judicial authority (they were allowed to keep one-third of the fines collected), was to represent the landlord in the community, which meant responsibility for collecting all rents due them. As a consequence of their position, village mayors in Poland and Hungary were often ennobled during the fourteenth century. During the fifteenth century, though, the office of village mayor became an object of greed. *Nobiles* sought to make the thriving economic operations of the village mayors the basis of their own agricultural enterprises, and the 1423 statute of the Warta gave them the opportunity to purchase the lands of village mayors. The law forced the village mayors to sell their lands under certain circumstances to the noble landlord at a price set by the court. The lord might then replace the hereditary mayor with a peasant appointed to supervise the community. We do not know how nobles made use of this possibility during the first half of the fifteenth century. At the end of the fifteenth century, however, the purchase of village mayors' lands was a frequent means of establishing demesne farms in Poland.

During the fourteenth and fifteenth centuries, peasants enjoyed a secure legal position in Poland, Bohemia and Hungary, thanks to German law. At the end of the fourteenth century, most Bohemian peasants, like those in Poland, farmed their hides on the basis of heritable usufruct, and in Hungary too, a free peasantry, the so-called *jobbágy*, had emerged. Their rights included freedom of movement, guaranteed rights of ownership, and firmly established rents and dues. These were generally fixed to prevent or eliminate competition among landlords over potential settlers. Numerous peasants achieved considerable prosperity, which is reflected in such statistics as the number of cattle and dependent labourers. However, this apparently favourable situation in comparison with that of western Europe changed over the course of the fifteenth century. Since no further migration from the west was to be expected, and landlords' income from rents was reduced by currency devaluation, the lords put increasing pressure on the productive power of the peasantry. The landed nobility used its growing political power to limit peasant autonomy and freedom of movement. At the same time, the lords attempted to increase peasant labour services. This development was associated with the gradual expansion of the direct exploitation of the land by the nobility, with their growing orientation toward European markets. Initially, this could only be achieved by increasing labour input. However, the edict of 1423 restricted corvée services to fourteen days a year. This notwithstanding, landlords attempted to increase the labour due to one day per week. And in order to escape this pressure, many peasants tried to abandon their land. That was generally prevented by noble majorities in the regional diets, and in the national diet of Piotrków in 1494, which tied the peasants to the soil.

Only in Bohemia does the position of the peasant population appear to have improved continuously during the fifteenth century, which gives the lie to previous claims by historians regarding a crisis of agriculture in pre-Hussite times. Corvée duties decreased, and by 1550 were no more than eighteen to twenty-four days a year. Labour rents were insignificant, especially since the number of self-operated demesnes also fell. The mobility of the peasant population is also surprising. Peasants accepted lands from the landlords, or even moved from one domain to another legally, or settled in the towns.[49]

In Hungary, by contrast, the nobility restricted the conditions for departure to the point that peasants could only leave their land with permission from the landlord after having fulfilled all obligations. Nonetheless, the development of the manorial economy was still in its early stages, and the great majority of peasants in east-central Europe paid their rents primarily in money or in kind, and not in corvée labour. Major peasant unrest was therefore rare in these areas, with the exception of the rebellions in Transylvania in 1437 and in Hungary in 1514, which had local or regional causes.[50] Less affected by the looming deterioration of the position of the peasantry was the sub-peasant population. The gardeners and landless villagers were an indispensable labour reserve for the agricultural economy. They settled sometimes in large numbers on outlying estates, or on the land of peasants or village mayors, and carried out all the labour required in the manorial economy that was performed neither by farm servants nor peasant farmers. As the labour burden on peasants became more onerous, the importance of these workers increased. Paid in kind for their work, and owing little in dues or statute labour, they were able to sell the produce of their gardens and in some cases to acquire considerable numbers of animals. This gave them the possibility of upward mobility into the peasant stratum.

6.5 Multicultural reality in east-central Europe

The multi-ethnic nature of east-central Europe led to the emergence of literary monuments in all languages. In the areas adjacent to the Greek Orthodox populations, Old Church Slavonic served as a lingua franca, which was also mutually comprehensible with Old Polish and Old Czech, for example. Later, in the Catholic areas, medieval literature was largely written in Latin. This included the chronicles, which began with the work of Cosmas of Prague in the twelfth century and culminated in the autobiography of Charles IV, the *Vita Caroli*. In Poland, a monk of French origin known as Gallus Anonymus, a contemporary of Cosmas, wrote the first history of the Polish state. A century later, the bishop of Cracow Vincent Kadłubek wrote a history of Poland, which he regarded mainly as an object lesson in living according to the laws of God and the Church. It was only at the time of the Jagiełłonians, however, that Poland produced a historian in John Długosz (1415–80), a member of the clientele of Cardinal Oleśnicki, who as a diplomat was familiar with contemporary politics and for the first time attempted a critical assessment of his sources. In Hungary, the first Latin authors were clerics of German or Italian origin who glorified the history of Christianisation and the life of King Stephen I (St Stephen). At the end of the twelfth century, another anonymous author wrote the first Hungarian chronicle, the *Gesta Hungarorum*, which was followed one hundred years later by another Latin chronicle from the pen of Simon Kézai. This work was continually updated and printed as the first Hungarian book in 1473. Especially in Hungary, Latin retained its status as the official language for a very long time; as late as the first half of the nineteenth century, the members of the Hungarian diet – as well as that of Croatia – spoke in Latin. Nonetheless, vernacular literature naturally appeared throughout the region; in Bohemia, books were published in both German and Czech. Preachers such as John Milíč Kroměříž composed their sermons in Latin, but delivered them in Czech or German. Jan Hus in particular provided important impulses for the Czech language and its literature, including vernacular translations of the

Bible from the Vulgate – as Martin Luther would do for German a hundred years later. His supporters and successors wrote vernacular devotional books for use in Christian households, which the Utraquists disseminated widely throughout Bohemia. The Slavs in Upper Hungary, known since the fifteenth century as Slovaks, neither used this literature nor developed their own. Cultural life in Upper Hungary in any case took place in the German-dominated towns; only with the Reformation in the sixteenth century did the Slovaks accept Czech as a Church language.

In addition to Czech, German was an important literary language especially among the nobility and the urban elites. Ottokar Přemysl sponsored troubadours such as Ulrich of Eschenbach at his court, and Wenceslas II even wrote love lyrics in German. At the court of Charles IV, his chancellor Johann of Neumarkt also wrote literature, and one product of the country's urban milieu, the popular novel *The ploughman of Bohemia* by Johannes of Tepl, is an important monument of German literary history. Compared with that in Bohemia, literary development in Poland was significantly slower. Apart from a few fragments such as the hymn to the Mother of God, *Bogurodzica*, the earliest surviving complete book in Polish is a psalter belonging to Queen Hedwig known as the St Florian Psalter. The next examples of Polish literature are translations from the Latin or Czech, and only in the fifteenth century did secular literature in Polish gradually begin to emerge. In Hungary, the text of the Gospels and several hymns had already been translated from Latin into Hungarian during the thirteenth century. Hungarian students studying abroad brought standard western European materials back to the country, including the *Alexander romance* and episodes from the Trojan wars, which were adapted by Hungarian-language authors. In Hungary, too, Hussite influence sparked an increase in vernacular religious writing, which involved the translation of texts from the Bible. Additional inspiration for literary activity came from the court of King Matthias Corvinus, who had himself and his rule lauded by paid humanists to compensate for his lack of origins in a great dynasty. The Hungarian court, like the Jagiełłonian court at Cracow, thus advanced to an avenue for the introduction of humanism and Renaissance culture into east-central Europe.[51]

Even in the first half of the fifteenth century, personalities around the royal chancery functioned as multipliers of humanistic ideas in Hungary. After studying and teaching in Padua, Florence and Bologna, Pier Paolo Vergerio (1370–1444) had met King Sigismund at the Council of Constance, and was hired to work in his Buda chancery. Although his surviving educational and historical works stem from his period in Italy, during his stay in Buda he does seem to have mediated contacts between Polish and Hungarian scholars on the one hand and Italian humanists on the other. These contacts would later be intensified by another member of the chancery, János Vitéz (*c.* 1408–72). Vitéz served in the royal chancery under Sigismund, Vladislav, the regent John Hunyadi and his son Matthias. He also maintained his own court, first as bishop of Varadi and later as archbishop of Esztergom. On numerous diplomatic missions, he made contact with other humanists such as Enea Silvio Piccolomini and Poggio Bracciolini, and corresponded with many others, so that his *Epistolae*, famous for their characteristic style, were published even during his lifetime. In the 'proto-academy' built around his library, he hosted meetings that included Gregory of Sanok from Poland, the Cypriot Filippo Podocataro and the papal legate Giuliano Cesarini. Other activities aimed at building an intellectual infrastructure in Hungary included the foundation of a university in Pressburg (Bratislava) known at the time as the *Academia Istropolitana*, the initiative to establish a printing press in Buda, and the sponsorship of Hungarians studying in Italy. The most successful student in Italy was a nephew of Vitéz's, who was celebrated there as a poet under the name of Janus Pannonius (1434–72). He had studied with Guarino Veronese, who gathered a group of students from throughout Europe around him in Ferrara to study Latin and Greek grammar and the ancient authors. His fame was based in particular on his epigrams in the style of Martial. After further study in Padua, he returned to Hungary, became bishop of Pécs and later vice chancellor under Matthias Corvinus. A diplomatic mission took him to Italy once more, where he met all of the leading humanists of his day, including Marsilio Ficino. In Hungary, he became a critic of the King, since, like his uncle, he refused to support his military actions against Bohemia and Austria. After being besieged in their episcopal see, he and his uncle died trying to flee in 1472.

Matthias Corvinus had now had enough of humanism for the time being, and only after marrying Beatrice of Naples and Aragón in 1476 did he again recruit Italian humanists to polish his royal image. The first result was the construction of a Roman line of succession for himself under the name Corvinus. In 1488, the Italian humanist Antonio Bonfini, who two years earlier had already flattered his way into the King's entourage with a text on the origins of the Corvini family known as *Libellus de Corvinianae domus origine*, received a contract to write a history of Hungary, the *Rerum ungaricorum decades*, while the Neapolitan ambassador Pietro Ranzano composed an *Epitoma rerum hungaricarum*. When the King died in 1490, the first sixteen books had been completed, and the new ruler, Vladislav II, had him continue the work. In 1492 he granted the author a noble title. The high point of the Jagiełłonian period was the foundation of a humanist academy, the *Sodalitas litteraria Hungarorum* in Buda, which was established on the initiative of Konrad Celtis almost simultaneously with the *Litteraria sodalitas Danubiae* in Vienna. Members included German, Polish, Bohemian, Hungarian and Italian humanists, and Viennese influence would increase further during the sixteenth century with Johannes Cuspinian and Wolfgang Lazius.[52]

Hungarian humanist influences, in turn, were palpable both in Bohemia and Moravia and in Poland during the fifteenth century. There, contact with humanist knowledge was provided by both travel to Italy and Hungarian mediation. Moravia in particular, with the bishopric of Olmütz (Olomouc), became a humanist centre. Johann of Neumarkt, the chancellor of Charles IV, who corresponded with Petrarch, was already active here during the fourteenth century. But not until 1457 would another humanist scholar, Protasius of Boskovic and Černahora, become bishop of Olmütz. During his studies in Vienna he had met Piccolomini, and through him made contact with Francesco Filelfo, Janus Pannonius and János Vitéz. He began to collect manuscripts, and summoned Franciscan Minorites to Moravia as teachers. The Moravian Johannes Filipec, who as bishop of Nagyvárad (Oradea) and confidant of Matthias Corvinus took over the administration of Olmütz in 1484, worked in a similar manner. His activities included founding a library and summoning German printers from Venice. Olmütz reached its pinnacle under Stanislas Thurzo, who, like his brother John, maintained libraries in Breslau, supported young poets and corresponded with such contemporary scholars as Erasmus. Another Moravian, Augustinus Olumucensis, known as Käsembrot (1476–1513), was a member of various humanist networks such as the *Sodalitates* in Vienna and Buda. He had studied in Carrara, where he composed such works as *Dialogus in defensionem poetices*. After his return, he became secretary to Vladislav II in Buda, and at the same time cathedral canon in Olmütz, and later in Brno and Prague. The bishopric of Olmütz seems to have been so attractive for humanists that Bohuslav Hasištejnský z Lobkovic (Bohuslav Lobkowitz of Hassenstein, 1461–1510) applied to assume it in 1493, albeit unsuccessfully. Bohuslav, who was independently wealthy, studied in Bologna and Ferrara and dedicated himself primarily to the study of humanities. After his return, he lived and wrote primarily at Hasištejn castle. He undertook numerous journeys to Strasbourg and Leipzig, as well as the Mediterranean region, travelling as far as Palestine and Egypt. His literary work includes lyric poetry, philosophical and political tracts, and an extensive correspondence. His splendid library of 750 volumes contained a large number of ancient authors, including seventy Greeks. With the establishment of a school at Hasištejn castle, humanist studies were widely disseminated for the first time among the Bohemian nobility and selected students from the towns.

A generation earlier, the Utraquist noble Jan of Rabštejn (Johann of Rabenstein, 1437–73), had already gained wide influence after completing his studies of jurisprudence as a doctor of both canon and civil law in Italy. His surviving major work, the disputation *Dialogus baronorum bohemorum*, is dedicated to his Padua teacher Giovanni Grassi. It exudes the spirit of Latin humanism, and refers at the same time to the confessional situation in Bohemia.[53]

Humanist ideas reached Poland at the beginning of the fifteenth century as a result of the travels of Polish clerics and diplomats to the papal court, and of Polish students to Italy. The Polish delegation to the Council of Constance also brought new information and manuscripts home with them. In exceptional cases, such as that of Francesco Filelfo, who in 1424 was invited to give the oration for the coronation of Jagiełło's fourth wife Sophia, Italian humanists also visited Poland. Moreover, Zbigniew Oleśnicki maintained an intensive correspondence with Enea Silvio Piccolomini in Vienna. Thus, even for the historian John Długosz, who was still entirely wedded to the Middle Ages, it was a matter of course to be familiar with such authors as Seneca, Livy, Caesar and Tacitus; his historiography was orientated toward Livy. On his Italian journeys, he met contemporary authors and acquired both their writings and valuable manuscripts. Długosz's contemporary Gregory of Sanok, after gaining his baccalaureate at Cracow, studied at a number of Italian universities and made a name for himself as a humanist with his commentaries on Virgil's *Eclogues*. During his activities as royal secretary and tutor to Hunyadi's sons in Hungary, he made contact with the Hungarian humanist circle around János Vitéz, and later, as archbishop of Lwów, turned his residence into a humanist centre. For this 'Callimachus Experiens' would later celebrate him in a panegyric biography. Callimachus (1437–94), whose real name was Philippo Buonacorsi, already had an adventurous career behind him when he settled in Cracow in 1472. Originally from San Gimigniano, he attracted attention in Venice as a poet of love elegies on the ancient model, and then received a position as a cardinal's secretary in Rome through the good offices of Pomponius Laetus, the founder of the Academia Romana. Accused together with Pomponius of plotting against Pope Paul II, he was forced to flee in 1467, reached Constantinople via Crete and Cyprus, and from there travelled to the court of Gregory of Sanok in Poland. Shortly thereafter, he rose to the position of royal secretary in Cracow, and promoted the dissemination of humanist learning at the university there. In addition to the typical humanist mixture of letters, elegies, *consilia* and biographies, his literary production included most notably political tracts calling for a Venetian-Polish alliance against the Turks. He participated in numerous diplomatic missions to Constantinople and Italy, but also addressed other current political issues such as the Bohemian succession of Vladislav, and the succession of his pupil John Albert to the Polish throne. In his *Consilia*, he presented theoretical political considerations in which he questioned Poland's move toward an aristocratic republic. He called for Poland to be ruled by a strong monarch, and for the abolition of the immunities enjoyed by the nobility. Although essentially a politician, in his correspondence with such important Florentine intellectuals as Marsilio Ficino, Angelo Poliziano and Giovanni Pico della Mirandola, Callimachus also raised basic philosophical issues such as the nature of sin and the relationship between body and mind. When he died, his Italian friends reported to their correspondents on his dignified funeral, and his tomb was the work of no less a sculptor than Veit Stoß.

Callimachus may also have attracted Konrad Celtis, who studied in Cracow in 1488 and would later teach there. This contact with other professors resulted in the idea of founding a *Sodalitas literaria Vistulana*, which may well have served as a model for later foundations in Vienna and Buda. The Cracow humanist community also included other persons who combined literary activities with court and diplomatic office. Maciej Drzewicki (1407–1535), chancellor of the University and a diplomat, wrote a *History of the bishops of Włoclawek*. The Danziger Jan Dantisgus (or Dantyszek, 1467–1535) served as royal secretary and also as ambassador to Vienna and Spain, was a friend of Erasmus, and later became bishop of Kulm (Chelmno) and Ermland (Warmia). In addition to moral poetry, he wrote the *Elegia armatoria* and an autobiography in Latin. Another Church official, Andrzej Krzycki (1482–1537), who after studying in Bologna rose through the Church hierarchy to the position of bishop of Płock and Gniezno, made a name for himself as a satirical Latin poet.

At the university, language teaching was improved with the aid of humanist grammars by Lorenzo Valla and Niccolò Perotti, and native teachers published epistolographic works in order to promote the humanistic culture of letter writing. A large number of humanist scholars such as the Swiss Rudolf Agricola Jr regularly held lectures on ancient literature at Cracow, a university also renowned for mathematics and astronomy.[54]

However, the Jagiełłonian University's most famous graduate, Nicholas Copernicus, never taught there. After studying law in Bologna and medicine in Padua and receiving a doctorate in canon law in Ferrara, he returned to the bishopric of Warmia and dedicated himself to the management of the episcopal domains.[55]

There are three major eras in the art history of east-central Europe that may be considered processes of cultural exchange on the European level: the Gothic period of the Luxembourgs in Bohemia, the Corvinian Renaissance, and the Jagiełłonian Renaissance. Thus under Charles IV, Prague rose to the status of a cultural centre of European significance. It underwent urban restructuring, through the building not just of the New Town and the Charles Bridge but also of many churches, including the Church of Our Lady before Tyn, and especially the reconstruction of the St Vitus Cathedral, which stimulated the development of a specific late-Gothic style and became a model for many German hall churches. Matthew of Arras had been called from Avignon to carry out the reconstruction of the St Vitus Cathedral on the model of the French high Gothic. With the prototype of the Pietà, his successor as master builder, Peter Parler, created a sculpture that would set a stylistic standard in many parts of Europe. Italian artists worked in Bohemia on the mosaics of the St Vitus Cathedral, as well as on the frescoes at Charles IV's residence at Karlstein.[56] However, such cultural symbioses, like humanist influences, would have no permanent future in Bohemia because of Hussite rule, nor were they revived during the period of stabilisation under George of Poděbrady. By contrast, Hungary, under another new arrival on the throne, advanced to a centre for the reception of the Renaissance. Matthias Corvinus can certainly be compared with Italian *condottieri* such as Federico da Montefeltro whose cultural investments served political ends. Even before King Matthias's time, though, there had been close artistic ties to Italy, which are often no longer visible because of the disruptions of the Turkish wars. In the first half of the fifteenth century, Italians such as Branda Castiglione or Andrea Scolari already held the position of master builder. Such Florentine artists as Manetto Amanatini and the famous Massalino da Panicale, who had worked on the Brancacci chapel, received commissions in Hungary. Matthias began to introduce his own Renaissance elements with a specific decorative programme in the Buda castle complex, which Sigismund had had rebuilt in the Gothic style. This included several statue groups and a Minerva fountain, which was presumably designed during his sojourn in Buda by Giovanni Dalmata, who also created the tomb of Pope Paul II at St Peter's in Rome. Other fountains included the Minerva fountain on the banks of the Danube much lauded in humanist literature and a Hercules fountain at the royal summer residence in Visegrád.[57] This, like the residence at Nyék, was designed as a villa in the antique style, and was built at approximately the same time as the Medici villa at Poggio a Caiano near Florence. In his attempts to install the entire repertoire of Renaissance art at his court, Matthias issued numerous commissions to Florentine masters such as Pollaiuolo and the goldsmith Caradosso, who, like the sculptor and intarsia artist Benedetto da Maiano, lived in Buda for a time.

He also had a passion for collecting codices and illuminated manuscripts, which were kept at the Bibliotheca Corviniana. From Buda, Renaissance art reached the courts of the bishops and the high nobility, although they also had direct contacts with Italy. Thus Cardinal Tamás Bakócz (1442–1521), who had studied in Italy and travelled there extensively, transplanted an Italian central-plan building as a chapel annex to Esztergom cathedral. The bishop of Vác, Miklós Báthory (1430–1506), also had his castle renovated by Italian master builders, while László Geréb, the bishop of Transylvania, collected Roman antiquities. In Moravia too, new Renaissance portal forms were integrated into buildings, probably by local craftsmen, for instance at the castles of the humanist noble Ladislas of Boskovic and Černahora at Třebová, or at Tobischau Castle (Tovacov).[58]

The Jagiełłonian Renaissance, too, adopted some elements from Buda; it is not true, however, as has long been claimed, that it represented a linear continuation of Corvinian architecture. Thus Vladislav II began his own construction programme in both Prague and Buda. In Prague, Vladislav originally resided in the Old Town, and in 1485 moved to Hradčaný Palace, which he sumptuously rebuilt as a royal residence. Benedikt Ried designed the Vladislav Hall by creating a vaulted ceiling over the interior in high Gothic style, and at the same time decorating the outer façade with Italianate Renaissance windows. Only in the 1490s did Vladislav move his residence from Prague to Buda. In Cracow, too, around 1500, the Gothic style was still an alternative chosen for both town houses and the interiors of religious buildings. Thus, for example, the bronze plate created by Veit Stoß for the grave of the humanist Callimachus followed the Gothic style, although the presentation was modelled after a humanist *studiolo*. The symbiosis of old and new styles is evident in the tomb of King John Albert in Wawel Cathedral (1502–05), which combines a large gravestone from Stoß's workshop with the architecture in the antique style of Francesco Fiorentino. Under a triumphal arch, the funerary niche is adorned with the classic ornaments of Italian sculptural art, including garlands, pilasters and trophies. Around the same time, the reconstruction of the royal

Figure 4 Bartolomeo Berrecci, Sigismund chapel in the Wawel Cathedral in Cracow.

castle complex on the Wawel hill began. Sigismund had Fiorentino, whom he had brought from Buda, build an arcade court in the Italian manner. The arcades followed the model that Brunelleschi had established with the foundling hospital in Florence; however, with the incorporation of several galleries with columns stacked one above the other, the structure achieved far greater heights.

Presumably the most influential structure of the Jagiełłonian Renaissance in Poland was the Sigismund chapel built by the Florentine Bartolomeo Berrecci (1517–33). This central-plan building with wall niches for portrait statues was inspired by the new Italian chapel style and the tomb of Cardinal James of Portugal in San Miniato del Monte in Florence. Berrecci may have participated in the project of the tomb of Pope Julius II in Rome, and he had worked in Cracow with the team of Italian artists who adorned the walls of the Sigismund chapel with mythological scenes.[59] It has long been assumed that Sigismund's patronage of Italian masters was associated with his second wife, Bona Sforza, whom he married in 1518. However, the introduction of new forms had already begun with his accession to the throne in 1506, which suggests a deliberate choice of Italian Renaissance elements for the purposes of royal representation.[60] In the years that immediately followed, the high nobility and high clergy were already emulating the King. Thus, for example, the royal chancellor Krzysztof

Szydłowiecki and the hetman Jan Tarnowski commissioned the Berrecci workshop to design a child's tomb for Szydłowiecki's small son Ludwik Mikołai at Opatów, as well as a tomb for Tarnowski's late wife Barbara at Tarnów. In Gniezno, Giovanni Cini and Bernadino de Gianotis, close associates of Berrecci, designed the tomb for the archbishop and humanist Andrzej Krzycki; they had previously also created the tomb for Krzysztof Szydłowiecki at Opatów. If no Italian artists were available, the nobility and high clergy at least incorporated Renaissance set-pieces into their palace architecture.[61]

The musical development of east-central Europe offers another example of intensive cultural exchange. The courtly life of the Přemyslid kings brought secular music to Bohemia. Poets and singers such as Reinmar Zweter and Ulrich of Eschenbach were active at the Prague court, and King Wenceslas II saw himself as a troubadour. During the reign of John of Luxembourg, Bohemian troubadour singing reached a high point under Heinrich of Mügeln and Mülich of Prague. The work of Guillaume de Machaut, who began his career as secretary to John of Luxembourg, and the compositions of the French *ars nova* were known in Prague. During the Hussite era, Czech songs began to crowd out Latin ones. Over the course of the fifteenth century, there was a revival of sacred music, as reflected in the art of organ building. Hans Peysinger of Kempten built an organ for the church of St Nicholas in Eger (Cheb) in 1498, while Jan Behaim of Dubrau built the organ for the Fugger chapel in St Anne's in Augsburg and for the church of St James in Innsbruck. Increasingly, Bohemian musicians and organists served as cantors in Saxony and other regions. It was only under Emperor Rudolf II, however, that the Prague court chapel would make the city on the Moldau a centre of court music.

Poland had an uninterrupted tradition of sacred music. Here, polyphonic music was already known during the fourteenth century, as extant monastic manuscripts indicate, and organs are documented for the thirteenth century. Organs were widespread from the late fourteenth century (Katy *c.* 1380, Kalisz *c.* 1403, Poznań in 1404, Lwów in 1409, Gniezno in 1417, Włocławek before 1429, Przeworsk, Kraśnik, Łowicz and Warsaw in 1462). By the sixteenth century, at the latest, a number of printers were busy meeting the demand for musical literature such as organ tablatures. The tablatures of the sixteenth century include Polish dances and songs, numerous fantasies, dances and songs of Italian, Flemish and German origin. Secular music is attested both at the courts and in the cities for weddings, baptisms, births and other festivities; in the fourteenth century, the Cracow municipal authorities addressed the large number of musicians in sumptuary laws. The journey of the Polish delegation to the Council of Constance brought further inspiration for the development of music, which was reflected in compositions for the royal court and for Cracow University as well as for urban demand. A fourteenth-century manuscript in the Krasiński Library mentions native composers such as Nicholas of Radom and Zacharias alongside French and Italian artists.

Because of its cultural orientation toward Italy and France, Hungarian musical culture also regularly profited from the influence of French singers such as Peire Vidal and Gaucelm Faidit, who had already sojourned at the Hungarian court during the twelfth and early thirteenth centuries. They were followed by such troubadours as Heinrich of Mügeln and Oswald of Wolkenstein. During the reign of Matthias Corvinus, the entire range of western European musical culture was represented in Hungary by such figures as Jacobus Barbireau, P. Bonnus, Stephano de Salerno and John de Stockhem. Instrumentalists were mainly recruited from Italy, while singers represented the Flemish style. In addition, the time Hungarian students spent in Paris, Bologna and Padua as well as Vienna and Cracow was also important for expanding musical horizons. The organist Anton of Kassa and the clavichord player Kasper of Eperjes, for instance, had studied in Cracow, while Hungarian court musicians, too, were sent to the imperial cities. In this manner, they, like the Hungarian itinerant musicians – primarily fiddlers – disseminated the popular dances long known under the name *Ungaresca*, which were even integrated into courtly culture.

Notes

1 Urban, *The Livonian crusade*; Murray (ed.), *Crusade and conversion on the Baltic frontier*.
2 Knoll, *The rise of the Polish monarchy*.
3 Wyrozumski, *Dzieje Polski piastowskiej*, 314–75.
4 Engel, *The realm of St Stephen*, 124–56.
5 Ibid., 157–73. See also 6.2.
6 Spěváček, *Jan Lucemburský*; Benešovská (ed.), *King John of Luxembourg*.
7 Svatoš (ed.), *Dějiny University Karlovy*, 27–100.
8 Polívka, 'The Political culture in the Bohemian kingdom of the Luxembourg period', 120–7, Hergemöller, *Maiestas Carolina*; Seibt, 'Zur Entwicklung der böhmischen Staatlichkeit', 478–80; Kejř, 'Die sogenannte Maiestas Carolina'.
9 Mezník, *Lucemburská Morava*, 250–301; Fajt, *Charles IV: Emperor by the grace of God*.
10 Davies, *God's playground*, 93–9.
11 Tiberg, *Moscow, Livonia and the Hanseatic League*; Frost, *The northern wars*.
12 Baczkowski, *Dzieje Polski*, 277–303.

13 Fudge, *The magnificant ride: The first reformation in Hussite Bohemia.*
14 Šmahel, *Die Hussitische Revolution*, II, 788–838.
15 Šmahel, *Die Hussitische Revolution*, I, 636–715, and II, 1032–70.
16 Seibt, 'Die Zeit der Luxemburger', 539–60.
17 Engel, *The realm of St Stephen*, 278–97.
18 Ibid., 298–322.
19 Sedlar, *East central Europe*, 270–3; Wyrozumski, *Dzieje Polski*, 365–7.
20 Fügedi, 'Castles and castellans', 49–65.
21 Górski, 'The origins of the Polish Sejm'; Russocki, '" Consilium baronum"'.
22 Seibt, 'Zur Entwicklung der böhmischen Staatlichkeit', 133–51; Sedlar, *East central Europe*, 285–6.
23 Bak, *Königtum und Stände*, 39–40.
24 Engel, *The realm of St Stephen*, 278–80, 314–18, 347–57.
25 Siemieński, 'Od sejmików', 449–51; Włodarczyk, 'Sejmiki łęczyckie', 32; Iwańczak, 'Political culture of the nobility in late medieval Poland', 101–11.
26 Zientara, 'Społeczeństwo polskie', 162–67; Russocki, 'Początki Zgromadzeń Stanowych'.
27 Boockmann, *Der Deutsche Orden*, 197–220.
28 Burleigh, *Prussian society and the German Order.*
29 Zientara, Mączak, Ihnatowicz and Landau (eds), *Dzieje gospodarcze Polski*, 88–9; Stone, *Polish-Lithuanian state*, 67–8.
30 Boháč, 'Postup osídlení'; Maur, 'Die demographische Entwicklung Böhmens'.
31 Hoffmann, *Land, liberties and lordship*, 286–90.
32 Engel, *The realm of St Stephen*, 102, 267–9, 328–30.
33 Still fundamental on this and what follows are Schlesinger (ed.) *Die deutsche Ostsiedlung*; and Higounet, *Les Allemands en Europe centrale.*
34 On the indigenous towns of the Slavic states see Jiří Macháček (ed.), *The rise of medieval towns and states in east-central Europe.*
35 Samsonowicz, 'Polish politics'.
36 Makkai, 'Die wirtschaftlichen Regionen'; Pach, *Hungary*, 244–56.
37 Zientara, 'Roskwit feudalizmu'; Biskup, 'Przeobrażenia w handlu i rzemiośle', and 'Gdańsk a Hanza'; Samsonowicz, 'Miejsce Gdańska' and 'Dynamciczny ośrodek handlowy'; North, 'Wirtschaft, Gesellschaft, Bevölkerung', 131.
38 Podlecki, *Wieliczka*; Molenda and Balczerak, *Metale nieżelazne.*
39 Spufford, *Money and its use*, 99–101.
40 Vlachovič, *Slovenská med' v 16. a 17. Storoči*; Westermann, 'Zur Silber- und Kupferproduktion'.
41 Ihnatowicz, Mączak and Zientara (eds), *Społeczeństwo polskie*, 153–60.
42 Mályusz, 'Hungarian nobles'.
43 Šmahel, *Die Hussitische Revolution*, I, 221–2.
44 Zientara, 'Społeczeństwo polskie', 97–225, 161.
45 Samsonowicz, 'Polish politics', 64–5.
46 Klassen, 'Hus, Hussites and Bohemia', 382; Polívka, 'A contribution to the problem of property differentiation of the lesser nobility in the pre-Hussite period in Bohemia', 331–60.
47 Engel, *The realm of St Stephen*, 334.

48 Ibid., 262.
49 Čechura, 'Die Bauernschaft', 293–6, and *Die Struktur der Grundherrschaften*, 126–9.
50 Pach, 'The development of feudal rent', and 'Der Bauernaufstand'.
51 Sedlar, *East central Europe*, 428–44.
52 Ritoók-Szalay, 'Der Humanismus in Ungarn'; Birnbaum, 'Humanism in Hungary'.
53 Šmahel, 'Die Anfänge des Humanismus'; Wörster, 'Breslau und Olmütz'.
54 Müller, 'Humanismus und Universität'.
55 Segel, *Renaissance culture in Poland*.
56 Legner, *Die Parler*; Drake, Boehm and Fajt (eds), *Prague, the crown of Bohemia*.
57 Bredekamp, 'Herrscher und Künstler', 254–61.
58 Kaufmann, *Court, cloister and city*, 39–48; Ritoók-Szalay, 'Der Humanismus in Ungarn', 168–70; Marosi, 'Die Corvinische Renaissance in Ungarn', 181–7; Balogh, 'Die Kunst der Renaissance'.
59 Bredekamp, 'Herrscher und Künstler', 268–76.
60 Kaufmann, *Court, cloister and city*, 52–4.
61 Kozakiewicz and Kozakiewicz, *Renesans w Polsce*, 34–8, 51, 54–8, 62–6.

7

South-east Europe

South-east Europe, which extends from the eastern Alps to the eastern Mediterranean region, was marked on the one hand by the culture of antiquity and the early reception of Christianity, and on the other by the invasions and settlements of Germanic and Slavic peoples and steppe nomads. In conflicts with the East Roman (Byzantine) Empire, large kingdoms and nations such as the Bulgarians, Serbs and Bosnians emerged, who felt the impact of Ottoman expansion beginning in the second half of the fourteenth century. In the course of attempts to defend against and push back Ottoman rule, such European dynasties as the Luxembourgs and the Habsburgs gained influence in the nations of south-east Europe.

7.1 The fall of the Byzantine Empire

The name Byzantium was first coined in 1557 by Hieronymus Wolf (1516–82) to refer to the state that called itself *Basileia ton Rhomaion* – the kingdom of the Romans – using the Latinised name *Byzantion*, an ancient Greek city on whose foundations the Emperor Constantine established 'his' city of Constantinople in 330. By that time, the Byzantine Empire had long since collapsed.

The Fourth Crusade, which – rather than bolstering Crusader rule in the Holy Land – under Venetian leadership conquered Constantinople in 1204, already spelled the end of the unified Byzantine Empire and created a power vacuum in the eastern Mediterranean. While this strengthened Venice's pre-eminent position, it initiated the disintegration of the Byzantine Empire. Since the Venetians and the other Crusaders were able to take Constantinople but were unable to re-establish the position of the East Roman Empire, only fragments emerged from the struggle. One of them,

Nicæa, became the point of departure for political reconstruction in the region.

The conquest of 1204 met with an economically and politically depleted empire, which had already lost major segments of its territory in Asia Minor after the defeats at the hands of the Seljuks at Manzikert in 1071 and at Myriocephalon in 1176. Thus the Fourth Crusade was primarily a loss of prestige for the once shining metropolis of the eastern Mediterranean. The legendary wealth and the immeasurable treasure of relics plundered by the Crusaders were to fill the treasure chambers of the West. Henceforth, the city's poverty rather than its magnificence would become a byword. The Venetians, too, however, were only able partially to stabilise the eastern Mediterranean. They decided upon the division of the Empire, and instead of Boniface of Montferrat, the leader of the Crusade, they installed Count Baldwin of Flanders as the Latin Emperor of Byzantium. He received approximately one-quarter of the empire, while the other Crusaders and Venetians divided up the rest. Baldwin controlled Thrace and north-western Asia Minor. The Venetians occupied areas in Epirus, Greece and on the Peloponnese, as well as other ports and islands. They exchanged Thessalonica, which Boniface of Montferrat received as a residence, for Crete. In addition to Boniface's kingdom, a number of small Frankish domains such as the principality of Achaia emerged.

After the conquest, the court and officials of the Byzantine Empire went into exile in Nicæa in Asia Minor, where they proclaimed the rival Emperor Theodore. The Greeks in Nicæa had time on their side, since the Latin monarch Baldwin suffered defeat in a war against Bulgaria in 1205. Baldwin's brother Henry concluded an armistice and, in 1214, a peace treaty with Nicæa. Under Michael Palaiologos, who pushed Theodore's successors aside and proclaimed himself Emperor, the reconquest of the capital in 1261 succeeded without major losses. Thus was the Byzantine Empire re-established from Nicæa. It had, however, to maintain itself in the face of numerous external foes. Especially in the Mediterranean area, Michael's rule in Constantinople sparked the revival of old anti-Byzantine resentments, and both Charles of Anjou and the Pope attempted to initiate another Crusade. In this situation, the Byzantine Empire bought time by proposing a Church union with Rome, a union that, in spite of being proclaimed at the Council of Lyons in 1274, was never actually implemented. Michael was more successful in his support for the Sicilian rebellion against Charles of Anjou, the so-called Sicilian Vespers, which forced Charles to suspend his military efforts against the Byzantines.[1]

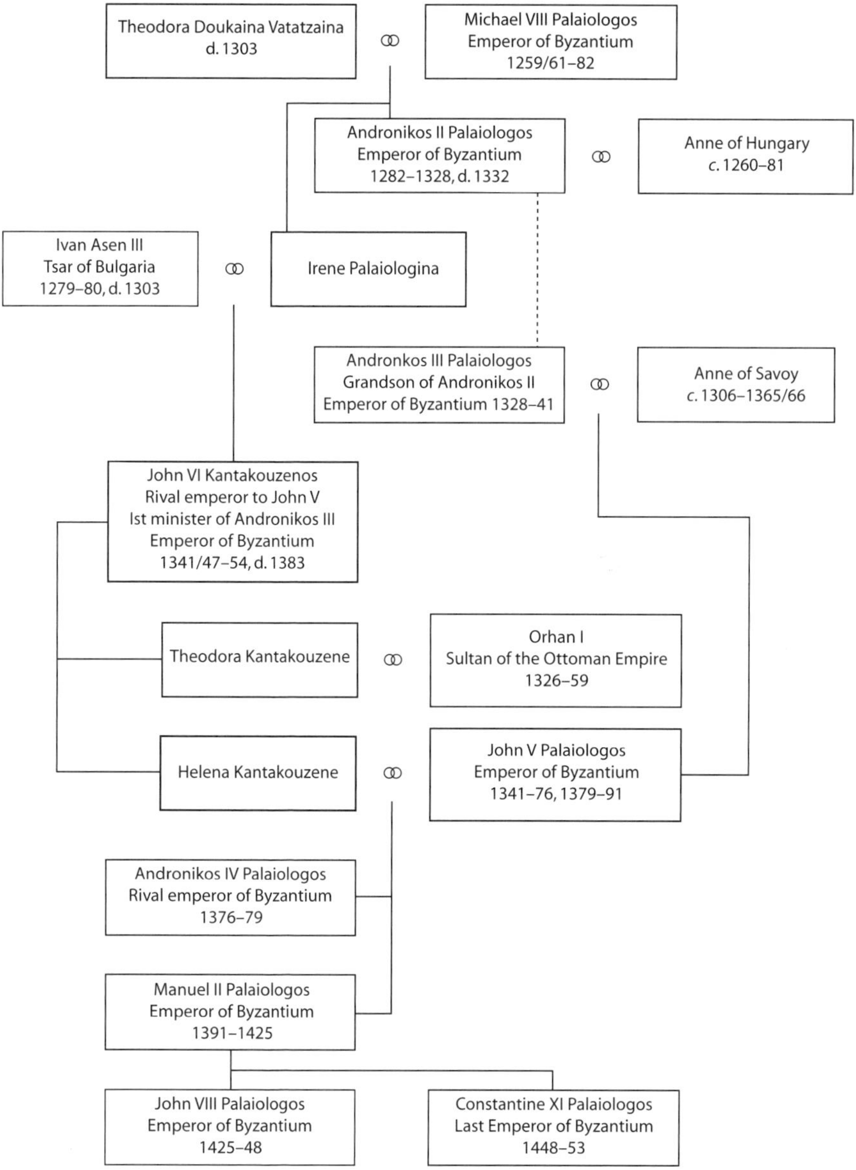

Genealogical table 6 The Palaiologan dynasty

Michael's successor, Andronicus II (1282–1328), was unable to maintain the status quo. The Turkish tribes had used the weakening of the Seljuks by the Mongol Ilkhans to expand into western Asia Minor and establish emirates; the Byzantines succeeded only in holding the coastal areas. In the west, the great Serbian kingdom was formed in the Balkans, and Tsar Stephen Dušan considered reuniting his empire with that of the Byzantines. After Dušan's death, the Serbian position deteriorated rapidly, so that after crossing the Dardanelles in 1369, Turkish troops laid siege to Adrianople and began to conquer the other small Serb kingdoms, which, after the Battle of Kosovo in 1389, became vassals of the Ottoman Empire. Four years later, the Ottomans also conquered the rest of the Bulgarian kingdom. The Byzantine Empire now mounted a frantic diplomatic campaign to mobilise its western European Christian coreligionists against the Muslims.

However, it was not the journeys of the Emperor to western and southern Europe or the support he gained as a result, but rather the victory of the Mongols under Tamerlane over the Ottomans that offered the Byzantine Empire some respite at the beginning of the fifteenth century. Since all Byzantine attempts at consolidation proved unsuccessful, though, it was only a matter of time before the Ottomans would return in full force, and finally take Constantinople. In this situation, western Europe demanded a union of both Churches in return for support against the Ottoman Empire. This union was concluded in 1439 at the Council of Ferrara and Florence. Nevertheless, the cultural relations established during Emperor John VIII's journey to Italy may have been more effective than any military support. From 1430, the decimation of the Byzantine Empire proceeded apace: the Ottomans first captured Thessalonica and Ioannina, and then laid siege to Constantinople in 1442.

Under the leadership of King Władysław III of Poland and Hungary and the voyevod of Transylvania, John Hunyadi (see 6.5), one last great attempt was made to mobilise European Christendom against Islam. It was initially successful, and an armistice was reached at Adrianople. Since the Pope urged the Hungarian King to continue the struggle, however, Sultan Murad II no longer felt bound by the armistice, and in 1444 utterly crushed the Christian army at Varna; Władysław III fell in the battle, earning him the honourable byname of *Warneńczyk*. The path to Europe was now open for the Ottomans. Accordingly, it was only a matter of time before the next assault on Constantinople. Murad's son Mehmed II ordered new siege instruments and cannon, and slowly cut the city off from its supply lines. Even the Church union, which was renewed in 1452, could do nothing to counter these measures. On the contrary, the pact with the

Latins, from whom no help could be expected in any case, discredited the Emperor. By 1453, the defenders of Constantinople had little with which to oppose the Turks. Although on 28 May 1453, on the eve of the conquest of the city, the Church union was once again confirmed in the Hagia Sophia, the de-Christianisation of this mother church and its transformation into a mosque could no longer be prevented. The centre of Orthodox Christianity would thus shift to Moscow, the so-called 'third Rome'. In the years that followed, the other Greek domains, such as Mistras in the Peloponnese and Trebizond on the Black Sea coast, would also fall to the Ottoman forces.[2]

7.2 Economic and demographic decline

While the Byzantine Empire fell into political decline, economic deterioration did not necessarily ensue everywhere, or at the same time. On the contrary, the Venetians and Genoese did good business in the region right up to the conquest of Constantinople. Many Byzantine landowners prospered into the middle of the fourteenth century, and even thereafter merchants profited from intermediary trade. In particular such agricultural products as oil, olives, wine, grain, currants, fish, cheese, honey and wax were traded to the Crusader states in exchange for wood, metal, cloth and other products.[3]

The economy of the Byzantine Empire was based on agriculture, and thus depended on shifts in the size of the population. Fifteenth-century sources from Mount Athos and Ottoman tax registers support the assumption that the population developed along roughly similar lines as that of western Europe. Until the arrival of the Black Death in 1347, the Byzantine Empire experienced long-term population growth; this was little affected by the wars against the Crusaders, the Ottomans or Bulgaria. The empire's European provinces in particular seem to have been so densely settled during the fourteenth century that there was relatively little mobility of land ownership. This primarily benefited the estate owners, who were thus able to demand higher rents from their peasants. However, 'tax evasion' by the great magnates and the so-called *pronoia* land grants, which deprived the state of revenues, meant that the state scarcely profited from growing agricultural production. Thanks to the Genoese Black Sea trade, the urban economy experienced an upswing into the fourteenth century.[4] In this area, the losses incurred in the Fourth Crusade seem to have been compensated for a century later. Under these circumstances, the plague negatively affected the Byzantine economy and rule. The plague claimed up to a third of the population of the Byzantine Empire, while the empire's Ottoman, Serbian and Bulgarian enemies suffered far smaller losses.[5]

In the century after the Crusaders captured Constantinople (1204), the Byzantine Empire experienced only a slow economic recovery. Increasingly cut off from Asia Minor, Constantinople, with a population of 50,000, was reduced to a safe port on the trade route into the Black Sea. Foreign observers noted the ruins, and no longer counted Constantinople among the great capitals of the Old World. Since the centres in the Greek provinces recovered more rapidly, the differences between them and the capital diminished. While the Black Death dramatically accelerated the empire's decline in power, that decline had already begun fifty years earlier. When he ascended the throne in 1282, Andronicus II could count some five million subjects; by the end of his reign in 1328, warfare and invasion had reduced the number of people he ruled to approximately two million. The empire's inability to defend its territory and islands against the Ottomans, Venetians and Genoese was the real cause of decline. For after the final conquest by the Ottomans in the fifteenth century, it became evident that the resources of the Balkan countries and Asia Minor would have sufficed to maintain the Byzantine Empire, since they were enough to support the Ottoman Empire.

The presence of westerners was increasingly noticeable in Byzantine society, although foreigners from the Caucasus, the area north of the Black Sea and the Balkan countries had always migrated to the empire. They had, however, integrated into the Byzantine cultural sphere. Italian merchants, in contrast, had lived in closed quarters since the twelfth century, and the Latins had assumed important positions in the army and the navy. With the aim of winning allies, the emperors had increasingly married western European princesses, who 'infected' the court with Latin influences. The *pronoia* system gained prominence in the late eleventh century. In return for the grant of income from land ownership, the *pronoiar* was required to provide military or other services, similar to western vassalage law. With time, the fiefdoms, which had originally been granted temporarily, were issued for life, and later even became hereditary. In this way, numerous Latins rose to the status of large landowners. They thus became opponents of the Byzantine nobility, which was in any case considerably less socially exclusive than that in the rest of Europe.[6] For here, nobility was not exclusively a status one inherited, but could also be acquired through recognition within noble society. Even upwardly mobile commoners and outsiders could rise to the highest offices and dignities. Since military capability permitted foreigners to rise socially, education became an important criterion for nobility among the Byzantine aristocrats. This education consisted of a symbiosis of ancient 'pagan' elements and components of the Christian faith. The society may have been deeply indebted to its own traditions, but it was more open than similar ones in western Europe. Byzantine culture and scholarship also reflected this mixture; on the one hand, it disseminated the ancient ideal of education within the Byzantine Empire and toward the west, and on the other, it radiated its influence toward Serbia, Bulgaria and Russia.

7.3 Cultural exchange

During the fourteenth and fifteenth centuries, Constantinople was the most cosmopolitan city in Europe. In addition to the Genoese quarter of Pera on the other side of the Golden Horn, there were Venetian and Pisan quarters, and smaller colonies of Provençal, Spanish, Florentine and Ragusan (Dubrovnik) merchants. Moreover, the Jewish community was involved in silk production and dyeing, as well as trade. They had a synagogue, just as the Muslims had a mosque. The court was particularly multiethnic as a result of marriages to foreign princesses. Of the last twelve Byzantine emperors, at least eight married foreigners – from Italy, Armenia, Germany, Bulgaria, Serbia and Russia, while their younger sons married into the Italian aristocracy. This reflects the political pressure under which the emperors found themselves. The emperors of the Palaiologan dynasty, for instance, were forced to travel to the west, for they could no longer wait for European princes or their ambassadors to come to Constantinople and pay their respects.[7]

John V travelled to Rome in 1369 to document his conversion to Catholicism. Manuel II journeyed to Italy, Paris and London in search of military support between 1399 and 1402. John VIII attended the Council of Ferrara in 1438/39 in the hope of building a defensive alliance against the Ottomans. In their travels, the emperors were inspired by European culture. John VIII spoke glowingly of French architecture and art, especially tapestries, and his visit to Ferrara provided Pisanello with the occasion to create the first Renaissance medal.

The Byzantine presence in the west brought the princes and artists of Europe into contact with Byzantine art. Byzantine icons had been piling up in Venice since the thirteenth century, from where they were disseminated to the rest of Europe. In Italy, northern artists such as Rogier van der Weyden in 1450 and Gossaert in 1508 were able to familiarise themselves with these works of art. In addition, the dukes of Burgundy, the French kings and the nobility of these regions acquired numerous icons. Extant

Figure 5 Gentile Bellini, *Sultan Mehmed II* (painting, 1480, oil on wood 70×52 cm).

inventories document them using the term *à la façon grèce*, although the items themselves have been lost. Sometimes, such icons were depicted and illustrated in books, before being disseminated in the form of woodcuts or copper etchings.[8] Of course, Netherlandish painters also made copies of these icons, painted under their inspiration, or integrated the motifs – such as the Virgin and Child – into their own imagery.

Although Vasari argues that Florentine art began with Cimabue, who watched Byzantine artists at work, visual commonalities in the Mediterranean area would appear to be a better explanation. Byzantine art and artists were incorporated into the visual culture of Italian trading posts, as evident in the cathedrals of St Mark in Venice and St Lawrence in Genoa. Italian humanists recognised the value of knowing Greek as early as 1400, when Manuel Chrysoloras, who taught Greek in Florence from 1397 to 1400, functioned as a source of inspiration. His students disseminated knowledge of the language and, like Niccolò Niccoli, collected large numbers of manuscripts. One of his sources was the Sicilian Giovanni Aurispa, who imported to Italy more than 200 manuscripts from the Byzantine Empire, which fell into the hands of numerous scholarly collectors.[9]

Byzantine-Islamic relations, too, were not characterised solely by religious disagreement, but also by an identity of interests among the elites in Anatolia. Members of the elite, feeling abandoned by the Byzantine Empire, entered Ottoman service and thus integrated elements of both cultures.[10] This cultural exchange would continue despite Turkish expansion in the eastern Mediterranean, for instance when Gentile Bellini painted a portrait of Sultan Mehmed II on a commission from Venice (see Figure 5).

7.4 Ottoman expansion in the Balkans

Migrating Turkic tribes had settled in Anatolia since the end of the eleventh century, and in smaller numbers in the Balkans. The defeat of the Byzantines by the Seljuks at Manzikert in 1071 and at Myriocephalon in 1176 meant that first eastern Anatolia, and in the thirteenth century virtually all of Anatolia, was settled by Turks. During the fourteenth century, Nicæa, the former capital of the Palaiologan dynasty, also fell into Ottoman hands. In the Balkans, the Seljuks and later the Ottomans ran up against South Slavic rulers who had only been partially successful in solidifying political rule over their territories. Under the Asen dynasty, the Bulgarian kingdom, with its capital at Trnovo, certainly succeeded in exploiting Byzantine weakness to expand its territory. In 1205, the Bulgars even defeated and captured Baldwin of Flanders, the first Latin Emperor. By 1231, Tsar Ivan Asen II (1218–41) had expanded his domain to include Macedonia, Albania, Serbia, southern Walachia and northern Greece, thereby founding the second Bulgarian empire after that of Symeon the Great (893–927) by proclaiming himself tsar and autocrat of the Bulgarians and the 'Romans' – i.e., the Byzantines – and restoring the autocephalous Bulgarian Orthodox Church with its own patriarchate. However, this second Bulgarian empire

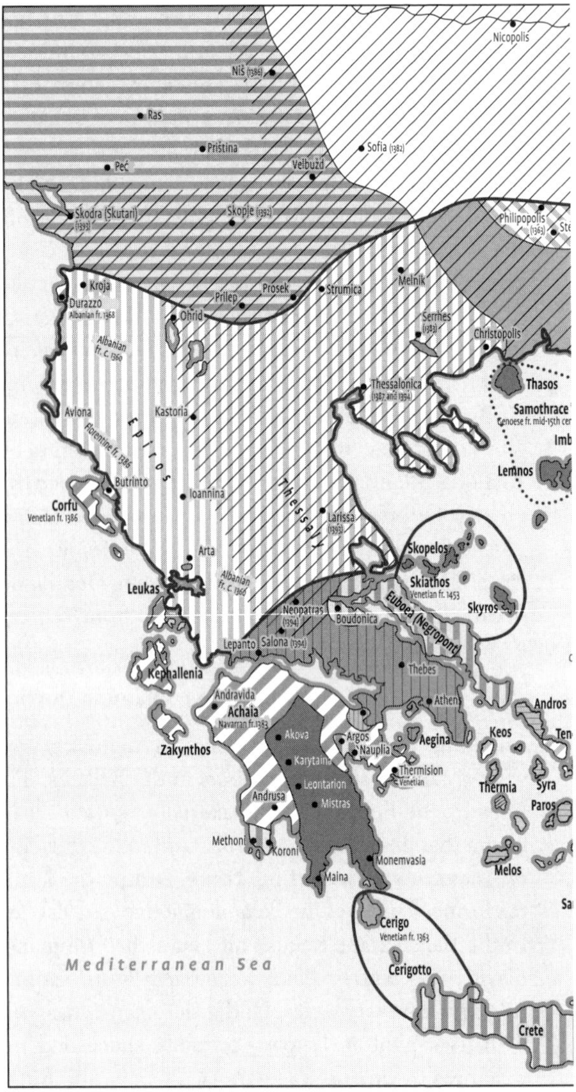

Nicopolis
Niš (1386)
Ras
Priština
Sofia (1382)
Peć
Velbužd
Skodra (Skutari) (1393)
Skopje (1392)
Philipopolis (1363)
Kroja
Durazzo
Albanian fr. 1368
Prilep
Prosek
Strumica
Melnik
Ohrid
Serrhes (1383)
Christopolis
Albanian fr. c. 1360
Thessalonica (1387 and 1394)
Thasos
Samothrace
Aviona
Kastoria
Epiros
Florentine fr. 1386
Lemnos
Butrinto
Ioannina
Thessaly
Corfu
Venetian fr. 1386
Larissa (1393)
Skopelos
Arta
Skiathos
Venetian fr. 1453
Leukas
Albanian fr. c. 1360
Neopatras (1394)
Boudonica
Euboea (Negropont)
Skyros
Lepanto
Salona (1394)
Thebes
Kephallenia
Andravida
Achaia
Navarran fr. 1383
Athens
Andros
Akova
Argos
Aegina
Keos
Zakynthos
Karytaina
Nauplia
Thermision
Venetian
Leontarion
Thermia
Syra
Andrusa
Mistras
Paros
Methoni
Koroni
Monemvasia
Melos
Maina
Cerigo
Venetian fr. 1363
Cerigotto
Mediterranean Sea
Crete

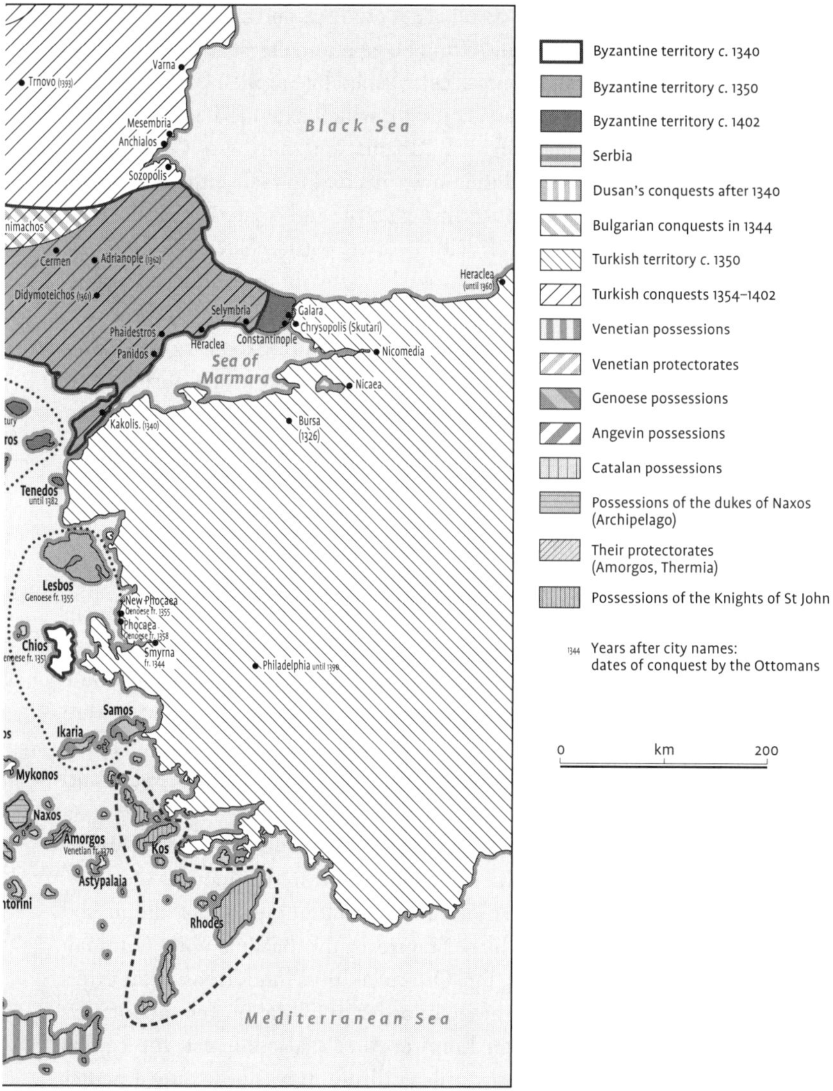

Map 13 The decline of the Byzantine Empire

did not survive the Mongol invasion of 1237 to 1242, and attempts to restore it thereafter proved unsuccessful. In 1330, its remnants were taken over by the rising Greater Serbian kingdom established by Stephen Uroš III (1321–31) and his son Stephen Dušan (1331–55), which extended across Serbia, Montenegro, Macedonia, Bulgaria, Albania and northern Greece. But here, too, ambitions exceeded the power needed to realise them. In 1346, Stephen Dušan followed the Bulgarian example and created an autocephalous Serbian Orthodox Church with its own patriarchate, and crowned himself Tsar of the Serbs and 'Romans'. His attempt to conquer Constantinople in alliance with Ragusa (Dubrovnik) and Venice failed, however. After the Tsar's death during the campaign, his empire disintegrated. The inner ties binding these states together were far weaker than Serbian and Bulgarian historians were long willing to admit. Ottoman expansion soon overwhelmed the disintegrating multiethnic kingdoms, exploiting the power vacuum both in Byzantium and in the South Slavic lands.

The Ottoman Empire had its roots in Osman I, who ruled a small emirate in north-western Anatolia around 1300, and took advantage of the decline of the Seljuk empire. In 1326, his son and successor Orhan (1326–62) conquered Bursa, which became the centre of the new Ottoman state. The conquest of the last Byzantine cities in Anatolia and an unbroken string of military successes attracted adventurers and supporters, some of whom became sultans of the rising Ottoman Empire. The latter were not necessarily Turkic or Turkish, for the Ottoman rulers often married Christian princesses in order to establish dynastic ties with southern and eastern Europe.

The growing number of warriors had to be kept occupied. Thus in 1345 the Byzantine usurper John Kantakouzenos hired numerous Ottoman soldiers as mercenaries to help him take Constantinople. He also attempted to overcome the Greater Serbian Empire in the Balkans with Ottoman assistance. During the 1350s, the Ottomans then undertook attacks on the Balkans, settling first in Thrace in order to fill the power vacuum left behind by the Greater Serbian Empire. After that conquest, the capital was moved from Bursa to Adrianople (Edirne). It was now only a matter of time before the other cities fell to Ottoman conquest. During the 1380s, the Ottomans conquered Bitolia (Monastir), Sophia, Niš, Thessalonica, Kolarovgrad (Šumen), Provadi and Novi Pezar in quick succession. In 1389 came the showdown between a coalition of Serbian, Bulgarian, Albanian and Bosnian princes and the superior forces of the Ottoman foe at Kosovo Polje ('field of the blackbirds'). In spite of some losses, the Ottomans continued their conquest of Serbian territory unhindered until

1392. They were supported not only by Christian warriors fighting on the Ottoman side, or who had changed sides, but also by princes and nobles who sought to make careers for themselves as clients of the Ottomans. Moreover, the Ottoman occupation and the resulting political stability benefited merchants and artisans, while the new rulers brought no change at all for the peasant population.[11]

The triumphal march of Islam appears interesting, for instance in Bosnia and Herzegovina, where it has been associated with the crypto-heretical heritage of the Bogomils in that region. Although the lack of Orthodox Church structures or the rivalry between Orthodox and Roman Catholic structures may have enhanced the local population's willingness to convert, Islamisation still proceeded very slowly. According to the tax register, in 1468/69 Muslims still made up less than 10 per cent of the population in Bosnia, and only in the late sixteenth and early seventeenth centuries did they constitute a majority here. Conversion to Islam certainly had its advantages for both official careers and improved legal status.

Slaves and serfs could obtain freedom by converting to Islam, which contributed to the growth of the new Muslim centres of Mostar and Sarajevo.[12] Moreover, such small states as Bosnia feared Hungary or Hungarian influence more than they feared the Ottomans. Consequently, virtually all Balkan domains fell under Ottoman control during the 1390s, at which time the Byzantine Empire consisted of nothing more than Constantinople and its immediate surroundings.

Only Ragusa (Dubrovnik), Montenegro, Hungarian Croatia and the islands of the eastern Mediterranean under Italian control, as well as the cities on the Dalmatian coast, were able to keep Muslim domination at bay, thanks to Venetian hegemony. Tamerlane's invasion of Anatolia from Central Asia provided the Balkan states with a short breathing spell, permitting them to shake off Ottoman domination. Nonetheless, Sultan Mehmed I (1413–21) was able to re-stabilise the Ottoman territories, for the peasants and merchants on the Balkans certainly had an interest in the reestablishment of a *pax ottomanica*. The Christian rulers of the Balkans turned to Hungary, which thanks to the successes of John Hunyadi was able to raise great hopes, but the victory of Sultan Murad II (1421–51) at Varna in 1444 and again at Kosovo in 1448 re-established the old power relationship, which finally sealed the fate of Constantinople.

During the following decades, the Ottomans occupied the former vassal states in Greece (1456–59), Bosnia (1463), Albania (1467–79), Herzegovina (1482–83), Montenegro (1499) and Belgrade (1521). Montenegro, Moldavia and Walachia were however able to retain a certain degree of autonomy as vassals of the Ottoman Empire. Between 1526 and 1528, Croatia, Transylvania and Hungary fell under Ottoman rule. The Venetian possessions in the eastern Mediterranean were not yet seriously threatened, but their inhabitants had to pay high taxes to finance the costs of defence. Here, a change of ruler appeared quite attractive to some.

On the Greek islands, too, the Orthodox Church felt less threatened by the Ottoman Empire than by Catholic priests. For the Ottomans, the Orthodox Church was thus an element separating the Christians on the Balkans from the Western world. Nonetheless, the Christian inhabitants of the Balkans had to pay higher taxes than Muslims, and also to contribute personnel for military levies. In the so-called *devshirme*, or 'collection (of boys)', children from the European parts of the empire were taken from their parents, raised as Muslim Turks, and trained in military schools as 'janissaries', or members of the elite military units. As military slaves of the Sultan, they were in a privileged service relationship, which often provided them with the opportunity to rise into high office, including that of grand vizier.

In the Ottoman Empire, the closing decades of the fifteenth century were marked by struggles over the succession after the 1481 death of Mehmed II, as well as by economic expansion into the Black Sea region. Sultan Bayazid attempted to strengthen economic contacts toward the north-west by occupying the ports of Kelly and Akkerman, which were frequented in particular by the Genoese. At the same time, the Venetian ports of Lepanto and Durazzo (Dures) in the eastern Mediterranean were conquered. That meant restrictions for western trade with the Black Sea ports. At the same time, the former Venetian outposts of the Ottoman Empire developed into ports in their own right. The Black Sea had become the domain of Islamic merchants, and soon of Sephardic Jews from the western Mediterranean as well. The Ottomans supported the settlement of Jewish traders after their expulsion from Spain in 1492, hoping to harness this imported know-how to strengthen the mercantile element in their port cities.

Notes

1 Schreiner, *Byzanz*, 26–30; Norwich, *Byzantium: The decline and fall*, 184–214.

2 Schreiner, *Byzanz*, 30–2; Norwich, *Byzantium: The decline and fall*, 410–43.

3 Laiou, 'The agrarian economy' 305–70.

4 Kislinger, 'Gewerbe im späten Byzanz'; Matschke, 'The late Byzantine urban economy', 454–86.

5 Jacoby, 'La population de Constantinople'; Treadgold, *A history of the Byzantine state*, 773–4, 840.

6 Schreiner, *Byzanz*, 37–8.
7 Evans (ed.), *Byzantium*, 5–15; Talbot, 'Revival and decline'.
8 Ainsworth, '"A la facon grèce". The encounter of northern Renaissance artists'.
9 Nelson, 'Byzantium and the rebirth of art'.
10 Redford, 'Byzantium and the Islamic world'.
11 Faroqhi, *The Ottoman Empire. A short history*, 73–5; Hösch, *Geschichte der Balkan-Länder*, 78–84; Kreiser, *Der Osmanische Staat*, 19–24.
12 Malcolm, *Bosnia*, 52–3, 65–7.

8

Russia

The history of Russia in the period from the twelfth century onward was characterised on the one hand by the decline of Kievan Rus', and on the other by a political shift of gravity toward the north-east. The Crusades and the decline of Constantinople already represented a severe setback to Kiev's dominant position, based as it was on control of key trading posts, and the Mongol invasion spelled the end of its political dominance. By contrast, the princes of the north, around Vladimir and Suzdal, were able to spread throughout the region by expanding their territories and later by the 'gathering' of Russian lands; Novgorod, initially their partner, later became their major competitor. This process laid the foundations of the early modern Muscovite state.[1]

8.1 The Mongol invasion and Mongol rule in Russia

While Russia appears as the principal European victim of the Mongol invasion, it was only the final link in a chain of conquests carried out by the Great Khan Temujin, or Genghis, during the first decade of the thirteenth century. After Siberia in 1207, and eastern Turkestan and north-western China between 1207 and 1211, the Mongols had conquered virtually all of China and Manchuria by 1215. Between 1218 and 1221, it was the turn of the Islamic realms of Khorezm in western Turkestan and Iran, and in 1223, the Kipchaks and the princes of southern Rus' were defeated at the battle of the Kalka. The Grand Prince of Kiev, Mstislav Romanovich, was killed in that battle. After the death of Genghis Khan in 1227, the Mongols planned new attacks in Asia and Europe. Their first victim was the kingdom of the Volga Bulgars in 1236, and in 1237 came the attack on the Russian principalities. Ryazan fell first, followed by Kolomna, Moscow, Vladimir and Suzdal and later Rostov, Yaroslavl and Tver. The advance to Novgorod in the north-west, as well as toward the north-east, was cancelled, presumably because of the impending thaw. However, in 1239/40, Chernigov, Pereyaslavl and Kiev were conquered and besieged. From here, the campaign proceeded westward; the Mongols overran Halych-Volhynia, Moldavia, the Bukovina and Transylvania, and thereafter defeated the Hungarian army under Bela IV and the German-Polish army at Liegnitz (Legnica) in Silesia in 1241. Only the death of the Great Khan Ögädäi and the fact that the victorious commander Batu had an interest in taking part in the consultation over his successor saved east-central Europe from incorporation into the Mongol empire. However, the Russian principalities of the former Kievan Rus' became subject to the Mongols, who ruled from Sarai on the Lower Volga. Faced with Mongol superiority, Novgorod, too, surrendered.[2]

The Mongols skilfully used the existing political structures to impose their might. The Russian princes were able to maintain their positions, but became vassals of the Mongol khans. They had to appear before the khan on the Volga to be confirmed in their rule. Even in this situation, the familiar succession struggles between a grand prince's sons and brothers after his death persisted. The principle of seniority remained in effect, except that the khan was now the arbitrator of such conflicts, since a precondition for occupying the throne of the grand principality was possession of a document of grace (*jarlyk*). For example, after the death of Grand Prince Yaroslav Vsevolodovich, his brother Svyatoslav and his sons Andrei and Alexander Nevsky vied for the throne. Alexander ultimately obtained it with Mongol support, and was enthroned as Grand Prince of Vladimir in 1250.

Mongol rule required tribute payments to permit the recruiting of auxiliary troops; presumably, this money was raised by a tax on households as well as commodities. In the late fourteenth century, the tribute paid was a fixed sum of 5,000 roubles; later, this was raised to 7,000 roubles.[3]

Even in the thirteenth century, the tribute payments had provoked an uprising of the Novgorod population. They forced Grand Prince Alexander Nevsky to visit the Mongol khan once again. When he died on his way home in 1263, no successor who ruled over several principalities was in sight. The Mongols now lacked a super-regional contact. As the khans searched for candidates for the grand prince's throne, the Khanate began to show signs of disintegration. The fourteenth century therefore witnessed constant conflicts over pre-eminence in Russia, with the khans acting as both participants and adversaries in the struggle.

8.2 The rise of Muscovy

The consolidation of rule varied in intensity. Especially in the north-eastern regions less affected by the Mongol attacks, signs of economic recovery were already noticeable during the second half of the thirteenth century. Some areas, including the city of Moscow, were in a favourable geographical position surrounded by protective swamps and forests, and at the same time linked by waterways to the major rivers. Many refugees and warriors from the south and south-east who had fought against the Mongols settled in northern Rus'. The growing population and their search for new sources of livelihood required territorial expansion. By the beginning of the fourteenth century, the Principality of Moscow had tripled its territorial expanse by incorporating numerous other principalities.[4] In the process, its interests collided with those of the principality of Tver, which had existed since 1254. Tver profited from its position on the Volga and its location in the far north preserving it from Tartar attacks and permitting it to consolidate a large comprehensive territory, including several cities. Muscovy now constituted a rival to Tver for pre-eminence, a potentially lucrative position because of the tribute collection that the Mongols assigned to native princes.

In filling the office of grand prince, the Khans' preference was guided by an assessment of which candidate promised to bring in the most tribute. The first dispute between Muscovy and Tver for pre-eminence erupted in 1304, when the last of Alexander Nevsky's sons died. According to the principle of seniority, his successor should have been his next younger brother, or that brother's heir. Accordingly, Michael Yaroslavich of Tver would have been the legitimate heir to the office of grand prince, but he was challenged by Yuri Danilovich of Moscow. Both sides reinforced their support bases, and sought the backing of the Golden Horde, which decided in favour of the legitimate successor. However, Michael still had to defend his title of grand prince against Moscow militarily. After his benefactor, Khan Tohtu, died, the situation was reversed. Renewed confirmation required a two-year stay in Sarai, during which time Michael's position of power in Russia deteriorated. Shortly after his return to Tver, Yuri succeeded in attaining the position of grand prince from the Khan. While Moscow was unable to enforce this militarily, Michael's attempt to obtain the office of grand prince by a renewed appearance before the Khan resulted in him being condemned and murdered. Yuri appeared to have emerged as the victor until Michael's son Dmitry succeeded, through denunciation, in returning the office of grand prince to Tver.

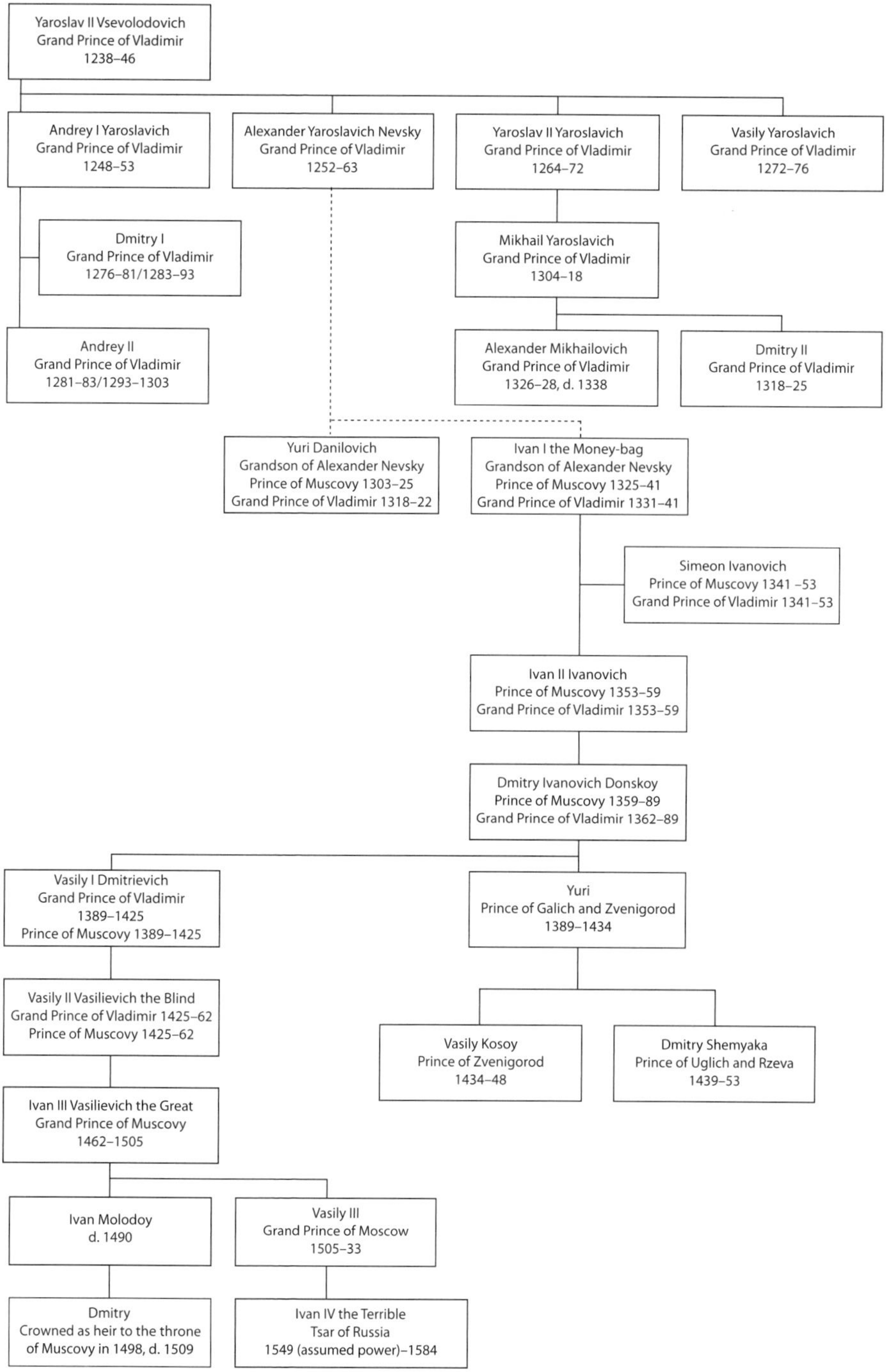

Genealogical table 7 The grand princes of Vladimir and Muscovy

However, neither Dmitry, who was executed shortly thereafter, nor his brother Alexander would be able to enjoy this office for long, since the Muscovites under Ivan Danilovich devastated Tver and other cities at the head of a Tartar army. Alexander fled to Pskov, and then to Lithuania, where he received the support of Lithuanian Grand Prince Gediminas. In 1337, Alexander even regained the title of grand prince in Tver, but during another visit to the Volga in the company of his son Fedor, both were murdered at the behest of Ivan of Moscow. This secured Muscovite pre-eminence, and the metropolitan, who had resided at Vladimir since the Mongol conquest of Kiev in 1299, acknowledged this state of affairs by moving his residence to Moscow. Thanks to his position as the tribute collector for the Golden Horde, Grand Prince Ivan (the Money-bag) was not only able to enrich himself and expand Muscovite territory, but also, as a supporter of Khan Özbeg, to permanently win the favour of the Golden Horde. His son Simon became grand prince with no major problems, but was increasingly forced to deal with Lithuanian expansion to the south and east.[5]

The Lithuanian principality first appeared on the political stage around 1250 under its ruler Mindaugas. He thrust southward to challenge the Tartars, and at the same time attempted to reach a modus vivendi with the Teutonic Knights in the west. His territory, which consisted of a number of small principalities, achieved unprecedented stability under the Gediminian dynasty, which would lay the foundations for the territorial expansion of the Lithuanian empire. The dynasty could rely on an emerging aristocratic stratum, which not only occupied castles but, as the core of the Lithuanian army, used military innovations to increase its combat effectiveness. The first objective under the new Grand Prince Gediminas (1316–41) was Kiev, which, like Smolensk shortly thereafter, was conquered and placed under Lithuanian rule. Marital ties with Poland and Halych-Volhynia led to territorial gains in northern Volhynia after the death of his son-in-law Boleslav Yuri II.[6] After Gediminas died, his son Algirdas succeeded in gaining recognition as a grand prince from his brothers, who ruled the smaller principalities. Like his father, he expanded his rule southward and to the south-east using both marital policy and war. He himself was married to the heiress of Vitebsk, which he annexed as a result. He married his daughters to petty Russian princes. Algirdas managed to defend his territorial gains against the Tartars at the Battle of Blue Waters. Previously, the Russian principalities of Chernigov, Novgorod-Seversk and Bryansk had been attached to his domain, which now incorporated approximately three-fifths of the former Kievan empire. As an ally of his brother-in-law Michael of Tver, he intervened in the conflict with Moscow, which he attempted to conquer in 1368 and 1370.

Since Lithuania's support for Tver remained half-hearted during the ensuing period, the Prince of Moscow Dmitry Donskoy, a grandson of Ivan Money-bag, was able to win a temporary victory over Tver. However, the Moscow metropolitan used Tver's alliance with the pagan Lithuanians to promote a religious mission by Moscow. At the same time, an alliance between Lithuania and the Golden Horde loomed, which Dmitry forestalled with his victory over the partners on the Don, which brought him the surname of Donskoy. The myth of the invincibility of the Golden Horde was thus shattered, even if it continued to maintain its suzerainty.[7]

Dmitry Donskoy attempted to further consolidate his Muscovite empire, which now embraced all of north-western Russia. For this reason, he introduced the system of primogeniture, and named his eldest son Vasily I as his successor. Thanks to Vasily's marriage to Sophia, daughter of Lithuanian Grand Prince Vytautas, Algirdas' nephew, the situation in the west was somewhat eased, especially since Vytautas's rival Jagiełło, Algirdas' son, entered into a union with Poland in 1385. However, this constellation did not prevent Vytautas from conquering Smolensk in 1404 and waging war on Moscow.

The crisis of the Muscovite state during the first half of the fifteenth century was self-imposed. When Vasily I named his minor son Vasily II as his successor, and Grand Prince Vytautas as his guardian, his brother Yuri, invoking the old system of seniority succession, refused to agree to the decision. After the death of Vasily's protector Vytautas, Yuri and his sons Vasily Kosoy (d. 1448) and Dmitry Shemyaka (d. 1453) began a battle for the position of grand prince. They repeatedly drove Vasily II (1425–62) out of Moscow. He was blinded (hence his byname *Tyomny*, the blind), and had his cousin Vasily Kosoy blinded in return. The Tartars too joined in these struggles, and not until 1450 could Vasily secure his position, in alliance with Tver, based on the marriage between his son and successor Ivan III and the daughter of Boris Alexandrovich of Tver. During the ensuing period, Vasily managed to strengthen his following greatly by installing trusted supporters to rule former principalities. Vasily also secured the position of grand prince for his son Ivan, and thus confirmed the principle of primogeniture, already raising him to the position of grand prince in 1448/49, to preclude struggles over the succession after his death.

Church policy during Vasily's reign was much affected by developments in Byzantium. While the Byzantine Empire saw an ecclesiastical union with Rome as the last possibility of warding off the Turkish menace by securing Christian support against the Ottomans, Moscow was decidedly sceptical about such a project. Metropolitan Isidor, who took part in the Council of Ferrara in 1439 against the wishes of the Grand Prince, and there gave his approval of the ecclesiastical union, was imprisoned by Vasily II after his return to Moscow, and brought to trial. While the Metropolitan did succeed, apparently with the approval of the Grand Prince, in fleeing to Italy, the fall of Constantinople in 1453 made ecclesiastical union a dead letter in any case. Moscow, which would not abandon the true faith, saw itself confirmed in its policy. Since the Byzantine patriarch was now under Ottoman rule, the Russian Church also became autocephalic. From 1461, Metropolitan Feodosy used the title Metropolitan of Moscow and all of Russia. However, it would be more than a century before the Russian metropolitan became a patriarch.

Around the middle of the fifteenth century, new prospects emerged for the implementation of Moscow's claim to power, for in spite of its temporary domestic paralysis, Moscow's external enemies had failed to take advantage of the situation. After finally securing his claim to leadership, Vasily II attempted to continue his territorial consolidation. His first objective was Novgorod, which had granted asylum to one of his enemies, Dmitry Shemyaka. The Republic, ruled by an aristocratic, or boyar, oligarchy (see 8.5), had been able to maintain a position of relative independence during the ascendancy of the Golden Horde, and Lithuanian attempts to incorporate Novgorod into their realm had proved unsuccessful. With the defeat of Tver by Muscovy and finally the alliance between the two former rivals, in the mid-fifteenth century Novgorod found itself without allies. As a result, Novgorod was forced by Moscow's winter campaign of 1455/56 to submit to Vasily and pay a contribution of 10,000 roubles. Henceforth, no one whom the Grand Prince considered a *persona non grata* could take refuge in Novgorod, and the Republic was barred from conducting an independent foreign policy. While in the ensuing period Novgorod attempted to withdraw from Moscow's embrace by moving closer to Poland-Lithuania, that kingdom was so preoccupied with its struggles with the Teutonic Knights and Bohemia-Hungary that it was unable to undertake any engagement on the Russian front. As a result, it was only a matter of time before Vasily's son and successor Ivan III solved the Novgorod problem to the benefit of Moscow. The occasion was the victory of the pro-Lithuanian party within the Novgorod aristocracy, which forged an alliance with Poland-Lithuania. Ivan III interpreted this procedure as Novgorod's abandonment of the true Orthodox faith, which gave him the pretext to renew the war with the Republic.

Novgorod's army was no match for the superior might of Russia, especially since no support was forthcoming from Poland-Lithuania. The leaders of the pro-Lithuanian party were executed; beyond that, the grand prince only demanded a contribution of 16,000 roubles, as well as payments of an unknown amount to Moscow's generals. The peace treaty cemented the status quo in the Novgorod-Moscow relationship, and in 1475 Ivan III once again marched his army to Novgorod in a demonstration of power. Two years later, unrest in the city directed against representatives of the Muscovite party caused Ivan III to undertake another march on Novgorod. This time, the Novgorodians were unable to retain even partial autonomy, and were forced to accept the rule of the Grand Prince over their city. In 1478, they swore eternal loyalty to Ivan, and the bell of the Novgorod *Veche*, the city's general assembly, was removed to Moscow. During the following period, Ivan visited Novgorod repeatedly to nip any opposition in the bud. Moreover, his promises to the contrary notwithstanding, he resettled thousands of Novgorod citizens on his manors, and in return granted confiscated aristocratic and Church lands in Novgorod to officials and associates from the Muscovite heartland. The final blow was the closure of the Hanseatic trading post, St Peter's Court, in 1494, which robbed the city of its last international connection.[8]

The annexation of Novgorod with its vast territories pushed Muscovy's borders northward to the White Sea and eastward to the Urals. The only remaining autonomous territories were now the small principality of Vereya-Beloozero, the principalities of Tver and Ryazan, and the Republic of Pskov. While Vereya-Beloozero could only withstand Muscovite pressure for a brief period, and the Muscovite influence in Ryazan was already very powerful, Michael Borisovich of Tver attempted to maintain his autonomy in alliance with Casimir IV of Poland. These efforts did not produce the hoped-for support, however, so that the prince was forced in 1484/85 to submit to a Muscovite diktat, which put an end to Tver's independence. Michael fled to Lithuania, the boyars changed sides, and the principality was incorporated into the grand principality. Without foreign support, Pskov was no longer viable. Since the beginning of the fifteenth century, the Republic had consistently elected Moscow's candidate as its own prince, which for Ivan III was sufficient confirmation of Moscow's influence. Only his son and successor, Vasily III, used the conflict between the citizens of Pskov and the prince in 1510 to eliminate the republican constitution and have the city ruled henceforth not by a prince selected by Moscow, but by Muscovite governors. Here, too, land confiscations and resettlements were used, which even affected the merchants, since Muscovite traders were settled in the city in place of native merchant families. The Hanseatic merchants, who had attempted to continue their trade from Pskov after the closing of their trading post in Novgorod, also temporarily left the city.[9]

Last in line was Ryazan. Here, the transition was unspectacular, since part of Ryazan's territory fell to Muscovy by inheritance. The rest was acquired by luring the Prince of Ryazan to Moscow in 1520 by a ruse, and arresting him. Now no more independent principalities stood in the way of the Grand Prince of Moscow. Only those principalities ruled by the Grand Prince's brothers could challenge his policies. Relations with the Golden Horde were largely friendly, particularly since the khanates of Kazan and Crimea split off as independent entities. As early as 1476, Ivan III had failed to obey the summons to Sarai, which the Khan, possibly encouraged by Lithuania, used as a pretext for war against the Grand Prince in 1480. However, there were no major battles that might have altered the status quo. In 1502, the Golden Horde was defeated by the rival khanate of Crimea, and thereby eliminated as a serious opponent.

After several attempts, Muscovy scored similar successes against Poland-Lithuania. At the centre of its interest were the Slavic Orthodox regions located between the two realms. The conflict was sparked by a change of rulers among the Orthodox boyars of these regions, who kept their lands, but aligned themselves with the grand prince of Moscow as their new suzerain. In a war lasting from 1500 to 1503, major areas were occupied, and the Lithuanian Grand Prince Alexander was able to hold only Smolensk. The six-year armistice confirmed Muscovy's territorial gains along the upper Daugava, and also a territory on the Desna, the so-called Severian principalities and Chernigov. Since Ivan III died in 1505, and Alexander in 1506, the situation did not change at first. Only in 1512 did Lithuania attempt to recoup its territorial losses, in alliance with the Crimean Tartars. Nonetheless, an armistice was reached which was extended several times during the ensuing period, ultimately leading to recognition of Smolensk as a Russian possession.[10]

Russia's conflict with Poland-Lithuania rendered it increasingly interesting for those European powers that were seeking alliances against the Jagiełłonian empire. Particularly during the period when Casimir IV and his sons ruled both Poland-Lithuania and Bohemia, Matthias Corvinus of Hungary attempted to push back the Jagiełłonians through an alliance with Ivan III. After the unexpected death of Corvinus in 1490, the Hungarian throne fell to the Jagiełłonian Vladislav II of Bohemia after all. The voyevod of Moldavia Stephen IV, too, attempted to forge an alliance

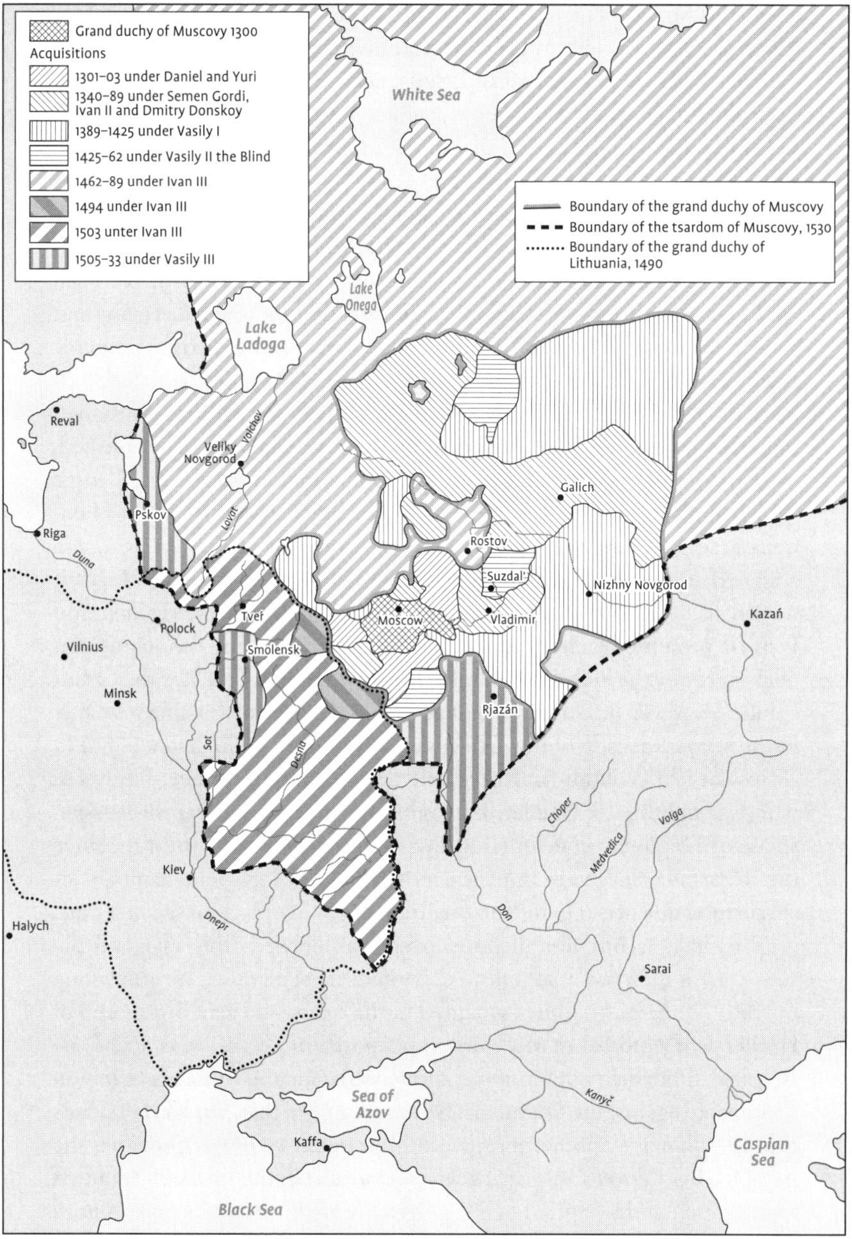
Grand duchy of Muscovy 1300
Acquisitions
1301–03 under Daniel and Yuri
1340–89 under Semen Gordi, Ivan II and Dmitry Donskoy
1389–1425 under Vasily I
1425–62 under Vasily II the Blind
1462–89 under Ivan III
1494 under Ivan III
1503 unter Ivan III
1505–33 under Vasily III
Boundary of the grand duchy of Muscovy
Boundary of the tsardom of Muscovy, 1530
Boundary of the grand duchy of Lithuania, 1490
White Sea
Lake Onega
Lake Ladoga
Reval
Veliky Novgorod
Volchov
Lovat
Pskov
Riga
Duna
Polock
Tver
Smolensk
Vilnius
Minsk
Sot
Desna
Kiev
Dnepr
Halych
Galich
Rostov
Suzdal'
Nizhny Novgorod
Moscow
Vladimir
Kazań
Rjazán
Choper
Medvedica
Volga
Don
Sarai
Kanyč
Sea of Azov
Kaffa
Black Sea
Caspian Sea

Map 14 The expansion of the grand duchy of Muscovy

against Lithuania, which he even sought to seal by marrying his daughter Elena to Crown Prince Ivan. However, Stephen remained neutral in the conflicts between Russia and Lithuania, and the alliance became obsolete once and for all when Ivan III expelled his Moldavian daughter-in-law and her son in 1502. In the period that followed, Moldavia became completely subordinate to the Ottoman Empire.

Faced with the Jagiełłonian expansion in central Europe, the Habsburgs were also desperately looking for partners, without knowing how to win over the Russian grand princes in case of need. The Breslau patrician Nicholas of Popplau, who had travelled many times through Germany and western Europe, rode from Breslau to Russia twice as the envoy of Emperor Frederick III, with the assignment of putting together alliances, and even broaching the subject of marriage ties with Ivan's daughters. Although this was viewed with great suspicion in Moscow, contact was established, and the Grand Prince sent a Greek-born diplomat in his service, George Triachaniot, to western Europe, where Frederick III and his son Maximilian received him in 1489. The imperial envoy Jörg of Thurn, who was assigned to accompany Triachaniot on his return journey to Moscow, was in fact successful in forging an alliance, in which Maximilian and Ivan III promised each other mutual support in securing the acquisition of Hungary by the Habsburgs, and in the re-conquest of Kiev by the Grand Prince. However, no common military action grew out of this alliance. Only in the second decade of the sixteenth century did Maximilian attempt to revive the old coalition and persuade the new Grand Prince, Vasily III, who was fighting for Smolensk, to support a Habsburg-Danish-Russian alliance. The treaty concluded in 1514 boosted Moscow's prestige, since the Russians managed to dupe the imperial envoy Jörg Schnitzenpaumer and use the title of tsar to refer to the Russian grand prince for the first time.

This led to countless disputes over rank between the Tsar and the Emperor in the years that followed. Moreover, Maximilian was unwilling to abide by the obligations contained in the treaty, and sent Sigismund of Herberstein (1516/18) to Moscow as an 'apostle of peace' to bring about a Russian-Lithuanian compromise, and to persuade the Russians to join in a campaign against the Ottomans. Nothing came of that, but Herberstein's travels – he made another journey to Moscow in 1526/27 – provided the basis for his *Rerum muscoviticarum commentarii*, the first well-founded and competent description of the geography, politics, religion and culture of the Muscovite empire.[11]

Russia's relationship with Livonia had changed as a result of its victory over Novgorod. Russian merchants depended on the Livonian towns as intermediaries in their trade with western Europe, and these cities often prevented the free passage of Russian and western European merchants to Moscow. With the establishment of the Ivangorod fort in 1492, Ivan created a potential threat to the Livonian city of Narva. In this situation, the Livonian branch of the Teutonic Knights, already embroiled in conflicts with the city of Riga, sought to adopt a cautious see-saw policy between Russia and Lithuania. Under its master Wolter of Plettenberg, the Order formed an alliance with Lithuania in 1501, and in 1502 defeated the Russian army. Thanks to internal Russian conflicts, the existence of Livonia was secured until the second half of the sixteenth century, when it became the object of direct Russian aggression.[12] Sweden was also confronted with Russia's new westward policy, when Russia unsuccessfully besieged Vyborg in 1496/97, in response to which the Swedes briefly occupied Ivangorod. In alliance with Denmark, Russia attempted to exert pressure on Sweden, leading to new areas of conflict during the sixteenth century.

8.3 Integration into the European system of long-distance trade

The devastation caused by the Mongol invasion decisively influenced Russia's economic development; at the same time, it opened up new possibilities for international trade under the *pax mongolica*, which created a unified economic area. Through its foreign-trade centres such as Pskov and Novgorod, Russia was affected by the European plague of 1349, and during the 1350s Moscow suffered many plague-related deaths. Even greater numbers fell victim to the plague of 1417/18, which again entered the country through Novgorod, and resulted in famine. As a consequence, most of the desertion of land and villages occurred during the first half of the fifteenth century, while the fourteenth century and the second half of the fifteenth century witnessed both economic growth and a greater density of settlements. The number of cities increased from twenty-eight *goroda* in the pre-Mongol period to sixty-eight during the fourteenth and fifteenth centuries, and the older towns expanded their economic potential. Nevertheless, only one of them, Novgorod, with 25,000 to 30,000 inhabitants during the second half of the fifteenth century, had a population comparable to that of European metropolises.

Rural settlements appeared in the areas less strongly affected by the Mongol attacks, and hitherto unsettled forest regions were colonised. In addition, settlers migrated northward from the heartlands between the Volga and the Oka. Here they encountered people of Finnish origin who became Russified with time, but the peasants opened up new lands toward the White Sea as well. The monasteries also undertook extensive internal colonisation on their growing landed property. They inherited not only occupied villages and operating farms, but also numerous abandoned sites, which the landowners viewed as relatively useless, and had therefore donated to the monasteries as a cheap means of attaining salvation. Proceeding from the inhabited settlements, the monasteries attempted to reoccupy these areas in a kind of internal colonisation process.[13] At the same time, individual monks would often abandon life in the monasteries and found hermitages in wilderness areas, which in turn became the core of colonisation efforts. Considering this monastic peasant context, it is no coincidence that the Russian word for peasant, *krestyanin*, derives from the word *christianin*, meaning Christian. Generally, Russian agriculture was marked by a large number of economic forms of ownership and usufruct rights. The average size of a peasant holding was nine to ten hectares of farmland, along with shares of common forest and pasture. The holdings would usually be passed on to an heir, with extended family use and communal cooperation, especially in the colonisation areas, being the rule. Here, land was made arable by fire clearance. Agriculture, animal husbandry and silviculture were closely interconnected.

Agricultural production initially grew thanks to the expansion of the land in use. Intensification with the aid of multi-field crop rotation is only attested from the beginning of the fifteenth century. During this period, ploughing presumably advanced from the simple hoe (*ralo*) to the double- or multi-bladed *socha*, which cut more deeply into the soil and permitted the application of fertilisers. The main cereal was rye; the only other grain cultivated in any quantity was oats. Linseed, hemp and poppies were also important crops. The raising of pigs, cattle and sheep was widespread. The use of natural resources included forest bee keeping and fishing, as well as woodworking and the preparation of forest products. Raw iron was another important ancillary source of income for the peasants. In the winter, peasants also participated in hunting, for furs were the most important export product of the Russian economy. Artisan production, in contrast, was almost exclusively to meet local needs in the domestic market. Accordingly, the principal trades were woodworking, leatherworking and clothesmaking. Moreover, Moscow developed as a centre of specialised commercial production, with particular settlements, the so-called *slobody*, specialising in the production of certain goods or services for the grand prince's court. The manors of the nobles and the Church were also integrated into commercial production. Thus, Moscow also became the most important trade centre, in no small part because it was unable to feed itself, and depended on imports of cereals from the south.

Long-distance trade was in the hands of the so-called *gosty*, who maintained contacts with the south and west by way of the north-west. The window to western Europe was Novgorod, where Hanseatic merchants primarily purchased wax, furs, flax and tallow. For example, the Veckinghusen merchant family exported some two million pelts between 1402 and 1411. In return, Russia imported textiles and salt, but also herring and especially precious metals. Since Russia had no silver deposits of its own, it relied on the flow of silver bars. Western European trading partners had to pay for a good part of purchases in bullion, because Russian exports greatly exceeded the value of imports. Thus in the mid-fourteenth century, Hermann and Johann Wittenborg paid for their purchases of furs and wax with shipments of silver. The Teutonic Knights, another major trader on the Russian market, also sent bullion to Russia as their only commodity. Silver flowed regularly to Novgorod in particular, with coins not replacing bars as the dominant means of payment until the fifteenth century. At that time, silver and gold exports were an issue debated in the Hanseatic diet, which in some cases even imposed restrictions. At the beginning of the sixteenth century, the Livonian cities expressed concern at the diets about the quality of the silver shipped from Lübeck, since the Russians were no longer accepting it in exchange for flax, hemp, tallow, furs and wax.[14]

The Muscovite pressure on Novgorod adversely affected the Hanseatic trade; after the closing of St Peter's Court, alternatives had to be found. Livonian Hanseatic cities such as Riga and particularly Reval profited from this, and at the end of the fifteenth and in the sixteenth century, their trade with Lübeck developed very dynamically. In addition to the western trade, the southern trade with the Black Sea area was also of major significance. Surozh and Kaffa (Feodosiya) were the main entrepôts, and a particular group of merchants in Moscow known as *surozhane* concentrated on commerce there. In addition to silk, through these ports in the Crimea weapons, wine and spices were obtained, while furs, wax and leather goods were delivered in return.[15]

8.4 Aristocratic society

The Russian social structure was dominated by the princes and the nobility, who ruled over the great mass of the peasant population. The concentration of nobles and princes in the north-east affected the nature of the Russian aristocracy. Originally, under the then prevailing seniority system, all princes of the Rurik dynasty had an equal opportunity to succeed to the position of grand prince. This changed, however, once the principalities of the north-east instituted primogeniture within their particular lines. The result was the pre-eminence, and ultimately dominance, of the north-eastern principalities over the rest of the country. It was also no longer possible to rise to the position of grand prince, or to have the office rotate from one principality to another. Opportunities for advancement were restricted to members of the Rurik dynasty. Princes without their own principalities sought positions at the courts of other princes, especially at that of the grand prince in Moscow. The princes of the western Russian territories under Lithuanian rule, such as the Severine principalities and Chernigov, also switched their allegiance in the fifteenth or sixteenth century and subordinated themselves to the grand prince of Moscow. At the same time, the Muscovite grand princes began appointing their brothers to rule the smaller principalities. The Russian nobility, which had emerged from the *druzhina*, the prince's retinue, and which had originally inhabited noble manors (*dvory*) around the prince's castle (*kreml*), is documented in Moscow since the fourteenth century.

The boyars constituted the highest stratum of the nobility. Since the 1330s, they had increasingly been establishing their courts in the emerging princely residence of Moscow. The boyars owned extensive heritable landed property, which they sought to expand by becoming supporters of the grand princes. In addition to the boyars, who were noble by birth, there was also a service nobility, a lower aristocratic stratum, which had been granted service manors (*pomestye*) by the princes or the grand prince. These were granted on a large scale from the mid-fifteenth century, particularly during the conflicts between the Muscovite grand princes and the principality of Tver. Later, service nobles and boyars were given land primarily in the conquered areas. Also considered members of the lower nobility were the so-called 'boyars' children' (*deti boyarskie*) mentioned in the sources, who were probably impoverished aristocrats. Generally, nobles and princes in Russia concluded contracts on the services to be rendered. At least theoretically, this gave boyars the possibility of switching from the service of one prince to that of another. Successions to the throne were one occasion when such service relationships could be terminated, and nobles could avail themselves of their right of departure.

In this way, through the restructuring of Muscovite territory, a boyar could find himself and his property in the realm of the grand prince or one of the petty princes. In order to prevent this from affecting the service relationship, freedom of movement and the guarantee of property had to be provided. During the fifteenth century, however, this developed into a one-way street leading to Moscow. For an aristocracy weakened by the division of inheritances, service for the Muscovite state became ever more attractive. The established service nobility attempted to defend itself with all available means against 'deserters' from other principalities. In order to prevent the self-destruction of the aristocracy, the so-called *mestnichestvo* system was created, in which Mongol influences played an important role.[16] It fixed the rank and offices available to every member of the aristocracy, taking into account descent, the services rendered by their ancestors, and their own service to the prince. Originally, *mestnichestvo* applied only to those persons who were mentioned in the official service list during the second half of the fifteenth century. With the migration of distinguished families to Moscow, they too had to be integrated into the existing Moscow boyar hierarchy. This led to strife over rank, in which one noble might refuse to serve under the command of another; here, only the grand prince was in a position to arbitrate.[17]

Unlike their counterparts in western and central Europe, the Russian nobility did not find Church office to be an attractive prospect. Thus a boyar serving the metropolitan was, under the *mestnichestvo* system, clearly inferior to one in the service of the prince, and the service nobles of the bishops were of course far below those of the metropolitan. To the extent one can judge from the inadequate sources, nobles consequently did not particularly aspire to positions in the Church, and nepotism and the purchase of ecclesiastical offices increased only in the sixteenth century. The fact that in Russia even bishops and abbots – unlike in western Europe – were barred from attaining positions of political power may have been a factor here.

The peasantry, who differed according to the quality of their land tenure, accounted for the mass of the population. In addition to the so-called free or 'black peasants' (*chernye krestyane*), who were settled on the land of the prince or the Muscovite state, another segment of the peasantry, the 'white peasants', lived on domain land. Many peasants in the old settlement areas, and also on Novgorod territory, became dependent on lords; in other words, 'black peasants' became 'white peasants', and were thus no longer subjects of the State. Grants, new settlements, abandoned land and bestowals of service manors reduced the number of 'black peasants', and hence their payments in money or kind.

The domain peasants, a group that also included those on Church and monastic lands, provided payment in kind and labour service to their lords. However, the latter involved mainly hauling service; corvée labour in the fields was still in its early stages. Because the peasants were increasingly unable to pay taxes, Ivan III attempted to enhance the state's peasant potential, for example by transferring the domain peasants of Novgorod to the status of 'black peasants'. Russian peasants were not yet tied to the land, and they were able to exercise their right of mobility after fulfilling all of their duties, and sometimes paying a departure fee. Nonetheless, some restrictions on the freedom of departure can be found, such as the fact that since 1460, in some principalities peasants could only exercise their right of departure during a period of one week before and after St George's Day in the autumn (November 26). In 1497, this rule was enshrined in the law code (*sudebnik*) for the entire grand principality. This was in the interest of the service nobility, since it ensured a regular income, which they needed in order to meet their own service requirements. Only in the second half of the sixteenth century were stricter measures concerning ties to the land introduced, which would then lead to the legendary institution of Russian serfdom.[18]

The lines between countryside and city were not clear-cut in Russia, since here, unlike in western Europe, no political or legal structures had emerged in the towns to distinguish them from the countryside. In Russia, it was thus impossible to move out of the domain of landlord rule into the realm of urban freedom. At the same time, the great mass of the urban population, the *chernye lyudi*, the artisans, small traders and day labourers, were certainly comparable to the 'black peasants'. They were obliged to pay taxes and provide other services for the prince, although they did enjoy personal freedom. After the aristocracy, merchants and long-distance traders occupied the top of the urban hierarchy. They were called *gosti*, a word derived from the term for foreign merchants; later the terms *kupchy* and *torgovye lyudi* were added. In Moscow and other cities, such designations as *surozhane*, i.e., merchants from Surozh or those who traded there, and *sukonniki*, for those who traded in western cloth, also existed. However, by the end of the sixteenth century these special names were replaced by more general terms.[19] Even in the specific cases of the urban republics of Novgorod and Pskov, social structures did not fundamentally differ from those in other Russian cities. Novgorod, for instance, was dominated socially and politically by thirty to forty boyar families. They owned about one-third of all the land, but also engaged in long-distance commerce. According to contemporary descriptions, they included the *zhiti lyudi*, the prosperous people, who originated in the landowning merchant stratum and the artisan class, and occupied low-level municipal offices. Next came the *kuptsi*, the merchants who had originally belonged to the political and economic ruling elite, but had been pushed out by the boyar oligarchy. By this time, only the merchant contracts with the Hanseatic League referred to the *kuptsi* as a separate stratum. The lines between them and the *chernye lyudi*, the rest of the free, taxpaying citizens of the city, were fluid. This stratum of artisans, like the strata above it, could take part in the general assembly, the *veche*. Individual members of the *chernye lyudi* likewise used their economic opportunities to advance socially. Political upheavals and exchanges of elites, such as the replacement of the Lithuanian party by the Muscovite party, in particular, repeatedly offered possibilities for social mobility.[20]

8.5 The power of the princes and the *veche*

By the time of the erosion of the Golden Horde and the incorporation of the last principalities, the Russian grand prince was the unquestioned ruler of the country. The only challenges to his power came occasionally from rival family members. The aristocracy did not constitute a political counterweight, as was the case in some western European estate assemblies. There was, however, a consultative body of the high nobility, the so-called Boyar *Duma*, which met periodically when summoned by the ruler. This council of 'clever boyars' is attested since the thirteenth century, and fifteenth-century chroniclers blame even the misfortune of the Mongol invasion on a lack of consultation with the 'elders'. Princely consultation with the boyars was thus a type of customary rule, which the princes might use more or less frequently. It appears, however, that at the end of the fifteenth century, the consultative influence of the nobility had receded markedly in favour of strengthened autocratic rule, as statements by contemporaries suggest.[21] For instance, Maxim the Greek (Maksim Grek), while emphasising the duty of the ruler to heed his counsellors, also points to the virtually divine nature of the tsar, stemming from his monarchical virtues and omnipotence. Moreover, the boyars of the Boyar *Duma* were representatives of the high nobility, who usually also held other important positions at court or in the administration.[22] This evolved into a select privy council of ten to fifteen participants, the *Blizhnaya Duma*, while Vasily III worked with only a very small group of counsellors. While the membership of the body of counsellors appears to have shrunk gradually between the fifteenth and sixteenth centuries, Ivan IV evidently called upon a larger body than the Boyar *Duma*. The concrete influence of the boyar counsellors on day-to-day politics and society cannot be judged here, however.[23] In addition to the counsellors mentioned, in *c*. 1500 initial signs of a central administration began to appear, which attempted to unify the separate activities of the princely court administration. In the country, the princely regents (*namestniki*) and officials (*volosteli*) assumed appropriate tasks. To this end, they were provided with money and goods in kind by the 'black peasants' and the townspeople.

In addition to the princely officials, numerous forms of self-administration existed, ranging from individual village communities (*mir*) and communes composed of several villages (*obshchina*) to the *veche* of the city-states. As an assembly of the citizens, representing their interests, the *veche* has attracted the particular interest of historians. The institution presumably emerged during the eleventh century as a form of urban self-organisation directed against the princes. From the twelfth century until the Mongol invasion, the *veche* assemblies played an important role as contractual partners to the princes. After the Mongol invasion, which largely paralysed urban life, the *veche* assemblies were able to develop further as constitutional organs, especially in Novgorod and Pskov. The key factor here was that, until it was conquered by Muscovy, Novgorod had never been incorporated into a princely domain, and had selected its own prince for external representation and defence, as well as for judicial functions. The contractual party was in all cases the *veche*, the assembly of all free citizens of the city, who might summon this assembly themselves by ringing the *veche* bell. Decisions were arrived at by a majority of those present.

In addition to the princes, the *veche* also elected the highest officials, the *posadniki* and the *tysyatskie*, and appointed successors to ecclesiastical office, including that of archbishop, from the ranks of the monks. Below the general assembly were the five districts of the city, which administered themselves, elected their own officials, and delegated these to the *soviet gospod*, the council of lords. It was formed by the ruling high officials, the archbishop and the representatives of the princes, together with the above-mentioned delegates of the city's quarters. The *soviet gospod*, which in the second half of the fifteenth century consisted of some fifty persons, constituted the supreme legislative and executive instrument of rule of the *veche* republic, and was dominated by the leading boyar families.[24]

8.6 Icon painting and architecture

Russian art is generally associated with icon painting. This genre of religious art presumably reached Russia from Byzantium shortly after Christianisation in the eleventh century. The pictorial programme of the newly built churches, with their mosaics and frescoes, as well as their liturgy, may have been more significant in missionary terms, but distinct schools of icon painters were already beginning to emerge in the twelfth and thirteenth centuries. The schools of Novgorod and Pskov contended for influence over northern Russian art. Since not only the icons, but also particular types of icons ordained for certain places in religious ceremonies, the liturgy of worship services, and on the iconostases (walls of icons), were precisely determined, the possibilities of artistic variation and innovation were restricted. Nonetheless, from the late fourteenth century, Russian art was influenced by innovative impulses from Greek or Byzantine artists and their schools.

Theophanes the Greek (Feofan Grek, 1325–1404/15), who was born and trained in Constantinople, and reached northern Russia via the Crimean port of Kaffa, is considered the founder of the so-called 'Moscow school'. He worked for a lengthy period in Novgorod, and later in Nizhny Novgorod, Moscow, Kolomna and Pereslavl Zalesky, before settling permanently in Moscow. His outstanding works include the frescoes in the Spas Preobrazhenie church in Novgorod, as well as his iconostasis in the Cathedral of the Revelation (*blagoveshchenie*) in the Moscow Kremlin. Some icons, however, for example the Bogomater Donskaya, which is associated with the victory of Dmitry Donskoi, are merely attributed to him.

Theophanes the Greek introduced an element of expressiveness into the hitherto largely static imagery, which was to reach its peak under his disciple Andrej Rublev (*c.* 1360/70–*c.* 1427), a monk at the Andronikov monastery in Moscow. He is supposed to have worked with Theophanes on the Blagoveshchenie Cathedral in 1405, and later on the Cathedral of the Dormition in Vladimir, as well as on the Andronikov Monastery and the Church of the Trinity in the Sergei Monastery in Zagorsk. His masterpiece is the icon of the Holy Trinity, which the 'Council of the Hundred Chapters' of 1551 canonised as a type of depiction. The proclamation stated: 'Painters will reproduce the ancient models, those of the Greek icon painters, of Andrej Rublev, and other famous painters; in nothing will they follow their own fancy'.[25] Although other artists, such as Dionisy at the turn of the fifteenth to the sixteenth century, tested the limits of the prescribed possibilities of representation in his frescoes for the Cathedral of the Nativity of the Virgin in the Ferapont Monastery in northern Russia, the reception of Italian panel and wall painting, with its three-dimensional representation of figures and space, was not possible in Russia. Since religious functions continued to dominate Russian painting, secular representation could only be expressed through other media.[26]

Accordingly, architecture constituted a field of experimentation with whose aid the Muscovite grand princes, and especially Ivan III, sought to document their position of power. To this end, Ivan engaged the Italian architect and engineer Aristotle Fioravanti (*c.* 1415/20–*c.* 1486), who had previously worked for King Matthias Corvinus of Hungary through the mediation of Milan. When Ivan married the niece of the last Byzantine Emperor, Zoë Palaiologina, who had long lived in Rome under the protection of the Pope and had been educated by the humanist Cardinal Bessarion, the Russians, too, began to show more interest in Italy. In this climate – Zoë had brought her Italian court with her to Russia – Fioravanti was commissioned to build the Cathedral of the Dormition (*Uspensky Sobor*) in the Moscow Kremlin, after a Russian attempt to erect a new structure had just failed. It was to be orientated toward older prestigious buildings such as the Cathedral of Dormition in Vladimir, with which Grand Prince Andrey Bogolyubski had already set new standards during the twelfth century.

Despite some technical innovations, such as the use of harder bricks and cement, and changes in the design of façades, the cathedral in Moscow was closely modelled on that in Vladimir. Not until the beginning of the sixteenth century would Alessio (Alevisio) Novi introduce noticeably more northern Italian formal elements such as arches, pilasters and capitals in his design for the Archangel Michael Cathedral in the Kremlin.

Nonetheless, the basic Russian cathedral type did not change fundamentally. The Italian borrowings are more clearly visible in the fortifications of the Kremlin, one of the builders of which was Pietro Antonio Solario. The Palace of the Facets in the Kremlin also recalls Italian examples. However, there was no permanent redesign of the Kremlin in (Italian) Renaissance style. Such a project would not be realised until Peter the Great – influenced by Dutch, German and French models – engaged such architects as Andrea Trezzini (1670–1743), Bartolomeo Francisco Rastrelli (1675–1744), Jean Baptiste Alexandre le Blond (1669–1719) and Andreas Schlüter (1660–1714) to build his new capital in St Petersburg.[27]

Old Russian literature had a strong religious orientation. In addition to the *vitae* of saints and monks, such as the martyrs Boris and Gleb, or Abbot Theodosius of the Monastery of the Kiev Caves, numerous biographies were translated from the Greek and disseminated in Russia. During the fifteenth century, migrants from the Balkan countries, such as Pakhomy Logofet and Epiphany Premudry, composed new hagiographic literature based on Byzantine examples. Closely connected with these *vitae* or biographies were the chronicles. Thus, for example, the Kiev monk Nestor (eleventh–twelfth century) not only wrote a biography of Abbot Theodosius, but probably also compiled the first Russian chronicle, the *Povest vremmenych let*, extant in late medieval copies. The first Novgorod chronicle of the thirteenth century was also influenced by Nestor's chronicle. The popular tales of war, which recounted the battles against the Tartars since the thirteenth century, also followed the examples of hagiography and the chronicles. Translations of antique materials such as the Alexander romance and the Trojan legends were also known in Russia. During the fifteenth century, some men of letters joined in the published debates around Church reform – without, however, creating any specific literary forms. Only the liturgical hymns might be interpreted as poetry set to music. There seems to have been no reception of Italian or humanist thought in Russia, despite the presence of Maxim the Greek, an Italian-educated humanist. Born as Michael Trivolis in 1470 in Arta (Epirus), he studied in Italy from 1492 and was acquainted with Marsilio Ficino (1433–99) and Giovanni Pico della Mirandola (1463–94). In 1502, he entered the monastery of St Mark in Florence, which he left after one year, only to enter the Mount Athos Monastery some time later as an Orthodox monk. At the request of Grand Prince Vasily III, Maximos, to use his monastic name, was sent to Moscow in 1518 to undertake translations from Greek into Russian. Although he had long since left behind the neo-Platonic teachings of the Florentine humanists, Maxim the Greek was able here to draw on his knowledge of Latin and textual criticism. He translated the desired texts from Greek into Latin, and Russian interpreters then translated the Latin texts into Russian and dictated them to scribes. Apparently, scholars of Greek were impossible to find in Russia at the time. In the years that followed, Maxim the Greek revised numerous Russian liturgical texts based on the Greek sources, and participated with polemics in the debate on Church reform in Russia (see 13.4).[28]

Notes

1 Martin, *Medieval Russia.*
2 Morgan, *The Mongols*; Saunders, *History of the Mongol conquests.*
3 Martin, *Medieval Russia*, 147–51.
4 Choroškevič, 'Das Moskauer Fürstentum', 83–4.
5 Fennell, *The emergence of Moscow.*
6 Nikžentaitis, 'Litauen', 70–2; Rowell, *Lithuania ascending: A pagan empire within east-central Europe.*
7 Martin, *Medieval Russia*, 207–15.
8 Birnbaum, 'Did the 1478 annexation of Novgorod by Muscovy fundamentally

change the course of Russian history?', 37–50, and *Lord Novgorod the great.*
9 Nitsche, 'Die Mongolenzeit', 641–3.
10 Martin, *Medieval Russia*, 302–12.
11 Reichert, *Erfahrungen der Welt: Reisen und Kulturbegegnung im späten Mittelalter* (Stuttgart, 2001), 109–12.
12 Tiberg, *Moscow, Livonia and the Hanseatic League.*
13 Goehrke, *Die Wüstungen in der Moskauer Rus'*, 63–78.
14 Khoroshkevich, *Torgovlja Velikogo Novgoroda*, 281–8; North, 'Bilanzen und Edelmetall'; Martin, *Treasure of the land of darkness.*
15 Knackstedt, *Moskau*, 109–27.
16 Ostrowski, *Muscovy and the Mongols.*
17 Rüss, *Herren und Diener*, 259–85, 390–408.
18 Schmidt, *Leibeigenschaft im Ostseeraum*, 63–71.
19 Knackstedt, 'Moskauer Kaufleute'.
20 Leuschner, *Novgorod*, 32–43; Goehrke, 'Die Sozialstruktur'.
21 Bogatyrev, *The sovereign and his counsellors.*
22 Alef, *The origins of Muscovite autocracy*, 7–362, and *Rulers and nobles in fifteenth-century Muscovy.*
23 Rüss, *Herren und Diener*, 409–39, and *Adel und Adelsoppositionen*, 106–17.
24 Zernack, *Die burgstädtischen Volksversammlungen*, 180–3; Birnbaum, *Lord Novgorod the Great*, 45–6, 91–3; Fennell, *The crisis of medieval Russia,* 18–19.
25 Quoted in Kaufmann, *Court, cloister and city*, 29–39.
26 Rakova and Rjazancev, *Istorija russkogo iskusstva*, I, 57–62, 70–3.
27 Kaufmann, *Court, cloister and city*, 30–9.
28 Sinicyna, *Maksim Grek v Rossii.*

9

Scandinavia

The history of the Scandinavian countries Denmark, Norway and Sweden was characterised from the thirteenth century onward by growing centralisation and the consolidation of State authority by the kings, the Church and the nobility, on the one hand, and protracted countervailing developments on the other. Only in the fourteenth century did the 1319 union of Norway and Sweden and later the 1397 Union of Kalmar lead to broader associations between the countries. Whether these processes were dominated by centralising or de-centralising tendencies depended largely on the relative strength of monarchs, the Church and the nobility.

9.1 The path to union

In 1227, Danish expansion in the Baltic area ended with the defeat of Denmark at the hands of the northern German princes and cities in the Battle of Bornhöved. Around the same time, after the death of Valdemar II (1202–41), a process began in which Denmark, much like Poland around the same time, disintegrated into petty principalities. In his testament, Valdemar had provided each of his six sons with part of the kingdom, which gave them independence, but also set the stage for future conflict. Abel, for example, received the territory of Schleswig, while the eldest son, Eric IV, became king. Before long, the Duke and the King were at war, resulting, after the murder of Eric, in the brief reign of Abel. After his death, the third brother, Christopher I, succeeded him; however, members of Abel's line were constantly challenging his position.

The Church too, which in the twelfth century still stabilised the Danish monarchy, now went its own way and tried to intervene in the power struggle for leadership of the country. Moreover, the weakness of the monarchy fortified the position of the nobility. Increasingly, future kings were forced to accede to the demands of the aristocracy for electoral capitulations, as Eric V Klipping (1259–86) was forced to do in 1282, for example, with the *håndfæstning*, the first Danish constitution, in which he promised regularly to convoke the so-called *Danehof*, the supreme legislative and judicial body.

After Eric's violent death, the guardians of his son and successor Eric VI Menved (1286–1319) shook off the control of the Danehof; later, Eric Menved too would prefer a council of the realm to the so-called estate assembly. At the same time, by pursuing an active foreign policy in the southern Baltic area he sought to give the country a new international perspective. These enterprises so drained the treasury that the King and his brother, who succeeded him as Christopher II, were forced to mortgage large parts of the crown domain. Since tax increases would have sparked internal unrest, and could not have been imposed without the agreement of the Danehof, the sale and mortgage of land seemed the most favourable alternative.[1] The counts of Holstein, Gerhard of Rendsburg and John of Kiel, in particular, soon held major parts of the country in mortgage, in return for backing the King. The Swedish King Magnus IV Eriksson (1319–63) obtained Scania in 1332 by redeeming the mortgage held by John of Kiel. After the death of Christopher II in 1332, the mortgage holders saw no reason to have another king of Denmark elected. Only after the death of Gerhard during a rebellion in Jutland in 1340 was the time ripe for a new monarch. The choice fell upon Christopher's son, Valdemar, who was supported by Emperor Louis the Bavarian in his function as Margrave of Brandenburg, and also by the Hanseatic city of Lübeck. To bolster his power, Valdemar IV Atterdag (1340–75) had first to redeem the mortgaged lands. He succeeded in doing so by exerting political pressure. The foreign creditors were paid off from the proceeds of the sale of Estonia to the Teutonic Knights, as well by imposing extraordinary taxes. This formed the basis of a skilful foreign policy, which aimed to establish Danish predominance in the Baltic area through shifting alliances with the kings of Sweden and the northern German princes.[2]

One important step in this direction was to be the re-conquest of Scania and the island of Gotland, where the Danish king intended to tap the economic power of Visby and the Hanseatic trade. While Valdemar soon reached an agreement with King Magnus IV Eriksson, the 'suzerain' of Gotland, the Hanseatic cities prepared for war. They had considered even the taxes levied by Valdemar after the conquest of Scania to be an undue burden on their trade, and succeeded in forming an alliance both with the new Swedish King Albert of Mecklenburg (1364–89) – Magnus Eriksson had been deposed in the meantime – and with a number of Danish magnates. Their primary achievement, however, was to unify the hitherto loosely associated Hanseatic cities – from the towns of the Zuiderzee to Narva – in the Cologne Confederation in 1367, for the purpose of taking military countermeasures. This led in 1370 to the Peace of Stralsund, under which the Hanseatic cities were able to impose unhampered freedom of trade and shipping, and also to obtain payment of damages for the expenses of the war, in the form of a mortgage on two-thirds of the income from the castles of Helsingborg, Skanör, Falsterbo and Malmö for a period of fifteen years. When Valdemar died in 1375, he was succeeded by his fifteen-year-old grandson Olaf II, issue of the marriage between his daughter Margaret and the Norwegian King Haakon VI (1355–80). After Haakon's death, Olaf also inherited the Norwegian throne as Olaf IV. Thus the unification of the two countries, which would last until 1814, was concluded. Olaf's mother Margaret took over the regency, and was elected regent in both countries after Olaf's early death in 1387.

Norway, too, underwent a rapid succession of kings during the twelfth and thirteenth centuries, and for a long time it was unclear whether they should succeed by right of inheritance or by election. Only Haakon IV (1217–63) was able to consolidate the kingdom, which included not just the mainland, but also the Faroes, the Shetlands, the Orkneys, the Hebrides and the Isle of Man. In addition, Haakon incorporated Iceland and Greenland into his realm. In the far north, he reached an agreement with the Grand Prince of Novgorod in 1252, under which both rulers reserved the right to levy taxes upon the nomadic Lapps living between the Lyngen Fjord and the White Sea. Trade agreements with England and Lübeck strengthened Norway's economic position, although it remained dependent on Hanseatic grain shipments. Domestically, Haakon proclaimed a new rule of inheritance in 1260, which stipulated automatic succession within the royal family, beginning with the oldest legitimate son. These principles, which were later affirmed and which turned Norway into a hereditary monarchy while stabilising the kingship, could also lead to the dynastic extinction of the monarchy. Under his successor, Magnus VI Haakonsson the Law-Mender (1263–80), a uniform legal code was introduced throughout the country, and the establishment of ecclesiastical courts strengthened the Church. In foreign policy, Magnus ceded the militarily indefensible Hebrides and the Isle of Man to the Scottish King in 1266.

His successor Haakon V (1299–1319) selected Oslo as his residence and as the political administrative centre for the south-east of the kingdom, while the old royal residence at Bergen remained responsible for the western part of the mainland. The move of the capital reflected a change of perspective, away from the North Sea and toward Sweden and Denmark. Haakon had only one daughter, Ingeborg, from his marriage to Euphemia of Rügen. Ingeborg was married to a Swedish prince. Thus when Haakon died in 1319, their three-year-old son Magnus inherited the Norwegian crown.[3]

The personal union between Norway and Sweden after 1319 rendered Iceland ever more peripheral. Although Magnus shared the Norwegian kingdom with his son Haakon VI (1355–80) from 1343 to 1350, he reserved the revenues from Iceland, the Faroes, the Shetlands and northern Norway for himself. Thanks to the prosperous fishing industries of these areas, this income compensated at least in part for the losses caused by the decline in the number of taxable subjects in the wake of the Black Death. Under the subsequent Norwegian-Danish union, the Faroes, Shetlands, Orkneys, Iceland and Greenland fell to the Danish Crown. The Orkneys were retained until 1469 when they served as a dowry for the daughter of Christian I, who married James III of Scotland. Iceland remained in personal union with Denmark until 1944 (albeit as a sovereign state since 1918), while the Faroes received relative autonomy in 1948, and Greenland in 1979.

Swedish politics were dominated around the middle of the thirteenth century by Earl (*Jarl*) Birger, who conducted a very active foreign policy. Although the office of *Jarl* was only the most important position aside from the king, Birger in fact determined policy. This is evident from the fact that he was able to marry the daughter of King Eric XI Ericsson, and also to marry his children to spouses of high rank. His daughter was married to Haakon Haakonsson, co-king of Norway with his father, Haakon IV, and his son Valdemar married the daughter of Eric IV of Denmark. That ensured peaceful relations with his Scandinavian neighbours for a time. Hamburg and Lübeck were pacified with royal privileges, in order to promote the trade of Hanseatic merchants with Sweden. After Eric IV died childless in 1250, Birger's son Valdemar (1250/1266–75) succeeded him as king, although Birger ran the government until his death. His second son Magnus assumed the position of *Jarl* in 1266, and quickly began to usurp the duties of his royal brother.

During the 1270s, Magnus I Birgersson (1275–90), who forced his brother from the throne and succeeded him in 1275, was able to consolidate his power with the aid of the Church and of the peasants. His good relations with the Danish royal house were strengthened by double marital ties, but were called into question again at the beginning of the fourteenth century. His son King Birger Magnusson (1290–1318), crowned in 1302, was king in name only; Marshal Torgils Knutsson (1290–1318) was the real power behind the throne. At the same time, Birger's younger brothers, Eric and Valdemar, very soon established their own duchies in Sweden and Finland, and began to act independently on the Scandinavian stage, both politically and militarily. Eric, in particular, the son-in-law of Haakon V of Norway and brother-in-law of Eric Menved of Denmark, expanded his domain in Norway and Denmark. It was only a matter of time before Eric and Valdemar would depose their brother Birger and imprison him. In a compromise, Birger was finally granted Södermanland, Närke, Öster Götland with Gotland Island, and Viborg in Finland, while the dukes received the rest of the kingdom as fiefs with full royal authority and rights of inheritance. Although King Birger succeeded in 1317 in taking his brothers prisoner, he was unable to regain overall control of the kingdom. In May 1319, Haakon V of Norway died, leaving his kingdom to his three-year-old grandson Magnus, son of Duke Eric. In June of the same year, Magnus II Eriksson was elected King by the Swedish prelates and magnates,[4] who swore an oath of fealty to him before the *Drost* (seneschal) Matts Kettilmundsson. At the same time, a Charter of Liberties was issued in the king's name, which would later be termed the Magna Carta of Sweden. It confirmed the privileges of the prelates and of the nobility, as well as the right of consultation of the royal diet and the right of the individual provinces to approve taxes.[5]

When Magnus II Eriksson took power in 1331, he attempted to avoid the restrictions of the Charter of Liberties as much as possible. He married Blanche, daughter of the Count of Namur in the southern Netherlands, and conducted an expansive foreign policy at Denmark's expense. In 1332, he accepted the homage of a delegation of the estates of Scania led by the archbishop of Lund, and at the same time redeemed the mortgage on Scania, Halland and Blekinge. In 1343, he concluded peace with the new Danish king, Valdemar IV, who renounced his claim to Scania, Blekinge and southern Halland. That same year, Magnus attempted to settle the question of the succession by having his elder son Eric elected King of Sweden, and proclaiming his younger son Haakon King of Norway. He dedicated himself to new foreign-policy objectives, and from 1348 to 1351 waged war against Novgorod for control of the Novgorod trade. These costly and largely unsuccessful enterprises damaged his reputation considerably. The resistance of the Swedish magnates grew, with an Uppland noblewoman, the later St Bridget, becoming the voice of the opposition. In 1356, an open revolt broke out, and young Eric Magnusson was first proclaimed counter-king, and later, in agreement with Magnus, co-king, as Eric XII. However, this solution was soon rendered superfluous by Eric's early death in 1359, and by a military defeat at the hands of Valdemar IV of Denmark, who captured Scania and Gotland from Sweden. In 1362, Magnus's remaining son Haakon VI of Norway was elected Swedish co-king, and accepted by his father as such. The two kings accepted the loss of Scania, and confirmed the peace with Denmark through the marriage of Haakon to Margaret I of Denmark. This new alliance outflanked the opposition, which now sought a new candidate for the throne in Magnus's brother-in-law, Duke Albert of Mecklenburg. With Hanseatic support, Albert reached Stockholm and was elected King (1363–89). Magnus and Haakon fought in vain for their kingdom; Haakon was forced to retreat to Norway. The Swedish magnates were dissatisfied with Albert of Mecklenburg, however, since he not only imposed special taxes, but also appointed his followers from Mecklenburg to the highest offices. Therefore, in 1388 Albert's former supporters offered King Haakon's widow, Queen Margaret I of Denmark and Norway, the Swedish crown, which she obtained in 1389, also by military means.

Now all three Scandinavian kingdoms, together with their overseas and island territories from Greenland in the west to Finland in the east, were united under one queen. Margaret, who ruled her realm from Denmark, was interested in a rapid solution to the question of succession. In 1388, she arranged for the recognition of her grandnephew Bogislav of Pomerania as heir to the kingdom of Norway under the name of Eric XIII. In 1396, Eric was also accepted as successor in Denmark and Sweden. In order to provide the three kingdoms with a uniform structure and lend universal legal validity to the agreements reached thus far, Margaret summoned the prelates and magnates of the three kingdoms to an assembly at Kalmar. After Eric was crowned in 1397, the details of the future government and the foundations of the so-called Union of Kalmar were addressed, and established in two documents completed in July 1397, which are still extant today. Because of their contradictory nature, the so-called Act of Coronation and the Union Document are the most hotly debated sources in medieval Scandinavian history. While the Act of Coronation describes the monarchist programme of a 'royal regime' (*regimen regale*), the Union Document reflects aristocratic desires for a 'political regime' (*regimen politicum*). Since only the Act became legally binding, the Crown emerged as the victor from the constitutional struggles in Kalmar. The ideas of the nobility and the prelates contradicted those of the Queen, who did not affirm the Union Document. As a result, the Act of Coronation was the

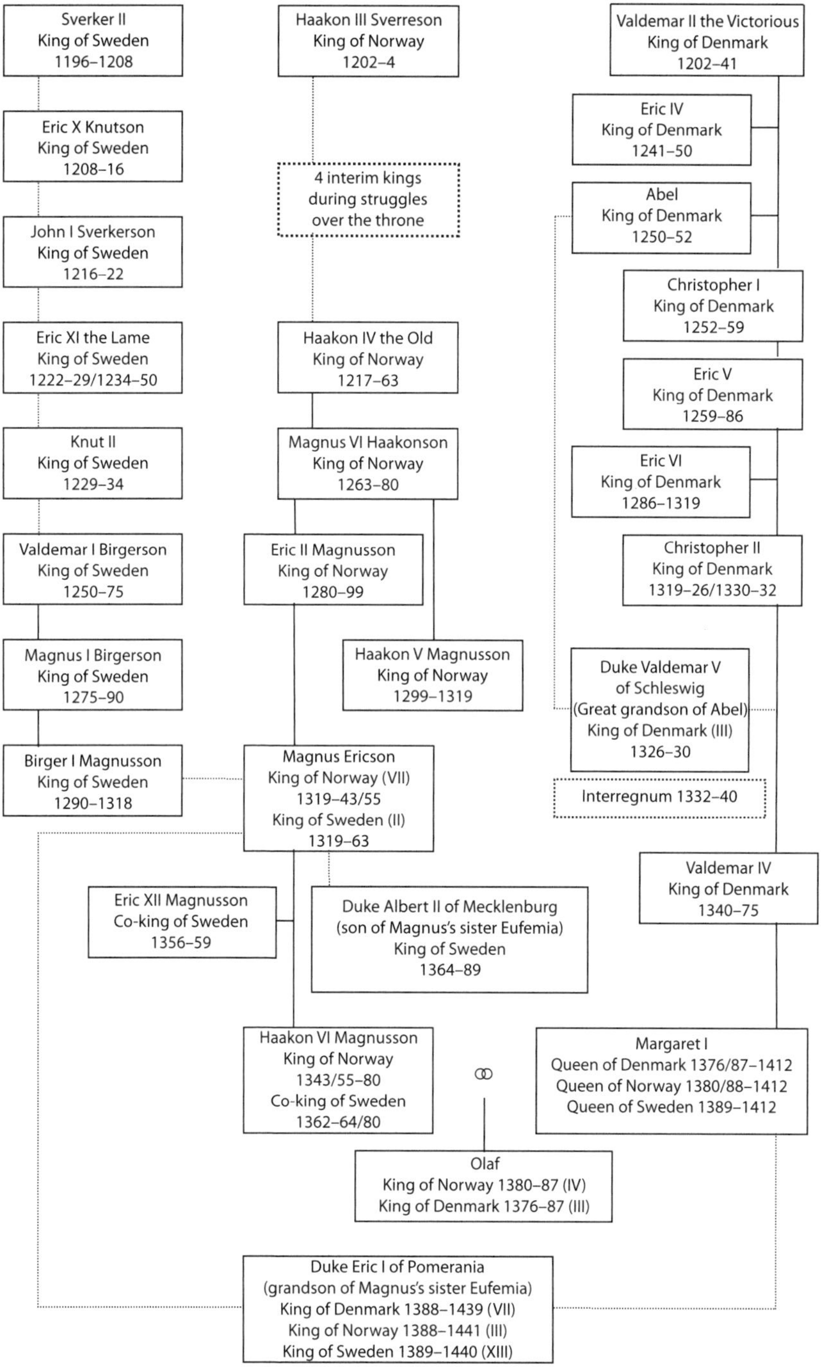

Genealogical table 8 Kings and queens in Scandinavia 1196–1441

legal basis for the rule of the newly crowned King Eric of Pomerania (Eric III in Norway, VII in Denmark and XIII in Sweden).[6]

The question of which form the union would take was to be addressed by the councils of the realm of the three kingdoms. However, neither Margaret nor her grandnephew wished to wait that long. Overall, even the traditionally anti-monarchist Swedish aristocracy accepted the strengthening of the monarchy, since the Mecklenburg threat was still present: Albert's forces continued to hold Stockholm, and had been able to withstand the siege of the new rulers with the support of the Hanseatic fleet. With their unhindered control of the royal castles, Margaret and Eric were able to impose a uniform government, and to implement closer ties between the kingdoms than had been provided for under the Union Document. As guardian and co-regent, Margaret continued to wield great influence in political affairs until her death in 1412. The government, concentrated in Denmark, profited from the augmentation of the royal finances, with Scania becoming possibly the most important asset of the Crown. The income from fiefs rose, as did that from extraordinary taxes; moreover, the restitution of crown land, too, increased the revenues of the royal treasury. Eric of Pomerania also had coins struck on the Lübeck model, the so-called *Witte* (white), which, thanks to their low silver content, were also profitable for the state coffers. Close connections to the churches of the kingdom and cooperation with the papacy with regard to the investiture of bishops also helped to fortify Margaret's rule. In this way, like her father, she intensified her influence in the Councils of the Realm, in which the bishops were the opinion-making leaders. The former Crown offices, and the offices of the *drost* (seneschal) in the three kingdoms, remained unoccupied, as did those of marshal for Denmark and chancellor of the treasury for Scania. When Eric came of age in 1400 and took over the government, the question of an international marriage alliance arose. From England came a proposal for a double marriage, in which Eric would marry Philippa, daughter of Henry IV, and Eric's sister Catherine would wed Henry, Prince of Wales (Henry V). This plan was only partially successful, in that Eric and Philippa did indeed marry in 1406, bringing Eric increased prestige beyond his united Nordic realm in the eyes of the imperial court. However, since that marriage remained childless, Eric attempted to arrange for the succession of his cousin Bogislav of Pomerania-Stolp, who was not yet of age.

Thus the question of the succession soon become an issue for his imperial policy in the Baltic region. Now, the Hanseatic cities were his partners; joint action against piracy in the Baltic helped to improve relations over the long term. In 1408/09, Hanseatic mediation was able to settle a conflict with the Teutonic Knights, who had occupied Gotland in 1398, supposedly armed with a mortgage from King Albert. Otherwise, Eric of Pomerania skilfully used the emerging competition of English and Dutch merchants in the Baltic area to play the Hanseatic cities, which were jealous of their privileges, off against one another. Moreover, he founded and privileged new cities, such as Landskrona on the eastern shore of the Sound, and extended the existing trade privileges of Malmö. Castles were built on the shores of the Sound, the most important strait between the North and Baltic Seas, to control trade and to take a share of the profits it brought. Beginning in 1429, a toll of one noble per ship, the so-called Sound dues, was collected from every ship passing through the straits. This fee, which was collected until 1857, would become the most important source of revenue for the Danish Crown in the centuries that followed.

However, the toll repeatedly led to conflicts with Lübeck, until the city received the privilege of toll-free passage through the Sound in 1435 (see 5.12). The problem of Schleswig also remained unresolved. Here, the counts of Holstein held major crown lands in mortgage, which they withheld from redemption and restitution. The counts of Holstein ignored a 1413 resolution of the Danehof, confirmed by Emperor Sigismund two years later, according to which Schleswig was to be returned to the suzerainty of the Danish Crown on the grounds of 'felony' (breach of trust to one's feudal lord). Since several military actions proved unsuccessful, Eric was forced in 1435 to grant an armistice to Duke Adolf VIII of Holstein, in which he confirmed him in his possession of Schleswig. The real conflicts, however, would erupt in Sweden. There, a revolt against the Danish seneschals broke out in the mining region of Dalarna in 1434 under the leadership of the mine owner Engelbrekt Engelbrektsson, which the Swedish magnates instrumentalised in their opposition to the monarchs.[7] To pacify the situation, Eric summoned an assembly of the union councils to Kalmar in 1436. A document of reconciliation was drawn up, based on a reinterpretation of the Union Document of 1397. It stipulated that all castles and offices were to be occupied by local notables, after consultation with the council of the realm of the respective country. The union with a single government was thus converted into a confederation of three independent kingdoms. However, it was already too late to implement the stipulations of Kalmar, since Eric was unwilling to leave his refuge in Gotland for more than a brief period. The Swedish estates assembled under the leadership of Marshal Karl Knutsson Bonde, and undertook the redistribution of the

Map 15 Scandinavia during the Kalmar Union

castles and offices. At the same time, they got rid of their allies by executing several leaders of the uprising.

Since Eric was still not interested in any accommodation with the Swedish estates, Karl Knutsson became the de facto ruler of the kingdom. Eric for his part sought support from the Teutonic Knights, the Prussian Hanseatic cities and his Pomeranian relatives, and for a time his position in Denmark seemed to improve, and there were even signs of a relaxation of tensions in his relationship with Sweden. However, the negotiations failed as a result of Eric's insistence that Bogislav of Pomerania be installed as his successor, or as regent in his place. In this situation, Eric withdrew to Gotland, and the Danish and Swedish councils agreed in July 1438 to a new Treaty of Union based on the Union Document of 1397. In Denmark, Eric's nephew Christopher of Bavaria was ready to assume the kingship, but was not elected regent until 1440. Thereafter, all that remained to Eric was his inherited kingdom of Norway, but the Norwegians too held fast to their union with Denmark and Sweden, and exerted pressure on Eric. The Swedish estates then also elected Christopher as king in 1440; in a privilege granted upon his accession, he accepted their demands. In 1441, he was proclaimed king in Stockholm, and later crowned in Uppsala Cathedral. Karl Knutsson was still the strong man behind the scenes, but Christopher was nevertheless able to build up an aristocratic clientele, even in Sweden. In June 1442, Christopher was crowned in Oslo, and on New Year's Day 1443 in Denmark, as Christopher III. Thus was the Nordic Union re-established, with Christopher of Bavaria as King of all three kingdoms, and the councils reinstalled as the actual rulers of each kingdom.[8] However, Christopher died in 1448 without an heir, so that the union was once again at issue. That same year, at the behest of Duke Adolf VIII of Holstein, Denmark elected his nephew Christian I of Oldenburg to the kingship, thus founding the dynasty that would rule Denmark until 1863. In Sweden, the upper nobility elected the strongman Karl Knutsson as king. Historians have interpreted this election as an expression of both a conflict between union and nationalism, and one between royal regime and political regime. The issue, however, was not so much nationalism, which is more a projection back into the fifteenth century of modern antagonisms between Sweden and Denmark, as the political power struggle between various noble groupings in Denmark and Sweden.[9]

Since both rulers had claims to Gotland and Norway, the union was in great danger. Karl Knutsson also succeeded in having himself crowned King of Norway, but since he could neither permanently conquer Gotland, nor maintain the upper hand in Norway, the Norwegian council of the realm declared his coronation invalid, so that the newly elected Christian could also be crowned at Trondheim in August 1450. At assemblies in Halmstad and Bergen, the Norwegian and Danish councils of the realm laid new groundwork for a union under which the two kingdoms would be united in a personal union, but would be autonomous and equal. In view of the Danish-Hanseatic alliance, Sweden was also willing to accept peace with the Danish-Norwegian union. During the 1450s, the balance of power shifted in Christian's favour. Numerous Swedish royal counsellors under the leadership of the Archbishop of Uppsala, Jöns Bentsson Oxenstierna, rebelled against Karl Knutsson, who was forced to flee to Danzig. In 1457, Christian I was elected King of Sweden after affirming the agreements hitherto arrived at in the constitutional guarantees. However, rebellions soon broke out against the new King, when he levied taxes, and Karl Knutsson Bonde returned to the throne in 1464/65 and in 1467.[10] After Knutsson's death in 1470, new perspectives opened up for Christian. The council of the realm was split, with the Oxenstierna party voting for Christian, and the rival party, led by Karl's nephew Sten Sture and supported by a number of inland provinces as well as by the citizens of Stockholm, calling for a Swedish solution. Although Christian was able to gain some support, Sten Sture was nonetheless considerably more popular among the Swedish population, and was able to mobilise enough troops to defeat Christian at the Battle of Brunkeberg near Stockholm in October 1471. In that struggle, many Swedish magnates such as the Oxenstiernas and the Vasas, as well as the peasants of Uppland, had fought on Christian's side, while Sture could count on the old Engelbrekt supporters – the mine owners, miners and peasants of Dalarna, as well as the citizens of Stockholm. Here, propaganda against the 'Danish-dominated union' fell on fertile ground. Since some members of the Swedish council of the realm still supported the idea of union, however, Christian and all succeeding Danish kings into the seventeenth century continued to maintain their claim to the Swedish throne.

Christian met with greater success in the southern part of his realm. When the Schauenburg family in Holstein died out, Christian was elected Duke of Schleswig and Count of Holstein by the knights in Ripen (Ribe) in 1460. The Treaty of Ripen stipulated the unity and indivisibility of Schleswig and Holstein, and the right of the knights of Schleswig-Holstein to participate in ruling the country. The phrase in the treaty '*up ewich ... ungedelt*' (united in eternity) was to become the basis for the constitutional structure of Schleswig-Holstein, especially after it was conjured back from oblivion during the Danish-German disputes of the nineteenth century. In fact, however, after Christian's death, his sons John and Frederick agreed to a division of Schleswig and Holstein, so that each of the duchies was divided into royal and ducal portions, which were not clearly delimited from one another. King John I (1481–1513) was recognised as king not only in the duchies, but also in all three kingdoms, but the modalities of the reintegration of Sweden into the union had not yet been settled.

In Sweden, the regent Sten Sture increased his power to such a degree during the 1470s that, in spite of the agreement reached at Kalmar in 1483 to elect John king of Sweden (as John II), he was able to prevent his assumption of government for several years. After Gotland had been conquered by Denmark in 1487, King John moved to solve the problem by military means. In an alliance reached in 1493 with Ivan III of Moscow, who sought to expand to Karelia, Sten Sture came under pressure in Finland. After this plan proved unsuccessful, and an armistice came into force in 1497, King John invaded Sweden with Danish and Norwegian troops, together with German mercenaries, and achieved his coronation by force of arms. When the Danish army suffered a serious defeat at the hands of the Frisian peasant republic of Dithmarschen at Hemmingsted in 1500, rebellion in Sweden broke out anew. In 1501 the council of the realm complained about foreign seneschals, illegal taxation and the threatened loss of Karelia to Russia. Against this Swedish opposition, John was able to hold only Kalmar and Borgholm Castle on the island of Öland. The death of Sten Sture in 1503 failed to alleviate the conflict, since the alliance of the peasants and mine owners of Dalarna with the citizens of Stockholm remained unshaken. Only the support of Lübeck appeared for a time to hold out the possibility of compromise with Sweden. However, after Lübeck and the other Wendish (i.e., north and north-east German) Hanse towns switched their support to Stockholm, the King lost his last bases of support in Sweden.

When King John died in 1513, the conflict erupted in earnest. His successor, Christian II, who had connections with the Low Countries, not only attempted to restrict the Hanseatic League with the support of Dutch shippers and merchants, but also to seize the Swedish throne by force. The latter enterprise was supported by the development of a pro-union group in the Swedish council of the realm, which, under the leadership of the new archbishop of Uppsala, Gustav Trolle, turned against the increasingly powerful Sture party. When the dispute between the archbishop and the regent Sten Sture escalated, Christian II saw a welcome opportunity to intervene. Initial attempts at military intervention in 1515 and 1518 failed, but in 1520, mobilising all the resources of the kingdoms of Norway and Denmark, Christian managed to conquer all of Sweden. This success was facilitated by the fact that Pope Leo X had placed a ban on Sten Sture the Younger, and an interdict on all of Sweden, for the imprisonment of the archbishop by Sten. In November 1520, Christian II was crowned king, and Archbishop Gustav Trolle pronounced the clerical, noble and urban supporters of Sten Sture to be heretics; some eighty of them were then executed on the Stortorg (great square) in Stockholm.

This 'Stockholm bloodbath' permanently undermined the King's position. The people of Dalarna rallied behind the young noble Gustavus Vasa, who had escaped from a Danish prison, and were joined by a large part of the Swedish lower nobility. In 1521, Vasa was elected regent, and in 1522 received the support of the Hanseatic cities, which permitted him to take the coastal fortresses which had hitherto remained faithful to Christian. In June 1523, the Swedish royal diet elected him king as Gustavus I, thus putting an end to the reconstitution of the union. In Denmark, Christian II had already been deposed by the Danish council of the realm in January 1523 after a rebellion by the nobility, and his uncle Duke Frederick I of Schleswig (1523–33) was elected king in his place. Christian fled to the Netherlands, where, while he failed to obtain an alliance, he was given money to hire ships and mercenaries. With these forces – despite their decimation in a storm – he besieged Akershus Fortress near Oslo in 1531. However, Frederick succeeded in preventing further conflicts by luring his nephew Christian to Denmark and keeping him imprisoned for the remaining twenty-eight years of his life.

9.2 Councils of the realm and offices

By the end of the thirteenth century, the legal and institutional foundations had been laid for all three Scandinavian kingdoms. The Code of Jutland, proclaimed by King Valdemar II in 1241, made the king the preserver of the law and at the same time the legislative authority. In 1274, Norway received its national law code, which was supplemented by the *Hirđskrá*, specifying the rights and duties of vassals. In 1296, with the Code of Uppland, Sweden also obtained a legal code. Another common feature of the Scandinavian kingdoms during the centuries that followed was the virtual absence of an estate system. Instead of large estate assemblies, or a parliament, as in England, the country was represented by a council of the realm, an assembly of prelates and magnates with a number of different functions.

In Denmark this assembly – known as the Danehof – initially met annually, and evolved into the highest legislative and judicial authority. Especially during periods of weaker royal authority, or of conflicts with the upper nobility, the kings were often forced in the documents (*håndfæstning*) they issued upon assuming power to guarantee the regular summoning of the Danehof. This body was thus not merely a legislative organ, but also a court at which nobles were tried, and the highest court of appeal. At the same time, a rival body appeared in the form of the royal council which, since the perpetual peace of 1377, in effect assumed the tasks of jurisprudence previously exercised by the Danehof. In Sweden, the 1319 Charter of Liberties certainly corresponded to the Danish electoral capitulations. Accordingly, the assembly of the nobility and the higher clergy evolved from a royal council (*concilium regis*) into a council of the realm (*concilium regni*). According to the royal electoral law, which was incorporated into the Swedish national law code in 1350, each new king could appoint his council of the realm. The eligible officials included the archbishop of Uppsala as well as the bishops and the secular nobility. The membership numbers changed up to the time when all Swedish bishops as council members and the Swedish council of the realm were declared irremovable. A precondition for participation was birth in the kingdom (*indygenat*, see Chapter 6).

In Denmark and Norway, the king could also appoint members of the council, while in Sweden, membership apparently required co-optation by the council. In Denmark, the bishops and certain abbots were automatically members of the council. After the Union of Kalmar, the power of the councils of the realm seems to have grown substantially, at least during the negotiations of 1397. However, Queen Margaret's successful policy caused their political influence to decline at first. While the councils of all three kingdoms were summoned to Kalmar in 1397, they now assembled for visits by the Queen to Sweden or Denmark, often at Helsingborg Castle. Generally, however, as in Norway, only those who could do so at short notice attended the assembly. Since the central administration continued to be located in Denmark, such issues fell outside the control of the councils of the realm.

Only after the Engelbrekt rebellion in Sweden and the deposition of Eric of Pomerania did the councils of the realm acquire new duties under Christopher of Bavaria. In the union of the three kingdoms that now developed, they held the leading position; they were no longer royal bodies, but rather institutions that both ruled the kingdom and represented its people. This altered the relationship between the council of the realm and the king in the various countries.

In Denmark, where the central governing apparatus continued to be located, the interests of the forty or more counsellors of the realm from the high nobility overlapped with those of the king. The councillors of the realm, who assembled several times a year at the king's invitation, were for the most part royal officials, who otherwise resided throughout the kingdom. Their gathering at court stimulated their sense of common identity, which was reinforced by the placement of trusted associates in the bishoprics. Accordingly, the older regional and state assemblies of Jutland, Zealand and Funen, known as *landsthings*, generally backed the king. In Norway, where the high nobility consisted of only a few families who depended on the other Scandinavian peers for marriage partners, Church representatives dominated the council of the realm, and during the second half of the fifteenth century they usually supported the policy of the Danish kings. Only in Sweden, where local candidates contended for power with the Danish kings, was conflict between the council of the realm and the royal authority endemic. Here, powerful noble parties and their clienteles determined policy, so that the kings were often only able to establish their authority by military force. Moreover, in the Swedish council of the realm, it was not the clerical but the secular nobility that dominated numerically.

The gentry of Finland, which was part of Sweden, rarely participated in assemblies, but were informed of the decisions, and if necessary assembled separately. What is more, the assembly of the council of the realm could be expanded to an assembly of all estates of the entire kingdom. This occurred in political crisis situations such as the 1430s, when the council of the realm summoned the nobles of the whole country, together with the representatives of the cities and rural communities, in order to fortify its position. From the 1460s, these assemblies could certainly be considered precursors to the royal diet (*Riksdag*). Several of these varied, not yet uniformly structured assemblies were even held in Åbo (Turku), Finland, such as that convoked in 1457 to confirm the election of the king; here, the nobility, the cities and the peasantry alike were included.

At the local level, the administrations in the Scandinavian kingdoms were very similar. The administration of the districts (*len*) was of interest to the king and the native nobility. The districts were of several types. Some of them could be bestowed by the treasury without regard for aristocratic approval, while others served as compensation granted by the Crown for real or fictitious services. The office-holder was the king's representative in military, fiscal and judicial matters, and could combine his office with his private domain. In Norway, too, those of the narrow aristocratic stratum often enhanced their domains by controlling royal land. Here, regional administration was in the hands of the castellans of Bergenhus and Akershus (Oslo), most of whom were not native Norwegians, and exercised their administrative authority with the aid of seneschals in the country. In Sweden, the most important castellan offices – such as Stockholm, Västerås, Kalmar, and also Åbo – proved to be prestigious positions of power for their incumbents, although they provided little in the way of economic profit. The tasks of office-holders included keeping the peace, overseeing tax collection and performing judicial duties.

Taxation developed in the Scandinavian kingdoms particularly in the twelfth and thirteenth centuries, and standard and regularly levied duties were established relatively rapidly. In Denmark and Sweden, these were based on the transformation of peasant military service into taxes. In Norway, peasant military service was retained but, around 1200, the fulfilment of that duty was transformed into a periodic tax. Although the peasants rebelled against this ever more frequently, a compromise was reached in 1270, to the effect that in peacetime, the tax would only be half the amount due in times of war. This permitted the maintenance of the emerging cavalry-based armies. Domestic considerations were also important, however. Since Viking raids no longer brought new wealth into the kingdoms in the form of plunder, the states had to rely on domestic financial resources. This led to a development that had already been concluded in most European countries, whose example the kings followed in their levying of extraordinary taxes. For example, Eric IV of Denmark attempted to introduce a plough tax in Scania in 1249, but was unsuccessful in the face of peasant insurrection. Extraordinary taxes could not be levied without the support of the nobility, which gave the emerging council of the realm numerous possibilities to lodge objections. During the ensuing period, only Queen Margaret seems to have succeeded in transforming the extraordinary Swedish taxes into regular taxes, payable in cash and in kind. To this end, she established a tax register for the entire country, possibly drafted by foreign officials, for the Danish Crown profited most from the information. As a result of this development, no extraordinary taxes were levied for some time. Around the middle of the fifteenth century, the Danes were increasingly burdened by extraordinary taxes, while Sweden, which was by now independent de facto, reduced its tax demands by one-third. This was the reason for which Karl Knutsson lost his crown when he demanded these taxes again. The Danish kings, too, faced resistance. Their financial basis continued to be the Danish districts as well as taxation of the cities, general consumption taxes and customs duties. Moreover, the Danish kings had direct access to the capital market through a money market known as the *Kieler Umschlag*, held once a year in Kiel.[11]

In addition to the financial administration, dispensing justice was an important local duty. In Denmark, it was carried out in the various provinces at the so-called *landsthings*, or provincial assemblies, chaired by an aristocratic judge, the *landsdommer*, often with aristocratic assistants. The *landsthings* had an important function in turning royal or council decisions into law. A royal decree could only come into force once it had been accepted by one of the prestigious *landsthings* of Lund (Scania), Ringsted (Zealand) or Viborg (Jutland). The judicial function in Denmark was thus assumed by the king, the justice of the realm, and the nobility, while in Norway, peasant society had its own system of justice. Here, the local *thing* was important as a court of law and as a place of assembly for the peasantry, or for negotiations between the peasants and royal representatives, with peasant assessors assisting the royal judges. In Sweden, the situation was different, since in place of a provincial *thing* there was an annual court date at which a bishop and a judge elected from the local nobility adjudicated in the king's name. There were variations from province to province, however. In Norrland, Finland and Dalarna, free peasants predominated and, as in Norway, held fast to their old *thing* system of justice.[12]

9.3 Losses of population and settlements

Our information on the demographic development of the Scandinavian countries, like that for the rest of Europe, is quite rudimentary. However, it is relatively clear that the population increased continually during the Viking period and thereafter, up to around 1330. Only for Norway can population development be estimated more precisely, since we can determine the number of farms there more precisely than elsewhere, from the settlement pattern of separate individual farms, the names of which have survived in many cases. At the end of the Viking period, there were approximately 31,500 peasant households in Norway, the average size of which, including slaves, can be estimated at between five and six persons. Presumably, no more than 1 or 1.5 per cent of the population made a living from pursuits other than agriculture at this time, yielding a total population of some 185,000 persons. Around 1330, Norway had 73,000 farmsteads, and the average household size may have been reduced to 4.5 persons, which would mean a peasant population of 328,500 persons. Assuming an additional non-peasant population of 5 per cent, this would mean a total of 345,000 inhabitants.[13] The population of Norway had been increasing continually since the Viking period, and the settlements had at any rate moved northward.

In Denmark and Sweden, the population also grew during this period, although exact calculations are impossible. Nonetheless, around 1300, the population of Denmark living within today's boundaries was probably between 600,000 and 700,000, but approximately 1,000,000 within the boundaries of the medieval Danish kingdom, which included Scania and Schleswig. Sweden without Finland may have had between 500,000 and 650,000 inhabitants at this time.

The Black Death and its impact on Norway have been closely studied. Presumably the plague arrived in late 1348 or early 1349, and spread rapidly along the coast from Bergen. Additional waves of plague are attested for 1370, 1371, 1379, and 1391/92, and then again in the fifteenth century, in 1452, 1459 and 1500. The loss of population was immense. Based on the tax register of 1520, it appears plausible that between one-half and two-thirds of the medieval farmsteads were abandoned, implying a population loss of between 30 and 60 per cent. Only in the sixteenth century would signs of population and settlement growth be seen again. In Denmark, the plague struck in 1350, although the exact losses cannot be calculated. Further epidemics are attested for 1360, 1368/69, 1379, 1412/13 and 1460. One symptom of the population decline is the abandonment of 143 churches by the end of the sixteenth century, most of them in Jutland, where one-third of churches were no longer in use. Here, the population seems to have recovered during the sixteenth century, but it was not until the seventeenth century that it appears to have returned to its level during the High Middle Ages.

The plague came to Sweden in 1349/50; outbreaks are also documented for 1359, 1412/13, 1420, 1422, 1439, 1450, 1455 and 1469. Even the royal family was not spared. However, the Swedish population had already begun to increase again during the fifteenth century, so that the levels of 1300 had been reached by around 1570. In Finland, only the coastal strip was affected by the plague, and the population rose continually from 1400 to the middle of the sixteenth century, when it reached between 250,000 and 300,000 inhabitants.[14] Iceland escaped the plague by cutting off its maritime ties with Norway; its population around 1300 was between 32,000 and 39,000 inhabitants. If any of them fell victim to the plague of 1402/04, the population probably recovered during the fifteenth century. The situation in Greenland is interesting, where 500 Scandinavian settlements, including 300 to 400 farmsteads, are attested for the Middle Ages. This population, estimated at 2,000 to 3,000 persons, died out entirely during the ensuing two centuries, without any sign of the plague or other diseases. The cause must therefore have been a different one: since the Scandinavian settlers in Greenland lived from animal husbandry, hunting and fishing, and had to import all of their grain, the loss of population appears to have resulted from an interruption in trade, isolation from the mother country and the collapse of agricultural resources in the face of a worsening climate.

Only Norway saw a similarly dramatic decline in settlement patterns. A Scandinavian research project on abandoned settlements conducted during the 1960s and 1970s produced a wealth of new findings.[15] Even though settlement losses of approximately 60 per cent can be ascertained here, the degree of abandonment differed from one region to the next. The regions most strongly affected were those with poorer natural resources for agriculture, where up to 80 per cent of farmsteads vanished. In the coastal regions, by contrast, fishing provided an alternative, which delayed the process of abandonment. Although the plague was long assumed to have been the main cause of the abandonment process, other factors also seem to have played a role. Between 1340 and 1365, for example, the climate in Scandinavia was particularly harsh, which affected agricultural activity, and may have forced the abandonment of farmsteads located inland at higher altitudes. Moreover, the separate farms of nuclear families, which were the dominant settlement form, were more strongly exposed to the plague and the impact of nature than the villages of other Scandinavian countries.

In Denmark, the process of abandonment seems to have been less pronounced, and to have differed in intensity from region to region. While in Jutland, the infertile areas west of Haderslev and Åbenrå in Schleswig were deserted, there were few abandoned villages in the fertile regions near Århus and on the islands of Zealand, Falster and Funen. Here, in the rare cases where villages or fields were deserted, the land was successfully used to raise oxen. Moreover, in the coastal areas, fishing and trade were important sources of livelihood. Scania, the most fertile region in Scandinavia, showed no signs of abandonment at all. However, less is known about the development of settlement in Sweden. While some 30 to 40 per cent of settlements in Småland were abandoned, only 16 to 21 per cent of those in Värmland, and only 5 to 10 per cent of the medieval farmsteads in Vester Götland and Södermanland were disused in 1550.

In addition to abandonment, however, colonisation and settlement also occurred in eastern and northern Scandinavia. In Finland, northward settlement proceeded apace. The division of holdings stimulated new settlement in forests and wilderness areas. Moreover, extensive new settlement took place in northern and southern Karelia, in the river valleys and along the coast of the Gulf of Bothnia. Kings Magnus IV Eriksson and Eric of Pomerania (Eric XIII) in particular promoted colonisation efforts with the aim of strengthening these regions in the face of the expansion of Novgorod and Moscow. The financial aspect was an important factor in all of these settlements, as it was in all land-development measures.[16] These undertakings were matched by corresponding efforts in Russia, where northward settlement pushed ahead in spite of minor outbreaks of disease.

9.4 Land distribution and economic structures

In Scandinavia, agriculture determined the feudal system to a far lesser degree than it did in western and central Europe. In pre-feudal systems of land use, both large landowners and small peasants could dispose freely of their land, pass it on to their heirs, or sell it. Generally, however, land was considered family or clan property, which limited the possibility of sale outside the family. Feudal elements were present nonetheless, as evident for example in the dispute in Denmark over whether Church lands were royal fiefdoms or not. In Denmark, the feudal system was more advanced than in the other Scandinavian countries.

The favourable system of land titles and inheritance was long regarded as an outgrowth of conditions in prehistoric Scandinavia. Nonetheless, inheritance law became differentiated during the Middle Ages. While legislation in Denmark, eastern Sweden and Norway favoured the division of holdings after 1274, single inheritance predominated in the fertile farming regions of central Sweden. The fact that land ownership was widespread in Scandinavia did not, however, mean that all owners, be they peasants or nobles, owned their land according to the same legal conditions. With the introduction of new military technology, particularly of cavalry armies, the traditional duties of the peasants to equip ships with crews and provisions was transformed into a land tax for the support of the cavalry. Only the

Table 3 Distribution of land in Scandinavia *c.* 1520 (per cent)

Region	*Freehold*	*Crown*	*Nobility*	*Church*
Danish realm	*c.* 15	10–12	35–40	35–40
Norway	30	7	15	48
Iceland	53	2	—	45
Sweden	45	6	24	25
Finland	93	1	3	3

Source: K. Helle (ed.), *The Cambridge history of Scandinavia*, vol. 1, p. 583.

landowners, who themselves performed service in the cavalry, were free of that duty. In this way, a privileged noble stratum emerged in all three kingdoms during the second half of the thirteenth century. Freedom from taxation was thus recognition of the performance of military service.

The distribution of land was nevertheless not homogeneous in the three kingdoms, and also changed over the course of the following centuries. At the beginning of the fourteenth century, the largest landowners were the Church, which owned 30 per cent of the land, the nobility with 20 per cent, and the king with 7 per cent. However, the free peasants held one-third of the land. Geographically, the land was distributed unevenly, inasmuch as Church and noble holdings were largely located in the central areas. In Denmark, the free peasants held one-quarter of the land, and the king only 5 per cent; the rest was divided between the Church and the nobility. Exact figures for Sweden and the other kingdoms are only available beginning in the sixteenth century. By that time, the proportion of free peasant land had declined in Denmark, while the landholdings of the king and the Church had increased at the expense of the lower nobility.[17] In Norway, on the other hand, the peasant proportion remained more or less unchanged. Only in Iceland, Sweden and especially in Finland did the free peasantry predominate.

After the growth phase of agricultural production, the plague brought dramatic changes, especially in Norway. Income from the land dropped, as did land prices, from which leaseholders and rural labourers alike profited. The free peasants, on the other hand, could hardly improve their situation; indeed, it even deteriorated, since they continued to be taxed by the king. Abandonment of settlements in Norway and Denmark led to an increase in the average size of peasant holdings, so that an upward levelling process of land ownership took place. The cottars disappeared during the late Middle Ages, becoming leaseholders. In Sweden and Finland the agrarian structure did not change, since here, subsistence agriculture continued to dominate. Only in Denmark and Norway did new production structures appear. The unfavourable development of cereal prices led to the promotion of animal husbandry in both countries, with demand in northern Germany and the Netherlands providing the impetus for the large-scale raising of oxen in Denmark. Horse-breeding, with an annual export of 4,000 animals, was also important for Jutland and Zealand in the late fifteenth and sixteenth centuries. At that time, some 20,000 head of cattle were shipped annually from Denmark to the Elbe region for sale. During the sixteenth century, annual exports of oxen would rise to 50,000 head.

Sweden's agricultural production, by contrast, was limited to a single export product, the famous butter sold in the Hanseatic cities. Other than that, the Scandinavian economy lived from the exploitation of natural resources, especially fishing and mining. In Denmark (Scania), Norway and later also Iceland, fish was long the most important export product. The Scanian fishing industry, the decline of which historians generally attribute to a relocation of the swarms of herring, continued unbroken up to the middle of the sixteenth century at Skanör, and especially at Falsterbo. Moreover, the shift of the herring banks to the Kattegat and the North Sea during the second half of the sixteenth century led to the emergence of two new centres of herring fishery and trade in Denmark-Norway. Henceforth, Ålborg, at the northern tip of Jutland, and Marstrand, off the Bohus coast, supplied the Baltic area with herring, to the extent that demand was not met by North Sea herring imported from the Netherlands. The fact that consumers in the Baltic area preferred the cheaper Ålborg herring to the higher quality Marstrand herring is confirmed not only by the deliveries to Riga carried out by the Holsten-Reimers company, but also by the boom in voyages to Ålborg by Lübeck ships toward the end of the sixteenth century.[18] In Norway and the offshore islands, fishing concentrated on cod, which, as dried stockfish, was sold on numerous markets. English customs sources of the early fourteenth century as well as the Lübeck customs book (*Pfundzollbuch*) of 1370 show that up to 80 to 90 per cent of both English and Lübeck imports from Bergen consisted of stockfish.[19] Around the turn of the sixteenth century, however, the market share of stockfish gradually dropped, since it could no longer compete with the cheaper fish from Iceland, cured cod, which was mostly exported on Hamburg ships.

Sweden's economy was dominated by the expanding mining and iron industries, and later by copper as well. Iron production began in Sweden in the late twelfth century, with the aid of technological imports from Germany. With time, annual iron exports rose from almost 300 tons around 1370 to more than 900 tons during the fifteenth century, reaching a peak of 1,100 tons in the 1490s. Iron was mined and processed in the mountainous areas of central Sweden, while copper was mined in Falun in the Dalarna region. Mining in Sweden was in the hands of free peasants and the lower nobility, who operated the mines as shareholders, while smelting was carried out in furnaces on the farms of the mine owners themselves. This involved a large number of wage labourers. It has been estimated that 20,000 persons, 3 per cent of the total population of Sweden, worked in the mining industry. This productive structure was the basis for the main export products, which were transported chiefly by ship along the route from Stockholm or Kalmar to Lübeck. According to the Lübeck customs books of 1492–95, copper accounted for 60 per cent of Stockholm exports, and iron for 30 per cent.[20] Commercial production in the cities, on the other hand, was primarily directed toward local and regional needs.

In addition to fishing and mining, peasant shipping and shipbuilding should not be overlooked, as they took place in more or less all of the coastal areas. Although the royal governments attempted to monopolise trade and shipping for the citizens of the towns, the interchange between the cities and surrounding countryside kept the commercial and shipping activities of the peasants intact and important. In Norway, for example, the coastal regions that engaged in fishing and the fish trade were among the most prosperous, and the fish traders there constituted the upper stratum of society.[21]

The peasants were not the only ones to engage in shipping and trade in the areas around the cities and along the coast; the nobility and the clergy, too, claimed the right to sell their own products, and in turn to satisfy their own needs, in the marketplace. Even an ecclesiastical institution such as Uppsala cathedral made only some 10 per cent of its expenditures in the city itself at the end of the fifteenth century, and did most of its business with Stockholm merchants.[22]

9.5 Nobles and peasants

The nobility in the Scandinavian countries had emerged by the thirteenth century, but it grew increasingly differentiated within the various countries with regard to both numbers and privileges over the course of the fifteenth century. While the privileges of the nobles were tightly restricted in Norway, Denmark was more orientated toward western European models. Sweden was somewhere between the other two kingdoms in this respect, as is already evident from the distribution of land. In Denmark, the nobility held the largest share of the land. The foundation for the emergence of the nobility and the conclusion of that process in Sweden were the statutes of Alsnö (*c.* 1280), in which the king freed not only his own vassals from taxation, but also all men who served the bishops or the secular lords and knights. No corresponding documents exist for Denmark, although the service nobility's exemption from taxation developed in a like manner there. Only in Norway was the freedom from taxation that King Magnus VI granted to his own vassals and those of the bishops in the 1270s very limited. In Norway, nobles were compensated for royal service by the bestowal of local offices that, unlike in Sweden and Denmark, often developed into fiefs. During the fourteenth century, the king finally also recognised the vassals of the secular nobility. The rise of a free peasant (*bonde*) into the lower nobility was possible, for a peasant who presented himself at the annual mustering of the nobility with a horse and arms could thereby attain the status of *frälse*. While the terminology for Denmark and Norway remained fairly imprecise, the Swedish statutes of the fourteenth century distinguish between knights and members of the royal council, *swenæ* (*milites*), a category of nobility equal to knighthood; squires, also known as *swenæ* or *militares*; and the common nobility (*frälse* or *alios armigeros*). During the fifteenth century, reference was made to knights, squires and 'commoners' (*frälse*), in accordance with this distinction. In Denmark, during the thirteenth century, there was at least a distinction between knights and the *herremænd* (lords, singular *herremand*), and in the fourteenth century between knights and squires.

The social and economic differences within the nobility were considerable. For instance, at the end of the fourteenth century the Swedish official Drost Bo Jonsson controlled half the royal castles. Another example is that of the Jutland magnate and royal counsellor Stig Andersen, whose Björnholm Castle in Djursland was certainly comparable to a royal residence. On the occasion of the death of his son, he had a requiem performed in the cathedrals of Lübeck, Århus and Viborg, as well as in the Dominican monasteries in Lübeck and Århus, and elsewhere. In addition, he donated a manor on Zealand to the Antvorskov monastery, and a chapel to the Dominican church in Lübeck.[23] Freedom from taxation encouraged the nobility in Denmark and Sweden to purchase land, which met with resistance from the Crown, since this meant the loss of taxpaying peasants (*bønder*). Queen Margaret therefore attempted to recover such lands by purchase or force. The nobility's freedom from taxation had been scrutinised thoroughly on an earlier occasion. A decree from Nyköping stated that all those who had attained freedom from taxation since 1363 would have to prove the legality of this privilege. During the fifteenth century, the king claimed the right of ennoblement. In Norway, the number of nobles even declined from the end of the fourteenth century, since the loss of population reduced their incomes. In these desperate straits, Norwegian nobles sought Swedish or other foreign peers as husbands for their daughters, who were then rapidly assimilated in Norway. Moreover, some petty nobles succeeded in rising into the high nobility.

In Denmark and parts of Sweden, the high nobility appears to have been strengthened at the cost of the lower nobility. It was able to consolidate its holdings toward the end of the fifteenth century, and to establish large manor complexes in Funen and Scania, and even in Zealand. Moreover, scattered holdings were exchanged with other nobles and with Church institutions, with peasant and petty noble properties being purchased on a large scale. Some petty nobles were then appointed as seneschals or administrators on the manors of the magnates. Conditions in Finland, where only a small service nobility was able to establish itself during the reign of Albert of Mecklenburg and his successors, were completely different. The Swedish nobility did not consider the Finnish gentry to be their peers, but rather merely a local nobility, and claimed the most important royal castles for themselves. The Finnish nobles were at least represented in the Swedish council of the realm, and in time they too received royal offices in Finland.[24]

The higher clergy was also of noble origin. In all three kingdoms, the canons came for the most part from the lower nobility, and in Denmark and Sweden some of the clergy were burghers from the towns. Some Danish and Swedish bishops were the offspring of high-magnate families, a tendency that, as elsewhere in Europe, was reinforced toward the end of the fifteenth century. In addition, it was possible even for burghers to rise to high office by means of university study and a position in the royal chancery. Examples include the archbishops Birger Gunnarsson of Lund and Jens Anderson Beldenak of Odense, whose appointment King John was able to arrange thanks to his good relations with the clergy. Since local universities were not founded until 1477 in Uppsala and 1479 in Copenhagen, Scandinavian students were obliged to study abroad. During the High Middle Ages, Paris was long the leading centre for Scandinavian theological study, and some students also studied Roman law and canon law at Bologna. During the fifteenth century, Scandinavian students increasingly frequented the newly founded German universities at Rostock and Greifswald on the southern shore of the Baltic Sea.[25] However, students accounted for only a small fraction of the Scandinavian clergy. In Norway, the palpable lack of priests was a function of demographic decline, in particular. For this reason, the Norwegian bishops persuaded the Pope to give them carte blanche to choose candidates for the priesthood, disregarding existing stipulations pertaining to age and origin. Low population density and a low degree of urbanisation meant that the number of monasteries in Scandinavia was very small. Few new monasteries were founded, and religious endowments largely flowed to the cathedrals. The only order to succeed in expanding were the Bridgettines, founded in Rome by the Swedish noblewoman canonised in 1391. The influence of Queen Margaret, who had been raised by one of St Bridget's daughters, stimulated the foundation of Bridgettine convents in Scandinavia.

The Scandinavian towns were small by European standards. No city had more than 10,000 inhabitants, and the Norwegian port city of Bergen, with 7,000 inhabitants, was probably the largest settlement in Scandinavia around 1500. Stockholm and Copenhagen, too, with 5,000 and 6,000 inhabitants respectively, were of modest size. Otherwise, only Malmö, with approximately 4,500 inhabitants, was somewhat more substantial. The next level of towns included Oslo, Trondheim, Ribe, Roskilde, Lund, Kalmar, Uppsala and Åbo (Turku). During this period, the vast majority of towns certainly had no more than a few hundred inhabitants.

The development of Scandinavian towns was closely associated with trade. While the centres of local commerce suffered considerably from population loss and the agrarian crisis, such international trading cities as Bergen, Copenhagen, Malmö, Stockholm and Kalmar prospered. Foreign merchants, particularly from the Hanseatic cities, but also from England, were involved in this development to a significant degree. English and later also Scottish merchants contributed considerably to the rise of Bergen as a North Sea port, since they exported stockfish in large quantities. In most Baltic port cities, on the other hand, Hanseatic merchants were the most numerous, an effect of the generous privileges granted by Sweden, Norway and Denmark (see 5.12). The strong presence of German merchants led to repeated discussions about whether they should only be accepted as guests, for instance during the trading season, or also during the winter. The former was the policy at least of the Danish Crown, while in Norway, year-round stays at the Hanseatic trading post at the German Bridge became the rule. In Sweden, too, the Germans were present permanently, accounting for up to a third of the population of Stockholm, Kalmar and Västerås, and constituting a major political force in the town councils. For this reason, German merchants were deeply involved in the political debates in Sweden. This went so far that Germans murdered Stockholm merchants in 1389, and 100 years later, after the victory of the Sture party over Christian I in 1471, they were driven out of the Stockholm town council.[26]

Council positions in the larger Swedish and Danish cities were reserved for members of the merchant class. In Denmark, a decree of 1422 even stipulated that no master artisan could be elected to a town council in Zealand. Only in Norway and the smaller Swedish cities could householders and artisans achieve positions of power in the town council, since the number of merchants was insufficient there. In any case, the corporative organisation of artisans in Scandinavia remained at a lower level overall than in western and central Europe. Only in Denmark were there artisans' and merchants' guilds, while in most Norwegian and Swedish cities, Stockholm being the exception, no craft guilds existed. The guilds formed in Bergen were associations of German artisans. Both in Bergen and in Stockholm, the shoemakers constituted the largest guild, followed by tailors, furriers, goldsmiths and bakers.

Regardless of their social status, rural landowners in Scandinavia differed in two respects from those in western Europe; first, in their unlimited right of ownership, and second, in their personal freedom. Nonetheless, the free peasants or leaseholders were not a homogeneous social stratum. The leaseholders of major farms were economically often better off than the owners of smallholdings. Leaseholders were also personally free in relation to their landlords, since after the expiration of a leasehold, they could either renew it or terminate it. Therefore, for many peasants it was more favourable to lease holdings from the Church or the Crown. Sometimes, peasants became leaseholders when the Crown repossessed land. In Denmark, where the large share of Church landholding is immediately apparent, ecclesiastical institutions began to lease out holdings in the early twelfth century, while the nobility started to do so only in the fourteenth century. The tenants of these holdings (*villici*) obtained very large domains of between 15 and 65 hectares, and had dependent peasant holdings (*colonia*) and so-called cottars (*inquilini*) subordinate to them. The *villici* paid their leases either in kind, with fixed amounts, or by so-called sharecropping, while the simple peasants had to perform four to eight days of labour service annually. The *inquilini* had to render approximately twenty days of labour service, and thus constituted the rural reserve labour force. During the fifteenth century, the owners of large farms with cereal and animal production as well as wood production, in particular, profited from the economic upturn, especially from the western European (Dutch) demand for grain. In many cases, they accumulated large fortunes, which they invested in the capital market.[27]

In Norway, alongside free peasants with small farms, there were also those who owned numerous holdings or parts of holdings, and leased them out, as well as many landless or land-poor cottars. Unlike in Denmark, though, no manorial system with large land complexes emerged in Norway. Icelandic society was dominated by a group of chieftains who controlled one or more farms, and used them as residences. In addition, there were subordinate peasant holdings. The majority of peasants leased holdings from the Church, the magnates or the rich peasant farmers, who were then provided with animal stock by the landlord in return for an additional rent payment. In Sweden and Finland, the extensive availability of unsettled land gave peasants the opportunity to colonise and expand. The manors of the local nobility and the Church were primarily located in the central provinces around Lake Mälar, west of Stockholm, which was farmed by wage labourers and also slaves (thralls), and from the fourteenth century was increasingly leased to peasants.

Slavery was widespread in Scandinavia during the High Middle Ages. Slaves were either captured abroad or purchased locally. They worked in the households of the Norwegian elite, and in Iceland on normal peasant holdings. In the long run, however, slavery declined. It was abolished before 1100 in Iceland and in the twelfth century in Norway, but survived longer in Sweden and Denmark. At the beginning of the thirteenth century, Archbishop Absalon of Lund and his successor Andreas Sunesen owned slaves. In Sweden, slavery was not abolished until a royal decree of 1335.[28]

Despite the peasant population's seemingly favourable situation, uprisings and even major peasant rebellions occurred regularly in Scandinavia, for example from 1255 to 1258 and again in 1328 in Zealand, in 1313 in Jutland, and in 1217 and again in 1227 in Norway. Most of the uprisings were in opposition to new – often extraordinary – taxes imposed by the Crown, as well as rent or tithe increases by the Church. During the civil war of the twelfth century, the Norwegian peasants rebelled, primarily against the nobility and the Crown. In Denmark, local and regional *thing* organisations fought attempts by the Crown and the Church to take over common lands, with entire village communities joining the insurrections. By contrast, the Estonian peasant rebellion of 1343 against the Danish Crown was largely preventative in character: The peasants knew that Denmark planned to sell parts of the country to the Teutonic Knights, and they rebelled against these prospective rulers. The tax policy of the government of Albert of Mecklenburg also sparked a rural uprising. Finally, during the 1430s, rebellion broke out all over Denmark, Norway and Sweden, the most widespread being the Engelbrekt Rebellion carried out by an alliance of mine owners, peasants and nobles. This unrest resumed during the 1460s in the course of the political struggles in Sweden. Hanseatic trade policies also elicited peasant resistance. In 1472 a peasant revolt erupted on the west coast of Schleswig when the Hanseatic League imposed a trade prohibition as part of its conflict with the Low Countries. Since King Christian I, who needed Hanseatic support for his war against Sweden, supported this measure, and banned the export of cereals from his kingdom, the peasants of Schleswig were directly affected. Moreover, they saw their trade in cereals with the Low Countries threatened by Hamburg privateers, and therefore openly rebelled against their rulers. Apart from the Engelbrekt

Rebellion, which was also directed against the policy of union, most of the uprisings were suppressed relatively quickly. Only the communally organised Frisian peasant republic of Dithmarschen, which was subordinate to the bishopric of Bremen-Verden, was able to resist subjugation until the middle of the sixteenth century.[29]

9.6 Nordic literature and culture

The beginning of Nordic literature is generally considered to be the *Edda*, which has come down to us in numerous different literary forms. Apart from the *Poetic Edda* and *Snorri's Edda*, a training manual for young *skalds* (court poets) written by Snorri Sturluson, the multifariousness of the saga literature is particularly impressive. Here, new literary forms, such as contemporary sagas, sagas of bishops and sagas of kings were composed on the model of the old family or clan sagas. The chivalric sagas also offered native adaptations of French or Anglo-Norman materials from the courtly context, as well as the translation of Latin *vitae* into sagas of saints. The courts of Haakon Haakonsson in Bergen in the thirteenth century and Haakon V in Oslo at the beginning of the fourteenth century, in particular, evolved into centres of literary production. The 'King's mirror' (*konungs skuggsjá*) and the sagas about King Haakon and his son Magnus VI the Law-Mender were products of the circle around the royal chancery. The transmission of courtly literature from western Europe to Scandinavia came through the courts of Bergen and Oslo, where courtly romances and ballads were composed in several castles belonging to the high nobility.[30]

The historic masterpiece of Old Norse, however, is the *Heimskringla*, composed by Snorri Sturluson between 1220 and 1241, on the basis of a number of older traditions. In this history of the Norwegian kings, from their mythological beginnings until the reign of King Sverre in the twelfth century, he interwove biography, rhetoric, verse and portraits and miracles of saints. Snorri's work stimulated others to compose a chronicle of the Danish kings, the *Knytlinga saga*, later in the century. However, the actual counterpart to the *Heimskringla* was the *Gesta Danorum* of Saxo Grammaticus. It was written during the first decades of the thirteenth century, commissioned by Archbishop Absalon of Lund and dedicated to his successor Andreas Sunesen. The work addressed an elite, literate audience, whom the author sought to impress with his references to and quotations from Roman literature. Although that hardly makes the chronicle easier to understand, it soon became a standard historical work, from which Shakespeare even drew the material for *Hamlet*. In Sweden, however, historiography was a later development. There, the fifteenth-century *Chronica regni Gothorum* by the Uppsala university professor Ericus Olai may be considered the first historical account, although its main purpose was to construct a claim for Uppsala as the successor to Jerusalem and Rome in the Christian narrative of salvation, and hence to portray Sweden as pre-eminent among both the Scandinavian and the non-Scandinavian countries. Later chronicles, such as the Swedish *Karlskrönikan* (*c.* 1450) and the Danish *Rimkrøniken* (rhymed chronicle) were less elaborate in form, and mainly served propaganda purposes, such as – in the case of the *Karlskrönikan* – the promotion of King Karl Knutsson. The Danish *Rimkrøniken* was published in Copenhagen in 1495 by Gottfried of Ghemen, who was originally from Gouda in the Netherlands. It was the first incunabulum in any Scandinavian language.

Also, in addition to these works, we should not underestimate the production of religious literature in Latin. It includes not only such rhymed saints' *vitae* as those of the most famous of the Nordic kings, Olaf II of Norway (St Olaf), or the Virgin Mary, but also the *Hexaemeron* by Andreas Sunesen, a creation theology abbreviated for didactic purposes. Other important works include the letters of the Swedish Dominican Petrus de Dacia to the mystic Christine of Strommeln, who suffered terrible tribulations of body and soul. More influential, however, was the Paris-trained Mathias Övedsson, the first confessor of the future St Bridget. Both Nicholas of Cusa and Bernardino of Siena were familiar with his commentary on the revelations of St John. Bridget's heavenly and earthly visions, as recorded in her *Revelationes*, themselves became a work of literature, and the convent at Vadsterna founded after her death became a centre of Latin study and literary production. Vernacular literature was comparatively meagre during the fourteenth and fifteenth centuries. Only a collection of Danish proverbs by Peter Laale and a few Swedish satires from the end of the fifteenth century have come down to us. Prior to the Reformation, the translation of Italian or western European literature into the Scandinavian languages seems to have been sporadic, and the reception of ancient authors also only began on a large scale after that period.[31]

Scandinavian architecture, in contrast, adopted western European influences as early as the twelfth century. As elsewhere in Europe, new cathedrals were built or existing churches reconstructed in Denmark, Norway and Sweden. While the twelfth-century cathedral of Lund still followed Lombard examples, inspired by Mainz and Speyer, in the thirteenth century the French style was chosen for the newly built Uppsala cathedral. For this reason, French builders and stonemasons were hired.

Since sandstone is rare in Scandinavia, this material was used only for columns, capitals and other details, and, by necessity, brick for the rest. Trondheim cathedral was begun in Romanesque style, but continued in Gothic style in the late twelfth century, influenced perhaps by the English exile of Archbishop Eystein from 1180 to 1183.

In Åbo (Turku), the construction of the cathedral, which still exists today, began at the end of the thirteenth century, after the episcopal see was established there. During the next century, the reconstruction or even demolition of Romanesque parish churches and their replacement with new buildings proceeded all over Scandinavia, perhaps because the old churches were frequently built solely of wood. It was then that the large Gothic stone churches appeared on the island of Gotland, which represent an independent tradition, and also bear witness to the high standard of stonemasonry. The interiors of the churches were decorated with frescoes and sculptures, in Norway often based on English models, and in southern Scandinavia on northern German models. But French stonemasons, too, left evidence of their work, as in Uppsala. Northern German influence is readily apparent especially in the construction of altarpieces in the late fourteenth and fifteenth centuries. The altar of the Kalanti church near Åbo, from the workshop of Master Franke in Hamburg, is one example; another is the altar at Trondenes, Norway, endowed by the Lübeck merchants who traded in Bergen. These two examples are but the tip of the iceberg of a vigorous trade in art, in the course of which the entire Baltic region was supplied with altarpieces through Lübeck. Generally, Scandinavian prelates and monasteries wishing to commission altarpieces turned to Lübeck merchants, who then made contact with workshops in Lübeck or elsewhere in northern Germany. Several years might pass between the order and the delivery of such works, for example five years in the case of the St Bridget retable for the Vadsterna convent. The established channels of art imports may have delayed the development of native schools of woodcarving in the Scandinavian towns.[32]

Nordic rulers also availed themselves of this service. The Swedish regent Sten Sture the Elder ordered a monumental sculpture group of St George slaying the dragon from the Lübeck woodcarver Bernt Notke to commemorate his victory over the Danish army at Brunkeberg in 1471. The purpose was not simply to decorate Stockholm's St Nicholas church (*Storkyrkan*, 'great church'), but also to immortalise himself as the rescuer of Sweden from the Danish dragon. Some sculptures also came from the Low Countries which, however, would only attain the status of a major provider of art objects for Scandinavia around the middle of the sixteenth century. Accordingly, the reception of the Italian Renaissance in the field of architecture also took place directly or indirectly through the southern Netherlands at the end of the sixteenth and into the seventeenth century.[33]

The sources on Scandinavian music of the period are quite sparse. While we know that as early as the High Middle Ages, princes and nobles hired musicians for the purposes of entertainment and prestige, and that during the fifteenth century, the musicians organised themselves in the towns, it is not clear what kind of music they played. With the establishment of schools in Denmark and Norway, and later also in Sweden and Finland, musical training seems to have progressed; however, the first known examples of notation in the *Liber daticus lundensis* refer to existing European melodies. For this period, there are indications of the existence of organs and of the use of polyphony in religious contexts. St Bridget opposed this 'new custom', and banned it in her order. Instead, the Bridgettines attempted to disseminate a *cantus sororum*, with new texts set to old melodies, even beyond the borders of Scandinavia.

Notes

1 Skovgaard-Petersen, 'The Danish kingdom'.
2 Bracke, *Die Regierung Waldemars IV.*, 19–39.
3 Helle, 'The Norwegian kingdom'.
4 Rosén, *Striden mellan Birger Magnusson och hans bröder*; Christensen, *Kalmar-unionen*, 12.
5 Schück, 'Sweden under the dynasty'.
6 Etting, *Queen Margrete I.*; Bøgh, 'On the causes of the Kalmar Union', 9–30.
7 Bøgh, 'Sociale oprør i Sverige-Finland', 138–67; Katajala, *Northern revolts*.
8 Olesen, 'Inter-Scandinavian relations', 740, and 'Christopher of Bavaria, King of Denmark, Norway and Sweden', 109–36.
9 Olesen, *Rigsråd – Kongemagt – Union*, and 'Die doppelte Königswahl'.
10 Olesen, 'Oprør og politisering i Sverige'.
11 Poulsen, 'Kingdoms on the periphery of Europe'.
12 Schück, 'The political system', 702–6.
13 Benedictow, 'Demographic conditions'.
14 Olesen, 'Die Verbreitung des Schwarzen Todes'; Benedictow, *Plague in the late medieval Nordic countries*.
15 Gissel, Jutikkala, Österberg, Sandnes and Teitsson, *Desertion and land colonisation in the Nordic countries*.
16 Vahtola, 'Population and settlement'.
17 Poulsen, 'Land mobility in Denmark'.
18 Jahnke, *Das Silber des Meeres*.
19 Nedkvitne, 'Handelssjøfarten', 73–4, 87.
20 Orrman, 'The condition of the rural population'.

21 North, *Geldumlauf und Wirtschaftskonjunktur*, and 'Bilanzen im Lübecker Schwedenhandel'; Kumlien, 'Stockholm, Lübeck und Westeuropa', 13.
22 Dahlbäck, 'en stad i staden'.
23 Ulsig, 'The nobility', 639.
24 Orrman, 'Den värdsliga frälsejordens lokalisering i Finland', 137–49.
25 Link, *Auf dem Weg zur Landesuniversität.*
26 Olesen, 'Der Einfluß der Hanse'.
27 Poulsen, 'Late medieval and early modern peasants'.
28 Orrman, 'Rural conditions', 308–11.
29 On this, see the good overview in Bøgh et al. (eds), *Til kamp for friheden*, especially the essays by Würtz Sørensen, 'Bøndernes oprørspraksis'; Olesen, 'Oprør og politisering i Sverige'; and Poulsen, 'Bonden overfor det europæiske marked'.
30 Bagge, *Da boken kom til Norge.*
31 Ståhle, *Medeltidens profana literatur*; Jansson, *Eufemiavisorna*; Pipping, *Den fornsvenska litteraturen*; Ronge, *Konung Alexander.*
32 Bonsdorff, 'Is art a barometer of wealth?', 29–43, and *Kunstproduktion und Kunstverbreitung.*
33 Roding, 'The North Sea coasts'.

PART II

Themes: Developmental tendencies in the state, the economy, society and culture

10

State and constitution

During the period that interests us here, Europe was characterised by a variety of types of political rule. The great monarchies that would shape European history from the late fifteenth century had not yet been consolidated.

Around 1300, only England's monarchy had a territorial base and institutions that allowed for the intensification of rule over at least part of the country. In the long run, in the British Isles only Scotland could resist this process and maintain its independence. France, which was also dominated for a time by English kings, developed into a national monarchy in the course of conflicts with England, whereby dynastic accident was also among the destabilising and stabilising factors. The integration of Brittany and Provence as well as the decline of Burgundy all contributed to gradual unification.

On the Iberian Peninsula, the various kings and princes were locked in protracted and bloody conflict, and only the marriage of Ferdinand, the future King of Aragón, and Isabella, the reigning Queen of Castile, created a personal if not yet an institutional union of the two kingdoms. In any case, the new union of the Catholic monarchs made it possible to conquer and incorporate the Moorish kingdom of Granada. The expulsion of the Jewish and Muslim population was regarded as an integrative measure here. Aragón's interests and possessions in Sicily and Naples also belonged to this composite monarchy, along with Castile's overseas possessions, which were just beginning to take shape at the time.

In Italy, long characterised by a great diversity of political rule, processes of concentration were also at work from the late fourteenth century. Alongside the republics of Genoa, Florence and Venice, the duchy of Milan, the Papal State and the kingdom of Naples emerged as major powers.

The situation was quite different in the heart of Europe as well as on the periphery. With the Holy Roman Empire, a confederation of princely states and cities under imperial sovereignty dominated central Europe, which revealed aspects of integration and disintegration in equal measure. Thus the Swiss Confederacy resisted integration into the empire, while the Hanseatic cities only joined the imperial fold in the course of the sixteenth century. In addition, the Netherlandish towns claimed relative autonomy in both the duchy of Burgundy and in the Holy Roman Empire.

In the kingdoms of Poland, Bohemia and Hungary dynastic coincidences meant that individual dynasties ruled several east-central European countries at the same time, thus contributing to the emergence of larger complexes of countries. The Polish-Lithuanian personal union of 1385, which became a real union in 1569, was the key power here, since the Jagiełłonians in the form of Casimir IV and his sons ruled Poland-Lithuania, Bohemia and Hungary. They had to share power there with the estates, however, which elected the kings and reshaped the monarchies as 'aristocratic republics'.

From the thirteenth century, the history of the Scandinavian countries Denmark, Norway and Sweden was characterised by growing centralisation and increasing state authority. However, there were also long-term developments in the opposite direction, and it was not until the fourteenth century that the first union between Norway and Sweden (1319) and later the Kalmar Union (1397) led to major transnational connections.

In Russia, the shaking off of Mongol rule and the 'gathering of the Russian lands' by the Grand Prince of Moscow led to political consolidation. The first objective was to annex the republic of Novgorod; with its huge territory, Moscow extended its northern frontiers to the Arctic Sea and its eastern borders to the Urals. In the period that followed the remainder of the principality of Vereya-Beloozero, the principalities of Tver and Ryazan and the Pskov Republic were also integrated into the realm of the Muscovite autocrat.

Although some of the kingdoms expanded well beyond their original frontiers, consolidation and stability were more significant in the long run. Thus the borders of Germany and Austria, France, England, Poland, Hungary, Czechia-Bohemia and Denmark as well as Portugal and Spain are not that different in the twenty-first century from what they were around 1400, although there were phases of expansion and disintegration.[1] This early consolidation cannot be attributed to the dynasties alone, although they proved surprisingly resilient. Thus, for example, the majority of the German reigning families forced to abdicate in November 1918 could be traced back to the twelfth century, and the ecclesiastical territories that arose in the Middle Ages existed until the *Reichsdeputationshauptschluss* of 1803, with which an imperial deputation resolved to redistribute territorial sovereignty in the Holy Roman Empire through a process of secularisation and mediatisation.

10.1 Forms of political representation

According to the tradition long dominant in German scholarship, forms of political representation developed on the territorial, monarchical or state level, which led to the *Ständestaat* (state of estates) or the dualism between monarch and estates becoming an ideal type.[2] In reality, however, this model, which was developed for the central European territories, applied neither to the period in question nor to many European countries. Autonomous organisational models played a role particularly in the urbanised regions of northern Italy or the coastal areas of north-western Europe, where territorial states and even monarchies exerted little influence. Aside from the city-states of northern Italy, one could include among them the cities of the Hansa or the league of Flemish towns.

In some electoral monarchies such as the Holy Roman Empire, Poland-Lithuania, Bohemia or Hungary, the initiative for representation as a basis for financial assistance proceeded from the king or emperor on the one hand and the nobility on the other. There was also self-organisation from below, such as we find in the Swiss Confederacy or southern Germany.

In the most highly evolved representative body, the English Parliament, too, in the thirteenth century the initiative came equally from the king's advisers and the nobility. They resolved that in future, a parliament of fifteen royal councillors and twelve representatives of the barons would assemble three times yearly. In the period that followed, these parliaments became an arena for the king and the leaders of the baronial party, who at least once summoned parliaments simultaneously to Windsor and St Albans, respectively. After 1325, representatives of the shires and towns (boroughs and cities) were accordingly summoned regularly to Parliament, where they constituted the Commons, in contrast to the upper nobility and clergy, who were summoned personally. While Parliament in England developed into a legislative body also responsible for approving taxes, in France the *parlement* evolved into a judicial body. Here, the estates-general claimed the right to authorise taxes, without this authorisation being binding, since the provincial estates continued to have the last word on taxation. The estates-general nonetheless played a significant role in the national integration of the country.

The *cortes* of Aragón went back to the thirteenth century and retained substantial power into the seventeenth century. The financial needs of the kings in the fourteenth century led to frequent convocations of the *cortes*, which even succeeded in enforcing a control of tax collection by the estates. These were the earliest beginnings of a contractual regulation, later known as *pactismo* or *pactisme*, of the estates' right to a say in all important matters, which would take effect above all during Alfonso V's long absence in his new capital at Naples, and even become the subject of debates in political theory. In Castile and León, where the monarchy was generally stronger than in Aragón, the position of the *cortes* proved weaker. *Cortes* were already held here in the twelfth century, when representatives of the clergy, nobility and cities assembled under royal protection. Unlike in Aragón, the kings of Castile began circumventing the *cortes* in the fourteenth century by introducing new taxes outside the jurisdiction of the estates. In the late fifteenth century, the *cortes* repeatedly assembled on the summons of the Catholic monarchs for purposes of counsel and the acclamation of royal laws. Alongside them, beginning in the fourteenth century, the Spanish towns formed so-called *hermandades* intended to serve as independent associations for the preservation of their privileges.

In Scandinavia, the assemblies of the temporal and clerical nobility developed into a council of the realm, from a *concilium regis* to a *concilium regni*. According to the mid-fourteenth-century Swedish statute on the election of the monarch, a new king was to elect his council of the realm. The importance of the councils of the realm in Sweden, Denmark and Norway increased with negotiations on a union. Their power, however, rested on consultation to Queen Margaret and her successors. While in Denmark, the seat of the central government, the concurrence of interests between the councillors of the realm, who came from the upper nobility, and the monarch was extensive, in Sweden, where various candidates vied for the throne, conflicts regularly ensued with the council of the realm, which was dominated by powerful noble parties and their clientele.

Relations between the estates and the king took on a very different quality in the east-central European electoral monarchies of Bohemia, Poland, Lithuania and Hungary. Here, in order to gain recognition for the succession of his sons, King Jagiełło had to concede extensive privileges to the Polish nobility, ranging from personal inviolability to economic prerogatives. Wars could be begun only with the consent of the regional assemblies, which had to be consulted before the levy en masse. This strengthened the status of the regional assemblies (*sejmiki*) dominated by the lower nobility and led to the emergence of a parliamentary system out of the regional and general assemblies. In the late fifteenth century, the regional assemblies deliberated first on suggestions by the king, then the general assembly convened. The latter took far-reaching decisions in 1494 such as that binding peasants to the land. In 1504/05 the regional assemblies adopted the *nihil novi* act or constitution, which stipulated that no new laws could be passed without the assent of the senate and the representatives of the regional assemblies. This occurred on the initiative of the magnates, who represented one-third of deputies to the regional assemblies in 1504.[3] This paved the way for the aristocratic republic, for in Hungary (1505) and Bohemia (1500) territorial legal codes also laid down the primacy of the estates.[4]

In the Holy Roman Empire, the course was set for institutionalised cooperation between the king/emperor and the imperial estates in the late fifteenth century. This development had roots in a number of elements. In the mid-fourteenth century, only the electors who chose the king had a function in the imperial constitution, which they used for the first time in order to assume responsibility during the captivity of King Wenceslaus in 1394. They gathered at a 'kingless assembly', which was followed by additional assemblies summoned by the prince-electors during the Hussite Wars in 1422 and the Council of Basle in 1438. Another element was the *Hoftag*, the assembly of the vassals or magnates of the empire, whom the king summoned on certain occasions.

The imperial diet or *Reichstag* – a name used for the first time in 1495 – developed as a customary law symbiosis between the 'kingless assembly' and the *Hoftag*. Apart from the electors, princes and imperial cities, the lesser powers of counts, knights and prelates were integrated here into the process of securing the peace of the empire. Without the assent of the imperial diet, or after 1500 of the so-called imperial estates, kings could neither begin wars nor make any alliances to the detriment of the empire. The estates' further-reaching ideas, however, such as the establishment of an imperial council (*Reichsregiment*), to which Maximilian had to bow in 1500 in return for the estates' subsidies to the empire (*Reichshilfe*), could not be implemented in the long term. The briefly established estate government contributed more to the 'continuation and concentration of imperial policy', and thus did not necessarily correspond to the interests of the powerful imperial estates.[5]

Apart from this institutional consolidation of the formerly 'open' empire, diverse forms of communal representation evolved in the urban networks on its southern and north-western frontiers as well as in the Swiss Confederacy.

The earliest beginnings of municipal government can already be found in twelfth-century Genoa, where merchants, ship owners and mariners joined forces to resolve daily municipal and economic issues and established representative bodies. This included a consulate, whose free election the Emperor affirmed in 1162.[6]

In Venice, the Great Council represented the commune. In 1297 its membership was expanded to more than 1,000, and they elected all of the city's officeholders. At the same time, the Great Council closed its ranks, a process completed by 1320. Henceforth, only those who had been members for at least four years would belong. Although a small circle of old families who had reserved the lion's share of offices for their kinsmen before 1297 continued to enjoy the greatest prestige in the Republic, networks and clientele relationships extending beyond these families now became important in filling offices. The Doge, whose freedom of action the Republic further curtailed in the course of the fifteenth century, could shape Venetian policy only in cooperation with his peers.[7]

In Florence, the commune, or *popolo*, was represented by a guild elite. Power lay with the seven major guilds, the *arti maggiori*, which included lawyers and notaries as well as international cloth exporters, bankers, moneychangers, and silk and cotton merchants. Even in the leading guilds, however, only a few masters held the important positions. These *popolani grassi* occasionally adopted the demands of simple guild members, but their main objective was to consolidate their own position among the city's leaders.

Flanders, which was also heavily urbanised, represents yet another example of communal traditions. By the thirteenth century, many Flemish cities had obtained privileges to organise their own municipal governments, which at the same time curtailed the rights of the counts. The counts for their part frequently supported the autonomy of the powerful cities in order to weaken the nobility. In the fourteenth century the artisan strata successfully sought to participate in municipal politics and underlined their claims with a permanent representation of the guilds in the municipal government. Although conflicts repeatedly broke out between the guilds and the patriciate as well as between individual guilds, the autonomy of the Flemish cities grew. A contributing factor in the fourteenth and fifteenth centuries was the institutional relationship between the three large cities of Bruges, Ypres and Ghent, which met regularly with representatives of the Bruges countryside (*Brugse Vrije*) as the 'four members of Flanders' (*Vier*

Leden van Vlaanderen) and determined Flemish policy. They presented a united political front to the territorial ruler, and small towns and rural regions also regularly called upon the 'four members' for legal or diplomatic assistance. The cities' main concerns were trade regulations, the settlement of legal disputes, coinage and fiscal policy as well as foreign relations, and later taxation and defence.[8] It is thus not surprising that the Flemish cities put up considerable resistance to the intensification of rule by the dukes of Burgundy in the fifteenth century, resistance that sometimes could only be broken by military means.

The Hanseatic cities referred to for the first time in 1358 as *de Stede van der Dudeschen hense* represent a special case of communal and municipal organisation. They had already begun to gather on significant occasions in the thirteenth century, mainly to discuss trade matters. In the mid-fourteenth century, regular assemblies to which the member cities sent deputies established themselves as the highest Hanseatic authority. Regional assemblies bringing together the Hanseatic towns of a certain region (quarter) were also founded. At these regional assemblies, a number of Hanseatic towns discussed current problems and sometimes also decided which towns should represent the region at the next Hanseatic assembly. Below these regional assemblies were the town councils of the individual cities, which articulated their interests through the regional and Hanseatic assemblies. Although the individual towns enjoyed equal legal status, size and economic importance more strongly influenced their roles, or their resulting claims to leadership in the Hansa as a whole. Thus the pre-eminent position of Lübeck or of the Lübeck town council as the head of the Hanseatic League was only challenged in the late fifteenth century, for example by Cologne. Hanseatic politics focused on preserving trade privileges and urban liberties, and generally sought to resolve conflicts peacefully. War, which threatened trade, was treated as a last resort.[9]

Yet another variant of self-organisation and representation could be found in the Swiss Confederacy, although it certainly shared comparable organisational principles with the Hansa. The Confederacy consisted of a system of individual republics that had joined forces. These republics emerged from the thirteenth century in a process of communalisation based on the purchase of freedom from nobles and monasteries. The popular assemblies that organised the shared use of land evolved into the *Landsgemeinde*, the precursor to the cantonal assembly. It decided all of the important matters affecting a given *Land* and also elected the leaders, such as the chief magistrate (*Landammann*).[10] In the Swiss Confederacy, representatives of the *Orte* (precursors to the cantons) met at least once a year for the *Tagsatzung* or Swiss Assembly, whose decisions became legally binding through ratification in the individual *Orte*.

10.2 Administration

Most monarchs had a council of vassals and a royal household to handle everyday matters. The royal household or court (*curia*) developed with time into administrative units that no longer accompanied the ruler on his travels. The court offices contributed to this growing autonomy, although the process of diversification proceeded differently in the various European countries. Key elements of administrative development were the chancery on the one hand and the treasury or financial administration on the other.

In England, the Chancery began to emerge as a stabilising factor in the thirteenth century, and distributed several thousand documents a year. Next to the chancellor, the treasury or Exchequer, which drew up the budget and controlled the accounts of the tax collectors as well as the expenses of the commanders of the army, became the most important administrative agency. The Wardrobe, as the finance and accounting office, also funded the royal household and at times warfare as well. This was particularly important in the fourteenth and the early decades of the fifteenth century, when English kings spent long periods on the Continent. New sources of income were tapped to satisfy the growing need for funds that resulted from these enterprises. Since the income from the royal domains no longer sufficed and even fell in the wake of the Black Death, the State resorted to direct and indirect taxation, which Parliament generally authorised up to the mid-fifteenth century to finance military enterprises. Indirect taxes on imports and exports, particularly on the export of wool and later woollen cloth, played an important role here.[11]

In France the royal household, which consisted of the six offices of *paneterie*, *échansonnerie*, *cuisine*, *fruiterie*, *écurie* and *chambre* was referred to as the *hôtel du roi*. The chamber and chamberlain or *chambellan* served the most important functions. The *hôtel* was constantly growing, leading to the emergence of a multiplicity of competences, which in turn were gradually centralised. Power became concentrated in the royal officers, the secretaries, who were responsible above all for maintaining financial order in the kingdom. The chamber of accounts or *chambre des comptes* mainly administered the extraordinary taxes such as the *aides* and *subsides*. New taxes were introduced in 1355 and 1370, adding the *gabelle* on salt and the *traites* as import and export duties alongside the *aides*.

The royal *taille* was also levied as a hearth tax. The new system of taxation created a direct relationship between the king and his subjects. At the same time, four tax administrations arose for Languedoc, Languedoïl, Normandy and Paris, reflecting at once the interests of the central government and the regions. The highest royal court, the *parlement*, in contrast, was established initially at Paris as a judicial organ for the entire country. It comprised three chambers, the *grande chambre* (chamber of appeals), the *chambre des enquêtes* (chamber of inquiries), and the *chambre des requêtes* (chamber of petitions), which met in certain rooms in the Palais de la Cité in Paris and were staffed with professional councillors. In the second half of the fifteenth century, the growing flood of legal cases was channelled through the newly founded provincial *parlements* of Toulouse (1443), Grenoble (1456), Bordeaux (1462), Dijon (1477), Rouen (1499), Aix (1501) and Rennes (1554).

Following the French model, Burgundy also introduced chambers of accounts in Flanders (1382, transferred to Lille in 1386), Burgundy (Dijon) and Brabant (Brussels), although the financial administration of the large Flemish cities may have been more important here. In the fifteenth century, the Burgundian rulers established a common chancery for the duchy, although some territories such as Brabant maintained independent chanceries. Nicolas Rolin, the outstanding chancellor of Philip the Good, lent the Burgundian chancery a particular political weight.

In the Holy Roman Empire, the influence of a chancery also depended strongly on the person of the chancellor, as is evident from the example of the Bohemian court chancery of Charles IV under Johann of Neumarkt. The court of the German kings originally consisted of loosely assembled bodies from which emerged the institutions of the aulic council (*Hofrat*), the court chancery (*Hofkanzlei*) and the high court of justice (*Hofgericht*). The aulic council performed tasks of governance. Alongside the court chancery, which was already quite well organised under Ruprecht of the Palatinate, a second chancery was added in the fifteenth century. Frederick III correspondingly organised the chanceries according to their orientation into an imperial court chancery and an Austrian court chancery. The royal exchequer (*Hofkammer*) and thus the financial system, in contrast, was far less institutionalised than it was in England or France, or in the financial administrations of cities in Germany, the Netherlands or northern Italy.[12] At least as important as the rudiments of central administration was the establishment of territorial administrations. In most German territories so-called *Ämter* (offices) arose in the fourteenth century as the lowest level of territorial rule. They were charged with managing dues and taxes, administering justice and policing. On the highest level, the chanceries endeavoured to compile in so-called cartularies the legal titles to which the territories were entitled or laid claim. This development had advanced furthest in the territories of the electoral prince-bishops of the Rhine. The fifteenth century also saw a consolidation of feudal relationships between territorial rulers and vassals, and the beginnings of the establishment of central territorial administrations.

In Hungary and Poland, too, the kings were at first mainly peripatetic, and part of the court travelled with them. The most important officials such as the paladin/voivode, chancellor and treasurer were present in the country, however, and often met with the members of the royal council only at the king's behest. Since the paladin or voivode represented the king in judicial matters as well as in commanding the army, this court office developed into the king's deputy in his lands. The central office of castellan was also created within the government hierarchy, along with castellans in the provinces to staff the royal fortresses. With the establishment of the capital at Cracow, the royal chancellors and vice-chancellors became the most important officeholders who, like the Cracow Chancellor Zbigniew Oleśnicki, exerted a defining influence on Jagiełłonian politics. At the same time, the court chancery evolved into a cultural centre that proved significant for the reception of humanist achievements.

This development is comparable to that of the Castilian court chancery, which played a key role in the evolution of a Castilian administrative idiom alongside Latin and consequently contributed to the emergence of Castilian Spanish as a national language. In the Italian cities, a permanent staff of trained notaries handled foreign correspondence, and notaries were also employed in the various areas of a diversifying municipal administration. In addition, the communes as well as merchants, ship owners and mariners had access to the services of a number of public notaries. In most states, the administrations were expanded and sometimes even inflated. A prime example is the administrative and judicial organisation of Milan, which was partly independent of the ruler. With its courts for the western and eastern provinces and several courts of appeals, the demand for university-educated lawyers in the ducal government and judiciary rose. In Naples, Alfonso V of Aragón established a court of appeals with a staff of six jurists as salaried judges. At the papal court, the College of Cardinals served as a council. As it grew, the Pope relied more and more on a smaller circle of cardinals and secretaries. The popes also increasingly entrusted the Papal State's many administrative offices to their nephews.

The financial administration was particularly highly developed, and took a similar path in many of the large Italian cities. All those cities linked by common republican traditions, such as Venice, Genoa, Florence, Siena or Lucca, imposed compulsory loans on their citizens according to their means. The communes then consolidated the proceeds from these forced loans in a municipal debt with stable interest payments. The cities also took on additional loans guaranteed by wealthy owners of capital. Special agencies were founded to administer the municipal debt. In 1345 Florence established a *Monte comune*, which was supposed to consolidate public debts at a rate of 5 per cent. In Genoa, the investors in municipal bonds formed a consortium, the *Casa delle compere di San Giorgio*, which set a uniform interest rate for public borrowing of 7 per cent. For the next four centuries, this institution would form the heart of Genoese finance by administering municipal taxes and the acquisition of new municipal revenues. Sometimes the *Monte* shared the administration of a bond with the banking and insurance business; in Florence the *Monte* of 1415 was given money to hold in trust, and that of 1423 paid investors a life annuity. The *Monte doti* (dowry *monte*) of 1424 was more inventive: If the investors married within the next seven and a half or fifteen years, they received 250 or 500 per cent, respectively, of their initial investment; if they died beforehand or did not marry, the sum went to the public coffers. As in Florence, the Venetian financial administration, the *Camera degli imprestiti* (bond office), was a public institution. It nevertheless differed from the *Monte comune* in that the Venetian state sought to amortise and reduce the debts. In Florence, in contrast, the debt was consolidated in the long term with high interest rates, so that one may speak of a redistribution of the taxes from Florentine citizens and the surrounding countryside in favour of wealthy creditors.[13]

The sale of municipal annuities also played an important role in northern France, the Netherlands and numerous German cities. They represented a long-term investment for their buyers, the lenders, which could always be recapitalised if necessary. At the same time, this also strengthened citizens' identification with their urban polity,[14] although, as in the Hansa, outside investors also put their capital in Lübeck or Hamburg municipal annuities.

10.3 Warfare

In the courtly chivalric environment, war was glorified as an honourable adventure into the fifteenth century. Such idealisation, however, contrasts sharply with the brutalisation of war by the mass armies of this era. War was waged to assert or defend real or imagined feudal, corporative, dynastic or so-called historic rights or claims. The enforcement of 'divine justice' could also be a *casus belli*. Finally, it was also a matter of extending territory (*contado*), for example that of the northern Italian city-states and principalities, and thus of very concrete economic resources. Nevertheless, such ambitions (e.g., the Florentine Republic's struggle against 'Milanese tyranny') could be dressed in the elegant humanist trappings of a defence of republican liberty. Wars of religion or ideology, in contrast, were waged only on the margins of Europe, in the Balkans against the Turks, in Prussia and Livonia against the Lithuanians, on the Don against the Tartars or in Andalucía and North Africa against the Moors. In core Europe, the focus was on conflicts between states and dynasties. They led to a transformation of warfare and, gradually, to the establishment of standing armies and thus, of necessity, to the centralisation of military administration.[15]

Changes occurred in England and France in the wake of the Hundred Years War and in an Italy marked by constant power conflicts and rivalries. The Hundred Years War had revealed that the contingent of noblemen enlisted in case of war was ill-suited to a protracted war of attrition, and that the French nobility, with their aspirations toward glory on the battlefield, were no match for the disciplined tactics of the English. The armoured French cavalry, reinforced by Italian and Spanish mercenaries, had already suffered a heavy defeat against the foot troops of the Flemish towns and the peasants of eastern Flanders at the 1302 battle of Kortrijk. At the battles of Crécy and Poitiers, English archers and the dismounted English cavalry once again took the French noble force by surprise with a tactical innovation. The blind King John of Bohemia, for example, had allowed himself to be led into the battle of Crécy in order to die a hero's death. At Agincourt in 1415, too, the superior fighting morale and discipline of the English longbowmen and men-at-arms, who were united by a common language, helped them to vanquish the feudal French troops. Christine de Pizan comforted the widows of the fallen knights that their deaths had at least made them 'martyrs of God'.[16]

Although in the long run military developments favoured the infantry, the cavalry continued to play an important role in fifteenth-century warfare despite the above-mentioned defeats. The victory at Agincourt and the expansion of English holdings on the Continent, however, necessitated the permanent presence of an English army there, which had not been the case during the expeditions of Edward III or the Black Prince in the fourteenth century.

The early death of Henry V (1422) meant that the English could not indefinitely back their presence on the Continent militarily. Instead, the new French King, Charles VII, deployed advanced military forms of organisation to recapture the English-occupied lands. While in the 1420s he already relied on Piedmontese and Scottish mercenaries, he now used the consolidation of the royal finances with the help of the hearth tax, the *taille*, to set up units known as *compagnies d'ordonnance* as a preliminary step to establishing a standing army. The aim of the military reforms (*ordonnances*) undertaken in 1439 was to either integrate the groups of mercenaries wandering the country or render them superfluous. The *compagnies d'ordonnance* encompassed a good 7,000 professional soldiers including cavalry, long- and crossbowmen and foot soldiers with light arms, who were assigned quarters in towns in strategically favourable locations. Through regular payment, the king created a highly loyal elite force, which allowed him to monopolise war and peace.[17] At the same time, he built up his royal artillery, which he deployed successfully to capture the fortified English strongholds in Normandy and Gascony.

Charles VII could rely for his reforms not just on Italian personnel, but also on organisational models from Italy, whose military had already undergone a structural transformation. There, the disinclination of town and country people to fulfil their military duties – that is, the demilitarisation of urban society – led in the thirteenth century to city-states recruiting mercenaries from all over Europe on a contract basis for brief military campaigns.

In the fourteenth century, the city-states and other powers went over to hiring larger companies of mercenaries for longer periods. These mercenary troops became autonomous with time and waged war independent of their employers, who dared not dismiss them. The aggressive Papal State proved to be a haven for the mercenary troops, when in doubt deploying them against their former masters. One example of such shifting loyalties is the much-feared English *condottiere* John Hawkwood. In 1372, during a period of idleness, he plundered the Florentine countryside, and in 1375, during the war between Florence and the papacy, he refused obedience to the latter. Two years later he entered the service of the Florentine Republic, to which he remained loyal until his death in 1394. His fame and reputation are reflected in Paolo Uccello's fresco in the *Duomo* in Florence, which was commissioned by the city.

At the turn of the fifteenth century, the Italian powers sought to solve the problem of frequently switching loyalties by forming long-term associations with Italian mercenary leaders. Territorial expansion provided the necessary means to growing states such as Milan, Florence and Venice in the north, and the Papal State and Aragón-Naples in the south. Reliable personnel, garrisons and fortresses were also needed to defend territorial acquisitions. Accordingly, the states entered long-term contracts (*condotte*) with the *condottieri*, who kept the standing armies for their customers, especially the cavalry, under arms. This was how the Italian states stabilised their military system. At the same time, many *condottiere* were permanently integrated into their employers' territories through grants of land and privileges. The Italian states in turn had to establish a bureaucratic and administrative apparatus to supply and pay the standing armies. Milan and Venice led the way, and were most successful in disciplining the hired mercenary companies, while in Florence substantial reservations remained concerning standing mercenary armies.

The structure of armies also changed in the course of the fifteenth century. The proportion of infantry grew continuously, along with increasing numbers of arquebusiers with firearms and artillery trains.[18] Thus, for example, Charles the Bold of Burgundy sought to bring his army up to date by adopting French and Italian innovations. Following the French model, in 1471 he created twelve standing companies with a larger proportion of infantry, which he expanded in 1476 with additional companies of infantry and light cavalry. Charles's reforms stressed training and exercises. The professional Italian cavalry were supposed to spur on the Burgundian knightly levies tactically. In addition, the army experimented with infantry formations trained to make the most effective use of the new hand firearms. The newly formed Burgundian army nevertheless failed to survive its first deployments, succumbing to the pikes and halberds of the Swiss.

While in their fourteenth-century victories over the Habsburg lords (Morgarten 1315, Sempach, 1386) Swiss tactics initially consisted only of the exploitation of the terrain, in the fifteenth century the Swiss *Orte* further perfected their infantry tactics. The halberdiers formed the core of the Swiss square formations known as *gevierthaufen*, and were surrounded by several ranks of soldiers carrying pikes up to five metres long. With these last they could crush any cavalry attack. The prerequisites were discipline and fighting spirit, achieved by constant drill and the use of units from a single region. In this way the Swiss military entrepreneurs or 'pension lords' were able to raise more than 20,000 soldiers within a very short period of time and to deploy them in several (no more than three) square formations of 7,000 to 8,000 men each.

The victory of the Swiss over the Burgundians at the battles of Grandson and Murten (1476) as well as at Nancy (1477) made them popular military instruments for European rulers. Louis XI of France had Swiss mercenaries (known as *Reisläufer*) under contract, and Maximilian of Habsburg also rebuilt his army of foot soldiers on the new model. The prerequisite for this system was an oversupply of suitable men in Switzerland.[19] The Swiss defeat of Maximilian and the Swabian League, in particular, led Georg of Frundsberg to model the organisation and training of mercenary armies on the Swiss example. The innovations were not limited to the infantry in field warfare. The Catholic monarchs, for example, trained an infantry armed with swords and shields to storm the Moorish fortresses in Andalucía, supported by gunners and artillery. Elsewhere, too, most of the cannon cast in the fifteenth century were used to attack or defend fortresses. Changes in fortress architecture were also part of this development, for instance the erection of bastions and ramparts, first in Italy but also on Rhodes. There, people feared the successful deployment of cannon such as the Ottomans had practiced during the conquest of Constantinople.

Naval warfare should not be ignored in this context. Thus in the Mediterranean, galleys generally served as warships, although they were also used to transport luxury goods in the Venetian Orient trade. In 1284 Genoa destroyed the Pisan fleet, thus eliminating a maritime rival. Genoa and Venice regularly engaged in naval warfare against one another – Venice controlled the Adriatic and Genoa the Tyrrhenian Sea – until the fifteenth century, when they reached a balance of interests. At this period the two maritime powers already had to defend themselves regularly against the Ottoman Empire, which is why ever more ships of the galley fleets were equipped with cannon. Nevertheless, by 1475 Genoa had lost nearly all of its possessions in the eastern Mediterranean, and the Venetian outposts along the Greek coast had also fallen into Ottoman hands.

The Hanseatic towns regularly equipped warships for the conflicts in north-western Europe and above all in the Baltic region. The naval blockade was a particular strategic method that the Hansa had already imposed on Norway in 1284 to achieve trade-policy objectives. As in the wars against Valdemar IV (from 1368), troops also repeatedly landed by ship in Denmark. Open sea battles, in contrast, were rare, while privateer wars were frequently waged over trade policy, for example against the Dutch, but also against pirates.[20]

Notes

1 Blockmans, *A history of power in Europe*, 170.
2 Hintze, 'Typologie der ständischen Verfassungen'.
3 Russocki, 'Początki Zgromadzeń Stanowych', 178.
4 Ihnatowicz et al., *Społeczeństwo polskie*, 162–7.
5 Schmidt, *Geschichte des Alten Reiches*, 39.
6 Blickle, *Kommunalismus*, II, 27–8.
7 Rösch, *Der venezianische Adel.*
8 Blockmans, 'Representation', 55–7; Dumolyn and Haemers, 'Patterns of urban rebellion'.
9 Puhle, 'Organisationsmerkmale der Hanse'.
10 Blickle, *Kommunalismus*, II, 85–99.
11 Ormrod, 'England in the Middle Ages'.
12 Moraw, 'Verwaltung des Königtums'.
13 Felloni, 'Kredit und Banken'; Pezzolo,' Bonds and government debt', and *Il fisco dei veneziani*, 11–70.
14 Boone, Davids and Janssens (eds), *Urban public debts.*
15 Allmand, 'War'.
16 Blockmans, *A history of power in Europe*, 170.
17 Contamine, *Guerre, état et société*, 278–97.
18 Covini, 'Political and military bonds'; Mallett, *Mercenaries and their masters*, and 'The art of war'; Mallett and Hale (eds), *The military organization.*
19 Schmidtchen, 'Aspekte des Strukturwandels'; Peyer, 'Die wirtschaftliche Bedeutung'.
20 Lane, *Venetian ships and shipbuilders*; Fritze and Krause, *Seekriege der Hanse.*

11

The economy

Unlike the present day, when – with or without the approval of the people – a census is carried out from time to time, the development of the population in the Middle Ages and early modern period can be reconstructed only from a narrow base of sources and in many cases only very roughly estimated. If they exist at all, the sources of demographic history usually served fiscal or administrative purposes and thus offer only indirect information about the population in a given place at a particular time.

The earliest figures come from property inventories such as that compiled by Abbot Irminon of St Germain-des-Prés (Paris), which shortly before 829 registered the complete households of the land users, including the names of their children. According to these inventories, the average household size was 3.6 persons.

Land surveys such as the English Domesday Book of 1086 were the exception. In Italy, the first population records were assembled in the thirteenth century. Similar documents were compiled in Castellón de la Plana (Spain) in 1438, Nuremberg in 1449, Nördlingen in 1459, Fribourg (Switzerland) in 1444–48 or Ypres in 1412, 1437 and 1491 to 1506. Household size ranged from between 3.5 and 3.7 persons in Castellón de la Plana to between 4.1 and 5.5 in Ypres and the German towns. Other sources consulted for demographic studies include poll or hearth tax rolls, although tax exemptions and non-payers can distort the picture here. In addition, lists of citizens and town books (registers of new citizens) provide insight into horizontal mobility. Church registers, which can be used to reconstruct family structures for the early modern period because of their data on baptisms, marriages and deaths, survive in only fragmentary form for the Middle Ages. Thus many population estimates provide general orientation at best. Nonetheless, the analysis of various regional sources

Table 4 Estimated population of Europe, 1000–1500 (in millions)

Territory	*1000*	*1340*	*1450*	*1500*
Greece and the Balkans	5	6	4.5	7
Italy	5	10	7.5	10.5
Iberian Peninsula	7	9	7	6.8
France – Netherlands	6	19	12	18.6
British Isles	2	5	3	3.9
Germany – Scandinavia	4	13	8	10
Russia	6	8	6	9
Poland – Lithuania	2	2.5	3.5	7.5
Hungary	1.5	2	3.5	7.5
Europe as a whole	**38.5**	**74.5**	**55**	**80.8**

Source: J. C. Russell, *Late ancient and medieval population,* p. 148; with corrections, especially for Italy, based on K. J. Beloch, *Bevölkerungsgeschichte Italiens,* III, pp. 344–52, and for the Balkans using J. C. Russell, 'Late medieval Balkan and Asia Minor population', pp. 269–70, as well as J. De Vries, 'Population', 1–50, esp. Table 1, 13.

provides some rough outlines of medieval demographic development.

The population grew most rapidly in the high Middle Ages, from 950 in Italy and later in central and north-western and possibly eastern Europe as well. With the highest growth rates around 1150/1200 and 1300, the population in northern Italy and central and northern Europe tripled. For the first time, population centres such as Paris, London or Cologne passed the 30,000 mark. The increase was only slower in eastern Europe, particularly in the Russia of the Golden Horde. By 1300, however, the limits of growth had been reached in many parts of Europe. Most forests had already been felled, and the marginal soils produced sufficient yields only under optimal conditions. Europe suffered first from famine and then from the plague. This epidemic appeared for the first time in 1331/32 in central Asia and spread from Kaffa in the Crimea to the Mediterranean region via the Genoese trade network. One port city after another succumbed to the contagion. After Cairo and Constantinople, the plague broke out in the Sicilian port of Messina in October 1347. From there it spread in early 1348 to Pisa, Genoa, Venice, Marseilles and Barcelona and then in April to Florence. By June it had appeared in Dorset in south-west England, spreading as far north as Scotland in the course of 1349.

The epidemic crossed the Alps into Bavaria, Swabia and the Rhineland. It spread to Calais, Bergen, Cologne, Copenhagen, Lübeck and

Novgorod with the Hanseatic ships. Not all towns and regions were affected, however. Thus the plague bypassed Milan, Nuremberg and Würzburg, and Brabant, Flanders, Hainaut, Bohemia, Moravia, Silesia and Poland also appear to have been spared. In the early years (1348–50) the mortality rate was around 25 per cent, but high birth rates compensated for it. Subsequent epidemics killed a smaller percentage of the population, although the young were disproportionately affected (the so-called children's plague). By 1380 the overall population of the Holy Roman Empire had fallen by about 40 per cent, and many regions would long continue to stagnate, at best.[1]

Thus in England, whose population had fallen to *c.* 3.2 million from 3.7 million around 1300, signs of recovery did not become evident until 1500. In Flanders, Brabant and Hainaut, which had scarcely been touched by the plague, the population fell from 1.4 million in 1375 to 1.25 million in 1500. In Florence, the most important source, the *Catasto*, reveals long-term demographic stagnation. The same number of people – 128,000 – were counted in the city and its environs in 1470 as in 1427, and only in 1490 did the figure rise to 137,000. Thereafter the population of northern and southern Italy alike exploded. In England, too, the population nearly doubled between 1500 and 1600. In the northern and southern Netherlands, the population also grew substantially up to the 1560s, when demographic conditions were fundamentally altered by migration from the south to the north in the wake of the Dutch Revolt.

Along with mortality, age at marriage and fertility determined demographic development. In respect to marriage, fertility and family structure, what John Hajnal has called the European marriage pattern emerged across the Continent. In this pattern, young couples typically did not marry into the families of their spouses, but instead established homes of their own. Since they only married when they had saved enough money, the marital age in western and northern Europe was relatively high. Although Hajnal's conclusions are based on research on the modern period, this marriage pattern probably applied in the Middle Ages as well. The monastic villications had already been inhabited primarily by parent-child groups (nuclear families), and with the settlement of the east and the so-called hide constitution (*Hufenverfassung*), this family model spread eastward to a line stretching from St Petersburg to Trieste. Only in the Byzantine region, the Balkans, southern Italy and Moorish Spain did other agrarian systems and thus family models persist. Because of the lower age at marriage, birth rates were significantly higher there than in western, central and east-central Europe, where late marriage cut short women's period of fertility.[2]

Since founding a separate household, marrying and leaving the family of origin deprived the parental home of labour and financial means, permission to marry was tied to the consent of the head of household. In many cases marriage was also dependent on the agreement of the feudal lord, the city and the Church or the authorities more generally. The authorities demanded that a man who wished to marry was able to support his family, thus excluding journeyman artisans, servants and farm labourers from the marriage market. Inheritance law had the opposite effect. At least in regions with a form of partible inheritance (*Realteilung*) where each heir had the right to a piece of land of equal size, the regulation of inheritance gave many heirs the possibility of – albeit limited – economic independence, and thus fostered population growth more strongly in south-western Germany than in the north German regions with primogeniture, in which the farm was passed on intact to a single heir, and the other heirs compensated.

Conception roughly followed the rhythms of agrarian labour. Most children were born in late winter, and the fewest during the peak work periods in summer, when mothers could not look after their children. Assuming that every third child died in infancy, and that 10–20 per cent of marriages ended with the premature death of one of the partners, a decline in population could only be avoided if the brief period between late marriage and the menopause was used intensively for reproduction, including the contracting of second marriages.

When analysing the average life span, it is important to distinguish between life expectancy at birth and the life expectancy of those who survived childhood. While according to English observations up to the year 1300, and again in the fifteenth century, average estimated life expectancy at birth was around thirty, older children could expect to live a good deal longer. In the intervening period, diseases and the plague had lowered life expectancy to less than twenty years. We have more precise figures for Florence based on the *Catasto*. Thus in the early fourteenth century, the average Florentine could expect to live to the age of forty. From the plague years up to the end of the fourteenth century, life expectancy fell to about twenty, and only stabilised at around forty again in the second half of the fifteenth century. Demographic incursions also influenced marital age and the contraction of marriage. Thus as a result of the plague, the age at first marriage fell markedly for both men and women, and only gradually rose when the population began to grow again. While before the plague the average age at marriage for men in Florence was thirty, in the surviving records for the period between 1351 and 1400 men married at twenty-four.

In the fifteenth century, however, the age of marriage had returned to thirty. Florentine women, much like their contemporaries in Prato, delayed the time of marriage in the fifteenth century, only marrying at nearly twenty-one years (average age 20.8) rather than at eighteen (average age 17.6) as they had earlier.[3]

There are also many examples of elderly persons in positions of power in the Middle Ages, however. In the seventh century, Theodore of Tarsus only became bishop of Canterbury at the age of sixty-seven, and lived for another twenty-one years. Doge Enrico Dandolo led the Fourth Crusade when he was over eighty years old, and despite the low average life expectancy, many bishops lived extremely long lives. The European ruling dynasties, in contrast, appear to have suffered from shorter life spans in the late Middle Ages owing to the stresses of life at court and in the tournaments. Many men already held important offices at the age of twenty-one or twenty-two. Accordingly, by the age of fifty, Emperor Charles V, but also theologians such as Martin Luther or John Calvin, already felt exhausted and decrepit. The life expectancy of women in the Middle Ages and the early modern period was significant lower than men's. Frequent childbirth and hard physical labour sapped women's energies and made them more susceptible to disease.[4] The glorification of the feminine in chivalric romances and *Minnesang* did little to change that. Girls were already more likely to be neglected in childhood than boys, as the Florentine example shows.[5] Female infants were abandoned more frequently than male, so that in 1419 the commune of Florence decided to establish the foundling hospital later built by Brunelleschi.[6]

11.1 The feudal system and agrarian production

Three factors defined agriculture in pre-industrial Europe: social organisation, demographic development and biogeographic conditions. The last included the division of Europe into two climate zones, which were separated approximately by the Loire and the Alps. In the northern zone, with its naturally damp climate, summer cereals were planted, while in the southern zone a water shortage and dry summers were typical. Here, cereals could only be cultivated with the aid of artificial irrigation.

The dominant forms of social organisation were the manorial system and feudalism, which in many regions persisted into the nineteenth century. In the feudal system, the feudal lord, who was obliged to provide military services in the form of armour and horses in case of war, did not work the land personally, but delegated this labour to dependent peasants (*grundhold*, *villein*) who offered the lord dues and services (socage) and received protection in exchange. The feudal system was organised in *villicationes* or manors with scattered holdings, whereby the *villicatio* was composed of a demesne (*terra salica*), which was worked by bonded farm labourers and dependent peasants, and peasant land (hide land).

The feudal system developed into a fixed economic and legal system in the Carolingian period, when individual manors took shape as comparatively self-sufficient economic units, which scarcely depended on the market for their own needs. Degrees of autarchy differed. Alongside large *villicationes* with extensive economic autarchy in the heartland of the Carolingian kingdom between the Loire and the Rhine, other feudal manors served mainly as collecting points for peasant dues. During the ninth and tenth centuries, increasing numbers of free peasants became dependent as a result of the expansion of the feudal system through clearing, the suppression of formerly free peasants but also voluntary submission to influential protectors, although the degree of dependency varied from manor to manor and region to region.

In all those areas where particular skills were needed, for example embanking or draining land, peasants retained or regained their freedom. At the same time, peasants gained more freedoms with the dissolution of the *villicatio* system and the inland colonisation of the high Middle Ages beginning in the eleventh century. The causes of these changes were strong population growth, advances in agricultural productivity – for example through the introduction of the plough and three-field crop rotation – as well as an upswing in trade and commerce, which made possible a division of labour between town and countryside.

The cultivation of the lord's demesne using serf labour was replaced either by forming peasant holdings or granting larger enclosed sections of the demesne to a peasant farmer. Socage was replaced by payments in money and kind, which gave peasant farms greater autonomy. Their production for the emerging urban market grew and gave them the opportunity to earn money. The manorial lords, who now received money rents from their peasants, could also purchase the necessities on the urban markets, since urban artisans produced goods better and cheaper than the lord's villeins had done. The former services on the demesne also became superfluous and were replaced by cash payments.[7]

The dissolution of the manorial system and the accompanying development of money rents proceeded quite unevenly in Europe, as the following examples illustrate. In Italy, where the manorial system was already less firmly established than in western and central Europe, its dissolution ran parallel to the wave of urbanisation between the eleventh and thirteenth centuries. Peasants moved to the cities, villages became towns; the commercialisation of peasant production, that is, market orientation, was in full swing from the twelfth century. Thus in 1196, a feudal lord in Arquà could already boast that he had the best peasant in the village because the man had loaned him money. Feudal dues, which in mid-thirteenth-century Tuscany consisted of cereals, money and pepper, point to peasants' close contacts to the market, since they had to buy the pepper.[8]

Moreover, by the twelfth century systems of fixed-term leases had become established, which gradually supplanted long-term use at a fixed rent, since Italian feudal lords seem to have been the first to recognise that indefinitely tying land use to a fixed rent would diminish their incomes in the long run because of the devaluation of coinage, which progressed more quickly there than elsewhere in Europe. The manorial lords preferred the already long-established *mezzadria* (share-cropping) system, in which lord and tenant each received 50 per cent of the agricultural produce, whether in cereals, olives or cattle. One could, of course, regard this as a return to the barter economy, but it was more the successful attempt of lords to participate directly in rising prices for agricultural products at a time of increasing monetary depreciation.

In the rest of Europe, share-cropping played a dominant role in the cultivation of large estates only in Flanders, the most economically and monetarily advanced region after Italy. In France and Germany, the majority of peasants held land tenancies based on heritable rents (*Erbzinsrecht*) with payment in money and kind. It is impossible to generalise about the types of rents, although certain regional trends are evident. Thus in twelfth-century Roussillon, for example, peasants largely paid their rent in kind, although this was replaced by money rents there, as in Picardy, Normandy, Languedoc, Poitou or Burgundy, in the late twelfth and particularly the thirteenth century.

In the German lands, feudal labour services were largely supplanted by rents in money and kind in the twelfth and thirteenth centuries and lands were let for hereditary rents. Payments in money and kind often played equal roles, as was the case in the 'records of customs' (*Weistümer*) of Werden Abbey in the Ruhr. Thus one cannot simply say that in the long term, money replaced payment in kind. Even if the *Weistümer* and leases stipulated monetary payments, the lords also seem to have accepted payment in kind when the peasants lacked cash.

In the territories of northern, central and eastern Germany, the monetary economy only gradually penetrated rural society in the thirteenth and fourteenth centuries. Inland colonisation and the settlement of the east made early contributions to monetarisation. Peasants who participated in reclamation by clearing and embanking land received their holdings in hereditary tenancy and, after a stipulated rent-free period had elapsed, had to pay a fixed money rent and make payment in kind. Apart from these calculable payments, the larger plots of land, hereditary tenancy rights and judicial autonomy were attractive to settlers and encouraged them to participate in colonisation enterprises in the lower and middle Elbe regions and later in the Mark Brandenburg, Mecklenburg, Pomerania, Prussia, Pomerelia and Schleswig-Holstein. Colonisation had a number of advantages for the German and Slavic princes and feudal lords in the new areas of settlement, who attracted settlers with the help of settlement entrepreneurs known as locators. Not only could they expand the land under cultivation, but for the first time they also had a dependable source of money, instead of relying on the agricultural and artisanal services of the Slavic population to meet their basic everyday needs.

Nevertheless, inland colonisation and population growth could not continue indefinitely. By about 1300, the land resources were exhausted in many places. First famine (1315–26) and then the plague (1349–51) descended upon a densely populated Europe. The population decline led to an agrarian crisis that left large segments of land desolate. In order to use the land at all, some regions went over to specialised crops and intensified cultivation, while others switched to extensive agriculture, converting fields of grain to pasture and grazing land for cattle. Thus sheepherding was expanded in England and Spain, as was viniculture in Burgundy or along the Rhine and the Moselle. There was also more room now for specialised crops (flax, madder, woad, hops, fruit and vegetables). No fundamental change in agricultural production could be expected, however, given the inadequacy of fertilisation, irrigation and drainage methods. Yields remained correspondingly meagre. One grain sown produced an average of only three to four grains, and the yield by acre did not change much either. On the demesne of the bishop of Winchester between 1208 and 1452, 11 bushels of grain were harvested per acre. This was the case although, owing to the use of fertilisers and other measures, land productivity had been higher in the period of strong demand for cereals before the plague than afterward, when the demographic losses no longer offered any incentive to intensify agriculture.[9] The demographic revival of the late fifteenth century also brought agricultural recovery, but it was based largely on the extensive expansion of acreage rather than intensification and heightened productivity.

11.2 The trades and manufacturing

Although agriculture was doubtless the dominant economic sector in terms of output and the population involved, manufacturing represented a far greater part of aggregate output than the number of persons employed in it would lead us to expect. While cereals were largely consumed by the producers and their feudal lords, only industrial production was more strongly commercialised. Even in an underdeveloped country such as England, the proportion of grain in aggregate output around 1300 has been estimated at less than 40 per cent. The significance of manufactures in the more highly developed and urbanised European regions such as Lombardy, Tuscany or Flanders thus appears all the greater.[10]

In the early Middle Ages, the crafts were centred around the noble and princely courts and the royal domains (*villicationes*). Peasants generally produced their own clothing and tools. In the Slavic regions of east-central Europe specialised craftsmen who made high-quality products (weapons, metal work or clothing) for princes and manorial lords worked in service settlements. The rise of cities in the high and late Middle Ages represented an important caesura, leading to a growing division of labour between town and countryside. Although wheel- and cartwrights as well as cobblers, tailors and members of the victual trades (bakers) continued to work in the villages, the rest of craft production shifted permanently to the towns.

In the cities, artisans organised themselves in occupational organisations, the guilds, whose statutes were issued by the town authorities or town council. The guilds were associations of independent master craftsmen and exercised a monopoly as well as regulating competition within the trade. Anyone who produced particular artisanal products was obliged to join the corresponding guild (guild coercion), and was only allowed to ply that trade within the city (*Bannmeile*). Within the guild, regulation or the removal of competition ensured that all members had an equal chance to earn a living. To this end, the guilds limited the number of workshops, journeymen and apprentices, restricted working and opening hours and stipulated the prices as well as the quality of products in detail. As production processes grew more complex, the guilds also became increasingly diversified. Thus, for example, textile workers such as weavers, fullers, shearers and sometimes also dyers organised their own separate guilds.

The trades boomed with the rise in the number of towns in the high and late Middle Ages, quickly taking artisanal production beyond the limits of local demand. The products of urban craftsmen were not only sold in the environs; certain commodities, such as textiles, soon conquered foreign markets as well. The urban trades organised, diversified and specialised. The good reputation of cloth from Stamford or Arras, for instance, meant that it was imitated in other towns. A key factor in the development of textile exports was the introduction of the horizontal foot treadle loom in the eleventh and twelfth centuries, which allowed for both complicated patterns and higher production. The use of new raw materials in textile manufacturing and dyeing led to innovations and a broader range of products. Cotton and silk fabrics became more popular, while the trend shifted from heavy woollens to lighter textiles and blended fabrics. English worsteds and the new lighter draperies from the Netherlands captured the markets. Apart from high-quality textiles, demand also grew for standardised mass products, whose quality was guaranteed by trademarks and cloth seals.

European cloth manufacturing was centred in the Flemish towns, from where production also shifted in the late Middle Ages to Brabant, Holland and England. Cloth was the most important commodity traded at the fairs in Champagne, and went mainly to Italy, but also to central Europe. The supply of wool, which Flanders drew mainly from England, was a key factor here. Flanders, where smaller towns (Dixmude, Langemark, Hondschoote and Poperinge) increasingly became known for their own production alongside major urban centres such as Ypres or Ghent, is remarkable for the wide range of cloth on offer.[11] Thus in his account book, the Hamburg merchant Vicko von Geldersen (1367–92) mentions forty different types of Flemish and French cloth.

Another cloth merchant who plays an outstanding role in the literature was Francesco Datini. His enterprise and its branches in the Mediterranean region devoted much attention to the purchase of wool from local production, weaving and cloth sales. He bought wool from England but above all from the Balearic Islands, for Italian textile manufacturers depended on shipments of Spanish wool. Thus it may have been problems with the supply of raw material in Italy that led to a boom in fustian weaving. Fustian, a blended fabric made by weaving cotton wefts on a linen warp, which was pleasant to wear in both warm and cold weather, originated in the Near East, spread via Sicily in the twelfth century and became well established in Bologna, Venice, Piacenza and Milan in the thirteenth. In the fourteenth century, demand for Italian fustian was so robust in Germany that south German merchants bought it on a grand scale. In the mid-fourteenth century, cotton purchases by German merchants in Venice document the establishment of a fustian industry in southern Germany as well. Cities such as Ravensburg, Regensburg, Constance, Basle, Ulm or Augsburg converted their traditional linen production to fustian and thus became dependent on deliveries of raw materials from Venice. The south German product became an export hit and was sold first in central Europe and later chiefly at the fairs of Brabant.[12]

In Italy, silk gained ground alongside fustian. By the twelfth century, in the silk centre of Lucca silk was already being produced for export, for example to Bruges. For many years, however, it was impossible to acquire the necessary raw material for silk production from mulberry trees in northern Italy. Accordingly, raw silk had to be imported from Asia Minor, Andalucía and Sicily. Only in the fifteenth century did significant Florentine silk manufacturing emerge, and Venice came to surpass Lucca. At the same time, Genoa was successful with velvet, another silk product greatly in demand for Renaissance fashion.[13]

While in the late Middle Ages Flanders, northern Italy and southern Germany dominated European textile production, from the sixteenth century those regions would be replaced by England, the northern Netherlands and later France. The south German region managed to maintain its pre-eminent status in the manufacture of metal products and above all in large-scale mining and metalworking enterprises. Like agriculture, mining belongs to the primary sector of the economy, since it uses natural resources. Because of its close relationship with metallurgy and smelting, however, it must also be regarded as a processing sector. The first mining boom was dominated by silver and began in the Rammelsberg mine near Goslar, although silver yields in the Vosges and the southern Black Forest also played a role. This boom peaked in the twelfth and thirteenth centuries with discoveries of silver in Trent, Montieri and Massa Marittima in Tuscany, Iglesias on Sardinia, Friesach in Carinthia and Freiberg in the Erzgebirge. In the thirteenth century, additional mines were opened in Iglau (Jihlava, Moravia), Kuttenberg (Kutná Hora, Bohemia) and the Hungarian mining towns. This era ended in the fourteenth century when the veins were exhausted and many mines flooded, in part for climatic reasons. Despite temporary yields of silver in Bosnia and Serbia (Srebrenica, Trepa, Novo Brdo), mining only revived around 1460. Driven by a shortage of silver, 'a second mining boom emerged from the interplay between long-distance merchants willing to invest and interested in mining and metallurgy, princes open to new forms of organising capital and labour and ready to grant the corresponding privileges and, not least, hardworking miners'.[14] The boom continued – in different regions at different times – into the late sixteenth century and was marked by the mining and smelting of silver and copper.

Flooded mines were restored to productivity with pumps driven by waterwheels and new shafts driven to depths of up to 400 metres. Innovative smelting methods such as the Saiger technique, which used lead to separate silver from copper, improved yields of precious metals. This fundamentally altered the forms of enterprise involved, since these innovations required investments that exceeded the means of the miners' guilds. The deeper the mines, the greater the influence of merchant capital on mining and the greater the concentration in the hands of a few providers of capital became. The miners, heretofore skilled craftsmen, became wage labourers and the south German merchant companies like the Fuggers organised mining and smelting as vertically concentrated large enterprises or at least as a putting-out system. Key factors were the coordination of a production process requiring many workers and work steps on the one hand, and the organisation of material, provisions, transport and sales on the other.

The most significant deposits were now those at Schwaz in the Tyrol, the silver fields of Schneeberg, Annaberg and Buchholz on the Saxon side of the Erzgebirge and the Joachimstal silver mine discovered in 1518 on its southern slope. In this connection one must also mention the argentiferous copper deposits in Neusohl (Banská Bystrica) and the county of Mansfeld, from which both copper and silver could be extracted using the Saiger method. This proved so successful that at the height of their productivity in the 1520s, the silver output of the Saiger smelteries at Eisleben and Hettstedt exceeded even that of the Saxon deposits at Schneeberg, Annaberg and Buchholz, without, however, being able to touch that of the Schwaz fields, which were exploited by the Fuggers and surpassed all others. If one adds together the production figures for the various regions, the massive expansion of central European silver production becomes evident. It doubled between the 1470s and 1520s, and peaked in the decade that followed. Thereafter, silver mining declined more or less sharply in the various mining regions.

Silver was transported from the mining regions to the bullion markets, among which the trade fair city of Frankfurt occupied a central position. The European silver dealers met in Frankfurt, and it was here that the mints acquired their supply of the valuable raw material, which they paid for in gold. Silver also flowed through commerce to the Netherlands, England and above all Italy and the Levant, since there was still a trade deficit with the south.[15]

The mining of iron ore, the most significant industrial raw material apart from wood, was also important. Iron was mined in the Upper Palatinate, the Siegerland and the Dillenburg region but above all in Sweden. The new smelting-furnace technology, which spread from northern Italy in the late Middle Ages, substantially increased the production of crude iron. Crude iron was either cast into pots, kettles or stove plates or worked with hammers and then processed by nail-, black- or gunsmiths or turned into wire. The largest European iron-producing region was the Upper Palatinate, centred in Amberg and Sulzbach.

11.3 The expansion of trade

We need to distinguish between the various levels and organisational forms in trade – and accordingly between various forms of marketplace. The lowest level was local trade. It was conducted within a town or between the town and its environs or various centres of production. The goods involved were foodstuffs and other everyday necessities, which were sold either by small shopkeepers or tradesmen (bakers, butchers, etc.) in their shops or by them and other producers (peasants) at weekly markets. Markets were generally held once or twice a week, usually in the city, but also in rural market towns.

While weekly markets served the local trade, the long-distance trade concentrated on the fairs that were held several times a year in certain cities with the permission and under the protection of the authorities. The dates of fairs were set so that merchants could visit one after the other in neighbouring cities. Historians accordingly look to certain changes in long-distance trade as indicators of the development of European commerce. The first of these occurred around AD 800, when Europe entered into commercial relations with the artisanally and commercially developed Muslim countries of the Mediterranean rim; a second phase of upheaval was the so-called commercial revolution of the thirteenth century.[16]

In the eleventh century, the Italian coastal cities increasingly entered the Mediterranean trade. The Crusades in the Holy Land and the *Reconquista* in Spain continually extended the dominance of Latin Christendom. The Mongol conquests (*pax mongolica*, *c.* 1200/50–1350), which stretched from Lithuania and Hungary to Peking, also opened up new trade relations with the empires of the Golden Horde in Europe and Asia. As the example of Marco Polo shows, commercial voyages to India, central Asia and China were nothing unusual for Italian merchants. Northern and central European goods also reached the Italian markets, however, with the fairs of

Champagne held on six fixed dates in the towns of Lagny, Bar-sur-Aube, Provins and Troyes developing into a crossroads of trade between western Europe, Italy, the Orient and even eastern Europe.

The so-called commercial revolution of the thirteenth century (see Introduction) further stimulated development. The trade in luxury goods was joined by the trade in mass goods, which offered new opportunities for participation to producers in northern and eastern Europe (see 5.12). Instead of small quantities of luxury goods, mass goods such as fish, salt, grain, furs, wax, honey, wine, raw wool and cloth were transported over long distances, and merchants no longer made their money from the sale of a few products with a high profit margin, but instead from selling large quantities at a smaller profit.

The development of Nuremberg's eastern trade and the intensification of economic relations with Venice in the fourteenth century brought about a shift in the continental trade system, whose centre the Frankfurt fairs now became. There the Nurembergers bought goods they sold to customers in the east: woollens from Hesse and the middle Rhine area, Flanders, Brabant and England and linen and fustian from southern Germany. They also brought precious and non-ferrous metals as well as Oriental goods imported via Venice to the Frankfurt fairs (see 5.3). Thus Frankfurt benefited to the same degree as the emerging world market of Antwerp from the rise in the continental trade during the second half of the fifteenth century.[17] By the beginning of the fifteenth century, the twice-yearly Brabant fairs in Antwerp and Bergen op Zoom developed into hubs for the trade in English woollens. They were imported, for example by the English Company of Merchant Adventurers, as semi-finished goods to Brabant, where they were dyed and glazed and sold as finished goods to Hansa merchants and soon to south Germans as well. The south German demand for cloth, like the Antwerp market for silver, attracted the expanding commerce of Nuremberg and Augsburg merchants in silver, copper and fustian to the Scheldthe. Here they met not just Englishmen, but also the Portuguese with their Asian trade and African gold and ivory; the Portuguese, in turn, depended on south German metal goods as well as copper and silver for their own trade with Africa and India. Thus Antwerp's rise to a 'European world market' in the late fifteenth century was founded on English cloth, south German metals and Portuguese spices (see 5.15).

11.4 Money and currency

The period between the second half of the twelfth and the middle of the fourteenth centuries was characterised by the geographical and social expansion of the money economy. While international trade and payment transactions intensified in the wake of the commercial revolution in southern Europe and the founding of cities in the Baltic region, money also reached broader segments of the population through the expansion of peasant production for the market in west and east. New mints were opened, new coins were struck in silver and – for the first time in centuries – in gold, and the bill of exchange developed as an instrument of cashless payment. On the geographical and social level, the new basis for increasing monetarisation was the tapping of fresh sources of precious metals, such as the exploitation of the silver fields of Freiberg, Friesach, Iglau and above all Kuttenberg. The European mints that purchased the new silver in ingot form as a raw material began by increasing their traditional production of small silver coins (known variously as *denier*, penny and other names derived from the Latin *denarius*). In the course of the thirteenth and fourteenth centuries they then began striking coins of larger denominations when needed. The demand for larger coins was strongest in Italy, the most economically advanced region in Europe; it was here, after all, that the Carolingian *denier*, which originally weighed 1.7 g, evolved into light coins with an infinitesimal silver content (0.1 to 0.2 g). Thus in 1194 Venice began minting a larger silver coin, the *grosso*, with a weight of 2.19 g. Genoa, Venice's rival in the Mediterranean trade, followed in the early thirteenth century along with the other northern Italian city-states. At the same time, the minting of larger silver coins to the value of several *deniers* also began north of the Alps. France commenced in 1266 with the minting of the *gros tournois* to the value of twelve *deniers*, which found imitators and still dominated the circulation of coinage in north-western Germany in the late fourteenth century. Bohemia followed around 1300 with the introduction of the Prague *groschen* minted of Kuttenberg silver. In England, the Low Countries and the German territories the time was not yet ripe for a coin of this size, which was too large for the requirements of local transactions. Only in the course of the fourteenth century were the English groat, various Flemish *groschen*, the Meißen *groschen* and, in the fifteenth century, the north German shilling valued at twelve pennies introduced. Equally important to the history of money as the establishment of the *groschen* was the resumption of gold coinage through the introduction of the *genovino* and the *fiorino* by Genoa and Florence, respectively, in

1252. There were several reasons for the revival of gold coinage. One was that the city-states needed gold coins for their trade with southern Italy, Spain and Sicily, and another was that for the first time, trade with North Africa brought in sufficient African gold to mint coins. The *genovino* and the *fiorino* were minted of 3.53 g and 3.54 g of pure, twenty-four-carat gold, respectively. Soon the new gold coin was circulating as a recognised means of payment in Italy, France, England and the Levant. Hungary minted the first *fiorini* or florins north of the Alps in 1325. In the German territories, the Rhenish electors adopted the minting of florins (known as *gulden*) on the Florentine model in the 1340s. They used the transit duties levied on the Rhine and its navigable tributaries as sources of gold. In this way, the Rhenish florin issued by the electors as their common currency from 1386 became the anchor currency in the empire and western Europe in the late Middle Ages. Apart from the *fiorino* or florin, we must also mention the ducat (3.54 g, twenty-four carats), minted in Venice of Hungarian gold from 1284. With the ducat, Venice created a gold coin that supplanted the silver money previously used in the city's Orient trade. It would become the dominant trade coin in the Near and Middle East in the second half of the fourteenth century. In the fifteenth century, Venice exported some 300,000 ducats annually for the purchase of spices and other goods in the Near East. By the fifteenth century, the ducat was already being imitated in both the eastern and western Mediterranean region. The fifteenth century also saw the gradual establishment of the ducat in central and western Europe.[18]

The monetarisation of the economy and society continued in the fourteenth century, although the bullion shortages of the fourteenth and fifteenth centuries saw repeated setbacks in the use of money. Central European silver mining came to an almost complete standstill in the fourteenth century. The flow of African gold also slowed to a trickle. The European mints reduced production where they did not stop it altogether. It has been estimated that European coin production fell by about 80 per cent between 1331/40 and 1491/1500.[19] The decline was not uniform, however, since phases of stronger coin shortages alternated with periods of revived coin production, and there were also regional differences. Thus England and Castile, for instance, were less affected than other countries by the shortage of precious metals because of their export income. The money supply fell overall, especially because Europe's permanent trade deficit with the Levant led to a constant flow of precious metals in that direction. The money supply also continued to lose coins to wear and hoarding.[20]

In the second half of the fifteenth century people not only began to pump out flooded mines and put them back into operation, but also discovered several new silver veins in rapid succession (see 11.2). The silver was brought to the bullion markets from the mining regions, and mints starved by the famine of precious metals now devoured it. The growing silver supply was visible in the coins themselves, since large silver coins were now produced for the first time. Venice led the way, striking a silver coin weighing 6 g in 1472. Milan and the Swiss cities followed. The actual minting of large silver coins or taler proceeded from the mining territories themselves, though. Archduke Sigismund 'the Rich' of the Tyrol took advantage of the Schwaz silver deposits to introduce a fundamental coinage reform. After the *pfundner* and the half-guldiner in 1486 Sigismund created the first taler coin in the *guldiner*, which had the same value as a gold florin. This prototype had as yet no importance as currency, however. Only the production of the mints in Schneeberg, Annaberg, Buchholz and above all Joachimstal made the taler a universally recognised means of payment. In this early phase, the taler was still referred to as a *guldengroschen* ('a groschen for a gulden'), until the extensive coinage from the Joachimstal mint gave the taler its name.[21]

11.5 Credit and banking

The central characteristics of banking – a word derived from *bancus*, the table used by money changers (*bancherii*) – are lending with the aid of equity and investment capital, payment on behalf of creditors and money exchange. These services were not necessarily always offered by the same firm, and even today banks differ in the services they provide. In the early Middle Ages, a master coiner such as St Eligius could function equally as a moneychanger, dealer in precious metals, goldsmith and money lender, and it was only in the course of the late Middle Ages that the various categories of banking emerged in Italy: international merchant bankers, local cambists and bankers as well as pawnbrokers. From here, institutions such as public exchange banks and public pawn offices (*monti di pietà*) developed.

International merchant bankers combined long-distance trade with exchange transactions. By 1200, Italian merchants were already lending money to other merchants who travelled to the fairs in Champagne in exchange for obligations (promissory notes – *instrumenta ex causa cambium*), which fell due at the fairs. The fairs thus became a market for goods, money and information and a clearinghouse for claims and debts. The *instrumentum* evolved into the bill of exchange. It allowed money to be accepted in one city or country and paid back in another city or country, or transferred from one country to another. This was associated with currency conversion at a set rate. In the next century, the bill of exchange established itself in Italian trade with the western Mediterranean and western Europe, and only when large trade deficits arose were they settled in precious metals. The bill of exchange served a second purpose as well: to circumvent the widespread ban on usury. Since canon law prohibited lending money for interest and threatened usurers with hellfire, interest rates could not be declared publicly or set in advance. By concealing interest behind the exchange rate, which fluctuated on the European money markets according to supply and demand, the creditor nevertheless benefited from his loan. Otherwise, the Italian merchant houses would doubtless not have made such transactions one of their lines of business.

The leading European financiers ('the Rothschilds of the thirteenth century') were the Bonsignori of Siena, followed in the age of the commercial revolution by Florentine family companies such as the Bardi, the Peruzzi and the Acciaiuoli. They drew their company capital (*corpo*) from family members, kinsmen and third parties and divided the profits and losses proportionately to the investments, although the liability of each individual was not limited by law. The companies had branches throughout Europe; the Peruzzi, for example, had fifteen stretching from London to Cyprus. The societies functioned as papal collectors, tax farmers and lenders to princes and also engaged in long-distance trade and bill transactions. In the early 1340s the houses of Bardi and Peruzzi failed because they had overextended themselves providing credit to the city of Florence and above all to King Edward III, who stopped his payments of interest and principal. New, smaller companies that organised their branch offices on the basis of separate partnerships took their place.

Examples include Francesco di Marco Datini, the renowned merchant of Prato, and the Medici bank. The Medici began in the late fourteenth century with investments in woollen and silk manufacturing as well as in a small but very successful bank in Florence. Branches were opened in Geneva (later Lyons), Bruges, Pisa, London, Avignon, Milan and Basle (during the Council). The most successful branch by far was that in the Roman curia, which also followed the Pope to his other residences. After the death of Cosimo de' Medici in 1464, however, economic decline set in here as well. Unauthorised credits to the English Crown and Charles the Bold of Burgundy and the collapse of the Lyons branch were among the contributing factors. Outside Italy, the outstanding merchant bankers included Jacques Coeur of Bourges, financier and purveyor by appointment to the French Crown, and the Fuggers, who represented the south German type of commercial and banking house with their widely ramified investments in productive sectors, notably mining.

Beneath the level of the international merchant bankers were the local moneychangers or bankers. The moneychangers or cambists were experts in recognising the various local and foreign coins; they knew the exchange rates and alloys, and could distinguish between genuine and counterfeit coins. Apart from this they also accepted deposits – in Genoa from the twelfth century – in current accounts (*conto corrente*) that private individuals or merchant companies could open with them. From this current account the moneychanger transferred funds on oral instructions from one account to another, or to the accounts of other moneychanger banks. To the degree that customers used cashless payments in bank money or deposit money – i.e., no longer withdrew their deposits – the capital available to the moneychanger grew. This allowed him to offer overdraft credits to his customers as well as small loans to merchants, tradesmen and the State.

Moneychangers' accounts had particular significance for the settlement and thus the intensification of bill transactions. The issuer of a bill of exchange, for example, drew it on his moneychanger, who paid the bill from the issuer's account when it became due by crediting the amount to the account of the beneficiary of the bill of exchange. In the thirteenth and early fourteenth centuries, the great significance of bank or deposit money in payment transactions, which allowed for a rational treatment of available precious metals, was still limited to northern Italy, where the higher than average money supply and degree of monetarisation guaranteed the encashment at any time of deposit money in the form of coins. In the regions of western and central Europe where monetarisation proceeded more slowly, the introduction of cashless payment was accordingly more sluggish. To be sure, in the twelfth and thirteenth century every town had municipal moneychangers who converted foreign coins into local currency, traded in precious metals and sometimes minted coins as well, but in Bruges, as in the Rhineland or southern Germany, there is no evidence of private exchange offices performing banking functions before the second half of the fourteenth and the fifteenth century.

Moneychangers and exchange banks often became the instigators and victims of crises when customers suddenly plundered their accounts in times of monetary panic. As a result, many exchange offices did not survive the great bullion shortage of the late fourteenth and early fifteenth century. Municipal governments were thus compelled to establish public exchange and deposit banks (the *taula de canvi*, founded in 1401 in Barcelona and 1408 in Valencia, and the Casa di San Giorgio founded in 1407 in Genoa), many of which also struggled with liquidity problems. Only those institutions founded in the late sixteenth century proved successful: they included the Banco di San Giorgio in Genoa (1586), Banco della Piazza di Rialto in Venice (1587), Banco di Messina (1587), Banco di Sant'Ambrogio in Milan (1593), etc. In the seventeenth century, they served as models for the establishment of municipal exchange banks in Amsterdam, Hamburg or Nuremberg.[22]

The most important form of credit on the lower level was pawnbroking, which helped to alleviate cash and food shortages during the annual cycle of agricultural production. The poor needed credit for their bare survival, and pawned a blanket, for instance, while the wealthy left jewels as pledges to finance the consumption of luxury goods. The business of giving loans for pledges was left to Jews, who as non-Christians were banned from the craft guilds as well as the ownership of real property, so that they invested their capital in the credit business. Both the seasonal shortage of money and grain and the difficulty of turning grain into cash in time to make interest payments opened a market niche for Jewish moneylenders. Italian cities and villages virtually invited Jews to set up pawn offices. In exchange for lowering the interest rate (to 15–20 per cent), the authorities guaranteed certain families a monopoly as well as the freedom to practice their religion, including kosher butchering. Cities and villages used such privileges to try to break the dominance of Christian usurers in the local money market (see 4.4).

The Christian usurers were primarily so-called Lombards, Piedmontese merchants from Asti and Chieri, as well as Cahorsins from Cahors in south-western France. The Lombards were already established in western Europe in the mid-thirteenth century, and soon made themselves indispensable with their novel financial practices. In contrast to the Tuscan merchant bankers, they limited their activities to lending small and middling sums, and only succeeded in entering the field of political finance in the regions between the Maas and the Rhine. While theologians were still debating whether the Tuscan merchant houses and local moneylenders were engaged in usury or illicit lucre (*turpe lucrum*), everyone agreed that pawnbroking plainly violated the so-called canonical prohibition of interest, which was based on Aristotelian ethics (which criticised as unnatural 'the birth of money from money') and the Sermon on the Mount ('lend, hoping for nothing in return'). For that reason pawnbroking, while officially banned and prosecuted, was also approved and specially licensed by territorial rulers and town councils, since it meant an additional source of revenue as well as credit for cities and territories.

In their campaign against 'infidel usurers' in fifteenth-century Italy, the Franciscan preachers invented the *monte di pietà*, i.e., the public pawn office. The *monte di poveri* founded in Perugia in 1462 is considered the oldest of its kind. Not long afterward, pawn offices popped up everywhere in northern and central Italy. They were of two types. In the cities, the *monti di pietà* gave credit to anyone who could leave his or her personal property as a pledge. They demanded a modest rate of interest (3 per cent) and the sum had to be repaid within a certain period. In the countryside, the *monti frumentari* provided wheat for sowing, which would be replaced after the harvest. Originally, the Church supported the pawn offices with donations, which were supplemented by endowments and public subsidies. Since the demand for loans clearly outstripped the capital resources, leading to credit shortages, in 1515 Pope Leo X issued a bull allowing the pawn offices to accept interest-bearing deposits and to calculate the interest costs when giving credit. This decision increased the capital base of the pawn offices, although it did not put an end to the canon-law discussion on the charging of interest by the *monti di pietà*. The idea of the *monte di pietà* – similar institutions also existed in fifteenth-century Spain – spread to western Europe, where public pawn offices were set up in the sixteenth century in Ypres (1534) and Bruges (1573) after the departure of the Lombards from those cities.[23]

Notes

1 Benedictow, *The black death 1346–1353*; Cohn, *The black death transformed*.

2 Mitterauer, *Warum Europa?*, chap. 3.

3 Herlihy and Klapisch-Zuber, *Tuscans and their families*, 78–92.

4 Russell, *Population in Europe*.

5 Klapisch-Zuber, *La maison et le nom*; Idem (ed.), *A history of women in the West*, II; Idem, *Women, family and the ritual*.

6 Herlihy and Klapisch-Zuber, *Tuscans and their families*, 145–6.

7 Jenks, 'Von den archaischen Grundlagen'.

8 Jones, 'Medieval agrarian society', 402; Cherubini, *Agricoltura e società rurale*, 45–61.

9 Campbell, 'Land, labour, livestock'; Thornton, 'The determinants of land productivity'.

10 Epstein, *Freedom and growth*.

11 Munro, 'Medieval woollens'.

12 Stromer, *Die Gründung der Baumwollindustrie*.

13 Cavaciocchi (ed.) *La seta in Europa*; Goldthwaite, *The economy of Renaissance Florence*, 282–95; Molà, *La comunità dei lucchesi a Venezia*.

14 Westermann, *Das Eislebener Garkupfer*, 249–50.
15 Suhling, *Der Seigerhüttenprozeß*; Westermann, *Das Eislebener Garkupfer*, 247, 251; Attman, *The bullion flow*, 61–7.
16 For an overview, see Spufford, *Power and profit*.
17 Jenks, 'Von den archaischen Grundlagen', 71–2.
18 Spufford, *Money and its use*; Lane and Mueller, *Money and banking*, 276–84, 373–9.
19 Day, 'The great bullion famine', and 'The question of monetary contraction', 20.
20 North, *Das Geld und seine Geschichte*, 34–44.
21 Ibid., 70–6.
22 Van der Wee, 'European banking', 74–116.
23 Mueller, 'Les prêteurs juifs de Venise'; Reichert, 'Lombarden', 188–223; Soetaert, *De 'Berg van Charitate'*; Menning, *Charity and state*.

12

Society

12.1 Divine *ordo*

According to the Church fathers, God created the world as an *ordo*. *Ordo* here meant both the order of the world and of each individual estate to which God had assigned human beings. This model of 'harmony through inequality', however, was but one of the competing ordering principles of medieval society. Thus one may understand medieval society as a structure composed of various orders or estates (clergy, nobility, craftsmen, peasants, paupers, etc.), but also of groups such as family, kinship, household and dynasty. Voluntary associations such as fellowships, guilds, peasant communities or urban communes also represented an important element of collective identities.[1]

12.2 The world of the nobility

Around 1200, the ideology of knighthood or chivalry was widespread among warriors throughout Europe. To contemporaries it was clear that knights (*milites*, *bellatores*) or the knightly estate (*ordo militaris*) differed from all other estates. All those who fought in armour on horseback in this period adhered to the chivalric ideal, which they shared with kings and princes. It provided the aristocracy with an instrument of self-definition and distinction from other groups.[2] Distinctions of rank also emerged within the aristocracy, however, and these are reflected in such medieval legal codes as the *Sachsenspiegel* (*c.* 1225), the *Schwabenspiegel* (*c.* 1270) or the *Siete partidas* (*c.* 1260) of Alfonso X. The process of social closure was a protracted one, stretching over several centuries in the various countries of Europe. It occurred earliest in France (1250). Here, the *milites* drew revenues as lords (*domini*) from the dependent peasantry or lived in fortified houses from the feudal rents of their peasants.

By 1300 the French nobility as a group had attained a distinct legal status, since the *parlement* in Paris had confirmed their exemption from taxes as well as the hereditary nature of their estate. Great differences of property, wealth and power persisted between the simple knights and the great lords, and these differences would grow greater rather than smaller over time. In England, the transition from knights to lords proceeded in a similar manner, whereby great manorial lords provided their knightly clients with land. In contrast to their French counterparts, however, the English nobility did not enjoy tax exemption, although the Magna Carta of 1215 limited their duties as vassals.

In the Holy Roman Empire the noble ranks were replenished with formerly unfree ministerials, who soon received a heritable economic basis in the form of a land grant (fief). They acquired noble status with the heritable right to a coat of arms and the concentration of the family in one or more castles. In the course of the thirteenth century the imperial ministerials, who had become masterless with the extinction of the Hohenstaufen dynasty, attained their independence and, together with the *Edelfreie* (independent noblemen), formed the so-called *Herrenstand* (lordly estate).[3] As members of the lower nobility, the lower ministerials became knights – that is, a professional estate was transformed into a hereditary estate, with princes, counts and lords above them. 'The idea of knighthood required a new social location',[4] and found it in tournaments, coats of arms, heralds and *Minne* at the courts.

In comparison to this stratum of the nobility, which was most influential in the countryside, the aristocracy of northern and central Italy was far more urban and commercially orientated. The urban aristocracy already documented there by 1100 also ruled the surrounding regions. Finally, in the thirteenth century, the Italian communes were dominated by a patriciate with roots in both the rural nobility and the rich merchant class. They lived in fortified towers in the cities, but continued to draw revenues from their landed property.

Certain analogies existed between Italy and Castile, where in the thirteenth century the upper nobility of so-called *ricos hombres* set themselves apart from the 'poorer' *hidalgos* and *caballeros villanos*, the latter mainly in the cities. Since the *ricos hombres* gradually died out in the course of the fourteenth century, this allowed the *caballeros* to rise into the upper nobility and representation in the *cortes*. The *Reconquista* offered a further opportunity for upward mobility. At the same time, the fourteenth century, with the plague and the agrarian crisis, meant a setback for the nobility, since their revenues from the land and thus their livelihood came under pressure.

Noble status had to be defended above all against social climbers, which led to a boom in coats of arms and family trees. Increasingly, the question of the origins of noble quality was raised. Thus in the late fourteenth century, the first works, such as the *grant coustumier*, a work of customary law compiled around 1388 by Jacques d'Ableiges (*bailli d'Évreux*), pointed out that entry into the nobility occurred through either birth or ennoblement.[5]

While this contribution was limited to France, in the fifteenth century the Castilian nobleman Diego de Valera (*c.* 1412–88) penned the treatise *Espejo de verdadera nobleza* (Mirror of true nobility, 1441), in which he discussed the future of the nobility in the various European countries. Despite variations in the different countries, he noted that the nobility, for example in Germany, would continue to exist as long as they lived honourably and did not stoop to unseemly pursuits.[6]

The various measures taken to preserve the noble estate included, most notably, the endowment of chivalric orders, as well as ennoblement and representation at court. Despite shared characteristics, noble society differed greatly from one European country to the next, as is evident from the quantitative estimates of Philippe Contamine. Thus for France he has calculated that nobles (from princes of the blood to lords) made up 1.5 to 2 per cent of the population, with strong regional variations. In England around 1500, the sixty peers with their families and the 6,300 families of the gentry probably represented about 1.2 per cent of the total population of 2.5 million. Castile, in contrast, had 100,000 noble families of all ranks (*grandes*, *caballeros*, *hidalgos*, *donceles*, etc.) out of a population of five million, meaning that nobles constituted some 10 per cent of society, a proportion otherwise probably only attained in Poland.[7] The more strictly the nobility's generative behaviour adhered to the rules of pure blood, the greater the likelihood that they would die out. While this held out the possibility for other families to take their place, the fear of extinction forced noble families to relax their code of conduct and adapt to the new circumstances (university studies, professional training, princely service).

Non-nobles had a variety of opportunities to rise into the nobility, although in many European countries, as Karl-Heinz Spieß has noted, 'the ideal path from non-noble to noble status was the acquisition of landed property, the "*chemin de la terre*"'. 'The individual who wished to rise acquired a landed estate, lived there and gradually integrated into the noble milieu with the aid of socio-economic osmosis.'[8] In such cases, the acquisition of sovereign rights and, frequently associated with it, taking the name of one's estate, were manifest evidence of social mobility. Other possibilities included military service. While in Italy successful *condottieri* could become princes, in the Holy Roman Empire or France non-noble mercenaries could grow into the (knightly) aristocracy. The demand for soldiers in the Hundred Years War created quite favourable conditions for this kind of upward mobility. In France, closeness to the king was already a vehicle of social mobility, since those who occupied royal office belonged to the administrative aristocracy of the *noblesse de robe*.

In the Holy Roman Empire, in contrast, this status was attained only by certain individuals who, after their university studies, were able to rise into the nobility based on their position in the royal chancery. One example is Emperor Sigismund's chancellor Casper Schlick, who came from the elite of Eger and even married the daughter of a duke. More prominent still was the Burgundian chancellor Nicolas Rolin, with roots in the citizenry of Autun, who as Philip the Good's chancellor controlled the fate of Burgundy for nearly forty years beginning in 1422. After the death of his first wife he married into the lower nobility and, when widowed again, into the Burgundian upper nobility, which together with his position as chancellor brought him the elevation into the knighthood in 1424. He documented this status with numerous endowments, of which the Hôtel-Dieu hospital in Beaune with Rogier van der Weyden's *Last Judgement* altarpiece remains unique.

The example of Rolin nevertheless also points to some general characteristics of the vertical mobility of potential nobles. A key factor was the social acceptance of the new nobleman by his fellow nobles, which he could attain by marrying into the corresponding stratum. In the case of patricians and the landed nobility this was generally unproblematic because of their numerous ties of marriage. Those who came from the guild milieu, in contrast, or who wished to rise quickly, required additional accelerating instruments. This included being knighted, which could be easily arranged during the coronation of the king in Aachen or the emperor in Rome, or a pilgrimage to the Holy Sepulchre in Jerusalem. As long as it was recognised by one's peers, an imperial *Wappenbrief* (document granting a coat of arms) or patent of nobility could promote individual upward mobility. At approximately 200, the number of persons ennobled by the emperors in the fifteenth century remained rather modest. The nearly 1,900 patents of nobility issued by the French kings between 1290 and 1483 appear a good deal more impressive, especially because they were in addition to ennoblements by the dukes of Brittany and Burgundy as well as the collective ennoblements by town councils, fief holders and the *noblesse de robe*.[9] Perhaps the prospect of exemption from taxation additionally increased the demand for noble titles in France as well as Spain, although those who did not live in a manner befitting their rank could forfeit their status. In Germany or England, in contrast, freedom from taxation played a smaller role as motivation. The number of people who rose into the gentry was accordingly modest, and entrance to the parliamentary peerage, if it occurred at all, was strictly limited by the king. Between 1388 and 1424, for instance, no such elevations occurred at all.[10]

12.3 Rural society

In pre-industrial Europe, 80–90 per cent of the population lived in the country and from agriculture, although the figures varied from region to region. For that reason, economic and social but also political developments occurred first of all in the countryside. The Black Death represented a significant caesura in the history of rural Europe and has thus tended to overshadow many other phenomena in the view of many historians. From this perspective, the agricultural depression, peasant unrest, the decline of the knightly estate and with them the so-called crisis of the late Middle Ages were all consequences of the plague. Alternative explanations inquire into signs of economic depression by the early fourteenth century (before the outbreak of the plague) as well as the causes of the agrarian expansion that was still evident in some regions of Europe in the fourteenth and fifteenth centuries (see Chapter 14).

Great variations existed between peasant societies in the different regions of Europe, but also within a single territory or even village. The peasants in a village could be subject, and thus owe services to, different lords. They also differed in regard to the size of the land they worked and their market quota. While the majority of European peasants engaged in subsistence farming, some regions produced for the market. The foundation of the peasant economy was the hide (*Hufe*, *mansus*), a unit within the *villicatio* system that became widespread in western and central Europe through this system and other colonisation processes. Although the size of the hide differed from region to region, the ties between hide and house made it 'a key structuring principle of rural society'.[11] This did not change even when the demographic growth of the high Middle Ages in the early fourteenth century meant that ever fewer peasants worked a full plot of thirty to forty hectares, and instead had to make do with one-half or one-quarter of that amount of land. At this period, about half of the peasant population did not even have the four hectares that were the minimum for subsistence, and had to seek other means of livelihood.[12]

The hide system and the ties of units of land to the house meant that peasant households generally consisted of a nuclear family, in which husband and wife engaged in agricultural work as a couple. Although wives were under the guardianship of their husbands, who also administered their assets, the working relationship was egalitarian, with the woman responsible for dairying and the husband for working the fields. This only changed with the professionalisation of dairy farming, for example cheese-making in parts of the Swiss Confederacy. Men now took charge of this export-oriented business as herdsmen and dairymen, as well as of harvesting using the scythe, a newly introduced tool. Up to that point, men and women had both harvested grain using sickles.[13]

Within the village community there were social distinctions, with a village aristocracy at the top (millers, sheriffs, innkeepers). They determined the use of common, especially grazing, lands and differed from other villagers in their larger landholdings and number of servants. In the course of the fourteenth century, however, the plague led to serious social and economic upheavals and a fall in population density. More land must have come on the market and eased the situation. It is worth recalling, however, that very few European peasants actually owned the land they worked and could dispose of it freely. The majority had only usufruct, and paid their manorial lords rents in kind, money and labour services. Although the greater part of the peasantry gained personal freedom when the *villicationes* were dissolved, in England only the Black Death ended serfdom for one-third of rural households.

As a consequence of the crop failures of 1315–23 and the years that followed, however, the population had already fallen in accordance with the available food supply even before the plague descended on Europe.[14] Both events reduced the numbers of rural consumers and producers alike. Although the sub-peasant population was able to take over a portion of the land that became free, villages and fields remained deserted, some of them permanently. Thus a village could be abandoned or extinct while the inhabitants of a neighbouring village worked its fields. People also increasingly moved to areas with better soils. The fertile marshlands saw the least desolation, and in France, with its generally dense population, far less land fell fallow than in sparsely settled Scandinavia or eastern German territories such as Brandenburg and Mecklenburg.[15] Rural rent payments fell, as did the demand and prices for agricultural products.

Manorial lords reacted differently to their altered revenues, especially because the degree to which income situations changed varied. While manorial lords all over Europe complained of poverty and the monasteries also lost revenues from their lands, only those lords with no other income were actually hard pressed by the decline in rents. Revenues from offices, as in France, could provide an alternative, as could mercenary service or specialisation in robber barony. In France such revenues did not suffice to maintain income levels, which had risen almost continually in the high Middle Ages as a result of inland colonisation. The oversupply of land forced lords to lower rents if they could even find peasants willing to work the land. At the same time, some manorial lords reduced the cultivation of their own demesne to avoid the rising cost of wages. Other factors such as the Hundred Years War and increased tax pressures counteracted this apparently favourable situation for peasants, however, and France only recovered economically and demographically when they disappeared in the mid-fifteenth century.

The situation in England was similar. Although tax pressures were absent, it was not until the sixteenth century that population figures truly recovered from the Black Death, while in southern Europe they had already reached pre-plague levels by this time. Castile, which had not been as devastated by the plague in the first place, witnessed an expansion and concentration of noble, seigniorial landownership. Some latifundia such as that of the Marquis de Villena extended over 25,000 square kilometres, so that the cultivation of the demesne and participation in the *mesta* with thousands of sheep played an important role.

While in various regions of western Europe manorial lords reduced the cultivation of their demesne or used their land extensively, the lords of eastern Europe made a virtue of necessity and took over the management of otherwise fallow land, which would lead in the long run to the greater dependence of peasants in the system of *Gutswirtschaft* (manorial economy), and the direct exploitation of land by the lords.[16] In many parts of western Europe, in contrast, relations of dependency eased. Serfdom declined, and peasants gained their personal liberty. Whether they profited from this economically depended on a variety of factors such as proximity to markets and market quota, feudal burdens, tax pressures, etc. While small producers, as subsistence farmers, were scarcely touched by the fall in agricultural prices, they did affect middle-size farms. The latter, however, if they were near a town, had the possibility of specialising in products for the urban market such as wine, vegetables, fruit and milk, and thus of tapping new sources of income. The level of duties and taxes, however, was decisive for their situation.

12.4 Urban society

With its population growth, the thirteenth century was the great era of urban expansion: old cities grew, new ones were founded and all types of towns became more distinct in character and function from their environs. The division of labour between town and country increased, and non-agricultural activities became dominant in the towns. At the same time, different types of city emerged: capitals (Paris, London), episcopal cities (Lincoln, Rouen), university towns (Oxford, Bologna), port cities (Marseilles, Genoa, Pisa, Venice, Lisbon, Bordeaux, Lübeck) and centres of commerce and manufacturing (Florence, Bruges, Ghent, Ypres). A common characteristic of all cities, however, was the dominance of the trades and wage work, with the exercise of the same trade or organisation in the same guild often determining where people lived in the town. Shared geographical origins, nationality or confession could also be decisive factors here.

Apart from organisation in a corporation, the exercise of a trade or a certain regional origin, other elements also served to create or differentiate status. Chief among them was citizenship. Although in Germany and on the Iberian Peninsula the principle that 'town air makes a person free' (*Stadtluft macht frei*) long guaranteed unimpeded movement from the countryside to the towns, migrants did not necessarily acquire the rights of citizens. Moreover, some cities demanded an oath affirming the individual's free status. Citizenship generally depended on long residence; in the Tuscan cities, this could mean up to thirty years. An entry fee and an oath of citizenship were also required. They could be coupled with additional preconditions such as ownership of real estate, property or guild membership. Cities varied in the 'liberality' of their policies. While in Frankfurt into the fifteenth century there was virtual freedom of trade even for non-citizens, who could also acquire land, and in Cologne it was possible to become a member of a guild without citizenship, Hamburg, Lübeck or Nuremberg demanded minimum assets for both guild membership and citizenship.[17] Once a man had acquired citizenship he could pass it on to his wife and children. This also applied to the English equivalent, the so-called freedom of the borough, which could be acquired by inheritance but also by apprenticeship in the craft workshop of a burgess. This enabled apprentices from the countryside to become freemen of London and establish themselves there. London became more restrictive in the fourteenth century, demanding six guild members as guarantors for citizenship and at the same time prohibiting non-freemen from practising a trade.[18]

In general, older cities, which sought to preserve their citizens' opportunities to earn a livelihood, were more restrictive in granting citizenship, while new or economically expanding cities tended to be more liberal. Thus as a rule fewer than half of townspeople were citizens, the prerequisite for participation in political power. Nonetheless, moving to town appears to have been attractive to many people even without the rights of citizenship. The city offered more and better paid work than the country, and the chance of social mobility for future generations. From settling in the city and acquiring citizenship, guild membership, real property and wealth, this could lead over several generations to a position on the town council. The stages people had to go through are evident from surviving contemporary sources on social stratification such as those from late fifteenth-century Nuremberg. Economic activities and social rank were closely linked here with political privileges such as membership in the small or greater council. The following picture emerges:

1 the old families of the urban aristocracy (patricians), who choose the small council
2 wholesale merchants, if they are *nominati* (*Genannte*) of the greater council, as well as craft entrepreneurs and university-educated men in municipal service
3 merchants and traders who, while *nominati* of the greater council, conduct smaller, less distinguished businesses and serve as managers (*Faktoren*) for other merchants, as well as the tradesmen of the small council
4 traders who have only been independent for a few years or are managers and do not belong to the *nominati*, as well as shopkeepers, tradesmen and commercial employees
5 common shopkeepers and tradesmen and all others.[19]

Thus social mobility demanded that the individual first rise from the status of wage labourer or journeyman to independent tradesman or shopkeeper, before members of the family's second generation could perhaps become wholesalers or craft entrepreneurs, and the third had a chance to ascend into the patriciate or ally itself with the local nobility through land acquisition and marriage. Apart from economic success, marrying into the 'right' family and membership in one of the distinguished confraternities, which served as reservoirs of mobility for career-minded young merchants, were also important for social mobility.[20] Alongside individual social mobility, economic expansion, the plague or the guild conflicts of the fourteenth and fifteenth centuries frequently provided entire generations with opportunities to rise collectively into the political elite and participate in political power. Although there were differences here in respect to the economic base, size, function and charters of the various towns, the basic lines of development in European cities were quite comparable.

In most European cities, the elite were a patriciate or urban aristocracy, although the Latin term *patricii* was not widely used until the sixteenth century. Next to the patriciate, which as a hereditary estate modelled its way of life on that of the landed nobility, was a stratum of notables composed of long-distance merchants who served as a reservoir for the political elites and could be co-opted when needed into the patriciate or the town council. Both groups invested in land inside and outside the city in addition to trade, which represented not simply an investment in social prestige, but also – given the risks of commerce – a sensible diversification of their portfolios. Thus, few urban families who bought into the nobility in the Holy Roman Empire, France or Spain immediately gave up their business activities. This occurred only when these collided with noble codes of conduct such as the prohibition on labour. On the other hand, alongside aristocrats who already lived in cities (Italy, Castile), nobles – for example members of the English gentry – also purchased land in town. In Italy, the increased power of urban nobles led to them usurping functions on the town council or exerting influence on elected individuals (straw men). In this way, the Visconti dominated Milan (1277–1450), and Cosimo de' Medici controlled the Florentine Republic without ever having to hold office. In contrast, from the fourteenth century Venice possessed a closed oligarchy in the 400 members of the Great Council, which however was larger than any patriciate in relation to the population. In the Holy Roman Empire the urban elites either closed themselves off (Nuremberg 1521), prevented their own extinction by adding new blood (Augsburg 1538) or retained their relative openness (the Hanseatic cities). Thus in fifteenth-century Cologne, for instance, newcomers could still be elected to the town council, and in the centuries that followed, a portion of seats on the Hamburg and Lübeck councils were always occupied by migrants.[21]

Below the stratum of the patriciate and notables it was above all the nature of one's business and the goods with which one traded as well as the prestige of one's craft that determined social position in the city. Thus the cloth-makers of Flanders, who manufactured a high-quality product for export, enjoyed a much higher reputation than those of the inland towns of France or Germany. In addition, the wool merchants who provided the cloth-makers with wool and dyes dominated the guilds of Flanders, which indicates the broad social range within a guild. In the Cologne silk weavers' guild (*Seidamt*), a female guild, the social spectrum extended from the upper-class silk merchant married to a long-distance trader to the poor woman who worked on a putting-out basis.[22] The women's guilds in Cologne were a special case, whose only counterpart existed in the Parisian silk industry. As a rule, husbands and wives worked together in a trade as a couple. In the course of professionalisation, specialisation emerged and wives came to be viewed as helpers in the craft business. Widows carried on their late husbands' craft and also commercial businesses for a certain period of time. Merchants' wives frequently became used to running the business during their husbands' absence, as documented in the intensive correspondence between Margarethe Veckinchusen in Lübeck and her husband Hildebrand Veckinchusen, who spent the years 1422–25 in debtors' prison in Bruges. Francesco Datini also wrote hundreds of letters to his wife Margherita between 1384 and 1400, when the couple lived largely apart. Datini saw to his branch offices in Florence or Pisa while his wife ran the household in Prato.[23]

In the towns, the hierarchy of occupations was outwardly illustrated by the order in which their members walked in the frequent processions. Thus in large European cities the victual trades such as the butchers of Paris and the fishmongers of London assumed a prominent place. In the coastal towns of the North Sea and the Baltic the brewers rose within the urban hierarchy to the extent that beer became an export product.

Below the independent guild members – regardless of the large social distinctions within a guild and between the guilds – were the dependent employees of the lower classes. They included not just journeymen but also maid- and manservants, who represented up to one-fifth of the population in larger towns. Under them were the unskilled workers in commerce (porters, haulers and drivers) as well as the many day-labourers in the building trades and agriculture, who often worked in town only seasonally. The many women who dealt in second-hand goods or who hawked beer, bread, fish or poultry from trays or market stalls also belonged to this group. The prostitutes had a special status. In Italy and France they generally lived and worked in brothels. Since the brothels were under the supervision of the council, their food, lodging, clothing, payment and medical care were usually regulated by the authorities. Although excluded from citizenship, prostitutes were integrated into urban society through participation in festivities and other events. They faced discrimination all the same, being identified by certain colours or relegated to a location on the edge of the city near the place of execution.[24] The paupers occupied the lowest rank in society, although the lines that separated them from simple maids, manservants and unskilled workers were permeable.

Religious and ethnic minorities constituted a particular group in urban and sometimes rural society. Apart from the Iberian Peninsula with its large Muslim population, Jews were the most widespread of these population groups in Europe. Their situation was precarious, and ranged from expulsion and pogroms to privileged status. Thus the Jews were expelled from England in 1290, and in 1306 Philip IV expelled some 100,000 Jews from France. Only in the county of Provence did vibrant Jewish life develop, but it was brought to an end by expulsion in the late fifteenth century when the region fell to the French Crown. In the Holy Roman Empire the Jews were under the King's protection as 'servants of the royal chamber', and paid a personal tax known as the *goldner opferpfennig*. In the wake of pogroms in the fourteenth century, a substantial portion of the Jewish population fled to Poland and Lithuania to escape persecution. In the period that followed nearly all imperial cities banished the Jewish population from their territory. Casimir the Great of Poland gave refuge to the persecuted Jews by granting them legal privileges and the opportunity to acquire houses and land. In Poland, whose princes began to promote the settlement of Jews in the fourteenth century as an infrastructural measure, the Jewish communities in the cities grew rapidly from the second half of the fourteenth century. In most cities 'Jewish streets' emerged, and soon Jewish quarters, which offered some protection from Christian assaults. Despite this relative safety, the Jewish population was subject to repeated attacks, above all in the fifteenth century (see 6.4).

In Italy cities and villages virtually invited Jews to set up pawn offices to combat the credit shortage. The climate only became harsher in the fifteenth century, when the Franciscans preached against Jewish usurers and founded the *monte di pietà*, a public pawn institution, to replace the services provided by Jews. Nevertheless, a flourishing Jewish life had developed in the cities by that time, so that Italy appeared as an attractive place of exile for Jews expelled from the Iberian Peninsula. The confessionalised Catholic Church pursued a restrictive policy against Jews in the sixteenth century, although the process of ghettoisation – the first ghetto arose in 1516 in Venice – had begun earlier. In Castile and Aragón, policy toward Jews and Muslims changed radically when the Catholic monarchs ascended the throne. Old ideas of segregating the Jewish and Muslim population, known as *apartamiento*, were put into practice, and Jews and Muslims were enclosed in *juderías* and *morerías* respectively. At the same time, the Inquisition took an increasing interest in the way of life of the *conversos*,

Jews who had converted to Christianity. Many of them had attained positions of power, and laws on the purity of blood (*limpieza de sangre*) were introduced in 1449 and 1467 to prevent them becoming public (municipal) officeholders and dignitaries. Since the regulations proved unsuccessful, in 1492 the remaining Jews were presented with the alternative of conversion or exile. In this way, Spain destroyed the largest Jewish community in Europe, for an estimated 50,000 to 70,000 Jews left the country (see 3.5).

Poverty was another widespread phenomenon of urban society.[25] On the one hand, in relation to poor (bonded) peasants, 'poor' meant both unfree and 'of lesser rights'. On the other, the medieval period already used the term 'poverty' to refer to a lack of property.[26] People were poor because of accidents of fate such as illness, disability, crop failure or famine. Thus in times of crisis, poverty became a mass phenomenon. Structural causes associated with the phenomenon of labour also played a role, however.[27] The old and sick, widows and orphans depended on outside support because they were unable to work enough, or at all. Tradesmen and their families fell into poverty because of insufficient income or work. Those who lacked the will to work became beggars, thieves (pickpockets) or vagrants, joining the ranks of the 'shameless' poor.[28]

As a rule, Church and municipal poor relief helped only those who had fallen into poverty or lived below the subsistence level through no fault of their own, the so-called 'shamefaced' poor, who were ashamed to carry the 'beggar's staff'. They represented about one-fifth of the urban population and could not survive without the aid of the convents and hospitals as well as private donations. Providing relief for the shamefaced or house poor was a part of everyday urban life, especially because paupers repaid donors' alms by praying for the salvation of their souls. At the same time, the fifteenth century saw changes in the treatment of the 'shameless' poor, above all the sturdy beggars who could have worked and the hungry outsiders regularly driven from the city, but who usually soon returned.

In the fourteenth and fifteenth centuries the concept of 'dishonourability' – that is, of social marginalisation, too – was used more strongly for purposes of exclusion. In the process, the repertoire of dishonourable trades was increasingly extended beyond the hard core of executioners, hangmen, knackers, gravediggers and itinerants to include beadles, shepherds, millers, tower watchmen, barber-surgeons, prostitutes, sow gelders, street sweepers and latrine cleaners.[29] The main driving force behind this process were the guilds, chiefly in northern and eastern Germany, which hereby developed an instrument of marginalisation, alongside discrimination against illegitimate birth – often against the will of the more magnanimous town council. Since the criterion of legitimate and honourable birth, as a precondition for guild membership, could also be applied to the wives of masters and their apprentices, it served to exclude potential competitors in times such as the fifteenth century when there was an oversupply of tradesmen, and was also deployed in the struggle with other guilds over honour and prestige.[30]

12.5 Revolts

The fourteenth and fifteenth centuries experienced various types of revolts, which did not differ fundamentally from those of the sixteenth or seventeenth centuries. Tax increases in particular led to peasant revolts. Peasant resistance in itself was nothing new. It ranged from the refusal to pay dues and perform services to passive resistance, from absconding and migration to armed uprisings, which could extend beyond the manorial estate to the territorial ruler. The most successful attempts of this kind included the self-assertion of the Dithmarschen peasants (republic) against the archbishops of Bremen and the struggle of the Swiss Confederacy against the Habsburgs. A spontaneous but nonetheless temporarily successful major peasant uprising was the so-called *Jacquerie*. In 1358, northern French peasants, oppressed by growing tax burdens and the pillaging of the Hundred Years War, joined forces to destroy the castles and manor houses of the nobility whom they blamed for their plight. The English peasants, in contrast, who rose up under Wat Tyler in 1381 and were influenced by the teachings of Wycliffe and supported by segments of the urban population, were fighting concretely against fiscal pressure and for the abolition of serfdom.[31] They largely achieved this latter aim, despite the crushing of the revolt in the course of the fifteenth century. In the Holy Roman Empire, too, peasant revolts became more frequent in the fifteenth century, and at the end of the century peasant associations assumed a superregional character. The so-called *Bundschuh* conspiracies, which broke out repeatedly above all on the Upper Rhine from 1493, were remarkable for their organisation and the radicality of their demands (freedom to hunt and fish, the abolition of rent payments, lowering of the Church tithes, etc.).[32] The 'Poor Conrad' insurgents of 1513/14 in Württemberg, who began by opposing new taxes and the despotism of ducal officials, took up these demands again, and they would continue to be raised until the great Peasants' War of 1525.

In the cities, in addition to bread riots and pogroms against outsiders (Jews), there were conflicts between various factions as well as tax revolts and political rebellions. The majority of rebellions were directed against the tax policies of the city's overlord, to whom most European cities were subject or into whose political sphere of influence they were integrated. Although there were independent city-states such as Genoa or Venice, even great centres such as Paris were under royal control, against which the Parisians rebelled in 1358, for example, under the leadership of Etienne Marcel. The Flemish towns that had joined forces in the *Leden* were also regularly compelled to defend their economic interests against the counts of Flanders or the dukes of Burgundy, which led in the years 1338–49, 1379–85 and 1482–92 to rule by the cities rather than the central power. Aside from these conflicts, we should also not underestimate the social and political struggles within the Flemish towns.[33] These led to the guilds assuming control of municipal finances instead of the patriciate. At the same time, heated conflicts arose between the individual trades, for example between weavers and fullers. After the central power of the Burgundian state regained its might in the fifteenth century, new alliances emerged. A segment of the urban elites now married into noble families and took over ducal offices. This reduced municipal autonomy, on the one hand, and put the urban lower classes in their place, on the other.[34]

Social unrest broke out in connection with the Peasant Revolt in 1380 in London, or was accompanied by political demands as in the case of the 1378 revolt of the *ciompi* in Florence. The rebellion of the wool carders, in which the *sottoposti* such as dyers, fullers and finishers also participated, targeted the establishment of the woollen merchants' guild, the *Arte della lana*, which refused them membership. In response to pressure from the street, three new guilds were established alongside the seven upper and fourteen lower guilds, which satisfied the demands of the *sottoposti*, but instigated a renewed revolt of the *ciompi*. The uprising collapsed in 1382. The Florentine oligarchy had learnt their lesson and in future excluded the middle classes from municipal office.

The rebellions known as *Schichten* or *Aufläufe* that erupted in numerous German cities from the fourteenth century were responses to questions of power and the municipal constitution. Critiques always centred on the town council's conduct of office and abuses of power, with poor finance policy, socially inequitable taxes, nepotism, irregularities in council elections and costly foreign policy entanglements being the structural causes or concrete occasions for revolts.

In many cities the craftsmen who had attained power and influence succeeded in reorganising the municipal constitution to replace a patrician regime with a system based on a guild constitution. Thus the Cologne constitution (*Verbundbrief*) of 1396 placed the municipal government on a broader basis and to that end formed guildlike organisations known as *Gaffeln*. Henceforth, seventeen of the twenty-two *Gaffeln* represented one or more craft guilds and five represented the merchants. In future, thirty-six of the forty-nine council members were elected in the *Gaffeln* and the rest were co-opted. When this council, too, became more restrictive in the fifteenth century, the middle classes in the guilds pushed for stronger representation, which they were granted in a revision of the *Verbundbrief* after the failed rebellion of 1481/82 and renewed unrest in 1512/13. For the first time, the municipal constitution guaranteed the personal domestic peace (*Hausfriede*) of the citizen.[35]

In this period around the year 1500, urban unrest already acquired a new quality through its intersection with rural revolts. It was no longer directed against the authorities alone, but, through the participation of burghers and peasants, transcended social lines and frequently regional ones as well.[36]

Notes

1 Morsel, *L'aristocratie médiévale*, 154–7; Oexle, 'Die funktionale Dreiteilung', and 'Stand, Klasse', 183–96.
2 Morsel, 'Inventing a social category'.
3 Spieß, 'Ständische Abgrenzung'.
4 Paravicini, *Die Ritterlich-höfische Kultur*, 22.
5 Laboulaye and Dareste (eds), *Jacques d'Ableiges, le grand coutumier de France*; cf. Contamine, *La noblesse au royaume de France*.
6 Contamine, 'The European nobility', 90–1.
7 Ibid., 96–7.
8 Spieß, 'Aufstieg in den Adel', 12; Arriaza, 'Le statut nobiliaire', 418–19.
9 Spieß, 'Aufstieg in den Adel', 23.
10 Nicholas, *The transformation of Europe*, 114.
11 Mitterauer, *Warum Europa?*, 69.
12 Fossier, *Peasant life in the medieval west*, 146.
13 Wunder, '"Jede Arbeit ist ihres Lohnes wert"'.
14 Campbell, *English seigniorial agriculture*, 1–10.
15 Rösener, *The peasantry of Europe*.
16 North, 'Entstehung der Gutswirtschaft'.
17 Isenmann, *Die deutsche Stadt*, 258–9.
18 Nicholas, *Urban Europe*, 120–1.
19 Isenmann, *Die deutsche Stadt*, 249; Bog, 'Reichsverfassung und reichstädtische Gesellschaft'.
20 Graßmann, 'Sozialer Aufstieg in Lübeck', 106–7.
21 Wensky, 'Städtische Führungsschichten', 27.
22 Wensky, *Die Stellung der Frau in der stadtkölnischen Wirtschaft*, 83–186.

23 Irsigler, 'Alltag einer hansischen Kaufmannsfamilie'; Origo, *The merchant of Prato*, 145, 161–80.
24 Trexler, 'La Prostitution florentine'; Schuster, *Das Frauenhaus.*
25 Geremek, *Poverty: A history*; Mollat, *The poor in the Middle Ages.*
26 Palme, 'Städtische Sozialpolitik', 45–7.
27 Jütte, *Obrigkeitliche Armenfürsorge*, 13–14.
28 Irsigler and Lasotta, *Bettler und Gaukler*, 24–6.
29 Hergemöller (ed.), *Die Randgruppen.*
30 Isenmann, *Die deutsche Stadt*, 264–5.
31 Hilton, *Bond men made free.*
32 Rösener, 'Peasant revolts in late medieval Germany', 17–42; Blickle, *The revolution of 1525.*
33 Blockmans, 'Alternatives'.
34 Dumolyn and Haemers, 'Patterns of urban rebellion'.
35 Ennen, *Stadt des Mittelalters*, 237–8.
36 Blickle, 'Unruhen in der ständischen Gesellschaft', 21–5.

13

Culture and Religion

13.1 Humanism

Like nearly all innovations of the period, humanism emerged in the late thirteenth century in northern Italy in such cities as Padua, Bologna or Milan. It was propagated by members of the rising liberal professions such as judges, notaries, schoolmasters and chancery clerks, who initially occupied themselves with rhetoric, only to draw instruction and inspiration from the authors of antiquity. The humanists were convinced that the study of the ancient languages and literature was an indispensable element of cultivation, since it afforded them access to the superior civilisation of classical antiquity.[1]

Although the term 'humanism', like 'the Renaissance', is a nineteenth-century invention, by the late fifteenth century – i.e., some 200 years after this development began – the term *humanista* was in use at Italian universities. It referred to a scholar who devoted himself to the humanities (*studia humanitatis*), that is, to grammar, rhetoric, poetics, history and moral philosophy, in particular, and thus broke down the rigid medieval system of the seven liberal arts (grammar, logic and rhetoric, arithmetic, geometry, astronomy and music). According to Leonardo Bruni (1369–1444), the new humanist studies perfected the human being, whom they would not merely render more learned, but also improve morally.

Similar ideas had already been attributed to Francesco Petrarch (1304–74), who is generally considered the first humanist, although scholars like the Padua judge Lovato Lovati (1241–1309) had been promoting the revival of ancient authors since the late thirteenth century. In ancient culture, Petrarch saw potential solutions to the moral problems of his day. Accordingly, he corresponded with many personalities whom he offered solicited or unsolicited advice. Above all, he polemicised against anyone and everyone, against medical doctors as well as critics of Italy or his concept of humanism. He also shone as the author of love sonnets, while his intellectual ambitions took him many places, from the papal court at Avignon to the service of northern Italian city tyrants as well as to the republic of Florence.

Florence, where Giovanni Boccaccio (1313–75), among others, promoted humanism, became the most important centre of northern Italian humanism beginning in the late fourteenth century. Boccaccio, who like his friend Petrarch was always on the lookout for manuscripts by ancient authors, promoted the study of the Greek language, which was permanently established in the city when the Florentine chancellor Coluccio Salutati (1331–1406) hired a Byzantine Greek scholar to teach at the university. Florentine statesmen like Salutati propagated the model of the Florentine city-state and its institutions with references to antiquity, particularly to the Athens ruled by free citizens or to republican Rome. Salutati placed his gifts as an author and rhetoretician at the disposal of the Florentine Republic, so that at the end of the fourteenth century the city's military enemy, Giangaleazzo Visconti of Milan, was compelled to note enviously that a letter by Salutati could counter the fighting force of one thousand knights. Salutati's successor Leonardo Bruni further developed the legend of Florence by lauding the active political life of Florentine citizens in the service of the commonweal as well as the city's beauty and the fairness of its institutions.

Hans Baron has referred to this variant of political humanism with some exaggeration as 'civic humanism'[2] and devoted a monograph to the subject. An identity located between humanist learning and the State was not a Florentine speciality, however.[3] In Rome, Milan, Venice or the kingdom of Naples, too, humanists entered the service of the State, regardless of its princely, republican, temporal or ecclesiastical constitution.

The productivity of Italian humanists grew by leaps and bounds over the course of the fifteenth century. The exodus of numerous Byzantine scholars, in particular, energised Italian humanism. The search for ancient texts above all in monastic libraries proved successful, and people began to take an interest in archaeology, epigraphics and numismatics. Out of their study of the works of classical antiquity, authors like Lorenzo Valla (1407–57) and Angelo Poliziano (1454–94) developed a historical-philological brand of textual critique. Libraries were endowed, and manuscripts and soon printed books as well were collected. Booksellers like Vespasiano da Bisticci (1421–98) disseminated the manuscripts as copies and through their European customers contributed significantly to the spread of humanism outside Italy. The interests and profiles of humanists became blurred in this stream of rising humanist scholarship and productivity. They published in a range of literary genres: poetry, orations, dialogues, commentaries and translations, did research in the various areas of the *studia humanitatis* and also devoted themselves more generally to other branches of knowledge such as medicine, Roman law or theology and philosophy.

The diffusion of humanism outside Italy took a number of paths.[4] On the one hand, humanists corresponded with European monarchs, as Petrarch did with Emperor Charles IV, while on the other noblemen such as Humphrey, Duke of Gloucester became patrons of Italian humanists.[5] The number of northern and central European travellers to Italy rose enormously, and encompassed pilgrims, soldiers, clerics, merchants, diplomats, artists and students. The last studied above all in Padua, but also in Bologna, Pavia or Ferrara. Other foreigners, such as diplomats, met Italian humanists in Florence and bought books on the local market. The abovementioned da Bisticci recorded foreign customers such as the Bishop of Ely, William Grey; the Archbishop of Esztergom, János Vitéz; or the Spanish nobleman Nuño de Guzmán, whose book purchases we can thus still reconstruct today. Apart from private book lovers, 'public' institutions such as the library of the University of Vienna bought manuscripts and books by Italian humanists.[6]

In central Europe, the courts in particular acted as centres for the diffusion of humanism. Thus at the court of Buda, the Hungarian King Matthias Corvinus (1458–90), perhaps inspired by the Archbishop of Esztergom, János Vitéz, promoted the study of antiquity and founded the so-called Bibliotheca Corvina with one of the largest collections of ancient authors.[7] The humanists of the Buda court had their greatest influence in east-central Europe, where they furthered the spread of the new intellectual current. They developed close contacts with Cracow and Vienna, the latter of which became the centre of humanism in the Holy Roman Empire.[8] Here, Enea Silvio Piccolomini disseminated Italian ideas in the empire during the ten years he worked in the chancery of Frederick III, so that by the mid-fifteenth century professors at the University of Vienna were giving humanist-influenced lectures. The most significant humanist north of the Alps was Konrad Celtis (1459–1508), whom Frederick III crowned with laurels in Nuremberg in 1487.[9] After studying in Heidelberg under Rudolf Agricola (1444–85) and teaching poetics at Erfurt, Rostock and Leipzig, he deepened his studies in Padua, Ferrara, Bologna, Florence, Venice and Rome, only to accept a professorship of rhetoric and poetics in Vienna in 1497 after additional sojourns in Cracow, Prague, Nuremberg, Ingolstadt and Regensburg.

These were the sources of so-called northern humanism, which emerged on the threshold of the sixteenth century and was dominated by Desiderius Erasmus (*c.* 1469–1536). This development, which is associated with scholars such as Johannes Reuchlin (1455–1522) in Germany, Thomas More (1479–1535) in England and Guillaume Budé (1467/68–1540) in France, and which made effective use of the new medium of the book, shows the lasting influence of humanist ideas as manifested in the founding of new humanist schools. Thus St Paul's School was established in London in 1509, and the Collegium Trilingue (for the classical languages Latin, Greek and Hebrew) in Louvain in 1517. While some bulwarks of scholasticism in France – such as the Sorbonne – or in Spain rejected the new teachings, new universities like Wittenberg, Marburg or Leiden were founded with a humanist orientation.[10]

Humanism inspired not just the study of ancient texts but nearly all disciplines. Translations from the Greek (Euclid, Archimedes, Hippocrates and Galen) placed mathematics and medicine on a new footing, and metaphysics and cosmology gained new impetus from the reception of Aristotle. The study of politics and historiography, too, would have been inconceivable without the authors of antiquity, and Justus Lipsius (1547–1606), who would later attain great renown in this field, was influenced equally by Seneca and Tacitus. The importance of humanism for the visual arts remains outwardly visible to this day, and is usually associated with the notion of the Renaissance.

13.2 The Renaissance

Like humanism, which has been understood thus far in the narrower sense of *studia humanitatis*, the term Renaissance, also coined in the nineteenth century, is rather imprecise. The meaning of the Renaissance as an epoch was first emphasised by the French historian Jules Michelet, and then above all by Jacob Burckhardt in his monumental *Civilisation of the Renaissance in Italy*.[11] When Burckhardt spoke of the Renaissance, he was referring to the unified culture of Italy between the fourteenth and sixteenth centuries, which he regarded as the very wellspring of the modern world. According to Burckhardt, aspects of this new epoch included political life in the city-states and principalities, the emergence of the individual or the modern human being, the confrontation with classical antiquity in humanism and the discovery of the world and the human being through travel, scholarship and literature. Sociability, combined with a refinement of life, and changes in religiosity were also central themes. Surprisingly, Burckhardt's book largely ignores art and architecture, which had played such an important role in his earlier work *Cicerone*, on art in Italy from antiquity to his own day. Although the Renaissance is now no longer viewed as a caesura along the way to the modern age, and scholars have taken issue with Burckhardt's 'italocentrism', the revival of antiquity continues to play a major role in most definitions of the Renaissance.

At the same time, the concept of a Renaissance in which the departure from the Gothic does not seem nearly as abrupt as Burckhardt assumed shows that epochal breaks in the fifteenth century are relatively random. Nevertheless, we can divide the Renaissance into an early Renaissance between 1300 and 1480/90, a high Renaissance between 1490 and 1530 and a late Renaissance, which continued into the seventeenth century.

There are many parallels here between the Italian high Renaissance and the era that Johan Huizinga characterised in the Franco-Flemish, urban courtly context as the 'autumn of the Middle Ages' in his 1919 book of the same name. Huizinga accordingly saw the fourteenth and fifteenth centuries as a period of 'ripeness' rather than preparation for a Renaissance or modern era. Moreover, in the landscape of western European cities and courts, the fifteenth century appears as an era of creativity comparable to the Italian Renaissance. Thus in the Burgundian Netherlands between 1420 and 1440 a fundamentally novel form of painting emerged in the work of Jan van Eyck, Robert Campin and Rogier van der Weyden, which overcame previous representational and genre conventions and enriched stylised Gothic modes of expression with new and – it was long believed – more realistic depictions.[12]

Through merchants, artists and the courts, the new Flemish inventions became known in southern Europe just as the achievements of the Italian Renaissance were disseminated in the north. At the same time, many only apparently Italian innovations developed in confrontation with the Byzantine world, and above all the late Renaissance represents a large-scale process of adaptation in northern and central Europe.

Just as Petrarch is regarded as the founder of humanism, Giotto di Bondone (*c.* 1266–1337) may be considered the founder of the new painting in Italy. Dante and Petrarch praised their contemporary, whom Boccaccio acknowledged for having brought to light art buried for centuries. Giotto, and his teacher Cimabue before him, distinguished themselves from their predecessors particularly in the expressiveness and three-dimensionality of their representation. Although the reception of classical antiquity is still barely noticeable in fourteenth-century art, it becomes all the more evident in the early fifteenth century. Vitruvius was not the only rediscovery. 'A small group of creative individuals who knew one another well',[13] including the architects Filippo Brunelleschi and Leon Battista Alberti, the sculptors Donatello and Lorenzo Ghiberti and the painter Masaccio, influenced Florentine art in confrontation with classical antiquity. Among the works now considered Renaissance inventions are the structures planned by Brunelleschi (the churches of San Lorenzo and Santo Spirito, the foundling hospital, the Pazzi chapel and the dome of the cathedral) as well as the bronze doors of the baptistery (Ghiberti), the statues of Donatello and Masaccio's *Trinity*. The latter are repeatedly cited as examples of the internalisation of perspective (see 4.5).

A growing private and public demand for art stimulated the production of these artistic innovators and the countless painters from the artisan milieu. Corporate patrons such as the *Arte della Lana* (woollen merchants' guild) played a role, as did the religious confraternities, which as sociable organisations were often associated with a church and endowed works of art for its adornment. The Florentine Republic bestowed public commissions such as the building of the aforementioned foundling hospital or later Michelangelo's *David*. 'Private individuals' such as Lorenzo de' Medici also became patrons of the arts, for example commissioning Botticelli's painting *Primavera*. This shows that artistic taste was gradually becoming secularised – that is, secular themes were growing increasingly popular.[14]

In the course of the fifteenth century, Florentine innovations were adopted in other parts of Italy, particularly at the courts of Rome, Naples, Mantua and Ferrara, and Medici sponsorship often had a stimulating effect. Artists played a central role alongside humanist schools and scholars. Thus Ludovico Gonzaga, as a margrave who only became a prince rather late and had a good deal of catching up to do as a patron, invited both Alberti and Mantegna to Mantua. The latter stayed more than forty years and embellished the palace. Also popular at court were Antonio Pisano (called Pisanello), the inventor of the medal that immortalised Ludovico Gonzaga, Lionello d'Este and Alfonso of Aragón and thus created a new medium for glorifying princes on the model of ancient Roman coins. Another important court was that of Federico da Montefeltro in Urbino, who had earned the means for his cultural activities as a military entrepreneur. Around 1476 he commissioned a portrait of himself and his son from Joos van Wassenhove, which shows him wearing a suit of armour and reading a book to illustrate his passion for collecting and his literary pursuits. He decorated his study with portraits of figures of classical antiquity, the Church fathers, the scholastic philosophers Thomas Aquinas and Duns Scotus as well as Dante and Petrarch, thereby placing them in a line of tradition.

In the late fifteenth century, the Republic of Venice finally developed its own contribution to the Renaissance. Important figures here were the brothers Gentile and Giovanni Bellini, both of whom studied the Orient. Venice was also a centre for the transmission of Renaissance innovations to the region north of the Alps.[15]

At the same time, papal building projects – especially the work on the new Saint Peter's – made Rome increasingly attractive for artists. The enthusiasm for ancient sculpture grew.[16] New excavations such as that of the Apollo Belvedere or the Laocoon group (1506) made collecting ancient sculptures fashionable not only in Rome. Pope Julius II had a courtyard for sculptures laid out at the Vatican and began to fill the papal collections with antiquities. It was thus only a matter of time before demand for antiquities and works in the classical style grew outside Italy as well. Princes of the Church in particular played a pioneering role with their passion for collecting. Cardinal Tamás Bakócz, for example, erected a chapel in the Florentine style in the cathedral of Esztergom in Hungary and followed the enthusiasm for the Renaissance of his monarch, Matthias Corvinus. Cardinal Georges d'Amboise had a château built in Gaillon with a loggia and a *studiolo*, and Thomas Wolsey filled Hampton Court Palace with a wealth of antiquities. The French King Charles VIII made things a good deal easier for himself, plundering paintings, statues and tapestries during his Italian campaign (1495), thus stimulating a taste for Italian art in France. His successor Francis I, however, spared no expense in attracting Italian artists such as Leonardo da Vinci and Benvenuto Cellini to his court.[17]

We should not underestimate the importance of humanist travellers to Italy, as well as central and western European merchants who traded with the country, as collectors and disseminators of antiquities. Thus it is not surprising that sixteenth-century Europe witnessed a vigorous trade in antiquities and the founding of private and princely collections of such objects.

13.3 Universities

The history of the European universities begins around 1200, with foundations in Bologna and Paris. Schools of law had already formed in the eleventh century in Bologna, attracting students (scholars) from near and far. Around the middle of the century, a decree by Frederick Barbarossa placed them under imperial protection against communal intervention. From this emerged student corporations in the form of sworn associations (*coniuratio*, *universitas*), which became the germ cell of the two Bologna universities of law. These institutions, which first appear in the sources around 1250, were divided in regard to their geographical sphere of influence into a *universitas legistarum citramontanorum* for students from Italy and a *universitas legistarum ultramontanorum* for students from beyond the Alps. In addition, the students of the *artes* and medicine joined forces in a *universitas artistarum et medicorum*. Only in the late thirteenth century, however, were these corporations (*universitates*) institutionalised by papal privileges such as the *Libertas scholarium*.

Alongside the institutionalisation in Bologna, the papacy also established a European centre for theology in Paris. The Church could draw here on the presence of various monastic orders as well as the prestige of the cathedral school of Notre Dame. In Paris, the growing streams of scholars had to be organised, and to this end a single *universitas* was established, in contrast to the practice in Bologna. The founding bull of 1231, which confirmed the liberties of members of the university, served as a model for many other European universities. The Pope also confirmed the right of the Parisian graduates (*magisters*) to teach anywhere.[18]

By the thirteenth century, the new educational model of the university had proved a success. Thus masters and scholars from Bologna established a *Studium generale* in Padua in 1222, and the Paduans founded a university at Vercelli in 1228. The Italian communes and later towns everywhere in Europe engaged in a veritable competition to attract scholars and magisters. As a result, into the early modern period the departure of the latter from one university town led to the founding of new universities. Thus a segment of the masters from Oxford University, which had been privileged in 1214 on the Parisian model, founded Cambridge in 1225. Montpellier, in contrast, had already been training students in medicine and jurisprudence before receiving its charter in 1220, which adopted models from both Bologna and Paris. Monarchs also founded universities to train their own jurists. They included Emperor Frederick II at Naples in 1224 or the kings of Castile at Salamanca in 1218/19.

University foundations were focused in the south, where they began operations in Orléans in 1235, in Piacenza (1248), Seville (1254/60), Valladolid and Lisbon (*c.* 1290). This changed little in the fourteenth century, when Avignon (1303), Rome (1303), Perugia (1308), Treviso (1318), Cahors (1332), Grenoble (1339) and Pisa (1343) followed. Emperor Charles IV founded the first university in central Europe north of the Alps at Prague in 1348. With this university, for the first time the 'newer Europe' surpassed the 'older Europe' rooted in the legacy of classical antiquity. Cracow (1364), Vienna (1365), Pécs (1367), Erfurt (1379), Heidelberg (1386), Cologne (1388) and Buda (1395) followed in quick succession, although in the south the programme of universities continued in a series of new and re-established institutions: Florence (1349), Perpignan (1350), Huesca (1354), Arezzo (1355), Siena (1357), Pavia (1361) and Lucca (1369). These foundations cannot, however, be compared to the established mass universities of their day such as Bologna or Paris, which had more than one thousand students, but also not to Padua, Perugia, Montpellier or Oxford.

Structurally they were broadly similar, since nearly all universities adopted the Parisian model of four faculties. Before they could enter the prestigious faculties of theology, law or medicine, all students had first to pass through the liberal arts as preparation. This prestige was distributed differently among the universities and their faculties. Thus Bologna and the study of law ranked higher than Paris with theology, which meant that a newly matriculated student of the law faculties in Bologna or Orléans ranked higher than a magister of the liberal arts and even of the theological faculties of Paris or Prague.[19]

The common student, the *scholaris simplex*, studied only at the faculty of arts without taking a final examination, while another widespread type of liberal arts student at least attained the first degree of *baccalareus*. If he continued his studies to the degree of magister he was permitted to enter the higher faculties. At the same time, however, as a magister he could also earn his living by teaching. Only a small minority continued studying until they had earned the doctorate.[20]

In this early phase, university teaching still took place very much within the knowledge system of scholasticism. This had been canonised on the basis of Aristotelian writings by scholars such as Albertus Magnus (*c.* 1200–80), Bonaventure (1217–74) and Thomas Aquinas (1225–74), for example in the latter's *Summa theologiae*. Nonetheless, new approaches, such as those introduced by John Duns Scotus (1265–1308), Roger Bacon (1214–92) or William of Ockham (1285–1348), expanded the knowledge system and ultimately led to its dissolution. With their more practical and professional orientation, law and medicine, in particular, could not adopt the scholastic scheme and with it a unified medieval system of scholarship. These fields were empirical, while theologians used the interpretation and exegesis of ancient and modern texts to produce introductions, commentaries and textbooks.

Masters and professors or doctors made significant contributions to the exchange of knowledge through teaching, reading, discussion and disputation. Scholarly exchange was conducted through both verbal communication in the university setting and the dissemination of notes and manuscripts. With time, university personnel and not just students began to wander from one university to another, and the Church infrastructure played an essential role here, as it did in the exchange of manuscripts and later of books as well.[21] This would intensify above all in the fifteenth century, when clerical dignitaries functioned not just as collectors and buyers of manuscripts but also as founders of universities and academies. In so doing, they counteracted a development that Peter Moraw has referred to as the territorial age of the European university. The rulers who now founded universities had only a limited interest in promoting scholastic education. Instead, they regarded the university as a producer and storehouse of knowledge for their own political needs. It was no longer a matter of universal knowledge, above all on behalf of the Church, but of legitimising and expanding territorial rule and training loyal subjects for princely service. Thus even the lower echelons of the central administration, for instance, employed graduates of the arts faculties as chancery clerks, and there is also evidence of an academisation of local administration.

Professors were now generally recruited from within the country and its academically notable families or clans. Clerical and secular rulers increasingly took the initiative in founding universities – for which, however, Church approval remained necessary. While the founding of the University of Würzburg by the bishop (1402) failed after only ten years, Turin (1404), Leipzig (1409), Aix-en-Provence (1409), St Andrews (1411), Parma (1412/20), Rostock (1419), Dole (1422), Louvain (1425), Poitiers (1431), Caen (1432), Bordeaux (1441), Catania (1444) as well as Gerona (1446) and Barcelona (1450) proved successful.

The second half of the century saw a boom in university foundings, which now spread as far as northern Europe: Glasgow (1451), Valence (1452), Trier (1454), Greifswald (1456), Freiburg im Breisgau (1457), Basle (1459), Nantes (1460), Bourges (1464), Pressburg (Bratislava) (1465), Venice (1470), Genoa (1471), Ingolstadt (1472), Saragossa (1474), Copenhagen (1475), Mainz (1476), Tübingen (1476), Uppsala (1477), Palma de Mallorca (1483), Sigüenza (1489), Aberdeen (1493), Frankfurt an der Oder (1498), Alcalá (1499), Valencia (1500), Wittenberg (1502), Seville (1505/16) and Toledo (1521). Humanist influences are evident in the later foundations, and the Reformation and confessionalisation would soon provide a further impetus for new waves of university foundations.

Humanist influences were reflected in teaching, as the Italian universities restructured their curriculum in the fifteenth century in keeping with the *studia humanitatis* (see 13.1). The universities north of the Alps profited from this only gradually, through students returning home or the circulation of books and manuscripts, which now inspired new writings.[22] Medicine was also placed on a broader textual basis with new editions of the works of Galen, which in the sixteenth century were published first in Greek and later in Latin translation. The field of jurisprudence was influenced by the historical-philological method, which developed a specifically humanist understanding of the law. It was not merely associated with a preference for secular Roman law; the attendant historicisation also contributed to increased attention being paid to the traditional bodies of law of various countries. This set the stage for the evolution of national legal cultures.

The number of scholarly publications from the universities increased markedly with the spread of the printing press in the late fifteenth century, although the printing houses long had trouble keeping up with the demand for textbooks. At the same time, the efflorescence of humanist epistolary culture, together with an improvement in postal services, increased exchanges among professors both within and between countries, although communication was no longer restricted to a closed circle of learned men. It was not until the late sixteenth century, however, that empirical and experimental approaches to science found a place at the university.

13.4 The Church

The ecclesiastical structures of the thirteenth to fifteenth centuries were shaped by the Avignon exile of the popes and the Great Schism as well as by endless reform debates in the Church. Although it appeared at first that the curia had finally won the battle between empire and papacy after the deposition of Frederick II at the Council of Lyons in 1245 and the collapse of Hohenstaufen rule in southern Italy, new and superior opponents emerged in the confrontation with the nascent national kingdoms. The coming struggles would play out above all between Pope Boniface VIII and the French King Philip IV, the Fair, who brooked no papal influence in his territory. In the conflict over the taxation of the French clergy and the charges brought against Bishop Bernard Saisset of Pamiers by royal officials, the Pope upheld papal supremacy in the bull 'Unam sanctam'. The primacy of the papacy was attacked in writing by the royal keeper of the seals Guillaume de Nogaret, and reduced to the absurd by the Roman Colonna family, who had the Pope held captive in 1303 (see 2.1).[23]

The next Pope but one, Clement V (1305–14), took up residence at Avignon in 1309, and in the years that followed the College of Cardinals became largely French, guaranteeing continuity of personnel. Up to 1376, six further popes would rule in succession from Avignon, accompanied above all by a strengthening of the papal administration and a lavish expansion of the bishops' palace into a papal residence. Although the papacy considered a return to Rome, for many years the means of imposing administrative rule in the Papal State were lacking. The reorganisation of the curial financial administration, particularly under John XXII (1316–34), made it easier to collect the money due the Pope in exchange for distributing prebends and benefices. The sums accumulated in this manner, which papal collectors gathered in the provinces and transferred to the curia with the aid of Italian bankers, allowed the popes not merely to hold court sumptuously at Avignon, but eventually to return to Rome.[24] Thus Gregory IX (1370–78) went back to Rome two years before his death. Now a Roman was to be elected pope, but in the event it was a compromise candidate, the former Archbishop of Bari (Urban VI, 1378–79) who emerged from the conclave. Since he displayed an unexpectedly reformist attitude, the cardinals had him declared unfit to rule and elected a new candidate, Clement VII (1379–94). In the meantime, Naples had come to support Urban VI, so that Clemens VII was ultimately forced to leave Rome and reside in Avignon. The Great Schism began.[25] While the 'Romans' enjoyed the support of Naples, other Italian states and central and eastern Europe, France, Burgundy, Savoy, Castile and Aragón and, with time, the German states as well became clients of Avignon. Since both camps were of roughly equal size it took a huge mutual political effort to restore the unity of the Church.

Ideas on the institutional unity of the Church combined here with questions of the unity of faith and notions of ecclesiastical reform such as were constantly being articulated from above and below. Initiatives for religious and spiritual renewal in particular repeatedly came from below, for example from the Cathar and Waldensian communities, the religious orders or the midst of the universities, as in the cases of Wycliffe, Hus or Luther. The Cathars – also known as Albigensians, after their centre in Albi – became prominent victims of the Church's persecution of heretics, although they were but one group among many. The Cathars were particularly dangerous for the Catholic hierarchy, however, because they viewed the earth as a hell and all reality, especially wealth, as the devil's work, and organised a counter-Church. They confronted the institutional Church with an unworldly, morally exemplary ideal of poverty and a dualist

'Christian' mythology based on the opposition between the earthly/evil and the heavenly/good.[26]

Since the Albigensian Crusade only drove the Cathars underground it was left to the Inquisition, which was established in 1233 in Languedoc, to wipe out the heretics. At first, however, the Cathars attracted new adherents. Only the strengthening of the Inquisition by Philip IV of France and the resultant execution of Cathar preachers, including Pierre Autier (d. 1311), led to a collapse of communication among the Cathars. The gap the Cathars left behind was partially filled by the Waldensians, who based their creed on Christianity but preferred different forms of worship and opposed the institutional Church. In seeking, like their founder Pierre Valdès, to return to the early Christian ideal of poverty, they attracted a large following and challenged the Church hierarchy.[27]

After the Waldensians had gone underground, above all in the rural and mountainous regions of southern France and Piedmont, but also of southern Germany, only the mendicant orders still represented the Church's ideal of poverty. The Dominicans and Franciscans, who picked up where the 'missionary successes' of the Cathars had left off, spread quickly throughout western Christendom in the thirteenth century, with the Dominicans acquiring new tasks as the Inquisition expanded. The Franciscans, in contrast, sought to move people to repentance not through preaching (or torture) but through the example of poverty. The ideal of poverty they demanded of the Church often proved a bone of contention. Thus the so-called *Fraticelli* or Franciscan Spirituals provoked the curial adminstration with their references to the poverty of Christ, and were inevitably threatened with the Inquisition by John XXII, the successful reorganiser of the papal finances. While the Franciscan order capitulated, the *Fraticelli* went underground.

The Church hierarchy exerted pressure on the structures of other orders as well, for instance by uniting the existing orders of hermits in the Augustinian Hermits. Congregations of nuns were institutionalised alongside orders of monks, and would henceforth be present in the cities both socially and culturally. This did not silence the ideas of Church reform, however. At the University of Oxford, in particular, the poverty of Christ continued to be a topic of discussion. The Irish theologian Richard FitzRalph (1295–1360) criticised abuses within the mendicant orders and addressed for the first time the problem of the relationship between dominion and divine grace. In this he inspired John Wycliffe, who mainly grappled with papal rule and propagated the sale of Church property to ameliorate the situation of the poor. Like Luther after him, Wycliffe also questioned the dominant sacramental understanding of penitence, arguing that contrition and true penitence could not be mediated by a priest or sacrament. His theories found support within the gentry, among whom the idea of secularisation, in particular, fell on fertile soil.[28]

Among those who cited Wycliffe were the protagonists of the English Peasant Revolt (1381), who had misunderstood him and thereby discredited his teachings and their dissemination by the so-called Lollards.[29] The influence of the English Bible translation he instigated persisted, and his writings were naturally known elsewhere as well, for example in Bohemia.

Thus it was Wycliffe's teachings that brought the Prague priest and university teacher Jan Hus, who also advocated translating the Bible into the vernacular, to the Council of Constance where he was condemned as a heretic and burnt at the stake (see 6.1).[30] Hus had gone a step farther than Wycliffe, conceiving of the Church as a community of the elect and calling for a chalice for the laity as its symbol, that is, for Communion in both kinds. Confronted with such provocative ideas, the Council of Constance sought to adopt the *causa fidei*, *causa unionis* and *causa reformationis* in broad consensus. At first, the primary focus was on Church unity, since the explosive nature of Wycliffe's teachings only became truly apparent through their dissemination by Hus, and there were now not just two popes but three at the helm of their dioceses. To be sure, the 1409 Council of Pisa had deposed both Gregory XII in Rome and Benedict XIII in Avignon, and elected a new Pope, Alexander V, who was succeeded in 1410 by John XXIII. Since Benedict XIII was still recognised in Spain, however, and Gregory XII also had his adherents, it appeared that only a general council could resolve the situation. When King Sigismund called a council for November 1414 in Constance, he could be assured of support from the German electors and princes as well as France, England, Burgundy, Poland, Hungary and Denmark. Only Benedict's supporters in Castile, Aragón and Scotland sent no representatives.

The council met with a very positive response at most European universities. Even before the Council of Pisa, the University of Paris, the alma mater of theology, had prepared an opinion on overcoming the schism and was now represented by its chancellor, Jean Gerson, one of the leading conciliar theologians of his day. Following university custom, the council was divided for the purposes of consultation and voting into four *nationes* (English, French, German and Italian), each of which represented several countries (the German nation brought together Germans, Poles, Bohemians, Hungarians and Danes). Voting by nation was intended to counteract the Italian majority of heads (mitres).

In the course of negotiations, the council succeeded first in deposing John XXIII (1415) and convincing Gregory XII to give up his office. In exchange for admitting a Spanish nation to the council, Benedict XIII was also deposed in 1417, leaving the delegates free to elect the Roman Oddo Colonna as the new Pope Martin V. This accomplished one of the central tasks, restoring the unity of Christendom. The unity of the Church and the restoration of its hierarchy had been demonstrated, even if it was attained by conciliar means. The unity of faith – *causa fidei* – was also ostensibly restored by the ban on Wycliffe's doctrines and writings as well as the condemnation and execution of Jan Hus. There was little progress in the matter of the *causa reformationis*, with the only agreement being that councils would be held periodically (five years after the Council of Constance concluded). The councils would nevertheless become the reform institutions of the future.[31]

Martin V convoked the next council in 1423 at Pavia, but only the University of Paris sent a substantial delegation. He accordingly moved the council to Siena, and then dissolved it in 1424. Martin V, who proved himself an able reorganiser of the Papal State and restorer of the papacy's temporal territorial power, then convoked the next council at Basle in 1431, in keeping with the rhythm set down at Constance. His successor, the Venetian Eugene IV (1431–47), did not feel bound by this agreement and tried to dissolve the council, which was at first still dominated by Parisian scholars and members of central European universities. The result was a veritable boom in conciliarism.[32] The council responded with the decree 'Haec Sancta', in which it affirmed the autonomy of the councils and stipulated in 'De Stabilimento Concilii' that councils could only be moved or dissolved with the consent of their members.

Since more and more bishops and representatives of the European monarchies arrived in Basle over the course of 1432, the papal legate Giuliano Cesarini was able to convince the Pope to relent. The military successes of the Hussites, who destabilised central Europe militarily and religiously in the wake of the condemnation of their idol, gave the Emperor and the German princes a powerful interest in reaching an accord with their moderate representatives. A council was necessary for this purpose, which provided great support for the conciliarists. The council opened negotiations with the Hussites and tackled an extensive programme of reform. The Pope was deposed again, and the council assumed a portion of his duties, such as deciding contested episcopal elections, tax collection and the distribution of offices to loyal clients.

Although the council reached an agreement with moderate Hussites and also brokered the 1435 Peace of Arras between France and Burgundy, the reorganisation of Church governance remained bogged down. The council became increasingly enmeshed in a Franco-Italian conflict that the Pope ultimately decided in his own favour by means of a foreign-policy gambit. Thus he succeeded in convincing representatives of the Greek Orthodox Church, which was under pressure from the Turks and thus sought dialogue with Rome, to come to a council in Ferrara (1439), and to unite with the Roman Catholic Church in Florence. The European powers continued to support the papacy of Eugene IV and at the same time adopted those Basle reform resolutions consonant with their own interests. For example, in the 1438 'Pragmatic Sanction of Bourges' Charles VII of France altered the decrees concerning the right to make appointments to Church offices and the payment of taxes to the curia in a manner beneficial to himself. After this success, the French, who had hitherto dominated the council, sometimes in concert with the German delegates, withdrew.[33]

In the 1439 'Acceptation' of Mainz the German princes also adopted the Basle resolutions, which were then 'watered-down' a few years later in the 'Concordat of Vienna' (1448) between King Frederick III and Eugene IV's successor Nicholas V, and henceforth defined the imperial Church's relationship to the curia.[34]

With his successes in what proved to be the short-lived union with the Greek Church, which was followed by further agreements with Armenians, Copts and Syrian Christians, Eugene IV had drawn leading protagonists of the council such as Giuliano Cesarini and Nicholas of Cusa over to his side. Representation at the council waned. In 1448 – after the concordat between the Empire and the curia – the 'remains' of the council proceeded to Lausanne and dissolved themselves one year later. Since the Emperor did not pursue the conciliar matter after his coronation at Rome in 1452, the German princes drew up the *Gravamina* (grievances) of the 'German Nation' in 1456. These were directed against papal appointments to benefices and interference in elections and the papal mode of raising money in Germany by granting expectatives, levying annates and selling indulgences. The princes were anxious to see the Basle reforms implemented and therefore demanded the regular holding of general and national councils.

Although the conciliar idea persisted, it was overshadowed by the foreign-policy successes of papal diplomacy, the emergence of the papal quasi-monarchy and Rome's development into the cultural centre of the Renaissance. Since popes such as Sixtus IV and Alexander VI shamelessly used their position for the aggrandisement of their families, on whom they bestowed cardinal's hats, benefices and temporal territories, reform impulses could only come from foreign rulers. Thus the last attempt to convoke a general council to weaken the Pope was undertaken by Louis XII of France, among others, and a group of oppositional cardinals in 1511 in Pisa. The Pope's response was to call the fifth Lateran or Vatican Council in Rome in 1512, with Spanish support. These efforts notwithstanding, the call for a council as well as reforms continued to be articulated and took on new meaning in the Reformation era. In the fifteenth century, this desire came together with imperial reforms such as those that would be undertaken by Frederick III and above all by Emperor Maximilian I.

There were also reform efforts on the lower echelons, which aimed at returning monks and nuns to the discipline and spirituality of their monastic Rules. In the case of the orders, they had Rome's support, as the German sojourn of the papal legate Nicholas of Cusa in 1451–2 affirmed.[35] The mendicant orders in particular, which in the light of urban cultural developments may have appeared as relics of the past, faced the necessity of reform. This process frequently saw orders split into the so-called observants, who strictly followed the Rules, and the conventuals, whose motto might be described as 'live and let live'. In the case of the Augustinian Hermits and the Carmelites, reform congregations embracing renewal emerged from those monasteries.[36]

New orders, for instance the Minims of Francis de Paula (1436–1507), arose or attracted new members in the fifteenth century, as was the case with the originally Swedish Bridgettine Order. Even old orders like the Benedictines came together to establish centres of reform, for example Santa Giustina in Padua, Subiaco near Rome, Kastl in the Upper Palatinate, Melk in Austria and Bursfelde on the River Weser. For the Augustinian canons regular, Windesheim was the centre from which they spread their reforms to the north German plain as far as Saxony and Thuringia.[37]

The Carthusians, whose excellent reputation was reflected in no fewer than 106 new monasteries in the fourteenth century, served as a bellwether. They inspired the lay movement of *devotio moderna*, in particular.[38] Thus Geert Grote (d. 1384), the son of a Deventer patrician family who had studied in Paris for more than ten years, was reputedly converted to the ideal of the simple life and above all fraternal communal life by the Carthusians of Monnikhuizen near Arnheim. He founded this new movement by establishing houses in his home city for young women and men where they could live a spiritual life of shared devotions without vows or enclosure.

This lay movement also sought to reach ordinary, less educated people through pastoral activities, spiritual songs and a popular style of preaching. The laity orientated themselves toward monastic ideals, which they emulated in the brother and sister houses of the 'Brethren of the Common Life'. They focused on disseminating books, schools and teachers, at first in the IJssel River towns of Kampen, Deventer and Zwolle, from where they gradually radiated out into other regions of the Holy Roman Empire. Their efforts centred on developing the Christian individual's 'new inwardness' on the way to a personal relationship with God, and took up the traditions of medieval mysticism.[39] Although the *devotio moderna*, unlike humanism and later the Reformation, did not challenge dominant theological doctrine and religious culture as it was practised, it nevertheless had a lasting influence on the spread of so-called Christian or biblical humanism in the Netherlands. The latter arose as a symbiosis of Italian scholarly humanist methods and the Christian spiritual ideals propagated by the *devotio moderna*.

Christian humanism grew from the seeds sown by the *devotio* movement with its Latin schools especially in the IJssel towns. It spread quickly from the far north-east of the Netherlands through the province of Holland to Brabant and Flanders, and found its most outstanding representative in Desiderius Erasmus (1469–1536). He was concerned with moral regeneration and Christian piety (*Enchiridion or manual of a Christian knight*, 1503) as well as reforming the Church as an institution (*The praise of folly*, 1511).[40]

Apart from the spiritual inwardness of the *devotio moderna*, the fifteenth century was also the heyday of popular piety. The cities demanded learned preachers and the villages good pastors, and religious foundations devoured huge sums of money saving souls. Pilgrimages, in particular, became a mass phenomenon, sometimes to the point of mass hysteria. New places of pilgrimage sprouted like weeds and attracted unprecedented numbers of the faithful, who spared no expense or effort in search of salvation, preferring to make too many pilgrimages and donations rather than too few. Academic theology did take note of this popular piety, especially when a prominent conciliar theologian such as Jean Gerson also became a propagator of *Frömmigkeitstheologie* (a form of theology that focused on the personal conscience and spirituality) in his lectures, treatises, letters and speeches.[41]

These reform movements were not restricted to Latin Christendom. Russia was also repeatedly gripped by waves of criticism of the Church. The followers of a movement that appeared in the late fourteenth century in Novgorod and the early fifteenth century in Pskov and thus at the same time as Wycliffe and Hus were known as *strigol'niki* (from *strich*, to shear), a name that referred both to their shorn heads and to the cloth-shearers among them. They fought above all against simony, the sale of ecclesiastical offices, and with it against the Church hierarchy, from whom they demanded the right to preach for all believers. Although the first supporters of the movement had already been executed in the 1370s, this heresy persisted in Pskov into the early fifteenth century. In the mid-fifteenth century a new movement arose in Novgorod, the so-called Judaisers, who built on the ideas of the *strigol'niki*. The Judaisers, as their opponents called them, also rejected the secularisation of the institutional Church, whose chief motivation they believed to be the accumulation of landed property. The target of the criticisms of this movement, which was dominated by the lower clergy of Novgorod and their followers, was the Archbishop of Novgorod and with him the entire oligarchical system of government. In Moscow, in contrast, members of court society also sympathised with the Judaisers, and even Grand Prince Ivan III found this movement rather convenient during the integration of Novgorod into his territory and the annexation of Novgorod church property. The Church opposed the Judaisers, but also felt compelled to respond to the challenge. Thus one of the harshest critics, Archbishop Gennady of Novgorod, took the Judaisers' translation of individual books of the Old Testament from the Hebrew as an occasion to commission the first translation of the Bible into Church Slavonic, based on the Latin Vulgate.

With their call for poverty in the Church, the Judaisers found common ground with another Church-reform movement, the *nestiazhateli* (non-possessors), as the followers of Nil Sorsky (*c.* 1433–1508) were known. After several years in search of tranquillity and inwardness on Mount Athos – influenced by the Byzantine mystical movement – Nil Sorsky had returned to the north, 'beyond the upper Volga', where he propagated the ideal of Christian virtue. This included not just monastic selflessness, chastity and obedience, but also the voluntary renunciation of ecclesiastical, especially monastic, landownership. His adversary was Abbot Joseph of Volokolamsk (Volotsky, 1439–1515), who advocated a different path to reform. As he saw it, monastics could only perform one of their main duties, caring for the poor and the sick, if their monasteries were adequately funded. The two viewpoints clashed when fundamental matters of Church structure were discussed at the Moscow Synod of 1503. While the synod agreed, under pressure from the territorial ruler, to abolish the traditional payments upon appointment to Church office and thus do away with simony, the Grand Prince's wishes regarding the secularisation of ecclesiastical lands went unfulfilled. Although Nil Sorsky, who had been invited to the synod, tried to persuade the synodals to relinquish their lands, they stubbornly refused

– and were supported in this by the boyars. Even Grand Prince Ivan III dared not force poverty on the Church. Whether this was a victory for the position of Joseph of Volokolamsk, with his support for a powerful institutional Church, as some historians claim, appears doubtful. At first, the Church apparatus had resisted the ruler, and it would take additional dynastic fortuities before a symbiosis between Church and State could emerge in the mid-sixteenth century.[42]

Notes

1 The literature on humanism is vast. For a good introduction, see Rabil, *Renaissance humanism*. For a useful collection of sources, see Mout (ed.), *Die Kultur des Humanismus*.
2 The term first appeared in a review of F. Engel-Jánosi's 'Soziale Probleme der Renaissance'. See Baron, *The crisis of the early Italian renaissance*, and *In search of Florentine civic humanism*.
3 Hankins (ed.), *Renaissance civic humanism*.
4 Helmrath, Muhlack and Walther (eds), *Diffusion des Humanismus*; Goodman and MacKay (eds), *The impact of humanism*.
5 Saygin, *Humphrey, duke of Gloucester*.
6 Burke, 'The spread of Italian humanism'; Nauert, *Humanism*, 95–123.
7 Klaniczay and Jankovics (eds), *Matthias Corvinus*.
8 Strnad, 'Die Rezeption', 71–135.
9 Machilek, 'Konrad Celtis'; Segel, *Renaissance culture*, 83–106.
10 Grafton and Jardine, *From humanism to the humanities*.
11 Burckhardt, *Civilisation of the Renaissance in Italy*.
12 Borchert, 'Introduction', in *Jan van Eyck's workshop*, 9.
13 Burke, *The European Renaissance*, 34.
14 Burke, *The Italian Renaissance*, 90ff.
15 Aikema and Brown (eds), *Renaissance Venice*.
16 Haskell and Penny, *Taste and the antique*.
17 Burke, *The European Renaissance*, 79–81.
18 Verger, 'Patterns', 35–64.
19 Moraw, 'Einheit und Vielfalt', 19–20.
20 Schwinges, 'Europäische Studenten' and *Artisten und Philosophen*.
21 Weber, *Geschichte der europäischen Universität*, 35–42, 63–70.
22 For Germany, see Overfield, *Humanism and scholasticism*, 102–20.
23 Favier, *Philippe le Bel*, 250–88, and *Histoire de France*, II, 244–52.
24 Mollat, *The popes at Avignon*; Renouard, *La Papauté à Avignon*.
25 Ullmann, *The origins of the Great Schism*; Brandmüller, 'Zur Frage nach der Gültigkeit'.
26 Hamilton, 'The Cathars and Christian perfection'.
27 Hamilton, 'The Albigensian crusade and heresy'; Costen, *The Cathars and the Albigensian crusade*.

28 Catto, 'Wycliff and Wycliffism'; Hudson and Wilks (eds), *From Ockham to Wyclif*, 281–330.
29 Rex, *The Lollards*.
30 Fudge, *The magnificent ride*.
31 Brandmüller, *Das Konzil von Konstanz*.
32 Brandmüller, 'Der Übergang', 85–110; Tierney, *Foundations of the conciliar theory*.
33 Bove, *Le Temps de la guerre de Cent Ans*, 406–12.
34 Helmrath, *Das Basler Konzil*; Müller, *Die Franzosen, Frankreich und das Basler Konzil*.
35 Meuthen, 'Die deutsche Legationsreise des Nikolaus von Kues', 472–6.
36 Weinbrenner, *Klosterreform im 15. Jahrhundert*.
37 Mertens, 'Monastische Reformbewegungen'; Saak, *High way to heaven*.
38 Angenendt, *Geschichte der Religiosität*, 75–6; Post, *Kerkelijke verhoudingen*; Lourdaux, 'Les dévots modernes'; Vauchez, *The laity in the Middle Ages*.
39 McGinn, *The harvest of mysticism in medieval Germany*.
40 Screech, *Erasmus*, 228–40; North, *De geschiedenis van Nederland*, 35–40.
41 Angenendt, *Geschichte der Religiosität*, 71–5; Hamm, 'Frömmigkeit'.
42 Stökl, 'Das Echo'; Skrynnikov, 'Kirchliches Denken'; Martin, *Medieval Russia, 980–1584*, 259–66; Ostrowski, 'Church polemics and monastic land acquistion', 335–79.

PART III

Debates and research problems

The authors of existing overviews of the literature[1] have sought to provide a brief outline of as many research approaches as possible. I shall take a different path here, and concentrate on a few issues that have been addressed in several European countries. My selection consciously follows my own interests, with a focus on economics and culture, which tend to receive less attention.

Note

1 For German examples, see Dirlmeier, Fouquet and Fuhrmann, *Europa im Spätmittelalter*; Meuthen, *Das 15. Jahrhundert*.

14

The 'crisis of the late Middle Ages'

One of the phenomena that have attracted attention in nearly all European countries is the crisis of the late Middle Ages. While some historians like Edouard Perroy, František Graus or Ferdinand Seibt have treated the question more generally,[1] the majority of scholars have focused on the economic crisis or the so-called depression of the late Middle Ages. There are several competing explanatory models. Apart from the various causes, historians have mainly examined divergent regional developments and different sectors of the economy. This yields new perspectives on the structural transformation of agriculture, industry and commerce. As to the term 'crisis', scholars at least agree that it was not a subsistence crisis of the old type, but rather a sales crisis or a depression. Explanations of the causes are influenced by two different schools of thought. While the neo-Malthusians or neo-Ricardians concentrate on developments in the real economy and population decline, and hold the plague, with attendant demographic losses, responsible for the crisis, the monetarists offer a quantitative (monetary) explanation that argues in terms of precious-metal production.

Proponents of the real economy model include Michael Postan, Wilhelm Abel and Georges Duby. Postan has proved the most influential, while Abel's work is known mainly in Germany, and has had scant impact on Anglo-American scholarship because little has been translated into English.[2] The three historians make quite similar arguments, however. They all assume that the drastic population decline in the fourteenth-century waves of plague altered the relationship between land and population. While the output per unit of land fell, the output per unit of labour rose. By stopping the cultivation of marginal soils and concentrating on good ones, relatively more grain could be produced with relatively less labour. At the same time, the number of agricultural labourers dropped, since the survivors either took over abandoned lands as peasant farmers or migrated to the towns. Agricultural prices fell because of the decreased demand for grain and the greater productivity of cultivation, allowing town dwellers to spend relatively less for basic foodstuffs and more on high-quality foods and craft products. Their prices also rose accordingly, as did the wages of those who made them. The 'golden age' of craft production began. According to this model, demographic changes were responsible for the elasticities of demand and the resulting differential development of prices for agrarian and craft products. Monetary historians, however, would also acknowledge that changes in relative prices are a result of varying elasticities of demand. The monetarists draw our attention to different phenomena. W. C. Robinson opened the discussion in 1959 with the thesis that the drop in European silver mining in the fourteenth and fifteenth centuries and diminished stocks of money as a result were responsible for the economic crisis in late medieval Europe.[3] Postan soon responded with a devastating critique and offered key arguments for the influence of demographic developments on late medieval economic cycles.[4] Without denying that European silver mining declined, Postan nevertheless rejected the conclusion that European silver stocks had dwindled. On the one hand, no fall in production could substantially reduce the European stocks of bullion amassed over several centuries of economic expansion. On the other, trade and the balance of payments were already the main sources of bullion for the majority of European countries without precious-metal deposits of their own. Changes in the balance of trade did not follow trends in precious-metal mining temporally, so that for example transfers of bullion to England continued even in times when silver mining declined.

More important was Postan's theoretically grounded second argument that the 30–40 per cent drop in the European population in the fourteenth and fifteenth centuries must have improved per capita supply. Harry Miskimin further developed Postan's thesis by interpreting the deflationary effect of monetary factors alongside population decline as a second cause of the late medieval depression.[5] Not until the 1970s was fundamental doubt cast on the assumption that late medieval bullion reserves were large in relation to the population. C. C. Patterson, Marion Archibald and above all Nicholas Mayhew have drawn attention to the yearly shrinking of the money supply as a result of losses of weight owing to wear. In the fifteenth century, because of the decline in silver extraction – mining in Kuttenberg collapsed once and for all with the Hussite Wars – it became increasingly difficult to compensate for these losses through new emissions, so that a country's silver supply necessarily dwindled. John Day has aptly called this situation the 'great bullion famine'.[6] By comparing production figures from various mints, Day demonstrated that a similar decline occurred in England, the Low Countries, France, Italy (Florence, Genoa) and Spain (Aragón, Navarra) in the fourteenth and fifteenth centuries.

Between 1331/1340 and 1491/1500 global mint production fell by approximately 80 per cent. Day regards Europe's permanent trade deficit with the East, especially the Muslim Near East, as the most important cause of these declining mint figures.[7] The growing deficit in the Levant trade – Venetian imports rose by at least one-third – coincided with the collapse of European silver production and the diminished supply of Sudanese gold.[8] Bullion exports to the eastern Baltic region are an additional factor, which Day does not take into account.[9]

Apart from the decline in silver mining, the continual loss of weight and the flow of bullion to the Baltic region, the population's increasing tendency to hoard also reduced the money supply. Concealed coins were withdrawn from the money supply in the short or long term, or bullion disappeared from circulation permanently when it was fashioned into gold and silver objects, brocade fabrics, interior decoration and the like. Nevertheless, precious metals could be melted down and re-minted and thus brought back into circulation. If we follow the thesis of the 'great bullion famine', hoarding increased the deflationary effect of the depression because it removed additional precious metals from circulation. The price of silver rose and the amount of goods available for a unit of silver was constantly increasing.[10] Prices and profit margins fell, while credit became more expensive as a result of the money shortage and adversely affected the banking sector because of liquidity bottlenecks. Erik Aerts discusses this phenomenon in his recent case study of Genoa.[11] The silver trade never stopped, however, even in times of bullion shortages, and, as Reinhold C. Mueller has shown, merchants in international trade developed the option of barter and thus of a more sparing use of existing bullion.[12]

Many of the hypotheses outlined here suffer from a lack of reliable data. Thus neither can we follow with any precision the regionally diverse demographic developments in many parts of Europe – there were definitely regions of growth in a period of general population decline[13] – nor can we reconstruct the economically relevant money supply or the velocity of circulation, which is important for the demand for money. Price and wage movements also frequently resist precise determination. Nonetheless, scholars like John H. Munro have tried in recent years to reconstruct the various components of economic development, taking England and the southern Netherlands as examples. They are aided by the survival of nearly complete series of mint production statistics for England and especially the southern Netherlands, which make it possible to reconstruct monetary and mint policy. Similarly, the existing accounts of hospitals, Church and municipal institutions (Henry Phelps Brown, Sheila Hopkins, Herman Van der Wee und John H. Munro) make it possible to prepare price indexes for England and the Low Countries and get a more precise handle on long-term wage developments.[14] Munro has been able to demonstrate that both the Low Countries and England experienced monetary contraction from the fourteenth into the second half of the fifteenth century, repeatedly interrupted, however, particularly in the Low Countries, by temporary bouts of inflation brought on by wartime devaluation. The long-term price decline accordingly differed from country to country and decade to decade. War and famine, like devaluation, tended to increase prices. Likewise, there is no evidence for the general wage increase claimed by Postan and Abel.

While Gregory Clark shows a rise in (day) wages for agricultural labour (threshing) after the Black Death,[15] John Munro underlines the inflexibility ('stickiness') of wages in the building sector, which as a rule could not be negotiated freely and thus did not directly follow changes in the money supply or population.[16] Since labourers were not in a position to adjust their wages to rising prices in the post-plague era, there were even attempts, for example in the manors of the bishop of Winchester and elsewhere, to squeeze the wages of agricultural labourers. According to Munro, only the deflation that began in the 1390s helped labourers to gain a rise in real wages, since nominal wages remained stable. This continued in the fifteenth century, although numerous bouts of inflation temporarily reduced real wages.[17]

In Germany, the few available figures for wages in Hamburg in the second half of the fifteenth and the early sixteenth century reveal great stability. Wages there remained on the same level into the third decade of the sixteenth century, despite rising prices.[18] Based on the more extensive sources from southern Germany, Ulf Dirlmeier has pointed out that we cannot draw conclusions about long-term employment or rising incomes from the level of daily wages. Thus the rising urban living standards postulated by Abel, with a growth of per capita meat consumption to 100 kg annually, do not correspond to reality.[19]

If we turn our attention to northern Europe and Norway, the futility of applying either neo-Malthusian or monetarist models becomes apparent. Norway, for instance, witnessed not only severe population loss, land desertion and a return to the subsistence economy and rents in kind, but also a halt to coin production and a diminishing demand for coins.[20]

While economic historians have sought to review and refute the Abel/ Postan concept both from the monetary perspective and in detail, Marxist scholars reject this 'market-based model' a priori, if they take note of it at all. Critiques focus on the inadequate attention to the feudal mode of production and the appropriation of peasant products by feudal lords in Abel's model, which, as a classic equilibrium model, ignored these factors from the *ceteris paribus* perspective, that is, all other things being equal. Western European Marxist historians such as Rodney Hilton as well as the Russian E. A. Kosminsky thus no longer explained the agricultural crisis cyclically, but rather structurally as a crisis of the productive forces resulting from increased feudal pressure.[21] This approach was varied in the early work of František Graus and by Marian Małowist, who held the transition from one form of rent to another – from rents in labour and kind to money rents and back again – responsible for the manifestations of crisis in east-central Europe.[22] In later publications, however, Małowist contrasts the development of a crisis-ridden west with the economic flowering of east-central Europe in the fourteenth and fifteenth centuries, without citing the reasons, such as the absence of the plague in the latter region.[23]

This approach assumed greater significance in French scholarship through the work of Guy Bois, who, following the *crise seugneuriale*[24] formulated by Robert Boutruche, constructed a 'crisis of feudalism' using the example of eastern Normandy.[25] His model, which takes demographic developments quite seriously, places the structural origins of the crisis at the centre. While neglecting economic cycles as well as prices and wages, he analyses feudal rents as the key burdens on the peasant economy. He distinguishes here between seigniorial feudal rents (*prélèvement seigneurial*), public feudal rents such as taxes (*prélèvement public*) and wartime feudal rents (*prélèvement de guerre*). To be sure, the seigniorial proportion of feudal rents was falling, but from the fourteenth century, with the beginning of the Hundred Years War, the State and warlords more than made up for this. While in times of inland colonisation the land under cultivation was expanded and the number of those obliged to pay rents could also be increased, this was no longer possible in times of demographic decline. The Hundred Years War descended upon an increasingly impoverished peasantry, with lords and the State demanding new dues and taxes from the remaining peasants. The peasant economy lost its reproductive capacity, which ultimately led to a crisis of the feudal system. Although the final third of the fourteenth century was a phase of recovery for the rural population and labour productivity improved because of the expansion of productive land (improvement of the ratio between people and land owing to the abandonment of farms), war and crisis returned in the first half of the fifteenth century. Meanwhile, the volume of feudal rents sank, and feudal lords and the State tried to compensate for this by raising the feudal quota, which ultimately had a further negative impact on levies. A vicious circle ensued, from which peasants and feudal lords could only have freed themselves by reducing feudal levies or the seigniorial portion of feudal rents.[26]

Bois's local study appears useful for the French case of eastern Normandy as an explanation of manifestations of crisis and might also have explanatory potential for other regions of France. It remains for detail studies to show how far the model can be applied to other countries. Thus in England, for example, the tax burden was far lower, since wool-export duties represented the most important source of revenue for the kingdom not only in peacetime. Here, the levying of a new poll tax in 1381 already sparked the English Peasants' Revolt. Bois remains stimulating nevertheless if we look beyond the concrete level of levies or feudal pressure and regard his work as a possible new structural explanation for crises. In that case, the intensification of serfdom on the Upper Rhine and with it the increase in the proportion of peasant agrarian production that was owed to lords via the so-called *Todfallabgaben* or death duties would certainly fall within the context of the feudal lords' structural weakening of the feudal system.[27] The fiscal pressure exerted by a northern Italian city, for instance Florence, on the peasants of its territory also paralysed their economic power in the fifteenth century, and with it the economic recovery of Tuscany.[28] Bois's model appears extremely useful for Peter Kriedte's explanation of the unequal developments in western and east-central Europe in the sixteenth and seventeenth centuries,[29] but also for developments from the late fifteenth century. Michael North has explained the expansion of the manorial economy in Schleswig-Holstein as a 'makeshift solution as a result of deficient levy opportunities'. In addition, depending on the type and regional location of the estate, both cyclical and structural factors of the manorial system could also be held responsible for manifestations of crisis in the manorial economy.[30]

Viewed from this perspective, Bois would prove superior to the explanations of unequal agrarian development in Europe propagated by Robert Brenner, which fixate exclusively on class constellations. By juxtaposing the feudal development of eastern with the capitalist development of western Europe, Brenner claims that the shift from the traditional peasant economy toward self-supporting economic growth is closely associated with capitalist class constellations. In western Europe, they had been established in conflict with the landowners and had led to capitalist relations between landlords and tenants. Since east-central Europe lacked corresponding class conflicts as well as effective peasant resistance, the manorial feudal system had become solidified there.[31] The Brenner debate, however, reveals various deficiencies in this relatively static model. Brenner neither took adequate account of the strong communal structures that also existed in the eastern settlement regions nor was he able or willing to explain the economic development and consequent processes of transformation and social differentiation. What were the social and economic effects of the Black Death in Europe? How and under what circumstances did a capitalist tenant respond to market stimuli? Brenner shares his scant attention to the market and trade with many of his opponents, but also with other macroeconomic explanatory models, which acknowledge neither market access, institutional limitations and stimuli nor, for instance, the role of the towns in this process.[32] For that reason, Markus Cerman has quite rightly called for a comparative study of land markets in western and east-central Europe.[33]

Stephan R. Epstein takes a different approach, challenging the concentration of most explanatory models on cereal production, which according to him probably accounted for less than 40 per cent of the English gross national product around 1300.[34] In a case study based on his own fundamental research on Sicily, he not merely calls into question the widespread view of the economic superiority of northern Italy and Sicilian underdevelopment, but also intervenes in the debate on the economic development of Florence.[35] This debate juxtaposes positive evaluations of the economic dynamism of the Florentine economy in the fifteenth century by Richard Goldthwaite with the critical assessments of David Herlihy or Anthony Molho, which have revived the earlier debates between Robert Lopez and Carlo Cipolla.[36]

Epstein's comparison of Sicily with Florence and its *contado* or surrounding countryside is a sobering one, however. While it was not until the sixteenth century that Florence recovered demographically from the plague, in Sicily the population rose from 350,000 in the mid-fifteenth to 500,000–550,000 in the mid-sixteenth century. In order to explain this divergent development, Epstein cites institutional framing conditions and the resulting developmental potentials of the individual regions through market adaptation and specialisation. In the Florentine case, the city's dominant position hampered the economic development of its rural surroundings. Instead of profiting from their favourable location in the environs of an urban centre, fiscal pressure from the city of Florence negated all positive economic stimuli. The peasants fell into poverty, since they were bled, with the aid of taxes, by the Florentine elites, who sought to compensate for their own financial losses by exploiting the countryside. In this way, wealth was constantly being transferred from the country to the city on the Arno.

Competition between the Sicilian cities, in contrast, which did not benefit from tax payments from the surrounding countryside, led to economic specialisation that made use of the natural resources of the rural areas. Interregional trade also emerged as a result of customs exemptions introduced during the reign of Alfonso V. The goods included not just wine, oil and wood, but also the region's most important exports, silk and sugar produced for super-regional markets. According to Epstein, the only such specialisation in Florence was soap making and the Prato woollen industry. An additional factor was that the *mezzadria* (sharecropping) system offered no incentives for market production, specialisation and commercialisation, since half of agrarian produce went to the landlords, making it not worth the while of Tuscan tenant farmers to intensify cultivation for the nearby market. Instead of expanding production for the market, the tenants – whom Brenner regarded as progressive – returned to subsistence farming. Tenants by no means benefited from the demographic losses, for even after the plague they still had to give half of their produce to their manorial lords. Thus in comparison with other Italian regions, the political and cultural success of the Florentine Republic adversely affected the economy of its environs, while the Aragonese state, which permitted no strong cities in Sicily that dominated the countryside, furthered the island's economic development, at least in the fifteenth century. Epstein believes that Lombardy or the Venetian *Terraferma* was characterised by a greater pluralism of rulers and thus greater competition among economic and political interests.

This approach can be used to explain the diversity of development not just within Italy, but also in comparison to other European regions. Whether and in what ways rulers – that is, princes and towns alike – exploited their environs fiscally always appears to have been a decisive factor. Thus Holland owed its economic rise – compared to Tuscan circumstances – not primarily to direct access to the sea, but rather to 'institutional flexibility' as a consequence of the weak influence of feudal lords and the lack of artificial boundaries between town and countryside.[37]

Cities could, however, also access the resources of their hinterlands economically for regional and international trade, thereby facilitating economic development. Economic historians such as Herman Van der Wee have looked in this direction for a possible understanding of economic development in the crisis-ridden fifteenth century, with maritime overseas trade playing an important explanatory role. Thus Van der Wee shows that before and after the crisis, the growth of the Continental overland trade provided important stimulating effects for growth especially on the Italy–Netherlands route. The wartime congestion of these trade arteries from the second half of the fourteenth and into the fifteenth century led to the collapse of overland trade. Maritime trade proved to be the only outlet, which also offered the advantage of lower transport costs. Accordingly, the regions in Italy, the Low Countries, the North Sea and the Baltic area that specialised in the maritime trade and shipping may have been less affected by the crisis than the Continent's trade fair towns.[38] This would explain the upswing in the Hanseatic trade in the so-called age of crisis.

Viewed against this backdrop, the lesser effect on east-central Europe, where it was only through the Hussite Wars that the crisis reached Bohemia and Silesia, appears less unusual.[39] Thus Marian Dygo, among others, attributes the economic flourishing of this region in the fourteenth century to precious-metal mining, on the one hand, and participation in the Hanseatic trade and long-distance trade between the Baltic and the Black Sea, on the other.[40]

Alongside these analytical studies, a whole range of other publications address the 'crisis of the late Middle Ages' more generally. Most, however, remain rather imprecise or even muddled and dispense with a more exact definition. Among them, František Graus offers the most precise definition of 'crisis as the coincidence of diverse disturbances (so-called sub-crises) of an objective nature (qualitative upheavals, slumps, trend reversals)',[41] if they are accompanied by the shaking of former certainties or purported losses of values. He regards it as a task for future research to test whether the individual crisis phenomena appeared in clusters and whether 'their accumulation is purely accidental or not'.[42] Thus for him, the 'crisis of the Middle Ages' is a scholarly problem, not a confirmed fact.

Ferdinand Seibt is a good deal more daring, interpreting the crisis, much like Jacob Burckhardt in his *Force and freedom*, as a period of political upheaval.[43] Since the 'crisis of the late Middle Ages' culminated in the Reformation and thus represented the breakthrough to the modern era, Seibt would have us understand it as the experience of a disintegrating political order – i.e., as a phenomenon of consciousness. This sense of crisis emerged from the awareness of the political environment, which, according to Seibt, was characterised around 1400 by urban unrest, peasant uprisings, aristocratic revolts and regicide, evoking fears of the future among contemporaries. He does not, however, document the extent to which individuals experienced a break-up of the political order, and whether they regarded it as a divine order or questioned it at all. When criticism did arise, it was levied against officeholders or particular persons while institutions such as the monarchy, the empire or the papacy survived unscathed and even produced successful integration. Accordingly, such a fabricated crisis appears rather implausible, for contemporaries perceived even the plague as merely a repeatedly recurring mass death.[44] For that reason, all attempts to use the general crisis of the late Middle Ages as a *deus ex machina* to explain other phenomena remain highly speculative.

It is in this category that we must place the American art historian Millard Meiss's attempt to use the plague to explain an alleged rejection of Giotto's new naturalism and thus a return to traditional depictions of saints, without taking into account the different patrons or buyers of these paintings.[45] Meiss's thesis has also been rendered obsolete by the dating of the frescos of the Camposanto in Pisa to the period before the plague.[46]

Such an approach, which might be subsumed under the heading 'the individual as victim of the crisis', accordingly does not do justice to the many human activities of the fourteenth and fifteenth centuries that appear as innovations in the arts or as specialisation and commercialisation in trade, industry and agriculture. This necessarily takes us back to the subject of 'the economy', and allows us, with Stuart Jenks, to understand the late Middle Ages as a period of profound structural transformation in which the labour shortage created incentives to innovate, since the only means of compensating for it was to apply technology. 'The necessary capital came to a large, and perhaps even an overwhelming, degree from people with only modest resources. The establishment of capital-intensive large-scale manufacturing forced operators to sell their products in the international wholesale trade, for they could not otherwise have met the high costs of launching and running their businesses'.[47] Companies were now at the mercy of the globalisation of the European economy, and some lost out in the structural transformation of the late Middle Ages. Although this point of view may sound too modern, it does offer a good example of the way in which each generation develops its own approach to an epoch – of the changing constructions of European history, which each generation must tackle anew.

Notes

1 Perroy, 'A L'origine d'une économie contractée', 167–82; Seibt (ed.), *Europa im Hoch- und Spätmittelalter*; *Revolution in Europa*; Seibt and Eberhard (eds), *Europa 1400*; Graus, *Das Spätmittelalter*; *Pest-Geißler-Judenmorde.*

2 Postan, 'Note', 77–82; 'Some economic evidence', 221–46; 'The trade of medieval Europe', 119–256; Abel, *Agrarkrisen und Agrarkonjunktur*; Duby, *Rural economy.*

3 Robinson, 'Money, population, and economic change', 63–76.

4 Postan, 'Note', 77–82; 'Some economic evidence', 221–46; 'The trade of medieval Europe', 191–222.

5 Miskimin, 'Monetary movements', 470–90; 'The economic depression', 408–26.

6 Day, 'The great bullion famine', 3–54. For the best overview of this topic, see Spufford, *Money and its use*, 339–62. Only England and Castile, which as wool exporters had an active balance of trade, appear to have been less affected by the bullion shortage. Unlike the mints in most western European countries, the Tower mint remained in operation with lower production. On England, see Jenks, 'Hartgeld und Wechsel', 127–66. On Castile, see MacKay, *Money, prices and policies*, 23–41.

7 Day, 'The question of monetary contraction', 20.

8 Day, 'The great bullion famine', 36–40.

9 Attman, *The bullion flow*, 61–7.

10 See also Sprandel, *Das mittelalterliche Zahlungssystem*, 133.

11 Aerts, 'European monetary famine'.

12 Mueller, 'Alcune considerazioni', 77–84; 'Il baratto', 27–36.

13 Campbell and Overton, 'A new perspective', 38–105.

14 Brown and Hopkins, *A perspective on wages and prices*, 13–59; the two authors also published components of the index for the first time here (1981). See also Van der Wee, 'Prices and wages as development variables', 58–78; 'Globalization, core and periphery'; Munro, 'Mint outputs, money, and prices', 64–9, 'Urban wage structures', 65–78; 'Wage stickiness', 185–297.

15 Clark, 'The long march of history'.

16 Munro, 'Wage stickiness', 185–297.

17 For labour legislation, see Cohn, 'After the Black Death; Munro, 'Wage stickiness', 194–5; Beveridge, 'Wages in the Winchester manors', 27.

18 North, *Geldumlauf*, 195–6.

19 Dirlmeier, *Untersuchungen zu Einkommensverhältnissen und Lebenshaltungskosten*, and 'Materielle Lebensbedingungen', 59–87; Dirlmeier and Fouquet, 'Ernährung und Konsumgewohnheiten', 504–26, here 508.

20 Gissel, 'Payments in money and in kind in late medieval Scandinavia'; Skaare, 'Coinage and monetary circulation in Norway'.

21 Kosminsky, 'Voprosy agrarnoj istorii', 59–76; 'The evolution of the feudal rent', 12–36, here 22, 31–5.

22 Graus, 'Die Krise des Feudalismus', 65–121, here 115–21; 'Die erste Krise des Feudalismus', 582–9; Małowist, 'Zagadnienie kryzysu feudalizmu', 86–106.

23 Małowist, 'L'inégalité du développement économique', 39–62; *Wschód a Zachód Europy w XIII–XVI wieku.*

24 Boutruche, *La crise d'une société.*
25 Bois, *Crise du féodalisme*, and *The crisis of feudalism.*
26 Bois, *Crise du féodalisme*, 189–92, 246–360. For a thorough analysis of Bois's theses, see Kriedte, 'Spätmittelalterliche Agrarkrise', 42–68.
27 Ulbrich, *Leibherrschaft am Oberrhein*, 59–80, 109–13; Blickle, 'Agrarkrise und Leibeigenschaft', 39–55.
28 Epstein, 'Cities, regions', 3–50.
29 Kriedte, *Peasants, landlords and merchant capitalists.*
30 North, *Die Amtswirtschaften*; 'Die Entstehung der Gutswirtschaft', 43–59.
31 Brenner, 'Agrarian class structure', 30.
32 The institutional changes in English agriculture after the plague are interpreted in Campbell, *English seigniorial agriculture*, 24.
33 Cerman, 'Social structure and land markets'.
34 Epstein, *Freedom and growth*, 47; Van Bavel and van Zanden, 'The jump-start of the Holland economy'.
35 Epstein, *An island for itself*; 'Cities, regions and the late medieval crisis'.
36 Goldthwaite, *The building of Renaissance Florence*, 29–66, 397–425; Molho, 'Fisco ed economia', 807–44. With time, Herlihy reversed his initially positive assessment of the consequences of the plague for the individual peasant. Herlihy, 'Santa Maria Impruneta', 242–76. Cf. Mueller, 'Epidemie, crisi, rivolte', 564–5, 580. For an overview of the earlier debates, see also J. Brown, 'Prosperity or hard times in Renaissance Italy?'
37 Epstein, *Freedom und growth*, 71; Van Bavel and van Zanden, 'The jump-start of the Holland economy', 528.
38 Van der Wee and Peeters, 'Un modèle dynamique'; Van der Wee, 'Structural changes'.
39 Čechura, 'Die Bauernschaft'; Hoffmann, *Land, liberties, and lordship.*
40 Dygo, 'West-Ost-Gefälle?'; see also Wyrozumski, 'Was Poland affected by the late-medieval crisis of feudalism?'
41 Graus, *Pest-Geißler-Judenmorde*, 537.
42 Graus, *Pest-Geißler-Judenmorde*, 545.
43 Burckhardt, *Force and freedom, reflections on history.*
44 Graus, *Pest-Geißler-Judenmorde*, 550.
45 Meiss, *Painting in Florence and Siena.*
46 Baschet, 'Image et événement'.
47 Jenks, 'Von den archaischen Grundlagen', 111.

15

Political integration

The scholarship on integration forms a counterpoint to that on the notion of crisis. As with the theme of crisis, here, too, Ferdinand Seibt essentially laid out the direction of future research. His concern was to examine, from a comparative European perspective, which paths led out of the crisis. According to his hypothesis, the crisis necessarily produced new integration, and we need to differentiate between multiple – at times overlapping – processes of integration. Alongside the integration of states, in the face of the Turkish threat there were also attempts at integration within Christendom. Regional integration processes and associations of persons formed on the basis of shared consciousness also occurred. Among them Seibt includes aristocratic confederations as well as urban alliances and the religious and military orders endowed by European rulers. The latter possessed a clearly dynastic connection and are evidence of the integrative power of dynasties in the fifteenth century. This integrative power was increasingly communicated outwardly through numerous media such as festivities, processions, architecture and chronicles, and represented inwardly by individual princes' 'persistent sense of predestination'.[1] These frequently successful dynastic attempts at integration coexisted with those on a regional level, such as can be found in the Swiss Confederacy, the Flemish towns or the German territories. The disadvantage of Seibt's approach is that while he describes the various integration processes, he and his collaborators never actually define the term 'integration' itself.

We might draw here upon a model proposed by Hartmut Kaelble, whose usefulness for other epochs the present author has already demonstrated. According to this model, integration requires, first of all, centralised decision-making. In the historical context, this would mean shifting decision-making from the territorial to the general State level.

An accompanying shift of competences can occur in consensus with the participants, and need not necessarily be the result of military conquest. A second form of integration consists in the increase of political, economic and social interdependences. A third form comprises the emergence of common structures, institutions and values, which must be studied in terms both of their efficacy and of how they were perceived. Such perceptions and the published discussion on integration themselves constitute a further form of integration.[2]

Taking this definition as a basis, the authors of Seibt's essay collection offer only a few examples of forms of integration in fifteenth-century Europe. The most impressive among them are the case studies on the Burgundian Netherlands and the Flemish towns. Here, Jean-Marie Cauchies emphasises the integrative effects of the reign of Philip the Handsome (1494–1506), who – unlike his father and grandfather – drew upon the estates general to support his rule. In this way, a consciousness of shared interests evolved within the estates general.[3] Blockmans regards this as a consequence of the strong institutional tradition that had developed in the urbanised regions of Flanders. For that reason, they could be better integrated into the 'superstructure' of the Burgundian state than the rural and territorially fragmented regions of Luxembourg or Guelders, for example.[4]

In France in the second half of the fifteenth century the kings even used geographically decentralised institutions such as the regional estate assemblies and parliaments to further the integration of newly acquired territories such as Provence or the Dauphiné into the kingdom.[5] In this context, Guenée has specifically pointed to the interaction between processes of institutional centralisation and geographical decentralisation in France.[6]

In the Holy Roman Empire, historians have mainly studied aspects of territorial consolidation under the general heading of integration.[7] Otherwise, scholarly interest has focused on the electors' and princes' path to institutional participation in imperial government.[8] So-called German reunification in the period after 1989 in particular has inspired constitutional historians to search, under the overall theme of 'state unification', for the 'supporting and inhibiting elements in German history'.[9]

Peter Moraw has turned his attention to the political and organisational integration of the Holy Roman Empire in the late Middle Ages.[10] He locates a significant integrative advance in the imperial diet of Worms in 1495, at which 'a larger group of political experts' set the course for the institutional development of the empire. For Moraw, the most important element of integration was the 'undeniable advent of the imperial diet', which would henceforth distinguish itself from its predecessor, the royal

Hoftag, by its continuity, hard rules and stable circle of participants. The participation of the princes and free cities alongside the electors and imperial cities gave rise to a basic consensus that would not be questioned when the 'condensed' empire subsequently entered 'the phase of "institutionalised dualism"'.[11] The constitutional integration of the German territories varied in intensity. Thus, for example, the lands that resisted integration, like Switzerland, as well as Livonia, which appeared politically incapable of integration, were excluded from the 'Germany of the imperial diet'. The Habsburg emperors and territorial rulers also initially kept the 'Germany of the hereditary lands' away from the imperial diet, and in the later partition (1557) of the hereditary possessions dismantled it in favour of the Spanish Habsburgs.[12] As recent research has shown, the Hanseatic/Low German region, which had not participated in the empire's process of political-organisational condensation in the fifteenth century, and was thus frequently labelled as 'remote' from the king or the empire (*königsfern*, *reichsfern*), did, however, become integrated into the political system of the empire at the latest in the mid-sixteenth century. This occurred on the one hand because the peace and enforcement framework that emerged from the religious Peace of Augsburg rendered the empire attractive to the North, and on the other because defence against the Turks became an integrative factor.[13] 'Questions of Political Integration in Medieval Europe' have also been discussed by the Constance Association for Medieval History in one of its conferences held on the island of Reichenau, the papers from which were published in a volume edited by Werner Maleczek.[14] Although some historians still have problems with applying modern terminology to the Middle Ages and question the suitability of the term 'integration' for the medieval period, six criteria for integration emerge particularly in the summaries by Matthias Thumser and Heribert Müller: 1. Dynasty, 2. Noble elites, 3. Administration and jurisdiction, 4. Centre and periphery, 5. the Church, and 6. Communal consciousness.[15] Only the Swiss Confederacy resists categorisation in this catalogue of criteria. According to Müller, here, as for the empire, defence against external threats (Burgundian wars, Ottoman wars) should be cited as a further criterion of integration.[16]

Surprisingly, another project, the European Science Foundation's major research 'The Origins of the Modern State in Europe (Thirteenth to Eighteenth Centuries)', treats the topic of political integration only tangentially, with the period between the thirteenth and sixteenth centuries frequently being regarded as merely a predecessor to the development of the State. Only the volume *Resistance, representation and community* edited by Peter Blickle addresses the problem of the integration of the peasantry or peasant communities into the political system around 1500, for example in the Scandinavian kingdoms.[17] As a result, the differentiations undertaken by Hugues Neveux and Eva Österberg to distinguish among the various forms of integration such as functional integration, forced integration or integration through shared identity or consensus, refer mainly to Scandinavia beginning in the late sixteenth century.[18] Only in examinations of values as principles of social organisation do the authors refer to the self-identification of the south German peasantry as the 'common man' as early as the fifteenth century, and inquire into the realisation of this peasant ideal in Upper Germany, Switzerland and Sweden.[19]

The volume *Power elites and state building* edited by Wolfgang Reinhard also addresses various levels of integration, generally without explicitly mentioning them.[20] This volume is based on Reinhard's model of the growth of State power, which differentiates between and links developments on three levels. Although this linkage, which ultimately leads to the modern State, was accomplished only after the period that interests us here, the integration processes that occurred on the various levels began a good deal earlier. On the micro-level of social groups there arose dynasties on the one hand and power elites closely allied with them on the other, which were also informally connected with one another in social networks. Their ties to the dynasty allowed them to participate in the nascent power of states and thus contribute to their growth. On the meso-level of the political system, the growth of State authority was supported by certain groups, which facilitated wars both physically and materially, although the most important processes on this level occurred only in the sixteenth and seventeenth centuries. This also applies to the connection between the meso-level and the societal macro-level, as power elites created or manufactured consensus throughout society to strengthen their own power or State authority.[21] Into the late fifteenth century, such processes were generally limited to the Italian city-states, although similar approaches are also evident under Henry VII in England or the Catholic monarchs on the Iberian Peninsula.

Interestingly, some authors have studied integration processes in composite monarchies. Thus Anna Maria Rao and Steinar Supphellen have compared Aragón–Naples to Denmark–Norway. In these entities, specific mechanisms emerged with which the power elites in the centres (Aragón and Denmark) negotiated with the local elites in the dependent territories (Naples or Norway). Conditions differed fundamentally between Aragón–Naples and Denmark–Norway. In Naples, an international merchant elite composed mainly of Italian merchant-bankers, which integrated the markets of the region and supported the Aragonese conquest of Naples in 1442 with loans, attained office and influence and thus advanced to the position of a power elite. With time, however, the Catalan element asserted themselves in the Neapolitan economy and royal administration. In Denmark-Norway the legal equality of the two partners was initially stipulated in the Kalmar Union, but in reality Norway was far weaker than Denmark and in personnel terms, too, succeeded only in establishing a limited administration of its own. The king and the Danish power elite accordingly tried to capture the most important offices in Norway as well for Danish partisans of the Crown, which ultimately succeeded in 1536, when the Norwegian Council was abolished. Since the local Norwegian elite were no longer represented, 'integration into the overall state' went forward, although the Danish officeholders in Norway were obliged to obey Norwegian laws and rule and administer the country according to Norwegian custom.[22]

Notes

1 Seibt and Eberhard (eds), *Europa 1500*, 19.
2 North, 'Integration im Ostseeraum', 2; Kaelble, 'Die soziale Integration Europas', 304–5.
3 Cauchies, 'Die burgundischen Niederlande'.
4 Blockmans, 'Stadt, Region und Staat'.
5 Bulst, 'Die französischen General- und Provinzialstände'.
6 Guenée, 'Espace et état', 121–5.
7 Rösener, 'Landesherrliche Integration'; Störmer, 'Die innere Konsolidierung'; Tewes, 'Ständische Mitsprache und Modernisierung'.
8 Isenmann, 'Integrations- und Konsolidierungsprobleme'.
9 Brauneder, *Staatliche Vereinigung*.
10 Moraw, 'Zur staatlich-organisierten Integration'.
11 Ibid., 27.
12 Ibid., 24–7.
13 Schmidt, *Geschichte des Alten Reiches*, 348; 'Deutschland am Beginn der Neuzeit', 17; North, 'Integration im Ostseeraum', 3.
14 Maleczek (ed.), *Fragen der politischen Integration*.
15 Thumser, 'Zusammenfassung I', 544.
16 Müller, 'Zusammenfassung II', 569–70, 575–6.
17 Imsen and Vogler, 'Communal autonomy', 42.
18 Neveux and Österberg, 'Norms and values', 156.
19 Ibid., 174–7.
20 Reinhard (ed.), *Power elites*.
21 Reinhard, 'Das Wachstum der Staatsgewalt'; 'Introduction: Power elites'.
22 Rao and Supphellen, 'Power elites'.

16

The court

Unlike the State, which only began to form in the late Middle Ages, the court has been attracting a good deal of attention in Germany of late, which was not always the case. While English scholars have long been engaged in intensive research on the court, as reflected in the monographs of H. W. Ridgeway or Malcolm Vale, collections of essays on court culture, or the many editions of David Starkey's survey on the English court from the Wars of the Roses up to the Civil War, the German literature on the court is of comparatively recent vintage.[1] Fundamental works such as those that exist for Italy are absent in Germany. Gregory Lubkin's study of Milan under Galeazzo Maria Sforza, for example, unfolds a panorama of a court from the consolidation of rule, the formation of the princely presence through the creation of a princely style and the courtiers, servants and artists responsible for it.[2] Guido Guerzoni's studies of the personnel of the d'Este court at Ferrara supplement Lubkin's perspective.[3] The panorama of the Renaissance courts is sketched in particular detail in the essay collection by Sergio Bertelli and others as well as in their thorough overview of the historiography of the courts.[4] Françoise Piponnier's study of the court of King René in Provence adopts a similarly multi-perspective approach, since she not merely places the court in its contemporary context, but above all delves into material culture, especially court dress.[5]

Against the background of this scholarship, it is not surprising that Werner Paravicini, an expert on the Burgundian–French courtly tradition, has been trying successfully for some time now to stimulate research on the courts within the framework of the Göttinger Residenzen-Kommission, a programme of the Göttingen Academy of Sciences. Although Paravicini does not intend us to regard the influence of the Burgundian court on the development of other European courts as a model,[6] his research on and edition of the court ordinances of the dukes of Burgundy has nevertheless set standards in Europe.[7] In his programmatic volume in the series of the *Enzyklopädie der deutschen Geschichte* (Encyclopaedia of German history), he offers the following explanation for his scholarly interest in the subject: 'the court is no mere cultural phenomenon of concern solely to historians of literature, art and music, but rather *the* most important political, social and even economic (consumption) institution of the Middle Ages and the early modern period'.[8] According to Paravicini, the court was polyvalent, since it served to organise daily life, guarantee access and security, heighten princely prestige and integrate the power elite, and naturally also acted as a centre of government and administration. In order to do justice to all these tasks, the court required multiple mechanisms for social organisation and the distribution of means as well as a materially imposing framework. The latter aspect, in particular, is the focus of the international colloquia that Paravicini has been organising for some time now, which address topics such as 'Everyday life at court', 'Ceremonial and space', 'Courts and court ordinances' and 'The ladies' chamber'.[9] The European framework is especially evident in the volume on 'Courts and court ordinances'. Here we find not just a European cultural gradient in the communication of court ordinances from west to east or from south to north, but also relationship networks, which participated for instance in the exchange of court ordinances. For that reason, Paravicini believes that in future we should pay attention to 'dependencies, competing emulations, adaptations and rejections' if we are to write the history of the European courts one day.[10]

The third essay collection to appear in the series of the Göttinger Residenzen-Kommission on Courts was edited by Karl-Heinz Spieß and attempts to locate the theme of the court socio-historically from a dynastic perspective. In a contribution for a volume edited by Peter Moraw that came out of the 1992/93 colloquia on the German royal court in the late Middle Ages, Spieß already specifically queries the nobility's motives for being at court.[11] Although he concentrates on methodological issues of the high Middle Ages using the example of Frederick Barbarossa, his question is naturally also relevant to later centuries and has still not been exhaustively answered.

In Moraw's view, functions accrued to the court as the heart of the dynasty, as a distributor of rank and dignity, as the centre of government, administration, finances and military activity, as the centre of rule toward which elites and subjects alike were orientated, as well as the focus of dealings 'with all and sundry'.[12] In light of the widely varying and often vague descriptions of the court, Auge and Spieß have offered a more precise definition of the court 'as a spatially orientated action system based on integration, participation, delegation and obedience'.[13]

The multifunctional court drew its significance from the absence or only rudimentary existence of the State, whereby the court definitely reflected the importance of its 'supporting country'. The courts of southern and western Europe were accordingly more 'modern' than those of central and northern Europe. A court gained legitimation here primarily in confrontation with or in the comparative awareness of other courts.[14] Nevertheless, most of the works mentioned so far have focused on the inner structure (the narrower and broader court), the composition of personnel and the court's attractiveness.

Thomas Zotz and the participants in a Freiburg conference, in contrast, have undertaken to examine the princely courts from the perspective of their environment.[15] At the centre of interest is the 'court landscape' of the German south-west, which was characterised by a range of relationships of exchange. Apart from relations from court to court – women from outside (that is, from other courts) were integrated through marriage, along with their retinues[16] – the interaction between the court and its immediate environs is also a topic of research. Here, too, Karl-Heinz Spieß emphasises the role of counts and lords in their systems of relations with neighbouring princes.[17] Taking the example of episcopal courts (Strasbourg, Basle, Constance and Speyer), the authors also devote greater attention to relationships with towns and citizenry during the establishment of bishops' residences.[18] Paul-Joachim Heinig points to the problems of identity that could arise at court, especially the royal or imperial court, against the background of the regionalised empire. In his pivotal studies, he shows how the court of Emperor Frederick III had to bridge the various divides between the Austrian and the imperial court nobility.[19]

In this literature, the cultural importance of the courts frequently becomes apparent only on the margins. Thus Heinig concentrates mainly on court politics. Earlier historians, and more recently Werner Maleczek, however, have also studied material culture at the court of Archduke Sigismund of Tyrol.[20] The conferences on 'Ceremonial and space' and 'The ladies' chamber', too, address the spatial location of ceremonial forms and their changes dependent on space using examples from various European countries. At the same time, this literature also discusses the material trappings of ceremonial and space.[21] Compared to the scholarship on court collections, particularly sixteenth-century art collections and cabinets of curiosities, the role of the courts in cultural transfer remains largely unexplored (see below, Chapter 18). Recently, articles such as Helmut

Trnek's 'Schatzkunst und höfische Geschenke: Kontinuität im künstlerischen Austausch' (Decorative arts and courtly gifts: continuity in artistic exchange) and Karl-Heinz Spieß's 'Materielle Hofkultur und ihre Erinnerungsfunktion im Mittelalter' (Material court culture and its memorial function in the Middle Ages), 'Der Schatz Karls des Kühnen als Medium der Politik' (The treasure of Charles the Bold as a medium of politics) and 'Asian objects and western European court-culture in the later Middle Ages' point in a promising direction.[22]

Notes

1 Ridgeway, *The politics*; Vale, *The princely court*; Starkey, *The English court.*

2 Lubkin, *A Renaissance court.*

3 Guerzoni, *Le Corti estensi e la devoluzione*; 'The Italian Renaissance courts' demand for the arts'.

4 Bertelli, Cardini and Zorzi, *Italian Renaissance courts*; Mozzarelli and Olmi, *La corte nella cultura.*

5 Piponnier, *Costume et vie sociale.*

6 Paravicini, 'The court of the dukes of Burgundy'; Freigang and Schmitt (eds), *La culture de cour.*

7 See the literature in Asch and Birke, *Princes, patronage and the nobility*, 69.

8 Paravicini, *Ritterlich-höfische Kultur*, 66.

9 Paravicini, *Alltag bei Hofe*, *Zeremoniell und Raum*, *Höfe und Hofordnungen*, and *Das Frauenzimmer.*

10 Paravicini, 'Europäische Hofordnungen'. These issues have been partially taken up by Karl-Heinz Spieß (*Fürsten und Höfe im Mittelalter*, 17–24, 59–118) and Werner Rösener (*Leben am Hof*) in their new histories of the European princes.

11 Spieß, 'Der Hof Kaiser Barbarossas'.

12 Moraw, 'Über den Hof Kaiser Karls IV', 79.

13 Auge and Spieß, 'Hof und Herrscher'.

14 Moraw, 'Über den Hof Kaiser Karls IV', 80.

15 Zotz (ed.), *Fürstenhöfe und ihre Außenwelt.*

16 Spieß, 'Fremdheit und Integration'.

17 Spieß, 'Zwischen König und Fürsten'.

18 Weber, 'Eine Stadt und ihr Bischofshof'; Kälble, 'Bischöflicher Hof in Basel'; Bihrer, 'Ein Bürger als Bischof von Konstanz?'; Fouquet, 'Haushalt und Hof'. See also the monographs by Hirsch (*Der Hof des Basler Bischofs Johannes von Venningen*) and Bihrer (*Der Konstanzer Bischofshof).*

19 Heinig, *Kaiser Friedrich III*; 'Der regionalisierte Herrscherhof'.

20 Ortwein, *Der Innsbrucker Hof*; Maleczek, 'Die Sachkultur am Hofe Herzog Sigismunds von Tirol'.

21 As examples, see the following essays: Kress, 'Per honore della ciptà'; Kerscher, 'Die Perspektive des Potentaten'; Whiteley, 'Ceremony and space'; De Mérindol, 'Le Cérémonial et l'espace'; Boone and De Hemptinne, 'Espace urbain'. See also

Contamine, 'Espaces féminins'; Kress, 'Frauenzimmer der Florentiner Renaissance'; Franke, 'Bilder in Frauenräumen'; Weiss, 'Die Rolle der Damen'; and Märtl, 'Frauen im Umkreis der römischen Kurie'.

22 Trnek, 'Schatzkunst und höfische Geschenke'; Spieß, 'Materielle Hofkultur', 'Der Schatz Karls des Kühnen als Medium der Politik', and 'Asian objects and western European court-culture'.

17

The Renaissance and humanism

In older reviews of the literature on the Renaissance and humanism, terminology, and thus the debate over what the words 'Renaissance' and 'humanism' actually mean tend to be in the foreground. Many scholars who summarise the older literature, most recently Erich Meuthen,[1] for instance, have ventured answers. Our overview will thus concentrate on newer studies, or on research that has not yet received attention in this context. Of late, interest has centred on cultural transfer, that is, the diffusion and reception of the Renaissance and humanism in and even beyond Europe. A further emphasis in studies of the Renaissance is its social and economic location and thus the question of patrons, the art market and the demand for art. Although this field has established its own research tradition in the past fifteen to twenty years, the dominant scholarship, stressing intellectual history or aesthetic approaches, has not taken adequate account of the development.

Various sociological approaches have been tested for the reception of Italian Renaissance painting. We may distinguish here between macro-sociological, micro-sociological and (macro-) economic approaches. The macro-sociologists study the development of European society and associate particular artistic phenomena such as the Italian Renaissance with it. The micro-sociological approach, in contrast, places the 'changing material conditions under which art was commissioned and created in the past'[2] at centre stage. These include, among others, the study of painters' training, guild organisation and the relationship between painter and patron. Finally, the economic approach seeks the links between a period's artistic production and economic cycles.

The first instance of a macro-sociological approach to art history was Alfred von Martin's *Sociology of the Renaissance* (German original 1932,

English translation 1944).[3] Martin interprets the Renaissance as a 'bourgeois revolution' in which rational merchants displaced the nobles and clerics from their social positions, thereby promoting the breakthrough of a rational world-view. Frederick Antal's *Florentine painting and its social background*,[4] which appeared not long thereafter, in 1947, proved more influential. Studying the example of the Florentine painters Gentile da Fabriano and Masaccio, Antal distinguishes between two social groups of art buyers in the Florentine upper-middle class of the *quattrocento*. Dynamic, upwardly mobile elements commissioned works by the innovative Masaccio, while the overwhelmingly conservative majority of this social stratum preferred Fabriano with his traditional painting style. Thus according to Antal, there was 'no longer any artistic development in the strict sense of the word, but only the expectations and penchants of social classes, to which greater or lesser artists hastened to minister'.[5] In his *Social history of art*, Arnold Hauser expanded on Antal's approach,[6] asserting that the advent of bourgeois society explained the new developments in art. Thus the 'principles of unity, which now become authoritative in art, the unification of space and the unified standards of proportions … are creations of the same spirit which makes its way into the organization of labour, in trading methods, the credit system and double-entry book-keeping …'.[7]

Distancing himself from such models, which were difficult to test using documentary sources, Michael Baxandall set out to reconstruct, on the basis of workshop organisation and relations between artists and patrons, how Renaissance people might have looked at pictures and evaluated artistic work. He attributes a preference for the perspective and proportions of art to the Florentine merchants who did their daily accounts with the help of the Rule of Three. At the same time, he seeks to understand the visual culture of the Renaissance, what he calls the 'period eye', and tries to locate it in individual works of art.[8] Although this already contains elements of a micro-sociological point of view, he was more interested in what was specific to the era.

The purely micro-sociological approach, in contrast, tends to be more limited in space and less ambitious in its aims. Martin Wackernagel tested it for the first time in the 1930s in his studies of Florentine painters, with a focus on the workshop, patrons and the art market.[9] In his monograph *The Italian Renaissance*, Peter Burke demonstrates in a methodologically unique manner how rewarding a combination of macro-sociological reflection and micro-sociological analysis can be for the social history of art. Burke on the one hand studied artists from the perspective of their social origins, training, social status and relationships with buyers and patrons, and on the other analysed iconography, taste, the function of art works and the underlying world-view. On the question of the relationship between the bourgeoisie and realism in the Renaissance, Burke notes, 'If bourgeoisies are divided into merchants and craftsmen, their contributions to the arts may be distinguished as follows. The milieu from which most artists come is urban and dominated by craftsmen ... Merchants, on the other hand, are especially important as patrons, and often quick to take up new genres'.[10]

A further historical approach has sought to relate artistic developments to economic cycles, based on the unspoken assumption that cultural efflorescence coincided with economic upturns and general prosperity and pointing to the Italian merchant republics of the *quattrocento* and *cinquecento*. People were correspondingly surprised to discover that economic historians interpreted the late Middle Ages in Europe as a period of economic crisis or depression, thus pulling the ground from under the cultural heyday of the Renaissance. Robert Lopez, for example, asserted in a 1953 lecture at the Metropolitan Museum of Art that the best period for the Italian economy had been not the Renaissance but the thirteenth century – which, however, brought forth no notable artistic achievements.[11] This led him to postulate that 'hard times' or depressions were more likely than were periods of economic growth to stimulate cultural investments. While in times of general economic growth all available resources were invested to make profits from trade and industrial production, he suggested, it was only during depressions, when trade, industry and land yielded little profit, that sufficient funds were available for unproductive investments in art and architecture.

The so-called depression thesis not merely unleashed a controversy among Italian historians concerning economic development in late medieval Italy, but also helped focus attention on the various influences of economic cycles on art. On closer inspection, the crisis affected the individual sectors of the late medieval economy very differently. The overall economic development of Italy thus no longer appears to have been as negative as Lopez and his students assumed. Be that as it may, it is certainly 'worth noting that liquid assets are simply necessary in order to finance larger unproductive projects',[12] as Arnold Esch, who himself sees no direct influence of economic cycles on the development of the arts, writes. 'A high degree of economic development was certainly a prerequisite', but not sufficient in and of itself, otherwise Genoa, Milan or Venice, for example, would have developed in the arts in a manner comparable to that of Florence.[13]

The links between economic cycles and culture have not been studied for only the Italian Renaissance, however. With Lopez's depression thesis in mind, John Munro compared the economic development of Flanders and Brabant in the fifteenth century to the Netherlandish Renaissance.[14] The economy of the Low Countries in this period presents a similarly contradictory picture – the decline of the old traditional cloth-making trade, the rise of new industries and service sectors – to the one Johan Huizinga painted for Netherlandish art in this period, in which melancholy alternated with merriment, violence with tranquillity and pomp with simplicity. Other scholars, such as Wilfried Brulez in his overview *Cultuur en getal* (Culture in numbers) on the relationships between economics, society and culture, have noted that investments in art and culture were of only marginal importance within the economy as a whole. Cultural investments thus do not represent 'significant compensation during the economic depression, and investments in a burgeoning economy are no competition for investments in culture.[15] Brulez may well be correct as regards the volume of investment in the cultural sector, which was always minor in comparison to the investment needs of the economy.

The connections between economic cycles and culture appear in a different light, though, if viewed from the perspective of other sectors of the economy or the demand for works of art. Thus a market demand for art works that extended beyond the elites could only arise when a broad segment of the population already had access to the basic material necessities. This was more likely to be the case during upswings than during depressions. At the same time, in periods of hardship, patrons and collectors tried as long as possible not to reduce their investments in art.[16]

Overall, the work of Baxandall and Burke as well as the comparisons between artistic and economic development have powerfully stimulated the socio-economic study of art in recent decades. The perceived deficiencies of the macro-sociological and macro-economic viewpoints, in particular, have led scholars to shift their attention to new regions, new sources and other epochs. The art market on the one hand and relations between workshops/artists and patrons on the other have become special fields of interest. Thus Arnold Esch, for example, has not only summarised the perspectives for future research in reviews of the literature on Renaissance Italy and Europe,[17] but also tapped Roman customs records as sources for studying imports to Rome. He demonstrates that many merchants of Italian but also Flemish, Greek or German origin imported paintings, woodcuts and other decorative objects made of glass, crystal, enamel and majolica, alongside other goods.[18] Esch's analysis in other essays of the extensive source material yields ample evidence of the north–south cultural transfer we will treat in the next section.[19]

The Bruges art market, with its contacts in Italy, played an important role here, as Michael North and Wim Blockmans have shown.[20] The conferences on the European art markets organised by Michael North and David Ormrod, Marcello Fantoni, Louisa C. Matthew, Sara F. Mathews-Grieco and the Francesco Datini Institute in Prato have produced a wealth of new findings.[21] Although the focus was on the more readily reconstructed market for paintings, participants also paid attention to other objects, such as majolica, and above all sought to follow the different market segments.[22] Apart from the relatively accessible commissions for masterpieces, historians and art historians have also focused on the emerging mass markets, which produced objects and pictures as cheap imitations, as well as the second-hand markets for art.[23]

Patrons and relationships between workshops and patrons have also been studied systematically. While Bernd Roeck has analysed a variety of examples of patronage in Germany and Italy,[24] Peter Burke distinguishes systematically between several forms of patronage or relationships between patron and artist: alongside the household system, in which artists lived and worked in their patrons' homes, there was the made-to-measure system, in which the relationship to the art patron who commissioned the work ideally continued only until the commission had been completed. While the first two systems dominated in Renaissance Italy, at the same time a new form of the commercialisation of art began with the market system, through which art could be purchased ready-made. Other forms of support still in operation today, such as the academy system or the subvention system, had not yet been instituted.[25] Evelyn Welch, in contrast, who has systematically examined the conditions of artistic production and demand together with a team in the research project 'The Material Renaissance: Costs and Consumption in Italy, 1350–1650', defines the relationships between artists and patrons as either individual (for instance private endowments), institutional or court patronage.[26]

Studies by younger scholars paint a vivid picture of the diversity of artist–patron relationships. Thus by comparing measurements and material costs, Susanne Kubersky-Piredda has gained insight into the material and artistic value assigned to paintings. Her work shows that despite rising prices for pigments, such as the costly ultramarine and azurite, which were used in large quantities to paint landscape backgrounds, artists still had sufficient scope for negotiating prices with their patrons, since they adapted their products to patrons' wishes or the market situation. The artist's name and reputation also seem to have influenced the development of prices. Thus because of his rank and perhaps also that of his prestigious patron, in this case the Florentine municipal government, Filippino Lippi could command nearly three times as much for an altarpiece as his less prominent colleague Francesco Botticini could from a Florentine confraternity. Once an artist belonged to the small circle of elite painters he could solidify his artistic status by demanding increasingly high prices.[27] Michelle O'Malley's monograph offers fundamental new information on this subject. Based on a thorough analysis of surviving contracts between artists and patrons, she has reconstructed the wide diversity of the commissioning process and in some cases the protracted negotiations as well. Discussions among the patron's family and circle of friends of artists' drawings that were prepared as suggestions played an increasingly important role here in the late fifteenth century. O'Malley has taken this idea further in a recent essay in which she documents the existence of patronage networks, which often remain hidden to present-day observers.[28] Her remarks on pricing are interesting. Thus patrons paid less for art works in Florence and central Italy than elsewhere in Italy. This explains why, from the late fifteenth century, Florentine artists were so happy to accept the – especially lucrative – commissions of Roman customers and to work outside their home city.[29]

Guido Guerzoni's studies of artists at the d'Este court from the late fifteenth century offer examples. The court was constantly hiring new craftsmen, painters and musicians recruited from abroad. Regular purveyors and artisans from the surrounding region ensured deliveries of raw materials for artistic production. In addition, agents regularly purchased art objects and manuscripts for the *studiolo* and library on commission from the court.[30] Isabella d'Este (1474–1539), wife of Margrave Gian Francesco Gonzaga of Mantua (1466–1519), was also a major customer for art and luxury goods and thus, as Evelyn Welch shows in her recent monograph, participated actively in the phenomenon of 'Renaissance shopping', a phenomenon that crossed social strata. Princely buyers not merely competed with the urban elites and ecclesiastical dignitaries for valuable works of art, but also drove the price of second-rate antiquities to dizzying heights in the late fifteenth century.[31]

Maximiliaan P. J. Martens supplements the mainly Italian picture, which he contrasts with the case of the Bruges art workshops, with an emphasis on the patronage of religious confraternities there. Members of the confraternities like the guild *van den Droghen Boome* (of the dry tree) also included the painters Petrus Christus, Arnoud de Mol and later Gerard David as well as musicians and craftsmen, alongside the dukes of Burgundy, families of the Bruges upper classes and leading Italian merchants. This 'institutional' demand was probably the most important motor of artistic production in Bruges, along with the demand from foreign merchants through these confraternities.[32] When the foreign merchants began to buy less in the late fifteenth century in the wake of economic decline in the city, the Bruges masters were obliged to create more 'finished products' for the emerging anonymous market. For this purpose they used the so-called *panden* in Bruges and Antwerp, stalls set up to sell art works in cloister courtyards during the annual trade fairs.[33] No other European centre of production north of the Alps developed an art market that could compare to that of Bruges. As Jan von Bonsdorff has shown, only Lübeck and to a lesser extent Danzig played a particular role in supplying carved altarpieces for the Baltic region. Many monasteries and cathedral chapters in Scandinavia, for example, had regular agents who organised commissions and deliveries of altarpieces from Lübeck wood carvers.[34]

Another aspect of recent research is the problem of the demand for art, which also takes us to the early history of collecting. Here authors like Luke Syson and Dora Thornton as well as Richard Goldthwaite and Lisa Jardine seek to locate art and the objects of material culture in the new Renaissance world of goods. Thus Syson and Thornton devote attention to the variety of new objects such as paintings, statues, crystal vases, majolica, tapestries, and inlaid and painted furniture that came to dominate home furnishings and increase the prestige of their owners.[35] According to Goldthwaite, in this initial phase of cultural consumption, pictures became increasingly important as objects of home decor. While in fifteenth-century houses paintings often decorated beds, chests or wainscoting, in the course of this and the following century they attained their own independent status as wall decoration. Frames became more sumptuous, the content and form of paintings more varied, and the number of pictures in households increased. Whereas medieval rulers had demonstrated their wealth and power with their treasure chambers, people were now eager to display their cultivation and taste first, and their material prosperity only second. A painting or a picture thus acquired multiple meanings, for it was at once religious object, home furnishing, artwork and cultural document. By collecting, as well as by commissioning or donating a picture, one acquired social credit in the present and a claim to posthumous fame.[36]

Lisa Jardine seeks to contribute to a reassessment of the Renaissance by drawing greater attention to the new world of goods in place of texts, as well as by looking beyond the borders of Italy. Her study of Byzantium and the Ottoman Empire offers insights into where the Europeans located themselves, which she also sees reflected in the circulation of objects within the network of European powers. Thus, for example, she reconstructs the presence of Turkish carpets in paintings as well as probate inventories, although the restriction to the highest dignitaries (princes and cardinals) makes it difficult to generalise her conclusions. Also interesting is her examination of the emerging market in books and manuscripts in the fifteenth century, which shows that, in addition to the contents analysed by scholars of humanism, we also should not underestimate the form of manuscripts and their role as collectors' items in and outside Italy. London in particular evolved into a market for Italian book production.[37]

Paula Findlen and Pamela Smith open up a more comprehensive and at the same time nuanced perspective. Findlen's *Possessing nature* and their co-edited volume *Merchants and marvels* treat the appropriation of material worlds in Europe in the late fifteenth and early sixteenth centuries.[38] Findlen places collecting and the emergence of collectors in the context of identity formation, self-knowledge, and the aestheticising of the self from the Renaissance on. Travel, discoveries and collecting all contributed to the search for one's place in the world. Only by going forth into the world and bringing it home in the form of objects did individuals acquire the knowledge that served to constitute identity. The spectrum of objects here ranged from the significantly mythical to the economically relevant: from Dutch burghers' accumulations of goods to aristocratic and princely collections that could be turned into capital when necessary. Both types of collection also functioned within systems of gift exchange or the gift economy, and always possessed a socially representative character. The religious, moral, scholarly and practical professional purposes of the collections mixed with economic ones, and only gradually did collections themselves become economic objects, that is, commodities.

Notes

1 Meuthen, *Das 15. Jahrhundert.*
2 Gombrich, 'The social history of art'.
3 Martin, *Sociology of the Renaissance.*
4 Antal, *Florentine painting.*
5 Esch, 'Über den Zusammenhang von Kunst und Wirtschaft', 187.
6 Hauser, *The social history of art*, II: *Renaissance, mannerism, baroque.*
7 Ibid., II, 4–5.
8 Baxandall, *Painting and experience.* On Baxandall, see Roeck, *Das historische Auge*; Langdale, 'Aspects of the critical reception'.

9 Wackernagel, *Der Lebensraum des Künstlers.*
10 Burke, *The Italian Renaissance*, 249.
11 Lopez, 'Hard times and investment in culture'.
12 Esch, 'Über den Zusammenhang von Kunst und Wirtschaft', 221.
13 Ibid., 219.
14 Munro, 'Economic depression and the arts'.
15 Brulez, *Cultuur en getal*, 83.
16 Blockmans, 'The creative environment'; North, 'Introduction', 6, and North, *Art and commerce in the Dutch golden age.*
17 Esch, 'Sul rapporto fra arte ed economia', 3–49; 'Prolusione. Economia ed arte', 21–49.
18 Esch, 'Roman customs registers', 72–87.
19 Esch, 'Kölnisches in Römisches Archivalien', 21–36; 'Importe in das Rom der Renaissance', 360–453; 'Die Grabplatte Martins V', pp. 209–17.
20 Blockmans, 'The Burgundian court'; North, 'Art markets', 52–64.
21 North and Ormrod (eds), *Markets for art*; Fantoni, Matthew and Matthews-Grieco (eds), *The art market in Italy*; Cavaciocchi, *Economia e arte.*
22 Spallanzani, 'Maioliche ispano-moresche', 367–77.
23 Comanducci, 'Produzione seriale e mercato dell' arte', 105–14; and Welch, 'From retail to resale'.
24 Roeck, *Kunstpatronage in der frühen Neuzeit.*
25 Burke, *The Italian Renaissance*, 88.
26 Welch, *Art in Renaissance Italy*, 103–23; O'Malley and Welch (eds), *The material Renaissance*.
27 Kubersky-Piredda, 'Spesa della materia', and 'Immagini devozionali', 115–26.
28 O'Malley, *The business of art*, and 'Altarpieces and agency'.
29 O'Malley, *The business of art*, 254.
30 Guerzoni, 'The Italian Renaissance courts' demand for the arts'; 'Ricadute ocupazionali'.
31 Welch, *Shopping in the Renaissance*, 245–73, 277–303.
32 Martens, 'Artistic patronage', and 'Petrus Christus', 16.
33 Martens, 'Some aspects of the origins'; Vermeylen, *Paintings for the market.*
34 Bonsdorff, *Kunstproduktion und Kunstverbreitung.*
35 Syson and Thornton, *Objects of virtue*, 12–36, 229–61.
36 Goldthwaite, *Wealth and demand for art*, 244–5.
37 Jardine, *Worldly goods.*
38 Findlen, *Possessing nature*; Smith and Findlen (eds), *Merchants & marvels.*

18

Cultural transfer studies

Another shift of perspective is the fresh look at the Renaissance that Claire Farago undertakes in the essay collection *Reframing the Renaissance*. Farago and the authors of her volume challenge not just the Italocentric but also the Eurocentric concept of humanism and the Renaissance and draw attention to works of art and craftsmanship from outside Europe. These include the products of the Ottoman Empire already mentioned by Lisa Jardine (see Chapter 17), as well as objects from Africa, India and later the Americas. That they were already appreciated at fifteenth-century European courts before finding a place as exotica in European chambers of curiosities is evident from a survey of court inventories. At the same time, these objects themselves provided the material for artistic objects, such as goblets fashioned from coconut or nautilus shells or rhinoceros horns.[1] Part of Farago's volume is also devoted to the reception of the European Renaissance in Latin America, particularly the processes of communication underpinning this transfer.[2] In the process, the authors treat numerous questions of cultural transfer or exchange such as the circulation of an object in various value regimes.

The field of cultural transfer studies is currently experiencing a boom. Not only has the European Science Foundation established a project on 'Cultural exchange in Europe, 1400–1700';[3] the terms 'cultural transfer' and 'cultural exchange' are also omnipresent in discussions, seminars, conferences and countless publications.[4] The lively debate began in the 1980s, when Michel Espagne and Michael Werner coined the term *transfers culturels* to refer to the transfer of elements of a 'French national culture' to Germany and its reception there during the eighteenth and nineteenth centuries. Espagne, Werner and their followers focused on national cultures in order to avoid some of the shortcomings of comparative history by contextualising questions of transfer, reception and acculturation.[5] Michael Werner and Bénédicte Zimmermann, who developed the concept of *histoire croisée* for the analysis of historical processes that interact simultaneously on the global and local level, went a step further. Rather than discussing bilateral transfers, *histoire croisée* examines multilateral entanglements that occur in a temporal and spatial framework where many actors interact on different levels, moving in different directions. *Histoire croisée* illuminates the synchronic tangle of political, economic, intellectual, artistic and human dynamics involved in processes of cultural exchange.[6]

Several excellent studies that take a systematic approach to the problem of cultural transfer or exchange have been written on earlier periods as well, however.[7] Proceeding from a definition that divides cultural transfer into source culture, mediating institution and target culture, Wolfgang Schmale separates cultural commodities into 'structuremes' and 'culturemes'. Culturemes have personal and spatial connotations (identitary essences) – that is, identities that characterise them, for example, as 'English', 'Dutch' or 'aristocratic'. Schmale refers to cultural commodities of this type as 'cultural products'. Structuremes, in contrast, refer to non-material and material cultural commodities such as printing technology or an architectural style. As connotations regarding their origins were not, or were no longer, relevant or known, contemporary views of cultural commodities play a significant role here.[8] For the fifteenth-century context and cultural exchange, however, it is above all cultural commodities with a specific national or regional identity that are of interest to the extent that it can be reconstructed in a given case.

Peter Burke has formulated and to some extent already realised a further approach in his *European Renaissance*, which represents a thematic expansion on his *Italian Renaissance*.[9] In his systematic observations on cultural exchange, Burke is concerned not just with simple transfer processes, but also with conscious or unconscious changes in the meanings of the transferred culture. The question arises here of whether the potential modification of values or symbolic content is carried out deliberately by the source culture, or whether the change takes place in the target culture instead. Recently, Peter Burke has argued that the term 'transfer' itself does not really adequately describe what can be called the 'encounter' of cultures, in which information and objects may flow in different directions, even if unequally. Hence Burke suggests the use of 'cultural exchange', or even better 'cultural exchanges', although 'cultural exchange' might still imply that a cultural good is simply handed over, and remains more or less unchanged. In fact, studies ranging from sociology to literature have pointed out that reception is not a passive but an active process. Burke himself has noted that 'Ideas, information, artefacts and practices are not simply adopted but on the contrary, they are adapted to their new cultural environment. They are first decontextualized and then recontextualized, domesticated or "localized". In a word they are translated.'[10]

Furthermore, cultural exchange leads to cultural mixtures, which Burke refers to as *bricolage*. This is evident in frontier cultures, e.g., the Christian-, Jewish- and Muslim-influenced material and everyday culture of Spain in the fourteenth and fifteenth centuries as well as in the major cities of east-central Europe. But stylistic mixtures or 'contaminations' are also characteristic of the reception of Renaissance architecture in a Gothic setting.[11]

Numerous studies of artistic exchange have addressed cultural exchange. One occasion was the major exhibition project 'The age of Van Eyck: the Mediterranean world and early Netherlandish painting'. Conceptualised by Till-Holger Borchert, the exhibition and catalogue explored workshop practices, the mobility of painters and art markets more generally. A number of European art historians also systematically examined the migration of painters, the transfer of objects and the reception of the Flemish style in France, Florence, Genoa, the northern Italian courts, Naples and the kingdoms of Castile, Aragón and Portugal.[12] Paula Nuttall offers the most recent overview of art transfer in the Low Countries in her study of the art trade, the commissioning practices of Italian merchants in the Netherlands and the written reception of Flemish artists in Italy.[13] Individual case studies also document concrete transfers. An example is Michael Rohlmann's essay on citations of Flemish landscape motifs in Florentine *quattrocento* painting. He documents thirty-two paintings with landscape backgrounds in which Florentine painters such as Sandro Botticelli, Domenico Ghirlandaio, Filippino Lippi and Biagio d'Antonio borrowed motifs, whether background or individual details, from Flemish works extant in Florence.[14] At the same time, Netherlandish painters like Dirk Bouts and Petrus Christus became acquainted through travel or other modes of communication with the geometrically constructed perspective common in Italy, to learn which was also said to be the objective of Dürer's journey to Venice in 1506.[15] In particular, the cultural and mutually influential artistic relations between Venice and the North were studied systematically for the first time in the major exhibition project of 1999.[16]

The oeuvre of the French court painter Jean Fouquet, who created his own synthesis of the artistic experience of his Italian journey and Netherlandish traditions, represents *bricolage* in the best sense of the word.[17]

Another desideratum cited repeatedly, for instance by Anthony Cutler,[18] is an exploration of the confrontation with the visual influences of Byzantine culture in the Italian Renaissance, but also in central Europe. Helen C. Evans's New York exhibition project 'Byzantium: faith and power (1261–1557)'[19] attempts to address this issue. Following Belting, Robert S. Nelson conceptualises a commonwealth in the Mediterranean region in which Byzantine art and artists were incorporated into the visual culture of the Italian commercial centres.[20]

Within the Holy Roman Empire, many cultural transfers occurred through the migration of artists, art commissions involving large geographical areas and communication between artistic centres.[21] Alongside these fields, east-central and eastern Europe (Russia) have proved especially worthwhile areas for research on cultural-transfer processes. Thomas DaCosta Kaufmann, in particular, has done groundbreaking work here. In his most recent book, *Toward a geography of art*, as well as in several essays, he succeeds in picking up where older research – discredited by nationalist developments in Germany and central Europe – left off and calling for the insertion of regional phenomena into broader lines of development.[22] Some of the questions he poses here are to what degree art relates to the place where it is made, and is defined or influenced by it, how art in turn influences the place, to what extent it is identified with the people, culture, region, nation or state, how far art in various places is interrelated through diffusion or contact, and how to delimit the areas of study.[23] Confronting Earl Rosenthal's concept of diffusion,[24] Kaufmann himself has investigated the role of Italian sculptors outside Italy, particularly in central Europe, and found the diffusion of an Italian repertoire of forms through communication, circulation, reception and rejection. At the same time, however, he calls into question the underlying assumption of diffusion from the centre to the periphery. Kaufmann's concept of diffusion proves productive, since it encompasses above all cultural selection, appropriation and translation on the part of interpreters and illuminates the various gradations. Kaufmann has already done pioneering work here with his fundamental studies of the east-central European countries and Russia in *Court, cloister and city*.[25] He is able to show that only in the Hungary of Matthias Corvinus and in Jagiełłonian Cracow did Italian architects and sculptors produce new, autonomous works of art based on stylistic innovations. In Bohemia and Russia, as in most regions of central Europe, architects went no further than *bricolage*, merely integrating Renaissance elements into traditional structures. The reception of the Italian Renaissance on a grander scale began here only in the sixteenth century, via artists from the Low

Countries. Of late, scholars have come to apply the concept of diffusion to the spread of humanism as well. Although Paul Oskar Kristeller's essay on 'The diffusion of Italian humanism' appeared as long ago as 1962, it is only recently that scholars have begun to address the topic of diffusion somewhat more systematically.[26]

Once again, authors tend to presuppose a spatial diffusion outward from Italy as the centre to the periphery, with pivotal overviews such as the three volumes on Renaissance humanism edited by Albert Rabil, Jr focusing attention on Italian humanism, humanism outside of Italy and a systematic approach to certain areas of humanist scholarship.[27] In addition, numerous essay collections have appeared on heretofore little studied regions.[28]

Among these local or regional studies, one recent project, which systematically examines the diffusion of humanism through the national historiographies of many European states, particularly stands out. The researchers involved conclude that diffusion occurred via individual and group-based transfer processes. After an instructive introduction by Johannes Helmrath, one project volume highlights northern Italy, but also treats the Holy Roman Empire, Switzerland, France, England, Poland and Hungary.[29] The findings are stimulating: according to Gerrit Walther, the diffusion of humanism spawned a competition among nations for cultural representation and thus for orientation toward the same models. 'The spread of humanism consequently led to the emergence of a system of coordinates within which the past became subject to comparisons. It helped people to place their own traditions in relation to others, and thus allowed them to become the object of international competition in the first place. Humanist national historiography therefore perfectly embodies the international character of humanism. A nation became a nation in order to present itself as such to other nations: to be successful in the contest that took place in the medium of the national or the humanist discourse on nationality'.[30] National (or regional) competition offered humanists apparently brilliant prospects, but this was by no means always the case, as recent research in social history underlines. As Anthony Grafton has shown, even the multi-talented artist, writer, and scholar Leon Battista Alberti had to adapt his various interests and projects to demand in the Florentine Republic, the curia or the courts of Urbino and Rimini. The humanist Lapo da Castiglionchio found searching for employment in the 1430s more difficult still, despite his well-aimed use of the new humanist medium of the letter collection as well as his own translation of Plutarch. He sent the latter, along with dedicatory epistles, to potential employers such as Humphrey, Duke of Gloucester, Pope Eugene IV, Alfonso of Aragón, Cosimo de Medici and Cardinals Cesarini, Orsini and Colonna, which casts a rather different light on the humanists' 'scholarly' preoccupation with specific themes and genres.[31]

Notes

1 Spieß, 'Asian objects and western European court-culture', 9–28.
2 Farago (ed.), *Reframing the Renaissance.*
3 Muchembled (ed.), *Cultural exchange in early modern Europe*, 4 vols.
4 For an overview, see Kaufmann and North, 'Introduction – artistic and cultural exchanges'; North (ed.), *Kultureller Austausch.*
5 Espagne and Werner, 'Deutsch-Französischer Kulturtransfer', and 'La Constitution d'une référence culturelle'; Espagne, *Les transferts culturels franco-allemands.* See also the overview in Schmale (ed.), *Kulturtransfer.*
6 Werner and Zimmermann, 'Beyond comparison'; Werner, 'Penser l'histoire croisée', and *De la comparaison.*
7 Schmale (ed.), *Kulturtransfer.*
8 Ibid., 46.
9 Burke, *The European Renaissance*, and *The Italian Renaissance.*
10 Burke, 'Translating knowledge, translating cultures', and *Kultureller Austausch.* See also Campbell and Milner (eds), *Artistic exchange and cultural translation.*
11 Burke, *Kultureller Austausch*, 35. This volume exists only in German.
12 Borchert (ed.), *The age of van Eyck.*
13 Nuttall, *From Flanders to Florence.*
14 Rohlmann, 'Zitate flämischer Landschaftsmotive'.
15 Borchert, 'The mobility of artists', 33; Pauwels and Pauwels, 'Dirk Bouts' Laatste Avondmaal'; Ainsworth, 'The art of Petrus Christus', 43–53.
16 Aikema and Brown (eds), *Renaissance Venice and the north.*
17 Avril (ed.), *Jean Fouquet.*
18 Cutler, 'The pathos of distance'.
19 Evans (ed.), *Byzantium: Faith and power.*
20 Nelson, 'Byzantium and the rebirth of art', 515–23.
21 Schmid, 'Kunst und Migration', 315–50; 'Kunstlandschaft – Absatzgebiet – Zentralraum', 21–34; North, 'Kommunikation und Raumbildung', 507–25.
22 Kaufmann, *Toward a geography of art*, 1–13, 68–104, and 'Der Ostseeraum als Kunstregion', 9.
23 Kaufmann, 'Italian sculptors', and *Toward a geography of art*, 187–216.
24 Rosenthal, 'The diffusion'.
25 Kaufmann, *Court, cloister and city.*
26 Kristeller, 'The diffusion of Italian humanism', 1–20.
27 Rabil (ed.), *Renaissance humanism.*
28 Eberhard and Strnad (eds), *Humanismus und Renaissance in Ostmitteleuropa*; Wörster, *Humanismus in Olmütz*; Füssel and Pirożyński (eds), *Der polnische Humanismus.*

29 Helmrath, Muhlack and Walther (eds), *Diffusion des Humanismus*; Maissen and Walther (eds), *Funktionen des Humanismus*.
30 Walter, 'Nationalgeschichte als Exportgut', 445.
31 Grafton, *Leon Battista Alberti*; McCahill, 'Finding a job as a humanist'; Saygin, *Humphrey, duke of Gloucester*.

TIMELINE OF POLITICAL, CHURCH, CULTURAL AND ECONOMIC HISTORY

Political history

1250–1254 Reign of the last Hohenstaufen King Conrad IV
1256–1273 Interregnum in the Holy Roman Empire
1254–1257 League of Rhenish cities
1258 Treaty of Corbeil, Aragón loses all possessions in southern France except Montpellier; France renounces overlordship in the Marca Hispanica (Catalonia, county of Barcelona).
1270–1275 Seventh Crusade
1270–1291 King Rudolf I of Habsburg tries to enforce the restitution ('revindication') of alienated crown lands in the empire.
1278 Rudolf I defeats King Ottokar II of Bohemia at the battle of the Marchfeld.
1282 'Sicilian Vespers': Peter III of Aragón becomes King of Sicily.
1291 'Perpetual alliance' between the three Waldstätte (forest cantons) of Uri, Schwyz and Nidwalden
1297 A treaty between Portugal and Castile permanently fixes the border between the two kingdoms.
1333–1370 Casimir III unifies the Polish duchies into a single kingdom and in 1366 completes the annexation of the economically important principality of Ruthenia.
1337/38 Beginning of the Hundred Years War between England and France. As the grandson of Philip IV, Edward III of England lays claim to the French throne after the extinction of the direct Capetian line.
1338 The electoral assembly of Rhense determines that the electors alone choose the emperor, thus rejecting the papal right of ratification, confirmed in the Golden Bull 1356.
1340 Iberian Crusade against the Moors
1340–1382 King Louis 'the Great' extends Hungarian territory in the Balkans. He becomes King of Poland in 1370.
1356 John II of France falls into the hands of the English victors at the battle of Maupertuis.
1367/68–1370 War between the Hanseatic League and King Valdemar IV Atterdag of Denmark
1381 Wat Tyler's Rebellion in the southeast and east of England
1385 Act of Krewo, personal union between Poland and Lithuania
1386 The Swiss Confederates defeat the Habsburgs at Sempach.
1389 The Turks defeat the Serbs at the Battle of Kosovo.

1397	The Kalmar Union unites the three Nordic kingdoms.
1404	John the Fearless becomes Duke of Burgundy.
1410	The Teutonic Order is defeated by Poles at Tannenberg; in the 1411 First Peace of Thorn, the Order loses its claim to Samogitia.
1415	The Hundred Years War resumes. The English are victorious at Agincourt.
1418	Holland becomes a Burgundian possession, followed in 1428 by Zeeland and 1433 by Hainaut.
1426	The Taborite campaigns begin.
1433	Gil Eanes sails around Cape Bojador.
1453	Turkish conquest of Constantinople
1454–1466	Thirteen Years War between Poland and the Teutonic Order
1456	Defeat of the Turks at Belgrade
1466	Second Peace of Thorn. The Teutonic Order loses part of Prussia to Poland, known as Royal Prussia.
1467	Charles the Bold becomes Duke of Burgundy.
1476	The Swiss Confederates defeat Charles the Bold at Grandson and Murten.
1492	Spain occupies Granada and ends Muslim rule on the Iberian Peninsula.
1494	Treaty of Tordesillas settles conflicts between Spain and Portugal over their spheres of interests.
	Alexander, Grand Prince of Lithuania, recognises Ivan III as 'sovereign of all Rus'.
1495	The diet of Worms leads to the institutionalisation of the empire (imperial reform, perpetual peace, imperial chamber court).
1498	Vasco da Gama reaches India.
1498–1504	Columbus makes his third and fourth voyages to America.

Church history

1274	Second Council of Lyons
1296	Philip the Fair imposes a tax on the clergy.
1302	The bull 'Unam sanctam' postulates papal supremacy in both ecclesiastical and temporal matters.
1309	Pope Clement V takes up permanent residence in Avignon.
1311–1312	Council of Vienne. Suppression of the Order of Knights Templar
1356	The direct influence of the pope on the election of the kings of the Holy Roman Empire ends with the Golden Bull.
1378	Beginning of the Western Schism with the election of two popes: Urban VI (1378–1389) in Rome and Clement VII (1378–1394) in Avignon
1381	The English theologian and critic of the Church Wycliffe is forced to withdraw from public life.
1414–1418	Council of Constance
1415	Jan Hus is burnt at the stake in Constance.
1429	Appearance of the Maid of Orleans, who is executed in 1431
1431–1449	Council of Basle

1439	The Council of Ferrara issues a decree of union with the Eastern Church.
1449	Dissolution of the Basle rump council at Lausanne
1456	Pope Calixtus III obliges the Portuguese Order of Christ to undertake missionary activities in Africa and East Asia.
1471	A great Christian Congress is held to raise money for defence against the Turks.
1481	Beginning of religious persecutions in Spain, expansion of the Inquisition
1482	Spanish concordat (state influence on the Church)
1484	Pope Innocent VIII issues the 'Witch Bull'.
1487	The Dominican Heinrich Kramer (Institoris) publishes *Malleus Maleficarum*, triggering the persecution of witches.

Cultural history

1271	Marco Polo sets off for China.
1288	Founding of the University of Lisbon (moved to Coimbra 1308–1338, then returned to Lisbon)
1289	Founding of the University of Montpellier
1290/95	Giotto begins work on the frescoes in Assisi.
1311	Dante writes *De monarchia.*
***c.*1315**	Dante writes the *Divine comedy.*
1338	Francesco Balducci Pegolotti describes the Silk Road in his *Pratica della Mercatura.*
1338/39	Ambrogio Lorenzetti's frescoes in the Palazzo Pubblico in Siena
1347	The humanist and poet Petrarch is crowned poet laureate at Rome following the classical tradition.
1348	Founding of the University of Prague by Charles IV
1353	Boccaccio completes his *Decamerone.*
1388	Founding of the University of Cologne
1409	German professors leave Prague for Leipzig.
1424	Ghiberti finishes work on the baptistery door in Florence (begun 1402).
1430	Duke Philip the Good establishes the Order of the Golden Fleece.
1436	Completion of the dome of Florence Cathedral under Francesco Brunelleschi
1443	Rogier van der Weyden is commissioned by the Burgundian chancellor Rolin to paint the *Last Judgement* altarpiece.
1455/56	Gutenberg invents the printing press using movable type.
1459	Founding of the University of Basle
1470–1480	Botticelli paints pictures with mythological motifs, including the *Primavera.*
1475–1478	Hugo van der Goes paints the *Portinari altarpiece.*
1496/97	Leonardo's *Last Supper* at the church of Santa Maria delle Grazie in Milan ushers in the high Renaissance.
1498	Dürer's *Apocalypse* woodcuts and self-portrait
1501–1504	Michelangelo's *David*

Economic history

1252	Florence and Genoa begin minting gold coins.
1266	Louis IX decrees the introduction in France of the *gros tournois*, one of the first groat (thick silver) coins.
***c.*1270**	English woollen manufacturing for export begins. Bruges evolves into the most important commercial and financial centre.
1273	The *mestas* of León, Soria, Segovia and Cuenca combine into a royally sponsored sheep-breeding cooperative.
1284	Venice begins minting gold coins (ducats).
***c.*1300**	In Italy, some moneylenders start using double-entry bookkeeping.
***c.*1300**	Technological innovations in agriculture and the crafts (the reversible plough, spinning wheel, specialised cultivation)
1315–1317	Crop failures in the Low Countries, France and Germany; famine across Europe from 1316
1343	The minting of gold coins begins in England, Aragón and Hungary.
1343	Edward III's cancellation of debts leads to the ruin of the Florentine banking house of Peruzzi. The same fate befalls Florence's Bardi banking house in 1346.
1347	Alfonso XI of Aragón places sheep farming throughout his kingdom under royal oversight.
1347/48–1352	Plague ('the Black Death') returns to Europe. Anti-Jewish pogroms follow.
1356	Flanders begins to mint gold coins ('mouton d'or').
1357	First Hanseatic assembly (*Hansetag*); Scotland starts minting gold coins.
1386	The Rhenish prince-electors form a coinage union (introduction of the Rhenish florin or *gulden*).
1389	The first German paper mill is founded in Nuremberg.
1418	Portugal claims the Madeira archipelago.
1441	According to the Peace of Copenhagen, the Hanseatic League must open their ports to the Dutch.
From 1445	Portuguese settlement of the Azores
1459	The monk Fra Mauro prepares the first map of the world with a realistic depiction of Africa for the Portuguese King Afonso V.
1464/65	Edward IV devalues the currency, lowering the price of English woollen cloth on the Continent.
1482	São Jorge da Mina Castle (later Elmina) is erected on the Gold Coast.
1484	Sigismund of the Tyrol mints *pfundner*, *halb-guldiner* and *guldiner* coins.
1488	Bartolomeu Días sails around the Cape of Good Hope and discovers the sea route from Europe to Asia via Africa.
1490	The noble house of Taxis establishes the postal system of the Holy Roman Empire.
1492–1496	Columbus undertakes his first and second voyages in search of a western sea route to India. He discovers America in 1492.

BIBLIOGRAPHY

Introduction

Abulafia, D. (ed.), *The new Cambridge medieval history*, V, *c. 1198–c. 1300* (Cambridge, 1999)

Abulafia, D., 'Introduction: Seven types of ambiguity, *c.* 1100–*c.* 1500', in D. Abulafia and N. Berend (eds), *Medieval frontiers: Concepts and practices* (Aldershot, 2002)

Abulafia, D., *The discovery of mankind: Atlantic encounters in the age of Columbus* (New Haven and London, 2008)

Allmand, C. (ed.), *The new Cambridge medieval history*, VII, *c. 1415–c. 1500* (Cambridge, 1998)

Backman, C. R., *The worlds of medieval Europe* (New York, 2003)

Barraclough, G., *European unity in thought and action* (Oxford, 1963)

Behringer, W., *Im Zeichen des Merkur: Reichspost und Kommunikationsrevolution in der Frühen Neuzeit* (Göttingen, 2003)

Berg, D. and F. Autrand, *Auswärtige Politik und internationale Beziehungen im Mittelalter (13.–16. Jahrhundert)* (Bochum, 2002)

Black, A., *Political thought in Europe, 1250–1450* (2nd edn, Cambridge, 2000)

Blo, F. J. (ed.), *Trade, travel and exploration in the Middle Ages: An encyclopedia* (New York, 2000)

Blockmans, W. and P. Hoppenbrouwers, *Introduction to medieval Europe, 300–1550* (London, 2007)

Boia, L., 'Les frontières de l'Europe – réalités, imaginaire, idéologies', in S. Ghervas and F. Rosset (eds), *Lieux d'Europe: Mythes et limites* (Paris, 2008)

Boockmann, H., *Lebenslehren und Weltentwürfe im Übergang vom Mittelalter in die Neuzeit: Politik – Bildung – Theologie* (Göttingen, 1989)

Boockmann, H., *Mittelalter: Annäherung an eine fremde Zeit* (Regensburg, 1993)

Borgolte, M. (ed.), *Das europäische Mittelalter im Spannungsbogen des Vergleichs: Zwanzig internationale Beiträge zu Praxis, Problemen und Perspektiven der historischen Komparatistik* (Berlin, 2001)

Borgolte, M., *Europa entdeckt seine Vielfalt, 1050–1250* (Stuttgart, 2002)

Bosl, K., *Europa im Mittelalter* (Darmstadt, 2005)

Brady, T. A., H. A. Oberman and J. D. Tracy (eds), *Handbook of European history 1400–1600: Late Middle Ages, Renaissance and Reformation*, I: *Structures and assertions* (Leiden, 1994)

Brady, T. A., H. A. Oberman and J. D. Tracy (eds), *Handbook of European history 1400–1600: Late Middle Ages, Renaissance and Reformation*, II: *Visions, programs and outcomes* (Leiden, 1994)

Brunner, O., W. Conze and R. Koselleck (eds), *Geschichtliche Grundbegriffe: Historisches Lexikon zur politisch-sozialen Sprache in Deutschland* (8 vols, Stuttgart, 1974–1997)

Burke, P., 'Did Europe exist before 1700?', *History of European Ideas*, 1 (1981), 21–9

Burke, P., 'How to write a history of Europe: Europe, Europes, Eurasia', *European Review*, 14 (2006), 233–9

Commynes, P. De, *Memoiren: Europa in der Krise zwischen Mittelalter und Neuzeit* (Stuttgart, 1972)

Dictionary of the Middle Ages, ed. J. R. Strayer (13 vols, New York, 1982–89)

Dirlmeier, U., G. Fouquet and B. Fuhrmann, *Europa im Spätmittelalter 1215–1378* (Munich, 2003)

Dohrn-van Rossum, G., *Die Geschichte der Stunde* (Munich, 1992)

Dyer, C., *Making a living in the Middle Ages: The people of Britain 850–1520* (New Haven and London, 2002)

Eisenstein, E. L., *The printing press as an agent of change: Communications and cultural transformations in early modern Europe* (2 vols, Cambridge, 1997)

Erkens, F.-R. (ed.), *Europa und die osmanische Expansion im ausgehenden Mittelalter* (Berlin, 1997)

Erlen, P., *Europäischer Landesausbau und mittelalterliche deutsche Ostsiedlung: Ein struktureller Vergleich zwischen Südwestfrankreich, den Niederlanden und dem Ordensland Preußen* (Marburg, 1992)

Feldbauer, P. et al. (eds), *Vom Mittelalter zum Atlantik: Die mittelalterlichen Anfänge der europäischen Expansion* (Vienna, 2001)

Ferguson, W. K., *Europe in transition, 1300–1520* (Boston, 1962)

Fernández-Armesto, F., 'A European civilization: Is there any such thing?', *European Review*, 10 (2002), 3–14

Fischer, J., *Oriens-Occidens-Europa: Begriff und Gedanke 'Europa' in der späten Antike und im frühen Mittelalter* (Wiesbaden, 1957)

Fuhrmann, M., *Europa: Zur Geschichte einer kulturellen und politischen Idee* (Constance, 1981)

Gautier Dalche, P., *Carte marine et portulan au XIIe siècle: Le Liber de existencia riveriarum et forma maris nostri Mediterranei (Pise, circa 1200)* (Rome, 1995)

Haas, W., *Welt im Wandel: Das Hochmittelalter* (Stuttgart, 2002)

Hay, D., *Europe: The emergence of an idea* (2nd edn, Edinburgh, 1968)

Heimpel, H., 'Europa und seine mittelalterliche Grundlegung', *Die Sammlung*, 4 (1949), 13–26

Heinig, P.-J. (ed.), *Reich, Regionen und Europa in Mittelalter und Neuzeit: Festschrift für Peter Moraw* (Berlin, 2000)

Herzog, R. and R. Koselleck (eds), *Epochenschwelle und Epochenbewußtsein* (Munich, 1987)

Hiestand, R., '"Europa" im Mittelalter – vom geographischen Begriff zur politischen Idee', in H. Hecker (ed.), *Europa – Begriff und Idee: Historische Streiflichter* (Bonn, 1991)

Holmes, G. (ed.), *Europa im Mittelalter* (Stuttgart 1993)

Isidor of Seville, *Etymologiarum sive originum libri XX*, ed. W. M. Lindsay (2 vols, Oxford, 1911)

Jackson, P., 'William of Rubruck in the Mongol Empire: Perception and prejudices', in Z. van Martels (ed.), *Travel fact and travel fiction: Studies on fiction, literary tradition, scholarly discovery and observation in travel writing* (Leiden, 1993)

Jenks, S., 'Von den archaischen Grundlagen bis zur Schwelle der Moderne (ca. 1000–1450)', in M. North (ed.), *Deutsche Wirtschaftsgeschichte: Ein Jahrtausend im Überblick* (2nd edn, Munich, 2005)

Jones, M. (ed.), *The new Cambridge medieval history*, VI, *c. 1300–c. 1415* (Cambridge, 2000)

Karageorgos, B., 'Der Begriff Europa im Hoch- und Spätmittelalter', *Deutsches Archiv für Erforschung des Mittelalters*, 48 (1992), 137–64

Keller, H., K. Grubmüller and N. Staubach (eds), *Pragmatische Schriftlichkeit im Mittelalter: Erscheinungsformen und Entwicklungsstufen* (Munich, 1992)

Kersken, N., *Geschichtsschreibung im Europa der 'nationes': Nationalgeschichtliche Gesamtdarstellung im Mittelalter* (Cologne, 1995)

Kéry, L., 'Pierre Dubois und der Völkerbund. Ein "Weltfriedensplan" um 1300', *Historische Zeitschrift*, 283 (2006), 1–30

Laqueur, W. *The last days of Europe: Epitaph for an old continent* (New York, 2007)

Larner, J., *Marco Polo and the discovery of the world* (New Haven and London, 1999)

Latham, R. (ed.), *The travels of Marco Polo* (Harmondsworth, 1959)

Le Goff, J. *L'Europe est-elle née au Moyen Age?* (Paris, 2003)

Melis, F., 'Intensità e regolarità nella diffusione dell'informazione economica generale nel Mediterraneo e in Occidente alla fine del Medioevo', in F. Melis, *I trasporti e le comunicazioni nel Medioevo* (Prato, 1984)

Menut, A. D. (ed.), *Maistre Nicole Oresme: Le Livre de politique d'Aristote* (Philadelphia, 1970)

Mitterauer, M., *Warum Europa? Mittelalterliche Grundlagen eines Sonderweges* (Munich, 2003)

Monnet, P., 'Le projet de paix et d'union chrétiennes de Georges de Podiebrad en 1462–1464', in P. Boucheron, J. Loiseau, P. Monnet and Y. Potin (eds), *Histoire du monde au XVe siècle* (Paris, 2009)

Montanari, M., *Storia medievale* (Rome, 2002)

Motzo, R. B., *Il compasso da navigare: Opera italiana della metà del secolo XIII* (Cagliari, 1947)

Nicholas, D., *The evolution of the medieval world: Society, government and thought in Europe, 312–1500* (2nd edn, London, 1993)

Nicholas, D., *The transformation of Europe 1300–1600* (London, 1999)

Nicholas, D., *Urban Europe, 1100–1700* (Houndmills, 2003)

North, M., *Kommunikationsrevolutionen: Die neuen Medien des 16. und des 19. Jahrhunderts* (2nd edn, Cologne, 2001)

North, M., *Europa expandiert, 1250–1500* (Stuttgart, 2007)

Oberman, H. A., 'The long fifteenth century: In search of its profile', in T. A. Brady (ed.), *Die deutsche Reformation zwischen Spätmittelalter und Früher Neuzeit* (Munich, 2001)

Oberman, H. A. *The two Reformations: The journey from the last days to the New World* (New Haven, 2003)

Oberman, H. A., *Zwei Reformationen: Luther und Calvin – alte und neue Welt* (Berlin, 2003)

Oschema, K., 'Der Europa-Begriff im Hoch- und Spätmittelalter: Zwischen geographischem Weltbild und kultureller Konnotation', *Jahrbuch für Europäische*

Geschichte, 2 (2001), 191–235
Oschema, K., 'Europa in der mediävistischen Forschung': eine Skizze, in R. Schwinges, C. Hesse and P. Moraw (eds), *Europa im späten Mittelalter: Politik – Gesellschaft – Kultur* (Munich, 2006)
Oschema, K., 'Eine Identität in der Krise – Konstruktionen des mittelalterlichen Europa', in C. Dartmann and C. Meyer (eds), *Identität und Krise? Konzepte zur Deutung vormoderner Selbst-, Fremd- und Welterfahrungen* (Münster, 2007)
Oschema, K., 'L'idée d'Europe et les croisades (XI–XV siècles)', in B. Guenée and J.-M. Moeglin (eds), *Relations, échanges et transferts en Occident dans les derniers siècles du Moyen Age: Hommage à Werner Paravicini* (Paris, 2010)
Oschema, K., 'Medieval Europe: Object and ideology' (forthcoming)
Pegolotti, F. B., *La pratica della mercatura*, ed. A. Evans (Cambridge, MA, 1936)
Perroy, É., *Le Moyen Age: l'expansion de l'orient et la naissance de la civilisation occidentale* (Paris, 1993)
Piccolomini, E. S., 'Aufruf zum Kreuzzug (1454)', in R. H. Foerster (ed.), *Die Idee Europa 1300–1946* (Munich, 1963)
Polo, Marco, *The description of the world*, ed. A. C. Moule and P. Pelliot (2 vols, London, 1938)
Rachewiltz, I. de, 'Marco Polo went to China', *Zentralasiatische Studien*, 27 (1997), 34–92
Ramada Curto, D., A. Cattaneo, A. Ferrand Almeida (eds), *La cartografia europea tra primo Rinascimento e fine dell'illuminismo* (Florence, 2003)
Reichert, F., *Begegnung mit China: Die Entdeckung Ostasiens im Mittelalter* (Sigmaringen, 1992)
Reichert, F., *Fernreisen im Mittelalter* (Berlin, 1998)
Reichert, F., *Erfahrungen der Welt: Reisen und Kulturbegegnung im späten Mittelalter* (Stuttgart, 2001)
Reuter, T., 'Medieval ideas of Europe and their modern historians', *History Workshop*, 33 (1992), 176–80
Rubies, J.-P., *Travel and ethnology in the Renaissance: South India through European eyes, 1250–1625* (Cambridge, 2000)
Schmale, W., *Geschichte Europas* (Vienna, 2001)
Schneidmüller, B., 'Die mittelalterlichen Konstruktionen Europas: Konvergenz und Differenzierung', in H. Duchhardt and A. Kunz (eds), *'Europäische Geschichte' als historiographisches Problem* (Mainz, 1997)
Schwinges, R. C., C. Hesse and P. Moraw (eds), *Europa im späten Mittelalter: Politik – Gesellschaft – Kultur* (Munich, 2006)
Seibt, F. and W. Eberhard (eds), *Europa 1400: Die Krise des Spätmittelalters* (Stuttgart, 1984)
Seibt, F. (ed.), *Europa 1500: Integrationsprozesse im Widerstreit: Staaten, Regionen, Personenverbände, Christenheit* (Stuttgart, 1987)
Seibt, F. (ed.), *Handbuch der europäischen Geschichte*, part 2: *Europa im Hoch- und Spätmittelalter* (Stuttgart, 1987)
Skalweit, St., *Der Beginn der Neuzeit: Epochengrenze und Epochenbegriff* (Darmstadt, 1982)
Verdon, J., *Travel in the Middle Ages* (Notre Dame, IN, 2003)

Verlinden, C., 'Boudewijn van Hennegouwen, een onbekende reiziger door Azië uit de dertiende eeuw', *Tijdschrift voor geschiedenis*,65 (1952), 122–9

Verlinden, C. and E. Schmitt (eds), *Die mittelalterlichen Ursprünge der europäischen Expansion* (Munich, 1986)

Wieczorek, A. and H.-M. Hinz (eds), *Europe's centre around AD 1000* (2 vols; Stuttgart, 2000)

William of Malmesbury, *Gesta Regum Anglorum*, ed. and transl. A. B. Mynors, R. M. Thomsen and M. Winterbottom (2 vols, Oxford, 1998–1999)

Zeeden, E. W., *Europa vom ausgehenden Mittelalter bis zum Westfälischen Frieden 1648* (Stuttgart, 1981)

Chapter 1 The British Isles

Allmand, C., *The Hundred Years War: England and France at War c. 1300–c. 1450* (Cambridge, 1994)

Allmand, C., *Henry V* (2nd edn, New Haven and London, 1997)

Apfel, E., *Studien zur Satztechnik der mittelalterlichen englischen Musik* (2 vols, Heidelberg, 1959)

Bailey, M., 'Demographic decline in late medieval England: Some thoughts on recent research', *Economic History Review*, 49 (1996), 1–19

Baker, J. H., *The legal profession and the common law: Historical essays* (London, 1986)

Barron, C. and N. Saul, *England and the Low Countries in the late Middle Ages* (New York, 1995)

Barron, C. M., 'London 1300–1540', in D. M. Palliser (ed.), *The Cambridge urban history of Britain*, I: *600–1540* (Cambridge, 2000)

Barrow, G. W. S., *Robert Bruce and the community of the realm of Scotland* (3rd edn, Edinburgh, 1988)

Barry, T. B., R. Frame and K. Simms (eds), *Colony and frontier in medieval Ireland: Essays presented to J. F. Lydon* (London, 1995)

Bolton, W.F., *The Middle Ages* (London, 1993)

Britnell, R. H., *The commercialisation of English society, 1000–1500* (2nd edn, Manchester, 1996)

Britnell, R. H., *The closing of the Middle Ages? England: 1471–1529* (London, 1997)

Brown, A. L., 'Parliament, *c.* 1377–1422', in R. G. Davies and J. H. Denton (eds), *The English parliaments in the Middle Ages* (Manchester, 1981)

Brown, A. L., *The governance of late medieval England 1272–1461* (London, 1989)

Brown, J. M. (ed.), *Scottish society in the fifteenth century* (London, 1977)

Burns, J. H., 'Fortescue and the political theory of "dominium"', *Historical Journal*, 28 (1985), 777–97

Caenegem, R. C. van, *The birth of the English common law* (Cambridge, 1973)

Campbell, B. M. S., *English seigniorial agriculture, 1250–1450* (Cambridge, 2000)

Campbell, B. M. S., 'England: Land and people', in S. H. Rigby (ed.), *A companion to Britain in the later Middle Ages* (Oxford, 2003)

Campbell, B. M. S., 'The land', in M. Ormrod and R. Horrox (eds), *Social history of England, 1200–1500* (Cambridge, 2006)

Campbell, B. M. S. and M. Overton, 'A new perspective on medieval and early modern agriculture: Six centuries of Norfolk farming *c.* 1250–*c.* 1850', *Past & Present*, 141 (1993), 38–105

Campbell, J., 'England, Scotland and the Hundred Years War in the fourteenth century', in J. R. Hale, J.R.L. Highfield and B. Smalley (eds), *Europe in the late Middle Ages* (London, 1965)

Carpenter, C., *The Wars of the Roses: Politics and the constitution in England, c. 1437–1509* (Cambridge, 1997)

Carus-Wilson, E. M., *Medieval merchant venturers* (2nd edn, London, 1967)

Carus-Wilson, E. M. and O. Coleman, *England's export trade, 1275–1547* (Oxford, 1963)

Chrimes, S. B., C. Derek Ross and R. A. Griffiths (eds), *Fifteenth-century England 1399–1509: Studies in Politics and Society* (Manchester, 1972)

Chrimes, S. B., *Henry VII* (2nd edn, London 1987)

Coldstream, N., 'Architecture', in B. Ford (ed.), *The Cambridge guide to the arts in Britain*, II: *The Middle Ages* (Cambridge, 1988)

Contamine, P., C. Giry-Deloison and M. H. Keen (eds), *Guerre et société en France, en Angleterre et en Bourgogne, XIVe–XVe siècle* (Lille, 1991)

Coss, P. R., *Heraldry, pageantry and social display in medieval England* (Woodbridge, 2002)

Coss, P. R., 'An age of deference', in R. Horrox and W. M. Ormrod (eds), *A social history of England, 1200–1500* (Cambridge, 2006)

Crane, S., *The performance of self: Ritual, clothing, and identity during the Hundred Years War* (Philadelphia, 2002)

Davies, R. G. and J. H. Denton (eds), *The English parliament in the Middle Ages* (Manchester, 1981)

Davies, R. R., *The first English Empire: Power and identities in the British Isles, 1093–1343* (Oxford, 2000)

Duffy, P. J., D. Edwards and E. Fitzpatrick (eds), *Gaelic Ireland c. 1250–c. 1650: Land, lordship and settlement* (Dublin, 2001)

Duncan, A. A. M., 'The war of the Scots, 1306–1323', *Transactions of the Royal Historical Society* (6th Series), 2 (1992), 125–51

Dyer, A., *Decline and growth in English towns 1400–1640* (Cambridge, 1991)

Dyer, C., *Standards of living in the later Middle Ages: Social change in England c. 1200–1520* (Cambridge, 1993)

Dyer, C., *Everyday life in medieval England* (London, 1994)

Dyer, C. *Making a living in the Middle Ages: The people of Britain 850–1520* (New Haven and London, 2002)

Ellis, S. G., *Tudor Ireland: Crown, community and the conflict of cultures 1470–1603* (London, 1985)

Ellis, S. G., *Reform and revival: English government in Ireland 1470–1534* (Woodbridge, 1986)

Fleming, P., *Regionalism and revision: The Crown and its provinces in England, 1250–1650* (London, 1998)

Ford, B. (ed.), *Cambridge guide to the arts in Britain*, II: *The Middle Ages* (Cambridge, 1988)

Fortescue, J., *De laudibus legum Angliae*, ed. S. B. Chrimes (Cambridge, 1942)

Fortescue, J., *On the laws and governance of England*, ed. S. Lockwood (Cambridge, 1997)

Fryde, E. B. and N. Fryde, 'Peasant rebellion and peasant discontents', in *The agrarian history of England and Wales*, III: *1348–1500*, ed. E. Miller (Cambridge, 1991)

Given-Wilson, C., *The English nobility in the late Middle Ages: The fourteenth-century political community* (London, 1987)

Goldberg, P. J. P., *Women in England, c. 1275–1525: Documentary sources* (Manchester, 1995)

Griffiths, R. A., *The reign of King Henry VI* (2nd edn, Stroud, 1998)

Gross, A., 'Unending conflict: The political career of Sir John Fortescue', in A. Gross, *The dissolution of the Lancastrian kingship: Sir John Fortescue and the crisis of monarchy in fifteenth-century England* (Stamford, 1996)

Hallam, H. E., *The agrarian history of England and Wales*, II: 1042–1350 (Cambridge, 1988)

Harriss, G. L., *King, parliament and public finance in medieval England to 1369* (Oxford, 1975)

Hatcher, J., *Plague, population and the English economy 1348–1530* (Houndmills, 1977)

Hatcher, J., 'Mortality in the fifteenth century: Some new evidence', *Economic History Review* (2nd Series), 39 (1986), 19–38

Hatcher, J. and M. Bailey, *Modelling the Middle Ages: The history and theory of England's economic development* (Oxford, 2001)

Haverkamp, A. and H. Vollrath (eds), *England and Germany in the high Middle Ages: In honour of Karl J. Leyser* (Oxford, 1996)

Hibbert, C., *The English: A social history 1066–1945* (London, 1989)

Hicks, M., *Bastard feudalism* (London, 1995)

Hilton, R. H., *Class conflict and the crisis of feudalism: Essays in medieval social history* (London, 1985)

Hilton, R. H., *Bond men made free: Medieval peasant movements and the English rising of 1381* (1973; London, 2003)

Hughes, A., 'Fifteenth-century polyphony discovered in Norwich and Arundel', *Music and letters*, 59 (1978), 148–58

Jackson, W. T. H., *The literature of the Middle Ages* (New York, 1962)

Keen, M. H., *England in the later Middle Ages: A political history* (5th edn, London, 1995)

Keene, D., 'London from the post-Roman period to 1300', in D. M. Palliser (ed.), *The Cambridge urban history of Britain*, I: *600–1540* (Cambridge, 2000)

Kermode, J., 'The greater towns 1300–1540', in *The Cambridge urban history of Britain*, I

Krieger, K.-F., *Geschichte Englands in drei Bänden*, I: *Von den Anfängen bis zum 15. Jahrhundert* (2nd edn, Munich, 1990)

Lambdin, L. C. and R. T. Lambdin (eds), *A companion to Old and Middle English literature* (Westport, CT, 2002)

Macdougall, N., *James III: A political study* (Edinburgh, 1982)

Macdougall, N., *James IV* (Edinburgh, 1989)

MacIntosh, M. K., *Controlling misbehaviour in England, 1370–1600* (Cambridge, 1998)

McFarlane, K. B., *The nobility of later medieval England* (Oxford, 1973)

McFarlane, K. B., *The nobility of later medieval England: The Ford lectures for 1953 and related studies* (Oxford, 1997)

Macpherson, A. G., 'Pre-Columbian discoveries and exploration of North America', in J. L. Allen (ed.), *North American exploration, I: A new world disclosed* (Lincoln, 1997)

Maurer, M., *Geschichte Englands* (Stuttgart, 2000)

Miller, E., *The agrarian history of England and Wales*, III: *1348–1500* (Cambridge, 1991)

Miller, E., *Medieval England: Rural society and economic change 1086–1348* (5th edn, London, 1992)

Myers, A. R., *England in the late Middle Ages* (8th edn, Harmondsworth, 1991)

Nicholls, K. W., *Gaelic and Gaelicised Ireland in the Middle Ages* (Dublin, 1972)

Niedhart, G. and H. Haan, *Geschichte Englands in drei Bänden*, II: *Vom 16. bis zum 18. Jahrhundert* (Munich, 1993)

North, M., 'The role of Scottish immigrants in the economy and society of the Baltic region in the sixteenth and seventeenth centuries', in W. Minchinton (ed.), *Britain and the northern seas: Some essays* (Exeter, 1988)

O'Brien, A. F., 'Politics, economy and society: The development of Cork and the Irish south-coast region, *c.* 1170–*c.* 1583', in P. O'Flanagan and C. G. Buttimer (eds), *Cork history and society: Interdisciplinary essays on the history of an Irish county* (Dublin, 1993)

Orme, N, 'The early musicians of Exeter cathedral', *Music and Letters*, 59 (1978), 395–410

Ormrod, W. M., 'State building and state finance in the reign of Edward I', in W. M. Ormrod (ed.), *England in the thirteenth century: Proceedings of the 1989 Harlaxton Symposium* (Stamford, 1991)

Palliser, D. M. (ed.), *The Cambridge urban history of Britain*, I: *600–1540* (Cambridge, 2000)

Platt, C., *Medieval England: A social history and archaeology from the conquest to 1600 AD* (1978; London, 1994)

Pollard, A. J. (ed.), *The Wars of the Roses* (Houndmills, 1995)

Pollard, A. J. (ed.), *Late medieval England 1399–1509* (Harlow, 2000)

Prestwich, M., *War, politics and finance under Edward I* (London, 1972)

Raftis, J. A., *Peasant economic development within the English manorial system* (Montreal, 1996)

Rexroth, F., *Deviance and power in late medieval London*, trans. Pamela E. Selwyn (Cambridge, 2007)

Richmond, C., 'The visual culture of fifteenth-century England', in A. J. Pollard (ed.), *The Wars of the Roses* (London, 1995)

Rigby, S. H., *English society in the later Middle Ages: Class, status and gender* (London, 1995)

Rigby, S. H., *Chaucer in context: Society, allegory, and gender* (Manchester, 1996)

Rigby, S. H. (ed.), *A companion to Britain in the later Middle Ages* (Malden, MA, 2003)

Rogers, C. J. (ed.), *The wars of Edward III: Sources and interpretations* (Woodbridge, 1999)

Rorke, M., 'English and Scottish overseas trade, 1300–1600', *Economic history review*, 59:2 (2006), 265–88

Sandon, N. and C. Page, 'Music', in B. Ford (ed.), *The Cambridge guide to the arts in Britain*, II: *The Middle Ages* (Cambridge, 1988)
Sayles, G. O., *The kings' parliament of England* (London, 1975)
Schoeck, R. J., 'Humanism in England', in *Renaissance humanism*, II: *Humanism beyond Italy* (Philadelphia, 1988)
Seymour, M. J., *The transformation of the North Atlantic world, 1492–1763* (Westport, CT, 2004)
Sharp, J. J., *Discovery in the North Atlantic: From the sixth to the seventeenth century* (Halifax, 1991)
Sicca, C. M., 'Consumption and trade of art between Italy and England in the first half of the sixteenth century: The London house of the Bardi and Cavalcanti company', *Renaissance studies*, 16:2 (2002), 163–201
Simms, K., 'Bards and barons: The Anglo-Irish aristocracy and the native culture', in R. Bartlett and A. Mackay (eds), *Medieval frontier societies* (Oxford, 1989)
Spufford, P., *Origins of the English Parliament* (London, 1967)
Stacey, R. C., 'Parliamentary negotiation and the expulsion of the Jews from England', *Thirteenth-century England*, 6 (1997), 77–101
Taylor, J. and W. Childs (eds), *Politics and crisis in fourteenth-century England* (Gloucester, 1990)
Thomson, J. A. F., *The transformation of medieval England 1370–1529* (2nd edn, London, 1986)
Tscherpel, G., *The Importance of Being Noble: Genealogie im Alltag des englischen Hochadels in Spätmittelalter und Früher Neuzeit* (Husum, 2004)
Vale, M., *The Angevin legacy and the Hundred Years War, 1250–1340* (Oxford, 1990)
Whittle, J., *The development of agrarian capitalism: Land and labour in Norfolk, 1440–1580* (Oxford, 2000)
Wormald, J., *Court, kirk and community: Scotland, 1470–1625* (London, 1981)
Wormald, J., *Lords and men in Scotland: Bonds of manrent, 1442–1603* (Edinburgh, 1985)
Wormald, J., 'Scotland 1406–1513', in *The new Cambridge medieval history*, VII: *c. 1415–c. 1500* (Cambridge, 1998)

Chapter 2 France

Allmand, C., *The Hundred Years War: England and France at war c. 1300–c. 1450* (Cambridge, 1994)
Allmand, C. (ed.), *War, government and power in late medieval France* (Liverpool, 2000)
Arabeyre, P., 'La France et son gouvernement au milieu du XVe siècle d'après Bernard de Rosier', *Bibliothèque de l'Ecole des Chartes*, 150 (1992), 245–85
Aubert, M., *Cathédrales et trésors gothiques de France* (Paris, 1958)
Autrand, F., 'Noblesse ancienne et nouvelle noblesse dans le service de l'Etat en France: les tensions du debut du XVe siècle', in A. Guarducci (ed.), *Gerarchie economiche e gerarchie sociali sec. XII–XVIII* (Prato, 1990)
Autrand, F., *Christine de Pizan: une femme en politique* (Paris, 2009)
Avril, F. (ed.), *Jean Fouquet: Peintre et enlumineur du XVe siècle* (Paris, 2003)

Barber, M., *The trial of the Templars* (Cambridge, 1978)
Bautier, R.-H., 'Les Foires de Champagne', in *La Foire* (Brussels, 1953)
Beaune, C., *Naissance de la nation France* (Paris, 1985)
Beaune, C., *Jeanne d'Arc: Vérités et légendes* (Paris, 2008)
Bergier, J.-F., *Les Foires de Genève et l'économie internationale de la Renaissance* (Paris, 1963)
Bois, G., *Crise du féodalisme* (Paris, 1976)
Bouchard, C. B., *'Strong of body, brave and noble': Chivalry and society in medieval France* (Ithaca and London, 1998)
Boutruche, R., *La Crise d'une société: Seigneurs et paysans du Bordelais pendant la Guerre de Cent Ans* (1947; Strasbourg, 1963)
Bove, B., *Le temps de la guerre de Cent Ans 1328–1453* (Paris, 2009)
Boyer-Xambeu, M.-T., G. Deleplace and L. Gillard, *Monnaie privée et pouvoir des princes: L'économie des relations monétaires à la Renaissance* (Paris, 1986)
Bulst, Neithard, 'Die französischen General- und Provinzialstände im 15. Jahrhundert. Zum Problem nationaler Integration und Desintegration', in F. Seibt and W. Eberhard (eds), *Europa 1500: Integrationsprozesse im Widerstreit: Staaten, Regionen, Personenverbände, Christenheit* (Stuttgart, 1987)
Bulst, N., *Die französischen Generalstände von 1468 und 1484: Prosopographische Untersuchungen zu den Delegierten* (Sigmaringen, 1992)
Carpentier, E. and M. Le Mené, *La France du XIe au XVe siècle: Population, société, économie* (Paris, 1996)
Cassagnes-Brouquet, S., *La Passion du livre au Moyen Age* (Rennes, 2003)
Chenu, M.-D., 'Dogme et théologie dans la bulle "Unam sanctam"', *Recherches de science religieuse*, 40 (1952), 307–17
Christine de Pizan, *Le Livre des trois vertus*, ed. C. C. Willard and E. Hicks (Paris, 1989)
Collard, F., *Pouvoirs et culture politique dans la France médiévale Ve–XVe siècles* (Paris, 1999)
Contamine, P., *La Guerre de Cent Ans* (3rd edn, Paris, 1977)
Contamine, P., *De Jeanne d'Arc aux guerres d'Italie: Figures, images et problèmes du xv siècle* (Orléans-Caen, 1994)
Contamine, P., *La Noblesse au royaume de France de Philippe le Bel à Louis XII* (Paris, 1997)
Contamine, P., *Le Moyen Âge: Le roi, l'église, les grands, le peuple, 481–1514* (Paris, 2002)
Coste, J., 'Les Deux missions de Guillaume de Nogaret en 1303', *Mélange de l'Ecole Française de Rome/Moyen Age*, 105:1 (1993), 229–326
Demurger, A., *Temps de crises, temps d'espoirs XIVe–XVe siècle* (Paris, 1990)
Demurger, A., *Vie et mort de l'ordre du Temple* (Paris, 1998)
Denis, A., *Charles VIII et les Italiens: Histoire et mythe* (Geneva, 1979)
Derville, A., *La société française au Moyen Âge* (Villeneuve d'Ascq, 2000)
Duby, G. (ed.), *Histoire de la France rurale* (Paris, 1975)
Duby, G., *The age of the cathedrals: Art and society 980–1420*, trans. E. Levieux and B. Thompson (Chicago and London, 1981)
Duby, G., *Le Moyen Âge: De Hugues Capet à Jeanne d'Arc 987–1460* (Paris, 1987)
Ehlers, J., *Geschichte Frankreichs im Mittelalter* (Stuttgart, 1987)
Epstein, S. R., 'Regional fairs, institutional innovation, and economic growth in late

medieval Europe', *Economic History Review* (New Series) 47:3 (1994), 459–82
Evergates, T., *Aristocratic women in medieval France* (Philadelphia, 1999)
Favier, J., *Philippe le Bel* (Paris, 1978)
Favier, J., *La Guerre de Cent Ans* (Paris, 1980)
Favier, J., *Histoire de France*, II: *Le Temps des principautés 1000–1515* (Paris, 1992)
Favier, J., *La France féodale* (Paris, 1995)
Fraioli, D., 'The literary image of Joan of Arc: Prior influences', *Speculum*, 56:4 (1981), 811–30
Gascon, R., *Grand commerce et vie urbaine au XVIe siècle: Lyon et ses marchands* (2 vols; Paris, 1971)
Gaussin, P.-R., *Louis XI, un roi entre deux mondes* (Paris, 1976)
Gauvard, C., *La France au Moyen Age du Ve au XVe siècle* (Paris, 1996)
Gazzaniga, J.-L., *L'église de France à la fin du Moyen Age: Pouvoirs et institutions* (Boldbach, 1995)
Genet, J.-P. (ed.), *La Genèse de l'état moderne: Culture et société politique en Angleterre* (Paris, 2003)
Genet, J.-P., 'France, Angleterre, Pays Bas: L'état moderne', in P. Boucheron, J. Loiseau, P. Monnet and Y. Potin (eds), *Histoire du monde au XVe siècle* (Paris, 2010)
Goldsmith, J. L., *Lordship in France 500–1500* (New York, 2003)
Grafton, A., *Commerce with the classics: Ancient books and Renaissance readers* (Ann Arbor, 1977)
Guenée, B., 'Etat et nation en France au Moyen Âge', in B. Guenée, *Politique et histoire au Moyen Âge* (Paris, 1981)
Guenée, B., *Un Meurtre, une société: L'assassinat du duc d'Orléans 23 novembre 1407* (Paris, 1992)
Guenée, B., *L'opinion publique à la fin du Moyen Âge d'après la 'Chronique de Charles VI' du religieux de Saint-Denis* (Paris, 2002)
Guillot, O., A. Regaudière and Y. Sassier, *Pouvoirs et institutions dans la France médiévale*, 2 vols (Paris, 1994)
Huizinga, J., *The autumn of the Middle Ages*, trans. R. J. Payton and Ulrich Mammitzsch (Chicago, 1996)
Kerhervé, J., *Histoire de la France: La naissance de l'état moderne 1180–1492* (Paris, 1998)
Knecht, R. J., *The rise and fall of Renaissance France, 1483–1610* (London, 1996)
Krumeich, G., *Jeanne d'Arc in der Geschichte: Historiographie-Politik-Kultur* (Sigmaringen, 1989)
Le Goff, J., *Saint Louis*, trans. G. E. Gollrad (Notre Dame, IN, 2009)
Le Roy Ladurie, E., *Peasants of Languedoc*, trans. J. Day (Champaign, IL, 1977)
Le Roy Ladurie, E., *L'état royal de Louis XI à Henri IV: 1460–1610* (Paris, 1987)
Leguai, A., 'Emeutes et troubles d'origine fiscale pendant le règne de Louis XI', *Le Moyen Age*, 73 (1967), 447–87
Leguai, A., 'Les 'états princiers' en France à la fin du Moyen Âge', *Annali della fondazione italiana per la storia amministrativa*, 4 (1967), 133–67
MacFarlane, J., *Antoine Vérard* (1900; Geneva, 1971)
Macpherson, 'Pre-Columbian discoveries and exploration of North America', in J. L. Allen (ed.), *North American exploration*, I: *A new world disclosed* (Lincoln, 1997)

Mieck, I., *Die Entstehung des modernen Frankreichs 1450 bis 1610* (Stuttgart, 1982)
Mollat, G., *The popes at Avignon 1305–1378* (London, 1963)
Mollat, M., *Jacques Coeur ou l'esprit d'entreprise au XVe siècle* (Paris, 1988)
Müller, M., 'Die Tradition als subversive Kraft: Beobachtungen zur Rezeption italienischer Renaissanceelemente im französischen und deutschen Schloßbau', in N. Nußbaum, C. Euskirchen and St. Hoppe (eds), *Wege zur Renaissance: Beobachtungen zu den Anfängen neuzeitlicher Kunstauffassung im Rheinland und den Nachbargebieten um 1500* (Cologne 2003)
Neveux, H., J. Jacquart and E. Le Roy Ladurie, *Histoire de la France rurale*, II: *L'âge classique, 1340–1789* (Paris, 1975)
North, M., 'Von den Warenmessen zu den Wechselmessen: Grundlagen des europäischen Zahlungsverkehrs in Spätmittelalter und Früher Neuzeit', in P. Johanek and H. Stoob (eds), *Europäische Messen und Märktesysteme in Mittelalter und Neuzeit* (Cologne, 1996)
Paravicini, W. (ed.), *Savoir-vivre et savoir-faire: civilisation courtoise et civilisation technique dans les relations entre la France et l'Allemagne du Moyen Age aux temps modernes* (Sigmaringen, 1995)
Paviot, J. and J. Verger (eds), *Guerre, pouvoir et noblesse au Moyen Âge: Mélanges en l'honneur de Philippe Contamine* (Paris, 2000)
Pernoud, R., *La Spiritualité de Jeanne d'Arc* (Paris, 1990)
Pernoud, R. and M.-V. Clin, *Joan of Arc: Her story*, trans. J. D. Adams (New York, 1999)
Perroy, É., *La Guerre de Cent Ans* (Paris, 1945)
Perroy, É., 'Social mobility among the French noblesse in the later Middle Ages', *Past & Present*, 21 (1962), 25–38.
Potter, D., *A history of France, 1460–1560: The emergence of a nation state* (New York, 1995)
Reyerson, K. L., *Jacques Coeur: Entrepreneur and king's bursar* (New York, 2005)
Rice, Eugene F., Jr, 'Humanism in France', in A. Rabil, Jr (ed.), *Renaissance humanism: Foundations, forms and legacy*, II: *Humanism beyond Italy* (Philadelphia, 1988)
Rioux, J.-P. and J.-F. Sirinelli (eds), *Histoire culturelle de la France* (Paris, 1997)
Rorke, M., 'English and Scottish overseas trade 1300–1600', *The Economic History Review*, 59, 2 (2006), 265–88
Roset, J., *Josquin des Prez 1440–1521: Prince de la musique* (Saint-Quentin, 1996)
Roux, S., *Paris au Moyen Âge* (Paris, 2003)
Schmitt, J.-C. and G. O. Oexle, *Les tendances actuelles de l'histoire du Moyen Âge en France et en Allemagne* (2nd edn, Paris, 2003)
Schnerb, B., *Les Armagnacs et les Bourguignons: La sale guerre* (Paris, 1986)
Seymour, M. J., *The transformation of the North Atlantic world, 1492–1763* (Westport, CT, 2004)
Sharp, J. J., *Discovery in the North Atlantic: From the sixth to the seventeenth century* (Halifax, 1991)
Thomas, H., 'Beiträge zur Geschichte der Champagne-Messen im 14. Jahrhundert', *Vierteljahrschrift für Sozial- und Wirtschaftsgeschichte*, 64 (1977), 433–67
Thomas, H., 'Die Champagnemessen', in Hans Pohl (ed.), *Frankfurt im Messenetz Europas* (Frankfurt, 1991)
Vale, M. G. A., *The origins of the Hundred Years War: The Angevin legacy 1250–1340*

(2nd edn, Oxford, 1996)
Vaughan, R., *John the Fearless: The growth of Burgundian power* (Woodbridge, 2002)
Vaughan, R., *Philip the Bold: The formation of the Burgundian state* (Woodbridge, 2002)
Vaughan, R., *Philip the Good: The apogee of Burgundy* (Woodbridge, 2002)
Willard, C., *Christine de Pizan: Her life and works* (New York, 1984)
Wright, N., *Knights and peasants: The Hundred Years War in the French countryside* (Woodbridge, 1998)
Zink, M., *Littérature française du Moyen Age* (Paris, 2001)

Chapter 3 The Iberian Peninsula

Abulafia, D., *A Mediterranean emporium: The Catalan kingdom of Majorca* (Cambridge, 1994)
Abulafia, D., 'Neolithic meets medieval: First encounters in the Canary Islands', in D. Abulafia and N. Berend, *Medieval frontiers: Concepts and practices* (Aldershot, 2002)
Ackerlin, S. R., *King Dinis of Portugal and the Alfonsine heritage* (New York, 1990)
Alves Conde, M. S., *Tomar medieval: O espaço e os homens* (Cascais, 1996)
Alves Conde, M. S., *Horizontes do Portugal medieval: Estudos históricos* (Cascais, 1999)
Anderson, J. M., *The History of Portugal* (Westport, CT, 2000)
Auacleto, R., 'El arte en Portugal en la época de Isabel la Católica', in P. Navascués Palacio (ed.), *Isabel la Católica: Reina de Castilla* (Barcelona, 2002)
Bermejo, E., 'Pintura de la epoca de Isabel la Católica', in P. Navascués Palacio (ed.), *Isabel la Católica: Reina de Castilla* (Barcelona, 2002)
Bernecker, W. and H. Pietschmann, *Geschichte Portugals: Vom Spätmittelalter bis zur Gegenwart* (Munich, 2001)
Birmingham, D., *A concise history of Portugal* (Cambridge, 1993)
Boxer, Ch. R., *The Portuguese seaborne empire 1415–1825* (Lisbon, 1991)
Burkholder, M. A. and L. L. Johnson, *Colonial Latin America* (Oxford, 2001)
Cabrillana, N., 'La crisis del siglo XIV en Castilla: La peste negra en el obispado de Palencia', *Hispania*, 28 (1968), 246–58
Caetano, M., *A Crise nacional de 1383–1385* (Lisbon, 1984)
Camillo, O. di, 'Humanism in Spain', in A. Rabil, Jr (ed.), *Renaissance humanism: Foundations, forms and legacy*, II: *Humanism beyond Italy* (Philadelphia 1988), 55–108
Carrasco, J. (ed.), *Historia de las Españas medievales* (Barcelona, 2002)
Carrère, C., *Barcelone: Centre économique à l'époque des difficultés, 1380–1462* (2 vols, Paris, 1967)
Castro Brandão, F. de, *História da expansão portuguesa 1367–1580: Uma cronologia* (Odivelas, 1995)
Cawsey, S. F., *Kingship and propaganda: Royal eloquence and the Crown of Aragon, c. 1200–1450* (Oxford, 2002)
Chueca, F. and P. Navascués, 'Arquitectura isabellina', in P. Navascués Palacio (ed.), *Isabel la Católica: Reina de Castilla* (Barcelona, 2002)
Coelho, A. Borges, *A Revolução de 1383* (Lisbon, 1965)

Comin, F., M. Hernández and E. Llopis (eds), *Historia económica de España, siglos X–XX* (Barcelona, 2002)
Constable, O. Remie, *Trade and traders in Muslim Spain: The commercial realignment of the Iberian Peninsula, 900–1500* (Cambridge, 1996)
Constable, O. Remie (ed.), *Medieval Iberia: Readings from Christian, Muslim, and Jewish sources* (Philadelphia, 1997)
Costa Gomes, R., *The making of a court society: Kings and nobles in late medieval Portugal* (Cambridge, 2003)
Deyermond, A. (ed.), *Edad media* (Barcelona 1991)
Di Camillo, O., 'Humanism in Spain', in A. Rabil, Jr. (ed.), *Renaissance humanism: Foundations, forms and legacy* (3 vols, Philadelphia, 1988)
Diffie, B. W. and G. D. Winius, *Europe and the world of expansion*, I: *Foundations of the Portuguese Empire, 1415–1580* (Minneapolis, 1977)
Disney, A. R., *A History of Portugal and the Portuguese Empire*, 2 vols (Cambridge, 2009)
Echevaria, A., *The Fortress of faith: The attitude towards Muslims in fifteenth-century Spain* (Leiden, 1999)
Edwards, J., 'Expulsion or indoctrination? The fate of Portugal's Jews in and after 1497', in T. F. Earle and N. Griffin (eds), *Portuguese, Brazilian and African studies: Studies presented to Clive Willis on his retirement* (Warminster, 1995)
Edwards, J., *The Spain of the Catholic monarchs 1474–1520: A history of Spain* (Oxford, 2002)
Elliott, J. H., *The Old World and the New 1492–1650* (Cambridge, 1992)
Emmer, P. C. (ed.), *Wirtschaft und Handel der Kolonialreiche* (Munich, 1998)
Engels, O., *Reconquista und Landesherrschaft: Studien zur Rechts- und Verfassungsgeschichte Spaniens im Mittelalter* (Paderborn, 1989)
Fernández, J. J., *Los concilios medievales compostelanos, 1120–1563* (Salamanca, 2000)
Fernández-Armesto, F., *Before Columbus: Exploration and colonisation from the Mediterranean to the Atlantic, 1229–1492* (London, 1987)
Fisher, J. R., *The economic aspects of Spanish imperialism in America, 1492–1810* (Liverpool, 1997).
Fuson, R. H., 'The Columbian voyages', in J. L. Allen (ed.), *North American exploration*, I: *A new world disclosed* (Lincoln, 1997)
Gerbet, M.-C., *Les noblesses espagnoles au Moyen Âge, XIe–XVe siècle* (Paris, 1994)
Giertz, G., *Vasco da Gama: Die Entdeckung des Seewegs nach Indien: Ein Augenzeugenbericht 1497–1499* (Berlin, 1990)
Glick, T. F., *From Muslim fortress to Christian castle: Social and cultural change in medieval Spain* (Manchester, 1996)
González Jiménez, M., *Alfonso X el Sabio* (Barcelona, 2004)
Hart, J., *Comparing empires: European colonialism from Portuguese expansion to the Spanish-American War* (New York, 2003)
Heine, H., *Geschichte Spaniens, 1400–1800* (Munich, 1984)
Hook, D. and B. Taylor, *Cultures in contact in medieval Spain: Historical and literary essays presented to L. P. Harvey* (London, 1990)
Kagay, D. J. and J. T. Snow (eds), *Medieval Iberia: Essays on the history and literature of medieval Spain* (New York, 1997)

Kasper, M., *Baskische Geschichte* (Darmstadt, 1997)
Klein, J., *The mesta: A study in Spanish economic history, 1273–1836* (Port Washington, 1964)
Knighton, T., 'Ritual and regulations: The organization of the Castilian royal chapel during the reign of the Catholic monarchs', in E. Casares and C. Villanueva (eds), *De Musica Hispana et Aliis: Miscelánea en honor al Prof. Dr José López-Calo*, I (Santiago, 1990)
Krus, L., *Passad, memória e poder na sociedale medieval portuguesa: estudos* (Cascais, 1994)
Ladero Quesada, M. A., *Castilla y la conquista del reino de Granada* (Granada, 1987)
Ladero Quesada, M. A., *La España de los Reyes Católicos* (Madrid, 1999)
Ladero Quesada, M. A. and M. González, *Diezmo eclesiástico y producción de cereale en el reino de Sevilla (1408–1503)* (Seville, 1979)
Lalinde Abadía, J., 'El pactismo en los reinos de Aragón y de Valencia', *El pactismo en la historia de España* (Madrid, 1980)
Liedl, G., *Zur Geschichte der spanisch-arabischen Renaissance in Granada*, Part 2: *Dokumente der Araber in Spanien* (Vienna, 1993)
Lomax, D. W., *The Reconquest of Spain* (London, 1978)
Lunenfeld, M., *The Council of the hermandad: A study of the pacification forces of Ferdinand and Isabella* (Florida, 1970)
MacKay, A., *Spain in the Middle Ages: From frontier to empire 1000–1500* (London, 1977)
Macpherson, A. G., 'Pre-Columbian discoveries and exploration of North America', in J. L. Allen (ed.), *North American exploration*, I: *A new world disclosed* (Lincoln, 1997)
Maravall, J. A., *El concepto de España en la Edad Media* (4th edn, Madrid, 1997)
Maroto, P. S., 'Flanders and the kingdom of Castile', in T.-H. Borchert (ed.), *The age of van Eyck 1430–1530: The Mediterranean world and early Netherlandish painting* (Ghent, 2002)
Marques, A. H. R. de O., *History of Portugal* (2 vols, New York, 1972–73)
Martz, L., 'Relations between conversos and old Christians in early modern Toledo: Some different perspectives', in M. D. Meyerson and E. D. English (eds), *Christians, Muslims, and Jews in medieval and early modern Spain.*
Meyerson, M. D. and E. D. English (eds), *Christians, Muslims, and Jews in medieval and early modern Spain: Interaction and cultural change* (Notre Dame, IN, 2000)
Meyn, M. (ed.), *Der Aufbau der Kolonialreiche* (Munich, 1987)
Mitre Fernández, E., *La España medieval: Sociedades, estados, culturas* (Madrid, 1979)
Monsalvo Antón, J. M., *La baja Edad Media en los siglos XIII–XV* (Madrid, 2000)
Moxó, S. de, 'De la nobleza vieja a la nobleza nueva: La transformación nobiliaria castellana en la baja Edad Media', *Cuadernos de historia*, 3 (1969), 1–210
Moxó, S. de, *Repoblación y sociedad en la España cristiana medieval* (Madrid, 1979)
Muñoz Machado, S., *Los grandes procesos de la historia de España* (Barcelona, 2002)
Navascués Palacio, P. (ed.), *Isabel la Católica: Reina de Castilla* (Barcelona, 2002)
Neuman, H. F., *Introducción a la música española del Renacimiento* (Barranquilla, 1990)
Newitt, M., *A history of Portuguese overseas expansion, 1400–1668* (Abingdon, 2005)

O'Callaghan, J. F., *The learned king: The reign of Alfonso X of Castile* (Philadelphia, 1993)

Oliveira Martins, J. P., *Historia de la civilización ibérica* (2nd edn, Malaga, 1993)

Pearson, M. N., *The Portuguese in India* (Reprint, Cambridge, 2001)

Pollmann, L., *Spanische Literatur zwischen Orient und Okzident* (Tübingen, 1996)

Porfirio, J. L., 'Portugal and the north', in T.-H. Borchert (ed.), *The age of van Eyck 1430–1530: The Mediterranean world and early Netherlandish painting* (Ghent, 2002)

Portela Sandoval, F. J., 'La escultura española en el reinado de Isabel I', in P. Navascués Palacio (ed.), *Isabel la Católica: Reina de Castilla* (Barcelona, 2002)

Reilly, B. F., *The Medieval Spains* (Cambridge, 1993)

Reinhard, W., *Geschichte der europäischen Expansion*, I: *Die Alte Welt bis 1818* (Stuttgart, 1983)

Reinhartz, D. and O. L. Jones, 'Hacia el Norte! The Spanish Entrada into North America, 1513–1549', in J. L. Allen (ed.), *North American exploration, I: A new world disclosed* (Lincoln, 1997)

Rico, F. and A. Deyermond (eds), *Historia y critica de la literatura Espanola*, I: *Edad Media* (Barcelona, 1991)

Rodríguez, J. L. M., *Historia de Espana*, V: *Baja Edad Media* (Barcelona, 1994)

Ruiz, T. F., *Spain's centuries of crisis: 1300–1474* (Malden, MA, 2007)

Russell, P. E., *Portugal, Spain, and the African Atlantic, 1343–1490: Chivalry and crusade from John of Gaunt to Henry the Navigator* (Aldershot, 1995)

Russell, P. E., 'Prince Henry the Navigator', in *Portugal, Spain and the African Atlantic*

Russell-Wood, A. J. R., *The Portuguese Empire, 1415–1808: A world on the move* (Baltimore, 1998)

Saraiva, A. J. and Ó. Lopes, *Historia da literatura portuguesa* (Porto, 1995)

Saraiva, J. H., *História de Portugal* (5th edn, Lisbon, 1998)

Schmidt, P. and P. A. Barceló, *Kleine Geschichte Spaniens* (Stuttgart, 2002)

Seymour, M. J., *The transformation of the North Atlantic world, 1492–1763* (Westport, CT, 2004)

Sharp, J. J., *Discovery in the North Atlantic: From the sixth to the seventeenth century* (Halifax, 1991)

Smith, P. H. and P. Findlen, 'Commerce and the representation of nature in art and science', in P. H. Smith and P. Findlen (eds), *Merchants and marvels: Commerce, science, and art in early modern Europe* (New York, 2002)

Sturtz, R., *Writing women in late medieval and early modern Spain* (Philadelphia, 1995)

Suárez Fernández, L., *Judíos españoles en la Edad Media* (Madrid, 1980)

Subrahmanyam, S., *The Portuguese Empire in Asia, 1500–1700: A political and economic history* (London, 1993)

Treppo, M. de, *I Mercanti cataloni e l'espansione della corona d'Aragona nel secolo XV* (Naples, 1972)

Valdeón Baruque, J., *Enrique II de Castilla: La guerra civil y la consolidación del regimen (1366–1371)* (Valladolid, 1966)

Valdeón Baruque, J., *Pedro I, el Cruel, y Enrique de Trastámara: La primera guerra civil española* (Madrid, 2002)

Vicens Vives, J. and J. Nadal Oller, *An economic history of Spain*, trans. F. M. López-Morillas (Princeton, 1969)
Vilar, P., 'Le déclin catalan du bas Moyen Âge: Hypothèses sur sa chronologie', *Estudios de historia moderna*, 6 (1956–59), 1–68
Watt, W. M. and P. Cachia, *A history of Islamic Spain* (Edinburgh, 1996)
Weddle, R. S., 'Early Spanish exploration: the Caribbean, Central America, and the Gulf of Mexico', in J. L. Allen (ed.), *North American exploration* (Lincoln, 1997)
Winius, G. D., *Studies on Portuguese Asia, 1495–1689* (Aldershot, 2001)
Yarza Luaces, J. J., 'Flanders and the kingdom of Aragón', in T.-H. Borchert (ed.), *The age of van Eyck 1430–1530: The Mediterranean world and early Netherlandish painting* (Ghent, 2002)
Yarza Luaces, J. J., *La nobleza ante el rey: Los grandes linajes castellanos y el arte en el siglo XV* (Madrid, 2003)
Yun Casalilla, Bartolomé, *Marte contra Minerva: El precio del imperio español, c. 1450–1600* (Barcelona, 2004)

Chapter 4 Italy

Atlas, A. W., *Music at the Aragonese court of Naples* (Cambridge, 1985)
Bagnoli, A. (ed.), *Duccio: Alle origini della pittura senese* (Milan, 2003)
Barr, C. M., *The monophonic lauda and the lay religious confraternities of Tuscany and Umbria in the late Middle Ages* (Kalamazoo, MI, 1988)
Bellomo, S., 'Dante e l'Europa', in G. Belloni and R. Drusi (eds), *Il Rinascimento italiano e l'Europa*, II: *Umanesimo ed educazione* (Vicenza, 2007)
Bellosi, L., *Cimabue* (Milan, 1998)
Benvenuti, G., *Le repubbliche marinare: Amalfi, Pisa, Genova e Venezia* (Rome, 1989)
Braccesi, S. A. and M. Ascheri (eds), *Politica e cultura nelle repubbliche italiane dal medioevo all'età moderna: Firenze, Genova, Lucca, Siena, Venezia* (Rome, 2001)
Branca, V., 'Boccaccio e l'Europa', in Belloni and R. Drusi (eds), *Il Rinascimento italiano e l'europa*, II: *Umanesimo ed educazione* (Vicenza, 2007)
Bredekamp, H. *Bau und Abbau von Bramante bis Bernini* (Berlin, 2000)
Bredekamp, H., *La fabbrica di San Pietro: Il principio della distruzione produttiva* (Turin, 2005)
Brown, J. C. and R. C. Davis (eds), *Gender and society in Renaissance Italy* (London, 1998)
Brucker, G. A., 'The Ciompi Revolution', in N. Rubinstein (ed.), *Florentine studies: Politics and society in Renaissance Florence* (London, 1968)
Brucker, G. A., *Renaissance Florence: Society, culture, and religion* (Goldbach, 1994)
Burckhardt, J., *The civilization of the Renaissance in Italy* (London, 1990)
Burke, P., *The Italian Renaissance: Culture and society in Italy* (Princeton, 1999)
Castelfranchi Vegas, L., 'Der künstlerische Austausch im Mittelmeerraum', in E. Carbonell et al. (eds), *Das Zeitalter der Renaissance: Kunst und Kultur und Geschichte im Mittelmeerraum* (Darmstadt, 2003)
Cherubini, G., *L'Italia rurale del basso Medioevo* (Rome, 1996)
Chiappa Mauri, L. (ed.), *L'età dei Visconti: il dominio di Milano fra 13. e 15. secolo* (Milan, 1993)

Chittolini, G., *La formazione dello stato regionale e le istituzioni del contado: Secoli XIV e XV* (Turin, 1979)
Chittolini, G., A. Molho and P. Schiera (eds), *Origini dello stato: Processi di formazione statale in Italia fra medioevo ed età moderna* (Bologna, 1994)
Cohen, E. S. and T. V. Cohen, *Daily life in Renaissance Italy* (Westport, CT, 2002)
Cracco, G. and G. Ortali (eds), *Storia di Venezia: Dalle origini alla caduta della serenissima*, II: *L' età del commune* (Rome, 1995)
Dean, T., *Land and power in late medieval Ferrara: The rule of the Este, 1350–1450* (Cambridge, 1988)
De Roover, R., *The Rise and decline of the Medici bank 1397–1494* (Cambridge, 1963)
Epstein, S. R., 'Cities, regions and the late medieval crisis: Sicily and Tuscany compared', *Past & Present*, 130 (1991), 3–50
Epstein, S. R., *An island for itself: Economic development and social change in late medieval Sicily* (Cambridge, 1992)
Epstein, S. R., 'The Rise and decline of Italian city-states', in M. H. Hansen (ed.), *A comparative study of thirty city-state cultures* (Copenhagen, 2000)
Esch, A., *Aspetti della vita economica e culturale a Roma nel Quattrocento* (Rome, 1981)
Fischer, K. von, 'Musica italiana e musicisti oltremontani nell'Italia del Trecento e del primo Quattrocento', *Rassegna Veneta di studi Musicali*, 1 (1985), 7–18
Forcheri, G., 'Dalle Regulae costituzionali del 1413 alla riforma del 1528', *La Storia dei Genovesi*, 4 (1984), 7–26
Franceschi, F., R. A. Goldthwaite and R. C. Müller, *Il Rinascimento Italiano e l'Europa*, IV: *Commercio e cultura mercantile* (Vicenza, 2007)
Gatto, L., *Medioevo quotidiano: Motivi e modelli di vita* (Rome, 1999)
Giusti, G. P., *Visconti e Sforza: I signori di Milano* (Pavia, 1997)
Goff, J. Le, *L'Italia nello specchio del Medioevo* (Turin, 2000)
Goldthwaite, R. A., *Wealth and the demand for art in Italy, 1300–1600* (Baltimore, 1993)
Goldthwaite, R. A., *The economy of Renaissance Florence* (Baltimore, 2009)
Gouwens, K. (ed.), *The Italian Renaissance: The essential sources* (Oxford, 2003)
Grubb, J. S., *Firstborn of Venice: Vicenza in the early Renaissance state* (Baltimore, 1988)
Guerzoni, G., 'The demand for arts of an Italian Renaissance court: The case of d'Este of Ferrara (1471–1560)', in M. North and D. Omrod (eds), *Art markets in Europe, 1400–1800* (Aldershot, 1998).
Hale, J. R., *Italian Renaissance painting from Masaccio to Titian* (Oxford, 1977)
Hardt, M., *Geschichte der italienischen Literatur: Von den Anfängen bis zur Gegenwart* (Düsseldorf, 1996)
Hausmann, F.-R., 'Anfänge und Duecento', in V. Kapp (ed.), *Italienische Literaturgeschichte* (Stuttgart, 1992)
Hausmann, F.-R., 'Quattrocento', in V. Kapp (ed.), *Italienische Literaturgeschichte* (Stuttgart, 1992)
Herlihy, D. and C. Klapisch-Zuber, *Tuscans and their families: A study of the Florentine catasto of 1427* (New Haven and London, 1985)
Hösle, J., *Kleine Geschichte der italienischen Literatur* (Munich, 1995)
Huck, O., *Die Musik des frühen Trecento* (Hildesheim, 2005)
Hyde, J. K., *Padua in the age of Dante* (New York, 1966)

Il tumulto dei Ciompi: Un momento di storia fiorentina ed europea. Convegno Internazionale di Studi (Firenze, 16–19 settembre 1979), Published by Istituto Nazionale di Studi sul Rinascimento (Florence, 1981)

Jacoby, D., 'Genoa, silk trade and silk manufacture in the Mediterranean region (*c.* 1100–1300)', in *Commercial exchange across the Mediterranean: Byzantium, the crusader Levant, Egypt and Italy* (Aldershot, 2005)

Jones, P., 'Communes and despots in late-medieval Italy', in B. G. Kohl and A. A. Smith (eds), *Major problems in the history of the Italian Renaissance* (Lexington, 1995)

Jones, P., *The Italian city-state: From commune to signoria* (Oxford, 1997)

Kohl, B. G., *Padua under the Carrara* (Baltimore, 1998)

'La pittura in Italia', *Il Quattrocento*, ed. F. Zeri (Milan, 1987)

Labanca, N., *Oltremare: Storia dell'espansione coloniale italiana* (Bologna, 2002)

Lane, F. C., *Venice: A maritime republic (*Baltimore, 1973)

Lane, F. C., *Venetian ships and shipbuilders of the Renaissance* (Baltimore, 1992)

Lane, F. C. and R. C. Mueller, *Money and banking in medieval and Renaissance Venice*, I: *Coins and money of account* (Baltimore, 1985)

Leydi, S., 'Le armi', in F. Franceschi, R. A. Goldthwaite and R. C. Mueller (eds), *Il Rinascimento Italiano e l'Europa* (Venice, 2007)

Lopez, R., 'Quattrocento Genovese', *Rivista storica italiana*, 75 (1963), 709–27

Lütteken, L., *Guillaume Dufay und die isorhythmische Motette: Gattungstradition und Werkcharakter an der Schwelle zur Neuzeit* (Hamburg, 1993)

Maginnis, H. B. J., *Painting in the age of Giotto: A historical reevaluation* (University Park, PA, 1997)

Maire Vigueur, J.-C., *Comuni e signorie in Umbria, Marche e Lazio* (Turin, 1987)

Martin, J. J., *The Renaissance: Italy and abroad* (London, 2003)

Martin, J. and D. Romano, *Venice reconsidered: The history and civilization of an Italian city-state, 1297–1797* (Baltimore, 2000)

Massa Piergiovanni, P., *Lineamenti di organizzazione economica in uno stato preindustriale, La repubblica di Genova* (Genoa, 1995)

Mueller, R. C., 'The Jewish moneylenders of late Trecento Venice: A revisitation', *Mediterranean Historical Review*, 10 (1995), 202–17

Mueller, R. C., *Money and banking in medieval and Renaissance Venice*, II: *The Venetian money market: Banks, panics, and the public debt, 1200–1500* (Baltimore, 1997)

Mueller, R. C., '"Veneti Facti Privilegio": Stranieri naturalizzati a venezia tra XIV e XVI secolo', in D. Calabi and P. Lanaro, *La città italiana e i luoghi degli stranieri XIV–XVIII secolo* (Rome, 1998)

Nigro, G. (ed.), *Francesco di Marco Datini: The man, the merchant* (Florence, 2010)

Nuttall, P., *From Flanders to Florence: The impact of Netherlandish painting 1400–1500* (New Haven and London, 2004)

Oertel, R, *Early Italian painting to 1400* (New York, 1968)

Origo, I., *The merchant of Prato: Francesco di Marco Datini* (London, 1992)

Partner, P., *The Papal State under Martin V: The administration and government of the temporal power in the early fifteenth century* (London, 1958)

Pinto, G., *La Toscana nel tardo medioevo: Ambiente, economia rurale, società* (Florence, 1982)

Raveggi, S., M. Tarassi, D. Medici and P. Parenti, *Ghibellini, guelfi e popolo grasso:*

I detentori del potere politico a Firenze nella seconda metà del Dugento (Florence, 1978)

Reinhardt, V., *Überleben in der frühneuzeitlichen Stadt: Annona und Getreideversorgung in Rom 1563–1797* (Tübingen, 1991)

Reinhardt, V., *Rom: Kunst und Geschichte 1480–1650* (Freiburg, 1992)

Reinhardt, V., *Die Medici: Florenz im Zeitalter der Renaissance* (2nd edn, Munich, 2001)

Reinhardt, V., *Geschichte Italiens: Von der Spätantike bis zur Gegenwart* (Munich, 2003)

Reinhardt, V., *Der unheimliche Papst: Alexander VI. Borgia 1431–1503* (Munich, 2005)

Rösch, G., *Venedig: Geschichte einer Seerepublik* (Stuttgart, 2000)

Rubinstein, N., *The government of Florence under the Medici (1434 to 1494)* (2nd edn, Oxford, 1997)

Ryder, A., *Alfonso the magnanimous, King of Aragon, Naples and Sicily, 1396–1458* (Oxford, 1990)

Shaw, C., 'Principles and practice in the civic government of fifteenth-century Genoa', *Renaissance Quarterly*, 58 (2005), 45–90

Stinger, C. L., *The Renaissance in Rome* (Bloomington, 1985)

Toscano, G., 'Nápoles el Mediterráneo', in *El Renacimiento Mediterráneo: Viajes de artistas e itineraries de obras entre Italia, Francia y España en el siglo XV* (Madrid, 2001)

Toubert, P. and A. Paravicini Bagliani (eds), *Federico II e le città italiane* (Palermo, 1994)

Vaini, M., *Ricerche gonzaghesche (1189–inizi sec. XV)* (Florence, 1994)

Varanini, G. M. (ed.), *Gli Scaligieri* (Verona, 1988)

Chapter 5 Holy Roman Empire

Aerts, E. 'The stock exchange in medieval and early modern Europe: The origins of a concept in the southern Netherlands', in F. Daelemans and A. Kelders (eds), *Miscellanea in memoriam Pierre Cockshaw (1938–2008): Aspects de la vie culturelle dans les Pays-Bas méridionaux (XIVe–XVIIIe siècle)* (Brussels, 2009)

Aerts, E., P. Rion and A. Vandenbulcke, *La Cour des comptes entre tradition et innovations: Histoire d'une institution de contrôle* (Tielt, 1999)

Angermeier, H., *Die Reichsreform 1410–1555: Die Staatsproblematik in Deutschland zwischen Mittelalter und Gegenwart* (Munich, 1984)

Annas, G., *Hoftag – Gemeiner Tag – Reichstag: Studien zur strukturellen Entwicklung deutscher Reichsversammlungen des späten Mittelalters (1349–1471)*, II: *Verzeichnis deutscher Reichsversammlungen des späten Mittelalters (1349 bis 1471)* (Göttingen, 2002)

Arnade, P. *Realms of ritual: Burgundian ceremony and civic life in late-medieval Ghent* (Ithaca, 1996)

Arnade, P. 'City, court and public ritual in the late-medieval Burgundian Netherlands', *Comparative Studies in Society and History*, 29:2 (1997), 296–314

Arnade, P. 'Urban elites and the politics of public space in late-medieval Low Countries cities', in M. Carlier et al. (eds), *Core and periphery in late-medieval urban society* (Louvain, 1997)

Beer, E. J. and N. Gramaccini (eds), *Berns große Zeit – Das 15. Jahrhundert neu entdeckt* (Berne, 1999)

Berg, D., *Deutschland und seine Nachbarn 1200–1500* (Munich, 1997)

Bergier, J.-F., *Die Wirtschaftsgeschichte der Schweiz: Von den Anfängen bis zur Gegenwart* (Zurich, 1983)

Bierende, E., *Lucas Cranach d. Ä. und der deutsche Humanismus: Tafelmalerei im Kontext von Rhetorik, Chroniken und Fürstenspiegeln* (Munich, 2002)

Blendinger, F., 'Versuch einer Bestimmung der Mittelschicht in der Reichsstadt Augsburg vom Ende des 14. bis zum Anfang des 18. Jahrhunderts', in E. Maschke and J. Sydow (eds), *Städtische Mittelschichten: Protokoll der 8. Arbeitstagung des Arbeitskreises für südwestdeutsche Stadtgeschichtsforschung, Biberach 14.–16. November 1969* (Stuttgart, 1972)

Blickle, P., *Kommunalismus: Skizzen einer gesellschaftlichen Organisationsform*, II: *Europa* (Munich, 2000)

Blickle, P., *Von der Leibeigenschaft zu den Menschenrechten: Eine Geschichte der Freiheit in Deutschland* (Munich, 2003)

Blockmans, W. P., 'Alternatives to monarchical centralisation: The great tradition of revolt in Flanders and Brabant', in H. G. Koenigsberger (ed.), *Republiken und Republikanismus im Europa der Frühen Neuzeit* (Munich, 1988)

Blockmans, W. P., 'De vorming van een politieke unie (14de–16de eeuw)', in J. C. H. Blom and E. Lamberts (eds), *Geschiedenis van de Nederlanden* (Rijswijk, 1993)

Blockmans, W. P., 'The economic expansion of Holland and Zeeland in the fourteenth-sixteenth centuries,' in E. Aerts et al. (eds), *Studia historica oeconomica: Liber amicorum Herman Van der Wee* (Louvain, 1993)

Blockmans, W. P., 'Der holländische Durchbruch in der Ostsee', in S. Jenks and M. North (eds), *Der Hansische Sonderweg? Beiträge zur Sozial- und Wirtschaftsgeschichte der Hanse* (Cologne, 1993)

Blockmans, W. P., 'The Burgundian court and the urban milieu as patrons in fifteenth-century Bruges', in M. North (ed.), *Economic history and the arts* (Cologne, 1996)

Blockmans, W. P., *Emperor Charles V. 1500–1558* (London, 2002)

Blockmans, W. P., 'Von der Stratifikation zur Gestalt: Der Pradigmenwechsel in der Stadtgeschichte der Niederlande', in H. Duchhardt and W. Reininghaus (eds), *Staat und Region: Internationale Forschungen und Perspektiven. Kolloquium für Peter Johanek* (Cologne, 2005)

Blockmans, W. P. and N. Mout (eds), *The world of Emperor Charles V* (Amsterdam, 2004)

Blockmans, W. P. and W. Prevenier, *The Burgundian Netherlands* (Cambridge, 1986)

Blockmans, W. P. and W. Prevenier, *The promised lands: The Low Countries under Burgundian rule, 1369–1530* (Philadelphia 1999)

Bodmer, J. -P., *Chroniken und Chronisten im Spätmittelalter* (Zurich, 1976)

Bonsdorff, J. von, *Kunstproduktion und Kunstverbreitung im Ostseeraum des Spätmittelalters* (Helsinki, 1993)

Boone, M. 'The Dutch revolt and the medieval tradition of urban dissent', *Journal of Early Modern History*, 11 (2007), 351–75

Boone, M. and M. Prak, 'Rulers, patricians and burghers: The great and the little traditions of urban revolt in the Low Countries', in K. Davids and J. Lucassen (eds), *A miracle mirrored: The Dutch Republic in European perspective* (Cambridge, 1995)

Borchert, T. -H. (ed.), *The age of van Eyck 1430–1530: The Mediterranean world and early Netherlandish painting* (Ghent, 2002)

Bracker, J., V. Henn, R. Postel (eds), *Die Hanse: Lebenswirklichkeit und Mythos* (2nd edn, Lübeck, 1998)

Brown, A., *The Valois dukes of Burgundy* (Oxford, 2002)

Die Burgunderbeute und Werke burgundischer Hofkunst. Exhibition, Bernisches Historisches Museum, 18 May–20 September 1969 (Berne, 1969)

Busch, R. von, 'Studien zu deutschen Antikensammlungen des 16. Jahrhunderts' (PhD dissertation, University of Tübingen, 1973)

Carl, H., *Der Schwäbische Bund 1488–1534. Landfrieden und Genossenschaft im Übergang vom Spätmittelalter zur Reformation* (Leinfelden, 2000)

Carson, P., *James van Artevelde, the Man from Ghent* (Ghent, 1980)

Cauchies, J. -M., *Philippe le Beau: Le dernier duc de Bourgogne* (Brepols, 2003)

Cramer, T., *Geschichte der deutschen Literatur im späten Mittelalter* (Munich, 1990)

Diestelkamp, B., *Das Reichskammergericht: Der Weg zu seiner Gründung und die ersten Jahrzehnte seines Wirkens (1451–1527)* (Cologne, 2003)

Dollinger, P., *The German Hansa* (London, 1999)

DuBoulay, F. R. H., *Germany in the later Middle Ages* (London, 1983)

Dumolyn, J. and J. Haemers, 'Patterns of urban rebellion in medieval Flanders', *Journal of Medieval History*, 31 (2005), 369–93

Fiala, D., 'Les musiciens étrangers de la cour de Bourgogne à la fin du XVe siècle', *Revue du Nord*, 84 (2002), 367–87

Fouquet, G., *Das Speyerer Domkapitel im späten Mittelalter (ca. 1350–1540): Adlige Freundschaft, fürstliche Patronage und päpstliche Klientel* (Mainz, 1987)

Franke, B. and B. Welzel (eds), *Die Kunst der burgundischen Niederlande: Eine Einführung* (Berlin, 1997)

Franke, B., 'Herrscher über Himmel und Erde: Alexander der Große und die Herzöge von Burgund', *Marburger Jahrbuch für Kunstwissenschaft*, 27 (2000), 121–69

Franke, B., 'Zwischen Liturgie und Zeremoniell: Ephemere Ausstattung bei Friedensverhandlungen und Fürstentreffen', in N. Bock et al. (eds), *Kunst und Liturgie im Mittelalter: Akten des internationalen Kongresses der Bibliotheca Hertziana und des Nederlands Instituut te Rome, Rom, 28–30 September 1997* (Munich, 2000)

Fritze, K., *Am Wendepunkt der Hanse: Untersuchungen zur Wirtschafts- und Sozialgeschichte wendischer Hansestädte in der ersten Hälfte des 15. Jahrhunderts* (Berlin, 1967)

Fudge, J. D., *Cargoes, embargoes and emissaries: The commercial and political interaction of England and the German Hanse 1450–1510* (Toronto, 1995)

Fuhrmann, B., *Konrad von Weinsberg: Ein adliger Oikos zwischen Territorium und Reich* (Wiesbaden, 2004)

Göttmann, F., *Handwerk und Bündnispolitik: Die Handwerkerbünde am Mittelrhein vom 14. bis zum 17. Jahrhundert* (Wiesbaden, 1977)

Graus, F., 'Randgruppen der städtischen Gesellschaft im Spätmittelalter', *Zeitschrift für Historische Forschung*, 8 (1981), 385–437

Groten, M., *Köln im 13. Jahrhundert: Gesellschaftlicher Wandel und Verfassungsentwicklung* (Cologne, 1995)

Head, R. C., *Early modern democracy in the Grisons: Social order and political language in a Swiss mountain canton, 1470–1600* (Cambridge, 1995)

Hechberger, W., *Adel, Ministerialität und Rittertum im Mittelalter* (Munich, 2004)

Heinig, P. -J. (ed.), *Kaiser Friedrich III. (1440–1493) in seiner Zeit* (Cologne, 1993)

Helmrath, J., 'Vestigia Aeneae imitari. Enea Silvio Piccolomini als "Apostel" des Humanismus: Formen und Wege seiner Diffusion', in J. Helmrath, U. Muhlack and G. Walther (eds), *Diffusion des Humanismus: Studien zur nationalen Geschichtsschreibung europäischer Humanisten* (Göttingen, 2002)

Herbers, K. and H. Neuhaus, *Das Heilige Römische Reich: Schauplätze einer tausendjährigen Geschichte (843–1806)* (Cologne, 2005)

Herborn, W., *Die politische Führungsschicht der Stadt Köln im Spätmittelalter* (Bonn, 1977)

Hergemöller, B. -U., *Fürsten, Herren und Städte zu Nürnberg 1355/56: Die Entstehung der "Goldenen Bulle" Karls IV.* (Cologne, 1983)

Hergemöller, B. -U. (ed.), *Randgruppen der spätmittelalterlichen Gesellschaft: Ein Hand- und Studienbuch* (2nd edn, Warendorf, 1994)

Hirschfelder, G., *Die Kölner Handelsbeziehungen im Spätmittelalter* (Cologne, 1994)

Hödl, G., *Albrecht II. Königtum, Reichsregierung und Reichsreform (1438–1439)* (Cologne, 1978)

Hoffmann, E., 'Lübeck und die Erschließung des Ostseeraums', in J. Bracker, V. Henn and R. Postel (eds), *Die Hanse: Lebenswirklichkeit und Mythos* (2nd edn, Lübeck, 1998)

Holbach, R., *Stiftsgeistlichkeit im Spannungsfeld von Kirche und Welt: Studien zur Geschichte des Trierer Domkapitels und Domklerus im Spätmittelalter* (Trier, 1982)

Hoppenbrouwers, P. and J. L. van Zanden (eds), *Peasants into farmers? The transformation of rural economy and society in the Low Countries (Middle Ages–nineteenth century) in light of the Brenner debate* (Turnhout, 2001)

Huizinga, J., *The autumn of the Middle Ages*, trans. R. J. Payton and U. Mammitzsch (Chicago, 1996)

Im Hof, U., *Die Schweiz: Illustrierte Geschichte der Eidgenossenschaft* (Stuttgart, 1984)

Isenmann, E., *Die deutsche Stadt im Spätmittelalter: 1250–1500. Stadtgestalt, Recht, Stadtregiment, Kirche, Gesellschaft, Wirtschaft* (Stuttgart, 1988)

Isenmann, E., 'The Holy Roman Empire in the Middle Ages', in R. Bonney (ed.), *The rise of the fiscal state in Europe, c. 1200–1815* (Oxford, 1999)

Jenks, S., 'Die "Carta mercatoria": Ein "hansisches Privileg"', *Hansische Geschichtsblätter*, 108 (1990), 45–86.

Jenks, S., *England, die Hanse und Preußen: Handel und Diplomatie, 1377–1474* (3 vols, Cologne, 1992)

Jenks, S., 'Von den archaischen Grundlagen bis zur Schwelle der Moderne (ca. 1000–1450)', in M. North (ed.), *Deutsche Wirtschaftsgeschichte: Ein Jahrtausend im Überblick* (2nd edn, Munich, 2005)

Johanek, P., 'Weltchronik und regionale Geschichtsschreibung im Spätmittelalter', in H. Patze (ed.), *Geschichtsschreibung und Geschichtsbewußtsein im späten Mittelalter* (Sigmaringen, 1987)

Jörn, N., R. -G. Werlich and H. Wernicke (eds), *Der Stralsunder Frieden von 1370: Prosopographische Studien* (Cologne, 1998)

Jörn, N. and H. Wernicke (eds), *Beiträge zur hansischen Kultur-, Verfassungs- und Schiffahrtsgeschichte* (Weimar, 1998)

Jörn, N., D. Kattinger and H. Wernicke (eds), *Genossenschaftliche Strukturen in der Hanse* (Cologne, 1999)

Kaufmann, T. DaCosta, *Court, cloister, and city: The art and culture of central Europe 1450–1800* (Chicago and London, 1995)

Kerler, D. (ed.), 'Deutsche Reichstagsakten unter Kaiser Sigmund: Erste Abtheilung 1410–1420', in *Deutsche Reichstagsakten ältere Reihe*, VII (Munich, 1878)

Kießling, R. and S. Ullmann (eds), *Das Reich in der Region während des Mittelalters und der frühen Neuzeit* (Konstanz, 2005)

Kossmann-Putto, J. A. and E. H. Kossmann, *Die Niederlande: Geschichte der nördlichen und südlichen Niederlande* (Rekkem, 1995)

Krieger, K.-F., *König, Reich und Reichsreform im Spätmittelalter* (Munich, 1992)

Krieger, K.-F., *Die Habsburger im Mittelalter: Von Rudolf I. bis Friedrich III.* (Stuttgart, 1994)

Lademacher, H., *Geschichte der Niederlande: Politik, Verfassung, Wirtschaft* (Darmstadt, 1983)

Lahrkamp, H., 'Das Patriziat in Münster', in H. Rössler (ed.), *Deutsches Patriziat 1430–1740* (Limburg, 1968)

Lecuppre-Desjardin, E., *La ville des cérémonies: Essai sur la communication politique dans les anciens Pays-Bas bourguignons* (Brepols, 2004)

Lloyd, T. H., *England and the German Hanse 1157–1611: A study of their trade and commercial diplomacy* (Cambridge, 1991)

Martens, M. P. J., 'Artistic patronage in Bruges institutions, c. 1440–1482' (PhD dissertation, University of California at Santa Barbara, 1992)

Martens, M. P. J. (ed.), *Bruges et la Renaissance: De Memling à Pourbus* (Bruges, 1998)

Moraw, P., 'Die Verwaltung des Königtums und des Reiches und ihre Rahmenbedingungen', in *Deutsche Verwaltungsgeschichte*, I: *Vom Spätmittelalter bis zum Ende des Reiches* (Stuttgart, 1983)

Moraw, P., *Von offener Verfassung zu gestalteter Verdichtung: Das Reich im späten Mittelalter 1250 bis 1490* (Berlin, 1985)

Moraw, P., 'Fürstentum, Königtum und "Reichsreform" im deutschen Spätmittelalter', in W. Heinemeyer (ed.), *Vom Reichsfürstenstande* (Cologne, 1987)

Moraw, P., 'Königliche Herrschaft und Verwaltung im spätmittelalterlichen Reich (ca. 1350–1450)', in R. Schneider (ed.), *Das spätmittelalterliche Königtum im europäischen Vergleich* (Sigmaringen, 1987)

Muhlack, U., 'Das Projekt der Germania illustrata: Ein Paradigma der Diffusion des Humanismus?' in Johannes Helmrath, Ulrich Muhlack and Gerrit Walther (eds), *Diffusion des Humanismus: Studien zur nationalen Geschichtsschreibung europäischer Humanisten* (Göttingen, 2002)

Münch, P., *Lebensformen in der Frühen Neuzeit 1500–1800* (Frankfurt, 1992)

Munro, H., 'Medieval woollens: Textiles, textile technology and industrial organisation, *c.* 800–1500' and 'Medieval woollens: The Western European woollen industries and their struggles for international markets, *c.* 1000–1500', in D. Jenkins (ed.), *The Cambridge history of western textiles*, I (Cambridge, 2003)

Murray, J. M., *Bruges, cradle of capitalism, 1280–1390* (Cambridge, 2005)

Nicholas, D., 'Economic reorientation and social change in fourteenth-century Flanders', *Past & Present*, 70 (1976), 3–29

Nicholas, D., *Medieval Flanders* (London, 1992)

North, M., *Geldumlauf und Wirtschaftskonjunktur im südlichen Ostseeraum an der Wende zur Neuzeit (1440–1570)* (Sigmaringen, 1990)

North, M., 'The German Hanse', in W. Blockmans, *Man on the move: The roots of western civilization* (Hilversum, 1993)

North, M., 'Von den Warenmessen zu den Wechselmessen: Grundlagen des europäischen Zahlungsverkehrs in Spätmittelalter und Früher Neuzeit', in P. Johanek and H. Stoob (eds), *Europäische Messen und Märktesysteme in Mittelalter und Neuzeit* (Cologne, 1996)

North, M., 'Die Entstehung der Gutswirtschaft im südlichen Ostseeraum', *Zeitschrift für Historische Forschung*, 26 (1999), 43–59

North, M., *Geschichte der Niederlande* (3rd edn, Munich, 2008)

Obenaus, H., *Recht und Verfassung der Gesellschaften mit St. Jörgenschild in Schwaben: Untersuchungen über Adel, Einung, Schiedsgericht und Fehde im fünfzehnten Jahrhundert* (Göttingen, 1961)

Petri, F., I. Schöffer and J. J. Woltjer, *Geschichte der Niederlande: Holland, Belgien, Luxemburg* (Munich, 1991)

Pölnitz, G. Freiherr von, *Die Fugger* (6th edn, Tübingen, 1999)

Prietzel, M., *Das Heilige Römische Reich im Spätmittelalter* (Darmstadt, 2004)

Reincke, H., 'Hamburgs Bevölkerung', in H. Reinicke (ed.), *Forschungen und Skizzen zur Hamburgischen Geschichte* (Hamburg, 1951)

Reinle, C., *Ulrich Riederer (ca. 1406–1462) Gelehrter Rat im Dienste Kaiser Friedrichs III.* (Mannheim, 1993)

Reisner, W., *Die Einwohnerzahl deutscher Städte in früheren Jahrhunderten mit besonderer Berücksichtigung Lübecks* (Jena, 1903)

Rill, B., *Friedrich III., Habsburgs europäischer Durchbruch* (Graz, 1987)

Rösener, W., *Bauern im Mittelalter* (2nd edn, Munich, 1986)

Rupprich, H., *Die deutsche Literatur vom späten Mittelalter bis zum Barock*, I: *Das ausgehende Mittelalter, Humanismus und Renaissance, 1370–1520* (2nd edn, Munich, 1994)

Samsonowicz, H., 'Die Handelsstraße Ostsee-Schwarzes Meer im 13. und 14. Jahrhundert', in S. Jenks and M. North (eds), *Der Hansische Sonderweg? Beiträge zur Sozial- und Wirtschaftsgeschichte der Hanse* (Cologne, 1993)

Sauter, A., *Fürstliche Herrschaftsrepräsentation: Die Habsburger im 14. Jahrhundert* (Ostfildern, 2003)

Schauerte, T. U., *Die Ehrenpforte für Kaiser Maximilian I. Dürer und Altdorfer im Dienst des Herrschers* (Munich, 2001)

Scheftel, M., *Gänge, Buden und Wohnkeller in Lübeck: Bau- und sozialgeschichtliche Untersuchungen zu den Wohnungen der ärmeren Bürger und Einwohner einer Großstadt des späten Mittelalters und der frühen Neuzeit* (Neumünster, 1988)

Schildhauer, J., 'Zur Verlagerung des See- und Handelsverkehrs im nordeuropäischen Raum während des 15. und 16. Jahrhunderts: Eine Untersuchung auf der Grundlage der Danziger Pfahlkammerbücher', *Jahrbuch für Wirtschaftsgeschichte*, 4 (1968), 187–211

Schmid, P., *Der gemeine Pfennig von 1495: Vorgeschichte und Entstehung, verfassungsgeschichtliche, politische und finanzielle Bedeutung* (Göttingen, 1989)

Schmidt, G., *Der Städtetag in der Reichsverfassung: Eine Untersuchung zur korporativen Politik der freien und Reichsstädte in der ersten Hälfte des 16. Jahrhunderts* (Stuttgart, 1984)

Schmidt, G., *Geschichte des Alten Reiches: Staat und Nation in der Frühen Neuzeit 1495–1806* (Munich, 1999)

Schneidmüller, B. and S. Weinfurter (eds), *Heilig, römisch, deutsch: Das Reich im mittelalterlichen Europa* (Dresden, 2006)

Schubert, E., *Einführung in die Grundprobleme der deutschen Geschichte im Spätmittelalter* (Darmstadt, 1992)

Schubert, E., *Fürstliche Herrschaft und Territorium im späten Mittelalter* (Munich, 1996)

Schulz, K., *Handwerksgesellen und Lohnarbeiter: Untersuchungen zur oberrheinischen und oberdeutschen Stadtgeschichte des 14. bis 17. Jahrhunderts* (Sigmaringen, 1985)

Schwinges, R. C. (ed.), *Berns mutige Zeit: Das 13. und 14. Jahrhundert neu entdeckt* (Berne, 2003)

Scott, T., *Society and economy in Germany, 1300–1600* (Basingstoke, 2002)

Seifert, D., *Kompagnons und Konkurrenten: Holland und die Hanse im späten Mittelalter* (Cologne, 1997)

Soly, H. and W. P. Blockmans (eds), *Charles V and his time: 1500–1558* (Antwerp, 1999)

Spading, K., *Holland und die Hanse im 15. Jahrhundert: Untersuchungen die Ursachen des Vordringens der Holländer in der Ostsee und der Zerfall der Zwischenhandelsmonopols der wendischen Städte* (Greifswald, 1968)

Spading, K., *Holland und die Hanse im 15. Jahrhundert: Zur Problematik des Übergangs vom Feudalismus zum Kapitalismus* (Weimar, 1973)

Spieß, K.-H., 'Ständische Abgrenzung und soziale Differenzierung zwischen Hochadel und Ritteradel im Spätmittelalter', *Rheinische Vierteljahrsblätter*, 56 (1992), 181–205

Spieß, K.-H., *Familie und Verwandtschaft im deutschen Hochadel des Spätmittelalters, 13. bis Anfang des 16. Jahrhunderts* (Stuttgart, 1993)

Spieß, K.-H., 'Aufstieg in den Adel und Kriterien der Adelszugehörigkeit im Spätmittelalter', in K. Andermann and P. Johanek (eds), *Zwischen Nichtadel und Adel* (Stuttgart, 2001)

Sprandel, R., 'Die Konkurrenzfähigkeit der Hanse im Spätmittelalter', *Hansische Geschichtsblätter*, 102 (1984), 21–38

Sprandel, R., *Von Malvasia bis Kötzschenbroda: Die Weinsorten auf den spätmittelalterlichen Märkten Deutschlands* (Stuttgart, 1998)

Stabel, P., B. Blondé and A. Greve (eds), *International trade in the Low Countries (14th–16th centuries): Merchants, organisation, infrastructure*, Proceedings of the International Conference Ghent-Antwerp, 12–13 January 1997 (Garant, 2000)

Stauber, R., 'Nürnberg und Italien in der Renaissance', in H. Neuhaus (ed.), *Nürnberg: Eine europäische Stadt in Mittelalter und Neuzeit* (Nuremberg, 2000)

Stauber, R., 'Hartmann Schedel, der Nürnberger Humanistenkreis und die "Erweiterung der deutschen Nation"', in J. Helmrath, U. Muhlack and G. Walther (eds), *Diffusion des Humanismus: Studien zur nationalen Geschichtsschreibung europäischer Humanisten* (Göttingen, 2002)

Stein, R. (ed.), *Powerbrokers in the late Middle Ages: The Burgundian Low Countries in a European context. Les courtiers du pouvoir au bas Moyen Âge: Les Pays-Bas bourguignons dans un contexte européen* (Turnhout, 2001)

Stettler, B., *Die Eidgenossenschaft im 15. Jahrhundert: Die Suche nach einem gemeinsamen Nenner* (Zurich, 2004)

Stoob, H., 'Albert Krantz (1448–1517) Ein Gelehrter, Geistlicher und Hansischer Syndikus zwischen den Zeiten', *Hansische Geschichtsblätter*, 100 (1982), 87–109

Strohm, R., *Music in late medieval Bruges* (Oxford, 1985, rev. edn 1990)

Stromer, W. von, *Oberdeutsche Hochfinanz 1350–1450, I–III* (Wiesbaden, 1970)

Stromer, W. von, 'Die ausländischen Kammergrafen der Stephanskrone unter den Königen aus den Häusern Anjou, Luxemburg und Habsburg, Exponenten des Großkapitals', *Hamburger Beiträge zur Numismatik*, 27/29 (1973/75), 85–106

Stromer, W. von, *Die Gründung der Baumwollindustrie in Mitteleuropa* (Stuttgart, 1978)

Thomas, H., *Deutsche Geschichte des Spätmittelalters 1250–1500* (Stuttgart, 1983)

Thomas, H., *Ludwig der Bayer (1282–1347) Kaiser und Ketzer* (Regensburg, 1993)

Toch, M., *Die Juden im mittelalterlichen Reich* (Munich, 1998)

Toch, M., *Peasants and Jews in medieval Germany: Studies in cultural, social, and economic history* (Burlington, 2003)

Trautz, F., *Die Könige von England und das Reich: 1272–1377* (Heidelberg, 1961)

Ulbrich, C., *Leibherrschaft am Oberrhein im Spätmittelalter* (Göttingen, 1979)

Van Bavel, B. J. P. and J. L. van Zanden, 'The jump-start of the Holland economy during the late medieval crisis, *c.* 1350–*c.* 1500', *Economic History Review*, 57, 3 (2004), 503–32

Van der Wee, H., *The growth of the Antwerp market and the European economy (14th–16th Centuries)* (3 vols, The Hague, 1963)

Van der Wee, H., 'Structural changes and specialization in the industry of the southern Netherlands, 1100–1600', *Economic History Review*, 28:2 (1975), 203–21

Van der Wee, H., 'The Low Countries in transition: From the Middle Ages to early modern times' and 'Trade in the southern Netherlands, 1493–1587', in *The Low Countries in the Early Modern World* (London, 1993)

Van Uytven, R., 'Splendour or wealth: Art and economy in the Burgundian Netherlands', *Transactions of the Cambridge Bibliographical Society*, 10:2 (1992), 101–24

Van Uytven, R., 'Stages of economic decline: Late medieval Bruges', in J. M. Duvosquel and E. Thoen (eds), *Peasants and townsmen in medieval Europe: Studia in Honorem Adriaan Verhulst* (Ghent, 1995)

Vaughan, R., *Valois Burgundy* (London, 1975)

Vaughan, R., *Charles the Bold: The last Valois duke of Burgundy* (Woodbridge, 2002)

Vaughan, R., *Philip the Good: The apogee of Burgundy* (Woodbridge, 2002)

Von den Brincken, A.-D., 'Martin von Troppau', in H. Patze (ed.), *Geschichtsschreibung und Geschichtsbewußtsein im späten Mittelalter* (Sigmaringen, 1987)

Walder, E., *Das Stanser Verkommnis – Ein Kapitel eidgenössischer Geschichte neu untersucht: Die Entstehung des Verkommnisses von Stans in den Jahren 1477 bis 1481* (Stans, 1994)

Wefers, S., *Das politische System Kaiser Sigmunds* (Wiesbaden, 1989)

Wernicke, H., *Die Städtehanse 1280–1418: Genesis, Strukturen, Funktionen* (Weimar, 1983)

Wernicke, H., *Studien zum Verhältnis der Städtehanse zum norddeutschen Fürstentum und zum Reich* (Greifswald, 1984)
Wiesflecker, H., *Kaiser Maximilian I. Das Reich, Österreich und Europa an der Wende zur Neuzeit*, I: *Jugend, burgundisches Erbe und Römisches Königtum bis zur Alleinherrschaft 1459–1493* (Vienna, 1971)
Wiesflecker, H., *Kaiser Maximilian I.*, II: *Reichsreform und Kaiserpolitik, 1493–1500: Entmachtung des Königs im Reich und in Europa* (Munich, 1975)
Willoweit, D., 'Die Entwicklung und Verwaltung der spätmittelalterlichen Landesherrschaft', in *Deutsche Verwaltungsgeschichte*, I: *Vom Spätmittelalter bis zum Ende des Reiches* (Stuttgart, 1983)
Witthöft, H., *Die Lüneburger Saline: Salz in Nordeuropa und der Hanse* (Rahden, 2010)
Wolf, A., 'Das "Kaiserliche Rechtsbuch" Karls IV. (sogenannte Goldene Bulle)', *Ius Commune* 2 (1969), 1–32
Wood, C. S., 'Maximilian I as archeologist', *Renaissance Quarterly*, 58, 4 (2005), 1128–74
Worstbrock, F. J., 'Hartmann Schedels "Index Librorum": Wissenschaftssystem und Humanismus um 1500', in J. Helmrath and H. Müller (eds), *Studien zum 15. Jahrhundert: Festschrift für Erich Meuthen*, II (Munich, 1994)
Wunder, G., *Die Bürger von Hall: Sozialgeschichte einer Reichsstadt, 1216–1802* (Sigmaringen, 1980)
Wunder, H., *Die bäuerliche Gemeinde in Deutschland* (Göttingen, 1986)
Wunder, H., '"Jede Arbeit ist ihres Lohnes wert": Zur geschlechtsspezifischen Teilung und Bewertung von Arbeit in der Frühen Neuzeit', in K. Hausen (ed.), *Geschlechterhierarchie und Arbeitsteilung: Zur Geschichte ungleicher Erwerbschancen von Männern und Frauen* (Göttingen, 1993)
Würgler, A., 'The league of the discordant members and how the old Swiss Confederation operated and how it managed to survive for so long', in A. Holenstein, T. Maissen and M. Prak (eds), *The republican alternative: The Netherlands and Switzerland compared* (Amsterdam, 2008)

Chapter 6 East-central Europe (Poland, Hungary, Bohemia)

Alexander, M., H. Hecker and M. Lammich (eds), *Der russische Staat in Mittelalter und früher Neuzeit: Ausgewählte Aufsätze* (Wiesbaden, 1981)
Baczkowski, K., *Dzieje Polski późnośredniowiecznej (1370–1506)* (Cracow, 1999)
Bak, J. M., *Königtum und Stände in Ungarn im 14.–16. Jahrhundert* (Wiesbaden, 1973)
Bak, J. M. and B. Király (eds), *From Hunyadi to Rákóczi: War and society in late medieval and early modern Hungary* (New York, 1982)
Balogh, J., 'Die Kunst der Renaissance in Ungarn', in *Matthias Corvinus und die Renaissance in Ungarn 1458–1541*, exhibition catalogue (Vienna, 1982)
Benešovská, K. (ed.), *King John of Luxembourg (1296–1346) and the art of his era*, Proceedings of the International Conference, Prague, 16–20 September, 1996 (Prague, 1998)
Birnbaum, M. D., 'Humanism in Hungary', in A. Rabil, Jr (ed.), *Renaissance humanism: Foundations, forms, and legacy*, II, *Humanism beyond Italy* (Philadelphia, 1988)
Biskup, M., *Historia Pomorza*, I (Poznań, 1969)

Biskup, M., 'Przeobrażenia w handlu i rzemiośle', in E. Cieślak (ed.), *Historia Gdańska*, I: *Do roku 1454* (Gdańsk, 1978)

Biskup, M., 'Gdańsk a Hanza w połowie XV stulecia' in E. Cieślak (ed.), *Historia Gdańska*

Boháč, Z., 'Postup osídlení a demografický vývoj českých zemí do 15. Století', *Historická demografie*, 12 (Prague, 1987), 59–87

Boockmann, H., *Der Deutsche Orden: Zwölf Kapitel aus seiner Geschichte* (Munich, 1981)

Boockmann, H. (ed.), *Die Anfänge der ständischen Vertretungen in Preußen und seinen Nachbarländern* (Munich, 1992)

Bredekamp, H., 'Herrscher und Künstler in der Renaissance Ostmitteleuropas', in J. Helmrath, U. Muhlack and G. Walther, *Diffusion des Humanismus: Studien zur nationalen Geschichtsschreibung europäischer Humanisten* (Göttingen, 2002)

Burleigh, M., *Prussian society and the German Order: An aristocratic corporation in crisis c. 1410–1466* (Cambridge, 1984)

Čechura, J., 'Die Bauernschaft in Böhmen während des Spätmittelalters: Perspektiven neuer Orientierung', *Bohemia*, 31 (1990), 283–311

Čechura, J., *Die Struktur der Grundherrschaften im mittelalterlichen Böhmen unter besonderer Berücksichtigung der Klosterherrschaften* (Stuttgart, 1994)

Davies, N., *God's playground. A history of Poland*, I: *The origins to 1795* (New York, 2005)

Drake, B., D. Boehm and J. Fajt (eds), *Prague, the crown of Bohemia, 1347–1437* (New Haven, 2005)

Engel, P., *The realm of St Stephen: A history of medieval Hungary, 895–1526* (London, 2001)

Fajt, J., *Charles IV emperor by the grace of God: Culture and art in the reign of the last of the Luxembourgs, 1347–1433*, exhibition catalogue, Prague Castle, 16 February–21 May 2006 (Bamberg, 2006)

Feicht, H., *Studia nad muzyką polskiego średniowiecza* (Cracow, 1975)

Feicht, H., 'Liturgical music in medieval Poland', in *Polish Musicological Studies*, 1 (Cracow, 1977)

Frost, R. I., *The northern wars: War, state and society in northeastern Europe, 1558–1721* (Harlow, 2000)

Fudge, T. A., *The magnificent ride: The first reformation in Hussite Bohemia* (Aldershot, 1998)

Fügedi, E., 'Castles and castellans in Angevin Hungary', in S. B. Vardy (ed.), *Louis the Great* (Boulder, 1986)

Górski, K., 'The origins of the Polish Sejm', *Slavonic and East European Review*, 44 (1966), 122–38

Graus, F., *Dějiny venkovského lidu v Čechách v době předhusitské* (2 vols, Prague, 1953–57)

Graus, F., *Eastern and western Europe in the Middle Ages* (London, 1970)

Halperin, C. J., *Russia and the Golden Horde: The Mongol impact on medieval Russian history* (3rd edn, Bloomington, 1987)

Hecker, H., 'Juden im mittelalterlichen und frühneuzeitlichen Polen und Rußland: Versuch eines Vergleichs', in E. Hübner, E. Klug and J. Kusber (eds), *Zwischen Christianisierung und Europäisierung* (Stuttgart, 1998)

Hergemöller, B.-U., *Maiestas Carolina: Der Kodifikationsentwurf Karls IV. für das Königreich Böhmen von 1355* (Munich, 1995)

Higounet, C., *Les Allemands en Europe centrale et orientale au Moyen Âge* (Toulouse, 1989)

Hoensch, J. K., *Die Luxemburger: Eine spätmittelalterliche Dynastie von gesamteuropäischer Bedeutung 1308–1417* (Stuttgart, 2000)

Hoffmann, R. C., *Land, liberties, and lordship in a late medieval countryside: Agrarian structures and change in the duchy of Wrocław* (Philadelphia, 1989)

Ihnatowicz I., A. Mączak and B. Zientara, *Społeczeństwo polskie od X do XX wieku* (Warsaw, 1979)

Iwańczak, W., 'Political culture of the nobility in late medieval Poland', in *Political culture in Central Europe (10th–20th century)*, I (Warsaw, 2005), 101–11

Jaworski, R., C. Lübke and M. G. Müller, *Eine kleine Geschichte Polens* (Frankfurt, 2000)

Kahk, J. and E. Tarvel, *An economic history of the Baltic countries* (Stockholm, 1997)

Kaufmann, T. DaCosta, *Court, cloister, and city: The art and culture of Central Europe 1450–1800* (Chicago and London, 1995)

Kaufmann, T. DaCosta, 'Will the Jagiellonians again have their day? The state of scholarship on the Jagiellonians and art in the Hungarian and Czech lands', in R. Suckale and D. Popp (eds), *Die Jagiellonen: Kunst und Kultur einer europäischen Dynastie an der Wende zur Neuzeit* (Nuremberg, 2002)

Kejř, J., 'Die sogenannte Maiestas Carolina: Forschungsergebnisse und Streitfragen', in F. B. Fahlbusch and P. Johanek (eds), *Studia Luxemburgensia, Festschrift H. Stoob* (Warendorf, 1989)

Klassen J., 'Hus, the Hussites and Bohemia', in C. Allmand (ed.), *The new Cambridge medieval history*, VII: *c. 1415–c. 1500* (Cambridge, 1998)

Knoll, P.W., *The rise of the Polish monarchy: Piast Poland in east central Europe, 1320–1370* (Chicago, 1972)

Kozakiewicz, H. and S. Kozakiewicz, *Renesans w Polsce* (Warsaw, 1976)

Kriedte, P., *Peasants, landlords, merchant capitalists: Europe and the world economy, 1500–1800* (Cambridge, 1983)

Kubinyi, A., 'Die Wahlkapitulationen Waldislaws II. in Ungarn (1490)', in R. Vierhaus (ed.), *Herrschaftsverträge, Wahlkapitulationen, Fundamentalgesetze* (Göttingen, 1977)

Kubinyi, A., 'Stände und Staat in Ungarn in der zweiten Hälfte des 15. Jahrhunderts', *Bohemia: A Journal for Central European History*, 31 (1991), 312–25

Legner, A., *Die Parler und der schöne Stil: 1350–1400: Europäische Kunst unter den Luxemburgern: Ein Handbuch zur Ausstellung des Schnütgen-Museums in der Kunsthalle Köln* (3 vols, Cologne, 1978)

Lübke, C., *Das östliche Europa* (Munich, 2004)

Macháček, J., *The rise of medieval towns and states in east central Europe: Early medieval centres as social and economic systems* (Leiden, 2010)

Makkai, L., 'Die wirtschaftlichen Regionen Ungarns zur Zeit des späten Feudalismus', in V. Zimányi (ed.), *Studien zur deutschen und ungarischen Wirtschaftsentwicklung (16.–20. Jahrhundert)* (Budapest, 1985)

Mályusz, E., 'Hungarian nobles of medieval Transylvania', in J. M. Bak (ed.), *Nobilities in central and eastern Europe: Kinship, property and privilege* (Budapest, 1994)

Mandelova, H. (ed.), *Europa im späten Mittelalter. Böhmen zur Zeit der Luxemburger Herrscher: Die Entstehung der Länder des Königsreiches Böhmen* (Brühl, 1994)

Marosi E., 'Die Corvinische Renaissance in Ungarn und ihre Ausstrahlung in Ostmitteleuropa', in J. Helmrath, U. Muhlack and G. Walther (eds), *Diffusion des Humanismus: Studien zur nationalen Geschichtsschreibung europäischer Humanisten* (Göttingen, 2002)

Martin, J., *Medieval Russia 980–1584* (Cambridge, 1999)

Maur, E., 'Die demographische Entwicklung Böhmens in vorhussitischer Zeit (1346–1419)', in E. Maur, *Gutsherrschaft und "zweite Leibeigenschaft" in Böhmen: Studien zur Wirtschafts-, Sozial- und Bevölkerungsgeschichte (14.–18. Jahrhundert)* (Munich, 2001)

Mezník, J., *Lucemburská Morava 1310–1423* (Prague, 1999)

Militzer, K., *Die Geschichte des Deutschen Ordens* (Stuttgart, 2005)

Molenda, D. and E. Balczerak, *Metale nieżelazne na ziemiach polskich od XIV do XVIII wieku* (Wrocław, 1987)

Müller, R. A., 'Humanismus und Universität im östlichen Mitteleuropa', in W. Eberhard and A. A. Strnad (eds), *Humanismus und Renaissance in Ostmitteleuropa vor der Reformation* (Cologne, 1996)

Murray, A. V. (ed.), *Crusade and conversion on the Baltic frontier 1150–1500* (Aldershot, 2001)

Murray, A. V. (ed.), *The clash of cultures on the medieval Baltic frontier* (Farnham, 2009)

North, M., 'Wirtschaft, Gesellschaft, Bevölkerung', in E. Opgenoorth (ed.), *Handbuch der Geschichte Ost- und Westpreußens*, II/1: *Von der Teilung bis zum Schwedisch-Polnischen Krieg 1466–1655* (Lüneburg, 1994)

North, M., *From the North Sea to the Baltic: Essays in commercial, monetary and agricultural history, 1500–1800* (Aldershot, 1996)

Nowak-Dluzwski, J., *Okolicznosciowa poezja polityczna w polsce: sredniowiecze* (Warsaw, 1963)

Pach, Z. P., 'The development of feudal rent in Hungary in the fifteenth century', *Economic History Review*, 19:1 (1966), 1–14

Pach, Z. P., 'Der Bauernaufstand vom Jahre 1514 und die "zweite Leibeigenschaft"', in G. Heckenast (ed.), *Geschichte der ostmitteleuropäischen Bauernbewegungen im XVI.–XVIII. Jahrhundert* (Budapest, 1977)

Pach, Z. P., *Hungary and the European economy in early modern times* (Aldershot, 1994)

Pauly, M. (ed.), *Johann der Blinde, Graf von Luxemburg, König von Böhmen 1296–1346* (Luxembourg, 1997)

Perz, M. and H. Kowalewicz (eds), *Sources of polyphony up to c. 1500* (Warsaw, 1976)

Podlecki, J., *Wieliczka: das königliche Salzbergwerk* (2nd edn, Cracow, 2001)

Polívka, M., 'A contribution to the problem of property differentiation of the lesser nobility in the pre-Hussite period in Bohemia', *Hospodárské dejiny/Economic History*, 2 (1978), 331–60

Polívka, M., 'The political culture in the Bohemian kingdom of the Luxembourg period (from the beginning of the 14th century until the outbreak of the Hussite revolution of 1419)', in H. Manikowska, J. Pánek and M. Holý (eds), *Political culture in Central Europe (10th–20th century)*, Part I: *Middle Ages and early modern era* (Prague, 2005)

Rady, M., *Nobility, land and service in medieval Hungary* (Basingstoke, 2000)

Rhode, G., *Kleine Geschichte Polens* (3rd edn, Darmstadt, 1965)

Ritoók-Szalay, Á., 'Der Humanismus in Ungarn zur Zeit von Matthias Corvinus', in J. Helmrath, U. Muhlack and G. Walther (eds), *Diffusion des Humanismus: Studien zur nationalen Geschichtsschreibung europäischer Humanisten* (Göttingen, 2002)

Rowell, S. C., *Lithuania ascending: A pagan empire within east-central Europe 1295–1345* (Cambridge, 2000)

Russocki, S., 'Początki zgromadzeń stanowych w Europie Środkowej', *Przegląd Historyczny*, 66 (1975), 171–88

Russocki, S., '"Consilium Baronum" en Pologne médiévale', *Acta poloniae historica*, 35 (1977), 5–19

Samsonowicz, H. 'Miejsce Gdańska w gospodarce europejskiej w xv w', in *Historia Gdańska*, II: *1454–1655* (Gdańsk, 1982)

Samsonowicz, H., 'Dynamciczny ośrodek handlowy', in *Historia Gdańska*, II.

Samsonowicz, H., 'Polish politics and society under the Jagiellonian monarchy', in J. K. Fedorowicz (ed.), *A republic of nobles: Studies in Polish history to 1864* (Cambridge, 1982)

Schlesinger, W. (ed.), *Die deutsche Ostsiedlung des Mittelalters als Problem der europäischen Geschichte: Reichenau-Vorträge 1970–1972* (Sigmaringen, 1975)

Sedlar, J. W., *East central Europe in the Middle Ages, 1000–1500* (Seattle, 1994)

Segel, H. B., *Renaissance culture in Poland: The rise of humanism, 1470–1543* (Ithaca, 1989)

Seibt, F., 'Die Zeit der Luxemburger und der hussitischen Revolution', in K. Bosl (ed.), *Handbuch der Geschichte der böhmischen Länder*, I: *Die böhmischen Länder von der archaischen Zeit bis zum Ausgang der hussitischen Revolution* (Stuttgart, 1967)

Seibt, F., 'Zur Entwicklung der böhmischen Staatlichkeit 1212 bis 1471', in H. Patze (ed.), *Der deutsche Territorialstaat im 14. Jahrhundert*, II (2nd edn, Sigmaringen, 1986)

Seibt, F., 'Zur Entwicklung der böhmischen Staatlichkeit 1212–1471', in F. Seibt, *Hussitenstudien: Personen, Ereignisse, Ideen einer frühen Revolution* (2nd edn, Munich, 1991)

Siemieński, J., 'Od sejmików do sejmu 1454–1505', in *Studia historyczne ku czci Stanisława Kutrzeby*, I (Cracow, 1938)

Šmahel, F., 'Die Anfänge des Humanismus in Böhmen', in W. Eberhard and A. A. Strnad (eds), *Humanismus und Renaissance in Ostmitteleuropa vor der Reformation* (Cologne, 1996)

Šmahel, F., *Die Hussitische Revolution* (2 vols, Hanover, 2002)

Spěváček, J., *Jan Lucemburský a jeho doba 1296–1346: K prvnímu vstupu českých zemí do svazku se západní Evropou* (Prague, 1994)

Spufford, P., *Money and its use in medieval Europe* (Cambridge, 1988)

Stone, D., *The Polish-Lithuanian state, 1386–1795* (Seattle, 2001)

Svatoš, M. (ed.), *Dějiny University Karlovy*, I: *1347/48–1622* (Prague, 1995)

Tarvel, E., 'Genesis of the Livonian town in the thirteenth century', in *Prusy – Polska – Europa: Studia z dziejów sredniowiecza i czasów nowożytnych*, ed. A. Radziminski and J. Tandecki (Toruń, 1999)

Tiberg, E., *Moscow, Livonia and the Hanseatic league 1487–1550* (Stockholm, 1995)

Tichomirov, M. N., *Srednevekovaja Moskva v XIV–XV vekach* (Moscow, 1957)
Tichomirov, M. N., *Srednevekovaja Rossija na mezhdunarodnych putjach (XIV–XV vv.)* (Moscow, 1966)
Urban, W., *The Livonian crusade* (2nd edn, Chicago, 2004)
Vlachovič, J., *Slovenská med' v 16. a 17. Storoči* (Bratislava, 1964)
Westermann, E., 'Zur Silber- und Kupferproduktion Mitteleuropas vom 15. bis zum frühen 17. Jahrhundert: Über Bedeutung und Rangfolge der Reviere von Schwaz, Mansfeld und Neusohl', *Der Anschnitt*, 38 (1986), 187–211
Włodarczyk, J., 'Sejmiki łęczyckie do początku XVI w', *Czasopismo Prawno-Historyczne*, 12:2 (1960), 9–46
Wojciechowski, M. and R. Schattkowsky, *Historische Grenzlandschaften Ostmitteleuropas im 16.–20. Jahrhundert: Gesellschaft – Wirtschaft – Politik. Studiensammlung* (Toruń, 1996)
Wörster, P., 'Breslau und Olmütz als humanistische Zentren vor der Reformation', in W. Eberhard and A. A. Strnad (eds), *Humanismus und Renaissance in Ostmitteleuropa vor der Reformation* (Cologne, 1996)
Wyrozumski, J., *Dzieje Polski piastowskiej (VIII wiek–1370)* (Cracow, 1999)
Zientara, B., 'Roskwit feudalizmu (XIII–XV w.)', in B. Zientara et al. (eds), *Dzieje gospodarcze Polski do roku 1939* (Warsaw, 1973)
Zientara, B., 'Społeczeństwo polskie XIII–XV wieku', in I. Ihnatowicz, A. Mączak and B. Zientara, *Społeczeństwo polskie od X do XX wieku* (Warsaw, 1979)
Zientara, B., A. Mączak, I. Ihnatowicz and Z. Landau (eds), *Dzieje gospodarcze Polski do roku 1939* (Warsaw, 1973)

Chapter 7 South-east Europe (including Byzantium)

Ainsworth, M. W., '"A la façon grèce". The encounter of northern Renaissance artists with Byzantine icons', in H. C. Evans (ed.), *Byzantium: Faith and power (1261–1557)* (New Haven and London, 2004)
Ashtor, E., *East-west trade in the medieval Mediterranean* (London, 1986)
Ashtor, E., *Technology, industry and trade: The Levant versus Europe, 1250–1500* (London, 1992)
Babinger, F., *Mehmed the Conqueror and his time* (Princeton, 1978)
Baynes, N. H. and H. S. L. B. Moss, *Byzantium: An introduction to East Roman civilization* (Oxford, 1948)
Božilov, I. and V. Gjuzelev, *Istorija na srednovekovna Bălgarija: VII–XIV vek* (Sofia, 1999)
Browning, R., *The Byzantine Empire* (2nd edn, Washington, D.C., 1992)
Bryer, A. and M. Ursinus (eds), *Manzikert to Lepanto: The Byzantine world and the Turks, 1071–1571* (Amsterdam, 1991)
Cardini, F., *Europe and Islam* (Oxford, 2001)
Ćirković, S., *La Serbie au Moyen Age* (Saint-Léger-Vauban, 1992)
Evans, H. C. (ed.), *Byzantium: Faith and power (1261–1557)* (New Haven, 2004)
Faroqhi, S., *The Ottoman Empire: A short history* (Princeton, 2009)
Fine, J. V. A. Jr., *The Bosnian church, a new interpretation: A study of the Bosnian church and its place in state and society from the thirteenth to the fifteenth centuries* (Boulder, 1975)

Gill, J. S. J., *Byzantium and the papacy 1198–1400* (New Brunswick, NJ, 1901)

Gjuzelev, V., *Bulgarien zwischen Orient und Okzident: Die Grundlagen seiner geistlichen Kultur vom 13. bis zum 15. Jahrhundert* (Vienna, 1993)

Hösch, E., *Geschichte der Balkan-Länder: Von der Frühzeit bis zur Gegenwart* (2nd edn, Munich, 2002)

Inalcik, H., *The Ottoman Empire: The classical age 1300–1600* (London, 1973)

Jacoby, D., 'La population de Constantinople', *Byzantion*, 31 (1961), 81–109

Jacoby, D., *Trade, commodities and shipping in the medieval Mediterranean* (Aldershot, 1977)

Kafadar, C., *Between two worlds: The construction of the Ottoman state* (Berkeley, 1995)

Kaser, K., *Südosteuropäische Geschichte und Geschichtswissenschaft: Eine Einführung* (Vienna, 1990)

Kazdhan, A. and G. Constable, *People and power in Byzantium: An introduction to modern Byzantine studies* (Washington, DC, 1982)

Kislinger, E., 'Gewerbe im späten Byzanz', in H. Kühnel (ed.), *Handwerk und Sachkultur im Spätmittelalter* (Vienna, 1988)

Kreiser, K., *Der Osmanische Staat 1300–1922* (Munich, 2001)

Krekić, B., *Dubrovnik: Italy and the Balkans in the late Middle Ages* (London, 1980)

Laiou, A. E., 'The agrarian economy, thirteenth–fifteenth centuries', in A. E. Laiou, *The economic history of Byzantium*, I (Washington, DC, 2002)

Laiou, A. E. and R. P. Mottahedeh (eds), *The Crusades from the perspective of Byzantium and the Muslim world* (Washington, DC, 2001)

Lilie, R. -J., *Byzanz: Geschichte des oströmischen Reiches 326–1453* (Munich, 1999)

Malcolm, N., *Bosnia: A short history* (London, 1994)

Matschke, K. -P., 'The late Byzantine urban economy: thirteenth–fifteenth centuries', in A. E. Laiou, *The economic history of Byzantium*, II.

Matschke, K. -P. and F. Tinnefeld (eds), *Die Gesellschaft im späten Byzanz: Gruppen, Strukturen und Lebensformen* (Cologne, 2001)

Matuz, J., *Das Osmanische Reich: Grundlinien seiner Geschichte* (2nd edn, Darmstadt, 1990)

Nelson, R. S., 'Byzantium and the rebirth of art and learning in Italy and France', in H. C. Evans (ed.), *Byzantium: Faith and power (1261–1557)* (New Haven, 2004)

Nicol, D. M., *The last centuries of Byzantium, 1261–1453* (2nd edn, Cambridge, 1993)

Nicol, D. M., *The Byzantine lady: Ten portraits 1250–1500* (Cambridge, 1994)

Norwich, J. J., *Byzantium: The apogee* (London, 1993)

Norwich, J. J., *Byzantium: The decline and fall* (London, 1996)

Ostrogrosky, G., *History of the Byzantine state*, trans. J. M. Hussey (New Brunswick, NJ, 1969)

Papacostea, Ş., 'Die politischen Voraussetzungen für die wirtschaftliche Vorherrschaft des osmanischen Reiches im Schwarzmeergebiet (1453–1484)', *Münchner Zeitschrift für Balkankunde*, 1 (1978), 217–45

Prinzing, G. and M. Salomon (eds), *Byzanz und Ostmitteleuropa 950–1453* (Wiesbaden, 1999)

Redford, S., 'Byzantium and the Islamic world, 1261–1557', in H. C. Evans (ed.) *Byzantium: Faith and power (1261–1557)* (New Haven, 2004)

Runciman S., *The fall of Constantinople 1453* (Cambridge, 1965)

Runciman, S., *Mistra: Byzantine capital of the Peloponnese* (London, 1980)
Schreiner, P., *Byzanz* (2nd edn, Munich, 1994)
Schreiner, P., 'Schein und Sein: Überlegungen zu den Ursachen des Untergangs des byzantinischen Reiches', *Historische Zeitschrift*, 266 (1998), 625–47
Steindorff, L., *Kroatien: vom Mittelalter bis zur Gegenwart* (Regensburg, 2001)
Steindorff, L., 'Zar Stefan Dušan von Serbien', in M. Löwener (ed.), *Die "Blüte" der Staaten des östlichen Europa im 14. Jahrhundert* (Wiesbaden, 2004)
Sugar, P F., *Southeastern Europe under Ottoman rule, 1354–1804* (Seattle, 1977)
Talbot, A.-M., 'Revival and decline: Voices from the Byzantine capital', in H. C. Evans (ed.), *Byzantium: Faith and power (1261–1557)* (New Haven, 2004)
Treadgold, W., *A history of the Byzantine state and society* (Stanford, 1997)
Werner, E., *Die Geburt einer Großmacht. Die Osmanen (1300–1481): Ein Beitrag zur Genesis des türkischen Feudalismus* (4th edn, Weimar, 1985)
Zernack, K., *Osteuropa: Eine Einführung in seine Geschichte* (Munich, 1977)

Chapter 8 Russia (including the Baltic countries)

Alef, G., *Rulers and nobles in fifteenth-century Muscovy* (London, 1983)
Alef, G., *The origins of Muscovite autocracy: The age of Ivan III* (Berlin, 1986)
Bessudnova, Marina, 'Die Schließung des hansischen Kontors in Novgorod im Jahre 1494 im Kontext der Beziehungen des Großfürsten von Moskau zu Maximilian von Habsburg', *Hansische Geschichtsblätter*, 127 (2009), 69–100
Birnbaum, H., *Lord Novgorod the Great: Essays in the history and culture of a medieval city-state* (Columbus, OH, 1981)
Birnbaum, H., 'Did the 1478 annexation of Novgorod by Muscovy fundamentally change the course of Russian history?', in L. Hughes (ed.), *New perspectives on Muscovite history* (London, 1993)
Bogatyrev, S., *The sovereign and his counsellors: Ritualised consultations in Muscovite political culture, 1350s–1570s* (Helsinki 2000)
Fennell, J. L. I., *The crisis of medieval Russia, 1200–1304* (London, 1983)
Fennell, J. L. I., *The emergence of Moscow, 1304–1359* (London, 1968)
Garleff, M., *Die baltischen Länder: Estland, Lettland, Litauen vom Mittelalter bis zur Gegenwart* (Regensburg, 2001)
Goehrke, C., 'Die Sozialstruktur des mittelalterlichen Novgorod', in *Untersuchungen zur gesellschaftlichen Struktur der mittelalterlichen Städte in Europa, Reichenau-Vorträge 1963/64* (Konstanz, 1966)
Goehrke, C., *Die Wüstungen in der Moskauer Rus': Studien zur Siedlungs-, Bevölkerungs- und Sozialgeschichte* (Wiesbaden, 1968)
Goehrke, C., *Russischer Alltag: Eine Geschichte in neun Zeitbildern*, I: *Die Vormoderne* (Zurich, 2003)
Halbach, U., *Der russische Fürstenhof vor dem 16. Jahrhundert* (Stuttgart, 1985)
Hamilton, G. H., *The art and architecture of Russia* (Harmondsworth, 1975)
Haumann, H., *Geschichte Rußlands* (Munich, 1996)
Hellmann, M., 'Das Großfürstentum Litauen bis 1569', in M. Hellmann (ed.), *Handbuch der Geschichte Russlands*, I: *Bis 1613: Von der Kiever Reichsbildung bis zum Moskauer Zarentum* (Stuttgart, 1989)

Hellmann, M., *Grundzüge der Geschichte Litauens und des litauischen Volkes* (4th edn, Darmstadt, 1990)

Kahn, H. W., *Die Deutschen und die Russen: Geschichte ihrer Beziehungen vom Mittelalter bis heute* (Cologne, 1984)

Kaufmann, T. DaCosta, *Court, cloister and city: Art and culture in central Europe, 1450–1800* (Chicago and London, 1995)

Khoroshkevich, A. L., *Torgovlja Velikogo Novgoroda s Pribaltikoj i zapadnoj Evropoj v XIV–XV vekach* (Moscow, 1963)

Khoroshkevich, A. L., 'Das Moskauer Fürstentum unter Ivan Kalita (1325–1389) und Dmitrij Donskoj (1359–1389)', in M. Löwener (ed.), *Die "Blüte" der Staaten des östlichen Europa im 14. Jahrhundert* (Wiesbaden, 2004)

Klug, E., *Das Fürstentum Tver, 1247–1485: Aufstieg, Selbstbehauptung und Niedergang* (Wiesbaden, 1985)

Knackstedt, W., *Moskau: Studien zur Geschichte einer mittelalterlichen Stadt* (Wiesbaden, 1975)

Knackstedt, W., 'Moskauer Kaufleute im späten Mittelalter: Organisationsformen und soziale Stellung', *Zeitschrift für Historische Forschung*, 3:1 (1976), 1–17

Leuschner J., *Novgorod: Untersuchungen zu einigen Fragen seiner Verfassungs- und Bevölkerungsstruktur* (Berlin, 1980)

Martin, J., *Treasure of the land of darkness: The fur trade and its significance for medieval Russia* (Cambridge, 1986)

Martin, J., *Medieval Russia, 980–1584* (Cambridge, 1995)

Misāns, J. and H. Wernicke (eds), *Riga und der Ostseeraum: Von der Gründung 1201 bis in die Frühe Neuzeit* (Marburg, 2005)

Morgan, D., *The Mongols* (Malden, 2007)

Nikžentaitis, A., 'Litauen unter den Großfürsten Gedimin (1316–41) und Olgerd (1345–77)', in M. Löwener (ed.), *Die "Blüte" der Staaten des östlichen Europa im 14. Jahrhundert* (Wiesbaden, 2004)

Nitsche, P., 'Die Mongolenzeit und der Aufstieg Moskaus (1240–1538)', in M. Hellmann (ed.), *Handbuch der Geschichte Rußlands*, I: *Bis 1613: Von der Kiever Reichsbildung bis zum Moskauer Zarentum* (Stuttgart, 1989)

North, M., 'Bilanzen und Edelmetall im hansischen Rußlandhandel', in E. Hübner, E. Klug and J. Kusber (eds), *Zwischen Christianisierung und Europäisierung: Beiträge zur Geschichte Osteuropas in Mittelalter und Früher Neuzeit, Festschrift für Peter Nitsche zum 65. Geburtstag* (Stuttgart, 1998)

Ostrowski, D., *Muscovy and the Mongols: Cross-cultural influences on the steppe frontier, 1304–1589* (Cambridge, 1998)

Pickhan, G., *Gospodin Pskov: Entstehung und Entwicklung eines städtischen Herrschaftszentrums in Altrußland* (Berlin, 1992)

Rakova, M. M. and I. B. Rjazancev, *Istorija russkogo iskusstva*, I – *iskusstvo X – pervoj poloviny XIX veka* (Moscow, 1991)

Reichert, F., *Erfahrungen der Welt: Reisen und Kulturbegegnung im späten Mittelalter* (Stuttgart, 2001)

Rowell, S. C., 'Unexpected contacts: Lithuanians at western courts, *c.* 1316–*c.* 1400', *The English Historical Review*, 111:442 (1996), 557–77

Rowell, S. C., *Lithuania ascending: A pagan empire within east-central Europe 1295–1345* (Cambridge, 2000)
Rüss, H., *Adel und Adelsoppositionen im Moskauer Staat* (Wiesbaden, 1975)
Rüss, H., 'Das Reich von Kiev', in M. Hellmann (ed.), *Handbuch der Geschichte Rußlands*, I: *Bis 1613: Von der Kiever Reichsbildung bis zum Moskauer Zarentum* (Stuttgart, 1989)
Rüss, H., *Herren und Diener: Die soziale und politische Mentalität des russischen Adels, 9.–17. Jahrhundert* (Cologne, 1994)
Sach, M., *Hochmeister und Grossfürst: Die Beziehungen zwischen dem Deutschen Orden in Preussen und dem Moskauer Staat um die Wende zur Neuzeit* (Stuttgart, 2002)
Saunders, J. J., *History of the Mongol conquests* (London, 1971)
Schmidt, C., *Leibeigenschaft im Ostseeraum: Versuch einer Typologie* (Cologne, 1997)
Sinicyna, N. V., *Maksim Grek v Rossii* (Moscow, 1977)
Stökl, G., *Osteuropa: Geschichte und Politik* (Opladen, 1979)
Stökl, G. (ed.), *Der russische Staat im Mittelalter und früher Neuzeit: Ausgewählte Aufsätze* (Wiesbaden, 1981)
Stökl, G., *Russische Geschichte: Von den Anfängen bis zur Gegenwart* (5th edn, Stuttgart, 1990)
Tiberg, E., *Moscow, Livonia and the Hanseatic League 1487–1550* (Stockholm, 1995)
Zernack, K. *Die burgstädtischen Volksversammlungen bei den Ost- und Westslaven: Studien zur verfassungsgeschichtlichen Bedeutung der Veče* (Wiesbaden 1967)
Zernack, K., *Osteuropa: Eine Einführung in seine Geschichte* (Munich, 1977)

Chapter 9 Scandinavia

Alnæs, K., *A history of Norway in words and pictures* (Oslo, 2001)
Bagge, S., *Da boken kom til Norge* (Oslo, 2001)
Benedictow, O. J., *Plague in the late medieval Nordic countries: Epidemiological studies* (Oslo 1996)
Benedictow, O. J., 'Demographic conditions', in K. Helle (ed.), *The Cambridge history of Scandinavia*, I: *Prehistory to 1520* (Cambridge, 2003)
Benedictow, O. J., *Norges historie, V: 1448–1536* (Oslo, 1977)
Bergsland, K., 'Om middelalderens Finnmarker', *Historisk Tidsskrift*, 49 (1970), 365–409
Bøgh, A., 'On the causes of the Kalmar Union', in D. Kattinger et al. (eds), *'huru thet war talet i kalmarn': Union und Zusammenarbeit in der nordischen Geschichte: 600 Jahre Kalmarer Union (1397–1997)* (Hamburg, 1997)
Bøgh, A., '"Med Guds og Sankt Eriks hjælp". Sociale oprør i Sverige-Finland 1432–38', in A. Bøgh, J. W. Sørensen and L. Tvede-Jensen (eds), *Til kamp for friheden: Sociale oprør i nordisk middelalder* (Ålborg, 1988)
Bøgh, A., S. J. Würtz and L. Tvede-Jensen (eds), *Til kamp for friheden: Sociale oprør i nordisk middelalder* (Ålborg, 1988)
Bonsdorff, J. von, *Kunstproduktion und Kunstverbreitung im Ostseeraum des Spätmittelalters* (Helsinki, 1993)
Bonsdorff, J. von, 'Is art a barometer of wealth? Medieval art exports to the far north

of Europe', in D. Ormrod and M. North (eds), *Art markets in Europe, 1400–1800* (Aldershot, 1998)

Bracke, N., *Die Regierung Waldemars IV.* (Frankfurt, 1999)

Christensen, A. E., *Kalmarunionen og nordisk politik, 1319–1939* (Copenhagen, 1980)

Dahlbäck, G., 'En stad i staden: Om domkyrkans ekonomiska betydelse för Uppsala under senmedeltiden', in N. Cnattingius and T. Nevéus (eds), *Från Östra Aros till Uppsala: Ein samling uppsatser kring det medeltida Uppsala*, VII (Uppsala, 1986)

Derry, K. T., *A history of Scandinavia: Norway, Sweden, Denmark, Finland and Iceland* (8th edn, Minneapolis, 1996)

Dey, R., *Skandinavien: Dänemark, Norwegen, Schweden, Finnland; Kultur - Geschichte - Landschaft; von steingewordener Vergangenheit bis zur lebendigen Gegenwart* (12th edn, Cologne, 1989)

Ersgård, L. (ed.), *Rescue and research: Reflections of society in Sweden 700–1700* (Stockholm, 1992)

Etting, V., *Queen Margrete I, 1353–1412, and the founding of the Nordic Union* (Leiden, 2004)

Gissel, S., E. Jutikkala, E. Österberg, J. Sandnes and B. Teitsson, *Desertion and land colonisation in the Nordic countries c. 1300–1600: Comparative report from the Scandinavian research project on deserted farms and villages* (Stockholm, 1981)

Helle, K. (ed.), *The Cambridge history of Scandinavia*, I: *Prehistory to 1520* (Cambridge, 2003)

Helle, K., 'The Norwegian kingdom: Succession disputes and consolidation', in K. Helle (ed.), *Cambridge history of Scandinavia*, I

Henn, V., *Norwegen und die Hanse: wirtschaftliche und kulturelle Aspekte im europäischen Vergleich* (Frankfurt, 1994)

Hørby, K. et al., *Danmarks historie*, V: *Velstands krise og tusind baghold, 1250–1400* (Copenhagen, 1989)

Hørby, K. et al., *Danmarks historie*, II, 1: *1340–1559* (Copenhagen, 1980)

Jahnke, C., *Das Silber des Meeres: Fang und Vertrieb von Ostseehering zwischen Norwegen und Italien (12.–16. Jahrhundert)* (Cologne, 2000)

Jansson, V., *Eufemiavisorna: en filologisk undersökning* (Lund, 1945)

Jutikkala, E., *Geschichte Finnlands* (2nd edn, Stuttgart, 1976)

Kan, A. S., *Geschichte der skandinavischen Länder: (Dänemark, Norwegen, Schweden)* (Berlin, 1978)

Katajala, K., *Northern revolts: Medieval and early modern peasant unrest in the Nordic countries* (Helsinki, 2004)

Kaufhold, M., *Europas Norden im Mittelalter: Die Integration Skandinaviens in das christliche Europa (9.–13. Jahrhundert)* (Darmstadt, 2001)

Krötzel, C., *Pilger, Mirakel und Alltag: Formen des Verhaltens im skandinavischen Mittelalter (12.–15. Jahrhundert)* (Helsinki, 1994)

Kumlien, K., 'Stockholm, Lübeck und Westeuropa', in *Hansische Geschichtsblätter*, 71 (1952), 9–29

Link, A., *Auf dem Weg zur Landesuniversität: Studien zur Herkunft spätmittelalterlicher Studenten am Beispiel Greifswald (1456–1524)* (Stuttgart, 2000)

Lizska, T. R. and L. E. M. Walker (eds), *The North Sea world in the Middle Ages: Studies in the cultural history of north-western Europe* (Dublin, 2001)

McCuire, B. P. (ed.), *The birth of identities: Denmark and Europe in the Middle Ages* (Copenhagen, 1996)
Nedkvitne, A., 'Handelssjøfarten mellom Norge og England i høymiddelalderen', *Søfartshistorisk årbok*, 1976 (Bergen 1977)
Nicholas, D., *The northern lands: Germanic Europe, c. 1270–c. 1500* (Chichester, 2009)
North, M., 'Bilanzen im Lübecker Schwedenhandel (14.–16. Jahrhundert)', in R. Bohn (ed.), *Gotlandia Irredenta: Festschrift für Gunnar Svahnström zu seinem 75.* Geburtstag (Sigmaringen, 1990)
North, M., *Geldumlauf und Wirtschaftskonjunktur im südlichen Ostseeraum an der Wende zur Neuzeit (1440–1570)* (Sigmaringen, 1990)
Olesen, J. E., *Rigsråd – Kongemagt – Union: Studier over det danske rigsråd og den nordiske kongemagts politik 1439–1449* (Aarhus, 1980)
Olesen, J. E., 'Oprør og politisering i Sverige 1463–1471', in A. Bøgh, J. W. Sørensen and L. Tvede-Jensen (eds), *Til kamp for friheden: Sociale oprør i nordisk middelalder* (Ålborg, 1988)
Olesen, J. E., 'Christopher of Bavaria, King of Denmark, Norway and Sweden (1440–1448): Scandinavia and southern Germany in the fifteenth century', in W. Paravicini (ed.), *Nord und Süd in der deutschen Geschichte des Mittelalters* (Sigmaringen, 1990)
Olesen, J. E., 'Die doppelte Königswahl 1448 im Norden', in W. Paravicini (ed.), *Mare Balticum: Beiträge zur Geschichte des Ostseeraums in Mittelalter und Neuzeit* (Sigmaringen, 1992)
Olesen, J. E., 'Der Einfluß der Hanse auf die Gestaltung des Bürgertums in den skandinavischen Ländern im Spätmittelalter', in J. Tandecki, *Die Rolle der Stadtgemeinden und bürgerlichen Genossenschaften im Hanseraum in der Entwicklung und Vermittlung des gesellschaftlichen und kulturellen Gedankengutes im Spätmittelalter* (Toruń, 2000)
Olesen, J. E., 'Inter-Scandinavian relations', in K. Helle (ed.), *Cambridge history of Scandinavia*, I: *Prehistory to 1520* (Cambridge, 2003)
Olesen, J. E., 'Die Verbreitung des Schwarzen Todes in Skandinavien und Finnland', in T. Fischer and T. Riis (eds), *Tod und Trauer: Todeswahrnehmung und Trauerriten in Nordeuropa* (Kiel, 2006)
Orrman, E., 'Den värdsliga frälsejordens lokalisering i Finland under medeltiden och 1500-talet', in H. Ilsøe and B. Jørgensen (eds), *Plov og pen: Festskrift til Svend Gissel 4. Januar 1991* (Copenhagen, 1991)
Orrman, E., 'Rural conditions', in: K. Helle (ed.), *The Cambridge history of Scandinavia*, I: *Prehistory to 1520* (Cambridge 2003), 250–311
Orrman, E., 'The condition of the rural population', in K. Helle (ed.), *The Cambridge history of Scandinavia*, I: *Prehistory to 1520* (Cambridge, 2003), 592–7
Pipping, R., *Den fornsvenska litteraturen* (Stockholm, 1943)
Poulsen, B., 'Bonden overfor det eurpæiske marked: Et slesvigsk oprør 1472', in A. Bøgh, J. W. Sørensen and L. Tvede-Jensen (eds), *Til kamp for friheden*
Poulsen, B., 'Kingdoms on the periphery of Europe: The case of medieval and early modern Scandinavia', in R. Bonney (ed.), *Economic systems and state finance* (Oxford, 1995)
Poulsen, B., 'Land mobility in Denmark', in S. Cavaciocchi (ed.), *Il mercato della terra sec. XIII–XVIII* (Florence, 2004)

Poulsen, B., 'Late medieval and early modern peasants of west Jutland and their markets', in M. Guldberg, P. Holm and P. K. Madsen (eds), *Facing the North Sea: West Jutland and the world* (Esbjerg, 1993)
Riis, T. (ed.), *Das mittelalterliche dänische Ostseeimperium* (Odense, 2003)
Roding, J. G., 'The North Sea coasts, an architectural unity?', in J. G. Roding and L. H. van Voss (eds), *The North Sea and culture (1550–1800)* (Hilversum, 1996)
Ronge, H. H., *Konung Alexander: Filologiska studier i en fornsvensk text* (Uppsala, 1957)
Rosén, J., *Striden mellan Birger Magnusson och hans bröder* (Lund, 1939)
Sawyer, B. and P. Sawyer, *Medieval Scandinavia, ca. 800–1500* (Minneapolis, 1993)
Schück, H., 'Sweden under the dynasty of Folkungs', in K. Helle (ed.), *Cambridge history of Scandinavia*, I: *Prehistory to 1520* (Cambridge, 2003)
Schück, H., 'The political system', in K. Helle (ed.), *Cambridge history of Scandinavia*, I: *Prehistory to 1520* (Cambridge, 2003)
Scott, F. D., *Sweden: The nation's history* (7th edn, Carbondale, IL, 1997)
Skovgaard-Petersen, I., 'The Danish kingdom: Consolidation and disintegration', in K. Helle (ed.), *Cambridge history of Scandinavia*, I: *Prehistory to 1520* (Cambridge, 2003)
Ståhle, C. I., *Medeltidens profana literatur* (Stockholm, 1955)
Ulsig, E., 'The nobility of the late Middle Ages', in K. Helle (ed.), *Cambridge history of Scandinavia*, I: *Prehistory to 1520* (Cambridge, 2003)
Vahtola, J., 'Population and settlement', in K. Helle (ed.), *Cambridge history of Scandinavia*, I: *Prehistory to 1520* (Cambridge, 2003)
Würtz Sørensen, J., 'Bøndernes oprørspraksis i nordisk middelalder', in A. Bøgh, J. W. Sørensen and L. Tvede-Jensen (eds), *Til kamp for friheden: Sociale oprør i nordisk middelalder* (Ålborg, 1988)

Chapter 10 State and constitution

Allmand, C., 'War', in C. Allmand (ed.), *The New Cambridge medieval history*, VII, *c. 1415–c. 1500* (Cambridge, 1998)
Benedictow, O. J.. *The Black Death, 1346–1353: The complete history* (Woodbridge, 2004)
Blickle, P. (ed.), *Landgemeinde und Stadtgemeinde in Mitteleuropa: Ein struktureller Vergleich* (Munich, 1991)
Blickle, P., *Kommunalismus: Skizzen einer gesellschaftlichen Organisationsform* (2 vols, Munich, 2000)
Blockmans, W., *A history of power in Europe: Peoples, markets, states* (Antwerp, 1997)
Blockmans, W., 'Representation (since the thirtheenth century)', in C. Allmand (ed.), *New Cambridge medieval history*, VII, *c. 1415–c. 1500* (Cambridge, 1998)
Boone, M., K. Davids and P. Janssens (eds), *Urban public debts: Urban government and the market for annuities in western Europe (14th–18th centuries)* (Turnhout, 2003)
Cohn, S. K., *The Black Death transformed: Disease and culture in Renaissance Europe* (London, 2003)
Contamine, P., *Guerre, état et société à la fin du Moyen Age: Etudes sur les armées des rois de France* (Paris, 1972)
Contamine, P., *War in the Middle Ages* (Oxford, 1984)

Covini, M. N., 'Political and military bonds in the Italian state system, thirteenth to sixteenth centuries', in P. Contamine (ed.), *War and competition between states* (Oxford, 2000)

Dumolyn, J. and J. Haemers, 'Patterns of urban rebellion in medieval Flanders', *Journal of Medieval History*, 31 (2005), 369–93

Felloni, G., 'Kredit und Banken in Italien, 15.–17. Jahrhundert', in M. North (ed.), *Kredit im spätmittelalterlichen und frühneuzeitlichen Europa* (Cologne, 1991)

Fritze, K. and G. Krause, *Seekriege der Hanse: Das erste Kapitel deutsche Seekriegsgeschichte* (Berlin, 1997)

Hansen, M. H., *A comparative study in thirty city-state cultures: An investigation conducted by the Copenhagen Polis Centre, 1999 Symposium on the concepts of city-state and city-state culture* (Copenhagen, 2000)

Herlihy, D. and C. Klapisch-Zuber, *Tuscans and their families: A study of the Florentine catasto of 1427* (New Haven and London, 1985)

Hintze, O., 'Typologie der ständischen Verfassungen des Abendlandes', *Historische Zeitschrift*, 141 (1930), 229–48, reprinted in G. Oestreich (ed), *Otto Hintze. Staat und Verfassung: Gesammelte Abhandlungen zur allgemeinen Verfassungsgeschichte*, I (Göttingen, 1962)

Ihnatowicz, I., A. Mączak, B. Zientara and J. Żarnowski, *Społeczeństwo polskie od X do XX wieku* (3rd edn, Warsaw, 1996)

Lane, F. C., *Venetian ships and shipbuilders of the Renaissance* (Baltimore, 1992)

Mager, W., *Die Entstehung des modernen Staatenbegriffs* (Mainz, 1968)

Mallett, M. E., *Mercenaries and their masters: Warfare in Renaissance Italy* (London, 1974)

Mallett, M. E., 'The art of war', in T. A. Brady, H. A. Obermann and J. D. Tracy (eds), *Handbook of European history, 1400–1600: Late Middle Ages, Renaissance and Reformation*, I: *Structures and assertions* (Leiden, 1999)

Mallett, M. E. and J. R. Hale, *The military organization of a Renaissance state: Venice, c. 1400–1617* (Cambridge, 1984)

Manikowska, H. and J. Pánek (eds), *Political culture in central Europe (10th–20th century)*, I, *Middle Ages and early modern era* (Prague, 2005)

Mitteis, H., *Der Staat des hohen Mittelalters: Grundlinien einer vergleichenden Verfassungsgeschichte des Lehnszeitalters* (11th edn, Cologne, 1986)

Moraw, P., 'Die Verwaltung des Königtums und des Reiches und ihre Rahmenbedingungen', in *Deutsche Verwaltungsgeschichte*, I, *Vom Spätmittelalter bis zum Ende des Reiches* (Stuttgart, 1983)

Ormrod, W. M., 'England in the Middle Ages', in R. Bonney (ed.), *The rise of the fiscal state in Europe, c. 1200–1815* (Oxford, 1999)

Paravicini, W. and K. F. Werner (eds), *Histoire comparée de l'administration (IVe–XVIIIe siècles)* (Munich, 1980)

Peyer, H. C., 'Die wirtschaftliche Bedeutung der fremden Dienste für die Schweiz vom 15. bis zum 18. Jahrhundert', in H. C. Peyer, *Könige, Stadt und Kapitel: Aufsätze zur Wirtschafts- und Sozialgeschichte des Mittelalters* (Zurich, 1982)

Pezzolo, L., *Il fisco dei veneziani: Finanza pubblica ed economia tra XV e XVII secolo* (Verona, 2003)

Pezzolo, L., 'Bonds und government debt in Italian city-states, 1250–1650', in W. N.

Goetzmann and K. G. Rouwenhorst (eds), *Of value: The financial innovations that created modern capital markets* (Oxford, 2005)
Puhle, M., 'Organisationsmerkmale der Hanse', in J. Bracker, V. Henn and R. Postel (eds), *Die Hanse: Lebenswirklichkeit und Mythos* (Lübeck, 1998)
Rösch, G., *Der venezianische Adel bis zur Schließung des Großen Rats: Zur Genese einer Führungsschicht* (Sigmaringen, 1989)
Russocki, S., 'Początki zgromadzeń stanowych w Europie Środkowej', *Przegląd Historyczny*, 66 (1975)
Schmidt, G., *Geschichte des Alten Reiches: Staat und Nation in der Frühen Neuzeit 1495–1806* (Munich, 1999)
Schmidtchen, V., 'Aspekte des Strukturwandels im europäischen Kriegswesen des späten Mittelalters und ihre Ursachen', in F. Seibt and W. Eberhard (eds), *Europa 1500. Integrationsprozesse im Widerstreit: Staaten, Regionen, Personenverbände, Christenheit* (Stuttgart, 1987)
Schneider, R. (ed.), *Das spätmittelalterliche Königtum im europäischen Vergleich* (Sigmarinen, 1987)
Strayer, J. R., *Die mittelalterlichen Grundlagen des modernen Staates* (Cologne, 1975)
Watts, J., *The making of polities: Europe, 1300–1500* (Cambridge, 2009)

Chapter 11 The economy

Abel, W., *Agrarkrisen und Agrarkonjunktur: Eine Geschichte der Land- und Ernährungswirtschaft Mitteleuropas seit dem hohen Mittelalter* (2nd edn, Hamburg, 1966)
Abel, W., *Strukturen und Krisen der spätmittelalterlichen Wirtschaft* (Stuttgart, 1980)
Abulafia, D., 'Asia, Africa and the trade of medieval Europe', in M. M. Postan and E. Miller (eds), *The Cambridge economic history of Europe*, II, *Trade and industry in the Middle Ages* (Cambridge, 1987)
Arnoux, M. and P. Monnet (eds), *Le technicien dans la cité en Europe occidentale 1250–1650* (Rome, 2004)
Attman, A., *The bullion flow between Europe and the East 1000–1750* (Göteborg, 1981)
Beloch, K. J., *Bevölkerungsgeschichte Italiens*, III: *Die Bevölkerung der Republik Venedig, des Herzogtums Mailand, Piemonts, Genuas, Corsicas und Sardiniens: Die Gesamtbevölkerung Italiens* (Berlin, 1961)
Benedictow, O. J.. *The Black Death, 1346–1353: The complete history* (Woodbridge, 2004)
Bruce, S. G., *Ecologies and economies in medieval and early modern Europe: Studies in environmental history* (Boston, 2010)
Campbell, B. M. S., *English seigniorial agriculture, 1250–1450* (Cambridge, 2000)
Campbell, B. M. S., 'Land, labour, livestock, and productivity trends in English seigniorial agriculture, 1208–1450', in B. M. S. Campbell and Mark Overton (eds), *Land, labour and livestock: Historical studies in European agricultural productivity* (Manchester, 1991)
Cavaciocchi, S. (ed.), *La seta in Europa secoli XIII–XVIII* (Florence, 1993)
Cherubini, G., *Agricoltura e società rurale nel Medioevo* (Florence, 1972)
Cipolla, C. M (ed.), *Fontana economic history of Europe* (6 vols, London, 1972–76)
Cohn, S. K., *The Black Death transformed: Disease and culture in Renaissance Europe* (London, 2003)

Day, J., 'The great bullion famine of the fifteenth century', *Past & Present*, 79 (1978), 3–54

Day, J., 'The question of monetary contraction in late medieval Europe', *Nordisk Numismatisk Årsskrift* (1981), 12–29

De Vries, J., 'Population', in T. A. Brady, H. A. Obermann and J. D. Tracy (eds), *Handbook of European History 1400–1600: late Middle Ages, Renaissance and Reformation*, I: *Structures and assertions* (Leiden, 1994)

Epstein, St. A., *An economic and social history of later medieval Europe, 1000–1500* (Cambridge, 2009)

Epstein, St. R., *Freedom and growth: The rise of states and markets in Europe, 1300–1750* (London, 2000)

Fritze, K. and G. Krause, *Seekriege der Hanse: Das erste Kapitel deutsche Seekriegsgeschichte* (Berlin, 1997)

Ganshof, F. L. and A. Verhulst, 'Medieval agrarian society in its prime. 1: France, The Low Countries, and Western Germany', in M. M. Postan (ed.), *The Cambridge economic history of Europe*, I: *The Agrarian Life of the Middle Ages* (2nd edn, Cambridge, 1966)

Goldthwaithe, R. A., *The economy of Renaissance Florence* (Baltimore, 2009)

Herlihy, D. and C. Klapisch-Zuber, *Tuscans and their families: A study of the Florentine catasto of 1427* (New Haven, 1985)

Howell, M. C., *Commerce before capitalism in Europe, 1300–1600* (New York, 2010)

Hunt, E. S. and J. M. Murray, *A history of business in medieval Europe 1200–1550* (Cambridge, 1999)

Jenks, St., 'Von den archaischen Grundlagen bis zur Schwelle der Moderne (ca. 1000–1540)', in M. North (ed.), *Deutsche Wirtschaftsgeschichte: Ein Jahrtausend im Überblick* (2nd edn, Munich, 2005)

Jones, P., 'Medieval agrarian society in its prime, 2: Italy', in M. M. Postan (ed.), *Cambridge economic history of Europe*, I (Cambridge, 1966)

Klapisch-Zuber, C. (ed.), *Women, family and the ritual in Renaissance Italy* (Chicago, 1987)

Klapisch-Zuber, C., *La maison et le nom: Stratégies et rituels dans l'Italie de la Renaissance* (Paris, 1990)

Klapisch-Zuber, C., *A history of women in the west*, II: *Silences of the Middle Ages* (Cambridge, MA, 1992)

Lane, F. C., *Venetian ships and shipbuilders of the Renaissance* (Baltimore, 1992)

Lane, F. C. and R. C. Mueller, *Money and banking in medieval and Renaissance Venice* (Baltimore, 1985)

Lopez, R. S., *The commercial revolution of the Middle Ages 950–1350* (Englewood Cliffs, NJ, 1971)

Lopez, R. S., 'The trade of medieval Europe: The south', in M. M. Postan and Edward Miller (eds), *The Cambridge economic history of Europe*, II: *Trade and industry in the Middle Ages* (Cambridge, 1987)

Macháček, J., *The rise of medieval towns and states in east central Europe: Early medieval centres as social and economic systems* (Leiden, 2010)

Menning, C. B., *Charity and state in late Renaissance Italy: the Monte di Pietà of Florence* (Ithaca, 1993)

Mitterauer, M., *Warum Europa? Mittelalterliche Grundlagen eines Sonderwegs* (Munich, 2003)

Molà, L., *La comunità dei lucchesi a Venezia: immigrazione e industria della seta nel tardo Medioevo* (Venice, 1994)

Mueller, R. C., 'Les prêteurs juifs de Venise au Moyen Âge', in *Annales*, 30 (1975), 1277–302

Munro, J. H., 'Medieval woollens: The Western European woollen industries and their struggles for international markets, *c.* 1000–1500', in D. Jenkins (ed.), *The Cambridge history of western textiles*, I (2 vols, Cambridge, 2003)

North, M., *Kredit im spätmittelalterlichen und frühneuzeitlichen Europa* (Cologne, 1991)

North, M., *Das Geld und seine Geschichte vom Mittelalter bis zur Gegenwart* (Munich, 1994)

North, M., 'Die Entstehung der Gutswirtschaft im südlichen Ostseeraum', *Zeitschrift für Historische Forschung*, 26 (1999), 43–59

North, M., *Kleine Geschichte des Geldes: Vom Mittelalter bis heute* (Munich, 2009)

Oexle, O. G., 'Die funktionale Dreiteilung als Deutungsschema der sozialen Wirklichkeit in der ständischen Gesellschaft des Mittelalters', in W. Schulze (ed.), *Ständische Gesellschaft und soziale Mobilität* (Munich, 1988)

Postan, M. M., 'The trade of medieval Europe: The North', in M. M. Postan and E. Miller (eds), *The Cambridge economic history of Europe*, II (Cambridge, 1987)

Pounds, N. J. G., *An economic history of medieval Europe* (2nd edn, London, 1994)

Reichert, W., 'Lombarden zwischen Rhein und Maas', *Rheinische Vierteljahrsblätter*, 51 (1987), 188–223

Russell, J. C., *Late ancient and medieval population* (Philadelphia, 1958)

Russell, J. C., 'Late medieval Balkan and Asia Minor population', *Journal of Economic and Social History of the Orient*, 3 (1960), 265–74

Russell, J. C., *Population in Europe 500–1500* (London, 1969)

Russell, J. C., 'Population in Europe 500–1500', in C. M. Cipolla (ed.), *The Fontana economic history of Europe*, I: *The Middle Ages* (London, 1972)

Soetaert, P., *De 'Berg van Charitate' te Brugge, een stedelijke leenbank (1573–1795)* (Brussels, 1974)

Spufford, P., *Money and its use in medieval Europe* (Cambridge, 1988)

Spufford, P., *Power and profit: The merchant in medieval Europe* (London, 2003)

Stromer, W. von, *Die Gründung der Baumwollindustrie in Mitteleuropa* (Stuttgart, 1978)

Suhling, L., *Der Seigerhüttenprozeß: Die Technologie des Kupferseigerns nach dem frühen metallurgischen Schrifttum* (Stuttgart, 1976)

Thornton, C., 'The determinants of land productivity on the bishop of Winchester's demesne of Rimpton, 1208 to 1403', in B. M. S. Campbell and M. Overton (eds), *Land, labour and livestock: Historical studies in European agricultural productivity* (Manchester, 1991)

Tracy, J. D. (ed.), *The political economy of merchant empires* (Cambridge, 1994)

Van der Wee, H., *The growth of the Antwerp market and the European economy (fourteenth–sixteenth centuries)* (3 vols, Louvain, 1963)

Van der Wee, H., *The Low Countries in the early modern world* (Aldershot, 1993)

Van der Wee, H., 'European banking in the Middle Ages and early modern times (476–1789)', in H. van der Wee and G. Kurgan-Van Hentenryk (eds), *A history of*

European banking (Antwerp, 2000)
Van der Wee, H. and J. H. Munro, 'The western European woollen industries, 1500–1750', in D. Jenkins (ed.), *The Cambridge history of western textiles*, I (Cambridge, 2003)
Van Zanden, L. J., *The long road to the industrial revolution: The European economy in a global perspective, 1000–1800* (Leiden, 2009)
Westermann, E., *Das Eislebener Garkupfer und seine Bedeutung für den europäischen Kupfermarkt 1460–1560* (Cologne, 1971)

Chapter 12 Society

Areford, D. S., *The viewer and the printed image in late medieval Europe* (Farnham, 2010)
Arriaza, A., 'Le Statut nobiliaire adapté à la bourgeoisie: mobilité des statuts en Castille à la fin du Moyen Age', *Le Moyen Age*, 100 (1994), 413–38 and 101 (1995), 89–101
Autrand, F., *Pouvoir et société en France, XIVe–XVe siècles* (Paris, 1974)
Bak, J. M. (ed.), *Nobilities in central and eastern Europe: Kinship, property and privilege* (Budapest, 1994)
Ben-Sasson, H. H. (ed.), *A history of the Jewish people* (Cambridge, MA, 1985)
Blamires, A., *The case of women in medieval culture* (Oxford, 1997)
Blickle, P. *The revolution of 1525: The German Peasants' War from a new perspective* (Baltimore, 1985)
Blickle, P., 'Unruhen in der ständischen Gesellschaft 1300–1800', *Enzyklopädie deutscher Geschichte*, I (Munich, 1988)
Blickle, P., *Communal reformation: The quest for salvation in sixteenth-century Germany* (Atlantic Highlands, NJ, 1992)
Blickle, P., *Von der Leibeigenschaft zu den Menschenrechten: Eine Geschichte der Freiheit in Deutschland* (Munich, 2003)
Bock, G., *Women in European history*, trans. Allison Brown (Oxford, 2002)
Bog, I., 'Reichsverfassung und reichsstädtische Gesellschaft: Sozialgeschichtliche Forschungen über reichsständische Residenten in den Freien Städten, insbesondere in Nürnberg', *Jahrbuch für fränkische Landesforschung*, 18 (1958), 325–99
Blockmans, W. P., 'Alternatives to monarchical centralisation. The great tradition of revolt in Flanders and Brabant', in H. G. Koenigsberger (ed.), *Republiken und Republikanismus im Europa der Frühen Neuzeit* (Munich, 1988)
Boockmann, H., *Fürsten, Bürger, Edelleute: Lebensbilder aus dem späten Mittelalter* (Munich, 1994)
Braudel, F., *The structures of everday life: The limits of the possible* (London, 2002)
Brunner, O., *Sozialgeschichte Europas im Mittelalter* (2nd edn, Göttingen, 984)
Campbell, B. M. S., *English seigniorial agriculture, 1250–1450* (Cambridge, 2000)
Contamine, P., *La noblesse au royaume de France de Philippe le Bel à Louis XII* (Paris, 1997)
Contamine, P., 'The European nobility', in C. Allmand (ed.), *New Cambridge medieval history*, VII: *c. 1415–c. 1500* (Cambridge, 1998)
Czermak, G., *Christen gegen Juden: Geschichte einer Verfolgung* (Frankfurt, 1991)

Dewald, J., *The European nobility, 1400–1800* (Cambridge, 1996)
Dumolyn, J. and J. Haemers, 'Patterns of urban rebellion in medieval Flanders', *Journal of Medieval History*, 31 (2005), 369–93
Ennen, E., *Die europäische Stadt des Mittelalters* (Göttingen, 1987)
Erler, M. C. and M. Kowaleski (eds), *Gendering the master narrative: Women and power in the Middle Ages* (Ithaca, 2003)
Fossier, R., *Peasant life in the medieval west* (Oxford, 1988)
Geremek, B., *Poverty: A history*, trans. Agnieska Kolakowska (Oxford, 1994)
Graßmann, A., 'Sozialer Aufstieg in Lübeck um 1500', in G. Schulz (ed.), *Sozialer Aufstieg: Funktionseliten im Spätmittelalter und in der Frühen Neuzeit* (Munich, 2002)
Greive, H., *Die Juden: Grundzüge ihrer Geschichte im mittelalterlichen und neuzeitlichen Europa* (Darmstadt, 1992)
Harksen, S., *Die Frau im Mittelalter* (Leipzig, 1974)
Hergemöller, B.-U. (ed.), *Die Randgruppen der spätmittelalterlichen Gesellschaft* (Warendorf, 2001)
Hilton, R., *Bond men made free: Medieval peasant movements and the English rising of 1381* (London, 1993)
Hindley, A. (ed.), *Drama and community: People and plays in medieval Europe* (Turnhout, 1999)
Ihnatowicz, I., A. Mączak and B. Zientara, *Społeczeństwo polskie od X do XX wieku* (Warsaw, 1979)
Irsigler, F., 'Der Alltag einer hansischen Kaufmannsfamilie im Spiegel der Veckinchusen-Briefe', *Hansische Geschichtsblätter*, 103 (1985), 75–99
Irsigler, F. and A. Lasotta, *Bettler und Gaukler, Dirnen und Henker. Außenseiter in einer mittelalterlichen Stadt: Köln 1300–1600* (Munich, 1989)
Isenmann, E., *Die deutsche Stadt im Spätmittelalter: 1250–1500. Stadtgestalt, Recht, Stadtregiment, Kirche, Gesellschaft, Wirtschaft* (Stuttgart, 1988)
Jütte, R., *Obrigkeitliche Armenfürsorge in deutschen Reichsstädten der Frühen Neuzeit: städtisches Armenwesen in Frankfurt am Main und Köln* (Cologne, 1984)
Klapisch-Zuber, C., *Women, family and ritual in Renaissance Italy* (Chicago, 1987)
Klapisch-Zuber, C., *A history of women in the West*, II: *Silences of the Middle Ages* (Cambridge, MA, 1992)
Kotowski, E.-V., *Länder und Regionen* (Darmstadt, 2001)
Laboulaye, E. and R. Dareste (eds), *Jacques d'Ableiges, le grand coutumier de France* (Paris, 1868)
Lilley, K. D., *Urban life in the Middle Ages 1000–1450* (Basingstoke, 2002)
McGee, T. J. (ed.), *Instruments and their music in the Middle Ages* (Farnham, 2009)
Mitterauer, M., *Warum Europa? Mittelalterliche Grundlagen eines Sonderwegs* (Munich, 2003)
Mollat, M., *The poor in the Middle Ages: An essay in social history* (New Haven and London, 1986)
Moore, R. I., *Die erste europäische Revolution: Gesellschaft und Kultur im Hochmittelalter* (Munich, 2001)
Morsel, J., 'Inventing a social category: The sociogenesis of the nobility at the end of the Middle Ages', in B. Jussen (ed.), *Ordering medieval society: Perspectives on*

intellectual and practical modes of shaping social relations (Philadelphia, 2001), 200–38

Morsel, J., *L'aristocratie médiévale: La domination sociale en occident (Xe–XVe siècle)* (Paris, 2004)

Mueller, R. C., 'Les prêteurs juifs de Venise au Moyen Âge', *Annales*, 30 (1975), 1277–302

Nicholas, D., *The transformation of Europe 1300–1600* (London, 1999)

Nicholas, D., *Urban Europe, 1100–1700* (Houndmills, 2003)

North, M., 'Die Entstehung der Gutswirtschaft im südlichen Ostseeraum', *Zeitschrift für Historische Forschung*, 26 (1999), 43–59

Oexle, O. G., 'Die funktionale Dreiteilung als Deutungsschema der sozialen Wirklichkeit in der ständischen Gesellschaft des Mittelalters', in W. Schulze (ed.), *Ständische Gesellschaft und soziale Mobilität* (Munich, 1988)

Oexle, O. G., 'Stand, Klasse (Antike und Mittelalter)', in O. Brunner, W. Conze and R. Koselleck (eds), *Geschichtliche Grundbegriffe: Historisches Lexikon zur politisch-sozialen Sprache in Deutschland*, VI (Stuttgart, 1990)

Oexle, O. G., 'Versuche der kategorialen Erfassung der ständischen Gesellschaft', in W. Schulze (ed.), *Ständische Gesellschaft und soziale Mobilität* (Munich, 1998)

Origo, I., *The merchant of Prato: Francesco di Marco Datini 1335–1410* (London, 1992)

Palme, R., 'Städtische Sozialpolitik bis zum 16. Jahrhundert', in H. Pohl (ed.), *Staatliche, städtische, betriebliche und kirchliche Sozialpolitik vom Mittelalter bis zur Gegenwart* (Stuttgart, 1991)

Paravicini, W., *Die ritterlich-höfische Kultur des Mittelalters* (Munich, 1994)

Pernoud, R., *Visages de femmes au Moyen Age* (Saint-Léger-Vauban, 1998)

Pernoud, R., *Women in the days of cathedrals*, trans. and ed. A. Coté-Harriss (San Francisco, 1998)

Petkov, K., *The kiss of peace: Ritual, self and society in the high and late medieval west* (Leiden, 2003)

Power, E., *Medieval women* (Cambridge, 1997)

Rösener, W., *Bauern in der europäischen Geschichte* (Munich, 1993)

Rösener, W., *The peasantry of Europe* (Oxford, 1994)

Rösener, W., 'Peasant revolts in late medieval Germany and the Peasants' War of 1525', in K. Haarstad and A. Mikkelsen (eds), *Tretvik Bonder, jord og rettigheter: Rapport fra agrarhistorisk symposium* (Trondheim, 1996)

Schuster, P., *Das Frauenhaus: Städtische Bordelle in Deutschland 1350 bis 1600* (Paderborn, 1992)

Scott, T. (ed.), *The peasantries of Europe from the fourteenth to the eighteenth centuries* (London, 1988)

Spieß, K.-H., 'Aufstieg in den Adel und Kriterien der Adelszugehörigkeit im Spätmittelalter', in K. Andermann and P. Johanek (eds), *Zwischen Nichtadel und Adel* (Stuttgart, 2001)

Spieß, K.-H., 'Ständische Abgrenzung und soziale Differenzierung zwischen Hochadel und Ritteradel im Spätmittelalter', *Rheinische Vierteljahrsblätter*, 56 (1992), 181–205

Thrupp, S. L. (ed.), *Change in medieval society: Europe north of the Alps, 1050–1500* (New York, 1964)

Toch, M., *Die Juden im mittelalterlichen Reich* (Munich, 1998)

Toch, M., *Peasants and Jews in Medieval Germany: studies in cultural, social and economic history* (Burlington, 2003)

Trexler, R. C., 'La prostitution florentine au XVe siecle', *Annales*, 36 (1981), 983–1015

Veltri, G. (ed.), *An der Schwelle zur Moderne: Juden in der Renaissance* (Leiden, 2003)

Vitullo, J. and D. Wolfthal (eds), *Money, morality, and culture in late medieval and early modern Europe* (Farnham, 2010)

Ward, J. C., *English noblewomen in the later Middle Ages* (London, 1992)

Wensky, M., *Die Stellung der Frau in der stadtkölnischen Wirtschaft im Spätmittelalter* (Cologne, 1980)

Wensky, M., 'Städtische Führungsschichten im Spätmittelalter', in G. Schulz (ed.), *Sozialer Aufstieg: Funktionseliten im Spätmittelalter und in der frühen Neuzeit* (Munich, 2002)

Wunder, H., '"Jede Arbeit ist ihres Lohnes wert": Zur geschlechtsspezifischen Teilung und Bewertung von Arbeit in der Frühen Neuzeit', in K. Hausen (ed.), *Geschlechterhierarchie und Arbeitsteilung: Zur Geschichte ungleicher Erwerbschancen von Männern und Frauen* (Göttingen, 1993)

Chapter 13 Culture and religion

13.1/13.2 Humanism and Renaissance

Aikema, B. and B. L. Brown (eds), *Renaissance Venice and the north: Crosscurrents in the time of Dürer, Bellini and Titian* (Milan, 1999)

Ames-Lewis, F., *The intellectual life of the early Renaissance artist* (2nd edn, New Haven, 2002)

Aston, M., *The panorama of the Renaissance* (London, 1996)

Baron, H., *The crisis of the early Italian Renaissance: Civic humanism and republican liberty in an age of classicism and tyranny* (2 vols, Princeton, 1955)

Baron, H., *In search of Florentine civic humanism: Essays on the transition from medieval to modern thought* (2 vols, Princeton, 1988)

Borchert, T.-H. (ed.), *The age of van Eyck 1430–1530: The Mediterranean world and early Netherlandish painting* (Ghent, 2002)

Burckhardt, J., *The civilization of the Renaissance in Italy* (London, 1990)

Burke, P., *The European Renaissance: Centres and peripheries* (Oxford, 1998)

Burke, P., *The Italian Renaissance: Culture and society in Italy* (Princeton, 1999)

Burke, P., 'The spread of Italian humanism', in A. Goodman and A. MacKay (eds), *The impact of humanism on western Europe* (London, 1990)

Campbell, G., *The Oxford dictionary of the Renaissance* (Oxford, 2003)

Chaix, G., *La Renaissance des années 1470 aux années 1560* (Paris, 2003)

D'Amico, J. F., *Roman and German humanism 1450–1550* (Aldershot, 1993)

Edgerton, S. Y., *The Renaissance rediscovery of linear perspective* (New York, 1975)

Engel-Jánosi, F., 'Soziale Probleme der Renaissance', *Historische Zeitschrift*, 132 (1925), 136–41

Gersh, S. and B. Roest (ed.), *Medieval and Renaissance humanism: Rhetoric, representation and reform* (Leiden, 2003)

Goodman, A. and A. MacKay (eds), *The impact of humanism on western Europe* (London, 1990)

Grafton, A. and L. Jardine, *From humanism to the humanities: Education and the liberal arts in fifteenth- and sixteenth-century Europe* (Cambridge, 1986)
Gramsch, R., *Erfurter Juristen im Spätmittelalter: Die Karrieremuster und Tätigkeitsfelder einer gelehrten Elite des 14. und 15. Jahrhunderts* (Leiden, 2003)
Hankins, J. (ed.), *Renaissance civic humanism: Reappraisals and reflections* (Cambridge, 2000)
Haskell, F. and N. Penny, *Taste and the antique: The lure of classical sculpture 1500–1900* (New Haven and London, 1998)
Helmrath, J., U. Muhlack and G. Walther (eds), *Diffusion des Humanismus: Studien zur nationalen Geschichtsschreibung europäischer Humanisten* (Göttingen, 2002)
Kallendorf, C. W. (ed.), *Humanist educational treatises* (Cambridge, 2002)
Klaniczay, T. and J. Jankovics (eds), *Matthias Corvinus and the humanism in Central Europe* (Budapest, 1994)
Lembke, S. and M. Müller (eds), *Humanisten am Oberrhein: Neue Gelehrte im Dienst alter Herren* (Leinfelden-Echterdingen, 2004)
Levi, A., *Renaissance and Reformation: The intellectual genesis* (New Haven, 2002)
Machilek, F., 'Konrad Celtis und die Gelehrtensodalitäten, insbesondere in Ostmitteleuropa', in W. Eberhard and A. A. Strnad (eds), *Humanismus und Renaissance in Ostmitteleuropa vor der Reformation* (Cologne, 1996)
McLaughlin, M. (ed.), *Bonae litterae: Current research on the studia humanitatis* (Oxford, 2003)
Melches, C., *Aspekte des Humanismus in Spanien* (Cuxhaven, 2003)
Mout, N. (ed.), *Die Kultur des Humanismus: Reden, Briefe, Traktate, Gespräche von Petrarca bis Kepler* (Munich, 1998)
Nauert, Ch. G. Jr., *Humanism and the culture of Renaissance Europe* (Cambridge, 1995)
Overfield, J., *Humanism and scholasticism in late medieval Germany* (Princeton, 1984)
Pellegrini, P. (ed.), *Dal medioevo all'umanesimo: la riscoperta dei classici* (Milan, 2001)
Rabil Jr., A., *Renaissance humanism: Foundations, forms and legacy* (3 vols, Philadelphia, 1988)
Reinhardt, V., *Die Renaissance in Italien: Geschichte und Kultur* (Munich, 2002)
Ruggiero, G., *A companion to the worlds of the Renaissance* (Oxford, 2002)
Saygin, S., *Humphrey, duke of Gloucester (1390–1447) and the Italian humanists* (Leiden, 2001)
Screech, M. A., *Erasmus: Ecstasy and the praise of folly* (2nd edn, London, 1988)
Segel, H. B., *Renaissance culture in Poland: The rise of humanism 1470–1543* (Ithaca, 1989)
Strnad, A. A., 'Die Rezeption von Humanismus und Renaissance in Wien', in W. Eberhard and A. A. Strnad (eds), *Humanismus und Renaissance in Ostmitteleuropa vor der Reformation* (Cologne et al., 1996)
Wilson-Okamura, D. S., *Virgil in the Renaissance* (New York, 2010)
Woolfson, J., *Reassessing Tudor humanism* (Basingstoke, 2002)

13.3 Universities

Cardini, F. (ed.), *Universitäten im Mittelalter: die europäischen Stätten des Wissens* (Munich, 1991)

Moraw, P., 'Einheit und Vielfalt der Universität im alten Europa', in A. Patschovsky and H. Rabe (eds), *Die Universität in Alteuropa* (Konstanz, 1994)

Pedersen, O., *The first universities: Studium generale and the origins of university education in Europe* (Cambridge, 2009)

Schwinges, R. C., 'Europäische Studenten des späten Mittelalters', in A. Patschovsky and H. Rabe (eds), *Die Universität in Alteuropa* (Konstanz, 1994)

Schwinges, R. C. (ed.), *Artisten und Philosophen: Wissenschafts- und Wirkungsgeschichte einer Fakultät* (Basel, 1999)

Verger, J., 'Patterns', in H. de Ridder-Symoens (ed.), *A history of the university in Europe*, I: *Universities in the Middle Ages* (Cambridge, 1991)

Weber, W. E. J., *Geschichte der europäischen Universität* (Stuttgart, 2002)

13.4 The Church

Angenendt, A., *Geschichte der Religiosität im Mittelalter* (Darmstadt, 1997)

Barraclough, G., *The medieval papacy* (London, 1968)

Benrath, G. A. (ed.), *Wegbereiter der Reformation* (Bremen, 1967)

Blickle, P., *Die Reformation im Reich* (3rd edn, Stuttgart, 2000)

Bove, B., *Le temps de la guerre de Cent Ans, 1328–1453* (Berlin, 2009)

Brandmüller, W., 'Zur Frage nach der Gültigkeit der Wahl Urbans VI.: Quellen und Quellenkritik', in W. Brandmüller, *Papst und Konzil im Großen Schisma (1378–1431): Studien und Quellen* (Paderborn, 1990), 3–41

Brandmüller, W., 'Der Übergang vom Pontifikat Martins V. zu Eugen IV.', in W. Brandmüller, *Papst und Konzil im Großen Schisma (1378–1431): Studien und Quellen* (Paderborn, 1990), 85–110

Brandmüller, W., *Das Konzil von Konstanz 1414–1418*, I: *Bis zur Abreise Sigismunds nach Narbonne* (Paderborn, 1991); II: *Bis zum Konzilende* (Paderborn, 1997)

Catto J. I., 'Wycliff and Wycliffism at Oxford, 1356–1403', in J. I. Catto and T. A. R. Evans (eds), *The history of the University of Oxford*, II: *Late mediaeval Oxford* (Oxford, 1992)

Costen, M., *The Cathars and the Albigensian crusade* (Manchester, 1997)

Erbstößer, M., *Religion und Klassenkampf im Spätmittelalter: Geißler, Freigeister und Waldenser im 14. Jahrhundert* (Leipzig, 1966)

Favier, J., *Philippe le Bel* (Paris, 1978)

Favier, J., *Histoire de France*, II: *Le Temps des principautés 1000–1515* (Paris, 1992)

Fine Jr., J. V. A., *The Bosnian Church: A new interpretation: A study of the Bosnian Church and its place in state and society from the thirteenth to the fifteenth centuries* (Boulder, 1975)

Fudge, T. A., *The magnificent ride: The first reformation in Hussite Bohemia* (Aldershot, 1998)

Hamilton, B., 'The Albigensian crusade and heresy', in D. Abulafia (ed.), *The new Cambridge medieval history*, V: *c. 1198–c. 1300* (Cambridge, 1999)

Hamilton, B., 'The Cathars and Christian perfection', in P. Biller and B. Dobson (eds), *The medieval Church: Universities, heresy and the religious life* (Woodbridge, 1999), 5–23

Hamm, B., 'Frömmigkeit als Gegenstand theologiegeschichtlicher Forschung: Methodisch-historische Überlegungen am Beispiel von Spätmittelalter und Reformation',

Zeitschrift für Theologie und Kirche, 74 (1977), 464–97
Helmrath, J., *Das Basler Konzil 1431–1449: Forschungsstand und Probleme* (Cologne, 1987)
Hösch, E., *Orthodoxie und Häresie im alten Rußland* (Wiesbaden, 1975)
Hudson, A. and M. Wilks (eds), *From Ockham to Wycliff* (Oxford, 1987)
Lourdaux, W., 'Les Dévots modernes, rénovateurs de la vie intellectuelle', *Bijdragen en mededelingen betreffende de geschiedenis der Nederlanden* 95 (1980), 279–97
Martin, J., *Medieval Russia, 980–1584* (Cambridge, 1995)
McGinn, B., *The harvest of mysticism in medieval Germany (1300–1500)* (New York, 2005)
Mertens, D., 'Monastische Reformbewegungen des 15. Jahrhunderts: Ideen - Ziele - Resultate', in I. Hlaváček and A. Patschovsky (eds), *Reform von Kirche und Reich zur Zeit der Konzilien von Konstanz (1414–1418) und Basel (1431–1449)* (Konstanz, 1996)
Meuthen, E., 'Die deutsche Legationsreise des Nikolaus von Kues 1451/1452', in H. Boockmann et al. (eds), *Lebenslehren und Weltentwürfe im Übergang vom Mittelalter zur Neuzeit: Politik - Bildung - Naturkunde - Theologie* (Göttingen, 1989)
Mollat, G., *The popes at Avignon: 1305–1378*, trans. Janet Love (London, 1963)
Müller, A. and K. Stöber, *Self-representation of medieval religious communities: The British isles in context* (Berlin, 2009)
Müller, H., *Die Franzosen, Frankreich und das Basler Konzil (1431–1449)* (2 vols, Paderborn, 1990)
North, M., *De geschiedenis van Nederland* (Amsterdam, 2008)
Ostrowski, D., 'Church polemics and monastic land acquisition in sixteenth-century Muscovy', *Slavonic and East European Review*, 64:3 (1986), 355–79
Post, R. R., *Kerkelijke verhoudingen in Nederland voor de Reformatie* (Utrecht, 1954)
Renouard, Y., *La Papauté à Avignon* (3rd edn, Paris, 1969)
Rex, R., *The Lollards* (New York, 2002)
Saak, E. L., *High way to heaven: The Augustinian platform between Reform and Reformation, 1292–1524* (Leiden, 2002)
Schwaiger, G., *Das Papsttum im Spätmittelalter und in der Renaissance: Von Bonifaz VIII. bis Klemens VII.* (Munich, 1957)
Skrynnikov, R. G., 'Kirchliches Denken und Kirchlicher Besitz zu Beginn des 16. Jahrhunderts', in E. Hübner, E. Klug and J. Kusber (eds), *Zwischen Christianisierung und Europäisierung: Beiträge zur Geschichte Osteuropas in Mittelalter und Früher Neuzeit (Festschrift für Peter Nitsche zum 65. Geburtstag)* (Stuttgart, 1998)
Stökl, G., 'Das Echo von Renaissance und Reformation im Moskauer Rußland', in G. Stökl, *Der Russische Staat in Mittelalter und Früher Neuzeit* (Wiesbaden, 1981)
Tierney, B., *Foundations of the conciliar theory: The contribution of the medieval canonists from Gratian to the Great Schism* (London, 1968)
Ullmann, W., *The origins of the Great Schism: A study in fourteenth-century ecclesiastical history* (London 1948, repr. 1967)
Vauchez, A., *The laity in the Middle Ages: Religious beliefs and devotional practices*, trans. Margery J. Schneider (Notre Dame, IN, 1993)
Weinbrenner, R., *Klosterreform im 15. Jahrhundert zwischen Ideal und Praxis: Der Augustinereremit Andreas Proles (1429–1503) und die privilegierte Observanz* (Tübingen, 1996)

Chapter 14 The 'Crisis of the late Middle Ages'

Abel, W., *Agrarkrisen und Agrarkonjunktur* (Berlin, 1978)

Aerts, E., 'The European monetary famine of the late Middle Ages and the Bank of San Giorgio in Genoa', in G. Felloni (ed.), *La Casa di San Giorgio: il potere del credito* (Genoa 2006), 27–62

Aston, T. H. and C. E. H. Philpin (eds), *The Brenner debate* (Cambridge, 1985)

Attman, A., *The bullion flow between Europe and the East 1000–1750* (Göteborg, 1981)

Baschet, J., 'Image et événement: l'art sans la peste (*c.* 1348–*c.* 1400)', in *La peste nera: dati di una realtà ed elementi di una interpretazione. Atti del XXX Convengo storico internazionale* (Todi, 1994)

Beveridge W., 'Wages in the Winchester manors', *Economic History Review*, 1, 7 (1936), 22–43

Blickle, P., 'Agrarkrise und Leibeigenschaft im spätmittelalterlichen deutschen Südwesten', in H. Kellenbenz (ed.), *Agrarisches Nebengewerbe und Formen der Reagrarisierung im Spätmittelalter und im 19./20. Jahrhundert: Bericht über die 5. Arbeitstagung der Gesellschaft für Sozial- und Wirtschaftsgeschichte* (Stuttgart, 1975)

Bois, G., *Crise du féodalisme* (Paris, 1976)

Bois, G., *The crisis of feudalism: Economy and society in eastern Normandy c. 1300–1550* (Cambridge, 1984)

Boutruche, R., *La Crise d'une société: Seigneurs et paysans du Bordelais pendant la Guerre de Cent Ans* (Paris, 1947; reprint 1963)

Brenner, R., 'Agrarian class structure and economic development in pre-industrial Europe', *Past & Present*, 70 (1976), 30–75

Brown, H. P. and S. Hopkins, *A perspective on wages and prices* (London, 1981)

Brown, J. C., 'Prosperity or hard times in Renaissance Italy?', *Renaissance Quarterly*, 42 (1989), 761–80

Burckhardt, J., 'Die geschichtlichen Krisen', in J. Oeri and E. Dürr (eds), *Gesammelte Werke, J. Burckhardt*, IV: *Weltgeschichtliche Betrachtungen über geschichtliches Studium* (Basle, 1978)

Burckhardt, J., *Force and freedom: Reflections on history* (New York, 1943)

Campbell, B. M. S., *English seigniorial agriculture, 1250–1450* (Cambridge, 2000)

Campbell, B. M. S. and M. Overton, 'A new perspective on medieval and early modern agriculture: Six centuries of Norfolk farming *c.* 1250–*c.* 1850', *Past & Present*, 141 (1993), 38–105

Čechura, J., 'Die Bauernschaft in Böhmen während des Spätmittelalters: Perspektiven neuer Orientierung', *Bohemia*, 31 (1990), 283–311

Cerman, M., 'Bodenmärkte und ländliche Wirtschaft', *Jahrbuch für Wirtschaftsgeschichte*, 2 (2004), 125–48

Cerman, M., 'Social structure and land markets in late medieval central and east-central Europe', in *Continuity and Change*, 23 (2008), 55–100

Clark, G., 'The long march of history: Farm wages, population, and economic growth, England 1209–1869', *Economic History Review*, 60:1 (2007), 97–135

Cohn, S., 'After the Black Death: Labour legislation and attitudes towards labour in late-medieval western Europe', *Economic History Review*, 60:3 (2007), 457–85

Day, J., 'The great bullion famine of the fifteenth century', *Past & Present*, 79 (1978), 3–54

Day, J., 'The question of monetary contraction in late medieval Europe', *Nordisk Numismatisk Årsskrift* (1981), 12–29

Dirlmeier, U., *Untersuchungen zu Einkommensverhältnissen und Lebenshaltungskosten in oberdeutschen Städten des Spätmittelalters* (Heidelberg, 1978)

Dirlmeier, U., 'Materielle Lebensbedingungen in deutschen Städten des Spätmittelalters: Äußerer Rahmen, Einkommen, Verbrauch', in R. Elze and G. Fasoli (eds), *Stadtadel und Bürgertum in den italienischen und deutschen Städten des Spätmittelalters* (Berlin, 1991)

Dirlmeier U. and G. Fouquet, 'Ernährung und Konsumgewohnheiten im spätmittelalterlichen Deutschland', *Geschichte in Wissenschaft und Unterricht*, 44 (1993), 504–26

Dirlmeier U., G. Fouquet and B. Fuhrmann, *Europa im Spätmittelalter 1215–1378* (Munich, 2003)

Duby, Georges, *Rural economy and country life in the medieval West*, trans. C. Postan (University Park, Pennsylvania, 1998)

Dygo, M., 'West-Ost-Gefälle? Krise und Blüte in Europa im 14. Jahrhundert', in M. Löwener (ed.), *Die 'Blüte' der Staaten des östlichen Europa im 14. Jahrhundert* (Wiesbaden, 2004)

Epstein, S. R., 'Cities, regions and the late medieval crisis: Sicily and Tuscany compared', *Past & Present*, 130 (1991), 3–50

Epstein, S. R., *An island for itself: Economic development and social change in late medieval Sicily* (Cambridge, 1992)

Epstein, S. R., *Freedom and growth: The rise of states and markets in Europe, 1300–1500* (London, 2000)

Fouquet, G., 'Haushalt und Hof, Stift und Adel: Bischof und Domkapitel zu Speyer um 1400', in T. Zotz (ed.), *Fürstenhöfe und ihre Außenwelt: Aspekte gesellschaftlicher und kultureller Identität im deutschen Spätmittelalter* (Würzburg, 2004)

Gissel, S., 'Payments in money and in kind in late medieval Scandinavia: Studies in agrarian rents', in J. S. Jensen (ed.), *Nordisk Numismatisk Årsskrift 1981: Nordic Numismatic Journal, Coinage and monetary circulation in the Baltic Area c. 1350–c. 1500* (Copenhagen, 1982)

Goldthwaite, R., *The building of Renaissance Florence: An economic and social history* (Baltimore, 1980)

Goldthwaite, R., *Wealth and demand for art in Italy, 1300–1600* (Baltimore, 1993)

Graus F., 'Die Krise des Feudalismus im 14. Jahrhundert', *Historický Sborník*, 1 (1953), 65–121

Graus F., 'Die erste Krise des Feudalismus', *Zeitschrift für Geschichtswissenschaft*, 3 (1955), 552–92

Graus F., *Pest-Geißler-Judenmorde: Das 14. Jahrhundert als Krisenzeit* (3rd edn, Göttingen, 1964)

Graus, F., *Das Spätmittelalter als Krisenzeit* (Prague, 1969)

Hatcher, J., *Plague, population and the English economy 1348–1530* (Houndmills, 1977)

Herlihy, D., 'Santa Maria Impruneta: A rural commune in the late Middle Ages', in N. Rubinstein (ed.), *Florentine studies* (London, 1968)

Hoffmann, R. C., *Land, liberties, and lordship in a late medieval countryside: Agrarian structures and change in the duchy of Wrocław* (Philadelphia, 1989)

Jenks, S., 'Hartgeld und Wechsel im hansisch-englischen Handel des 15. Jahrhunderts', in M. North (ed.), *Geldumlauf, Währungssysteme und Zahlungsverkehr in Nordwesteuropa 1300–1800* (Cologne, 1989)

Jenks, S., 'Von den archaischen Grundlagen bis zur Schwelle der Moderne (ca. 1000–1450)', in M. North (ed.), *Deutsche Wirtschaftsgeschichte: Ein Jahrtausend im Überblick* (2nd edn, Munich, 2005)

Kosminskij, E. A., 'Voprosy agrarnoj istorii v Anglii v XV veke', *Voprosy istorii*, 1 (1948), 59–76

Kosminskij, E. A., 'The evolution of the feudal rent in England from the XIth to the XVth centuries', *Past & Present*, 7 (1955), 12–36

Kriedte, P., 'Spätmittelalterliche Agrarkrise oder Krise des Feudalismus?', *Geschichte und Gesellschaft*, 7 (1981), 42–68

Kriedte, P., *Peasants, landlords and merchant capitalists: Europe and the world economy, 1500–1800* (Cambridge, 1984)

Leimus, I., 'Die spätmittelalterliche große Wirtschaftskrise in Europa – war auch Livland davon betroffen?', *Forschungen zur Baltischen Geschichte*, 1 (2006), 56–67

MacKay, A., *Money, prices and policies in fifteenth-century Castille* (London, 1981)

Małowist, M., 'Zagadnienie kryzysu feudalizmu w XIV i XV w. w świetle najnowszych badań (Próba krytyki)', *Kwartalnik Historyczny*, 60 (1953), 86–106

Małowist, M., 'L'inégalité du développement économique en Europe au bas Moyen Âge', in M. Małowist, *Croissance et régression en Europe XIVe–XVIIe siècles* (Paris, 1972)

Małowist, M., *Wschód a Zachód Europy w XIII–XVI wieku: Konfrontacja struktur społecznych i gospodarczych* (Warsaw, 1973)

Meiss, M., *Painting in Florence and Siena after the Black Death: The arts, religion and society in the mid-fourteenth century* (Princeton, 1951)

Meuthen, E., *Das 15. Jahrhundert* (3rd edn, Munich, 1996)

Miskimin, H. A., 'The economic depression of the Renaissance', *Economic Historical Review* (2nd Series), 14 (1962), 408–26

Miskimin, H. A., 'Monetary movements and market structures: Forces for contraction in fourteenth- and fifteenth-century England', *Journal of Economic History*, 24 (1964), 470–90

Molho A., 'Fisco ed economia a Firenze alla vigilia del Concilio', *Archivio storico italiano*, 148 (1990), 807–44

Mueller, R. C., 'Alcune considerazioni sui significati di moneta [contributo al tema "Economia naturale ed economia monetaria – un dibattito aperto"]', *Società e Storia*, 27 (1985), 77–84

Mueller, R. C., 'Epidemie, crisi, rivolte', in *Storia Medievale* (Rome, 1998)

Mueller, R. C., 'Il baratto in una terra soggetta a Venezia: l'esempio di Corfù nel Quattrocento', in P. Delogu and S. Sorda (eds), *La moneta in ambiente rurale nell'Italia tardomedievale, Atti dell'Incontro di Studio* (Rome, 2002)

Munro, J. H., 'Mint outputs, money, and prices in late-medieval England and the Low Countries', in E. van Cauwenberghe and F. Irsigler (eds), *Münzprägung, Geldumlauf und Wechselkurse* (Trier, 1984)

Munro, J. H., 'Urban wage structures in late-medieval England and the Low Countries: Work-time and seasonal wages', in I. Blanchard (ed.), *Labour and leisure in historical perspective, thirteenth to twentieth centuries* (Stuttgart, 1994)

Munro, J. H., 'Wage stickiness, monetary changes, and real incomes in late-medieval England and the Low Countries, 1300–1500: Did money matter?', *Research in Economic History*, 21 (2003), 185–297

North, M., *Die Amtswirtschaften von Osterode und Soldau: Vergleichende Untersuchungen zur Wirtschaft im frühmodernen Staat am Beispiel des Herzogtums Preußen in der zweiten Hälfte des 16. und der ersten Hälfte des 17. Jahrhunderts* (Berlin, 1982)

North M., *Geldumlauf und Wirtschaftskonjunktur im südlichen Ostseeraum an der Wende zur Neuzeit (1440–1570)* (Sigmaringen, 1990)

North, M., 'Die Entstehung der Gutswirtschaft im südlichen Ostseeraum', *Zeitschrift für Historische Forschung*, 26 (1999), 43–59

Perroy, É., 'A L'origine d'une économie contractée: Les crises du XIVe siècle', *Annales*, 4 (1969), 167–82

Postan, M. M., 'Some economic evidence of declining population in the later Middle Ages', *Economic History Review* (2nd Series), 2 (1950), 221–46

Postan, M. M., 'Note', *Economic History Review* (2nd Series), 12 (1959), 77–82

Postan, M. M., 'The trade of medieval Europe: The north', in M. M. Postan and E. Miller (eds), *The Cambridge economic history of Europe*, II: *Trade and industry in the Middle Ages* (Cambridge, 1987)

Robinson, W. C., 'Money, population, and economic change in late-medieval Europe', *Economic History Review* (2nd Series), 12 (1959), 63–76

Seibt, F., *Revolution in Europa: Ursprung und Wege innerer Gewalt: Strukturen, Elemente, Exempel* (Munich, 1984)

Seibt, F. (ed.), *Europa im Hoch- und Spätmittelalter*, II (Stuttgart, 1987)

Seibt, F. and W. Eberhard (eds), *Europa 1400: Die 'Krise des Spätmittelalters'* (Stuttgart, 1984)

Skaare, K., 'Coinage and monetary circulation in Norway from the middle of the 14th century till *c.* 1500', in J. S. Jensen (ed.), *Nordisk Numismatisk Årsskrift 1981: Nordic Numismatic Journal, Coinage and Monetary circulation in the Baltic Area c. 1350–c. 1500* (Copenhagen, 1982)

Sprandel, R., *Das mittelalterliche Zahlungssystem nach hansisch-nordischen Quellen des 13.–15. Jahrhunderts* (Stuttgart, 1975)

Spufford, P., *Money and its use in medieval Europe* (Cambridge, 1988)

Ulbrich, C., *Leibherrschaft am Oberrhein im Spätmittelalter* (Göttingen, 1979)

Van Bavel, B. J. P. and J. L. van Zanden, 'The jump-start of the Holland economy during the late-medieval crisis, *c.* 1350–*c.* 1500', *Economic History Review*, 57: 3 (2004), 503–32

Van der Wee, H., 'Prices and wages as development variables: A comparison between England and the southern Netherlands, 1400–1700', *Acta Historiae Neerlandicae*, 10 (1978), 58–78

Van der Wee, H., 'Structural changes in European long-distance trade, and particularly in the re-export trade from south to north, 1350–1750', in J. D. Tracy (ed.), *The rise of merchant empires: Long distance trade in the early modern world 1350–1750* (Cambridge, 1990)

Van der Wee, H., 'Globalization, core and periphery in the world economy of the late Middle Ages and early modern times', in P. Reill (ed.), *Theorizing the dynamics of core-periphery relations* (forthcoming)

Van der Wee, H. and T. Peeters, 'Un modèle dynamique de croissance interseculaire du commerce mondiale, XIIe–XVIIIe siècles', *Annales*, 15 (1970), 100–28

Wyrozumski, J., 'Was Poland affected by the late-medieval crisis of feudalism?', *Acta Poloniae Historica*, 78 (1998), 5–17

Chapter 15 Political integration

Blockmans, W. P., 'Stadt, Region und Staat: Ein Dreiecksverhältnis – Der Kasus der Niederlande im 15. Jahrhundert', in F. Seibt and W. Eberhard (eds), *Europa 1500: Integrationsprozesse im Widerstreit* (Stuttgart, 1987)

Brauneder, W., *Staatliche Vereinigung: Fördernde und hemmende Elemente in der deutschen Geschichte, Tagung der Vereinigung für Verfassungsgeschichte in Hofgeismar vom 13.–15.3.1995* (Berlin, 1989)

Bulst, N., 'Die französischen General- und Provinzialstände im 15. Jahrhundert: Zum Problem nationaler Integration und Desintegration', in F. Seibt and W. Eberhard (eds), *Europa 1500: Integrationsprozesse im Widerstreit* (Stuttgart, 1987)

Cauchies, J.-M., 'Die burgundischen Niederlande unter Erzherzog Philipp dem Schönen (1494–1506): Ein doppelter Integrationsprozeß', in F. Seibt and W. Eberhard (eds), *Europa 1500: Integrationsprozesse im Widerstreit* (Stuttgart, 1987)

Guenée, B., 'Espace et état en France au Moyen Âge', in B. Guenée (ed.), *Politique et histoire au Moyen Âge: Recueil d'articles sur l'histoire politique et l'historiographie médiévale (1956–1981)* (Paris, 1981)

Imsen, S. and G. Vogler, 'Communal autonomy and peasant resistance in northern and central Europe', in P. Blickle (ed.), *Resistance, representation, and community* (New York, 1997)

Isenmann, E., 'Integrations- und Konsolidierungsprobleme der Reichsordnung in der zweiten Hälfte des 15. Jahrhunderts', in F. Seibt and W. Eberhard (eds), *Europa 1500: Integrationsprozesse im Widerstreit* (Stuttgart, 1987)

Kaelble, H., 'Die soziale Integration Europas: Annäherungen und Verflechtungen westeuropäischer Gesellschaften seit dem Zweiten Weltkrieg', in E. Schremmer (ed.), *Wirtschaftliche und soziale Integration in historischer Sicht* (Stuttgart, 1996)

Maleczek, W. (ed.), *Fragen der politischen Integration im mittelalterlichen Europa* (Ostfildern, 2005)

Moraw, P., 'Zur staatlich-organisierten Integration des Reiches im Mittelalter', in W. Brauneder, *Staatliche Vereinigung: Fördernde und hemmende Elemente in der deutschen Geschichte, Tagung der Vereinigung für Verfassungsgeschichte in Hofgeismar vom 13.–15.3.1995* (Berlin, 1989)

Müller, H., 'Zusammenfassung II', in W. Maleczek (ed.), *Fragen der Politischen Integration im mittelalterlichen Europa* (Ostfildern, 2005)

Neveux, H. and E. Österberg, 'Norms and values of the peasantry in the period of state formation: A comparative interpretation', in P. Blickle (ed.), *Resistance, representation, and community* (New York, 1997)

North, M., 'Integration im Ostseeraum und im Heiligen Römischen Reich', in M. North and N. Jörn (eds), *Die Integration des südlichen Ostseeraumes in das Alte Reich* (Cologne, 2000)

Rao, A. M. and S. Supphellen, 'Power elites and dependent territories', in W. Reinhard (ed.), *Power elites and state building* (New York, 1996)

Reinhard, W., 'Das Wachstum der Staatsgewalt: Historische Reflexionen', *Der Staat*, 31:1 (1992), 59–75

Reinhard, W., 'Introduction: Power elites, state servants, ruling classes, and the growth of state power', in Reinhard (ed.), *Power elites and state building* (New York, 1996)

Reinhard, W. (ed.), *Power elites and state building* (New York, 1996)

Reinhard, W., *Geschichte der Staatsgewalt: Eine vergleichende Verfassungsgeschichte Europas von den Anfängen bis zur Gegenwart* (2nd edn, Munich, 2000)

Rösener, W., 'Landesherrliche Integration und innere Konsolidierung im württembergischen Territorialstaat des ausgehenden Mittelalters', in F. Seibt and W. Eberhard (eds), *Europa 1500: Integrationsprozesse im Widerstreit* (Stuttgart, 1987)

Schmidt, G., 'Deutschland am Beginn der Neuzeit: Reichs-Staat und Kulturnation?', in C. Roll (ed.), *Recht und Reich im Zeitalter der Reformation: Festschrift für Horst Rabe* (Frankfurt a. M., 1996)

Schmidt, G., *Geschichte des Alten Reiches: Staat und Nation in der Frühen Neuzeit 1495–1806* (Munich, 1999)

Seibt, F., 'Europa 1500: Integration im Widerstreit', in F. Seibt and W. Eberhard (eds), *Europa 1500: Integrationsprozesse im Widerstreit* (Stuttgart, 1987)

Störmer, W., 'Die innere Konsolidierung der wittelsbachischen Territorialstaaten in Bayern im 15. Jahrhundert', in F. Seibt and W. Eberhard (eds), *Europa 1500: Integrationsprozesse im Widerstreit* (Stuttgart, 1987)

Tewes, L., 'Ständische Mitsprache und Modernisierung in der kurkölnischen Zentralverwaltung während des 15. Jahrhunderts', in F. Seibt and W. Eberhard (eds), *Europa 1500: Integrationsprozesse im Widerstreit* (Stuttgart, 1987)

Thumser, M., 'Zusammenfassung I', in W. Maleczek (ed.), *Fragen der Politischen Integration im mittelalterlichen Europa* (Ostfildern, 2005)

Chapter 16 The court

Asch, R. G. and A. M. Birke, *Princes, patronage and the nobility: The court at the beginning of the modern age c. 1450–1650* (London, 1991)

Auge, O. and K.-H. Spieß, 'Hof und Herrscher', in W. Paravicini (ed.), *Höfe und Residenzen im spätmittelalterlichen Reich: Bilder und Begriffe* (Ostfildern, 2005)

Bertelli, S., F. Cardini and E. G. Zorzi, *Italian Renaissance courts*, trans. M. Fitton and G. Culverwell (London, 1986)

Bihrer, A., *Der Konstanzer Bischofshof im 14. Jahrhundert, Herrschaftliche, soziale und kommunikative Aspekte* (Ostfildern, 2005)

Bihrer, A., 'Ein Bürger als Bischof von Konstanz? Ulrich Pfefferhard (1345–1351), sein Hof und seine Stadt', in T. Zotz (ed.), *Fürstenhöfe und ihre Außenwelt: Aspekte gesellschaftlicher und kultureller Identität im deutschen Spätmittelalter* (Würzbug, 2004)

Boone, M. and T. de Hemptinne, 'Espace urbain et ambitions princières: les présences matérielles de l'autorité princière dans le Gand médiéval (12e siècle–1540)', in W. Paravicini (ed.), *Zeremoniell und Raum: 4. Symposium der Residenzen-Kommission der Akademie der Wissenschaften in Göttingen* (Sigmaringen, 1997)

Contamine, P., 'Espaces féminins, espaces masculins dans quelques demeures aristocratiques françaises, XIVe–XVIe siècle', in J. Hirschbiegel and W. Paravicini (eds), *Das Frauenzimmer: Die Frau bei Hofe in Spätmittelalter und früher Neuzeit, 6. Symposium der Residenzen-Kommission der Akademie der Wissenschaften in Göttingen* (Stuttgart, 2000)

De Mérindol, C., 'Le cérémonial et l'espace: L'exemple de l'hôtel Jacques-Cœur à Bourges', in W. Paravicini (ed.), *Zeremoniell und Raum* (Sigmaringen, 1997)

Fouquet, G., 'Haushalt und Hof, Stift und Adel: Bischof und Domkapitel zu Speyer um 1400', in T. Zotz (ed.), *Fürstenhöfe und ihre Außenwelt* (Würtzburg, 2004)

Franke, B., 'Bilder in Frauenräumen und Bilder von Frauenräumen: Imaginationen und Wirklichkeit', in J. Hirschbiegel and W. Paravicini (eds), *Das Frauenzimmer* (Stuttgart, 2000)

Freigang, C. and J.-C. Schmitt (eds), *La culture de cour en France et en Europe à la fin du Moyen Âge* (Berlin, 2005)

Guerzoni, G., 'The Italian Renaissance courts' demand for the arts: The case of d'Este of Ferrara (1471–1560)', in M. North and D. Ormrod (eds), *Art Markets in Europe, 1400–1800* (Aldershot, 1998)

Guerzoni, G., *Le corti estensi e la devoluzione di Ferrara del 1598* (Modena, 2000)

Heinig, P.-J., 'Der regionalisierte Herrscherhof: Kaiser Friedrich III. und das Reich in Fremd- und Selbstwahrnehmung', in T. Zotz (ed.), *Fürstenhöfe und ihre Außenwelt* (Würtzburg, 2004)

Heinig, P.-J. (ed.), *Kaiser Friedrich III. (1440–1493): Hof, Regierung und Politik* (Cologne, 1993)

Hirsch, V., *Der Hof des Basler Bischofs Johannes von Venningen (1458–1478): Verwaltung und Kommunikation, Wirtschaftsführung und Konsum* (Ostfildern, 2004)

Hirschbiegel, J. and W. Paravicini (eds), *Das Frauenzimmer: Die Frau bei Hofe in Spätmittelalter und früher Neuzeit, 6. Symposium der Residenzen-Kommission der Akademie der Wissenschaften in Göttingen* (Stuttgart, 2000)

Kälble, M., 'Bischöflicher Hof in Basel zwischen Stadt, Adel und Reich vom 12. bis zum 14. Jahrhundert', in T. Zotz (ed.), *Fürstenhöfe und ihre Außenwelt* (Würtzburg, 2004)

Kerscher, G., 'Die Perspektive des Potentaten: Differenzierung von "Privattrakt" bzw. Appartement und Zeremonialräumen im spätmittelalterlichen Palastbau', in W. Paravicini (ed.), *Zeremoniell und Raum* (Sigmaringen, 1997)

Kress, S., 'Frauenzimmer der Florentiner Renaissance und ihre Ausstattung: Eine erste "Spurensuche"', in J. Hirschbiegel and W. Paravicini (eds), *Das Frauenzimmer* (Stuttgart, 2000)

Kress, S., 'Per honore della ciptà: Zeremoniell im Florentiner Quattrocento am Beispiel des Besuchs Galeazzo Maria Sforzas im April 1459', in W. Paravicini (ed.), *Zeremoniell und Raum* (Sigmaringen, 1997)

Lubkin, G., *A Renaissance court: Milan under Galeazzo Maria Sforza* (Berkeley, 1994)

Maleczek, W., 'Die Sachkultur am Hofe Herzog Sigismunds von Tirol (gest. 1496)', in H. Appelt (ed.), *Adelige Sachkultur des Spätmittelalters: Internationaler Kongress Krems an der Donau 22. bis 25. September 1980* (Vienna, 1982)

Märtl, C., 'Le papesse: Frauen im Umkreis der römischen Kurie nach der Mitte des

15. Jahrhunderts', in J. Hirschbiegel and W. Paravicini (eds), *Das Frauenzimmer* (Stuttgart, 2000)

Moraw, P., 'Über den Hof Kaiser Karls IV', in P. Moraw (ed.), *Deutscher Königshof, Hoftag und Reichstag im späteren Mittelalter* (Stuttgart, 2002)

Mozzarelli, C. and G. Olmi, *La corte nella cultura e nella storiografia: immagini e posizioni tra le Otto e Novecento* (Rome, 1983)

Ortwein, M., *Der Innsbrucker Hof zur Zeit Erzherzogs Sigismund des Münzreichen: Ein Beitrag zur Geschichte der materiellen Kultur* (PhD diss., University of Innsbruck, 1936)

Paravicini, W., 'The court of the dukes of Burgundy. A model for Europe?', in R. G. Asch and A. M. Birke (eds), *Princes, patronage and the nobility* (London, 1991)

Paravicini, W., *Die Ritterlich-höfische Kultur des Mittelalters* (Munich, 1994)

Paravicini, W. (ed.), *Alltag bei Hofe: 3. Symposium der Residenzen-Kommission der Akademie der Wissenschaften in Göttingen, Ansbach, 28. Februar bis 1. März 1992* (Sigmaringen, 1995)

Paravicini, W. (ed.), *Zeremoniell und Raum: 4. Symposium der Residenzen-Kommission der Akademie der Wissenschaften in Göttingen, Potsdam, 25. bis 27. September 1994* (Sigmaringen, 1997)

Paravicini, W., 'Europäische Hofordnungen als Gattung und Quelle', in W. Paravicini and H. Kruse (eds), *Höfe und Hofordnungen 1200–1600: 5. Symposium der Residenzen-Kommission der Akademie der Wissenschaften in Göttingen* (Sigmaringen, 1999)

Paravicini, W. and J. Hirschbiegel (eds), *Das Frauenzimmer: die Frau bei Hofe in Spätmittelalter und früher Neuzeit: 6. Symposium der Residenzen-Kommission der Akademie der Wissenschaften in Göttingen, Dresden, 26. bis 29. September 1998* (Stuttgart, 2000)

Paravicini, W. and H. Kruse (eds), *Höfe und Hofordnungen 1200–1600: 5. Symposium der Residenzen-Kommission der Akademie der Wissenschaften in Göttingen, Sigmaringen, 5. bis 8. Oktober 1996* (Sigmaringen, 1999)

Piponnier, F., *Costume et vie sociale: La cour d'Anjou* (Paris, 1970)

Ridgeway, H. W., *The politics of the English royal court 1247–65, with special reference to the role of aliens* (Oxford,1983)

Rösener, W., *Leben am Hof: Königs- und Fürstenhöfe im Mittelalter* (Ostfildern, 2008)

Spieß, K.-H., 'Der Hof Kaiser Barbarossas und die politische Landschaft am Mittelrhein: Methodische Überlegungen zur Untersuchung der Hofpräsenz im Hochmittelalter', in P. Moraw (ed.), *Deutscher Königshof, Hoftag und Reichstag im späteren Mittelalter* (Stuttgart, 2002)

Spieß, K.-H., 'Fremdheit und Integration der ausländischen Ehefrau und ihres Gefolges bei internationalen Fürstenheiraten', in T. Zotz (ed.), *Fürstenhöfe und ihre Außenwelt* (Würtzburg, 2004)

Spieß, K.-H., 'Zwischen König und Fürsten: Das politische Beziehungssystem südwestdeutscher Grafen und Herren im späten Mittelalter', in K. Andermann and C. Joos (eds), *Grafen und Herren in Südwestdeutschland vom 12. bis ins 17. Jahrhundert* (Epfendorf, 2006)

Spieß, K.-H., 'Materielle Hofkultur und ihre Erinnerungsfunktion im Mittelalter', in C. Fey, S. Krieb, W. Rösener (eds), *Mittelalterliche Fürstenhöfe und ihre Erinnerungskulturen* (Göttingen, 2007)

Spieß, K.-H., *Fürsten und Höfe im Mittelalter* (Darmstadt, 2008)

Spieß, K.-H., 'Asian objects and western European court-culture in the later Middle Ages', in M. North (ed.), *Artistic and cultural exchanges between Europe and Asia, 1400–1900: Rethinking markets, workshops and collections* (Surrey, 2010)

Spieß, K.-H., 'Der Schatz Karls des Kühnen als Medium der Politik', in K. Oschema and R. Schwinges (eds), *Karl der Kühne von Burgund: Fürst zwischen europäischem Adel und der Eidgenossenschaft* (Zürich, 2010)

Starkey, D., *The English court: From the Wars of the Roses to the Civil War* (2nd edn, London, 1992)

Trnek, H., 'Schatzkunst und höfische Geschenke: Kontinuität im künstlerischen Austausch', in K. Herbers und N. Jaspert (eds), *'Das kommt mir spanisch vor': Eigenes und Fremdes in den deutsch-spanischen Beziehungen des späten Mittelalters* (Münster, 2004)

Vale, M., *The princely court: Medieval courts and culture in north-west Europe* (Oxford, 2001)

Weber, K., 'Eine Stadt und ihr Bischofshof: Straßburg im 13. Jahrhundert bis in die Zeit Bischof Konrads III. von Lichtenberg (1237–1299)', in T. Zotz (ed.), *Fürstenhöfe und ihre Außenwelt* (Würtzburg, 2004)

Weiss, S., 'Die Rolle der Damen am päpstlichen Hof von Avignon unter Papst Johannes XXII. (1316–1334)' in J. Hirschbiegel and W. Paravicini (eds), *Das Frauenzimmer* (Stuttgart, 2000)

Whiteley, M., 'Ceremony and space in the châteaux of Charles V, King of France', in W. Paravicini (ed.), *Zeremoniell und Raum* (Sigmaringen, 1997)

Zotz, T. (ed.), *Fürstenhöfe und ihre Außenwelt. Aspekte gesellschaftlicher und kultureller Identität im deutschen Spätmittelalter* (Würzburg, 2004)

Chapter 17 Renaissance and humanism

Antal, F., *Florentine painting and its social background* (London, 1947)

Baxandall, M., *Painting and experience in fifteenth-century Italy: A primer in the social history of pictorial style* (Oxford, 1972)

Blockmans, W., 'The creative environment: Incentives to and functions of Bruges art production', in M. W. Ainsworth (ed.), *Petrus Christus in Renaissance Bruges: An interdisciplinary approach* (New York and Turnhout, 1995)

Blockmans, W., 'The Burgundian court and the urban milieu as patrons in fifteenth-century Bruges', in M. North (ed.), *Economic history and the arts* (Cologne, 1996)

Bonsdorff, J. von, *Kunstproduktion und Kunstverbreitung im Ostseeraum des Spätmittelalters* (Helsinki, 1993)

Brulez, W., *Cultuur en getal: Aspecten van de relatie economie-maatschappij-cultuur in Europa tussen 1400 en 1800* (Amsterdam, 1986)

Burke, P., *The European Renaissance: Centres and peripheries* (Oxford, 1998)

Burke, P., *The Italian Renaissance: Culture and society in Italy* (Princeton, 1999)

Burke, P., *Kultureller Austausch* (Frankfurt a. M., 2000)

Cavaciocchi, S., *Economia e arte sec. XIII–XVIII* (Prato, 2002)

Comanducci, R. (ed.), 'Produzione seriale e mercato dell'arte a Firenze tra Quattro e Cinquecento', in M. Fantoni, L. C. Matthew and S. F. Matthews-Grieco (eds),

The art market in Italy (15th–17th Centuries): Il Mercato dell'arte in Italia (sec. XV–XVII) (Ferrara, 2003)

Esch, A. and D. Esch, 'Die Grabplatte Martins V. und andere Importstücke in den römischen Zollregistern der Frührenaissance', *Römisches Jahrbuch für Kunstgeschichte*, 17 (1978), 209–17

Esch, A., 'Importe in das Rom der Frührenaissance: Ihr Volumen nach den römischen Zollregistern der Jahre 1452–62', *Studi in memoria di Federigo Melis*, III (Naples, 1978)

Esch, A., 'Über den Zusammenhang von Kunst und Wirtschaft in der italienischen Renaissance: Ein Forschungsbericht', *Zeitschrift für Historische Forschung*, 8 (1981), 179–222

Esch, A., 'Importe in das Rom der Renaissance: Die Zollregister der Jahre 1470 bis 1480', *Quellen und Forschungen aus italienischen Archiven und Bibliotheken*, 74 (1994), 360–453

Esch, A., 'Roman customs registers 1470–80: Items of interest to historians of art and material culture', *Journal of the Warburg and Courtauld Institute*, 58 (1995), 72–87

Esch, A., 'Sul rapporto fra arte ed economia nel Rinascimento italiano', in A. Esch and C. L. Frommel, *Arte, Committenza ed Economia a Roma e nelle corti del Rinascimento 1420–1530* (Turin, 1995)

Esch, A., 'Prolusione: Economia ed arte: la dinamica del rapporto nella prospettiva dello storico', in S. Cavaciocchi (ed.), *Economia e arte sec. XIII–XVIII* (Prato, 2002)

Esch, A., 'Kölnisches in Römischen und Lucchesischen Archivalien des späten Mittelalters: Neue Belege für Waren- und Geldverkehr mit Italien', *Rheinische Vierteljahrsblätter*, 67 (2003), 21–36

Fantoni, M., *Il Rinascimento italiano e l'europa*, I: *Storia e storiografia* (Verona, 2005)

Fantoni, M., L. C. Matthew and S. F. Matthews-Grieco, *The art market in Italy (15th–17th centuries): Il Mercato dell'arte in Italia (sec. XV–XVII)* (Ferrara, 2003)

Findlen, P., *Possessing nature: Museums, collecting, and scientific culture in early modern Italy* (Berkeley, 2000)

Goldthwaite, R. A., *The building of Renaissance Florence: An economic and social history* (2nd edn, Baltimore and London, 1991)

Goldthwaite, R. A., *Wealth and the demand for art in Italy, 1300–1600* (Baltimore and London, 1995)

Goldthwaite, R. A., 'An entrepreneurial silk weaver in Renaissance Florence', *I Tatti Studies*, 10 (2005), 69–126

Gombrich, E. H., 'The social history of art', in E. H. Gombrich, *Meditations on a hobby horse and other essays on the theory of art* (3rd edn, London, 1978), originally published as a review of A. Hauser, *Social History of Art* (New York, 1951)

Guerzoni, G., 'Italian Renaissance courts' demand for the arts: The case of d'Este of Ferrara (1471–1560)', in M. North and D. Omrod (eds), *Art markets in Europe, 1400–1800* (Aldershot, 1998)

Guerzoni, G., 'Ricadute ocupazionali ed impatti economici della committenza artistica delle corti estensi tra Quattro e Cinquecento', in S. Cavaciocchi (ed.), *Economia e arte sec. XIII–XVIII* (Prato, 2002)

Hauser, A., *The social history of art* (New York, 1951)

Jardine, L., *Worldly goods: A new history of the Renaissance* (London, 1997)

Kubersky-Piredda, S., 'Spesa della materia und spesa dell'arte: Die Preise von Altartafeln in der Florentiner Renaissance', in S. Cavaciocchi (ed.), *Economia e arte sec. XIII–XVIII* (Prato, 2002)

Kubersky-Piredda, S., 'Immagini devozionali nel Rinascimento fiorentino: produzione, commercio, prezzi', in M. Fantoni, L. C. Matthew and S. F. Matthews-Grieco (eds), *The art market in Italy (15th–17th centuries): Il mercato dell'arte in Italia (sec. XV–XVII)* (Ferrara, 2003)

Langdale, A., 'Aspects of the critical reception and intellectual history of Baxandall's concept of the period eye', in A. Rifkin (ed.), *About Michael Baxendall* (Oxford, 1999)

Lopez, R. S., 'Hard times and investment in culture', in *The Renaissance: Six essays* (New York, 1962)

Martens, M. P. J., 'Artistic patronage in Bruges institutions, ca. 1440–1482' (PhD diss., University of California at Santa Barbara, 1992)

Martens, M. P. J., 'Petrus Christus: A cultural biography', in M. W. Ainsworth, *Petrus Christus, Renaissance master of Bruges* (New York, 1994)

Martens, M. P. J., 'Some aspects of the origins of the art market in fifteenth-century Bruges', in M. North and D. Ormrod, *Markets for art, 1400–1800* (Aldershot, 1998)

Martin, A. von, *Sociology of the Renaissance*, trans. W. L. Luetkens (London, 1944)

Meuthen, E., *Das 15. Jahrhundert*, rev. C. Märtl (4th edn, Munich, 2006)

Munro, J. H., 'Economic depression and the arts in the fifteenth-century Low Countries', *Renaissance and Reformation*, 19 (1983), 235–50

North, M., 'Introduction', in M. North (ed.), *Economic history and the arts* (Cologne, 1996)

North, M. and D. Ormrod, *Markets for art, 1400–1800* (Aldershot, 1998)

North, M., *Das Goldene Zeitalter: Kunst und Kommerz in der niederländischen Malerei des 17. Jahrhunderts* (Cologne, 2001)

North, M., 'Art Markets', in T.-H. Borchert (ed.), *The age of van Eyck 1430–1530: The Mediterranean world and early Netherlandish painting* (Ghent, 2002)

O'Malley, M., 'Altarpieces and agency: The altarpiece of the Society of the Purification and its "invisible skein of relations"', *Art History*, 28:4 (2005), 417–41

O'Malley, M., *The business of art: Contracts and the commissioning process in Renaissance Italy* (New Haven and London, 2005)

O'Malley, M. and E. Welch (eds), *The material Renaissance* (Manchester, 2007)

Riedel, V., *Antikerezeption in der deutschen Literatur vom Renaissance-Humanismus bis zur Gegenwart: Eine Einführung* (Stuttgart, 2000)

Roeck, B., *Kunstpatronage in der Frühen Neuzeit: Studien zu Kunstmarkt, Künstlern und ihren Auftraggebern in Italien und im Heiligen Römischen Reich (15.–17. Jahrhundert)* (Göttingen, 1999)

Roeck, B., *Das historische Auge: Kunstwerke als Zeugen ihrer Zeit* (Göttingen, 2004)

Segel, H. B., *Renaissance culture in Poland: The rise of humanism, 1470–1543* (Ithaca, 1989)

Smith, P. H. and Findlen P. (eds), *Merchants and marvels: Commerce, science and art in early modern Europe* (New York, 2002)

Spallanzani, M., 'Maioliche ispano-moresche a Firenze nei secoli XIV–XV', in S. Cavaciocchi (ed.), *Economia e arte sec. XIII–XVIII* (Prato, 2002)

Syson, L. and D. Thornton, *Objects of virtue: Art in Renaissance Italy* (London, 2001)

Vermeylen, F., *Paintings for the market: Commercialization of art in Antwerp's golden age* (Turnhout, 2003)

Wackernagel, M., *Der Lebensraum des Künstlers in der florentinischen Renaissance* (Leipzig, 1938)

Welch, E., *Art in Renaissance Italy 1350–1500* (Oxford, 1997)

Welch, E., 'From retail to resale: Artistic value and the second-hand market in Italy (1400–1550)', in M. Fantoni, L. C. Matthew and S. F. Matthews-Grieco (eds), *The art market in Italy (15th–17th centuries): Il mercato dell'arte in Italia (sec. XV–XVII)* (Ferrara, 2003)

Welch, E., *Shopping in the Renaissance: Consumer cultures in Italy 1400–1600* (New Haven and London, 2005)

Chapter 18 Cultural transfer studies

Aikema, B. and B. L. Brown (eds), *Renaissance Venice and the north: Crosscurrents in the time of Dürer, Bellini and Titian* (London, 1999)

Ainsworth, M. W., 'The art of Petrus Christus', in M. W. Ainsworth, *Petrus Christus, Renaissance master of Bruges*, exhibition catalogue, Metropolitan Museum of Art (New York, 1994)

Avril, F. (ed.), *Jean Fouquet: Peintre et enlumineur du XVe siècle* (Paris, 2003)

Borchert, T.-H. (ed.), *The age of Van Eyck 1430–1530: The Mediterranean world and early Netherlandish painting* (Ghent, 2002)

Borchert, T.-H., 'The mobility of artists: Aspects of cultural transfer in Renaissance Europe', in T.-H. Borchert (ed.), *The Age of Van Eyck* (Ghent, 2002)

Burke, P., *The European Renaissance: Centres and peripheries* (Oxford, 1998)

Burke, P., *The Italian Renaissance: Culture and society in Italy* (Princeton, NJ, 1999)

Burke, P., *Kultureller Austausch* (Frankfurt, 2000)

Burke, P., 'Translating knowledge, translating cultures', in M. North (ed.), *Kultureller Austausch in der Frühen Neuzeit* (Cologne, 2009)

Campbell, S. J. and S. J. Milner (eds), *Artistic exchange and cultural translation in the Italian Renaissance city* (Cambridge, 2004)

Cutler, A., 'The pathos of distance: Byzantium in the gaze of Renaissance Europe and modern scholarship', in C. Farago (ed.), *Reframing the Renaissance: Visual culture in Europe and Latin America 1450–1650* (New Haven and London, 1995)

Eberhard, W. and A. A. Strnad (eds), *Humanismus und Renaissance in Ostmitteleuropa vor der Reformation* (Cologne, 1996)

Espagne, M., 'Französisch-sächsischer Kulturtransfer im 18. und 19. Jahrhundert: Eine Problemskizze', *Comparativ*, 2 (1992), 100–21

Espagne, M., *Les Transferts culturels franco-allemands* (Paris, 1999)

Espagne, M. and W. Greiling (eds), *Frankreichfreunde: Mittler des französisch-deutschen Kulturtransfers (1750–1850)* (Leipzig, 1996)

Espagne, M. and M. Middell (eds), *Von der Elbe bis an die Seine: Kulturtransfer zwischen Sachsen und Frankreich im 18. und 19. Jahrhundert* (Leipzig, 1999)

Espagne, M. and M. Werner, 'Deutsch-Französischer Kulturtransfer im 18. und 19. Jahrhundert: Zu einem neuen interdisziplinären Forschungsprogramm des C.N.R.S', *Francia*, 13 (1985), 502–10

Espagne, M. and M. Werner, 'La constitution d'une référence culturelle allemande en France: Genèse et histoire (1750–1914)', *Annales*, 42 (1987), 969–92

Evans, H. C. (ed.), *Byzantium: Faith and power (1261–1557)* (New Haven and London, 2004)

Fajt, J. and M. Hörsch (eds), *Künsterlische Wechselwirkungen in Mitteleuropa* (Stuttgart, 2006)

Farago, C. (ed.), *Reframing the Renaissance: Visual culture in Europe and Latin America 1450–1650* (New Haven and London, 1995)

Füssel, S. and J. Pirożyńsky (eds), *Der polnische Humanismus und die europäischen Sodalitäten* (Wiesbaden, 1997)

Grafton, A., *Leon Battista Alberti: Masterbuilder of the Renaissance* (New York, 2000)

Helmrath, J., U. Muhlack and G. Walther (eds), *Diffusion des Humanismus: Studien zur nationalen Geschichtsschreibung europäischer Humanisten* (Göttingen, 2002)

Kaufmann, T. D., 'Italian sculptors and sculpture outside of Italy (chiefly in central Europe): Problems of approach, possibilities of reception', in Farago, C. (ed.), *Reframing the Renaissance: Visual culture in Europe and Latin America 1450–1650* (New Haven and London, 1995)

Kaufmann, T. D., *Court, cloister and city: Art and culture in central Europe, 1450–1800* (Chicago and London, 1995)

Kaufmann, T. D., *Toward a geography of art* (Chicago, 2004)

Kaufmann, T. D., 'Der Ostseeraum als Kunstregion: Historiographie, Stand der Forschung und Perspektiven künftiger Untersuchungen', in M. Krieger and M. North (eds), *Land und Meer: Kultureller Austausch zwischen Westeuropa und dem Ostseeraum in der Frühen Neuzeit* (Cologne, 2004)

Kaufmann, T. D. and M. North, 'Introduction – artistic and cultural exchanges between Europe and Asia, 1400–1900: Rethinking markets, workshops and collections', in M. North (ed.), *Artistic and cultural exchanges between Europe and Asia, 1400–1900: Rethinking markets, workshops and collections* (Farnham, 2010)

Kristeller, P. O., 'The diffusion of Italian humanism', *Italica*, 39 (1962), 1–20

Kristeller, P. O., 'Die Verbreitung des italienischen Humanismus in Europa', in P. O. Kristeller, *Humanismus und Renaissance*, II: *Philosophie, Bildung und Kunst* (Stuttgart, 1975)

Maissen, T. and G. Walther (eds), *Funktionen des Humanismus: Studien zum Nutzen des Neuen in der humanistischen Kultur* (Göttingen, 2006)

McCahill, E. M., 'Finding a job as a humanist: The epistolary collection of Lapo da Castiglione the Younger', *Renaissance Quarterly*, 57 (2004), 1308–45

Muchembled, R. (ed.), *Cultural exchange in early modern Europe* (4 vols, Cambridge, 2006–2007)

Nelson, R. S., 'Byzantium and the rebirth of art and learning in Italy and France', in H. C. Evans (ed.), *Byzantium: Faith and power (1261–1557)* (New Haven and London, 2004)

North, M., 'Kommunikation und Raumbildung', in R. C. Schwinges (ed.), *Neubürger im späten Mittelalter: Migration und Austausch in der Städtelandschaft des alten Reiches (1250–1550)* (Berlin, 2002)

North, M. (ed.), *Kultureller Austausch in der Frühen Neuzeit* (Cologne, 2009)

Nuttall, P., *From Flanders to Florence: The impact of Netherlandish painting 1400–1500* (New Haven and London, 2004)

Pauwels A. and H. Pauwels, 'Dirk Bouts' Laatste Avondmaal, een belangrijk keerpunt in de evolutie van de perspectief in de schilderkunst van de Nederlanden', in A. Bergmans (ed.), *Dirk Bouts' Leuven in de late middeleeuwen: Het laatste avondmaal* (Tielt, 1998)

Popp, D. and R. Suckale (eds), *Die Jagiellonen: Kunst und Kultur einer europäischen Dynastie an der Wende zur Neuzeit* (Nuremberg, 2002)

Rabil, A. Jr, *Renaissance humanism: Foundations, forms, and legacy* (3 vols, Philadelphia, 1988)

Rohlmann, M., 'Zitate flämischer Landschaftsmotive in Florentiner Quattrocentomalerei', in J. Poeschke (ed.), *Italienische Frührenaissance und nordeuropäisches Spätmittelalter: Kunst der frühen Neuzeit im europäischen Zusammenhang* (Munich, 1993)

Rosenthal, E., 'The diffusion of the Italian Renaissance style in western European art', *Sixteenth Century Journal*, 9 (1978), 33–44

Saygin, S., *Humphrey, duke of Gloucester (1390–1447) and the Italian humanists* (Leiden, 2002)

Schmale, W. (ed.), *Kulturtransfer: Kulturelle Praxis im 16. Jahrhundert* (Innsbruck, 2003)

Schmid, W., 'Kunst und Migration: Wanderungen Kölner Maler im 15. und 16. Jahrhundert', in G. Jaritz and A. Müller (eds), *Migration in der Feudalgesellschaft* (Frankfurt, 1988)

Schmid, W., 'Kunstlandschaft – Absatzgebiet – Zentralraum: Zur Brauchbarkeit unterschiedlicher Raumkonzepte in der kunstgeographischen Forschung vornehmlich an rheinischen Beispielen', in U. Albrecht and J. v. Bonsdorff (eds), *Figur und Raum: Mittelalterliche Holzbildwerke im historischen und kunstgeographischen Kontext* (Berlin, 1994)

Spieß, K.-H., 'Asian objects and western European court-culture in the later Middle Ages', in M. North (ed.), *Artistic and cultural exchanges between Europe and Asia, 1400–1900. Rethinking markets, workshops and collections* (Farnham, 2010)

Strohmeyer, A., 'Geschichtsbilder im Kulturtransfer: Die Hofhistoriographie in Wien im Zeitalter des Humanismus als Rezipient und Multiplikator', in A. Langer and G. Michels (eds), *Metropolen und Kulturtransfer im 15.–16. Jahrhundert: Prag – Krakau – Danzig – Wien* (Stuttgart, 2001)

Walter, G., 'Nationalgeschichte als Exportgut. Mögliche Antworten auf die Frage: Was heißt "Diffusion des Humanismus?"', in J. Helmrath, U. Muhlack and G. Walther (eds), *Diffusion des Humanismus: Studien zur nationalen Geschichtsschreibung europäischer Humanisten* (Göttingen, 2002)

Werner, M. and B. Zimmermann, 'Penser l'histoire croisée: entre empirie et réflexivité', *Annales H.S.S.*, 57 (2003) 7–34

Werner, M. and B. Zimmermann, *De la comparaison à l'histoire croisée* (Paris, 2004)

Werner, M. and B. Zimmermann, 'Beyond comparison: Histoire croisée and the challenge of reflexivity', *Religion and History*, 45 (2006), 30–50

Wörster, P., *Humanismus in Olmütz: Landesbeschreibung, Stadtlob und Geschichtsschreibung in der ersten Hälfte des 16. Jahrhunderts* (Marburg, 1994)

INDEX